Number	Chapter	Formula
12	6	$s_{\text{est } y} = s_y \sqrt{\dfrac{N(1 - r^2)}{N - 2}}$
13a	7	$\beta_1 = \dfrac{r_{Y1} - (r_{Y2} \cdot r_{12})}{1 - r_{12}^2}$
13b	7	$\beta_2 = \dfrac{r_{Y2} - (r_{Y1} \cdot r_{12})}{1 - r_{12}^2}$
14	7	$R = \sqrt{(\beta_1 r_{Y1}) + (\beta_2 r_{Y2})}$
15	9	$s_{\overline{x}} = \dfrac{s}{\sqrt{N}}$
16	9	$t = \dfrac{\overline{X} - \mu_{\overline{x}}}{s_{\overline{x}}}$
17a	9	upper limit of $\mu = \overline{X} + (t_{\text{crit}(\alpha)} \cdot s_{\overline{x}})$
17b	9	lower limit of $\mu = \overline{X} - (t_{\text{crit}(\alpha)} \cdot s_{\overline{x}})$
18	9	$t = \dfrac{r\sqrt{N - 2}}{\sqrt{1 - r^2}}$
19	10	$s_{\overline{x}_1 - \overline{x}_2} = \sqrt{\left(\dfrac{SS_1 + SS_2}{N_1 + N_2 - 2}\right)\left(\dfrac{1}{N_1} + \dfrac{1}{N_2}\right)}$
20	10	$t = \dfrac{(\overline{X}_1 - \overline{X}_2) - (\mu_1 - \mu_2)}{s_{\overline{x}_1 - \overline{x}_2}}$
21	11	$s_{\overline{d}} = \dfrac{s_d}{\sqrt{N_d}}$
22	11	$t = \dfrac{\overline{X}_d - \mu_{\overline{d}}}{s_{\overline{d}}}$

INTRODUCTORY STATISTICS FOR BEHAVIORAL RESEARCH

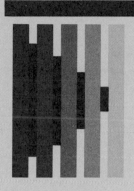

INTRODUCTORY STATISTICS FOR BEHAVIORAL RESEARCH

Ronald H. Nowaczyk

Clemson University

Holt, Rinehart and Winston, Inc.

New York   Chicago   San Francisco   Philadelphia
Montreal   Toronto   London   Sydney   Tokyo

For my parents Frances and Henry

Publisher   Susan Meyers
Acquisitions Editor   Susan Arellano
Senior Project Manager   Sondra Greenfield
Production Manager   Stefania Taflinska
Design Supervisor   Gloria Gentile
Cover Photographer   Clayton Price

Library of Congress Cataloging-in-Publication Data

Nowaczyk, Ronald H.
    Introductory statistics for behavioral research.

    Includes index.
    1. Social sciences—Statistical methods.   I. Title.
HA29.N779   1988   519.5   87–28672

ISBN 0-03-004043-4

Requests for permission to make copies of any part of the work should be mailed to:
Permissions
Holt, Rinehart and Winston, Inc.
111 Fifth Avenue
New York, NY 10003
PRINTED IN THE UNITED STATES OF AMERICA

8 9 0 1   0 3 2   9 8 7 6 5 4 3 2 1

Holt, Rinehart and Winston, Inc.
The Dryden Press
Saunders College Publishing

Preface

This book is written for the student enrolled in a statistics course in the behavioral sciences or in education. This type of statistics course is often the least popular because it frequently involves material with little direct application to subjects of interest to the student. Yet, the use of statistical procedures is a critical component in the advancement of knowledge in the behavioral sciences. An understanding of the underlying statistical concepts and procedures that are used in analyzing behavioral science and educational research is essential to further study in these areas. Much of what is known or discussed in later courses relies on research that incorporates statistical procedures in interpreting the findings.

This book attempts to bridge the separation between statistics and content often mentioned by students. Each chapter in this book begins with an example from a published research study. The intent is to use the chapter example as a vehicle for explaining statistical concepts and illustrating statistical procedures. Researchers use statistics to aid them in testing hypotheses, interpreting their findings, and adding to the body of knowledge in their discipline. Therefore, combining real research examples with the discussion of statistics provides a more complete picture of the use of statistics in behavioral science research.

A number of other texts also incorporate references or discussions of published studies; this book is different, however, in that the chapter examples are discussed throughout the chapter. Two examples are fully discussed and analyzed in each of the chapters describing statistical tests. In most cases, the examples are from the same study. In all cases, the findings of the statistical procedures are related back to the original research questions the researchers asked.

The examples are almost all from psychology although many have applications to other areas such as education or nursing. They were selected to be both interesting to the student and illustrative of the necessary statistical principles. I generated the data in each example; however, I was careful that the data provided findings very similar to those reported in the original study.

Providing a readable, interesting, and informative book for the student was the primary goal in preparing this book. In addition to using examples from the literature, other changes from many current statistics texts were incorporated. One important change is the integration of descriptive and inferential statistics in each chapter dealing with statistical tests. Many texts describe descriptive statistics in earlier chapters and then make little reference to their use in chapters dealing with inferential statistics. In this text the importance of integrating descriptive and inferential statistics is highlighted and reinforced by applying procedures (such as calculating measures of both central tendency and variability and introducing the use of graphing) to the examples in chapters on statistical tests. These chapters include sections on describing the data before sections on statistical testing.

Consistent with this approach of integrating statistical procedures is the numbering of formulas throughout the text. Definitional and computational formulas are included throughout the text. However, only computational (raw-score) formulas are numbered. Often, some students have difficulty deciding between several alternative forms of the same formula. To help these students, the definitional formula is presented and described but is not numbered. Only the formulas that should be used in calculating information, the computational formulas, are numbered. And in these cases, only the most general form is used, eliminating the need for the student to choose from several alternative computational formulas. As an example, formulas using frequency values are not included in this book. It has been my experience, both in my own work and in discussions with others, that seldom, if ever, does a researcher use computational formulas based on frequency distributions.

The computational formulas are included inside the front and back endpapers of the book. Chapter numbers of where the formulas are first introduced are included. Because of the integration of procedures across chapters, several formulas are used many times throughout the text. This is especially true for some of the formulas involved in calculating measures of central tendency and variability and in analyzing data using the analysis of variance. Rather than give the impression that certain formulas are appropriate in only limited applications, which might occur if formulas are numbered according to chapter, the numbering of formulas in this book shows the student the wide applicability of these formulas to numerous examples.

To make it easier for students to use the tables in Appendix E, they are labeled according to the statistic they list. For instance, Table T lists critical t values, Table F lists critical F ratios. This labeling scheme should be easier for the student who is trying to locate the appropriate table for a particular statistic.

There are two types of exercises at the end of many of the chapters. The first type involves questions about concepts or application of various procedures described in the chapter. The other type of exercise is a complete research problem similar to that discussed in the chapter. This problem requires the student to identify the research and statistical hypotheses, use descriptive and inferential statistics, and then relate the findings to the original research question. There are two problems like this included for every chapter dealing with inferential statistics. The answers for all the odd numbered questions and for the first of the complete research problems in each chapter are provided in Appendix D.

A workbook containing four additional problems for each statistical test is also available. These problems are identical to the complete research problems described above. The workbook also contains general instructions for using descriptive statistics and each type of statistical test. Appendix C at the back of the text includes the data from the chapter examples which can be used in conjunction with two popular computer programs, SAS and SPSS$_x$.

To the Instructor

This book follows the outline of many current texts in the field. It may be difficult to complete the entire text in a single semester. For that reason, some of the later chapters, Chapter 7 and Chapters 13 through 19, may be omitted depending on the time permitted, the goals of the course, and you and your students' interest. The nonparametric tests follow the same presentation order as the parametric tests, but the chapters are written so that a different order can be followed if so desired.

To the Student

This book is written for you. I hope that it develops and stimulates your interest in the behavioral sciences. It has been written so that the only mathematical knowledge needed is an understanding of basic high-school algebra. Appendix B provides a review of some concepts for those that feel they may need it. I intentionally kept the presentation as simple and straightforward as possible. As a result, in some instances, you may want to know more about a particular concept. I have included references throughout the text for further reading. The full references are included in the Reference's section at the back of the book. The references for the chapter examples are also included in the back. I encourage you to read at least one or two of the full articles that form the basis for the chapter examples. The articles will give you a better understanding of the research question and the findings of the study. Lastly, I encourage you to write to me with your comments. Since the book is written for you, I would like to know how it has worked and how it might be improved.

ACKNOWLEDGMENTS

There are a number of individuals who provided assistance in the development of this book. I would like to thank Jane Moulton, Richard Owen, and Gary Woodruff for their comments and suggestions in the early stages of the preparation of this book. I would also like to thank the following individuals who reviewed all or portions of this book in its manuscript form:

David E. Johnson, John Brown University; James Tromater, University of Richmond; Jeczy Karylowski, University of North Florida; Eric F. Ward, Western Illinois University; Jane L. Buck, Delaware State College; Leah Light, Pitzer College; Jack Kirschenbaum, Fullerton College; David Hess, Fredonia State University College; Michael Fishbein, Roosevelt University; Charles Reichardt, University of Denver; Gordon Allen, Miami University(Ohio); Marion (Tim) Gaines, Presbyterian College; Stephan Arndt, Notre Dame University; Paula Hertel, Trinity University; Henry Bernbach, Purdue University; Mary Jo Williams, San Jacinto Central College; Douglas Mandra, Francis Marion College; William Wozniak, Kearney State College; John A. Kennedy, Jr., New York University; Gordon Greenberg, University of Illinois; Susan Donaldson, University of Southern Indiana.

The staff at Holt, Rinehart & Winston was very helpful in the preparation and production of this text. I thank them for their help. I especially would like to thank Susan Meyers, Susan Arellano, and Sondra Greenfield for their guidance, suggestions, and expertise. I am also grateful to the literary executor of the late Sir Ronald A. Fisher, F. R. S. to Dr. Frank Yates, F. R. S. and to Longman Group Ltd. London, for permission to reprint Tables II, III, IV, and VII from their book *Statistical Tables for Biological, Agricultural and Medical Research*. (6th edition, 1974).

I would also like to thank Professors John C. Jahnke and Benton J. Underwood, both of whom instilled in me an appreciation for the rigors and methods involved in behavioral science research. Lastly, I most gratefully acknowledge the patience and understanding of my wife, Pat, who provided her love, encouragement, and support throughout the preparation of this book.

Contents

P A R T T H R E E : Understanding Inferential Statistics   159

P A R T F O U R : Interpreting Two-condition Experiments With Interval or Ratio Data   207

P A R T   F I V E :   Analyzing Multiple-condition Studies With Interval or Ratio Data   279

Introduction

TERMS DISCUSSED

research hypothesis

experiment

quasi experiment

correlational study

statistics

data

descriptive statistics

inferential statistics

population

sample

- representative sample
- random sample

In 1983, Lucinda McClain published an article in the Teaching of Psychology *that describes a study on the test-taking behavior of "A," "C," and "F" students. She observed that students often ask instructors for help with improving their performance on multiple-choice tests. She knew that past research had been concerned primarily with the effectiveness and wisdom of changing answers on multiple-choice tests and the strategy of skipping difficult questions until the end of the test. Based on her own observations and an investigation of what other researchers had published on the topic, McClain decided to conduct her own study to better understand test-taking behavior.*

She asked student volunteers to talk aloud into a tape recorder while taking a multiple-choice test for her introductory psychology course. She was interested in the students' performance level on three previous tests, that is whether they had received "As," "Cs," or "Fs." In addition, she measured several different behaviors. These included, (1) the number of alternatives read for each question, (2) the number of incorrect alternatives that were eliminated by stating the reasons that the alternatives were incorrect, and (3) the number of times students anticipated the correct answer after reading a question but before reading the multiple-choice alternatives. She believed that the different types of students ("A," "C," and "F") would not use the same strategies on the test.

She selected a sample of 60 students from 129 volunteers. Equal numbers of these students had averages greater than 90% (the "A" students), between 70 and 76% (the "C" students), or below 60% (the "F" students). All 60 students took the 70-item multiple-choice test on the same day as the other students in the class, but the subject students took the test individually in small rooms in which they could talk aloud as they completed the test. The students took a little longer to complete the test than those who took the test under normal conditions, but McClain reported that none of the students withdrew from the study and most were surprised at the ease with which they could talk aloud while taking the test.

This brief description of a study on test-taking behavior contains some of the important components in behavioral science research. Research in the behavioral sciences is based on the scientific study of behavior and social interaction. Not only do researchers in the behavioral sciences observe behavior, they often control environmental settings or situations in order to better understand factors influencing behavior. These researchers use the methods of scientific study in their accumulation of knowledge. And, they employ a number of techniques common among the scientific disciplines.

These techniques often include (1) observation, (2) theory and hypothesis formulation, (3) research and data collection, and (4) statistical analysis. Without guidelines and agreement among researchers in using these techniques for studying behavior, the accumulation of knowledge would be slowed and less organized. Professor McClain used these techniques in conducting her study. Although this book deals primarily with statistical analysis, it is important to understand the entire research cycle to appreciate the role statistical analysis plays.

DESCRIBING A RESEARCH CYCLE

Scientific research is cyclic, that is, it is a continuous process. Researchers in the behavioral sciences focus on a particular issue and identify what they believe are its important components. From their observations, researchers develop explanations for observed behaviors and predictions of how those behaviors will change in different settings. To be scientific, these predictions should be testable. The researcher can then conduct a research study and observe and collect information about behavior. This information is then subjected to statistical analysis. The findings of the analysis may support or refute the researcher's prediction. In many cases the findings lead to additional questions and, perhaps, a refinement of the researcher's prediction or hypothesis for the particular area of study. The research cycle is then repeated. Therefore, the findings of one study often lead to another, and so on. Figure 1.1 is a diagram of this research cycle. Let's look at one point on the research cycle, that of observation.

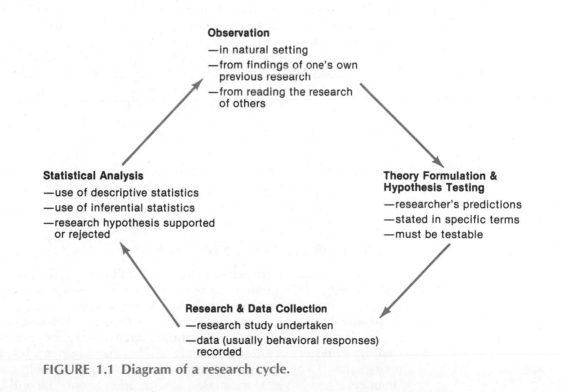

FIGURE 1.1 Diagram of a research cycle.

THE ROLE OF OBSERVATION

A beginning point in the scientific process is observation. Observation takes several forms. In one case, it may be the researcher observing behavior in the natural setting or real world. For instance, an educator may notice that students appear happier with one instructional system rather than another. Or, a sociologist may observe that solar homes are not as popular as conventional homes in terms of home sales. A psychologist might watch the way children play. For instance, Piaget, the Swiss psychologist, derived many of the important concepts in his theory of cognitive development from observing children as they played and interacted with each other. In other cases, the researcher may observe behavior in a controlled laboratory setting. In these instances, the environmental setting might be manipulated or controlled in a particular fashion in order to observe behavior. These observations often result from the researcher's own previous studies.

The observations made by researchers are more detailed than those of the lay person. A researcher is trained to critically examine events and to identify and isolate factors that may be contributing to the observed behaviors. Identifying the factors that influence behavior is important for meaningful research.

Another source of information is the work of other researchers. Behavioral science researchers frequently look to previous research in addition to their own in the study of behavior. By observing what others have found, a researcher is better prepared to focus on particular behaviors, settings, or situations in a research study. Researchers rely on talking with other researchers, reading reports of research findings in scientific journals and books, and attending professional conferences to learn about the research of others. McClain, in her research, relied on the findings of other studies in developing her study. She wanted to add to what was already known about test-taking behavior and did not want to repeat the study of a previous researcher.

Most college libraries have indexes to the written research reports and papers presented at conferences. These sources in the behavioral sciences include, *Social Science Citation Index*, *Education Index*, *ERIC*, *Psychological Abstracts*, and *Sociological Abstracts*. By referring to these sources, the researcher can determine what has been studied and researched on a given topic. The introduction in a research paper usually includes a summary of the relevant previous research.

HYPOTHESIS TESTING AND THEORIES

From observations from her own research and from that of other scientists, the researcher may predict the outcome of a proposed study. If a researcher feels she understands the relationship between some aspect of the environment and behavior, she should be able to predict what would happen in a study. The **research hypothesis** is the researcher's prediction about what the findings or results of a research study will be. For instance a researcher might predict that if a person finds himself alone, he will likely help another person in an emergency. Yet, if the person is with other people, he will be less likely to help a person in need. Or, as another example, he might predict that a person raised in a certain socioeconomic environment might value being famous or well known more than a person raised in a different environment. The research hypothesis is stated often in very specific terms and is based on past research or a theory.

Research hypotheses can develop from theories. Theories provide a way for organizing a body or set of research findings by tying together the findings of previous studies. The ability to explain what influences behavior is a critical function of theories in the behavioral sciences. They should tell us what factors or combinations of factors in the environment or within an individual influence behavior. An example of a current theory is the "set point" theory. This theory explains eating behavior to be under the influence of the hypothalamus, which acts like a thermostat in maintaining a person's weight at a particular "set point" (Keesey & Corbett, 1983).

In addition to providing an organizing framework for research findings and explaining behavior, theories must also be a source for additional research hypotheses and predictions. Theories must be testable. Through tests of these new research hypotheses, we can determine the limits and usefulness of a particular theory.

The research hypothesis itself must also be testable. This means that it should be stated in a way that allows the researcher to conduct a study and reject the hypothesis if it is wrong. For example, we currently don't have the technology to test the hypothesis that personal memories are stored in a specific location within the human cortex. The technology for mapping neuronal transmissions, neuron by neuron, does not exist at present. Therefore, this hypothesis would not now be testable. However, technological advances may enable researchers to test this hypothesis in the future.

Research hypotheses are stated in terms of predictions. This text will examine two types of research hypotheses. One is hypotheses that predict *differences* in behavior as a function of changes in some other variable. For example, one such hypothesis might predict that students using a study guide in an introductory sociology course will perform better than students not using a study guide.

There are also hypotheses that predict a *linear relationship* between a variable of interest and a behavior. An example of this type of hypothesis is the relationship between smoking behavior and the probability of developing lung cancer. The type of hypothesis used is important in determining the type of research study to be conducted.

THE RESEARCH STUDY AND DATA COLLECTION

Some research is designed to describe behavior with little or no intervention or control on the part of the researcher. This research may take the form of a survey, a study of public or historical records (often called archival research), or a case study (a study of an individual). There are, however, a large number of research studies in which the researcher intervenes in or controls aspects of the environment in order to study behavior. This text deals with analyzing the findings from these types of studies. Most of the examples in this book are taken from psychological research. However, the statistical techniques and ways of reasoning can be applied to a number of studies in biology, education, health research, political science, and sociology.

The research design which affords the greatest amount of control to the researcher is called an experiment. Basically, an **experiment** is a controlled research study designed to determine the effects of one variable on another variable. Control often requires the researcher to restrict what occurs in the environmental setting in order to allow certain other aspects or variables of the setting to change. In behavioral research, one of these variables is often some aspect of the environment or a characteristic of the subjects in the study, and the other variable is the behavior of the individuals being observed. The research hypothesis is often stated so as to predict differences in behavior depending on the environmental setting. For example, an experiment could be used to test the hypothesis that students' study habits are affected by the type of test they are to be given. Students who receive essay tests will study more than students who are given multiple-choice tests. Students in one section of an introductory sociology course might be given essay exams, and students in another section receive only multiple-choice exams. A researcher might record the number of hours each individual studied each night during the term. The number of hours of study would be the behavior being measured. Finding that students who were given essay exams studied more than those who received multiple-choice exams would support the research hypothesis.

Another example of an experiment is a study in which different therapies are administered to individuals complaining of stress-related problems (e.g., headaches, anxiety, inability to sleep). The different therapies would make up the aspect of the environment being studied. The behavior might be the number of stress-related symptoms reported by the individuals after being in therapy for a given period.

Other research designs provide the researcher with less control than experiments. A **quasi experiment** is a research study that has many of the characteristics of a true experiment except that total control on the part of the researcher is not possible. If the researcher cannot assign participants to particular conditions in a study then the researcher does not have total control and the research study would be a quasi experiment. For instance, in a study of gender differences, the researcher cannot "assign" a person to be male or female; the person is of a particular gender before participating in the study.

Another type of research design is the **correlational study** which is designed to identify relationships among variables in the environment and behavior. Correlational studies often are designed to identify the existence of *relationships* between the environment and behavior. An example of a correlational study would be a study testing the hypothesis that test grades are related to the number of hours people study. We might record (or observe) the number of hours that each person in a class studies before a test and then determine if the number of hours of study was related to the person's test score. Presumably, the more hours a person studies, the higher his test grade will be. Or a researcher might investigate the relationship between the amount of privacy your roommate provides you and how much you like her. It might be predicted that the more privacy you have, the more you like your roommate. Therefore, we would say a relationship exists between the amount of privacy you have and how much you like your roommate.

In many cases a correlational study is used because ethical considerations prevent the researcher from manipulating particular variables. For the example of smoking behavior, it would be wrong to "assign" people to smoking conditions in order to observe the occurrence of lung cancer. Therefore, much of our knowledge about the effects of smoking using humans is based on correlational studies. Later on we will discuss the notion of causality.

THE ROLE OF STATISTICAL ANALYSIS

The research hypothesis and research design of a study will influence the way its findings are analyzed. Certain procedures are appropriate when testing for differences or for linear relationships. The analysis of the research results is the focus of this book.

At this point, several terms need to be introduced. The first is statistics. **Statistics** encompasses the procedures for organizing and analyzing numerical information. Like geometry and algebra, statistics is a branch of mathematics. The numerical information collected is referred to as **data** (datum is singular, data is the plural form). When the data collection phase of a study is completed, the researcher organizes, summarizes, and analyzes the data. These procedures involve the use of statistics. In much of behavioral research, the data are a measure of some aspect of behavior.

Descriptive Statistics

There are two sets of procedures in statistics. **Descriptive statistics** organize and describe the data obtained in the study. For instance, a researcher might tabulate the number of different data values obtained (e.g., the number of people donating $5 to a particular charity). This procedure results in a frequency distribution for the data values. Many times instructors will provide a class with a frequency distribution of the number of people who got "A," "B," "C," "D," and "F" grades on a particular test. Along with constructing a frequency distribution, it is possible to transform original data values into percentile scores (for example, reporting that a test score is in the top 10% of the class or has a percentile rank of 90). Another procedure in descriptive statistics is the graphing of the results of a study. Graphs provide a pictorial description of the research data.

Descriptive statistics can involve summarizing a set of data values with a single value. There are two common types of values used. One is called a measure of central tendency. The most common measure of central tendency is the arithmetic average or mean. A measure of central tendency provides a description about the general location of a set of data values. For instance, a test with a mean (or average) score of 86 would have higher test scores than a test with a mean score of 47. The other type of value is called a measure of variability and it describes how spread out or dispersed the data are. The easiest measure of variability to calculate is the range, which is the difference between the high data value and the low data value. Again, instructors sometimes provide the class with the values for the highest and lowest scores on a test.

Inferential Statistics

Inferential statistics enable the researcher to determine whether her research hypothesis has been supported. Inferential statistics allow a researcher to extend or generalize the findings from a study to a larger set of individuals. In most studies, the researcher uses only a small subset of individuals. Yet, he may want to apply his findings to more than just those individuals who participated in the study. For example, drug companies test new pain-relieving drugs in controlled studies. Yet, they need to be able to conclude that their findings will apply to other similar people outside their studies. To be able to make this leap—from findings in one study to a more general statement about behavior—requires inferential statistics. The word *inferential* contains the word *infer*, which means to conclude or reason from something known. The researcher hopes to infer or conclude from the findings of one study that individuals similar to those in the study will react similarly.

Inferential statistics relies on probability and statistical tests. When the results of a study are reported to be significant, the behavioral science researcher is making a claim that the findings apply to more than just the subset of individuals who participated in the study. The researcher uses statistical tests in deciding whether or not the research hypothesis was supported. This decision involves the use of probability. Probability is used to identify the likelihood that the findings are the result of chance factors.

An example of the use of inferential statistics is an automobile company's statement that a research study showed its auto has "significantly fewer problems" than another. The manufacturer claims that purchasing one of its automobiles (not just the ones specifically tested in their study) will result in fewer repairs than if another company's auto had been purchased.

Some of the common procedures used in statistics are listed in Table 1.1.

TABLE 1.1 Listing of Some Common Statistical Procedures in Behavioral Science Research	
Descriptive Statistics	**Inferential Statistics**

1. frequency distribution
2. percentiles
3. graphs
4. measure of central tendency
5. measure of variability
	1. use of statistical tests
	   rely on probability
	   are needed in making conclusions based on
	     descriptive statistics
	   involve the concept of "statistical significance"
	2. used in estimating information about a
	   population from descriptive statistics

Once the statistical analysis is completed, the researcher takes note of the findings and conclusions that can be drawn from the study. These conclusions are presented in the discussion section for most behavioral science journals. As mentioned earlier, these conclusions serve as observations for future research and are often used in generating additional research hypotheses. And these conclusions can influence other researchers in terms of the direction they will pursue in their research.

POPULATIONS AND SAMPLES

This discussion of inferential statistics and its usefulness in extending the findings of a study illustrates the importance of two important terms in behavioral science research—population and sample. A researcher usually examines the behavior of a subset of individuals. This subset is called a **sample.** A sample is a segment or portion of some larger set of individuals. A researcher conducts a study and based on statistical tests, extends his study's findings to a larger set of individuals. This larger set is called the **population.** A population consists of all members or individuals that the researcher is interested in studying. A researcher's conclusions are extended to members of the population.

The membership of a population can differ depending on the researcher and the research study. For instance, a developmental psychologist may define her population as infants at the age of 6 months. A political scientist studying voter patterns may define a population as all registered voters. An educational psychologist may use children with a particular learning disability as the population of interest. The important point is that the population consists of *all* those individuals to whom a researcher wants to extend the findings of a study.

How a sample is selected from a population is important. A researcher wants the sample, or subset of the population, to be representative of the population. A **representative sample** is a sample that is unbiased. The members of the sample should accurately reflect the membership of the population. One way to increase the likelihood of having a representative sample is to select members randomly from the population. A **random sample** (specifically, a simple random sample) can be defined as a sample in which each member of the population has an equal chance of being selected. Furthermore, the selection process should be independent. That is, the selection of any one member should in no way influence the probability of another member being selected.

The larger the random sample, the more likely it is to represent the population. This should make sense intuitively. You would probably feel more comfortable making statements about the attitudes of students in your school if you were relying on a sample of 200 students rather than asking just one student for his or her attitudes.

THE McCLAIN STUDY

At this point, it will be helpful to examine the McClain study described in the beginning of this chapter. Using the research cycle presented earlier, we see that observation is a key point in the McClain study. McClain noted not only her observations of test-taking strategies of students in her class, but also a number of published studies on test taking. She mentioned studies investigating the wisdom of changing answers (not going with your first answer) and the time it takes students to complete a test. She commented that no studies have been published identifying what students do while taking a test. Based on her review of past literature and her observations in the classroom, she identified several test-taking behaviors to study.

Her hypothesis was that the students will differ in their test-taking strategies depending on how well they have done on previous tests. There is theoretical support for this hypothesis. Previous work in cognitive psychology has led to the position that success on memory tests is higher when a person learns the material in a manner that facilitates memory retrieval on a test. That is, reading and studying material for a multiple-choice test will result in better performance on a multiple-choice test than if an essay test is given unexpectedly. It is assumed that students often ask what type of test will be given because it influences how they will study. The student organizes material in a way that will help retrieval on the test. Because "A" students had performed better on previous tests than "C" or "F" students, McClain assumed that the "A" students may have organized the material differently from other students and may use different retrieval strategies on a test. Therefore, she decided to look for differences in how students answered the test.

Her sample consisted of students randomly selected from volunteers from her introductory psychology course. To extend her findings to all students in her class, she must have believed that her volunteers were representative of the population of students in her class and, perhaps, the typical college student. If she found differences in the test-taking strategies in her sample of "A," "C," and "F" students, then she would use statistical tests to determine the likelihood that the differences are the result of chance or sampling error. If the likelihood was small, then she would have concluded that the differences she found represent real differences in the population of students and that her research hypothesis was supported.

Researchers in most behavioral science studies want to extend the findings beyond the immediate population studied. For instance, McClain wanted to claim that the differences she found existed not only for students in her class, but also for all students in her university and, perhaps, for college students in general. To accomplish that, other researchers must believe that her sample was representative of the population of all college students. There are no statistical procedures that can test this assumption. Instead, researchers look at the way her students were selected and the type of students used. Researchers may also try to repeat or replicate her study to determine if the same differences are found with other samples of students at other universities. If the findings are consistent, then the scientific community is likely to assume that her findings represent true differences among college students. In the next chapter, we will use the McClain study again to illustrate some procedures in descriptive statistics.

ORGANIZATION AND GOALS OF THE BOOK

The chapters in this book are organized according to different statistical procedures. Chapters 2 through 4 explain the basic procedures used in descriptive statistics. Chapters 5 through 7 discuss procedures involved in interpreting correlational hypotheses. Chapters 8 and 9 provide the foundation for hypothesis testing and inferential statistics. And Chapter 10 begins the pre-

---

BOX 1.1 **Some Examples of the Use of Statistics in Newspaper and Magazine Reports**

"Wooing Older Consumers"—*New York Times* (Nov. 27, 1986)
—discusses grouping older people in one of three age groups (50–75, 75–85, and 85 and up) to describe purchasing patterns and consumer preferences.

"A Blood Test for Cancer"—*Newsweek* (Dec. 8, 1986)
—describes a "controlled" study of 331 people in which a blood test differentiated between individuals who did or did not have cancer.

"Poll Backs Ending Life Support in Some Cases"—*New York Times* (Nov. 29, 1986)
—reports on a survey that found 73% of the individuals surveyed would withdraw life support systems in certain instances. The article describes characteristics of those surveyed and the margin of error in the statistics.

"Poll: Most Americans Oppose Strict Bans of Sexual Materials"—*Associated Press* (Apr. 12, 1987)
—report of a poll of 1,402 adults concerning their views on sexually explicit material and pornography. The article describes a number of findings and reports margin of error in the statistics.

"Infant Mortality: Frightful Odds in Inner City"—*New York Times* (June 26, 1987)
—statistics and graphs reporting the incidence of infant deaths across the country. Rate of deaths for different areas are provided.

sentation of a number of statistical tests. Each of the chapters on experimental designs includes the integration of descriptive statistics with the appropriate inferential statistics.

The chapters begin with a description of an actual published study. Data consistent with what the researchers found are presented. The material in each chapter describes how and why the various statistical procedures are used. By demonstrating these statistical procedures for published research, I hope to impress upon you, the reader, the role statistics plays in data analysis and to show you that statistics is a necessary tool in behavioral science research.

This book provides an introduction to many of the basic statistical concepts and procedures used in behavioral science research. When you finish with this book, you should be able to understand and interpret many of the findings reported in the behavioral science literature. And, given a research study that corresponds to one of the designs discussed in this book, you should be able to analyze and interpret the data from that study.

This book may also provide an important fringe benefit if it makes you a more informed consumer of published information. Box 1.1 lists a number of examples taken from recent newspaper and magazine articles that illustrate the use of statistics. In our society, we rely on information in making daily decisions. To aid or influence us in our decision making, the news media, government, the scientific community, advertisers, and others provide statistics to bolster their positions and arguments. In many cases only a limited amount of statistical information is provided. The information and concepts presented in this book should help you in interpreting a number of these published statistics and in making informed and thoughtful decisions that affect your daily life.

SUMMARY

This chapter began with a brief description of the scientific process used in behavioral science research. This process includes observation, theory and hypothesis-formulation testing, research and data collection, and statistical analysis. This book is concerned with statistical analysis.

Statistical analysis involves procedures that organize, summarize, and analyze numerical information. In behavioral science research, this information is often a measure of some aspect of behavior and is referred to as data. Two common procedures in statistics are descriptive statistics and inferential statistics. Descriptive statistics involve describing a set or group of data values. Inferential statistics relies on using the laws of probability to extend the findings from a limited number of participants to a larger group. This larger group is called the population. A researcher includes only a small subset, or sample, of the population in the study. If each member of the population has an equal chance of being selected for the sample, then the sample is referred to as a random sample.

EXERCISES

1. How is a researcher's definition of *observation* different from that of a layperson?

2. List at least two index sources and their call letters from your library for use in research in your field of interest. These indexes should provide a listing of recent research on topics of interest to you.

3. What do you see as the differences between a theory and a hypothesis? Which one is the researcher's prediction in a study?

4. Statistics has been described in terms of various types of procedures. List several of them.

5. For each statement below, determine whether descriptive or inferential statistics is being used.
    a. the average or mean response rate was 10 responses per hour.
    b. the percentage of animals that recovered from surgery was 36.
    c. the difference between the two conditions was significant.
    d. the high score on the test was 96 and the low score was 47.
    e. the relationship between a student's SAT score and his or her first semester grade point average can be found not only for this sample of students but also for other college students.

6. What kind of statistics would you be using if you were to take a set of data values and graph the findings?

7. An instructor asks the students in the front row of his class to evaluate his lecture. Is this a representative sample of the class? Explain.

8. Find an example of statistics being presented in a newspaper or magazine article and identify specific uses or statements of descriptive or inferential statistics.

9. The use of probability and generalizing from a sample to a population involves what type of statistics?

10. Find a recently published research article in your field of interest and identify uses of statistics. From the introduction of the article can you determine the research hypothesis?

11. A researcher believes that the more confident a student is before taking a test the better his or her test performance will be. Students rate their confidence level before the test on a 7-point scale and test performance is measured by test score. What would be a measure of behavior in this type of study? Is the research hypothesis predicting a relationship between the variables in this study?

12. Provide an example of a television commercial or magazine advertisement that makes use of statistics.

Descriptive Statistics

OVERVIEW

Describing the data from a research study is the first task for the researcher after the data have been collected. In Chapter 2, the procedures for organizing and tabulating the number of values obtained for the study are discussed. These procedures result in the construction of frequency distributions. These distributions are reported in graphs or tables.

Chapter 3 focuses on procedures for summarizing a set of data with individual values. Two commonly reported types of values are measures of central tendency and measures of variability. Procedures in Chapter 4 use these measures in converting values into percentile ranks. Percentile ranks facilitate comparisons among values in different sets of values.

Frequency Distributions

TERMS DISCUSSED

variable
- values
- causal relationship
- independent versus dependent
- continuous versus discrete

scales of measurement
- nominal scale
- ordinal scale
- interval scale
- ratio scale

real limits

modality

symmetry

PROCEDURES DESCRIBED

constructing a frequency distribution

graphing a frequency distribution

frequency polygon

histogram

bar graph

The McClain (1983) study described in Chapter 1 investigated test-taking strategies. McClain sampled 60 students from 129 volunteers from her introductory psychology course. An equal number of students had performed at the "A," "C," or "F" level on previous tests in the course. McClain hypothesized that test-taking strategies would be different among the three different types of students.

Each student took a semester exam alone in a small room with a student experimenter who operated a tape recorder. The student was instructed to read each of the 70 multiple-choice question aloud and to verbalize all thoughts while answering the questions. Each question had four alternatives.

A number of different behaviors were analyzed once the students completed the exam. Among these behaviors was the number of alternatives read per question. The number of alternatives read per question could range from one to four (assuming that students read at least one of the alternatives before making a choice). For each student, the average number of alternatives read (based on all 70 questions) is shown in Table 2.1.

TABLE 2.1   The Average Number of Multiple-Choice Alternatives Read by Each Student in the McClain Study

Previous Performance Level of the Student		
"A"	"C"	"F"
4.0	2.5	1.8
3.5	1.3	1.5
3.8	1.8	1.4
3.8	1.8	1.8
4.0	1.2	1.5
3.9	1.9	1.4
3.6	3.1	1.3
3.1	1.9	1.7
4.0	2.0	1.6
3.4	2.1	1.6
3.6	1.4	1.5
3.0	1.6	1.7
4.0	1.1	1.5
4.0	2.4	1.6
3.9	1.4	.9
2.8	1.4	1.4
4.0	1.7	1.1
3.6	1.8	.7
3.4	2.2	1.5
4.0	1.8	2.1

Most behavioral science research, including the McClain study, is concerned with the identification of relationships between aspects of the environment and behavior. These aspects of the environment can include characteristics within an individual. For instance, McClain was interested in identifying the relationship between type of students and test-taking behavior. Behavioral scientists have specific terms for many of these aspects or characteristics they study. We will discuss a number of them in the next section.

THE CONCEPT OF A VARIABLE

Up to this point, our discussion on research studies has included terms such as aspects, characteristics, and behaviors. These terms are referred to as variables in a research study. The term **variable** is used to describe the characteristics and properties of a set of objects, events, behaviors, or environments, of interest to the researcher. The individual characteristics within the set are referred to as **values.** For example, in the McClain study "type of student" was a variable. Using McClain's way of segregating students, there can be at least five types of students: "A," "B," "C," "D," and "F" students. Each type of student is a value for the variable, type of student. Note that McClain was not studying all types of students in her study; she was studying only the "A," "C," and "F" students.

The different test-taking behaviors were also variables. Number of alternatives read for each question was a variable with values ranging from one to four alternatives per question. She also recorded the number of questions for which a student read the stem of the question and then generated a potential answer before reading the alternatives. Therefore, "the number of times an answer was generated by the student" was another variable in the study. Since there were 70 questions on the test, this variable could have values from 0 (when a student generated no answers) to 70 (when a student generated an answer for each question).

This distinction between a variable and a value is important. A variable consists of a set of values. Think of a variable as the term that describes what the values have in common. For instance, when you are given the values, January, February, March, and so on, you know that they represent the variable, months. In many studies, not all possible values of a variable will be included. Table 2.2 provides a number of examples of variables with corresponding values in the second column.

One common mistake of students learning about behavioral research is their assumption that a study contains more variables than it actually does. That is, students confuse values for variables. In the example for this chapter some students might conclude that the "A," "C," and "F" students represent three variables. They do not. The three groups of students represent values of the variable, type of student.

Researchers study relationships among variables. Some research designs

TABLE 2.2   Examples of Variables in Behavioral Research

Variable	Potential values	Scale of measurement	Continuous or discrete
		Variable Classifications	
type of teaching method	PSI, discussion, lecture	nominal	—
college football rankings	1, 2, 3, 4	ordinal	discrete
number of hours being deprived of sleep	1 hr, 8 hrs, 24 hrs	ratio	continuous
temperature in °F	−10°, 32°, 212°	interval	continuous
type of occupation	blue-collar, managerial, professional	nominal	—
number of children desired by newlyweds	0, 1, 2, 3, etc.	ratio	discrete
the way a student carries books	in briefcase/bag, under arm	nominal	—
educational level	h.-s. grad, jun. coll. grad, coll. grad., master's degree, etc.	ordinal	discrete
percentage of words recalled on a memory test	10%, 38%, 76%	ratio	continuous

and research hypotheses involve the study of noncausal relationships. In noncausal relationships, the researcher does not assume that values on one variable cause or influence the values on another variable. For example, many colleges and universities use an applicant's SAT score in deciding whether to admit or reject the applicant's college application. Many of these schools have found that a relationship exists between SAT score, a variable, and a student's grade point average in the freshman year, another variable. Students with high SAT scores tend to have higher grade point averages than students with low SAT scores. Although a relationship exists, it is not causal. In other words, it is incorrect to assume that SAT scores *cause* a student to have a particular grade point average. Rather, the colleges and universities assume that whatever skills or knowledge the SAT measures are the same as those that are needed in performing well in college. It should be mentioned that this relationship is not perfect. In other words, the SAT seldom predicts a student's *exact* grade point average. A number of studies have shown that this relationship between SAT scores and grade point average is not perfect; consequently many institutions rely on additional variables such as high-school courses taken and high-school rank in predicting college success.

Other research hypotheses involve the study of causal relationships. If the researcher has control over the variables in the research study, then it is possible to test for causal effects of one variable on another.

INDEPENDENT AND DEPENDENT VARIABLES

Researchers study causal relationships in an experiment. A **causal relationship** is one in which the values of one variable cause or influence particular values on another variable. In behavioral science research, most causal relationships take the form of a researcher's manipulation of some aspect of the environment, causing a particular behavior to occur.

These causal relationships are studied under conditions in which the researcher tries to control other variables. Controlling a variable can require keeping its value constant in the study i.e., ensuring that it doesn't change. For instance, McClain kept the testing environment constant. Every student took the test in a room alone with the experimenter. The number of other people in the room was always the same, one. Therefore, any differences in behavior could not be explained by saying that some students had more people in the testing room than others. In behavioral science experiments, controlling variables prevents the possibility of biasing the behaviors being studied.

Control can also involve the use of a control group, a group which is not subjected to the researcher's manipulation in a study. The behavior of a control group can be compared with that of other groups in an experiment. And, control can involve the manipulation of the environment itself. Researchers often exercise control by systematically changing some aspect of the environment (a variable) in order to study behavior.

Every experiment has two important kinds of variables, the independent variable and the dependent variable. The **independent variable** is that aspect of the experimental setting that the researcher manipulates or changes. The **dependent variable** in behavioral research is the variable that involves some aspect of behavior—how the participant responds or what the participant does or feels in response to the independent variable. The dependent variable can be viewed as the variable that "depends" on what the participant does.

A causal relationship in an experiment is based on the assumption that the independent variable causes or influences what is observed in the dependent variable. In behavioral science experiments, the researcher varies something in the environment, the independent variable, and looks for its influence on a behavior, the dependent variable.

Consider the example of an experiment investigating sleep. Let's assume that 40 volunteers who have trouble falling asleep are given a new drug that is supposed to help them fall asleep. A researcher might randomly assign 10 volunteers to a control group in which no drug is given; each participant drinks a neutral solution called a placebo. (The placebo solution ensures that it is the effect of the drug itself and not the volunteer's perception of receiving a drug that is critical to the results.) Ten other volunteers are given 25 ml of the drug, another 10 are given 50 ml, and the other 10 are given 100 ml. The drugs are given at the same time of night and the researcher assigns each participant to identical separate rooms in a hospital. The time it takes each participant to fall asleep following the drug is recorded.

The researcher is interested in the causal relationship between drug dosage and falling asleep. The drug dosage is the independent variable and the dosages of 0, 25, 50, and 100 ml are the levels. Researchers often refer to levels of the independent variable as conditions in the study. The dependent variable is the time it takes to fall asleep, with potential values of 0 min (falling asleep immediately), to whatever time it takes for the last participant to fall asleep. If other variables such as the immediate surroundings, how long the participants have been awake before the drug was administered, and so on are controlled, then any real difference in the time it takes to fall asleep can be attributed to the drug dosage.

The drug experiment is an example of a true experiment in that the experimenter manipulates the independent variable. The participants are randomly assigned to a particular level of the independent variable. In Chapter 1, quasi experiments were discussed. In a quasi experiment the experimenter may not have total control and cannot randomly assign participants to the values of the independent variable. Random assignment in a study means that a participant has an equal chance of serving in any one of the conditions in the study.

When studying characteristics of the participant as a variable, a researcher seldom has the opportunity to randomly assign participants to particular characteristics. For example, in studies of sex differences, a researcher cannot randomly assign an individual to be male or female. People come into the study as either women or men. Behavioral differences found between men and women are important. However, a researcher may have difficulty in attributing sex differences to particular biological or environmental factors because the researcher is unable to control the previous influence of these factors.

Quasi experiments are used because they may be the only type of study available to the researcher. When using a quasi experiment, a researcher must be careful about making causal statements.

The McClain study is a quasi experiment. The independent variable in a quasi experiment is referred to as a quasi-independent variable. The quasi-independent variable is the type of student with three values tested—"A," "C," and "F" grades on previous tests. McClain could not randomly assign students to one of the three values. The participants came into the study having performed at one of the three levels.

Because McClain could not randomly assign her subjects, she could not know if the differences between them were the result of differences in the amount they studied or differences in intellectual ability among other possibilities. McClain is restricted to reporting that the different types of students use different test strategies. Using the strategies of an "A" student does not ensure that a student will become an "A" student.

McClain predicted differences among these students in their test-taking strategies. Each behavior of test-taking behavior is a possible dependent variable. For the example in this chapter, the dependent variable is the number of alternatives read for each question. However, there were several additional dependent variables in the study, including number of correct answers students anticipated after reading the question and the number of questions students initially skipped.

Experiments, both true and quasi experiments, share certain features. The behaviors are represented by the dependent variables. An experiment may have more than one dependent variable. Also, there may be one or more independent or quasi-independent variables, which the researcher proposes are influencing the behaviors studied. The simplest type of experiment must have at least two values of the independent variable. Without two values of the independent variable, the researcher is unable to make comparisons in the behaviors. The use of particular statistical procedures and tests in behavioral science research depends on the type of study conducted and the values of the dependent variable. The values of a variable correspond to one of four scales of measurement.

SCALES OF MEASUREMENT

Every variable whether it is an independent or dependent variable can be classified on a particular scale of measurement. We will begin with the most basic and proceed to those that make more assumptions about the values of the variable. Figure 2.1 and the Table 2.2 provide examples for each type of scale of measurement.

Nominal Scale

A variable that has values on a nominal scale of measurement is often referred to as a nominal variable. The word *nominal* comes from the Latin word for name. It is a good word to use because a nominal variable has values

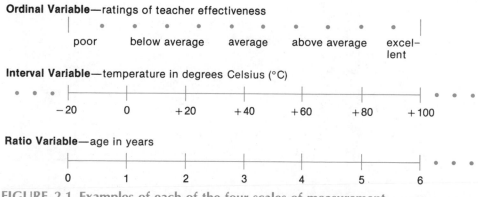

FIGURE 2.1 Examples of each of the four scales of measurement.

TABLE 2.3   Examples of a Regular Frequency Distribution and a Grouped Frequency Distribution

Regular Frequency Distribution (Number of Alternatives Read by "A" Students)	
Number of alternatives	Frequency
4.0	7
3.9	2
3.8	2
3.7	0
3.6	3
3.5	1
3.4	2
3.3	0
3.2	0
3.1	1
3.0	1
2.9	0
2.8	1

Grouped Frequency Distribution (Test Scores [70 Max.] From the McClain Example)	
Test score	Frequency
68–70	2
65–67	4
62–64	5
59–61	6
56–58	6
53–55	6
50–52	6
47–49	4
44–46	5
41–43	3
38–40	3
35–37	3
32–34	2
29–31	2
26–28	1
23–25	1
20–22	1

that could be viewed as names. There is no way of ordering these values on a numerical or quantitative scale. The values of a **nominal scale** are not related to each other on any type of numerical dimension or scale. Nominal variables include sex, color terms, names, and political party. Sex has two values, male and female. Political party can have several values, Democrat, Republican, Libertarian, and so on. In each case, the values are distinct, separate, and have no underlying numerical order.

Ordinal Scale

There are variables for which the values can be ordered on a dimension. Yet, the values may not be equally spaced on the dimension. Variables that have values that can be ordered but which are not equally spaced on a scale or dimension are referred to as **ordinal variables.** The word ordinal denotes order and nothing more. Grade received in a class could be considered an ordinal variable. The differences between an "A" and "B" may not be the same as the difference between a "C" and "D." The performance difference between a person with an "A" and one with a "B" may be very small, yet the difference between two people with a "C" and a "D" might be quite large.

Variables that have ranks as values are common ordinal variables in behavioral science research. If I asked you to rank your favorite top ten schools, the differences between the schools would probably not be equal. You could order the schools but the rank values would not accurately reflect the differences between schools.

Rating teachers from below average to excellent is another ordinal variable. It may take a truly outstanding teacher to get an "excellent" rather than an "above average" from you, but the difference between an "average" and "above average" teacher may not be as great.

Interval Scale

Variables that have values that can be ordered and have equal intervals between values are called **interval variables.** With interval variables it is possible to perform meaningful operations using addition and subtraction. An interval scale does not assume a real zero point. A real zero point means the absence of whatever the variable represents. Variables on an interval scale may have an arbitrary zero point. A good example is Centigrade temperature. Zero has been arbitrarily defined as the freezing point of water. It is not the absence of heat. We can describe the difference between the temperatures of 10°C and 15°C as being 5 degrees, and we know that this is equal to the temperature difference between 50°C and 55°C. Describing differences involves subtraction. Yet, because 0°C does not represent a real zero point, we cannot make what are called ratio comparisons—those involving multiplication and division. It doesn't make sense to say that 50°C is twice as warm as 25°C. All we can say is that it is 25 degrees warmer.

Some researchers use rating scales without a real zero and assume equal intervals between values. For instance, you might be asked to rate a movie on a 1–to–7 scale. If the person is making judgments using equal intervals, then the ratings can be assumed to be on an interval scale of measurement.

Ratio Scale

The last scale of measurement involves variables with values that are equally spaced and have a real zero point. With a ratio variable, it is possible to make ratio comparisons. Weight and age are two examples of ratio variables. Values are equally spaced on a number line and zero defines the absence of either weight or age. An individual who is 55 years old is 5 years older than someone 50 years old, the same as the difference between a person 15 and one 10. This is the same property found for interval variables. Yet, a ratio variable allows one to make ratio comparisons. A person who is 50 is 5 times older than a person 10 years old (50/10 = 5). This is a comparison that was not possible with the interval scale.

For statistical purposes, the distinction between an interval and a ratio variable is not critical. Most of the statistical procedures appropriate for a ratio variable will be appropriate for an interval variable. However, differences exist in statistical procedures between these variables and ordinal variables and between ordinal and nominal variables.

CONTINUOUS VERSUS DISCRETE VARIABLES

Another distinction between variables is the one between continuous and discrete variables. (The term *noncontinuous* is sometimes used by researchers instead of discrete.) This distinction does not involve the values for nominal variables. It is important only for variables that can be ordered on a number line, a dimension which lists values from lowest to highest. If the possible values of an interval or ratio variable can be arranged on a number line without any breaks or omissions in the number line, then the variable is **continuous.** If on the other hand, the possible values are from an ordinal variable or if there are breaks in the number line for an interval or ratio variable, then the variable is **discrete.** Figure 2.2 displays this concept. When talking about a continuous variable, the assumption is that *all* decimal or fractional values are possible. When only whole numbers or integers are possible, then the variable is discrete.

It should be emphasized that the decision about whether a variable is

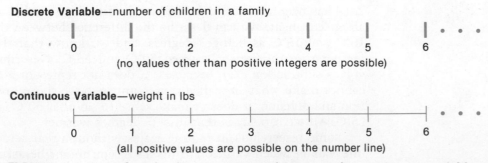

FIGURE 2.2 Examples of a discrete (noncontinuous) and a continuous variable.

continuous or discrete is based on *possible* values of the variable. You don't need to actually have all values on the number line represented in your data for a variable to be continuous. As long as the possibility exists, the variable would be classified as continuous.

CONSTRUCTING A FREQUENCY DISTRIBUTION

A basic procedure in descriptive statistics is organizing the findings of a study by tallying or counting the number of participants who responded with a particular value of a given variable. Organizing the behaviors of a sample of participants by counting the number of participants who behaved in a particular way provides the researcher with an interpretable picture of the findings. For example, you may have found it easier to understand your performance on a test when an instructor provides the number of students who scored within particular intervals. The tallying or counting of participants by each value on a variable results in a **frequency distribution.** There are a number of different types of frequency distributions.

REGULAR AND GROUPED FREQUENCY DISTRIBUTIONS

The most common types of frequency distributions involve two columns of information. The left column contains the values of the variable being summarized. These values can be listed separately or as groups of values called class intervals. The right column contains the number or frequency of participants who generated that particular value.

The goal in constructing a frequency distribution is to organize and summarize information in an understandable framework. Presenting the values as they occur in a study may not be very meaningful or interpretable. The data in Table 2.1 are presented in this fashion. They do not lend themselves to easy interpretation. In using a frequency distribution, the researcher organizes the data based on the values of the variable. Although there are no rigid rules in constructing a frequency distribution, most researchers tend to include no more than 20 values or class intervals. If the entire range of values is 20 or fewer, then each value represents a separate entry in the frequency distribution. This type of frequency distribution is called a regular frequency distribution. If, however, the range is greater than 20, then the researcher may decide to group several values together in each entry within the frequency distribution. These groupings or class intervals will enable the researcher to have a frequency distribution with fewer than 20 entries. Grouped frequency distributions have groups of values represented as class intervals. Table 2.3 provides an example of each type of distribution. The frequency distribution at the top represents the data for the "A" students from the chapter example in Table 2.1. The grouped frequency distribution at the bottom lists the overall test scores, the number of questions answered correctly, for the entire sample of students in the McClain study.

There are several important points to note. The first is that numerical values are arranged in descending order. If the values are nominal, then they are often arranged alphabetically. Second, all values between the high and low values are represented even if their frequencies are 0. This is done to provide a complete picture of the data. Notice that there were no participants in the top example of Table 2.3 who averaged either 3.7, 3.3, 3.2, or 2.9 alternatives read.

The grouped frequency distribution at the bottom of Table 2.3 has values presented in groups of three. Again, note that the the top interval and bottom interval include the highest and lowest values in the study. Also notice that all the intervals are of equal size. The number of intervals in an interval depends on the researcher's choice and the range of the values. In general, most grouped frequency distributions have between 10 and 20 equally sized intervals. Box 2.1 lists several guidelines for constructing grouped frequency distributions.

BOX 2.1   **Guidelines for Constructing a Grouped Frequency Distribution**

1. **Determine the range of values.**
   Subtract the lowest value from the highest value in the set of values. Then add 1 to this difference. This value represents the range for your distribution.

2. **Determine the interval size and number of intervals.**
   The grouped frequency distribution should have approximately 15 to 20 intervals. Divide the range obtained in Step 1 by an integer between 15 and 20. If possible, you should choose a value that will result in an answer with a whole number. For instance, if the range is 75, divide by 15 to get an interval size of 5; or if the range is 108, divide by 18 to get an interval size of 6. The number you divide by will determine the number of intervals. The resulting answer will be the interval size.

3. **Create the intervals beginning with the lowest interval.**
   The bottom interval will start with your lowest value. The highest value in that interval will be equal to the lowest value + interval size − 1. For example, if the lowest value is 12 and the interval size is 4, then the interval will contain values between 12 and 15 (12 + 4 − 1). Each succeeding interval will start with the next highest value. To determine the high value for each interval, add the interval size − 1 to the lowest value in the interval. Continue to create intervals until the highest value is included in an interval.

4. **Determine the frequencies in each interval.**
   Tally the number of occurrences of values within each interval. This tally serves as the frequency for that interval.

For regular and grouped frequency distributions, the right-hand column is often labeled f for frequency and lists the number of observations or participants with a particular value or within a particular interval of values. The sum of the frequencies should equal the total number of data values in the sample. The symbol N is used to denote the number of participants or observations in the sample.

RELATIVE FREQUENCY DISTRIBUTIONS

Another type of frequency distribution can be constructed using the information found in either a regular or grouped frequency distribution. This distribution is called a relative frequency distribution and has a third column labeled relative frequency or rel f. Relative frequency refers to the percentage of the sample found within each value or class interval. It is calculated by dividing the frequency for a particular value or interval by N, the total number of observations or participants in the sample. This value is then multiplied by 100. In Table 2.4, the frequency distribution for the "C" students from the chapter example is presented along with the relative frequencies. The relative frequency reports the percentage of the total number of obser-

TABLE 2.4 The Relative Frequency Distribution for the "C" Students from the McClain Study

Number of Alternatives	Frequency	Relative Frequency
3.1	1	5
3.0	0	0
2.9	0	0
2.8	0	0
2.7	0	0
2.6	0	0
2.5	1	5
2.4	1	5
2.3	0	0
2.2	1	5
2.1	1	5
2.0	1	5
1.9	2	10
1.8	4	20
1.7	1	5
1.6	1	5
1.5	0	0
1.4	3	15
1.3	1	5
1.2	1	5
1.1	1	5

vations within each value or interval. The sum of the relative frequencies must equal 100. The advantage of a relative frequency distribution over a frequency distribution is that you can compare the relative numbers of observations among values or intervals from a sample much more easily than if you have only frequencies.

CUMULATIVE FREQUENCY AND CUMULATIVE RELATIVE FREQUENCY DISTRIBUTIONS

The last two types of frequency distributions are extensions of the distributions just discussed. Rather than reporting the number of observations within an interval, it is possible to report the number of observations within that interval and all intervals below it. This results in a cumulative frequency distribution. The column label "cum f" is used to denote the number of observations within that interval and all intervals below it. At the left in Table 2.5, the data for the "F" students are shown in a frequency distribution. To calculate the cumulative frequency for each interval, the frequency for that interval is added to the frequencies of all intervals below it. Therefore, the bottom interval will have a cumulative frequency equal to the frequency for that interval, and the top interval will have a value of N, the total number of observations in the sample.

To create a cumulative relative frequency distribution, the cumulative

TABLE 2.5	The Cumulative Frequency and Cumulative Relative Frequency Distributions for the "F" Students from the McClain Study		
Number of Alternatives	**Frequency**	**Cumulative Frequency**	**Cumulative Relative Frequency**
2.1	1	20	100
2.0	0	19	95
1.9	0	19	95
1.8	2	19	95
1.7	2	17	85
1.6	3	15	75
1.5	5	12	60
1.4	3	7	35
1.3	1	4	20
1.2	0	3	15
1.1	1	3	15
1.0	0	2	10
.9	1	2	10
.8	0	1	5
.7	1	1	5

frequency values are divided by N and then multiplied by 100. These values will also increase from the bottom interval to the top interval. The top cumulative relative frequency must equal 100. The cumulative relative frequency distribution provides an important piece of information. These frequency values represent percentile ranks. You should be familiar with percentile ranks. A percentile rank refers to the percentage of individuals in a sample who have a particular value or a lower value. Therefore, if your percentile rank is 93, you know that 93% of the sample had a value equal to or less than your value. In the cumulative relative frequency distribution shown in Table 2.5, the percentile ranking for individuals who read an average of 1.6 alternatives was 75. This indicates that 75% of the "F" students read an average of 1.6 or *fewer* alternatives; 25% of the "F" students read more than 1.6 alternatives.

GRAPHING FREQUENCY DISTRIBUTIONS

The information contained in a frequency distribution can be represented in the form of a graph. There are different types of graphs depending on the scale of measurement of the variable and the type of frequency distribution used. For all distributions, the values of the variable are represented on the abscissa or x-axis of the graph. The frequencies are placed on the ordinate or y-axis.

The values of the variable are reported in ascending order on the x-axis. When the values are grouped in class intervals for grouped frequency distributions and for relative frequency distributions, researchers often report the midpoint of each interval. The midpoint is found by averaging the two extreme values for each interval.

Types of graphs

The graph of the grouped frequency distribution for the overall test scores in the chapter example is shown in Figure 2.3. As you can see, each interval is represented by the midpoint of the interval and the frequency for each interval is shown by a point. A graph in which the frequencies are represented as points and the points are then connected by lines is referred to as a **frequency polygon.** A frequency polygon is common when the variable on the x-axis is an interval or ratio variable that is continuous.

When the variable is discrete and in interval form, a histogram is often used. A **histogram** represents the frequencies for each value as bars with the bars touching each other. In Figure 2.4, a relative frequency distribution is shown for teacher ratings for a fictitious teacher. Students were asked to rate the teacher on a 1-to-7 scale, with 1 representing "very poor" and 7 representing "excellent." The majority of the students rated the teacher at a 4 or higher. Histograms are used when the researcher wants to convey to the reader that the values are discrete, that no possible values exist between those reported on the x-axis.

The last type of graph is called a bar graph. A **bar graph** uses bars that are separate and not touching to represent the frequencies of the values. A bar

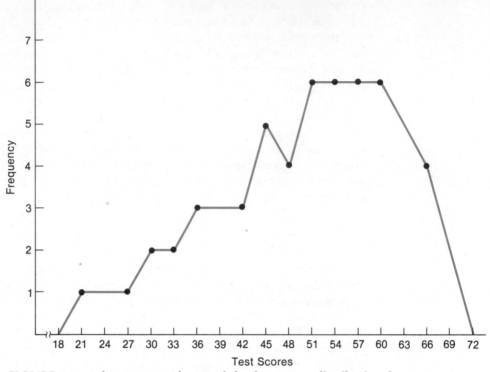

FIGURE 2.3 A frequency polygon of the frequency distribution for test scores from the chapter example.

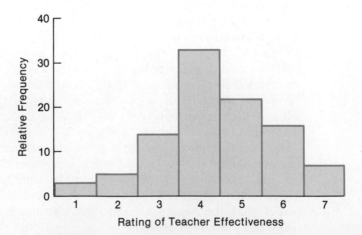

FIGURE 2.4 A histogram of the relative frequency distribution for ratings of teacher effectiveness.

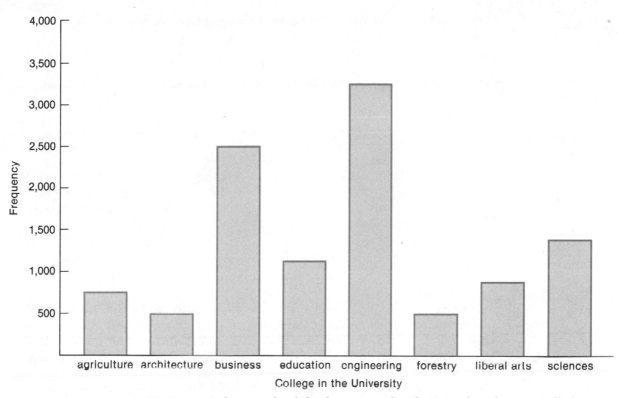

FIGURE 2.5 A bar graph of the frequency distribution of students enrolled in various colleges within a university.

graph is appropriate with nominal and ordinal variables. For nominal variables, the values can be ordered alphabetically. For ordinal variables, the values should be listed in ascending order. In Figure 2.5, a bar graph is shown for the number of students enrolled in different colleges at a particular university. Notice that the colleges are listed alphabetically. The bars should be of equal widths and the spacing between bars should be equal.

GRAPHING CUMULATIVE FREQUENCY DISTRIBUTIONS

The same procedures are followed for graphing cumulative frequency and cumulative relative frequency distributions. The only important difference is in listing the values on the x-axis for interval and ratio variables. The frequencies for these distributions represent the number of observations in a particular class interval and in all intervals below it. Therefore, the value reported on the x-axis must be the highest value in the interval. The midpoint will not be the highest value. In fact, the highest value for an interval is called the upper real limit. **Real limits** are the values that separate class intervals into equal intervals in a frequency distribution. They are halfway between

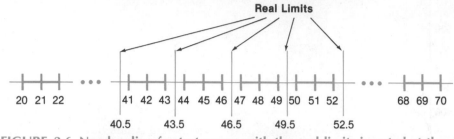

FIGURE 2.6 Number line for test scores with the real limits inserted at the midpoint between the defining values for the intervals. Note that the difference between the real limits is 3, which is the size of each interval.

the highest value listed in one interval and the lowest value listed in the next interval above.

In Figure 2.6, the number line lists some of the apparent test values for the frequency distribution of test scores from the chapter example (see Table 2.3). Note the gap between test values. The real limit for an interval is the midpoint between the high value in one interval and the low value in the next interval. Real limits exist at the lower and upper ends of every interval. For a regular frequency distribution, these limits are the midpoints between

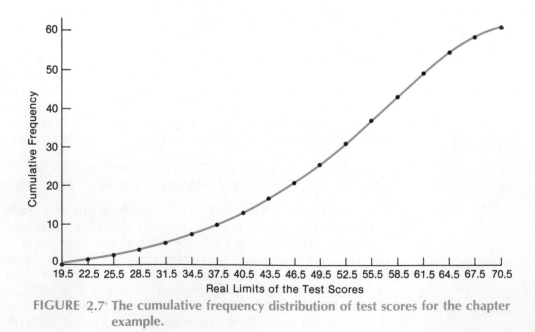

FIGURE 2.7 The cumulative frequency distribution of test scores for the chapter example.

each pair of values in the frequency distribution. The difference between the real limits at the two ends of an interval define the interval size. The difference between the real limits for each interval in Figure 2.6 is 3, which is the size of the interval.

The cumulative frequency distribution for the test scores from the McClain example is graphically represented in Figure 2.7. Note that the upper real limit is shown for each interval. By reporting the real limit, the researcher knows that the cumulative frequency includes all observations at or below that value.

In summary, frequency distributions have frequencies represented on the y-axis and values of the variable on the x-axis. For regular, grouped, and relative frequency distributions the value or midpoint of each interval is reported on the x-axis. For cumulative and cumulative relative frequency distributions, the upper real limit for each interval is reported on the x-axis. Guidelines for graphing frequency distributions are listed in Box 2.2.

BOX 2.2   Guidelines for Graphing a Frequency Distribution

1. The y-axis should be approximately ¾ the length of the x-axis.
2. Values of the variable in the distribution are listed on the x-axis.

   For nominal variables, values should be listed alphabetically; for all other variables, values should be listed in ascending order left-to-right.

   For grouped frequency distributions, list the midpoint of each interval.

   For cumulative frequency distributions, the upper real limits should be listed.

3. Frequencies and relative frequencies are listed on the y-axis.

   To determine the scale for frequencies, list your highest frequency (or relative frequency, cumulative frequency, or cumulative relative frequency) at the top and 0 at the bottom of the y-axis.

4. Label your axes with meaningful titles (i.e., the name of the variable on the x-axis and frequency, relative frequency, etc. on the y-axis)

5. Use the appropriate graph, bar graph, histogram, or frequency polygon.

   bar graph: nominal variables

   histogram: discrete variables

   frequency polygon: continuous variables

SHAPES OF DISTRIBUTIONS

Frequency distributions are described in terms of their shape. There are several common shapes that occur in the behavioral sciences. They are based on two properties of the distribution. The first is the modality. **Modality** describes the number of "humps" in the frequency distribution. Each hump or mode indicates an interval with a high frequency of observations. Distributions with one mode are called unimodal. The other property of distribution is symmetry. **Symmetry** occurs when the shape of the left half of the distribution is a mirror image of the right half.

A common frequency distribution is the normal distribution. It is bell-shaped and is shown in Figure 2.8a. Notice that it is unimodal (has one mode or high point) and is symmetric. In a normal distribution, the majority of the frequencies will occur near the middle values in the distribution and the frequencies decrease near the extreme values.

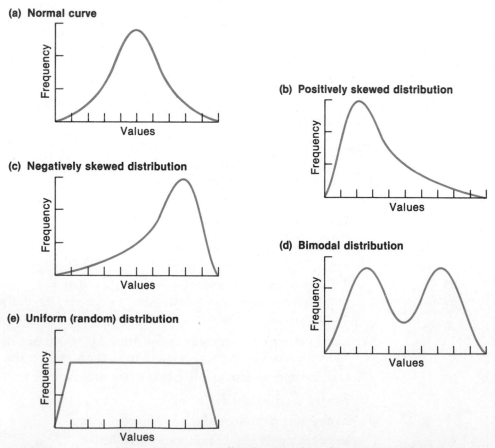

FIGURE 2.8 Examples of frequency distributions found in behavioral science research.

Figures 2.8b and 2.8c are examples of skewed distribution. A skewed distribution is unimodal but not symmetric. Figure 2.8b is a positively skewed distribution with greater frequencies for the lower values and fewer frequencies for the higher values. The "tail" of the distribution points in the "positive" direction. An example of a positively skewed distribution is an extremely difficult test in which there are few high scores and many low scores. A negatively skewed distribution (Figure 2.8c) has a greater number of values occurring at the upper end of the distribution and the tail of the distribution points in the negative direction.

Bimodal distributions also occur. In Figure 2.8d, the frequency distribution has two modes or humps. This can occur when the distribution is a combination of observations from two different populations. Finally, Figure 2.8e shows a uniform distribution. This occurs when the frequencies are equally distributed across all intervals.

A FINAL WORD ABOUT THE McCLAIN STUDY

McClain used a number of descriptive and inferential statistical procedures not described in this chapter. They will not be discussed now, but we will discuss her findings. She found that type of student was related to test-taking behaviors. "A" students differed in their test-taking strategies from "C" and "F" students. "A" students were more likely to read more alternatives than the other students. They also tended to anticipate correct answers before reading the alternatives and critiqued incorrect alternatives. They also skipped more questions when going through the test than the other students, and returned to the questions later. McClain does not argue that adopting an "A" student strategy will ensure better test performance, but she does suggest that "A" students were more thorough in considering each question than the other students. She feels confident that there are different test strategies used by good and poor students and that more research is needed to determine if the strategies of good students would help the poor student.

SUMMARY

A research study involves variables. A variable describes the characteristics or properties of a set of objects, events, behaviors, or environments of interest to the researcher. The values are the individual characteristics. Variables can be described in terms of their scale of measurement. The most basic scale is the nominal scale for which values are not ordered. An ordinal variable has ordered values that are not equally spaced. The interval and ratio variables have values that are equally spaced on a number line. The ratio variable also has a real zero point.

In an experiment, the researcher is interested in the causal relationship between the independent and dependent variables. The independent variable is often manipulated or controlled by the experimenter and the dependent variable is the participant's behavior. Research hypotheses are stated in terms of the independent variable influencing or causing the behavior measured by the dependent variable.

The behaviors that are recorded in a study can be represented in a frequency distribution. A frequency distribution includes the values of the variable and the frequencies or number of times each value occurred. When the frequencies are divided by N, the total number of observations in the study, a relative frequency distribution is formed. Cumulative frequency distributions report the number of observations for a particular interval or value and all intervals and values below it.

Frequency distributions can be represented graphically. The frequencies are listed on the y-axis and values or intervals of the variable are listed on the x-axis. Three types of graphs are used, frequency polygons, histograms, and bar graphs. The choice of graph depends on the variable in the distribution. Frequency distributions can be described in terms of modality and symmetry. Common shapes of frequency distributions include the normal curve, skewed distributions, bimodal distributions, and uniform distributions.

EXERCISES

1. Explain how a research study such as an experiment usually involves more than one variable.

2. In determining whether a variable is continuous or discrete, it is necessary to know the *values* for the variable. Explain.

3. State whether each item below is a variable or a value. If it is a variable, then list a possible value. If it is a value, then define the variable.
   a. red
   b. SAT test score
   c. 3:05 P.M.
   d. 25 mg of drug X
   e. Mary
   f. number of credit hours

4. For each experiment below, identify the independent variable, list its values, and identify the dependent variable.
   a. In order to measure the effectiveness of assertiveness training on self-esteem, at the beginning of a school semester 40 female college students are randomly assigned to one of four conditions, no assertiveness training, 1 week of training, 3 weeks of training, or 5 weeks of training. Two months into the semester, each student is given a personality test that measures her self-esteem from 0 (no self-esteem) to 30 (extremely high self-esteem).
   b. In order to determine if the results of surveys influence people, 60 shoppers are shown one of three different fictitious surveys. The surveys differ in terms of the listing of what is the most important problem in society today (e.g., crime, government budget, relationship with

the Soviet Union). After seeing the survey, the shoppers are asked what they consider to be the most important problem today.

    c. An educator is interested in determining if typed papers receive better grades than handwritten papers. The same 500-word essay is given to 80 school teachers to grade. For 40 of the teachers it is typed; for the other 40, the essay is handwritten. Each teacher is asked to grade the essay using the letter grades "A" through "F."

    d. To determine the effect of auditory distractions on driving skills, 90 senior, male high-school students are tested on an apparatus that measures the time it takes to press a brake pedal when a red light is flashed. For 30 of the students the test occurs in a quiet room. For another 30 students, a car radio playing popular music is on during the test. For each of the remaining 30 students, a person sits next to him and engages him in conversation during the test. The average response time (in sec) to press the brake pedal is measured for 20 trials on the machine for each student.

5. For each of the variables you identified in Exercise 4, determine the scale of measurement.

6. A relationship may exist between two variables, yet the relationship may not be a causal one. What is unique about a causal relationship?

7. A researcher studying smokers and nonsmokers finds a relationship between smoking and coffee drinking. Smokers drink more coffee than nonsmokers. Can the researcher conclude that smoking causes more coffee drinking? Explain.

8. IQ scores are designed so that the average or mean IQ is 100. The scale is developed on that assumption. The differences between IQ scores are designed to reflect differences in test performance. What type of scale of measurement does IQ score correspond to? Why?

9. For each variable below, identify the scale of measurement:

    a. the ranking of the instructors you have this semester in terms of the interest they generate in their courses.

    b. the number of classes missed by each student in your class this semester.

    c. satisfaction ratings of students in a residence hall using a 1–to–5 scale.

    d. the number of magazines you subscribe to.

    e. the hometown of each student in your class.

10. Determine whether each of the variables in Exercise 9 is continuous or discrete. Explain your answer in each case (using potential values if necessary).

11. Assume that you are constructing a frequency distribution for the variable "number of magazines subscribed to" for your class, with each student responding. Do you think a regular or grouped frequency distribution would be necessary? Why? What type of graph would be appropriate for this frequency distribution?

12. The number of siblings for each student at a small college is recorded. The distribution of values is shown below. Graph the frequency distribution. How would you describe the shape of the distribution?

Number of Siblings	Frequency
7	2
6	11
5	43
4	169
3	577
2	1,809
1	1,733
0	321

13. For the distribution in Exercise 12, construct a cumulative relative frequency distribution. What is the number of siblings that corresponds to the 50th percentile for this college?

14. An instructor informs you that the grades in a course are normally distributed with a low grade of 51, a high grade of 98, and an average grade of 75. How would you describe the distribution of grades in this course, that is, where would you expect most grades to be located?

15. For Exercise 12, what are the real limits for the two categories of 4 siblings and 3 siblings?

16. Thirty-six students are asked to estimate the probability that all types of cancer will have a cure by the year 2000. Each student's estimate is listed below. Construct the appropriate frequency and relative frequency distributions.

.80	.65	.70	.40	.00	.15
.25	.50	.50	.33	.67	.90
.95	.00	.35	.60	.65	.80
.25	.40	.50	.75	.50	.85
.50	.95	.20	.45	.70	.90
.33	.40	.85	.50	.55	.67

17. Graph the relative frequency distribution from Exercise 16. Which probability category has the highest frequency of response?

18. The following values were taken from a table of random numbers. The assumption is that each of the digits from 0 through 9 should be repre-

sented equally often. Construct the frequency distribution for these digits and then graph it. Which of the shapes from Figure 2.8 does it most closely resemble?

```
9 9 5 6 2 7 2 9 0 5
5 6 4 2 0 6 9 9 9 4
9 8 8 7 2 3 1 0 1 6
7 1 1 5 4 1 8 7 3 8
4 4 0 1 3 4 8 8 4 0
6 3 2 1 3 2 1 0 6 9
5 0 6 3 4 1 2 9 5 2
0 0 5 8 2 0 4 7 1 3
8 7 9 1 7 7 7 3 4 8
4 2 2 0 6 3 5 1 2 6
```

19. Listed below are three frequency distributions, the one on the left is normally distributed, the middle is skewed, and the one on the right is a uniform distribution. Construct a cumulative frequency distribution for each and graph it. How do the shapes of these cumulative frequency distributions differ?

X	A Frequency	X	B Frequency	X	C Frequency
9	1	9	3	9	7
8	2	8	19	8	7
7	6	7	18	7	7
6	14	6	10	6	7
5	17	5	6	5	7
4	14	4	4	4	7
3	6	3	2	3	7
2	2	2	1	2	7
1	1	1	0	1	7

20. An environmental psychologist asks residents to rate the attractiveness of a new monument located in the town square. She finds that the ratings are bimodally distributed. What does that mean?

CHAPTER
3

Measures of Central Tendency and Variability

TERMS DISCUSSED

measures of central tendency
- the mean ($\overline{X}$)
- the median (M_d)
- the mode (M_o)

measures of variability
- the range
- the variance
- the standard deviation

parameters and statistics

sum of the squared deviations

PROCEDURES DESCRIBED

statistical notation (ΣX and ΣX^2)

calculating the mean ($\overline{X}$)

determining the median (M_d)

determining the mode (M_o)

graphing a statistic

calculating the range

calculating the sum of the squared deviations (SS)

calculating the variance

calculating the standard deviation

*Two researchers, Elizabeth Loftus and John Palmer, published a study
in 1974 that investigated how accurate people were in making judgments
from memory. In reviewing the literature, they found that people often are
inaccurate in judging speed, time, and distance. To identify what might
cause these inaccuracies, they showed films of traffic accidents to college
students. They then asked each student several specific questions about
each accident. One of the questions concerned the speed of the cars at the
time of the accident. Of the 45 students in the study, 9 were asked, "About
how fast were the cars going when they hit each other?" Another nine of
the students were asked the same question but the verb "hit" was replaced
with "smashed, collided, bumped, or contacted." For example, nine
students were given the question, "About how fast were the cars going
when they contacted each other?" Therefore, although the students were
viewing the same accident, Loftus and Palmer were interested in
determining if the different verbs used in the question had an effect on the
students' estimates of the cars' speeds. The estimated speeds are listed in
Table 3.1.*

This study is an example of an experiment. Experiments are studies in
which the researcher is testing for a causal relationship between an independent and dependent variable. The simplest experiment must have at least two
values of the independent variable. Each value of the independent variable
can be thought of as a "condition" in the experiment. Often there are more
than two conditions in experiments. The Loftus and Palmer study had five
conditions, one for each of the five different verbs used.

For a causal relationship to be tested, it is important that the researcher
control the independent variable and any other variables that may influence

TABLE 3.1   Estimated Speeds (mph) by Students in the Loftus and Palmer Study

Verb Used in the Question				
"Smashed"	"Collided"	"Bumped"	"Hit"	"Contacted"
42	39	38	30	31
37	38	35	35	32
38	42	38	33	32
42	37	40	32	30
42	35	37	36	30
44	41	36	36	35
39	39	38	31	33
40	40	41	36	32
45	40	39	37	33

the behavior measured by the dependent variable. "Controlling" the independent variable can involve changing or manipulating values of the variable in order to observe changes in behavior. Participants are often assigned to a condition or value of the variable at random. That is, a participant has an equal chance of being assigned to any condition in the study. Random assignment avoids biases in assigning participants to conditions. This prevents, for instance, participants who serve in the early phases of the study or who are friendly or anxious from being assigned to one particular condition instead of another. Random assignment is designed to ensure that these personal characteristics are "balanced" equally across conditions.

The researcher observes and records some aspect of the participant's behavior which is the dependent variable. The purpose of an experiment is to determine what effect being exposed to or placed in a particular condition will have on a participant's behavior. In this example, Loftus and Palmer observed the effect the different verbs had on the college students' estimates of speed.

Loftus and Palmer's research hypothesis could be stated as "The particular verb used in the question will affect the student's estimate of speed; different verbs will produce different speed estimates." The "verb used in the question," the independent variable, should influence the "estimate of speed," the dependent variable.

MEASURES OF CENTRAL TENDENCY

Researchers often prefer to describe the data for each condition in a study with a single value. The data in each condition represent a sample. Describing a sample of values with a single value makes it easy to compare that sample to other samples.

One type of value that is used in describing a set of values is the measure of central tendency. The **measure of central tendency** provides information about the general location of a set of data values on a number line. The three common measures of central tendency are the mean, median, and mode. When an instructor reports that the average test score was 76, she is probably using the mean. The federal government often reports the median family income, which is the value that separates the top 50% of the families in the nation from the bottom 50%. When a poll reports that 58% of a sample favor a particular candidate, that 58% is the mode. They each use the set of data values in a different way to summarize the location of the set of values. We will look at each measure and then discuss when each is appropriate.

THE MEAN (OR ARITHMETIC AVERAGE), $\overline{X}$

The most frequently used measure of central tendency is the mean. It is identical to what many people refer to as the "average." However, because there is more than one type of average in mathematics, the term *mean* is used to identify the "arithmetic average." It is very easy to calculate. The **mean** is the sum of a set of values divided by the number of values in the set.

Calculating the $\overline{X}$

To express the mean mathematically, we rely on statistical notation. Several different symbols used in statistical notation will be introduced in this chapter and the next. The first statistical symbol is the Greek letter Σ or capital sigma. The capital sigma Σ is used as shorthand for "the sum of." Whatever follows Σ would be added or summed together. For instance,

$$\Sigma(3, 4, 8, 2) = 3 + 4 + 8 + 2 = 17$$

In most instances we do not list the values to be added in parentheses as in the above example. Rather, a *set* of values is indicated by a single letter (e.g., X, Y, Z) or different subscripts with the same letter (e.g., X_1, X_2, X_3). For instance, ΣX means sum all the values in the set defined as X. If X is the set of the four values 3, 4, 8, 2, then

$$\Sigma X = 3 + 4 + 8 + 2 = 17.$$

In the chapter example, there are five different sets of values, each representing a sample of estimated speeds to a different verb. Rather than assigning a different letter (e.g., A, B, C, D, and E) to each set, the same letter, X, could be used with each set having a different subscript. By using the same letter with different subscripts the researcher is indicating that the sets have something in common (they are all values from the same variable, the verb used). Numbers or words are frequently used as subscripts. In this example the verbs are used as subscripts to differentiate among the samples (i.e., X_{hit} would be the set of estimated speeds for those students saw the question with the verb *hit*).

In behavioral research it is common to use the letters X and Y to represent separate sets of values, although there is nothing preventing a researcher from using any letters one wishes to use. In many experiments, X is used to represent the independent variable and Y is used for the dependent variable. The other accepted notation is to use the letter N to represent the number of values in a particular set or sample. Thus, if you have nine values in a sample as we do in each of our five samples of estimated speeds, N would equal 9.

Knowing how to represent both the concept of adding a sample of values together and the number of values in a sample enables one to generate the following equation for calculating the mean,

$$\overline{X} = \Sigma X/N. \qquad [1]^*$$

The symbol $\overline{X}$, pronounced "X bar," is used to represent the mean for a sample. (Some research journals also use the symbol M to represent the sample mean.) Formula 1 would read as the "the mean equals the sum of the set of values represented by X divided by N, the number of values in Set X."

---

*Throughout this text, parenthetical numbers will be used for computational formulas and will be numbered without reference to particular chapters.

TABLE 3.2 **The Calculation of the Mean ($\overline{X}$) for Each Condition in the Loftus and Palmer Example**

Verb Used in the Question				
"Smashed"	*"Collided"*	*"Bumped"*	*"Hit"*	*"Contacted"*
42	39	38	30	31
37	38	35	35	32
38	42	38	33	32
42	37	40	32	30
42	35	37	36	30
44	41	36	36	35
39	39	38	31	33
40	40	41	36	32
45	40	39	37	33
$\Sigma X = 369$	$\Sigma X = 351$	$\Sigma X = 342$	$\Sigma X = 306$	$\Sigma X = 288$
$N = 9$	$N = 9$	$N = 9$	$N = 9$	$N = 9$
$\dfrac{\Sigma X}{N} = \dfrac{369}{9}$	$\dfrac{\Sigma X}{N} = \dfrac{351}{9}$	$\dfrac{\Sigma X}{N} = \dfrac{342}{9}$	$\dfrac{\Sigma X}{N} = \dfrac{306}{9}$	$\dfrac{\Sigma X}{N} = \dfrac{288}{9}$
$\overline{X} = 41$	$\overline{X} = 39$	$\overline{X} = 38$	$\overline{X} = 34$	$\overline{X} = 32$

Let's calculate the mean estimated speed for each of the five sets of values in the example. Each set of values is represented in Table 3.2. At the bottom of each column the sum of the values is presented by ΣX along with the number of values in the Set N. Below those values, Formula 1 was used to calculate the mean.

Although in these cases the calculations resulted in integer values, there are many cases in which the value calculated must be rounded to some number of digits. This often occurs when using calculators or computers that retain many digits in the calculations. Many researchers keep three digits beyond the original values and then round the value to two digits (e.g, when working with integers, use up to three decimal places and then round to two decimal places). A convenient rule in rounding the last digit is that if it is greater than 5, round up and if it is less than 5 round down. If it is 5 round so that the next-to-last digit is even. For example, if the original values were integers and the calculated value was 32.687, the reported value would be 32.69. Or if the calculated value was 1.065, then the reported value would be 1.06. If the original values were in tenths such as 0.6 or 0.4, then a calculated value of 0.3392 would be rounded to 0.339 (two digits beyond the original value). In many cases your instructor can help you or you can examine previous published research for guidance in determining the number of digits to report.

Properties of the $\overline{X}$

Note how this descriptive statistic $\overline{X}$ makes it easier to observe differences in the estimated speeds for the different verbs. The mean allows you to compare the sets of values very quickly and easily. It is unnecessary to compare each value in every set to see that there are differences in the estimated speeds. Many researchers use the mean as their primary measure of central tendency in describing a set of values.

The mean has several important properties. The first is that it is the only measure of central tendency for which every value in a set contributes equally in the calculations. Furthermore, the mean represents the arithmetic "balancing point" for a set of values. If you calculate how far each value of a set deviates from its mean $(X - \overline{X})$ and then add these deviations, $\Sigma(X - \overline{X})$, the sum would be zero. The mean is the only measure of central tendency that will always have 0 for the sum of the deviations. (See Box 3.1 for the mathematical proof.)

In addition, if the deviations from the mean were squared and then added together, $\Sigma(X - \overline{X})^2$, the resulting sum would be less than the sum for any other measure of central tendency. The mean minimizes the squared deviations for the set of values. This is an important property that will be used later in this chapter when calculating measures of variability.

THE MEDIAN (M_d)

The second measure of central tendency is called the median. The **median** is the value for the middle point of the distribution. The symbol M_d is used frequently to represent the median. Although there are a number of different

---

BOX 3.1   **Mathematical Proof that $\Sigma(X - \overline{X}) = 0$**

1. Distribute the summation sign Σ inside the parentheses.

$$\Sigma(X - \overline{X}) = \Sigma X - \Sigma\overline{X}$$

2. The $\overline{X}$ is a constant value. The summation of a constant is equal to N times the constant.

$$\Sigma X - \Sigma\overline{X} = \Sigma X - N \cdot \overline{X}$$

3. Substitute Formula 1 $(\Sigma X/N)$ for the $\overline{X}$.

$$\Sigma X - N \cdot \overline{X} = \Sigma X - N \,(\Sigma X/N)$$

4. Simplify by canceling the N values in the right side of the formula.

$$\Sigma X - N(\Sigma X/N) = \Sigma X - \Sigma X$$

5. The $\Sigma X - \Sigma X$ requires taking a sum and subtracting it which will always equal 0.

$$\Sigma X - \Sigma X = 0.$$

formulas and procedures for determining the median, we will use one of the simpler methods.

Calculating the M_d

The first step in calculating the M_d is to arrange the values in your distribution from highest to lowest. Then determine the middle point. Calculating $(N + 1)/2$ will provide the middle point for the distribution. (N is the total number of values in the distribution.) For example, if the number of values is odd such as 33, then $(N + 1)/2$ will result in $(33 + 1)/2$ or 17. The 17th value in your ordered set is the median. This procedure is illustrated at the top in Table 3.3 for two of the distributions from the chapter example. Prob-

TABLE 3.3 Calculating the Median (M_d) for Four Distributions

When N is Odd

"Smashed" Condition		"Bumped" Condition	
Unordered	*Ordered*	*Unordered*	*Ordered*
42	45	38	41
37	44	35	40
38	42	38	39
42	42	40	38
42	42 ⟵M_d	37	38 ⟵M_d
44	40	36	38
39	39	38	37
40	38	41	36
45	37	39	35

When N is Even

Height (in)		Grade Point Average	
Unordered	*Ordered*	*Unordered*	*Ordered*
62	71	3.19	3.68
58	69	3.64	3.64
71	62 ⎫	2.97	3.21
69	60 ⎬ $M_d = 61$	2.51	3.19
57	58 ⎭	2.33	3.05
60	57	1.98	2.97
		2.68	2.88 ⎫
		3.05	2.77 ⎬ $M_d = 2.82$
		1.70	2.68
		2.77	2.51
		2.88	2.43
		2.43	2.33
		3.21	1.98
		3.68	1.70

lem 3.6 at the end of this chapter requires calculating the median for the other three distributions from the chapter example.

If the distribution has an even number of values then using $(N + 1)/2$ will result in a fraction. For example, if there are 40 values, the median is the 20.5 value $((40 + 1)/2 = 20.5)$. It is then necessary to calculate the average of the 20th and 21st values in the ordered set of values. The bottom two distributions in Table 3.3 illustrate this procedure for two hypothetical distributions; one has 14 values and the other has 6 values.

Reasons for Using the M_d

The median (M_d) is reported less often than the mean. It is useful, however, in three particular situations. The first involves skewed distributions in which the values are not symmetrically distributed. These are distributions in which most of the values are grouped together with a few either extremely high or low values. An example is the positively skewed distribution of exam grades in which a midterm exam is difficult for the majority of students, with most grades between 60 and 75. However, a few students do quite well with grades between 95 and 100. In this situation, the $\overline{X}$ may be a misleading statistic. Because a few people did extremely well on the exam, the $\overline{X}$ may actually be an inflated measure of central tendency. For example, as shown in Table 3.4, the $\overline{X}$ is 74, yet perhaps two-thirds of the class had a score lower than 74.

The value of the M_d, on the other hand, is influenced only by the middle score(s) of the distribution. We might find that the 50th percentile score (the M_d) is 68; one-half of the class had scores above 68 and the other half had scores below 68. In this case, the M_d is actually giving us a better picture of the exam scores than the $\overline{X}$, because the $\overline{X}$ is influenced by the few extreme values. As shown in Figure 3.1, the mean is "pulled" toward the tail of a skewed distribution. When researchers find that the distribution of values is skewed, they may decide to report the M_d as the measure of central tendency rather than the $\overline{X}$.

Another instance in which the M_d is preferred over the $\overline{X}$ occurs when values for some participants are missing from the distribution. For instance, a researcher may be investigating problem-solving behavior. The measure of interest to her could be the amount of time it takes to solve a problem during a 30-minute session. She finds that 47 of her 51 participants solve the problem. Yet, four do not solve the problem. She is faced with a dilemma. Does she give them scores of 30 minutes (the maximum time limit), or some greater score, or does she drop them from the study? All of these options have some problems. By giving them a score of 30 minutes she is really underestimating the $\overline{X}$ time it took her participants to solve the problem. She really isn't justified in giving them some greater time value, because she's not sure how long it would have actually taken those four participants to complete the problem. And, if she excludes those four participants, she might be accused of biasing her findings by only including those participants who could solve the problem. She would probably decide that the best option is to report

TABLE 3.4 The Difference between the $\overline{X}$ and the M_d in a Positively Skewed Distribution

Test Scores
99
96
94
91
87
78
73
72
68 ⎫ $M_d = 68$
68 ⎭
67
65
65
65
64
61
60
59
$\Sigma X = 1332$
$N = 18$
$\overline{X} = 74$

the M_d for her set of scores. She would be justified in reporting the time for the "middle" person. That value would be the time it took the 26th person (51/2 + 0.5) to complete the problem.

Lastly, the M_d is used when the values arc from an ordinal scale of measurement. Remember that an ordinal variable does not assume equal inter-

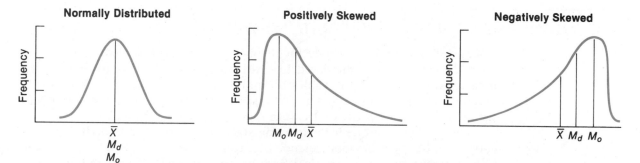

FIGURE 3.1 Relative locations of the three measures of central tendency for different frequency distributions.

vals between values. The M_d should be used as the measure of central tendency because adding values that are not equally spaced is inappropriate.

Therefore, the M_d is preferred over the $\overline{X}$ as the appropriate measure of central tendency when either (1) the distribution of values is skewed; (2) there are some values that are missing or cannot be calculated in the distribution; or, (3) the values are from an ordinal scale of measurement.

THE MODE (M_o)

The third measure of central tendency is the easiest to determine, but is least reported in the literature. The **mode** M_o is the most frequently occurring value in the distribution. To determine the mode, inspect your distribution and determine which value occurs more often than the other values. That value is the mode M_o. In distributions with few values, no one value may occur more frequently than others. In those instances, we would not report any M_o. An inspection of the values for the five distributions in our chapter example will reveal that the M_o for the different verbs is 42 mph for the "smashed" condition, 39 and 40 mph (bimodal, that is "two modes") for the "collided" condition, 38 mph for the "bumped" condition, 36 mph for the "hit" condition, and 32 mph for the "contacted" condition.

The M_o is seldom used as the sole measure of central tendency. It is, however, the appropriate measure of central tendency when the values come from a nominal variable, a variable with values that cannot be ordered. With a nominal variable the value(s) with the highest frequency in the distribution should be reported. For instance, if we were recording the home states of students in a class, it would be appropriate to report the state with the greatest number of students.

Another example, is found in polls and surveys. The results of a survey indicate which response was given most often (the M_o). "Yes," "no," and "no opinion" responses would be values from a nominal scale of measurement. If the results of a survey indicate that 52% said yes, 30% said no, and 18% had no opinion, the mode M_o response is "yes."

GRAPHING MEASURES OF CENTRAL TENDENCY

There are two basic methods for displaying measures of central tendency once they have been calculated in a research study. One is to present the measures in tabular form. Tables normally are designed with the conditions or groups listed across the top. The name or description of the dependent variable(s) is listed in the first column. (See the top of Figure 3.2.)

The other technique for displaying statistics is to draw a graph (which is called a figure in behavioral science literature). There are some basic rules to follow in graphing the statistical findings from a study. The first is that the values of the independent variable (the conditions or groups) are presented on the horizontal or x-axis (called the abscissa). The dependent variable (the behavioral response) is presented on the vertical or y-axis (called the ordinate).

	Verb Used in Question				
	Contacted	Bumped	Hit	Collided	Smashed
$\overline{X}$ Speed (mph)	32	38	34	39	41

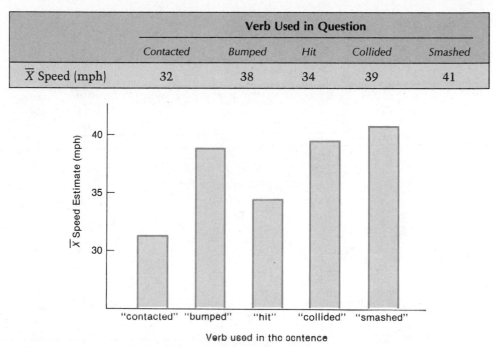

FIGURE 3.2 Reporting a descriptive statistic in a table (top) or in a figure (bottom). (The gap at the bottom of the y-axis indicates that the bottom interval is not drawn to scale.)

Each value of the independent variable is represented with a single statistic, most often the $\overline{X}$. The figure at the bottom of Figure 3.2 is based on the $\overline{X}$ speed estimates from the chapter example. Researchers seldom report the same information in both a table and a figure in a research report. Instead, they choose the one they feel best illustrates the findings of the study.

There are a number of common mistakes that students make in graphing the findings of a research study. Figure 3.3 illustrates some of the mistakes to be avoided. In Graph A the variables are on the wrong axes; the independent variable, hours of study, should be on the x-axis and the the dependent variable, the percentage correct, on the y-axis. In Graph B there are no labels for either axis. A reader would not know what the information refers to in this graph. In Graph C the y-axis is too compressed. Note that the highest reported $\overline{X}$ for the dependent variable is 10 weeks, yet the researcher has values of 15 and 20 included on the graph. The y-axis should be rescaled with the top value representing 10 weeks and with larger increments between 0 and 10 weeks. Graph D has two problems. The first is the bars are not of the same width. Bars should be of equal width and equally spaced. Second, the y-axis does not reflect equal intervals between values. The scale on the y-axis must incorporate the smallest and largest measures of central tendency to be graphed, and the scale must have equally spaced values.

There are two types of graphs commonly used in behavioral science research, line graphs and bar graphs. Graphs A and C in Figure 3.3 are line graphs, and Figure 3.2 and Graphs B and D of Figure 3.3 are bar graphs. A line

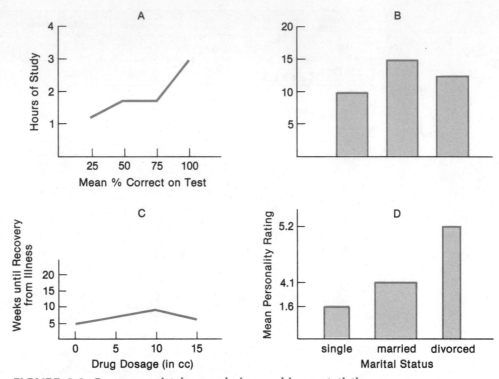

FIGURE 3.3 Common mistakes made in graphing a statistic.

graph is often used when the independent variable is an interval or ratio scale variable. General guidelines for using a line graph include: (1) ordering the values of the independent variable from lowest (left) to highest (right); (2) spacing the values to reflect their relative position on a number line; (3) representing the measure of central tendency for each value of the independent variable with a single point or dot; and (4) connecting the points from the point for the left-most value of the independent value to the point for the right-most value. An example of a line graph is Figure 3.4.

A bar graph (also called a bar chart) is used when the independent variable is a nominal or ordinal scale variable. The researcher needs to avoid giving the impression that a "trend" exists across values of the independent variable when the values cannot be ordered (nominal scale) or are not equally spaced (ordinal). Guidelines in constructing a bar graph are: (1) order the values of the independent variable on the x-axis alphabetically if the variable is nominal or by magnitude if it is ordinal; (2) represent the measure of central tendency for each value of the independent variable with bars of equal width without any lettering or information inside of the bars; and (3) space the bars an equal distance from each other.

The bar graph in Figure 3.2 was used for the Loftus and Palmer example because the verbs represent values on an ordinal scale of measurement. That is, the verbs describe different types of impact that can be ordered from mild ("contacted") to severe ("smashed"), but the values are not equally spaced.

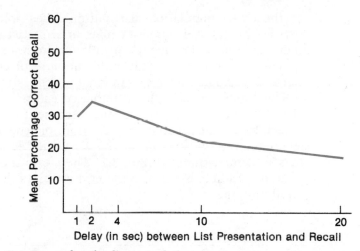

FIGURE 3.4 Example of a line graph from a short-term memory study. The independent variable is the delay before recalling a list of digits. The dependent variable is the percentage of digits correctly recalled.

As a word of caution, the guidelines listed for both the bar graph and line graph are *guidelines* only. There may be instances in which it makes sense to violate one of the guidelines. In those instances, look to see what other researchers have done in their reports. Remember, the reason for using a graph is to communicate your findings clearly and effectively.

PARAMETERS AND STATISTICS

When describing a set of values with a single value such as a measure of central tendency, researchers use different notation depending on whether the set of values is the population or a sample or a subset of values from the population. When a measure of central tendency or a measure of variability, which is discussed later in this chapter, is used to describe a population, the measure is referred to as a **parameter.** Parameters are represented by Greek letters. For instance, the mean of a population distribution is expressed by the Greek letter for m, μ (pronounced mu). If a researcher uses μ in reporting the mean, then we know that the set of values described is the entire population of values.

On the other hand, if the researcher is describing a sample, then the measures are called **statistics.** As mentioned earlier in this chapter, statistics are denoted with Arabic letters such as $\overline{X}$, M_d, M_o. Statistics include measures of central tendency and of variability that describe a sample.

In most behavioral science research, samples are used rather than entire populations. Therefore, researchers usually report statistics rather than parameters. However, the researchers often estimate what the parameters are for the entire population distribution based solely on the sample they selected. This is an example of inferential statistics in that the researcher is inferring information about a population from a sample.

For the most commonly used measure of central tendency, the mean, that is the sample mean $\overline{X}$, is in fact the best estimate of the population mean μ. The sample mean $\overline{X}$ is an unbiased estimate of the population mean μ. The $\overline{X}$ is an unbiased estimate of μ because if *all* samples of a particular size were taken from a population distribution and then if each sample $\overline{X}$ was calculated, the average of all the $\overline{X}$s would equal μ, the population mean. This is demonstrated in Box 3.2. Therefore, the $\overline{X}$ represents not only the mean of a sample but is also the best estimate the researcher has for the true population mean μ.

BOX 3.2   **A Demonstration that $\overline{X}$ Is an Unbiased Estimate of μ.**

1. Given a population of three values (1, 3, and 5), $\mu = 3$.
2. Select all possible samples of two values from the above population and calculate the $\overline{X}$ for each sample.

Sample	$\overline{X}$
1,1	1
1,3	2
1,5	3
3,1	2
3,3	3
3,5	4
5,1	3
5,3	4
5,5	5
Number of samples = 9	$\Sigma\overline{X} = 27$

3. Calculate the mean of all the sample $\overline{X}$s (sum of the $\overline{X}$s divided by the number of samples).

$$\text{Mean of } \overline{X}s = 27/9$$
$$= 3$$

4. The mean of the sample $\overline{X}$s, 3, is equal to μ, 3. Therefore, the sample $\overline{X}$ is an unbiased estimate of μ.

MEASURES OF VARIABILITY

Describing a set of values with only a measure of central tendency is usually insufficient. For example the two sets of values below have the same measures of central tendency.

$$A: 1 \quad 2 \quad 5 \quad 5 \quad 5 \quad 8 \quad 9 \qquad \overline{X}, M_d, \text{ and } M_o = 5$$

$$B: 4 \quad 4 \quad 5 \quad 5 \quad 5 \quad 6 \quad 6 \qquad \overline{X}, M_d, \text{ and } M_o = 5$$

Yet, the two sets are not the same. In Set A the "spread" of values is different from that in Set B. This difference of spread is described by another descriptive statistic, the measure of variability.

Measures of variability provide information about the dispersion or spread of values in a set of values. The greater the spread of values in a set, the larger the measure of variability will be. As was the case with measures of central tendency, there are a number of different measures of variability that can be reported. We will look at the most common measures used in behavioral science research.

THE RANGE

The easiest measure of variability to compute is the range. The **range** is the difference between the highest value in the set and the lowest value in the set:

$$\text{Range} = \text{highest value} - \text{lowest value} \qquad (2)$$

For instance, in the set of speed estimates for the "smashed" condition, the highest value is 45 and the lowest value is 37. The range is

$$8 = 45 - 37.$$

The "collided" and "hit" conditions have a range of 7 mph in estimated speed, and the "bumped" and "contacted" conditions have ranges of 6 mph and 5 mph respectively. Based on the range, the least variability in speed estimates occurred for students in the "contacted" condition. They gave the most similar estimates.

Although the range can be calculated quickly and easily, it does have a major drawback. It relies on only two values in the distribution, the highest value and the lowest value. Consider these two sets of values:

A: 95 90 84 82 79 73 71 60
B: 95 66 66 65 65 64 62 60

Notice that they both have the same range, 35. Yet, the spread of values in each distribution is different. In Set A, the spread for the majority of the scores is greater than that in Set B. However, because the range is based on only the two extreme scores, this difference is not shown. As a result, researchers rely on a more precise measure of variability in describing a distribution of values.

THE VARIANCE AND STANDARD DEVIATION

A more precise measure of variability would include every value in the entire set of values in its calculation. Two measures of variability, the variance and the standard deviation, use every value in the set. Both measures are based on the deviations of each value from the $\overline{X}$ of the set of values.

It is possible to determine how far each value deviates from a middle point in the set of values. The middle point that best fits this procedure is the $\overline{X}$. Calculating how far each value in the set deviates from the mean provides information about the spread or variability in the set of values. As you can see in Figure 3.5, if the differences are large then we can assume that the spread in the set of values is large; if the differences are small, then the spread is small. This logic is basic to understanding how the variance and standard deviation are calculated.

A Conceptual Framework for the Variance and Standard Deviation

It is important to understand how deviation values are determined. Table 3.5 lists the values of the "hit" condition that we will use to demonstrate the calculation of deviation values. These values along with the $\overline{X}$ are shown in the left-most column. To calculate deviation values, find the difference be-

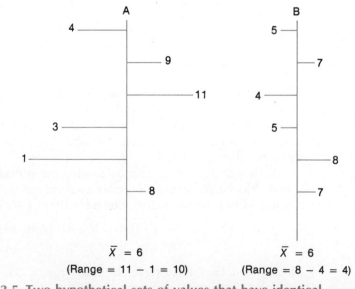

FIGURE 3.5 Two hypothetical sets of values that have identical
$\overline{X}$s ($= 6$) with different spreads of values (range of Set A $= 10$ and
the range of Set B $= 4$).

TABLE 3.5   Calculating Deviation Values for the "Hit" Condition

"Hit" Speeds	$(X - \overline{X})$	$(X - \overline{X})^2$
30	-4	16
35	$+1$	1
33	-1	1
32	-2	4
36	$+2$	4
36	$+2$	4
31	-3	9
36	$+2$	4
37	$+3$	9
$\overline{X} = 34$	$\Sigma(X - \overline{X}) = 0$	$\Sigma(X - \overline{X})^2 = 52$

tween each value and the $\overline{X}$, which is the arithmetic middle point for the set of values. These deviation values represented as $(X - \overline{X})$ are shown in the middle column of Table 3.5. You should recall that one property of the mean is that the sum of the deviation values $\Sigma(X - \overline{X})$ will always equal zero. Therefore, using this sum and dividing by N will always result in an average deviation value of 0.

To overcome this problem, each deviation value is squared *before* the sum is calculated. The right-most column in Table 3.5 shows these squared deviations, $(X - \overline{X})^2$. The negative values are eliminated by squaring each deviation value. Summing these squared deviation values results in a term we will use extensively, the **sum of the squared deviations** which is abbreviated as SS. The mathematical representation of SS is

$$SS = \Sigma(X - \overline{X})^2. \tag{Def}^*$$

Getting an average of the squared deviations involves dividing the SS by N, the number of values in the set. This results in the variance,

$$\text{Variance} = SS/N.$$

Using the values from Table 3.5, the variance is,

$$\text{Variance} = SS/N$$
$$5.78 = 52/9.$$

The **variance** is the mean of the squared deviation values. The variance will become important when we discuss certain tests in inferential statistics such as the analysis of variance. At this point, however, it is important that you realize that it is a measure of variability based on the *squared* deviation

---

*Formulas followed by (Def) are definitional formulas used to describe concepts and should not be used instead of computational formulas.

values. When comparing two sets of values, the set with the larger variance will have more variability (greater spread) among its values.

Because the variance is based on squaring deviation values, it is possible to reverse this procedure, so that the average deviation value is expressed in the same units as the $\overline{X}$ (rather than squared units). This operation is very simple. The square root of the variance is calculated. This value is called the standard deviation. The **standard deviation** is the square root of the variance.

$$\text{Standard Deviation} = \sqrt{\text{Variance}} \qquad \text{(Def)}$$

For the values in Table 3.5, the standard deviation would be,

$$\text{Standard Deviation} = \sqrt{\text{Variance}}$$
$$2.40 = \sqrt{5.78}.$$

In terms of measures of variability, the standard deviation is the preferred measure for a number of reasons. First, in contrast to the range, each value in the set contributes equally to the calculation of the standard deviation. Second, unlike the variance, the standard deviation is expressed in units identical to the original values in the data set. Third, the standard deviation is based on deviations from the $\overline{X}$, which is the best measure of central tendency to use in minimizing the sum of the deviation values. Fourth, as will be demonstrated in the next chapter, the standard deviation can be used in converting values from a normal distribution into percentile ranks. And lastly, like the other measures of variability, the larger standard deviations reflect greater variability in sets of values.

Computational Formulas for the Variance and Standard Deviation

Although the procedures outlined in the preceding section will give you the variance and standard deviation, there is a less time-consuming procedure that can and *should* be used. The major timesaver involves the calculation of SS. As shown in the previous example, calculating SS by (1) subtracting each X value from the $\overline{X}$ and then, (2) squaring the difference and, (3) adding these differences or deviations together was intentionally made to seem easy. A small set of values was used and the $\overline{X}$ and the X values were integers. Imagine the problems a researcher might face using this procedure if there were 60 or 70 values and these values went out to three decimal places. Calculating the deviations and squaring them would be exceedingly time-consuming and prone to error. (Try Problem 3.15 if you need to be convinced.)

Therefore, an alternative procedure for calculating SS has been developed. This procedure is illustrated using the same values included in the previous example from Table 3.5. Table 3.6 lists these values along with an additional column labeled X^2. The first step is to take each value and square it and list it in the right column. Then the sums of the two columns, ΣX and ΣX^2, are calculated. These sums are listed at the bottom of each column. The calculation of SS includes these two sums along with N, the number of values.

$$SS = \Sigma X^2 - \frac{(\Sigma X)^2}{N} \qquad (3)$$

TABLE 3.6 Calculating ΣX and ΣX^2 for the "Hit" Condition	
"Hit" Speeds (X)	X^2
30	900
35	1225
33	1089
32	1024
36	1296
36	1296
31	961
36	1296
37	1369
$\Sigma X = 306$	$\Sigma X^2 = 10456$

Note that ΣX^2 is not the same as the $(\Sigma X)^2$. For the example,

$$SS = 10{,}456 - \frac{(306)^2}{9}$$

$$- 10{,}456 - \frac{93{,}636}{9}$$

$$= 10{,}456 - 10{,}404$$

$$= 52.$$

This value agrees with the value calculated in the previous section when the definitional formula, $SS = \Sigma(X - \overline{X})^2$, was used.

CALCULATING THE POPULATION VARIANCE AND SAMPLE VARIANCE

As was the case with the mean, it is possible to discriminate between the population variance and sample variance (and standard deviations for each). The parameter σ^2 (small Greek letter sigma squared) represents the variance for a population distribution. And the statistic S^2 is commonly used to represent the variance for a sample. They are both based on dividing SS by N. If N represents the entire population, then the variance is represented by σ^2; if the distribution is a sample, then S^2 is used. And σ, the square root of the population variance, represents the population standard deviation, whereas S represents the sample standard deviation. Whereas μ and σ represent the parameters of a population distribution, $\overline{X}$ and S represent the statistics of a sample distribution.

CALCULATING THE ESTIMATE OF THE POPULATION VARIANCE, s^2

An important distinction must be made, however, when estimating the population variance (or standard deviation) from a sample. Recall that the sample mean $\overline{X}$ is an unbiased estimate of the population mean μ. The same is *not* true with regard to S^2 and σ^2. S^2 and S are biased estimates of σ^2 and σ. If one were to construct all the possible samples of a particular size from a population and calculate the variance for each sample, the average of the sample variances (S^2) would underestimate the true population variance σ^2. Therefore, an adjustment needs to be made in estimating the population variance. The adjustment involves the denominator in calculating the variance and standard deviation. Rather than dividing by N, the sum of the squared deviations is divided by $N - 1$. The estimate of the population variance is symbolized by s^2 and the estimate of the population standard deviation is represented by s. Box 3.3 shows that s^2 is a better estimate of σ^2 than S^2.

BOX 3.3   **A Demonstration that s^2 Is an Unbiased Estimate of σ^2 (and that S^2 Is a Biased Estimate).**

1. Given a population of three values (1, 3, and 5), $\sigma^2 = 2.67$.
2. Select all possible samples of two values from the above population and calculate S^2 (= SS/N) and s^2 (= SS/N − 1) for each sample.

Sample	S	s
1,1	0	0
1,3	1	2
1,5	4	8
3,1	1	2
3,3	0	0
3,5	1	2
5,1	4	8
5,3	1	2
5,5	0	0
N = 9	$\Sigma S^2 = 12$	$\Sigma s^2 = 24$

3. Calculate the mean of the sample variances S^2 and the mean of the estimates of the population variances s^2 (sum of the respective statistics divided by the number of samples).

$$\text{For } S^2: 12.00/9 = 1.33$$
$$\text{For } s^2: 24.00/9 = 2.67$$

4. The mean for the estimates s^2 is equal to σ^2 (both have a value of 2.67). The mean of the sample variance 1.33 underestimates σ^2. Therefore, s^2 is an unbiased estimate of σ^2.

The computational formula for the estimate of the population standard deviation is,

$$s^2 = SS / N-1. \tag{4}$$

And, the estimate of the population standard deviation is,

$$s = \sqrt{s^2}. \tag{5}$$

The calculations of s^2 and s are shown for two of the five conditions in the Loftus and Palmer study in Table 3.7. Notice that the variance and standard deviation are larger in the "smashed" condition than in the "bumped" condition. This indicates that the variability or spread of speed estimates is greater in the distribution for the "smashed" condition than in the "bumped" condition.

TABLE 3.7 The Calculation of s^2 and s for the "Smashed" and "Bumped" Conditions

"Smashed" Condition		"Bumped" Condition	
X	X^2	X	X^2
42	1764	38	1444
37	1369	35	1225
38	1444	38	1444
42	1764	40	1600
42	1764	37	1369
44	1936	36	1296
39	1521	38	1444
40	1600	41	1681
45	2025	39	1521
$\Sigma X = 369$	$\Sigma X^2 = 15187$	$\Sigma X = 342$	$\Sigma X^2 = 13024$

Using Formula 3: $SS = \Sigma X^2 - (\Sigma X)^2/N$

$SS = 15187 - (369)^2/9$	$SS = 13024 - (342)^2/9$
$= 15187 - 15129$	$= 13024 - 12996$
$= 58$	$= 28$

Using Formula 4: $s^2 = SS/N-1$

$s^2 = 58/8$	$s^2 = 28/8$
$= 7.25$	$= 3.50$

Using Formula 5: $s = \sqrt{s^2}$

$s = \sqrt{s^2}$	$s = \sqrt{s^2}$
$= \sqrt{7.25}$	$= \sqrt{3.50}$
$= 2.69$	$= 1.87$

CHOOSING THE APPROPRIATE MEASURE OF VARIABILITY TO REPORT

In the majority of studies, the set of values used represent a sample rather than a population. Because one of the goals of behavioral research studies is the ability to apply the findings beyond the sample used, researchers prefer to report s^2 and s, the unbiased population estimates as their measures of variability. The estimate of the population standard deviation s is preferred. Along with the $\overline{X}$, which is an unbiased estimate of the population mean, s provides the necessary information to describe the population distribution from which the sample in the study was selected.

The use of the sample standard deviation S would be appropriate in those limited instances in which the researcher wishes to describe only the sample and to make comparisons within the sample itself. In those circumstances in which the researcher is working with the entire population of values, then the calculation of σ^2 and σ are appropriate. When a researcher has the entire population of values, there is no reason to *estimate* the parameters because they can be calculated directly. As a final note, a number of calculators have keys for reporting these measures of variability. The key that has n as a subscript provides S (if a sample is used) or σ (if a population is used). The key with n − 1 provides s, the estimate of the population standard deviation.

A FINAL WORD ABOUT THE LOFTUS AND PALMER STUDY

In this chapter, data from the Loftus and Palmer study were summarized and described by calculating the measures of central tendency and of variability. Table 3.8 lists the $\overline{X}$ and s for each condition in the Loftus and Palmer study. As you should have noted, it appears that the verb used in a question did influence the students' estimates of speed. And, there was a little less variability in the speed estimates in the "bumped" and "contacted" conditions than in the "hit" and "smashed" conditions.

In behavioral research, we are required to carry our analysis a step further and perform the appropriate statistical test to determine how likely it is that

TABLE 3.8 $\overline{X}$ and s for Each of the Conditions in the Loftus and Palmer Study

	Verb Used in the Question				
	"Smashed"	"Collided"	"Bumped"	"Hit"	"Contacted"
$\overline{X}$	41.	39.	38.	34.	32.
s	2.69	2.12	1.87	2.55	1.58

these differences in estimated speed were the result of chance and not the experimental manipulation. We will deal with this type of question beginning in Chapter 8. However, to complete our discussion of this study, it should be reported that Loftus and Palmer's statistical tests revealed significant differences. The differences in speed among the conditions were very likely not the result of chance factors. They concluded that they were able to influence a student's recall about an accident by the way the question was worded.

SUMMARY

In describing a set of data values, researchers often rely on measures of central tendency and measures of variability. A measure of central tendency is a single value that describes the location of a set of data values. The most frequently reported measure of central tendency is the mean $\overline{X}$ or arithmetic average. The median M_d is another measure of central tendency and represents the 50th percentile value. It is used when the data set includes missing values, a set of values which is skewed, or values from an ordinal scale of measurement. The last measure of central tendency is the mode M_o which represents the most frequently occurring value in the set of data values. The mode is used for nominal variables.

Measures of variability provide information about the dispersion or spread of values in a set of data values. The easiest measure to calculate is the range, which is the numerical difference between the highest and lowest

---

BOX 3.4   **Measures of Central Tendency and of Variability Reported in Behavioral Science Research**

PARAMETERS

μ —Mean of a population distribution
σ^2 —Variance for a population distribution
σ —Standard deviation of a population distribution

STATISTICS

$\overline{X}$ —Unbiased estimator of μ and sample mean
s^2 —Estimate of variance for population distribution
s —Estimate of standard deviation for population distribution
M_d—Median for a distribution
M_o—Mode for a distribution
S^2 —Variance for a sample distribution
S —Standard deviation for a sample distribution

values in the set. The most frequently reported measure of variability is the standard deviation. It is based on the deviation of each score from the mean. The standard deviation is the square root of another measure of variability, the variance. The variance is the average of the squared deviations from the mean. This measure of variability is used in a number of tests involving inferential statistics.

In describing a distribution, a differentiation is made between population and sample distributions. Parameters, symbolized by Greek letters, are used to describe a population distribution. The two most common parameters used are μ, the population mean, and σ, the population standard deviation. Statistics are used to describe sample distributions and to estimate parameters. The symbol $\overline{X}$ represents the sample mean, which is an unbiased estimate of the population mean. The sample standard deviation is represented by S. The unbiased estimate of the population standard deviation is represented by s. These terms are listed in Box 3.4.

In graphing a statistic, a researcher often chooses between a bar graph and a line graph. The line graph is used when the independent variable is interval or ratio. The bar graph is used when the independent variable is nominal or ordinal. For both graphs, the independent variable is represented on the x-axis and the dependent variable, the measure of behavior, is represented on the y-axis.

SUMMARY FOR CALCULATING THE $\overline{X}$

1. Calculate ΣX and N
2. Calculate $\overline{X}$ using,

$$\overline{X} = \frac{\Sigma X}{N} \tag{1}$$

SUMMARY FOR CALCULATING s^2 and s

1. Calculate ΣX, ΣX^2, and N.
2. Calculate SS using,

$$SS = \Sigma X^2 - \frac{(\Sigma X)^2}{N} \tag{3}$$

3. Calculate s^2 using,

$$s^2 = \frac{SS}{N - 1} \tag{4}$$

4. Calculate s using,

$$s = \sqrt{s^2}$$ (5)

EXERCISES

1. What variable in an experiment (independent or dependent) is used in the actual calculations and statistical procedures? Explain using the example in this chapter.

2. Why are measures of central tendency and measures of variability called descriptive statistics? What are they describing?

3. The mean is considered an arithmetic "balancing point." Demonstrate that fact using the three samples below. (Hint: In each sample, calculate the $\overline{X}$ and then the difference between each score and the $\overline{X}$. Then compare the sum of these differences for scores above the $\overline{X}$ with the sum of the differences for the scores below the $\overline{X}$.)

Sample A	Sample B	Sample C
95	96	3.8
81	60	3.7
73	40	3.7
45	36	3.5
16	14	3.3
14	12	3.1
	12	2.8
	10	2.7
		2.6
		2.6
		2.3

4. For Sample B in Exercise 3, the M_d is 25. Why is there such a discrepancy between the $\overline{X}$ and the M_d for Sample B?

5. Why is the $\overline{X}$ preferred over the M_d by most researchers in the behavioral sciences? When would it be appropriate to report the M_d rather than the $\overline{X}$? When is the M_o the preferred measure of central tendency?

6. Calculate the M_d for the "collided," "contacted," and "hit" conditions from the Loftus and Palmer example in this chapter. Use Table 3.1.

7. After either reading about hunger in another country, seeing a film about hunger, or meeting a representative from a needy country, college students were asked to pledge a monetary donation for aid. Their pledges are listed below.

Type of Presentation		
Reading material	Film	Meet representative
$1.00	$2.00	$ 4.00
0.75	1.50	4.00
0.75	0.50	2.00
2.00	3.00	10.00
3.00	3.50	3.00
1.50	2.00	1.00
4.00	1.00	8.00
2.50	1.80	2.00
3.00	4.00	10.00
1.25	2.00	3.00

   a. Calculate the $\overline{X}$ and M_d for the data.
   b. Graph as separate graphs the $\overline{X}$ and M_d.
   c. Do the graphs provide the same general findings? If not, why not?
   d. Calculate the s values and describe what that tells you about each sample.

8. In a study on conformity, high-school students participated in groups in a perception experiment. Unknown to each student, all of the other participants in the group were confederates or "stooges" of the experimenter. On five critical trials these stooges gave an incorrect answer aloud. The experimenter was interested in whether or not the student went along with the incorrect answer. The independent variable was the size of the group, which varied from 1 other person to 10 other people. The number of times each student conformed to the group's incorrect answer is shown below.

Number of "Stooges" in the Group				
1	2	4	6	10
3	2	5	4	4
4	5	4	5	3
3	3	4	4	3
2	1	3	4	5
1	2	3	4	5
0	4	4	5	4

   Calculate an appropriate measure of central tendency and a measure of variability for each group, and graph the measure of central tendency.

9. To determine if questionnaire length influences whether a person decides to complete it or not, a study was undertaken at a large shopping mall on a Saturday afternoon. An interviewer stopped shoppers at random and asked if they would complete a questionnaire. Some shoppers were told that the questionnaire would take 2 minutes to complete. Others were told that it would take 5 minutes, 10 minutes, 15 minutes, or 30 minutes to complete. Fifty people were asked at each of the different times. The interviewer recorded the number of people who agreed to complete the questionnaire. The number of people giving the more frequent response, either yes or no, in each condition is reported below:

Time Given	More Frequent Response
2	45 said yes
5	38 said yes
10	28 said no
15	35 said no
30	50 said no

    a. What is the independent variable?
    b. What is the appropriate statistic to report? Why?
    c. Graph the findings of this study. (Hint: Be careful not to "mix" yes and no responses together in one graph.)
    d. Describe the findings of this study in your own words.

10. A study was conducted on perception and recognition of complex symbols. Forty complex symbols were constructed and tested equally often in each of five conditions. The conditions differed in terms of the length of exposure for the symbol, 0.5 , 1, 1.5, 3, or 5 seconds. After a symbol was shown on a screen, each participant was shown four symbols and was asked to pick the one that had just been shown. Five volunteers participated in all five conditions. The different exposure rates were varied randomly during the session. The number of correct recognitions for each condition is shown below:

Length of Exposure (in Seconds)					
Participant	0.5	1.0	1.5	3.0	5.0
A	0	1	3	6	7
B	1	0	3	7	8
C	0	1	2	6	6
D	1	2	3	8	8
E	0	1	1	5	8

    a. What are the independent and dependent variables and the levels for each variable?
    b. Calculate the three measures of central tendency for each exposure.

   c. In separate graphs, graph each of the three measures of central tendency.

   d. What should the researcher conclude about this study?

11. What information does a measure of variability provide that a measure of central tendency does not?

12. Which measure of variability could be described as the "mean of the squared deviations?" Which could be described as the "square root of the mean of the squared deviations?" Which measure of central tendency is the easiest to calculate? Which is the least preferred? Why?

13. Why is it necessary to square the deviation of each score from the mean, $(X - \overline{X})^2$?

14. A researcher finds that $\Sigma(X - \overline{X})^2 = 0$ for a set of 12 values. How can that happen?

15. Use both the conceptual approach and the computational formulas to calculate S for the following set of values:

$$\frac{A}{}$$

   4.672
   8.431
   5.008
   5.116
   3.924
   2.549

If your two Ss are not exactly the same, what explanation could you offer for the discrepancy?

16. Female college students were asked to rate financial security as a goal in life. They used a 1–to–5 scale with 1 meaning "not at all important" and 5 meaning "extremely important." Using the values below, determine the $\overline{X}$ and the three measures of variability (range, standard deviation, and variance).

3	4	2	2	1
2	2	2	4	2
5	1	3	3	3
2	1	2	3	2

17. A group of male college students were also asked to rate the importance of financial security. Calculate the same descriptive statistics as required in Problem 16.

2	5	3	3	4
3	4	2	1	3
1	4	2	2	2
4	3	5	3	3

18. Compare the information in Problems 16 and 17 and state your conclusion. Is financial security as a goal in life equally important to women and men? Does one group appear to be more similar in their values than the other?

19. A group of smokers were asked to record the number of cigarettes they smoked in a 7-day period. The number of cigarettes each smoked is reported below.
    a. Calculate the three measures of central tendency.
    b. Calculate the three measures of variability.
    c. Describe in words your conclusion regarding this set of values.

47	73	81	95	97	118	211
38	65	80	93	96	108	204
31	65	79	92	95	103	185
22	61	76	90	95	101	153
10	54	76	85	95	97	126

20. What would you conclude if another student told you that he calculated an s = −.28?

Standard Normal
Distribution

TERMS DISCUSSED

standard normal distribution

standard (z) scores

skewness

PROCEDURES DESCRIBED

calculating z scores

transforming values into percentile
ranks

converting percentile ranks into values

The Scholastic Aptitude Test (SAT) is widely used in the admissions' decisions at many colleges and universities across the country. The SAT was developed by Educational Testing Service (ETS) in Princeton, New Jersey and consists of three segments, verbal, quantitative, and analytic. Each segment is scored on a 200- to 800-point scale. The verbal and quantitative scores often are added together to provide a total SAT score. Obviously, students with higher SAT scores have a better chance of being accepted into the school of their choice.

Of importance in interpreting the SAT scores is the percentile rank associated with the SAT score. Tables are provided with the SAT scores to enable a student to determine his or her percentile rank on the test. These tables list SAT scores and the corresponding percentile rank. Each segment of the test was designed to provide a mean score of 500. The standard deviation was set to 100 points.

The SAT test and tests like it, such as the ACT (from the American College Testing program), are known to many college students. Performance on the test is one component often used by colleges and universities in admissions decisions. Although these tests have been the subject of debate concerning their appropriateness as a predictor of college performance, the focus of this chapter is on the scoring scale used for the SAT.

Each time the test is offered a large number of high-school students take it. Their scores represent a population of values. Using the scoring system devised by ETS, the mean score (μ) should be 500 with a standard deviation (σ) of 100. No one can have a score lower than 200 or higher than 800, scores which are three standard deviations (σ) from the mean. The test was designed so that the distribution of scores would be normal as shown in Figure 4.1. However, in a given year the scores may not fit the normal curve exactly because of the actual students' performances and adjustments which are made to allow comparisons across years of testing.

The SAT scores in themselves are not very meaningful to a student un-

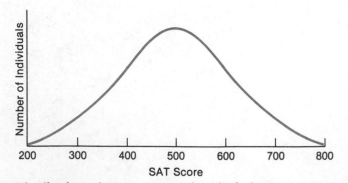

FIGURE 4.1 Distribution of SAT scores under ideal circumstances.

less they can be transformed into percentile ranks. A percentile rank identifies the percent of values at or below a particular value in a distribution. Students know more about their performance if they know that an SAT score of 600 represents the 84th percentile. Then we know that 84% of the students taking the test did as well or poorer than the student scoring a 600. Likewise, 16% had a higher SAT score.

In Chapter 2, the construction of frequency distributions included cumulative percentile ranks. One way to determine a percentile rank is to construct a cumulative frequency distribution and the corresponding percentile ranks. However, another method exists for distributions that are normal in shape. This method involves the use of standard scores.

STANDARD (z) SCORES

In a normal distribution, the three measures of central tendency, mean, median, and mode, have the same value. Therefore, if SAT scores are normally distributed, not only is the mean 500, but also the median and mode are 500. Since the M_d is the 50th percentile rank, we know that a score of 500 represents the 50th percentile.

THE STANDARD NORMAL DISTRIBUTION

One particular type of normal distribution is called a **standard normal distribution** (shown in Figure 4.2). The y-axis represents frequency or number of times each value occurred in the distribution. The scale on the x-axis is drawn to represent distance from the mean in terms of standard deviation units. These values are called standard scores or z scores. A **standard** (or **z**)

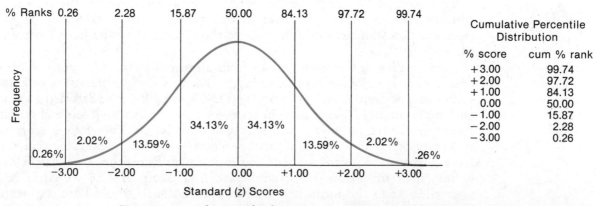

FIGURE 4.2 The standard normal distribution with a listing of the percentage of the distribution between standard scores.

score represents the difference between a value and the mean, divided by the standard deviation. For example, $+1$ indicates a value one standard deviation greater than the mean and -2 is two standard deviations less than the mean.

A standard normal distribution has two special properties. The first is that the mean of the distribution is 0. If all of the values (z scores) in this type of distribution were added together, the sum, Σz, would be 0. The second property is that the standard deviation and variance equal 1. SAT scores are designed to approximate the standard normal distribution (except for the scale) on the x-axis; the mean is 500 instead of 0 and the standard deviation is 100 points instead of 1.

In a standard normal distribution, almost all values (99.48%) will fall within three standard deviations of the mean. The areas under the distribution are divided according to these deviations from the mean. The percentages represent the percentage of the distribution found between any two standard deviation units. Notice in Figure 4.2 that these percentages sum to 100%. Also note that in this distribution 68.26% of the values will occur within one of the mean (34.13% above and 34.13% below the mean). And, 95.44% of the values in the distribution occur within two standard deviations of the mean (47.72% on each side of the mean). These percentages indicate that values are not equally distributed in a normal distribution. The majority occur near the mean and the frequency of occurrence of values decreases for extremely low or high values.

The scale at the top of Figure 4.2 represents percentile ranks. The percentile ranks are based on the area under the curve to the left of each standard deviation value. For comparison purposes, a cumulative percentile distribution similar to those constructed in Chapter 2 is shown to the right of Figure 4.2.

If a student had an SAT score of 200, 300, 400, 500, 600, 700, or 800 and the distribution of SAT scores is normal, it would be possible to determine the percentile rank by using Figure 4.2. For example, a score of 500 is the mean and the mean, in a normal distribution, has a percentile rank of 50. And since we know that the standard deviation is 100 points, a person with an SAT score of 400 would be one standard deviation below the mean, which corresponds to a percentile rank of 15.87. An SAT score of 700 would be 200 points or two standard deviations above the mean and would have a percentile rank of 97.72.

This ability to transform values from a normal distribution into percentile ranks is a major focus of this chapter. For this transformation of original values into percentile ranks, we must (1) know the difference between a value and the mean and (2) express it in terms of z scores. An SAT score of 600 is 100 points above the mean, or one standard deviation. Therefore, a score of 600 corresponds to a standard (or z) score of $+1$. The $+$ indicates that the score is above the mean. A $-$ before the value indicates the score was below or less than the mean. For example, an SAT score of 300, which is 200 points less than the mean (two standard deviations), would have a z score of -2.

CALCULATING z SCORES FROM ORIGINAL VALUES

There is a two-step formula for transforming original values into z scores. Without stating it explicitly, we've made use of the formula in the previous discussion. The first of the two steps involves calculating the difference between the original value and the mean. The second is transforming the difference into standard deviation units. This is accomplished by dividing the difference by the standard deviation. The formula is,

$$z = \frac{X - \overline{X}}{s}.$$

(6)

X refers to the original value. Formula 6 is designed to be used with the estimates of a population distribution, statistics you will be using most often. If, however, one has the entire population, as with the SAT scores, then μ is substituted for $\overline{X}$ and σ for s.

Formula 6 will provide the same z scores we calculated intuitively earlier in the chapter. It will also provide z scores for values that don't lend themselves to quick transformations. For example, an SAT score of 320 would result in the following z score,

$$z = \frac{X - \mu}{\sigma}$$

$$= \frac{320 - 500}{100}$$

$$= -1.80.$$

A person with an SAT score of 320 would be 1.80 standard deviation units below the mean. (z scores are usually reported with two decimal places.) To be sure that you know how to convert original values to z scores, use Formula 6 to confirm the following:

SAT of 580 has a z of +0.80
SAT of 410 has a z of −0.90
SAT of 760 has a z of +2.60.

TRANSFORMING z SCORES TO PERCENTILE RANKS

Once an original value has been converted to a z score it is necessary to determine the percentile rank associated with it. Figure 4.2 provides the percentile ranks for only the integer z values from −3 to +3. Percentile ranks for z scores to two decimal places are shown in Table Z in Appendix E.* A portion of Table Z is shown in Table 4.1.

*In Appendix E, tables are ordered according to the statistic represented. For instance, Table Z includes z scores.

TABLE 4.1 Part of Table Z which Lists the Proportion of Area Corresponding to Various Standard (z) Scores

(A) z	(B)	(C)		(A) z	(B)	(C)
0.00	.0000	.5000		1.00	.3413	.1587
0.01	.0040	.4960		1.01	.3438	.1562
0.02	.0080	.4920		1.02	.3461	.1539
0.03	.0120	.4880		1.03	.3485	.1515
0.04	.0160	.4840		1.04	.3508	.1492
0.05	.0199	.4801		1.05	.3531	.1469
0.06	.0239	.4761		1.06	.3554	.1446
0.07	.0279	.4721		1.07	.3577	.1423
0.08	.0319	.4681		1.08	.3599	.1401
0.09	.0359	.4641		1.09	.3621	.1379
0.10	.0398	.4602		1.10	.3643	.1357
0.11	.0438	.4562		1.11	.3665	.1335
0.12	.0478	.4522		1.12	.3686	.1314
0.13	.0517	.4483		1.13	.3708	.1292
0.14	.0557	.4443		1.14	.3729	.1271
•	•	•		•	•	•
•	•	•		•	•	•
•	•	•		•	•	•
0.85	.3023	.1977		1.85	.4678	.0322
0.86	.3051	.1949		1.86	.4686	.0314
0.87	.3078	.1922		1.87	.4693	.0307
0.88	.3106	.1894		1.88	.4699	.0301
0.89	.3133	.1867		1.89	.4706	.0294
0.90	.3159	.1841		1.90	.4713	.0287
0.91	.3186	.1814		1.91	.4719	.0281
0.92	.3212	.1788		1.92	.4726	.0274
0.93	.3238	.1762		1.93	.4732	.0268
0.94	.3264	.1736		1.94	.4738	.0262
0.95	.3289	.1711		1.95	.4744	.0256
0.96	.3315	.1685		1.96	.4750	.0250
0.97	.3340	.1660		1.97	.4756	.0244
0.98	.3365	.1635		1.98	.4761	.0239
0.99	.3389	.1611		1.99	.4767	.0233

In each segment of Table 4.1, Column A lists z scores. This column is used for both +z and −z scores. Because the normal distribution is symmetrical the shaded areas are of equal proportions on both sides of the mean for any z score. Column B lists the proportion of area from the mean to a particular z score. Column C lists the proportion of area from the z value to the tail. Notice that the proportions in B and C add to 0.50, which indicates that the mean divides the distribution into two segments of 50% each.

The information in Table Z is used in calculating percentile ranks. A percentile rank is the percentage of the distribution to the left of the z score. For a negative z score it will always be less than 50% because it is below the mean, and a positive z score will always have a percentile rank greater than 50%. The top example in Figure 4.3 shows a z score of −0.60 (which would correspond to an SAT score of 440). The percentile rank is the percentage of the shaded area. This corresponds to Column C in Table Z. Using Column C, we find a proportion of .2743 for a z score of 0.60. Proportions can be converted to percentages by multiplying by 100. Therefore, for negative z scores, a percentile rank is,

$$\text{Percentile rank} = 100 \cdot (\text{proportion in Column C}). \qquad (7a)$$

In our example, a z score of −0.60 corresponds to a percentile rank of 27.43. Therefore, a person with an SAT of 440 would have 27.43% of the population with the same or lower SAT score.

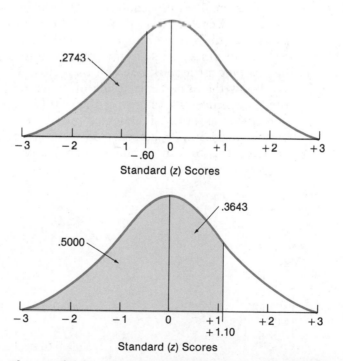

FIGURE 4.3 The standard normal distribution with the shaded areas indicating the proportion of the distribution to the left of the z score.

For positive z scores, the proportion in Column B is added to .50 before multiplying by 100. For example an SAT score of 610 would correspond to a z score of $+1.10$. As shown at the bottom of Figure 4.3, the shaded area is beyond the mean and would be greater than .50. In fact, the proportion is equal to .50 (for the area to the left of the mean) plus the area between the mean and the z score (Column B). Therefore, for a positive z score the following formula provides the percentile rank:

$$\text{Percentile Rank} = 100 \cdot (.50 + \text{proportion in Column B}). \qquad (7b)$$

For a z score of $+1.10$, the percentile rank is 100 times [.50 + .3643] (proportion in Column B) or 86.43. Therefore, 86.43% of the population had an SAT score of 610 or lower.

The conversion of values into percentile ranks is a two-step process when using the standard normal distribution. Formula 6 is used to transform the value into a z score, and then Table Z is used to convert the z score to a percentile rank. In the next section, the reverse situation is considered, how does one convert a percentile rank into a value?

TRANSFORMING PERCENTILE RANKS TO VALUES

Assuming you are given a percentile rank from a normal distribution, it is possible to transform the percentile rank into a value based on the original distribution. This procedure reverses the steps outlined in the previous section. The first step is to convert the percentile rank into a z score and then transform the z score into a "raw score" value.

For instance, let's assume that a college decides that a candidate must have a percentile rank of 85 on the verbal SAT to be accepted for admission. We know that a percentile rank of 85 would have a positive z score, because the percentile rank is greater than 50 (which has a z value of 0). In fact, a percentile rank of 85 is reflected in a distribution with 50 percent to the left of the mean and 35 percent (.35 in proportions) between the mean and the positive z score. This is shown graphically in Figure 4.4. Therefore, this pos-

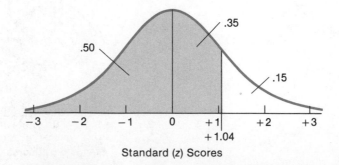

FIGURE 4.4 Proportions of the standard normal distribution for a z score of $+1.04$.

itive z score has .35 as the proportion between the mean and the z score and .15 beyond the mean. Applying this information to Columns B and C from Table Z (or see Table 4.1), a z score of 1.04 is found. The accepted practice is to use the z score with the closest values. By converting the percentile rank into proportions it is possible to use either Column B or C to identify the z score.

Once the z score is found, another form of Formula 6 is used to transform the z score into a raw score value. The alternative form, using estimates of the population distribution, solves for the value X rather than z.

$$X = \overline{X} + s(z) \tag{8}$$

Using the information we have about SAT scores, the following occurs

$$= 500 + [100 \times (+1.04)]$$
$$= 500 + 104$$
$$= 604$$

The cutoff SAT verbal score for admissions is 604. Anyone with a verbal SAT score equal or greater to 604 would have at least a percentile rank of 85.

IDENTIFYING THE PROPORTION OF A DISTRIBUTION BETWEEN TWO VALUES

Using the procedures outlined in the two previous sections, it is possible to estimate the proportion or percentage of a distribution between two values from a normal distribution. It is also possible to identify values that limit a proportion or percentage of the distribution. Let's examine an example of each.

Using the SAT distribution, a university official might want to know what percentage of those taking the test had SAT scores between 550 and 700. Let's assume that in the past at this university the majority of students who decide to attend had SAT scores in that range. The first step is to convert these scores to z scores. This can be accomplished through Formula 6,

$$z = \frac{\overline{X} - \mu}{\sigma} \tag{6}$$

$$= \frac{700 - 500}{100}$$

$$= +2.00.$$

And

$$= \frac{550 - 500}{100}$$

$$= +0.50.$$

The left-most distribution in Figure 4.5 shows these z scores along with the area of the distribution we need to determine. Using Table Z, it is possible

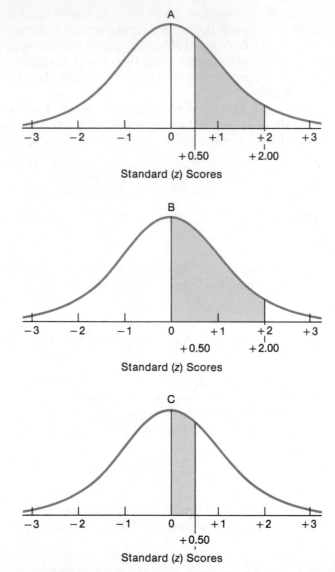

FIGURE 4.5 Standard normal distributions with shaded area representing
proportion of area between: (A) z scores of +0.5 and +2.0; (B)
mean and a z score of +2.0; and, (C) mean and a z score of +0.5.

to determine the proportion of area between the mean and each of the z
scores. These proportions are also shown in Figure 4.5. To determine the
proportion a z score of +0.50 and of +2.00, one needs to subtract the smaller
proportion, .1915, from the larger proportion, .4772. This results in a proportion of .2857, which is the area between an SAT score of 550 and 700. Therefore, .2857 (or 28.57%) of those taking the SAT should have scores between
550 and 700.

The procedure for determining the proportion between two values requires converting the values to z scores. Drawing the distribution and identifying the area needed is often helpful. Then using the proportions from Table Z appropriately, it is possible to determine the desired proportional area. In most instances, this involves either subtracting or adding proportions depending on the location of the area needed. Exercise 14 at the end of this chapter provides practice with this concept.

The second procedure to be discussed involves finding the values that partition a particular proportion or area of the distribution. For example, assume that a researcher is interested in determining the values that define the middle 95% of the SAT score distribution. This is shown in Figure 4.6. The shaded area represents the middle 95%. The proportion on each side of the mean is .475 (.475 + .475 = .95). The area beyond each of the z scores is .025. Using Table Z, the z score corresponding to these areas can be found. It is 1.96. Therefore, the two z scores −1.96 and +1.96 are the limits for the middle 95 percent of the distribution. Knowing these z scores and the mean and standard deviation of the distribution, the actual values can be found by using Formula 8

$$X = \mu + \sigma(z) \tag{8}$$
$$= 500 + [100 \times (+1.96)]$$
$$= 696.$$

And

$$= 500 + [100 \times (-1.96)]$$
$$= 304.$$

Therefore, the SAT scores of 304 and 696 define the middle 95% of the SAT distribution. Only 5% of those taking the tests should have a score lower than 304 or higher than 696.

To determine the values that define a particular proportion of a distribution, first find the z scores that limit the area. Then, use Formula 8 to convert the z scores into values. Box 4.1 reviews all of these procedures with another example.

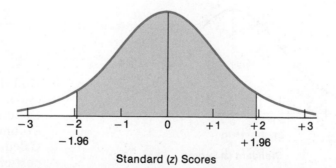

Standard (z) Scores

FIGURE 4.6 Standard normal distribution with shaded area representing the middle 95% of the total area.

BOX 4.1   Examples Using the Standard Normal Distribution

Assume that a test is given and the instructor reports that the mean is 76 and that the standard deviation is 8. This information along with the procedures described in the text could be used to answer the following questions.

A. What is the percentile rank for a student with a score of 89?

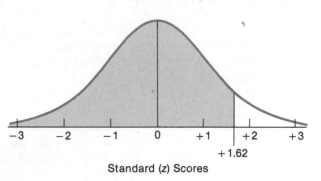

Standard (z) Scores

   a. Determine the z score (Formula 6):

$$z = \frac{X - \overline{X}}{s} = \frac{89 - 76}{8} = 1.625.$$

   b. Find the area between $\overline{X}$ and z (Table Z): $+z$ uses Column B (rounding to 1.62): .4474

   c. Determine percentile rank (Formula 7b):
$100 \times (.50 + .4474) = 94.74\%$

B. Students with scores in the bottom 12.5% of the distribution will receive "D"s or "F"s. What is the cutoff score for a "C" or better?

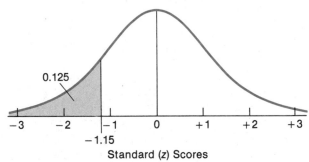

Standard (z) Scores

   a. Determine the z score corresponding to the percentile rank of 12.5%:
Use Column C of Table Z = -1.15

   b. Transform z into score (Formula 8):
$X = \overline{X} + sz = 76 + [8 \times (-1.15)]$
$= 66.8$
(rounded to 67)

C. If "D"s are given to students with scores above 60 and less than 67, what proportion of the class will receive "D"s?

Standard (z) Scores

   a. Determine the z scores (Formula 6):

$$z = \frac{X - \overline{X}}{s} = \frac{60 - 76}{8} = -2.00$$

$$z = \frac{X - \overline{X}}{s} = \frac{67 - 76}{8} = -1.125$$

   b. Find the area between $\overline{X}$ and z (Table Z):
Column B ($z = -2.00$): .4772
Column B ($z = -1.12$): .3686

   c. Calculate difference between proportions:
$.4772 - .3686 = .1086$

Always draw a figure if you are unsure of the procedure to be followed.

LIMITATIONS IN USING THE STANDARD NORMAL DISTRIBUTION

There are a couple of important issues to be considered before using the standard normal distribution to calculate proportions and percentile ranks. The first involves the shape of the original distribution. *The distribution of values must approximate the standard normal distribution.* Converting values into z scores will *not* make the original distribution normal. The shape of the distribution remains the same. Converting values into z scores is a transformation of the scale on the x-axis; it does not affect the shape of the distribution. In fact, using z scores with a skewed distribution will result in inaccurate proportions and percentile ranks.

It is possible to determine an index of skewness using the following formula:

$$\text{Index of Skewness} = \frac{3(\overline{X} - M_d)}{s}$$

This index is based on two measures of central tendency—the mean and median. You should recall that in a normal distribution, the two statistics should be identical. In a skewed distribution, the $\overline{X}$ will be pulled in the direction of the tail of the distribution. As a guideline, if the index of **skewness** for a distribution is between $-.50$ and $+.50$, then you may consider it symmetrical for most applications. If, however, it is beyond those values, then the distribution is skewed. If the index is negative, then the distribution is negatively skewed. Likewise, a large positive index of skewness indicates a positively skewed distribution. Chapter 16 includes a discussion of the chi-square test for goodness of fit, which allows one to test whether a distribution is not normal in shape.

A second concern is the number of values in the original distribution. To make meaningful use of the standard normal distribution, the original distribution must contain enough scores to permit accurate approximations of percentile ranks. As a guideline, distributions with at least 30 values are needed for the $\overline{X}$ and s to be useful in transforming values into z scores.

TRANSFORMATION OF VALUES TO A NEW SCALE

The transformation of values into z scores is only one of an infinite number of transformations that can be made for a set of values. It is possible to transform any set of values to conform to a new scale. The SAT scores are just one example; IQ scores are another. Some IQ tests are designed so that the mean IQ is 100 and the standard deviation is 15 IQ points (see Figure 4.7). Using the rule that almost all values will fall within three standard deviations on each side of the mean, it is possible to determine that almost all people have IQ values between 55 and 145, that is $100 \pm 3 \cdot (15)$.

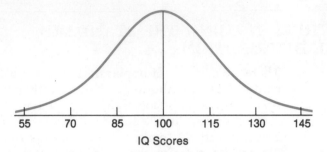

FIGURE 4.7 Distribution of IQ scores based on a normally distributed set of IQ scores with a mean of 100 and a standard deviation of 15.

Transformations are often made to make interpretation of values easier. For instance on a 25-question test, an instructor could record the number of questions answered correctly or "transform" the values so that each question is worth 4 points and the test scores can range from 0 to 100.

Transformation of values onto a new scale involves either adding, subtracting, multiplying, or dividing individual values by some new constant value. When an original value is modified by one or more of these operations, a new value will be obtained. These new values will result in different values for the measures of central tendency and of variability.

Adding or subtracting a constant to each value in a distribution will affect the $\overline{X}$ but not s^2 or s. This is demonstrated in the top and middle distributions of Figure 4.8. Adding or subtracting a constant to each value in effect "shifts" the distribution either to the left (for subtraction) or to the right (for addition). *The new mean is equal to the old mean plus (or minus) the constant.*

Multiplying or dividing each value by a constant will affect the mean, the variance, and the standard deviation. This is demonstrated in the bottom part of Figure 4.8. Multiplying each value by a constant not only shifts the mean to the right but also expands the scale. (Dividing by a constant will shift the mean to the left and contract the scale.) *When multiplying or dividing each value by a constant, the new mean will equal the former mean multiplied or divided by the constant.* The same is true for the standard deviation. *The new standard deviation will equal the original standard deviation multiplied or divided by the constant.* The new variance, which is the new standard deviation squared, is equal to the old variance multiplied or divided by the squared value of the constant. Therefore, it is possible to transform any distribution of values. These transformations will alter the scale on the x-axis but will not alter the relative standing (and percentile ranks) of the original values.

Lastly, transformations are useful when one wants to compare the relative standing in one distribution with that in another distribution. For instance, a student receives an 83 on one English test and an 86 on a second English test. If these tests do not have a similar $\overline{X}$ and s, then it may be inappropriate to say that the student performed better on the second test *relative* to the rest of the class. If the second test had a higher $\overline{X}$, for instance

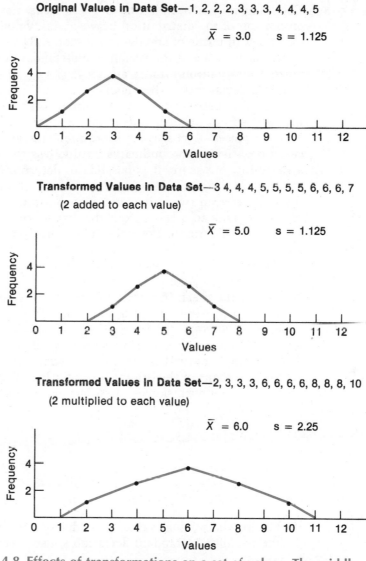

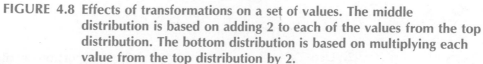

FIGURE 4.8 Effects of transformations on a set of values. The middle distribution is based on adding 2 to each of the values from the top distribution. The bottom distribution is based on multiplying each value from the top distribution by 2.

87, than the first test, whose $\overline{X}$ was 80, then performance on the first test was actually better than on the second test. Transforming both sets of test scores to a common scale, for instance z scores, permits meaningful comparisons across distributions. The score of 83 might have a z score of $+.50$, whereas the test score of 86 might have a z score of $-.17$ (this assumes that $s = 6$ for both tests). By comparing z scores, it is possible to determine that performance is better on the first test.

SUMMARY

The standard normal distribution is a frequency distribution for which the proportion of the distribution between any values can be defined. Values are expressed in terms of standard or z scores. The mean of the standard normal distribution is 0 and the variance and standard deviation are 1. In a standard normal distribution almost all (99.48 %) of all values will be within three standard deviations of the mean.

Given a distribution that is normal in shape, it is possible to transform the values from the distribution into z scores. All z scores are reported to two decimal places. A positive z score indicates a value greater than the mean, and a negative z score indicates a value less than the mean. By transforming a value into a z score, it is possible to determine the percentile rank for the value. It is also possible using z scores to determine the proportion of cases that fall between two values in a distribution. Lastly, transformations from a percentile rank to a value from the distribution are possible, enabling an individual to determine the value that corresponds to a particular percentile rank.

Transformation of values into z scores is one of a number of possible transformations. Adding or subtracting a constant to values in a distribution will affect the mean but not the standard deviation. Multiplying or dividing values in a distribution by a constant will change both the mean and the standard deviation.

Transforming values into z scores should only be used when the original distribution is normal in shape. The transformation into z scores will not change the shape of the original distribution. Therefore, the use of z scores is not appropriate with skewed distributions or distributions that do not appear normal.

SUMMARY FOR CALCULATING A PERCENTILE RANK USING A z SCORE

1. Having the original value X the distribution mean $\overline{X}$ and the estimate of the population standard deviation s, use Formula 6

$$z = \frac{X - \overline{X}}{s}. \tag{6}$$

2. Use Table Z to find the appropriate proportion of the distribution. Use the appropriate formula below to convert the proportion to a percentile rank.

For a negative z score:

$$\text{Percentile Rank} = 100 \cdot (\text{proportion in Column C}) \tag{7a}$$

For a positive z score:

$$\text{Percentile Rank} = 100 \cdot (0.50 + \text{proportion in Column B}) \tag{7b}$$

SUMMARY FOR CONVERTING A PERCENTILE RANK TO A VALUE

1. Use Table Z to determine the z score that corresponds to the percentile rank. It may help to sketch the standard normal distribution and plot the proportion/percentile rank.

2. Insert the z score along with the distribution $\overline{X}$ and s into Formula 8,

$$X = \overline{X} + s(z) \tag{8}$$

EXERCISES

1. If you were told that several persons scored four standard deviations above the mean on a test and that no one scored lower than one standard deviation below the mean, would you assume that the distribution is normal in shape? Explain.

2. For Exercise 1, what effect would transforming test scores to z scores have on the shape of the distribution? Would it "normalize" the test scores so that there are test scores with z scores less than -1.00?

3. A student down the hall from you in your dormitory is taking Introductory Psychology. He is a bit confused because his instructor converts all test scores to z scores. He tells you that on his last test, he was right at the average and was given a z score of 0.00. He feels that his studying hasn't been much of a help because he assumes that he would have gotten a 0.00 if he hadn't taken the test. What would you say to help alleviate this confusion?

4. You know that your score on a chemistry test in a large class was the sixth highest out of 200 (a percentile rank of 97). Yet, given the statistics from your instructor, you calculate that your test score results in a z score of 2.15, which indicates a percentile rank of 98.42. Why is there a discrepancy?

5. For each of the following, use the information to calculate the requested value:

   a. $z = -1.43$, percentile rank = ?
   b. $z = +.25$, percentile rank = ?
   c. $z = -1.88$, percent with higher z scores = ?
   d. $z = +.71$, percent with higher z scores = ?

6. Although the SAT is designed so that the mean is 500 with a standard deviation of 100, it often happens that the mean and standard deviation are slightly different (because ETS wants to allow for comparison of test scores from one year with those from previous years). Assume that a student has a verbal SAT of 620. What would be her percentile rank using the ideal statistics of a mean of 500 and a standard deviation of 100?

What would be her percentile rank if ETS reported that the actual mean of the distribution was 486 with a standard deviation of 92?

7. Transform the following set of values into z scores, then calculate the mean and standard deviation of the set of z scores. (The mean of the z scores should be 0 and the standard deviation should be 1.)

   SET OF SCORES: 1, 3, 4, 4, 5, 5, 5, 6, 7, 8

8. A particular university has a policy that students with a z score of -1.60 or lower on a placement test must take a remedial course. If the number of students taking the test is 3,500, approximately how many students will have to take the remedial course?

9. Given the same score of 63 on a test, from which class would you rather be, Class A with a $\overline{X}$ test score of 68 and an s of 8 or Class B with a $\overline{X}$ test score of 72 and an s of 16? Explain your answer.

10. Convert each of the following percentile ranks to a z score, and draw the standard normal distribution and shade in the appropriate area under the curve which corresponds to the percentile rank:
    (a) 95.15   (b) 44.83   (c) 2.87   (d) 97.93   (e) 86.43   (f) 10.56

11. A fellow student working with a sample of 13 values transforms each value into a z score and finds that she has 8 negative z scores, 1 z score of 0.00, and 4 positive z scores.

    a. Does it appear that this sample is normally distributed? Why?

    b. Would you assume that the median value has a negative, 0.00, or positive z value? Explain your answer.

12. An instructor decides that she will give approximately 10% "A"s, 25% "B"s, 50% "C"s, 10% "D"s, and 5% "F"s. Assuming that her final test averages are normally distributed, what would be the critical z values for each grade cutoff? Construct a standard normal distribution and shade in the areas under the curve for each letter grade. If she has 84 students in the class, how many "A"s, "B"s, "C"s, "D"s, and "F"s should be awarded? Using the above information, assume that the mean test average is 72 with a standard deviation of 9, determine the cutoff test values for each letter grade.

13. An instructor needs to "curve" his grades on a test. The test was exceedingly difficult and most grades were lower than expected. The mean on the test was 62 and the standard deviation was 10. He really would like the mean to be 74 with a standard deviation of 8. What would he have to do to the original test values to transform them to a set of values with the new mean and standard deviation?

14. For each pair of z scores determine the proportion of the distribution between the z scores:

    a. -1.20 and -0.45

    b. -1.65 and -0.83

    c. -1.40 and $+0.67$

    d. -0.28 and $+0.28$

    e. $+0.50$ and $+1.50$

    f. $+1.25$ and $+2.00$

15. On an IQ test, the top 10% of the distribution indicates "gifted" individuals. Assuming an IQ test with a mean of 100 and a standard deviation of 15, what would be the cutoff score for the gifted individuals.

16. The personnel officer of a large company believes that the top 40% of individuals who take a particular interest inventory test would be successful employees in her firm. Assuming that the test has a mean score of 54 with a standard deviation of 7, what would the cutoff value be for a "successful" employee?

17. Determine the z score(s) for each of the following:

    a. the scores that define the top 5% of the distribution

    b. the scores that define the bottom 1% of the distribution

    c. the scores that define the extreme 5% of the distribution

    d. the scores that define the extreme 1% of the distribution

    e. the scores that define the middle 99% of the distribution

18. The instructor for the student in Exercise 3 decides to stop using z scores because the students are confused by negative values. Therefore, he decides to transform his z scores into a different score called a T score, which has a mean of 50 and a standard deviation of 10. What would he need to do to each of his z scores to accomplish this transformation?

19. In each case below, determine whether the standard normal distribution is appropriate to use. Justify your answer.

    a. $\overline{X} = 25$, $M_d = 23$, $s = 6$, $N = 43$

    b. $\overline{X} = 46$, $M_d = 47$, $s = 9.16$, $N = 24$

    c. $\overline{X} = 91.65$, $M_d = 93.4$, $s = 17.3$, $N = 118$

    d. $\overline{X} = 70.97$, $M_d = 68.11$, $s = 4.38$, $N = 71$

20. A fellow student likes the idea of transforming original values into z scores to determine percentile ranks. He conducts a pilot study using 20 close friends. The friends complete a self-esteem test that he has developed, and he determines the percentile rank for each friend using the self-esteem scores. Another student recommends to him that he use the procedures outlined in Chapter 2 for determining percentile ranks rather than z scores. Who do you think is correct? Why?

Interpreting Correlational Research

OVERVIEW

Research in the behavioral sciences depends on finding, describing, and explaining relationships among variables. These variables most often include *observable* behaviors. Correlational hypotheses are used by researchers to predict relationships among variables and behaviors. The next three chapters describe statistical techniques used in describing some of these relationships.

The existence of a relationship between two variables does not imply causation. There are cases when a researcher cannot (or chooses not to) control the environment sufficiently to allow one to conclude that one variable causes a resulting behavior. For instance, ethical reasons prohibit a researcher from randomly assigning individuals to a smoking or nonsmoking condition in order to determine the causal relationship between smoking and a particular behavior. And, in many cases, controlling variables would create an artificial situation for which the results would be difficult to generalize to real-life situations. The researcher may decide to identify and describe the relationships among variables and behaviors.

In Chapter 5, the most common type of relationship, the linear relationship, will be examined. In a linear relationship, two variables are related in a fashion that can be described by a straight line. Chapter 5 focuses on identifying the existence of such a relationship, and Chapter 6 discusses the procedures for determining the equation for the best line to describe the relationship. Chapter 7 introduces you to more complex relationships when more than two variables are involved.

Correlational Research

An important area of research in social psychology involves interpersonal attraction. This research includes the identification of factors that predict whether or not a person will find another person attractive. Byrne, Ervin, and Lamberth (1970) described a study involving college students that simulated a computer dating service. A group of 420 introductory psychology students completed a 50-item attitude–personality questionnaire. The responses were compared for every student in order to construct every possible male–female couple in the class. From these responses, couples were "arranged" so that 20 couples had a low level of similarity or agreement in terms of attitude and personality, that is, from 24 to 40% of the responses were answered in the same way. Another 24 couples had a high level of similarity with 66 to 74% of their responses answered in the same way.

Each person in the couple was brought into a room to meet each other and the experimenter. They were told that the study was designed to create a situation like that of a computer date. They had completed a questionnaire and now the experimenter wanted them to spend a short time getting acquainted. They were asked to spend 30 minutes together on a "coke date" at the student union. The experimenter provided money for the date. After the 30 minutes the couple returned to the room to meet with the experimenter. At that time, each of the students used a scale to rate several aspects of the other person. Byrne et al. (1970) investigated a number of different measures of attraction. However, we will look at only two. One of the items was a 7-point rating scale involving the physical attractiveness of the other person, with a 7 representing a very attractive person. Another 7-point rating scale dealt with the other person as a potential date, with a 7 representing someone the person would very much like to date. It is reasonable to assume that these two variables would be related to each other. Physical attractiveness should be related to wanting to date the other person. The values on these two scales for the male students are shown in Table 5.1.

Byrne et al. (1970) were concerned with identifying factors which are related to interpersonal attraction. One of their research hypotheses was that the physical attractiveness of a potential date is related to a person's desire to date the individual. The assumption was that people like to date physically attractive people. To test this hypothesis it will be necessary to determine if the two variables, the physical attractiveness of another person and the desire to date the person, are related to each other.

If a relationship exists between two variables then knowing the value for one variable allows you to predict the value on another variable. Of course, the better or "stronger" the relationship, the better the prediction. In this chapter the focus will be on linear relationship. In a **linear relationship** the relationship between the two variables can be represented by a straight line. If a large value on one variable is related to a large value on another variable

TABLE 5.1 Ratings for the Chapter

Subject	Ratings Attractiveness	Potential Date
a	7	7
b	4	4
c	7	5
d	5	5
e	7	6
f	1	2
g	7	4
h	2	4
i	7	5
j	2	1
k	7	6
l	2	3
m	6	6
n	4	3
o	5	4
p	3	2
q	5	7
r	6	7
s	4	3
t	6	5
u	7	5
v	2	3
w	3	5
x	5	4
y	6	5
z	6	5
aa	3	4
bb	4	5
cc	5	4
dd	6	4
ee	7	5
ff	5	5
gg	5	4
hh	5	6
ii	2	4
jj	3	4
kk	2	1
ll	3	4
mm	4	5
nn	4	4
oo	5	7
pp	4	5
qq	4	5
rr	4	2

(and a small value is related to a small value) then the relationship is a **positive linear relationship**. In the example with dating, one would predict that the relationship is positive. If you rate a person as being unattractive (a small value on physical attractiveness) then you will not likely to want to date the person (a small value as a potential date). On the other hand, if you find the person physically attractive (a large value) then you will want to date that person (a large value).

There are linear relationships in which a large value for one variable is related to a small value on the other variable. In a **negative linear relationship** large values on one variable are related to small values on the other variable and vice versa. For instance, a negative linear relationship exists between the weight of an automobile and gas mileage. Light autos (a small value for auto weight) get better gas mileage (a large value for MPG, miles per gallon) than do heavy autos. Heavy autos have greater weight but lower gas mileage. Another example of a negative relationship is the amount of privacy children have relative to family size. Children who are the only child have more privacy at home than do children who have many siblings and who must therefore share space in the home. The amount of privacy one has decreases with increasing family size.

Examples of these types of relationships are shown in Figure 5.1. The graphs in Figure 5.1 represent scatterplots. A **scatterplot** is a graphic representation of the relationship between two variables. Each variable is represented on a separate axis and each point corresponds to the intersection of the two values for each individual in the study. (Of course, for auto weight and gas mileage, an "individual" is a particular type of auto.) Notice that in Scatterplots A and D the points in the plot are heading in an upward, positively sloped direction. This indicates that a positive linear relationship exists. In Scatterplots B and C the points are downward and negatively sloped. This indicates the existence of a negative linear relationship.

Scatterplot E is different in that the relationship appears to be shaped somewhat like an inverted U. This is an example of a curvilinear relationship. A **curvilinear relationship** is a nonlinear relationship and can best be described by a curved, rather than a straight, line. In the example in Scatterplot E the x-axis represents physiological and psychological arousal with low arousal near the origin and high states of arousal to the right. The y-axis represents test performance. In taking an exam or test in school there is an optimal level of arousal which will have a positive effect on test performance. This level for peak performance is some intermediate level of arousal. You want to be "up" for a test and ready for it. Lower levels of arousal may not enhance performance (the left part of the inverted U). And, having too high of a level of arousal leads to test anxiety and "freezing" on the test (the right part of the inverted U). Although there are specific tests for curvilinear relationships, this chapter will focus only on linear relationships, the most common type of relationships studied in the social sciences.

Finally, Scatterplot F in Figure 5.1 is an example of two variables that are not related. Notice that the points are scattered throughout the graph and there does not seem to be any pattern emerging from the plot. In this case,

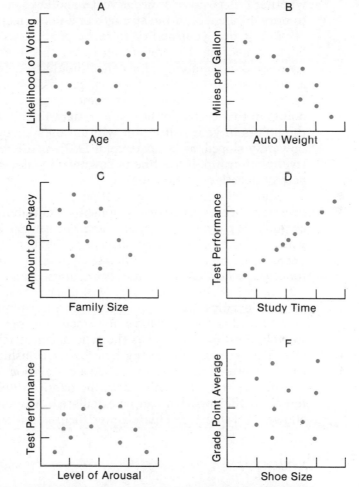

FIGURE 5.1 Examples of scatterplots. Scatterplots A and D show positive linear relationships, whereas B and C show negative linear relationships. Scatterplot E demonstrates a curvilinear relationship, and F indicates no relationship.

knowing the value of one variable will not help in predicting the value on the other variables. For Scatterplot F we find no relationship between shoe size and grade point average.

THE PEARSON *r* CORRELATION COEFFICIENT

A scatterplot is useful in visually representing a relationship. Inspecting scatterplots such as those in Figure 5.1 can aid in determining whether a relationship is linear or not (Scatterplots A through D versus E and F) and whether it is positive or negative, (A and D versus B and C). It is also possible to note differences in the strength of a relationship.

Recall that your ability to make predictions when two variables are related depends on the strength of the relationship. In Scatterplot D, your ability to predict memory performance should be excellent if you know how long a person studied the list of words. This is because the relationship between study time and memory performance is perfect in that example, all of the points in the scatterplot fall on a straight line. In a perfect linear relationship, the points in your scatterplot will fall on a single straight line. If the line is upwardly sloped, as in Scatterplot D, then the relationship is a perfect positive relationship. If the line is downwardly sloped, then the relationship is a perfect negative relationship.

Scatterplot D shows a perfect positive relationship, but Scatterplot A represents a weaker positive relationship. Your ability to predict *y* values is not as good. For a given *x* value, there are several individuals with different *y* values. There is no one-to-one correspondence. The points cannot be connected on a single straight line. Therefore, the *strength of a relationship is a function of how close the points or intersection of values come to falling on a straight line.* In Chapter 6 we will discuss how to draw the best fitting line for relationships such as those shown in Scatterplots A through D.

Up to this point we have discussed two important components for a linear relationship. The first is the type of linear relationship, positive or negative. The second is the strength of the relationship. Both of these components can be captured in a statistic called a correlation coefficient. Correlation coefficients are statistics which describe relationships. There are a variety of different coefficients that can be calculated. A number of these coefficients are shown in Table 5.2. This chapter focuses on two of these coefficients, the

TABLE 5.2 Different Correlation Coefficients Used in the Behavioral Sciences

Type of Coefficient	Appropriate Use
Pearson *r*	When both variables are on an interval or ratio scale of measurement
Spearman r_s	When both variables are ranks (and it is assumed that equal intervals exist between ranks)
Multiple *R**	When there are three or more variables all on an interval or ratio scale of measurement
Kendall's τ**	When variables are ranks on an ordinal scale of measurement
φ**	When both variables each have only two possible values
φ coefficient***	When both variables are on a nominal scale of measurement

*Discussed at an introductory level in Chapter 7.
**See Siegel (1956), *Nonparametric Statistics.*
***Discussed in Chapter 16.

Pearson product-moment correlation coefficient (Pearson r) and the Spearman rank-order correlation coefficient (Spearman r_s). These are the most commonly calculated coefficients in behavioral science research. Both have the same range of possible values. In fact, the Spearman r_s is another version of the Pearson r and is used when both variables are expressed as ranks. We will look at the Pearson r first.

INFORMATION CONTAINED IN THE PEARSON r

The Pearson r is a statistic with a range of possible values from -1.00 to $+1.00$ and is usually expressed as a two-decimal value. The Pearson r contains the two pieces of information needed to describe a linear relationship. The sign of the correlation coefficient describes the type of relationship, either positive or negative. The value of the coefficient describes the strength of the relationship. The larger the value, the stronger the relationship. A perfect relationship will have a coefficient of either -1.00, if it is a perfect negative relationship, or $+1.00$, if it is a perfect positive relationship. A correlation coefficient of .00 indicates that the two variables are not linearly related. The larger the absolute value of r for two variables, the more closely related they are and the stronger the relationship between the two variables. In Figure 5.1, Scatterplot A would have a coefficient of $+.29$ indicating a weak relationship. Scatterplot B, with a coefficient of .91, is a fairly strong negative relationship, and Scatterplot C, with a coefficient of $-.49$, describes a relationship of moderate strength, one that is stronger than that in Scatterplot A but weaker than that in Scatterplot B.

THE PEARSON r AS IT RELATES TO STANDARD SCORES

The Pearson r is an index of the linear relationship between two variables. If two variables are positively related then one would expect that a value that is above the mean of one variable would be related to a value above the mean of the other variable. And, if another value is below the mean of one variable, then it would be related to a value below the mean of the second variable. The opposite would be predicted for a negative relationship in that being above the mean of one variable would be related to a value below the mean of the second variable (for instance, a "heavy" car would have lower than average gas mileage).

One way the Pearson r demonstrates this concept is through the use of z scores. Recall from Chapter 4 that a z score provides information about the relative standing of a value in a distribution. It is possible to describe the relationship between two variables that are expressed in z scores. The relationship can be determined by the following formula:

$$r = \frac{\Sigma(z_x \cdot z_y)}{N}. \qquad \text{(Def)}$$

The values for each variable are transformed into z scores. Then the z scores for each pair of values are multiplied together, added, and then divided by N, the number of pairs of z scores.

At the top of Table 5.3 are two sets of values, one for Variable A and the other for Variable B. If you were to construct a scatterplot of these values, you would notice that a perfect linear relationship exists. Next to each value is the z score for the value calculated using Formula 6 from Chapter 4. When a perfect positive relationship exists, the identical z scores will be found for each pair of values. The rightmost column, labeled "$z_x z_y$," shows the results from multiplying the pairs of z scores. Using the sum of this column and dividing by N provides the Pearson r of $+1.00$.

In the middle of Table 5.3, the same sets of values are used but now the

TABLE 5.3	Examples of Three Relationships Using the Standard Score Formula for Pearson r				
	Variable A		**Variable B**		
X	Z_x	Y	z_y		$z_x \cdot z_y$
Positive Relationship					
1	-1.414	40	-1.414		2.00
2	-0.707	70	-0.707		0.50
3	0.00	100	0.00		0.00
4	$+0.707$	130	$+0.707$		0.50
5	$+1.414$	160	$+1.414$		2.00
$\overline{X} = 3$		$\overline{X} = 100$			$\Sigma z_x z_y = 5.00$
$\sigma = 1.414$		$\sigma = 42.426$			$r = 1.00$
Negative Relationship					
1	-1.414	160	$+1.414$		-2.00
2	-0.707	130	$+0.707$		-0.50
3	0.00	100	0.00		0.00
4	$+0.707$	70	-0.707		-0.50
5	$+1.414$	40	-1.414		-2.00
$\overline{X} = 3$		$\overline{X} = 100$			$\Sigma z_x z_y = -5.00$
$\sigma = 1.414$		$\sigma = 42.426$			$r = -1.00$
No Relationship					
1	-1.414	100	0.00		0.00
2	-0.707	160	$+1.414$		-1.00
3	0.00	40	-1.414		0.00
4	$+0.707$	70	-0.707		-0.50
5	$+1.414$	130	$+0.707$		1.00
$\overline{X} = 3$		$\overline{X} = 100$			$\Sigma z_x z_y = -0.50$
$\sigma = 1.414$		$\sigma = 42.426$			$r = -0.10$

highest value in Variable A is associated with the lowest value in Variable B and so on. The values for Variable B have been reversed. A scatterplot would reveal a perfect negative relationship. Now, z scores of opposite signs are paired together. Using the formula for the Pearson r in this example results in a coefficient of −1.00.

The last case shown at the bottom of Table 5.3 describes the situation in which no relationship exists. Using the z scores and the formula for the Pearson r, a coefficient of −.10 is obtained. This statistic indicates that the two variables are practically unrelated to each other.

It is important to note two things from this example. The first is that the two *original* variables do not have to be on *identical* scales. Remember that transforming values to z scores sets the mean of the variable at 0 and establishes the standard deviation as 1. This transformation does not change the relative standing of the values within the sample. The second point to note is that the z scores reflect deviations from the mean $(X - \overline{X})$. These deviations are expressed in terms of standard deviation units. The Pearson r coefficient is based on these deviation values. In a positive linear relationship, values that deviate from the mean on one variable are related to values that deviate in the *same direction* on the other variable. For a negative linear relationship, values that deviate in one direction on one variable are related to values that deviate in the *opposite direction* on the other variable.

CALCULATING THE PEARSON r FROM THE ORIGINAL VALUES

Although the formula using z scores can be used to calculate the Pearson r, an easier computational formula exists. It is based on the original values in the sample and does not require the initial transformation of values into z scores. The formula is based on the summary statistics for each variable and the sum of the products for each pair of values. The formula is,

$$r = \frac{\Sigma XY - \dfrac{\Sigma X \cdot \Sigma Y}{N}}{\sqrt{SS_x \cdot SS_y}}. \tag{9}$$

All of these terms except the first term in the numerator have been introduced earlier. The "ΣXY" is the sum of the multiplication of each pair of X and Y values. SS_x and SS_y refer to the sum of the squared deviations for each variable $[\Sigma (X - \overline{X})^2$ and $\Sigma (Y - \overline{Y})^2]$ which can be determined by using Formula 3.

Let us calculate the Pearson r for the chapter example. The data from Table 5.1 are reproduced in Table 5.4 along with the necessary summary statistics. At the bottom of each column for X and Y, the sum of the values and SS are shown. The last column represents the product of each pair of X and Y values with the ΣXY shown at the bottom of the column. The number of *pairs* of values (or individuals) in the sample is represented by N. In this example, N is 44. Substituting values into Formula 9 provides the following,

TABLE 5.4 Ratings and Calculation of Necessary Statistics for the Chapter Example

	Ratings		
Subject	Attractiveness (X)	Potential Date (Y)	$X \cdot Y$
a	7	7	49
b	4	4	16
c	7	5	35
d	5	5	25
e	7	6	42
f	1	2	2
g	7	4	28
h	2	4	8
i	7	5	35
j	2	1	2
k	7	6	42
l	2	3	6
m	6	6	36
n	4	3	12
o	5	4	20
p	3	2	6
q	5	7	35
r	6	7	42
s	4	3	12
t	6	5	30
u	7	5	35
v	2	3	6
w	3	5	15
x	5	4	20
y	6	5	30
z	6	5	30
aa	3	4	12
bb	4	5	20
cc	5	4	20
dd	6	4	24
ee	7	5	35
ff	5	5	25
gg	5	4	20
hh	5	6	30
ii	2	4	8
jj	3	4	12
kk	2	1	2
ll	3	4	12
mm	4	5	20
nn	4	4	16
oo	5	7	35
pp	4	5	20
qq	4	5	20
rr	4	2	8
	$\Sigma X = 201$	$\Sigma Y = 194$	$\Sigma XY = 958$
	$\Sigma X^2 = 1047$	$\Sigma Y^2 = 948$	$N = 44$
	$SS_x = 128.80$	$SS_y = 92.64$	

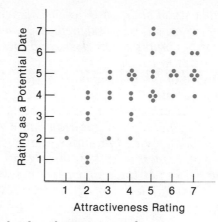

FIGURE 5.2 Scatterplot for chapter example.

$$r = \frac{\Sigma\, XY - \dfrac{\Sigma X \cdot \Sigma Y}{N}}{\sqrt{SS_x \cdot SS_y}}$$ (9)

$$= \frac{958 - \dfrac{201 \times 194}{44}}{\sqrt{128.80 \times 92.64}}$$

$$= \frac{958 - 886.23}{\sqrt{11932.03}}$$

$$= \frac{71.77}{109.23}$$

$$= +.66.$$

A positive relationship exists between the males' ratings of physical attractiveness and their ratings of the other person as a potential date. A scatterplot for the data in this example is shown in Figure 5.2. Note that the plot of the points depicts the positive relationship indicated by the Pearson r coefficient of $+.66$. In general, the more physically attractive a man rated a woman, the more desirable he rated her as a date. Let's look at a second example from this same study.

A SECOND EXAMPLE

Byrne et al. (1970) also used an unobtrusive measure of attraction in their study. An unobtrusive measure is one in which the subject is unaware that he or she is being observed or that a behavior is being recorded. When each couple of students returned from the "coke date," they met with the experimenter to receive the instructions to complete the final set of questionnaires. Unknown to the students, upon their return to the experimenter's room, the experimenter measured the physical distance the couple stood apart. A 0–to–5 scale was used. If the couple were touching each other, a 0 was assigned. A 5 was assigned if the couple stood at opposite corners of the desk, and intermediate values were assigned for distances in between. These distance values were compared with a measure of interpersonal attraction that was based on a final questionnaire. This questionnaire included two questions, one dealing with liking the other person and the other with working with the other person in an experiment. Each question had a 7-point scale. The sum of the two questions provided an index of attraction, with a 2 indicating the lowest level of attraction and 14 the highest level of attraction. Byrne et al. tested whether or not the unobtrusive measure of attraction was related to the questionnaire index of attraction. The values for the women in the study are shown in Figure 5.3.

Obviously if the two measures are recording the same behavior, then a relationship between the two variables should exist. Byrne et al. (1970) believed that a linear relationship exists between these two variables. In fact, it was hypothesized that a negative relationship exists between their distance measure and the questionnaire measure of attraction. The relationship is assumed to be negative because of the ordering of values on the two scales. Couples who have a strong attraction should stand close together, resulting in a low value on the distance measure (remember a 0 indicates a couple touching). On the other hand, the questionnaire measure of attraction is designed so that a high value indicates strong attraction. Therefore, a high level of attraction toward the other person would be indicated by a low value on the distance measure and a high value on the questionnaire measure. A low level of attraction would be indicated by the opposite, a high value on distance and a low value on the questionnaire.

Figure 5.3 contains not only the values for each female student but also the necessary statistics for calculating the Pearson r. At the right is the scatterplot for the sample data. Notice that there appears to be a negative relationship in that the trend of points is in the downward direction. Using Formula 9, the Pearson r as an index of this relationship can be calculated

$$r = \frac{\Sigma XY - \dfrac{\Sigma X \cdot \Sigma Y}{N}}{\sqrt{SS_x \cdot SS_y}} \tag{9}$$

$$= \frac{1278 - \dfrac{130 \times 448}{44}}{\sqrt{51.91 \times 302.55}}$$

$$= \frac{1278 - 1323.64}{\sqrt{15705.37}}$$

$$= \frac{-45.64}{125.32}$$

$$= -.36.$$

	Ratings		
Subject	Distance (Y)	Attraction (X)	X · Y
a	3	14	42
b	2	13	26
c	2	11	22
d	4	9	36
e	4	7	28
f	4	4	16
g	2	10	20
h	2	12	24
i	1	12	12
j	3	12	36
k	0	13	0
l	1	14	14
m	2	8	16
n	3	8	24
o	2	14	28
p	3	13	39
q	5	10	50
r	3	6	18
s	4	5	20
t	5	9	45
u	4	13	52
v	2	5	10
w	3	6	18
x	5	10	50
y	4	10	40
z	2	11	22
aa	3	9	27
bb	4	12	48
cc	4	8	32
dd	3	8	24
ee	2	13	26
ff	3	14	42
gg	3	10	30
hh	4	11	44
ii	2	13	26
jj	3	10	30
kk	2	10	20
ll	3	9	27
mm	4	9	36
nn	4	11	44
oo	2	12	24
pp	3	12	36
qq	3	11	33
rr	3	7	21

$\Sigma Y = 130$ $\Sigma X = 448$ $\Sigma XY = 1278$

$\Sigma Y^2 = 436$ $\Sigma X^2 = 4864$ $N = 44$

$SS_y = 51.91$ $SS_x = 302.55$

FIGURE 5.3 Data and statistics for second chapter example along with scatterplot.

A negative relationship exists between these two variables. However, it is not as strong a relationship as was found in the first example. The fact that the relationship exists tells us that the two measures share something in common. But the value of the Pearson r indicates that the points do not form a straight line. An inspection of the scatterplot in Figure 5.3 confirms this finding. For instance, notice that although a low value (4 to 6) on the questionnaire measure has correspondingly high values in distance, the values do vary from 2 to 4. For the highest value on the questionnaire measure, 14, distance values vary from 1 to 3. The Pearson r of $-.36$ indicates that although there is a general downward trend for the relationship, it is not as strong or precise a relationship as one might like. In fact, when the same relationship is tested for the men, a Pearson r of $-.48$ was found. This is indicative of a slightly stronger relationship between the two values for men. Remember that strength of a relationship is a measure of the predictability a researcher has. With a strong relationship, a researcher is more accurate in predicting a value on one variable given the value on the other variable.

Although we have looked at only two relationships in the Byrne et al. (1970) study, it should be noted that a number of additional relationships in identifying interpersonal attraction were studied. The researchers were able to conclude that the laboratory study of attraction provided consistent findings with the study of attraction in the field (or real world). Furthermore, they were able to conclude that their findings generalized to a population of students beyond those tested in this study. We have limited our discussion to identifying and describing relationships in this chapter. Later, in Chapter 9, we will discuss how researchers use this type of information to infer the existence of relationships in a population from what was observed in a sample.

LIMITATIONS AND CAUTIONS IN USING THE PEARSON r

There are a number of points that need to be addressed with regard to the Pearson r. One has already been discussed. The Pearson r will accurately measure only *linear* relationships. It will not be an accurate index for nonlinear relationships. In fact, it can underestimate the strength of nonlinear relationships such as curvilinear relationships.

There are two additional cautions with regard to using the Pearson r correlation coefficient. One involves the issue of causality. **Causality** assumes that when a relationship exists between two variables, one of the variables is causing or influencing the values obtained on the other variable. A correlational coefficient only shows that a relationship exists, which is a necessary but not sufficient condition for establishing causality. For instance, in the second example, it is clear that the physical distance measure and the questionnaire measure are related. Yet, based on the data from this study, it would be inappropriate to assume that either measure is *causing* the other. That is, it is unlikely that how close two people stand is the sole reason a person rates the other as attractive. Likewise, it is impossible to assume that the questionnaire measure causes the physical distance measure (especially since the questionnaire measure follows the distance measure in time).

A correlation coefficient shows if a relationship exists between Variables A and B, but does not indicate if A causes B or B causes A or if some third variable, C, causes A and B. In the chapter examples it is possible that some other variables, perhaps attitude similarity and how the "coke date" progressed, caused the values found on the two measures of attraction. Only when a researcher has conducted a study with sufficient controls and in a manner in which alternative explanations can be ruled out can the researcher conclude that a causal relationship exists.

The other caution involves the restricted range problem. A **restricted range** occurs when only a small portion of the values on one variable are sampled. A restricted range has a tendency to *reduce* or *minimize* the relationship between two variables. If two variables are linearly related and the

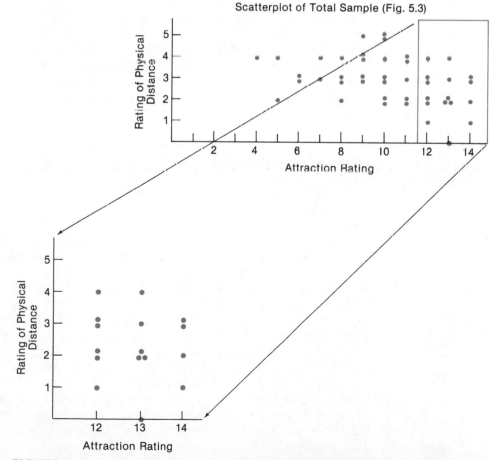

FIGURE 5.4 An example of a restricted range problem. Only those subjects who gave the other person an attractiveness rating of 12 or higher are included. The data are from the second chapter example.

range is restricted, the Pearson r coefficient will be smaller than it would be if the range were not restricted. For instance, in the second example the Pearson r for the relationship between the two measures of attraction was $-.36$. If, however, the range on the questionnaire measure was restricted to include only those individuals who rated the other person with at least a 6 on each of the two questions (summed values of 12, 13, or 14), then the Pearson r coefficient drops to $-.11$. Figure 5.4 is a scatterplot showing how this relationship would look.

Although the above example may appear trivial, there may be some important applications of the restricted range problem in other settings. For instance, one criticism of the SAT test as a predictor of college success is that the SAT score is not a strong predictor of performance in college. Yet, one must note that colleges tend to accept those students with the highest SAT scores. Therefore, colleges are restricting their sample to those individuals within a certain range of SAT values. The individuals with the low SAT scores are not accepted into college. Therefore, it is impossible to determine the relationship between SAT scores and college performance for those students. If all applicants, regardless of SAT score, were admitted to college and their subsequent performance measured, then a true measure of the relationship between SAT score and college performance could be obtained. Presently, a restricted range problem *may* result in our underestimating the true relationship between SAT score and college performance. Let us now look at the other correlation coefficient, the Spearman r_s.

THE SPEARMAN RANK-ORDER CORRELATION COEFFICIENT, r_s

The study of stress and its influence on an individual has been a major topic of study in recent years. Holmes and Rahe (1967) developed a scale of life change which has been shown to be related to physical illness. The scale involved 43 different life events that differ in the amount of stress involved. At the top of the list was "death of a spouse" and at the bottom was "minor violations of the law." A complete list of the events is shown in Table 5.5. In the original study Holmes and Rahe asked adults to rate the amount of social readjustment they perceived each event required. From these results, they developed the ranking of events shown in Table 5.5. The ranks in the first column are based on the adults in the Holmes and Rahe study. Ruch and Holmes (1971) tested whether the same ordering of events would be found if college students were used. The original study used adults of whom 48% were over the age of 30. Ruch and Holmes hypothesized that college students might not have experienced a number of the life events in the list and, therefore, their rankings might be different. They surveyed 211 college students and asked them to rate the events using the same procedure used earlier with the adults. The rankings for the college students are shown in the second column of Table 5.5.

TABLE 5.5 Rankings and the Differences between the Rankings for the Chapter Example Based on the Ruch and Holmes (1971) Study

Life Event	Adult Group Rank of Arithmetic Mean Value	Adolescent Group Rank of Arithmetic Mean Value	Difference in Ranks d	d^2
Death of spouse	1	1	0	0
Divorce	2	2	0	0
Marital separation	3	3	0	0
Jail term	4	8	−4	16
Death of a close family member	5	4	+1	1
Major personal injury or illness	6	6	0	0
Marriage	7	9	−2	4
Fired from work	8	7	+1	1
Marital reconciliation	9	10	−1	1
Retirement	10	11	−1	1
Major change in health of family member	11	16	−5	25
Pregnancy	12	13	−1	1
Sex difficulties	13	5	+8	64
Gain of a new family member	14	17	−3	9
Business readjustment	15	15	0	0
Change in financial state	16	14	+2	4
Death of a close friend	17	12	+5	25
Change to a different line of work	18	21	−3	9
Change in number of arguments with spouse	19	19	0	0
Mortgage over $10,000	20	18	+2	4
Foreclosure of mortgage or loan	21	23	−2	4
Change in responsibilities at work	22	20	+2	4
Son or daughter leaving home	23	25	−2	4
Trouble with in-laws	24	22	+2	4
Outstanding personal achievement	25	28	−3	9
Wife begins or stops work	26	27	−1	1
Begin or end school	27	26	+1	1
Change in living conditions	28	24	+4	16
Revision of personal habits	29	35	−6	36
Trouble with boss	30	33	−3	9
Change in work hours or conditions	31	29	+2	4
Change in residence	32	30	+2	4
Change in schools	33	34	−1	1
Change in recreation	34	36	−2	4
Change in church activities	35	38	−3	9
Change in social activities	36	32	+4	16
Mortgage or loan less than $10,000	37	31	+6	36
Change in sleeping habits	38	41	−3	9
Change in number of family get-togethers	39	37	+2	4
Change in eating habits	40	40	0	0
Vacation	41	39	+2	4
Christmas	42	42	0	0
Minor violations of the law	43	43	0	0

$$\Sigma d = 0 \qquad \Sigma d^2 = 344$$

Note. Reprinted with permission from *Journal of Psychosomatic Research, 15,* L. O. Ruch and T. H. Holmes, 1971, Pergamon Journals Ltd.

Ruch and Holmes were interested in determining if the two sets of rankings are related to each other. That is, do adults and college students perceive the same relative amounts of social readjustment for different life events. From an inspection of Table 5.5, it appears that there is a close correspondence, although there are a few discrepancies. For instance, "sex difficulties" are ranked as requiring more social readjustment by college students than by the adult sample. "Revision of personal habits," on the other hand, is ranked higher by the adults than the college students.

Although the Pearson r coefficient could be used to calculate an index of the relationship between the two sets of rankings, an easier formula exists. This formula results in the same coefficient as the Pearson r, but it takes into account that the sum of the ranks (ΣX and ΣY) is the same for both groups and so is the sum of the squared ranks (ΣX^2 and ΣY^2). Since both groups used the integers from 1 to 43 to rank their attitudes, they both must have the same sum and sum of the ranks squared. This makes the calculations of SS identical for both groups.

The correlation coefficient that measures the relationship between two sets of ranks is called the Spearman rank-order correlation coefficient, r_s. The formula assumes that both sets of values are ranks. If only one set is ranked, then the other set must be ranked before the formula is used. The formula requires that the differences between ranks be calculated and that these differences, d, be squared and summed. This is shown in the last two columns of Table 5.5.

The formula for calculating r_s is

$$r_s = 1 - \frac{6 \cdot \Sigma d^2}{N^3 - N.} \tag{10}$$

N refers to the number of pairs of ranks in the study. In this example there are 43. We have a pair of ranks for each life event. Using the information from Table 5.5, Formula 10 provides the following solution:

$$
\begin{aligned}
r_s &= 1 - \frac{6 \times 344}{43^3 - 43} \\
&= 1 - \frac{2064}{79464} \\
&= 1 - .03 \\
&= .97
\end{aligned}
$$

A very strong positive relationship was found between the ranks for adults and for college students. The adults and college students perceive the same relative ordering of life events with regard to the amount of social readjustment needed.

The Spearman r_s is an alternative form of the Pearson r and is interpreted the same way. The sign provides the direction of the relationship, either positive or negative, and the absolute value is a measure of strength. It is used when both of the variables are in the form of ranks and an alternative form of the Pearson r is desired.

A researcher should use the Spearman r_s when the values are in the form of ranks. Taking values and converting them to ranks because a researcher wants to use the easier Spearman r_s formula is inappropriate. Changing values to ranks can alter the character of the relationship of the original values.

SUMMARY

Two correlation coefficients are discussed, the Pearson r and Spearman r_s. Both coefficients measure the extent to which two variables are linearly related to each other. Neither will accurately measure nonlinear relationships. The correlation coefficient describes two aspects of the relationship—direction and strength. If a relationship is positive, then high values on one variable are related to high values on the other variable, and low values are related to low values. If the relationship is negative, then the opposite is true—high values on one variable are related to low values on the other variable.

Strength indicates the extent to which the relationship can be described by a straight line. It is possible to create a scatterplot for a relationship by plotting the points that represent each pair of X and Y values. If these points fall on a straight line, then a perfect linear relationship exists, and it is possible to predict exactly an X or Y value if the other value is known. If the points deviate from a straight line, then the relationship has less strength. A perfect linear relationship will have a correlation coefficient of either -1.00 (perfect negative) or $+1.00$ (perfect positive). A coefficient of .00 indicates that the two variables are not linearly related.

The Spearman r_s is an alternative form of the Pearson r and is used when both variables are in the form of ranks. Neither coefficient allows the researcher to determine causality. That is, the correlation coefficient indicates only if a relationship exists; it does identify either variable as the cause of the relationship.

A problem of restricted range can reduce the size of the correlation coefficient. If only a selected range of either variable is sampled, then it is possible that the full extent of the relationship between two variables may not be tested. This can result in the correlation coefficient having less strength than it would if the entire range of the variables was sampled.

SUMMARY FOR CALCULATING THE PEARSON r

1. For each of the two variables, calculate the sum (ΣX and ΣY) and the sum of the squared values (ΣX^2 and ΣY^2).
2. Multiply each pair of values ($X \cdot Y$) and sum these products (ΣXY).
3. Using Formula 3, calculate the sum of the squared deviations for each variable, SS_x and SS_y.
4. Use Formula 9 to determine the Pearson r.

$$r = \frac{\Sigma XY - \dfrac{\Sigma X \cdot \Sigma Y}{N}}{\sqrt{SS_x \cdot SS_y}} \qquad (9)$$

SUMMARY FOR CALCULATING THE SPEARMAN r_s

1. If either variable is not ranked, then rank the values.
2. Calculate the difference score d for each pair of ranks.
3. With N equal to the number of pairs of ranks, use Formula 10 to calculate r_s.

$$r_s = 1 - \frac{6 \cdot \Sigma d^2}{N^3 - N}.$$ (10)

EXERCISES

1. A student reads that the dosage of a particular drug is related to the number of hallucinations that occur during a 24-hour period. Can she assume that the Pearson r coefficient will reflect the strength and type of relationship between the drug dosage and the number of hallucinations? Explain.

2. If the student in Exercise 1 reads further that a positive linear relationship does exist, then what could she expect if she took a strong dosage of the drug? What if she took a weak dosage of the drug?

3. Given the following three situations determine which provides the least evidence of a linear relationship and which provides the best evidence of a linear relationship:
   (a) $r = -.61$　(b) $r = -.03$　(c) $r = +.44$
   Justify your answer.

4. For each of the following sets of data, create a scatterplot. Then estimate r for each of the sets based solely on the scatterplots.

A		B		C		D	
X	Y	X	Y	X	Y	X	Y
2	9	1	90	300	14	1	46
3	5	4	30	440	18	4	79
5	16	6	10	750	20	6	74
5	4	3	70	680	22	7	83
7	12	2	60	1000	30	8	90
9	7	5	10	900	26	8	91
10	6	1	70	600	15	9	95
11	15	7	10	1170	32	11	80
12	0	8	10	890	27	12	71
14	8	3	50	510	21	14	52

5. For Set B in Exercise 4, calculate r using all 10 sets of values. Then calculate r using only those sets of values for which $X < 5$. What happens to r? Explain in terms of what the scatterplot shows.

6. How would you describe the relationship for Set D in Exercise 4? Would you expect the Pearson *r* to accurately reflect this relationship? Explain.

7. For both of the variables below, convert each value to a *z* score. The transformations should be done separately for each variable. Create a scatterplot using the original values and a scatterplot using the *z* scores. Based on your scatterplots, what effect did the transformation have on the relationship between the two variables?

X	Y
91	18
17	62
46	57
92	28
14	83
34	63
70	42
53	7
76	56
64	59
8	76
27	89

$\overline{X} = 49.33$ $\overline{X} = 53.33$

$\sigma = 28.39$ $\sigma = 24.24$

8. Using the information from Exercise 7, calculate the Pearson *r* using the *z*-score formula, shown on page 101. Then calculate the Pearson *r* using Formula 9. Do the statistics agree?

9. A student believes that it is possible to alter a relationship by transforming the values in one or both of the variables (by adding or multiplying each value by a constant). Do you agree or disagree? Base your answer on the *z*-score formula.

10. Use the set of values from Exercise 7 to calculate *r*. Then multiply each value for Variable *X* by 3 and subtract 1 from each value for Variable *Y*. Recalculate *r* using these transformed values. What effect did the transformations have on the correlation coefficient? How would the scatterplots differ for the two sets of values?

11. A student believes that the Spearman r_s is easier to calculate than the Pearson *r* and concludes that since it is an alternative form of the Pearson *r*, it should be used whenever possible. Explain your response to this student.

12. A relationship ($r = +.42$) is found between the number of questions students ask in class and their final grades in the course. A teacher assumes that if instructors could get all students to ask more questions, their

grades would improve. Is this assumption correct given the correlational information above? Is the teacher violating any assumptions involved in correlational research? Explain your answer.

13. An employee complains to a personnel officer that her screening test is not a valid measure of job performance in that everyone at the company does well on a particular job and not everyone scored the same on the screening test. The personnel manager responds that it is true that the relationship between the test score and job performance is low at the company but that the company only hires people who score above 90 on the screening test. Is it unusual for the test and job performance to be unrelated given her sample of individuals? Explain.

14. Ten students are ranked by a faculty member in terms of the grades they earned in an introductory psychology course. Two years later the same 10 students are ranked by a faculty committee which reviewed their senior research theses. Using the ranks below, calculate the Spearman r_s to determine if performance in the introductory course is related to the quality of the theses. For both variables, a low rank indicates better performance.

Student	Introductory Course	Research Thesis
a	1	6
b	2	2
c	3	4
d	4	1
e	5	9
f	6	5
g	7	3
h	8	10
i	9	8
j	10	7

15. Using the ranks in Exercise 14, calculate the correlation coefficient using the Pearson r. Compare it with the Spearman r_s calculated in Exercise 14.

16. A social psychologist is studying the relationship between distance (in miles) from the person one is dating and one's rating of the relationship on a 1–to–100 scale. The hypothesis is that freshmen who are separated from people they are dating will rate their relationship lower as the distance between the couple increases. Eleven students in the class who are dating someone from out of town were asked to estimate the distance and to rate the relationship. The values are shown below. Use the Pearson r to estimate the strength of the relationship between these two variables. What are your conclusions about the psychologist's hypothesis?

Distance (in Miles)	Rating
50	85
75	90
30	80
200	60
375	55
140	75
100	95
180	70
500	45
110	83
390	62

17. Given the values in Exercise 16, it is possible to rank the values on each variable. For instance, the lowest distance could be given a rank of 1 and the largest distance a rank of 11. The lowest rating of 45 could be given a rank of 1 with the highest rating of 95 receiving a rank of 11. If the values were converted to ranks, then the Spearman r_s could be calculated. Is it the same as the Pearson r from Exercise 16? Explain. It might help to construct scatterplots for the original values and for the ranks. Does the conversion of values into ranks change the relationship?

18. An introductory-level course is being considered as a prerequisite for an advanced-level course. The grades of 15 students who took both courses are shown below. Determine if there is a relationship between the grades.

Student	Intro-level	Advanced-level
a	92	84
b	90	88
c	89	91
d	85	82
e	85	86
f	82	90
g	81	75
h	80	86
i	75	64
j	74	77
k	70	79
l	68	71
m	66	63
n	64	69
o	62	70

19. Assume that the introductory-level course described in Exercise 18 was used as a prerequisite with the further restriction that one must earn at least an 85 in the introductory-level course in order to take the advanced-level course. What would you predict would happen to the relationship between grades from the two courses? Would it be the same, stronger, or weaker than that found in Exercise 18 when all students from the introductory course were allowed to take the advanced-level course? Explain your answer.

20. You read a report that instances of pornography have increased in a particular town over the past 10 years. During that same time the number of sexual crimes has increased. A town council member concludes, based on a Pearson r of $+.67$, that the availability of pornography is causing people to commit sex crimes. Provide your comments based on limitations and cautions discussed in this chapter.

CHAPTER 6

Linear Regression and Prediction

TERMS DISCUSSED
linear regression
regression line
standard error of estimate $s_{est\ y}$
coefficient of determination r^2
coefficient of nondetermination k^2
homoscedasticity

PROCEDURES DESCRIBED
determining the regression line
calculating $s_{est\ y}$

One field of study within psychology is known as environmental psychology. Environmental psychology which developed from social psychology is the study of the environment and its effect on behavior. Gormley and Aiello published a study in 1982 that investigated roommate satisfaction and privacy in college residence halls. Sixty college students who were residing in either double- or triple-resident rooms completed a questionnaire. Among the statements asked were the student's satisfaction with one's roommate(s) and with the amount of privacy in the room. Roommate satisfaction was based on nine statements including ones such as "I like to spend time with my roommate" and "I am quite compatible with my roommate." The students indicated their level of agreement for each statement using a 1–to–5 scale, with 5 indicating greatest agreement. The privacy scale also consisted of statements rated on a 1–to–5 scale. For each student the mean rating given for each variable was calculated. For both variables, a high value indicated greater satisfaction.

Gormley and Aiello (1982) hypothesized that the two variables, roommate satisfaction and privacy, are related to each other. If a person were satisfied with the amount of privacy he had, then he was likely to be satisfied with his roommate(s). On the other hand, dissatisfaction with the amount of privacy was likely to be related to dissatisfaction with one's roommate(s).

TABLE 6.1   Summary and Descriptive Statistics for the Chapter Example

Descriptive Statistics

Satisfaction with privacy	Roommate satisfaction
$\Sigma X = 140.50$	$\Sigma Y = 150.70$
$\Sigma X^2 = 340.33$	$\Sigma Y^2 = 396.31$
$\overline{X} = 2.34$	$\overline{Y} = 2.51$
$SS_x = 11.33$	$SS_y = 17.80$
$s_x = .44$	$s_y = .55$

Calculation of Pearson r

$$\Sigma XY = 360.17, \text{N} = 60$$

$$r = \frac{\Sigma XY - \dfrac{\Sigma X \cdot \Sigma Y}{\text{N}}}{\sqrt{SS_x \cdot SS_y}} \qquad (9)$$

$$= \frac{360.17 - \dfrac{140.5 \times 150.7}{60}}{\sqrt{11.33 \times 17.80}}$$

$$= +.51$$

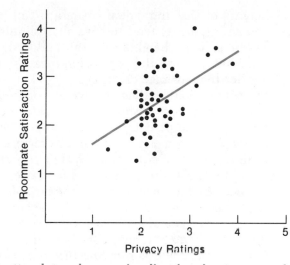

FIGURE 6.1 Scatterplot and regression line for chapter example.

This study by Gormley and Aiello (1982) has two variables of interest, room-mate satisfaction and satisfaction with the amount of privacy. Both variables have values that range from one—no satisfaction to five—a high level of satisfaction. The researchers are predicting that a relationship exists between the variables. In fact, they are predicting that the relationship is linear and positive. As satisfaction increases for one variable, satisfaction for the other variable will increase. Table 6.1 shows the summary and descriptive statistics for this example. The calculation of the Pearson r coefficient is shown at the bottom of the table. A Pearson r of $+.51$ was found indicating that a positive linear relationship exists between the two variables. This supports the hypothesis of the researchers.

In Figure 6.1, the scatterplot for the relationship is shown. Satisfaction with privacy is represented on the x-axis and roommate satisfaction is on the y-axis. Each point represents the intersection of the two satisfaction ratings for a student in the study. A line is drawn in this scatterplot which best represents this linear relationship. The focus of this chapter involves the procedure for determining the line for a linear relationship.

THE REGRESSION LINE

The statistical procedure for determining the line that best describes a linear relationship is called **linear regression.** Regression is a fairly complicated statistical concept. It is based on the fact that if two variables are not perfectly related (do not have an r of either $+1.00$ or -1.00), then values on a variable will tend to *regress* toward some central value.

We know, for instance, that the height of an individual is related to the heights of that individual's parents. Tall parents tend to have tall children and short parents tend to have short children. However, the relationship between parents' heights and the child's height is not perfect. As a result, regression toward the population mean height occurs. Tall parents will have a taller than average child, but it is likely that the child will be shorter than the parents (rather than the average of the parents' heights). Similarly, short parents may have a shorter than average child, but the child will likely be taller than the parents. The tendency is for the children to be influenced by the population mean height and to regress toward it rather than move away from it. Anytime two variables are not perfectly related, which is the case in most instances, the tendency is for extreme values on one variable to be influenced by the mean of the other variable. Rather than being more extreme, they regress, or draw closer, to the mean of the other variable.

The concept of regression applies to linear relationships and the determination of the line that best represents a linear relationship. For every linear relationship, there is *one* line that best describes the relationship. This line is called a **regression line.**

The regression line minimizes the sum of the squared deviations of points from this line. For every value of X, there is a Y value on the line which is represented by Y'. These values of Y' that are on the regression line are often referred to as the "predicted values of Y." The deviations of actual Y values from what is predicted by the regression line Y' can be determined. If these deviations $(Y - Y')$ are squared and then summed $\Sigma(Y - Y')^2$, the sum will be smaller for the regression line than for any other line that might be drawn to describe the linear relationship. This is often referred to as the "least squares" solution for fitting a line that best describes a linear relationship.

It is important to understand the difference between Y and Y' values. In behavioral research, Y values are obtained from a sample. Based on the sample, the researcher determines if a relationship exists between X and Y. Based on this relationship, a researcher or others may wish to predict the Y values for individuals not included but similar to those in the sample. For a given value of X it is possible to predict a Y value. That value is Y'. If a relationship exists but X is unknown, then the best predictor of Y' is $\overline{Y}$. For instance, in the chapter example, knowing nothing about a student's privacy rating, I would predict that his or her roommate-satisfaction rating would be equal to the mean satisfaction rating. But, if I know that the person is very satisfied in terms of privacy (high X), then I would predict that the roommate-satisfaction rating (Y') would also be high, that is above $\overline{Y}$. Using a regression line permits you to predict a specific value for Y'. As we will see, the stronger the relationship, the more accurate your prediction will be.

Figure 6.2 illustrates this concept. The top scatterplot represents a perfect negative linear relationship $(r = -1.00)$. Every actual value of Y falls on the regression line. Therefore, the sum of the squared deviations from the line is 0. For the middle scatterplot, the relationship is $+.76$. The deviations of actual Y values from the regression line are shown as dotted lines. The sum of these squared deviations is 712.69. No other line could be drawn for this

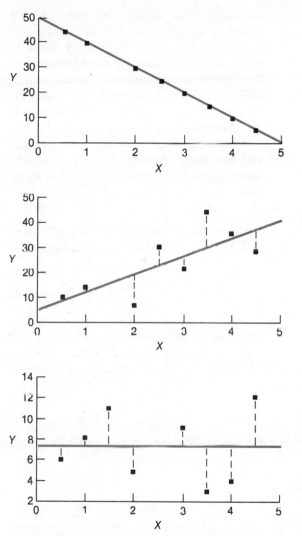

FIGURE 6.2 Three scatterplots with regression lines. Top scatterplot has $r = -1.00$; middle plot has $r = +.76$; and, bottom has $r = .00$. Dashed lines represent deviations from line.

relationship that would have a lower sum. The bottom scatterplot represents a situation in which there is no relationship between the two variables. In this case, the mean for Variable Y is the best predictor for all values of X and thus the regression line is a flat line corresponding to Y.

THE FORMULA FOR THE REGRESSION LINE

To determine the regression line for a linear relationship, it is helpful to review the general form of a straight line. Given two variables X and Y, the algebraic formula for a line is $Y = bX + a$. The letters a and b represent constants. The slope is represented by b, which shows how fast the line is rising or falling. The slope is based on the change in Y units as a function of a change in X units. A positive slope indicates that the line is going up; a negative slope indicates a line sloping downward. The larger the value of b, the greater the change in Y units for a given change in X units. As an example, a b value of $+3.0$ would indicate that a change in one unit on the x-axis results in a three-unit change on the y-axis. The a in the equation represents the y-intercept, the value of Y where the line crosses the y-axis.

The regression line for the Y variable consists of two variables X and Y' and two constants a and b. These constants can be determined with the statistics from Chapter 5. The general form of the regression line is

$$Y' = bX + a \tag{11}$$

The slope b is based on the the cross products of the deviations of the X and Y values and SS_x. The definitional formula for the slope is

$$b = \frac{\Sigma(X - \overline{X})(Y - \overline{Y})}{SS_x}. \tag{Def}$$

Note that the numerator is identical to that for the Pearson r. It is possible to simplify the calculation of b. An algebraic equivalent of the definitional formula exists using the Pearson r and the estimates of the population standard deviation for each variable s_x and s_y:

$$b = r\frac{s_y}{s_x}. \tag{11a}$$

Once the slope is known, the value for the y-intercept a is determined using the following formula:

$$a = \overline{Y} - b\overline{X}. \tag{11b}$$

Using the information from Table 6.1, it is possible to determine the regression line for the relationship between satisfaction with the amount of privacy and roommate satisfaction. Using Formulas 11a and 11b provides the following:

$$b = r\frac{s_y}{s_x} \tag{11a}$$
$$= .51\frac{.55}{.44}$$
$$= .64,$$

and

$$a = \overline{Y} - b\overline{X} \tag{11b}$$
$$= 2.51 - (.64 \times 2.34)$$
$$= 1.01.$$

Substituting these values for b and a into the regression line results in the following equation:

$$Y' = .64X + 1.01.$$

Using this equation for the regression line, it is possible to predict a student's satisfaction rating of a roommate Y' if you know the student's privacy rating X.

Graphing the regression line is fairly easy. To graph the line you must have two points. The easiest is the y-intercept. If $X = 0$, then the first term on the right of the equals sign disappears and the predicted value is a, the y-intercept. In the chapter example, this point corresponds to $(0, 1.01)$. The second point is the intersection of the two means $\overline{X}$ and $\overline{Y}$. The intersection of the two means must fall on the regression line. This is a good way to check your calculations for the regression line. Insert $\overline{X}$ for X and Y' must equal $\overline{Y}$. In the chapter example this corresponds to the point $(2.34, 2.51)$. Using these two points the regression line can be graphed as shown in Figure 6.1.

As a cautionary note, the regression line applies to the range of values found in the relationship. The point where the line crosses the y-axis, the y-intercept, is helpful for graphing purposes. Note that in the chapter example a 0 value cannot exist; the minimum value for both X and Y is 1. Therefore, extending the line beyond 1 or 5, the maximum value, is not warranted.

These procedures also work when using z scores. If, however, both X and Y are expressed in terms of z scores, then the means are 0 and the standard deviations are 1. Using this information in Formulas 11a and 11b results in b equalling r and a equalling 0. The regression line when working with z scores will pass through the origin $(0, 0)$ and the slope will equal r.

THE STANDARD ERROR OF THE ESTIMATE $s_{\text{est }y}$

The regression line provides the best predictions or estimates of Y for various X values. However, unless the relationship between X and Y is perfect, the estimates will not always be the same as the actual values obtained. There will be error in the estimated values, Y'. The extent of the error in the estimates depends on the strength of the relationship. The stronger the relationship, the less error.

The error in predicted values is based on the sum of the squared deviations of the actual values from the predicted values, $\Sigma(Y - Y')^2$. In fact, it is possible to calculate a standard deviation around the regression line. This standard deviation is called the **standard error of the estimate** and is abbreviated as $s_{\text{est }y}$. Recall from Chapter 3 that the larger the standard deviation, the greater the variability in values. This is the same for the standard error of the estimate. If the actual values are far from the regression line, then $s_{\text{est }y}$ will be large. When the actual values of Y are close to the regression line, the $s_{\text{est }y}$ will be small. The definitional formula for $s_{\text{est }y}$ is

$$s_{\text{est }y} = \sqrt{\frac{\Sigma(Y - Y')^2}{N - 2}}. \tag{Def}$$

Instead of calculating the squared deviation of each value from the mean, $(Y - \bar{Y})^2$, the squared deviation from the predicted value, $(Y - Y')^2$, is calculated. This difference if presented visually is the square of the distance of the actual Y values from the predicted Y' values.

The computational formula for $s_{est\ y}$ is

$$s_{est\ y} = s_y \sqrt{\frac{N\,(1 - r^2)}{N - 2}}. \tag{12}$$

Notice that $s_{est\ y}$ is a function of the estimate of the population standard deviation for the Y values s_y and the strength of the relationship r. If the relationship between X and Y is perfect, that is, $r = +1.00$ or -1.00, then the numerator under the square root is 0 and $s_{est\ y}$ is 0. There is no error in the predicted values because each value falls on the regression line. (See the top scatterplot in Figure 6.2.) The $s_{est\ y}$ reaches its maximum value when there is no relationship between X and Y; $r = .00$. This, of course, is the situation in which the best predictor of Y' is $\bar{Y}$ for all values of X (the bottom scatterplot in Figure 6.2).

Given that all other statistics are held constant, $s_{est\ y}$ will be smaller for stronger relationships than for weaker relationships. This should make intuitive sense. If there is a strong relationship between two variables, then using one of the variables to predict the value on the other variable should be more accurate and involve less error than if the relationship between the two variables is weak.

For the chapter example the $s_{est\ y}$ would be

$$s_{est\ y} = s_y \sqrt{\frac{N\,(1 - r^2)}{N - 2}} \tag{12}$$

$$= .55 \sqrt{\frac{60\,(1 - .51^2)}{60 - 2}}$$

$$= .55 \times .87$$

$$= .48.$$

The $s_{est\ y}$ can be interpreted in much the same way as s, the estimate of the population standard deviation, except that it applies to the population of predicted Y values, Y'. Recall from Chapter 2 that in a normally distributed population, approximately 68% of all values fall within one standard deviation above and below the mean, and approximately 95% of the values fall within two standard deviations of the mean. The $s_{est\ y}$ can be used to estimate the range of Y' values for a particular X value. (As we will see later this is true when the actual Y values are normally distributed around the regression line.) Although the regression line provides the best estimate Y' for a particular X value, it is likely that there will be some error in the prediction (unless, of course, if $r = +1.00$ or -1.00). The $s_{est\ y}$ is useful in determining the range of potential Y' values for a particular X value. Let's look at an example.

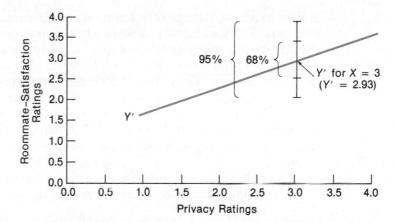

FIGURE 6.3 Predicting y' (roommate satisfaction) for a student with an x (privacy rating) of 3.00. The ranges of y' values for the 68% and 95% intervals are also shown.

Let's assume that a student is asked to rate his satisfaction with privacy. He has not already been tested but is from the same population of students used by Gormley and Aiello. He gives a rating of 3. Using the regression line developed earlier, it is possible to predict what his roommate-satisfaction rating would be.

$$Y' = .64X + 1.01$$
$$= .64(3) + 1.01$$
$$= 2.93.$$

We would predict that his rating of roommate satisfaction would be 2.93. Of course, since the relationship between privacy and roommate satisfaction is not perfect, it is possible that his rating would not be exactly 2.93.

We can use the $s_{est\ y}$ of .48 to determine that 68% of all students who give a privacy rating of 3 would have a roommate rating between 2.93 ± .48. Therefore, there is a 68% chance that the student would have a roommate-satisfaction rating between 2.45 and 3.41. Because 95% of the students would have ratings within $2s_{est\ y}$ values of Y', we know that there is a 95% chance that this student would have a roommate-satisfaction rating between 1.97, or $Y' - 2s_{est\ y}$, and 3.89, or $Y' + 2s_{est\ y}$. This is shown in the graph in Figure 6.3. Use Y' in conjunction with $s_{est\ y}$ to provide a range of Y' values. Given a particular s_y, the range will depend on r; the stronger the relationship the narrower the range.

EXPLAINING THE VARIATION FOR VARIABLE Y

When a relationship exists between two variables, then one of the variables can be used to *explain* or *account for* some of the variability associated with the other variable. For instance, in the chapter example we know that variability exists in ratings of roommate satisfaction. We know from the data that part of this variability is related to satisfaction with privacy. We can use the knowledge of this relationship to account for some of the variability in roommate satisfaction. However, although we know that this relationship exists, because of the nature of a correlational study, we don't know if privacy is causing the changes in roommate satisfaction (X causing Y); if roommate satisfaction is influencing consideration of another's privacy (Y causing X); or if some other third variable (Z), perhaps the number of friends in common, is influencing both roommate and privacy satisfaction (Z causing both X and Y).

The total variation in roommate satisfaction can be expressed in terms of the sum of the squared deviations from the mean.

$$\text{Total Variation} = \Sigma(Y - \overline{Y})^2.$$

To explain why some Y values are above $\overline{Y}$ and some are below $\overline{Y}$, we can look at the privacy ratings. Students who rate low privacy satisfaction tend to have low roommate satisfaction. High privacy satisfaction is likewise related to high roommate satisfaction. Therefore, knowing privacy satisfaction X explains some of the roommate satisfaction values. In fact, the regression line *predicts* how far above or below $\overline{Y}$ a Y value should be. This is the variation in Y values that can be explained.

$$\text{Explained Variation} = \Sigma(Y' - \overline{Y})^2.$$

This is depicted graphically in Figure 6.4.

When a Y value deviates from the regression line, it is the result of variables other than X. This is variability that cannot be explained by X and is called unexplained variation.

$$\text{Unexplained Variation} = \Sigma(Y - Y')^2.$$

This is also shown in Figure 6.4. Although X accounts for some of the variability in Y, there are other variables which have not been included and which account for some of the variability in Y. The variability resulting from these other variables is included in the unexplained variation.

Together the explained and unexplained variation sum to equal the total variation

$$\Sigma(Y - \overline{Y})^2 = \quad \Sigma(Y' - \overline{Y})^2 \quad + \quad \Sigma(Y - Y')^2.$$
Total Variation = Explained Variation + Unexplained Variation.

For perfect linear relationships, there will be no unexplained variation because every value will fall on the regression line and the $\Sigma(Y - Y')^2$ will equal 0. If $r = .00$, then no relationship exists and the regression line will be flat and correspond to $\overline{Y}$. In this case, $\overline{Y}$ could be substituted for Y' and the $\Sigma(Y' - \overline{Y})^2$ would equal 0. For relationships with r greater than 0.00 and less than $+1.00$ (or greater than -1.00), the explained variation will increase with increasing values of r.

Although the exact values of the explained and unexplained variation are

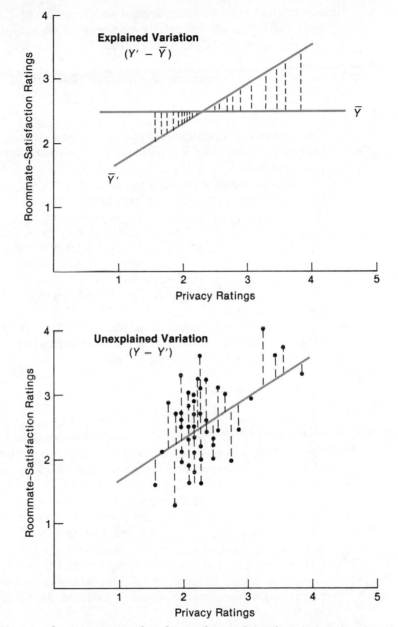

FIGURE 6.4 The top scatterplot shows the explained variation for the chapter
example (distance from line to mean). The bottom scatterplot
shows the unexplained variation (distance from value to line).

not critical because they depend on the scale of Y values, the proportion of explained and unexplained variation can be meaningfully interpreted. The proportion of explained variation is,

$$\text{Proportion of Explained Variation} = \frac{\Sigma(Y' - \overline{Y})^2}{\Sigma(Y - \overline{Y})^2}$$

$$= r^2.$$

The Pearson r coefficient squared is equal to the proportion of explained variation. This value is called the **coefficient of determination.** (Note that it is r^2 and not r.)

As you would expect, relationships with large absolute values of r will have a higher proportion of explained variation and this can be measured directly by squaring r. In the chapter example, privacy ratings explain .26 ($.51^2$) of the variation in roommate satisfaction. A perfect relationship results in total explained variation, 1.00 ($\pm 1.00^2$); whereas, no relationship results in no explained variation, 0.00 (0.00^2). Obviously, the function between the Pearson r and explained variation is not linear. While an r of .3 explains only .09 of the total variation, an r of .6 explains .36 and an r of .9 explains .81 of the total variation.

There is a coefficient of nondetermination as well as a coefficient of determination. The **coefficient of nondetermination,** abbreviated k^2, is equal to the proportion of unexplained variation,

$$\text{Proportion of Unexplained Variation} = \frac{\Sigma(Y - Y')^2}{\Sigma(Y - \overline{Y})^2}$$

$$k^2 = 1 - r^2.$$

The easiest way to calculate k^2 is to subtract r^2 from 1, since the proportion of explained variation and the proportion of unexplained variation must equal the total variation. In the chapter example, k^2 would equal 0.74 ($1 - 0.26$). Therefore, privacy ratings account for 26% of the variability in roommate satisfaction leaving 74% of the variability accounted for by other variables.

The coefficients of determination and nondetermination are useful in that they provide the researcher and reader with an estimate of how important a variable is in explaining variation in another variable. Obviously, it would be useful to identify all the variables and their contributions in explaining the variation in another variable. In Chapter 7, this topic will be briefly explored.

A SECOND EXAMPLE

The role of women in society has changed in the past decades, and researchers have tried to identify the impact of this change on individuals and society as a whole. Dambrot, Papp, and Whitmore (1984) investigated the attitudes of college women, their mothers, and their maternal grandmothers. These women were enrolled in an introductory psychology course at a midwestern state university. The women who volunteered to participate also solicited the participation of their mothers and maternal grandmothers. Each woman completed a 55-item questionnaire called the "Attitudes toward Women" scale (AWS). The scale required the students to indicate their feelings about such statements as "It is insulting to have the 'obey' clause remain in the marriage service" and "Women should worry less about their rights and more about becoming good wives and mothers." The women could score each item on a 0–to–3 scale, with 0 representing a traditional, conservative attitude and 3 representing a liberal, profeminist attitude. Therefore, AWS scores could vary from 0 to 165 with higher values representing liberal, profeminist attitudes. A total of 43 complete sets of questionnaires were collected. We will examine only the relationship between the college women and their mothers.

Dambrot et al. (1984) hypothesized that a relationship would exist between the attitudes of college women and their mothers but that the relationship might not be as strong as in earlier research when the roles of women were not changing as dramatically. Figure 6.5 shows the descriptive statistics for this study along with the scatterplot of the data. The X variable is the AWS scores of the college women, and the Y variable is the AWS scores of the women's mothers. Note that a positive relationship $r = +.34$ was found. Although the AWS scores are related, it is not a very strong relationship.

To determine the regression line for this example, the statistics in Figure 6.5 must be inserted into Formulas 11a and 11b,

$$b = r \frac{s_y}{s_x} \tag{11a}$$

$$= .34 \times \frac{22.83}{13.56}$$

$$= .57,$$

and

$$a = \overline{Y} - b\overline{X} \tag{11b}$$
$$= 100.00 - (.57 \times 106.19)$$
$$= 39.47.$$

These values can be inserted into Formula 11 to provide the following regression line:

$$Y' = bX + a \tag{11}$$
$$Y' = .57X + 39.47.$$

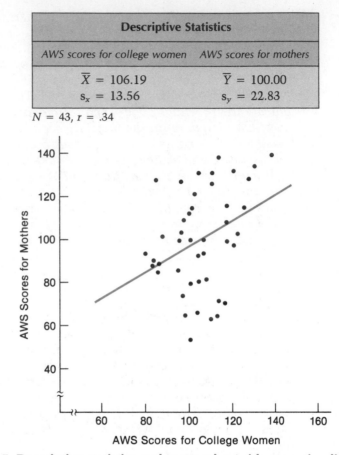

Descriptive Statistics	
AWS scores for college women	*AWS scores for mothers*
$\overline{X} = 106.19$	$\overline{Y} = 100.00$
$s_x = 13.56$	$s_y = 22.83$

$N = 43, r = .34$

FIGURE 6.5 Descriptive statistics and scatterplot (with regression line) for second chapter example.

To graph this regression line, we need two points; we know that one is the y-intercept, (0, 39.47). As a check of the calculations, $\overline{X}$ can be inserted into the equation and the result must be $\overline{Y}$, which is our second point, (106.19, 100.00). The regression line in Figure 6.5 is based on these calculations.

With the regression line, it is possible to predict the AWS score for the mothers of college women who are from the population sampled by Dambrot et al. (1984). With a student's score inserted into the equation, a Y', or predicted AWS score for the mother, can be calculated. However, because the relationship is not very strong, one could expect a relatively large error in the predicted scores. To determine the error in the estimates, $s_{\text{est } y}$ needs to be determined.

The standard error of the estimate $s_{\text{est } y}$ is the estimated population standard deviation for the regression line. Using Formula 12, the $s_{\text{est } y}$ for this example is

$$s_{est\ y} = s_y \sqrt{\frac{N\,(1 - r^2)}{N - 2}} \tag{12}$$

$$= 22.83 \sqrt{\frac{43 \times (1 - .34^2)}{43 - 2}}$$

$$= 22.83 \times 0.96$$

$$= 21.99.$$

The fact that the relationship is weak leads to a very small reduction in the amount of variability for $s_{est\ y}$ as compared with s_y. The proportional reduction is equal to 1 minus the value of the righthand component in Formula 12: $1 - .96 = .04$.

Knowing that 68% of the scores will fall within one standard deviation of a predicted score, we can see that the range of Y' scores is considerable. For example, if we knew that a college student had an AWS score of 120 using the regression line, we would predict that her mother's score would be

$$Y' = (.57 \times 120) + 39.47$$
$$= 107.87.$$

Although 107.87 would be our best single estimate, we would expect that 68% of the mothers who had daughters with AWS scores of 120 would themselves have AWS scores between 85.88 $(Y' - (1 \times s_{est\ y}) = 107.87 - 21.99)$ and 129.86 $(Y' + (1 \times s_{est\ y}) = 107.87 + 21.99)$. This is a range of almost 44 points, which is considerable. When a weak or moderate relationship between two variables exists, the amount of variability in the estimates $s_{est\ y}$ will not be much different from the amount of variability in the original values s_y.

We can conclude this example by identifying the proportion of explained variation in this study. Knowing the AWS scores for the college women or their mothers accounts for only .12 of the total variation in the AWS scores. The coefficient of determination r^2 for this example is $.34^2$, or .12. Since only 12% of the total variability in one variable can be explained by the other variable, the proportion of unexplained variability is quite large. The coefficient of nondetermination k^2 is .88 $(1 - r^2)$. The fact that the relationship between the AWS scores of the college students and their mothers is not strong is reflected in the low proportion of variability that can be accounted for by either variable and the high proportion of unexplained variability.

TWO ADDITIONAL ISSUES CONCERNING THE REGRESSION LINE

Before concluding this chapter there are two additional issues that must be discussed with regard to the regression line for a linear relationship. The first involves making predictions of X rather than Y. And, the second involves the variability of Y values around the regression line for different values of X.

THE REGRESSION LINE FOR THE X VARIABLE

The discussion in this chapter has focused on predicting values of Y using X values. The regression line in Formula 11 provided an estimated or predicted value of Y, Y'. This formula cannot be used for predicting a value of X, X'. The X and Y values in Formula 11 are not interchangeable.

An inspection of the calculation of the b and a constants for the formula (see Formulas 11a and 11b) reveals that they are a function of the means and estimates of the population standard deviations for both variables. If these statistics are not identical for both variables, then the regression lines for each variable will be different. The one situation in which the regression line for both X' and Y' is the same would be if the X and Y values are z scores. In this situation, the means for both X and Y would be 0 and the s would be 1.

Given that the regression line depends on the statistics of each variable, the easiest way to determine the prediction line for X would be to interchange the two variables in Formula 11 and then calculate the equation of the regression line. For instance, in the last example if one wanted to predict the college students' AWS scores based on the AWS scores of their mothers, then the AWS scores of the mothers should be considered as the X variable and the AWS scores of the college women as the Y variable. This information could then be inserted into Formula 11 to determine the regression line. (See Question 10 in the Exercises.) Care must be exercised when graphing the regression line if you retain the original X variable on the x-axis.

Also, it should be noted that $s_{est\,x}$ will not be the same as $s_{est\,y}$, because the standard error of estimate depends on the estimate of the population standard deviation. However, the coefficients of determination and nondetermination are the same whether predicting Y or X. These coefficients depend only on r and are not influenced by the individual statistics for either variable.

THE IMPORTANCE OF HOMOSCEDASTICITY

The standard error of the estimate $s_{est\,y}$ is based on the assumption that the variability of Y values around the regression line is the same for different X values. This assumption involves the principle of **homoscedasticity.** If this assumption is met and the Y values are normally distributed around the regression line, then one can use the techniques described earlier and in Chapter 2 to estimate the proportion of Y' values within certain distances of the $s_{est\,y}$ (such as 68% of the Y' values falling within one $s_{est\,y}$ of Y').

The principle of homoscedasticity is met in the top scatterplot of Figure 6.6. Note that the variability of Y values is similar across the different values of X. On the other hand, in the bottom scatterplot of Figure 6.6, the Y values vary much less for the lower values of X than for the higher values of X. There is much more variability among Y values when the X values are high. The bottom scatterplot does not meet the principle of homoscedasticity and, as a result, the $s_{est\,y}$ will not accurately estimate the error in prediction.

The easiest way to determine if the principle of homoscedasticity is met

A) Scatterplot satisfies the principle of homoscedasticity.

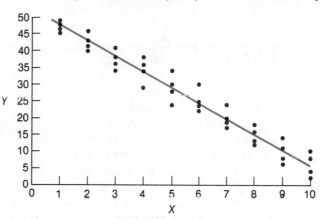

B) Scatterplot violates the principle of homoscedasticity.

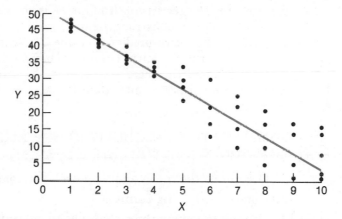

FIGURE 6.6 Top scatterplot meets the principle of homoscedasticity, but the bottom one does not. The y values vary more with high x values than with low x values in the bottom scatterplot.

for a relationship is to visually inspect the scatterplot with the regression line. If it appears that the variability among the Y values differs appreciably for different values of X, then one must be very cautious in using the $s_{est\ y}$ to estimate the error in Y'.

SUMMARY

The regression line for Y' is the line that minimizes the squared deviations of the Y values from the predicted values (Y') on the line. To determine the equation for the regression line, the slope, b, and y-intercept, a, must be calculated. Both rely on r and the X and s for each of the two variables. The general form of the line is $Y' = bX + a$.

The regression line can be used to predict Y values for those not in the original sample. Unless the relationship between X and Y is perfect, there will be error associated with the predicted values, Y'. The amount of error is given by the standard error of the estimate $s_{est\ y}$. It is a function of the strength of the relationship and the estimate of the population standard deviation for the Y variable s_y.

The coefficient of determination r^2 identifies the proportion of the variability for one variable that can be explained or accounted for on the basis of the relationship with another variable. If a perfect relationship exists between two variables, then the coefficient of determination is 1.00. If no relationship exists, then the coefficient is .00. The stronger the relationship between two variables, the greater the proportion of explained variance will be. The coefficient of nondetermination k^2 identifies the proportion of variability that cannot be explained by a relationship. It is equal to $1 - r^2$.

The regression line for Y' is not the same as that for X'. One method for determining the regression line for X' is to relabel the variables and to then use Formula 11 to construct the regression line for X'. When using the regression line and $s_{est\ y}$ to predict Y' values, it is important to consider the principle of homoscedasticity. Homoscedasticity assumes that the variability of Y values around the regression line is the same for different values of X. If this assumption is not met, then the $s_{est\ y}$ will not accurately indicate error in predicted Y'.

SUMMARY FOR CALCULATING THE REGRESSION LINE FOR Y'

1. Determine the mean and s for each variable. (Use Formulas 1 through 5.)
2. Determine r using Formula 9.
3. Use the following three formulas to determine the regression line:

$$b = r \frac{s_y}{s_x} \tag{11a}$$

$$a = \overline{Y} - b\overline{X} \tag{11b}$$

$$Y' = bX + a. \tag{11}$$

SUMMARY FOR CALCULATING $s_{est\ y}$

1. Determine N, r, and s_y.
2. Calculate $s_{est\ y}$ using the following formula:

$$s_{est\ y} = s_y \sqrt{\frac{N(1 - r^2)}{N - 2}}. \tag{12}$$

EXERCISES

1. Use the data from the first chapter example in Chapter 5 to determine the regression line for predicted ratings as a potential date. Much of the information you need can be found in Table 5.4.

2. Using the regression line calculated in Exercise 1, determine the predicted rating as a potential date for a person who is rated as 6 on the attractiveness scale. Would it be likely in your estimation that the student would ask this person for a date? Explain.

3. Given the data below, determine the regression line:

X	Y
$\overline{X} = 24$	$\overline{Y} = 48$
$s_x = 3.1$	$s_y = 5.4$

$N = 45 \quad r = -.60$

   Graph the regression line.

4. How would the regression line change in each of the following cases?
   a. r is $+.60$ instead of $-.60$
   b. $s_y = 2.7$ instead of 5.4
   c. $\overline{X} = 48$ and $\overline{Y} = 24$ instead of the values in Exercise 3.

5. Graph the regression lines for each of the three cases in Exercise 4 and compare them with the regression line graphed in Exercise 3.

6. Regression lines are often used by personnel officers in predicting the success of potential employees. Let's assume that a personnel officer knows that a particular personality inventory test (X) is related to the length of service in the firm (Y), $r = +.45$. This is based on data collection over a 10-year period. She now wants to use these data to construct the regression line for the relationship so that she can predict the length of service for future employees. Using the data below, determine the regression line and graph it.

   Personality test scores: $\overline{X} = 64.6$, $s = 10.0$
   Length of service in years: $\overline{Y} = 5.8$, $s = 1.2$

7. The personnel officer in Exercise 6 must select some job applicants for a new training program. In order to increase the chances that the company selects applicants who will remain with the company for some time, she wants only applicants who have predicted lengths of service of seven years or more. What would be the predicted score on the personality test? (Hint: You need only concern yourself with the minimum length of service—seven years.)

8. An instructor is counseling his class about their likelihood of succeeding in the course based on the results of their first exam. He has used alter-

native forms of the same tests for several years and knows that the relationship between the first exam and final course grades is $+.73$. Given that a passing grade is 70 (both on the first exam and in the course) and given the following data, should a person with a 66 withdraw from the course? Explain your answer.

First exam statistics (X) : mean $= 72.8$, $s = 8.1$

Final course statistics (Y): mean $= 76.4$, $s = 7.0$

9. The student in Exercise 8 wants more information from you. He wants to know the range of final course averages, so that he would be 68% confident getting a final average within the range. You should know, in addition to the information in Exercise 8, that the N for the original sample was 236.

10. Using the second chapter example, determine the regression line for predicting the college students' AWS scores given that you know the mothers' AWS scores. Graph this regression line and the regression line from the example on the same graph. Put the college students' scores on the x-axis.

11. In Exercise 10, the regression lines should cross. At what X and Y values do they cross? What is significant about those values?

12. A student is given data that were constructed by her instructor. She is puzzled because she knows that the r between the two variables is .40 and yet the $s_{est\ y}$ is 0. The N was 8. Can this situation occur? Explain.

13. Being provided with only this information $\overline{Y} = 8$ and $s_y = 2$, what would be your best guess as to the Y value for someone from this population? What would be the range of your guesses if you wanted to include 68% of the population values? Now you learn that Y is related to X ($r = .60$, $N = 16$) and that this person had an X score equal to $\overline{X}$. What would you predict the Y' to be and what would be the range for 68% of the population values? What effect did the information about the relationship have on your estimates?

14. For the first chapter example in Chapter 5, what proportion of the variability in ratings as a potential date could be accounted for by knowing the attractiveness rating? What proportion of the variability is unaccounted for?

15. Given the data from Exercise 1, what is the $s_{est\ y}$? How does it compare with s_y, which would be used in estimating error in predicting the ratings as a potential date if there was no relationship with attractiveness?

16. The data below indicate that the assumption of homoscedasticity has been violated. Explain where the violation occurs.

X	Y
1	10
1	12
1	11
1	12
2	14
2	17
2	16
3	19
3	20
3	21
4	26
4	22
4	30
4	30
5	19
5	27
5	36
5	30

17. In Exercise 16, if a person used the $s_{est\ y}$, which would be ill-advised, for which values of X would it tend to overestimate the range of Y' values and for which values would it tend to underestimate them?

18. Calculate the regression lines for X' and Y' for the two sets of ranks below and graph them. You can use the Spearman r_s instead of the Pearson r formula if you like.

X Ranks	Y Ranks
1	4
2	5
3	1
4	2
5	3

19. Are the regression lines in Exercise 18 the same or different? Explain your findings.

20. The data from the middle scatterplot in Figure 6.2 were transformed into z scores and are shown below. Determine the regression line and graph it. Compare it with the regression line and scatterplot in Figure 6.2. How do they differ?

X	Y
−1.51	−1.10
−1.15	−0.73
−0.44	−1.33
−0.09	0.48
0.27	−0.12
0.62	1.54
0.98	0.86
1.33	0.41

CHAPTER 7

An Introduction to Multiple Regression

TERMS DISCUSSED

multiple regression

criterion variable

predictor variables

correlation matrix

standardized partial regression
coefficient, β

the multiple R

PROCEDURES DESCRIBED

calculating β

calculating R and R^2

Getting into graduate school and successfully completing a graduate degree are the goals of an increasing number of undergraduate students. Universities with graduate programs are also concerned that they select the best students for their programs. Therefore, studies have been undertaken to identify or predict who the best undergraduates are for a graduate program.

Stricker and Huber (1967) investigated the performance of 37 graduate students in their clinical psychology program at Adelphi University in New York. Among the variables they studied was the student's grade point average in the graduate courses (GGPA). This was their criterion variable. They were interested in identifying other variables that are related to GGPA and which might be used in predicting a student's GGPA. As you might suspect, they studied a number of variables related to one's undergraduate education including overall GPA as an undergraduate, GPA for each of the four years, GPA in psychology courses, and the GRE scores.

They obtained the relevant data for each of their 37 students and then analyzed the relationships among these variables. They found two variables to be particularly important in predicting GGPA. These variables were the grade point average in undergraduate psychology courses (PGPA), and the combined GRE scores on the psychology and quantitative tests (GRE: P + Q). The Pearson r coefficients among these three variables are shown in the correlation matrix in Table 7.1.

The material in this chapter is an extension of the material discussed in the previous two chapters. In Chapters 5 and 6, linear relationships involving two variables were discussed. In this chapter, we will investigate the relationships among three variables. The identification of relationships among more than two variables involves **multiple regression**. Multiple regression can involve any number of variables. This chapter will focus on only three. (The

TABLE 7.1 Correlation Matrix Listing the Pearson *r* Coefficients for the Stricker and Huber (1967) Study

	Variable		
Variable	*GGPA (Y)*	*PGPA (X_1)*	*GRE: P + Q (X_2)*
GGPA		.52	.43
PGPA	.52		.30
GRE: P + Q	.43	.30	

Note. To read matrix, understand that the values represent the *r* coefficients for the variables identified by the column and row labels. Letters in parentheses are used to identify variables discussed in text.

study of the relationship between two variables, as in Chapters 5 and 6, is sometimes referred to as simple regression.)

In multiple regression, one variable is often identified as the criterion variable and can be designated with the letter Y. In Chapter 6 the criterion variable was designated with Y and took the form of Y' in the regression equation. You can think of the **criterion variable** as the variable for which the researcher is trying to predict the participant's value or score. For example, in a testing situation the criterion variable may be performance on a particular task.

The criterion variable also can be viewed as the variable that identifies the principal behavior of interest to the researcher. In a study of what factors are related to TV watching in children, for instance, the variable that describes TV watching would be the criterion variable. The other variables are often referred to as **predictor variables,** because they are used to predict values on the criterion variable. In some cases, researchers may also refer to the criterion variable as the dependent variable and predictor variables as independent variables.

In the chapter example, Stricker and Huber (1967) are interested in performance in graduate school. Specifically, their criterion variable is grade point average in graduate school (GGPA). They have two predictor variables, the GPA in psychology undergraduate courses (PGPA) and the combined GRE scores from the psychology and quantitative sections of the test (GRE: P+Q). The coefficients of the linear relationships are shown in Table 7.1. It is common to report the correlation coefficients in a matrix format as shown in that table. This matrix listing the coefficients of all of the combinations of variables is called a **correlation matrix.** The correlation matrix in Table 7.1 is a complete matrix in that the bottom portion below the diagonal contains redundant information and is a mirror image of the information above the diagonal. Matrices similar to this are sometimes included in computer printouts from statistical software.

It is obvious that these variables are positively related to one another, with the strongest relationship existing between GGPA and PGPA. The relationship between GGPA and GRE: P+Q is next in strength, followed by the relationship between PGPA and GRE: P+Q. To understand how multiple regression works, let's use this information and relate it to the concepts presented in Chapter 6.

A CONCEPTUAL APPROACH TO MULTIPLE REGRESSION

To begin this discussion the variability in GGPA is represented by the Venn diagrams in Figure 7.1. The area inside the circle in A represents the total variability in GGPA values. We can set this area to be 100% or to have a proportion of 1.00. Let's assume that all of this variability, as shown in Figure

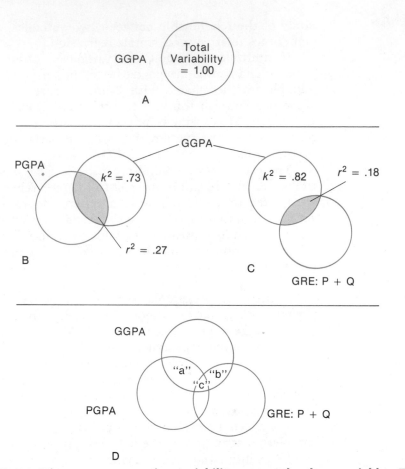

FIGURE 7.1 Diagrams representing variability among the three variables. The
top diagram shows total variability for GGPA. Diagrams B and C
show shared variability between GGPA and each of the other
variables (shaded areas), and the bottom diagram shows unique
variability between GGPA and each of the other variables (*a* and *b*)
and shared variability (*c*).

7.1(A), is unexplained, because we have no other variables yet that are related
to it.

In Figure 7.1(B) and (C), relationships between GGPA and PGPA and
GRE: P+Q are shown. Because there are relationships between these variables and GGPA, the circles overlap. The proportion of overlap in each corresponds to the proportion of explained variability r^2 for each relationship.
The remaining proportion of unexplained variability k^2, for GGPA is also
shown.

If the two variables, PGPA and GRE: P+Q, were unrelated to each other
(as shown in Figure 7.1(B) and (C)), then determining the proportion of explained variability for GGPA would be a simple matter. It would be the sum

of the two separate proportions of explained variability r^2 listed in Figure 7.1(B) and (C) (.27 + .18). However, PGPA and GRE: P+Q are related to each other, $r = .30$. Therefore, the correct depiction of the relationships among these three variables looks like that shown in Figure 7.1(D).

Because PGPA and GRE: P+Q are related to each other, they overlap in the proportion of explained variability for GGPA. Some of the factors that influence PGPA probably influence GRE: P+Q as well. Therefore, simply adding the two separate r^2 together will overestimate the proportion of explained variability in GGPA.

Instead, we need to determine (a) the unique contribution of PGPA to the proportion of explained variability; (b) the unique contribution of GRE: P+Q to the explained variability of G; and, (c) the shared contribution of PGPA and GRE: P+Q to the explained variability. To begin let's determine the total proportion of explained variability which is the sum of (a) + (b) + (c).

DETERMINING β, THE STANDARDIZED PARTIAL REGRESSION COEFFICIENT

The first step in calculating the total proportion of explained variability involves determining components of the multiple regression equation. As you might recall from Chapter 6, in determining the regression line for one X variable, it is necessary to calculate the slope b and the y-intercept a. If we were working with standardized scores (both X and Y are z scores), then b would equal r (because s_y and s_x would be 1), and a would be 0 (because both X and Y would be 0). The form of the regression line for one variable would be $z_{y'} = rz_x$. A similar situation exists with multiple regression if we use standard scores.

To simplify the discussion we will assume that all values have been standardized and converted to z scores. (Later Box 7.1 will briefly examine this example with original values.) The general form of the multiple regression equation with two predictor variables is

$$z_{y'} = (\beta_1 \, z_{x1}) + (\beta_2 \, z_{x2}).\qquad\text{(Def)}$$

The important components in the equation are β_1 and β_2. These values are called the standardized partial regression coefficients. They are often referred to as standardized beta weights. A **standardized partial regression coefficient** (or **standardized beta weight**) is a measure of the relationship between a predictor variable X and a criterion variable Y, with an adjustment made for the relationship(s) between the predictor variable and other predictor variables. For multiple regression equations with two X variables, the calculation of the standardized beta weight is

$$\beta_1 = \frac{r_{y1} - (r_{y2} \cdot r_{12})}{1 - r_{12}{}^2}\qquad\text{(13a)}$$

$$\beta_2 = \frac{r_{y2} - (r_{y1} \cdot r_{12})}{1 - r_{12}{}^2}.\qquad\text{(13b)}$$

These formulas may look formidable because of the subscripts. The subscripts refer to the particular Pearson r coefficients to be used from the correlation matrix. The relationship between the criterion variable Y and the predictor variable labeled X_1 is represented by r_{y1}. Likewise, r_{y2} represents the relationship between the criterion variable and the predictor variable labeled X_2. And, r_{12} is used to represent the relationship between two predictor variables, X_1 and X_2.

This last relationship is critical in adjusting the beta weights for the relationship (or overlap) between the two X variables. For instance, if the two X variables are unrelated, that is, $r_{12} = .00$, then the sum of the shaded areas in the middle panel in Figure 7.1(B) and (C) represents the relationships between the X variables and Y. And, as you can determine from Formulas 13a and 13b, the βs would equal the respective rs. However, since this rarely occurs, we will find that the standardized beta weights are smaller than the individual r values so as to adjust for the variance shared between the two predictor variables.

In the chapter example GGPA will substitute for Y and PGPA will replace X_1, with GRE: P+Q is used for X_2. Using Formulas 13a and 13b and the correlation coefficients from Table 7.1, we can determine the beta weights,

$$\beta_1 = \frac{r_{y1} - (r_{y2} \cdot r_{12})}{1 - r_{12}^2} \tag{13a}$$

$$= \frac{.52 - (.43 \times .30)}{1 - .30^2}$$

$$= \frac{.39}{.91}$$

$$\beta_{pgpa} = .43,$$

and

$$\beta_2 = \frac{r_{y2} - (r_{y1} \cdot r_{12})}{1 - r_{12}^2} \tag{13b}$$

$$= \frac{.43 - (.52 \times .30)}{1 - .30^2}$$

$$= \frac{.27}{.91}$$

$$\beta_{gre: \ p+q} = .30.$$

Notice that both beta weights, .43 and .30, are smaller than the respective rs, .52 and .43, because of the adjustment made for shared variability. The multiple regression equation for this example (in terms of standardized values) is

$$z_{ggpa} = .43(z_{pgpa}) + .30(z_{gre: \ p+q}).$$

THE CONCEPT AND CALCULATION OF THE MULTIPLE R

Once the beta weights are known then the multiple R can be determined. The **multiple R,** usually referred to as R, is the coefficient for the relationship between a criterion variable and a set of predictor variables. Unlike the Pearson r, however, it can only be positive. It has a minimal value of .00, indicating no relationship, and a maximal value of 1.00, which indicates a perfect relationship between the predictor variables and the criterion variable. The calculation of R for two predictor variables is

$$R = \sqrt{(\beta_1 \cdot r_{y1}) + (\beta_2 \cdot r_{y2})}. \tag{14}$$

For our example the calculations would result in

$$= \sqrt{(.43 \times .52) + (.30 \times .43)}$$
$$= \sqrt{.35}$$
$$R = .59.$$

This value of R indicates that the optimal combination of PGPA and GRE: P+Q values results in a linear relationship with a correlation coefficient of .59. A value of .59 indicates a moderate relationship.

As was the case with r, squaring the correlation coefficient results in the proportion of explained variability for the criterion variable. R^2 in this case would be $.59^2$, which equals .35. Therefore, the proportion of variability in GGPA that can be accounted for by knowing the PGPA and GRE: P+Q is .35. The remaining proportion of variability .65 cannot be accounted for by these two predictor variables.

IDENTIFYING THE UNIQUE CONTRIBUTIONS OF EACH PREDICTOR VARIABLE TO THE VARIABILITY OF THE CRITERION VARIABLE

Once R^2 is known, it is possible to begin "filling in" segments of the variability that was shown in Figure 7.1(D). Figure 7.1(D) is recreated at the top in Figure 7.2. The shaded area represents the proportion of explained variability which is equal to R^2. The remaining area $1 - R^2$ is in the clear area of the circle, "d." Obviously, the stronger the relationship and the higher the R value, the smaller this unexplained area will be.

The last task is to calculate the unique contributions for each of our two criterion variables. That is, we want to identify the "a" and "b" areas in Figure 7.2. The calculation for "a" and "b" is straightforward

$$\text{"a"} = R^2 - r_{y2}^2$$
$$\text{"b"} = R^2 - r_{y1}^2.$$

For each criterion variable, these formulas involve subtracting the variability associated with the other predictor variable from the total explained variability. Each of these values can be thought of as the increase in the proportion

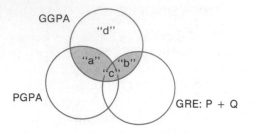

(A) Shaded area ("a", "b", & "c") represent proportion of GGPA that is accounted for by PGPA and GRE: P + Q. The proportion of variability unaccounted for by these two variables is represented by "d".

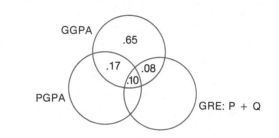

(B) Proportion of variability for each component in GGPA is included. Calculations are described in the text.

FIGURE 7.2 Diagram outlining the distribution of variability of GGPA for the chapter example.

of explained variability in the criterion variable when the respective predictor variable is added to the regression equation.

For our chapter example, these values correspond to

$$"a" = R^2 - r_{y2}^2$$
$$= .35 - .43^2$$
$$= .17,$$

and

$$"b" = R^2 - r_{y1}^2$$
$$= .35 - .52^2$$
$$= .08.$$

These values are included in Figure 7.2 at the bottom along with the calculation of "c." This area represents the proportion of explained variability of GGPA which is shared by both predictor variables. The calculation of "c" involves subtraction,

$$"c" = R^2 - "a" - "b"$$
$$= .35 - .17 - .08$$
$$= .10.$$

A SECOND LOOK AT THE STRICKER AND HUBER (1967) STUDY

Figure 7.2 is complete and shows in a visual fashion how the two predictor variables, PGPA and GRE: P+Q, are related to the criterion variable of GGPA. It is clear that the predictor variables are related to the graduate students' GPAs. These two variables when combined in an optimal fashion account for 35% of the variability in GGPA. The unique contributions of each variable is shown in the "a" and "b" areas in Figure 7.2. With regard to these two variables, PGPA made more of a contribution to predicting GGPA than did GRE: P+Q. Although these two variables are related to GGPA, it must also be mentioned that almost two-thirds of the variability in GGPA still remains unexplained. These points are discussed by Stricker and Huber (1967). They also warn against generalizing these findings too far. As they point out, these findings are based on a limited sample of 37 students from only one university. Studies such as this one, when combined with the findings of other studies using other students and schools, will help in providing a clearer picture about which variables best predict performance in graduate school. Box 7.1 uses this example to compare multiple regression with the concepts described in Chapter 6.

A SECOND EXAMPLE

In a somewhat different study on academic performance, Malloch and Michael (1981) investigated factors that would predict academic performance of students attending a community college. They had data from a sample of 71 full-time freshman and sophomore students attending a community college on the West Coast. Their criterion variable was the GPA for one academic quarter. They had a number of predictor variables. The two that will be the focus for this example were the student's academic ability and the student's expected GPA for the semester.

The student's academic ability (Aa) was based on scores from the ACT or SAT tests. A composite score was developed for each student. The student's expected grades (Eg) were based on the student predicting his or her final grade in each course registered for that quarter. This variable was included because a theoretical model of motivation (Vroom, 1964; 1965) predicted that an individual's expectations would influence motivated behavior. Malloch and Michael were interested in identifying the relationships among these variables as they relate to actual academic performance. The correlation matrix for these three variables is shown in Table 7.2.

As you can tell from Table 7.2, these three variables are related to each other. The relationships are positive, indicating that high values on a particular variable are related to high values on the other variables. And the overlap (or relationship) between the two predictor variables Aa and Eg is larger than in the previous example with PGPA and GRE: P+Q. This indicates that the shared contribution of these two variables to predicting GPA will be larger than in the first example.

BOX 7.1   **Comparison of Multiple Regression with Simple Linear Regression**

For illustration purposes, the Stricker and Huber (1967) study will be used to compare the procedures discussed in this chapter with those discussed in Chapter 6. Because the original study did not include descriptive statistics with regard to performance on the variables discussed in the chapter, statistics have been generated by the author. Although realistic values have been used, please do not assume that the information which follows for predicting grade point average in graduate school is applicable to any particular institution or program.

Let's assume that Stricker and Huber had found the following results from their sample of 37 students:

	GGPA	PGPA	GRE: P+Q
$\overline{X}$ =	3.05	3.20	575
s =	40	.25	80

It is possible to generate the separate regression lines using each of the predictor variables with these statistics and those reported in Table 7.1. Using Formulas 11a and 11b, the separate regression lines would be

$$\text{GGPA}' = [.832 \times (\text{PGPA})] + .39,$$

and,

$$\text{GGPA}' = [.002 \times (\text{GRE: P+Q})] + 1.90.$$

These prediction equations would be appropriate if you had a data value for only one of the predictor variables, PGPA or GRE: P+Q. For example, if a student reported a PGPA of 3.45, then the predicted grade point GGPA' would be 3.26. The standard error of the estimate $s_{est\,y}$ using Formula 12, would be .35. Therefore we could predict with 68% confidence (1 $s_{est\,y}$) that this student would have a GGPA' between 2.91 and 3.61 (3.26 ± 0.35).

In Figure 7.3, the diagram for the relationships among these variables is shown. As was the case in the previous example, the researchers would like to identify the proportion of explained variability in GPA, which is R^2, and the unique contributions of each predictor variable to GPA, "a" and "b," and the shared contribution, "c."

If, on the other hand, we had only the GRE: P+Q value of 650, then we would predict a GGPA' of 3.20. The $s_{est\ y}$ for this relationship would be .37. Therefore, we could be 68% confident that the person would have a GGPA' between 2.83 and 3.57 (3.20 ± .37).

Notice in both cases that we are predicting somewhere between a slightly lower than "B" average (2.83 to 2.91) to slightly lower than "A−" average (3.57 to 3.71). The $s_{est\ y}$ is slightly larger when using GRE: P+Q because the relationship between GRE: P+Q and GGPA is not as strong as that between PGPA and GGPA; rs are .43 and .52, respectively.

Knowing both a person's PGPA and GRE: P+Q should improve prediction based on the discussion of multiple regression. The text describes the regression equation only in terms of standardized scores. To transform the equation to use with original values involves transforming β values and defining the y-intercept. Transforming β values to B values, nonstandardized beta weights, is accomplished by multiplying each β by s_y and then dividing by s for that predictor variable (e.g., $B_{y1} = (B \cdot s_y)/s_1$). The y-intercept is equal to $\overline{Y} - (B_{y1} \cdot \overline{X}_1) - (B_{y2} \cdot \overline{X}_2)$. The multiple regression equation for this example is,

$$GGPA' = .688\ (PGPA) + .002\ (GRE: P+Q) - .30.$$

Using the data from the fictitious student, we would predict a GGPA' of 3.37. The $s_{est\ y}$ would equal .33. Therefore, we would be 68% confident that this student would have a GGPA between 3.04 and 3.70 (3.37 ± .33).

Because of the added knowledge that we acquired through multiple regression of the relationship between GGPA and the two predictor variables and the fact that our fictitious student was above average on both predictor variables, we are able to predict a higher GGPA than if we had data for only one variable, 3.37 versus 3.26 and 3.20. Furthermore, because the R^2 accounts for more variability than either r^2 alone, the $s_{est\ y}$ is less, .33 versus .35 and .37, and the range of predicted values is slightly smaller using multiple regression. Multiple regression increases the accuracy of the predictions in this example.

TABLE 7.2   Correlation Matrix Listing the Pearson *r* Coefficients for the Malloch and Michael (1981) Study

	Variable		
Variable	GPA (Y)	Aa (X₁)	Eg (X₂)
GPA		.58	.57
Aa	.58		.56
Eg	.57	.56	

Note. To read matrix, understand that the values represent the *r* coefficients for the variables identified by the column and row labels. Letters in parentheses are used to identify variables discussed in text.

IDENTIFYING β FOR EACH VARIABLE

To begin, let's determine the standardized partial regression coefficients (or beta weights) for each of the two predictor variables. Working with standardized values, we would expect that the multiple regression equation will take the following form:

$$z_{\text{gpa}}' = (\beta_{\text{Aa}} \times z_{\text{Aa}}) + (\beta_{\text{Eg}} \times z_{\text{Eg}}).$$

The determination of the beta weights follows from Formulas 13a and 13b (with GPA as Y, Aa representing Variable 1, and Eg as Variable 2),

$$\beta_1 = \frac{r_{y1} - (r_{y2} \times r_{12})}{1 - r_{12}^2} \tag{13a}$$

$$= \frac{.58 - (.57 \times .56)}{1 - .56^2}$$

$$= \frac{.26}{.69}$$

$$\beta_{\text{Aa}} = .38,$$

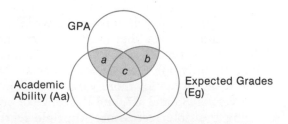

FIGURE 7.3 Diagram for the variability in GPA for the second chapter example. The shaded areas (*a*, *b*, and c) equal R^2.

and

$$\beta_2 = \frac{r_{y2} - (r_{y1} \cdot r_{12})}{1 - r_{12}^2}$$ (13b)

$$= \frac{.57 - (.58 \times .56)}{1 - .56^2}$$

$$= \frac{.25}{.69}$$

$$\beta_{Eg} = .36.$$

Knowing these values, it is possible to complete the multiple regression equation, so that for this study the equation that minimizes the differences between predicted GPA and actual GPA (in terms of standardized scores) is

$$z_{gpa}' = (.38 \times z_{Aa}) + (.36 \times z_{Eg}).$$

Notice that both of these beta weights are substantially lower than the r coefficients. As mentioned earlier, when two predictor variables are interrelated, the beta weights will be lower than the Pearson r coefficients.

CALCULATING R^2 AND THE UNIQUE CONTRIBUTIONS OF EACH VARIABLE

Once the beta weights have been determined, then the proportion of variability accounted for by the two predictor variables can be calculated. These calculations involve Formula 14 and the determination of R,

$$R = \sqrt{(\beta_1 \times r_{y1}) + (\beta_2 \times r_{y2})}$$ (14)

$$= \sqrt{(.38 \times .58) + (.36 \times .57)}$$

$$= \sqrt{.22 + .21}$$

$$= \sqrt{.43}$$

$$= .66.$$

The multiple R of .66 indicates the strength of the relationship between the combination of the two predictor variables Aa and Eg and the criterion variable GPA. This R is larger than either of the two predictor variables alone. Therefore, adding either variable improves the predictability of GPA compared with the case in which only one predictor variable is used.

Squaring the R value results in the proportion of GPA variability that is accounted for or shared with the two predictor variables. That value is $.66^2$ or .43. The shaded area in Figure 7.4 is equal to .43 of the total area in the circle representing GPA variability. The proportion of unaccounted variability is $1 - .43$, or .57. To determine the values for "a," "b," and "c" shown in Figure 7.4, the following calculations were performed:

$$\text{"a"} = R^2 - r_{y2}^2$$

$$= .43 - .57^2$$

$$= .11,$$

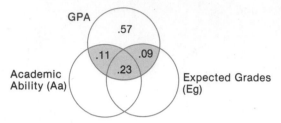

FIGURE 7.4 Diagram for the variability in GPA for the second chapter example with the proportions of variability included. The shaded areas equal R^2.

and

$$
\begin{aligned}
"b" = R^2 - r_{y1}{}^2 \\
= .43 - .58^2 \\
= .09.
\end{aligned}
$$

The value for "c" is found by subtracting "a" and "b" from R^2

$$
\begin{aligned}
"c" = R^2 - "a" - "b" \\
.23 = .43 - .11 - .09
\end{aligned}
$$

Figure 7.4 provides a visual description of the relationships among these three variables. Because Aa and Eg are strongly related to each other ($r = .56$), they share a substantial amount of variability with each other, especially in terms of their ability to account for variability in GPA. This shared variability is shown in "c." Given that these two variables overlap, the addition of either one in predicting GPA is not as substantial as one might expect. For example, if the researchers were using only Aa to predict GPA, then the proportion of explained variability would be ($r_{y1}{}^2$) .34. Adding Eg improves the proportion to (R^2) .43. This increase results from the "unique" contribution of Eg, which is .09 and is represented in "b." Obviously, when a predictor variable is highly related to other predictor variables, the unique contribution in prediction will not be as great as when the predictor variable is related to the criterion variable, but not to the other predictor variables.

Malloch and Michael (1981) concluded that these two predictor variables, academic ability and expected performance, are useful in predicting the academic performance of community-college students. Other variables that they studied contributed little, if at all, to predicting academic performance.

ADDITIONAL COMMENTS ABOUT MULTIPLE REGRESSION

These two examples provide just a brief introduction to the topic of multiple regression. A major goal of multiple regression is to identify how a number of variables are related to another variable. We have focused on the simplest case, two predictor variables and a criterion variable; however, many studies published today in the behavioral sciences involve more complicated analyses with several predictor variables. Fortunately, most of the calculations are left to the computer.

There are also different types of multiple regression analyses. You may encounter some of these different analyses in your reading of the scientific literature. This chapter dealt with examples in which the predictor variables were entered *simultaneously* into the multiple regression equation. That is, both predictor variables were treated equally in terms of their importance to the multiple regression equation.

Sometimes a researcher may have a theoretical reason for assuming that one variable may be more important than another in predicting the criterion variable. In these cases, the researcher may choose to use a *hierarchical* model of multiple regression. Such a model differs from the one discussed in terms of how the variability of the criterion variable is explained. It assumes that a series of multiple regression analyses are conducted, each one involving the addition of another predictor variable in a predetermined order. Such a model is beyond the scope of this text.

Lastly, some researchers rely on *stepwise regression*. This is empirically driven in that the analysis depends on the data obtained from the sample. Predictor variables are included one at a time in successive multiple regression analyses. However, unlike the hierarchical model, which has a predetermined order, the order of variables is determined on the basis of their strength with relation to the criterion variable. The most strongly related predictor variable (with the criterion variable) is included first, then the second strongest, and so on. Their relative contributions to the proportion of explained variability is a function of their location in the analysis. Because of the sophisticated and complicated nature of the analysis, stepwise regression is commonly performed using a computer.

SUMMARY

Multiple regression involves identifying the relationships of two or more variables, often called predictor variables, with another variable, the criterion variable. A multiple regression equation can be determined. This equation minimizes the squared deviations between the predicted values and the actual values of the criterion variable for a sample of data.

The equation contains values known as beta weights. These values are the partial regression coefficients that identify the relative weighting of a predictor variable with the criterion variable when an adjustment is made for the relationship of the predictor variable with other predictor variables. If the values of all variables have been standardized, then the symbol β is used. The β values are often less than the r values for a predictor variable, because predictor variables tend to be related to each other.

It is possible to calculate a statistic that is the coefficient for the relationship between the criterion variable and the combination of the predictor variables. This statistic is called the multiple R. Like the Pearson r, the larger its value, the stronger the relationship. Unlike the Pearson r, it is always positive and ranges from .00 to 1.00. The proportion of variability of the criterion variable that is accounted for by the optimal combination of predictor variables is represented by R^2.

There are a number of different analytic procedures available in multiple regression. Most are accomplished using computer programs written specifically for multiple regression.

SUMMARY FOR DETERMINING β WITH TWO PREDICTOR VARIABLES

1. Identify the r values for all relationships involving the predictor variables and the criterion variable.
2. Create a correlation matrix.
3. Use Formulas 13a and 13b to determine the β values

$$\beta_1 = \frac{r_{y1} - (r_{y2} \cdot r_{12})}{1 - r_{12}^2} \tag{13a}$$

$$\beta_2 = \frac{r_{y2} - (r_{y1} \cdot r_{12})}{1 - r_{12}^2}. \tag{13b}$$

SUMMARY FOR CALCULATING R AND R^2 FOR TWO PREDICTOR VARIABLES

1. Construct the correlation matrix and find the β values for each predictor variable.
2. Use Formula 14 to determine R (square R to get R^2),

$$R = \sqrt{(\beta_1 \cdot r_{y1}) + (\beta_2 \cdot r_{y2})}. \tag{14}$$

EXERCISES

1. Given the following correlation matrix, determine the β values for each predictor variable.

	Y	X_1	X_2
Y	—	.40	.20
X_1		—	.00
X_2			—

2. Explain the relationship between the r values and the β values found in Question 1.
3. If the r between X_1 and X_2 had been .50 in Question 1, how would the β values change? What would happen to R and R^2?

4. A personnel director knows that a particular test correlates with job performance. She has another test she knows is unrelated to the first test. However, this second test is also related to job performance. Should she use both tests in predicting job performance? Explain your answer in terms of proportion of explained variability.

5. Find a research study that uses multiple regression. Identify the R and R^2 in the article and the predictor and criterion variables.

6. A student knows that X_1 and Y are related ($r = -.30$). He knows that adding another variable X_2 and conducting a multiple regression analysis results in an R = .35. What possibilities exist in terms of the strength of the relationships among these three variables (specifically X_1 and X_2 and X_2 and Y) that can explain these findings?

7. A college admissions director knows that SAT scores account for 15% of the variability in the first semester GPAs for freshmen. The combination of SAT and with a second new test results in an R = .40 with first semester GPA. From a purely statistical viewpoint, should the director continue to use only the SAT in predicting GPA, or should this new test be required along with the SATs? Explain your answer.

8. A student contends that the b (in a simple regression equation from Chapter 7) will be the same as β if the correlation coefficients between the two predictor variables and between one predictor variable and the Y variable are .00. Is she correct? (Assume that all values have been standardized.)

9. Does it make sense to add an additional predictor variable to a multiple regression analysis if you know that the predictor variable is no more related to the criterion variable than the other predictor variables and that the new predictor variable is very strongly related to the other predictor variables? Explain.

10. Answer the same question as in Exercise 9 using the same information, except you should assume that the new predictor variable is not related to the other predictor variables.

11. The instructor of a psychology statistics course finds certain relationships in the performance of her students from the previous semester. Specifically, grade earned in the class is related to grades earned in a probability course offered from the math department, $r = .56$. The number of credit hours students register for during the semester they take the statistics course is negatively related to grades in the statistics course, $r = -.40$. Students with heavy course loads do not do well in the statistics course. The relationship between the number of credit hours and grades in the probability course is $-.10$. Construct the multiple regression equation (Assume the instructor wants to predict performance in the statistics course.) and determine R.

12. Using the information from Question 11, determine R^2. Construct a diagram for the variability in statistics grades and identify the various components of variability, "a," "b," and "c." Use Figure 7.4 as a model.

Understanding Inferential Statistics

OVERVIEW

The next two chapters introduce you to procedures involving inferential statistics. Up to this point, the discussion has centered on descriptive statistics. We have discussed frequency distributions, measures of central tendency, measures of variability, graphing, standard scores, and linear relationships. There is, however, a substantial portion of statistics in the behavioral sciences that extends beyond descriptive statistics. We have touched upon inferential statistics briefly when discussing unbiased estimators of population parameters $\bar{X}$ and s, but we will explore inferential statistics in greater detail in the next two chapters.

Researchers often extend their findings beyond the sample they examined in their studies. They want to generalize their findings to the population from which the sample was taken. The statistical procedures required to do this involve inferential statistics. Probability theory is at the base of these procedures and will be the focus of Chapter 8. In addition, Chapter 8 includes a discussion of the concepts of hypothesis testing.

Chapter 9 begins the presentation of statistical tests used by behavioral science researchers. We will examine the situation in which researchers determine the likelihood that a sample came from a particular population distribution. The topic of interval estimation is also examined. Although we know that $\bar{X}$ is the best estimate of μ, it is possible to generate a range of possible μ values from which a sample was selected. We will also discuss hypothesis testing involving linear relationships such as those discussed in Chapters 5 and 6.

CHAPTER
8

Probability and Hypothesis Testing

TERMS DISCUSSED

probability

independence

addition rule of probability

multiplication rule of probability

sampling with replacement

sampling distribution

hypothesis testing

concept of indirect proof

null hypothesis (H_0)

alternative hypothesis (H_1)

Although we have all been subjected to boring discussions, conversations, and lectures, there has been little empirical research on the components that are involved in boring interactions. Leary, Rogers, Canfield, and Coe (1986) reported the findings from three studies that investigated boring conversations. In the third of those studies, they presented tapes of different conversations to college students. The students were asked to rate individuals in these conservations on a number of personality characteristics.

The independent variable in this study was the type of individual rated, which Leary et al. (1986) referred to as the "target." Based on a screening of 64 tape recordings of different conversations, the conversations with the three most interesting and three most boring target individuals were selected for further testing. These conversations were presented to 72 undergraduates in a predetermined order. Each student listened to the conversation while following along with a typed transcript of the conversation. After hearing a conversation, the student rated the target individual in the conversation on a number of personality dimensions. These ratings constituted the dependent variables of the study. The ratings were based on either a 12-point or 7-point scale, with low values representing negative ratings and high values representing positive ratings.

The authors hypothesized that the type of target individual, either interesting or boring, would effect the ratings of personality characteristics. A partial listing of their findings is shown in Table 8.1.

This study by Leary et al. (1986) is an example of an experiment. It is one of the simplest designs, in that the independent variable, type of target, involves only two levels or conditions, interesting and boring target. There are a number of dependent variables observed. As you can see in Table 8.1, overall liking, overall impression, competence, and leadership are included among the different personality traits. We will not discuss the specifics of how the authors tested their particular hypotheses, but we will use this example to illustrate the roles of descriptive and inferential statistics in behavioral science research.

An inspection of Table 8.1 reveals a number of important pieces of information. The first is that the far left column lists some of the dependent variables used in the study. The next two columns list the mean ratings for each variable. These mean ratings constitute descriptive statistics for the study. Each sample of ratings is summarized and described by a single value. That single value is the mean, a measure of central tendency.

The last two columns provide statistics new to the discussion. The values under the column F lists statistics resulting from an inferential statistical test known as an analysis of variance. The F ratios in Table 8.1 are based on tests conducted for each dependent variable. We will postpone discussion on calculating F ratios until Chapter 13, but it should be noted that researchers rely on statistics such as these in reporting their findings.

TABLE 8.1   A Partial Listing of the Findings from Study 3 in the Leary et al. (1986) Study.

| Item | Mean Rating of Target | | | |
	Boring	Interesting	F	p <
Overall Liking[a]	6.3	7.1	30.00	.001
Overall Impression[a]	6.1	7.8	39.89	.001
Interesting[b]	3.4	4.6	53.06	.001
Enthusiastic[b]	3.4	5.4	374.83	.001
Competent[b]	4.3	4.4	2.56	ns
Leader[b]	3.4	4.4	54.92	.001

[a]Based on a 12-point rating scale
[b]Based on a 7-point rating scale
ns = not significant
Note: From "Boredom in interpersonal encounters: Antecedents and social implications" by M. R. Leary, P. A. Rogers, R. W. Canfield, and C. Coe, 1986, Journal of Personality and Social Psychology, 51, p. 973. Copyright 1986 by the American Psychological Association. Adapted by permission of the publisher and author.

The last column lists probability values. The use of inferential statistics depends on probability theory. Probability theory is used in determining if a research hypothesis is supported or not. In reading research articles, you may have already seen uses of probability theory in inferential statistics. Comments about "significant" or "nonsignificant" findings depend on probability. The first part of this chapter will review some of the basic aspects of probability theory as they apply to behavioral science research.

BASIC CONCEPTS IN PROBABILITY

Probability classically has been defined as the ratio between the number of ways a particular event can occur and the total number of events. It is most often reported as a proportion

$$\text{Probability} = \frac{\text{Number of Ways a Particular Event Can Occur}}{\text{Total Number of Possible Events}}.$$

The flipping of a coin is often used as an example. There are two possible events, heads and tails. Heads can occur only one way, therefore the probability of flipping a coin and getting heads is 1/2, or .50. Similarly, with a deck of cards there are 52 cards (or possible events). Thirteen of those cards are spades. Therefore, the probability of selecting a spade at random from a deck is 13/52 or .25.

Probability values are reported as proportions ranging from .00 to 1.00. The larger the probability value, the greater the likelihood that the event will occur. An event with the probability of .00 will not occur. Likewise, an event with a probability of 1.00 is certain to occur. Given the choice between betting on a coin coming up heads or selecting a spade from a deck of cards, it would be wiser to bet on the coin. The probability of heads is .50, whereas the probability of selecting a spade is only .25. Probability is often abbreviated with the letter p.

Although we could continue this discussion on probability by relying on coins and cards, it might be more useful to discuss the principles of probability using an example that is more closely related to behavioral science.

Let's assume that I asked each student in my class of 20 how many siblings (brothers and sisters) he or she has. Each student jots down the answer on a slip of paper. I could use these answers to represent the students. That is a student is represented by a value; the value refers to the number of siblings.

Figure 8.1 is a diagram representing the population of responses. Each of the students' responses is shown inside the circle. These responses represent the "events" in a discussion of probability as described earlier.

I could randomly sample from this population of responses. In other words, every response in the population has an equal chance of being selected. The probability of sampling one response from the population and having that response be "1" would equal the number of "1" values in the population (6), divided by the total number of responses in the population (20). Therefore the probability of randomly selecting a student who has one sibling (gave a response of 1) would be 6/20 or .30.

It is also worthwhile to talk about the complement of p, which is often abbreviated with the letter q. The probability of an event not occurring is represented by q. It can be viewed as the probability of "not p." For instance, given the example above, the probability of selecting a person who does not have 1 sibling (either 0, 2, 3, or 4) siblings is 14/20 or .70. The two probabilities p and q must equal 1, that is, $p + q = 1.00$. Therefore, $q = 1 - p$; in this example, $.70 = 1 - .30$.

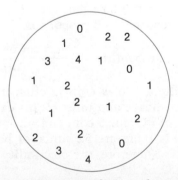

FIGURE 8.1 Diagram representing a population of 20 students. Values represent the number of other siblings in a student's family.

THE ADDITION RULE IN PROBABILITY THEORY

Probability is largely concerned with determining the likelihood of either one of a series of events occurring or the likelihood of the series of events itself occurring. These situations involve the combination of a number of different probability values, each for a particular event. The following discussion is limited to situations in which the events are independent of each other. **Independence** in probability theory indicates that the probability of one event occurring has no influence or effect on the probability of another event occurring. That is, one value being selected from a population will not influence the likelihood of another event occurring. If events influence each other, then the probabilities are not independent but are conditional and adjustments must be made in determining the probability. The use of probability in this text will not require conditional probabilities. (See Loftus & Loftus, 1982, or Runyon & Haber, 1984 for more on conditional probabilities.)

The first case to be examined involves the probability of *one* event occurring that can happen in a number of different ways. Assume that we want to know the probability of selecting one student from the population at random and that student has either 3 or more siblings. Using the diagram in Figure 8.1, we note that there are several individuals who reported having either 3 or 4 siblings. The probability of selecting a student with 3 or more siblings is equal to the sum of the probabilities for selecting a student with 3 siblings and for selecting a student with 4 siblings,

$$p \text{ (student with 3 or more siblings)} - p \text{ (3 siblings)} + p \text{ (4 siblings)}.$$

This is shown graphically in Figure 8.2. The probability of selecting a student with 3 siblings is 2/20, or .10, and the probability of selecting a student with 4 siblings is also 2/20, or .10. Therefore the probability of selecting a student with 3 or more siblings is .10 + .10, or .20. There are 4 ways that particular event (having 3 or more siblings) can occur out of 20 possible events. The probability is .20.

The **addition rule of probability** is used when determining the probability of one from a set of independent events occurring. When talking about the probability of one event *or* another event occurring, the correct procedure is to add the separate probabilities together. Question 5 in the Exercises provides practice with this concept using the data in Figure 8.1.

THE MULTIPLICATION RULE IN PROBABILITY

The other rule used in probability involves determining the probability of a *series* of events occurring. When determining the probability of a series of events occurring, the **multiplication rule of probability** is used. The probabilities for each event are multiplied together.

Using Figure 8.3, assume that we want to determine the probability of selecting the two students whose values appeared in small circles within the top circle. One student has 3 siblings and the other has 2 siblings. Further-

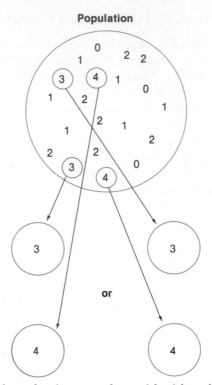

FIGURE 8.2 Diagram for selecting a student with either three or four siblings.

more, assume that we want to select the student with 3 siblings first and then select the student with 2 siblings. The probability for this series of two events occurring is equal to the two separate probabilities multiplied together

$$p \text{ (student ''3'' and then student ''2'')} = p \text{ (student ''3'')} \cdot p \text{ (student ''2'')}.$$

In the middle circle, the probability for selecting this student with 3 siblings is 1/20, or .05. This student is then returned to the population and then another student is selected. The probability for selecting the particular student with 2 siblings is also 1/20, or .05 (the bottom circle). The probability of selecting these two particular students in that particular order is .05 × .05, or .0025. That is, there is a .25% chance of selecting those two particular students in that order.

The rule as described assumes that each event is independent of each other and that sampling with replacement occurs. **Sampling with replacement** assumes that after an event is selected from the population of events (a sample is taken), that the event is returned to the population so that it could be sampled again.

The extremely low probability of selecting those particular two students in that order, .0025, can be noted when determining the probability of selecting *any* other pair of two students. The great majority of the time (99.75%,

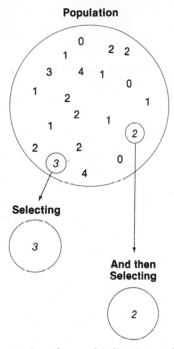

FIGURE 8.3 Diagram illustrating the multiplication rule. Example involves first selecting a student with three siblings and then selecting a second student with two siblings.

or $1 - p\%$) some other combination of two students will likely occur, assuming random selection.

AN EXAMPLE USING THE ADDITION AND MULTIPLICATION RULES TOGETHER

It is possible to use both of these rules when determining probabilities. For instance, let's determine the probability of selecting two students from our population; one has 3 siblings and the other has 4 siblings. The probability for this series of events is more complicated than just multiplying the probabilities of two events together as was just discussed. This is because the previous example involved two *particular* events (or students) selected in a *particular* order. Now you want the probability of selecting two students at random and one has 3 siblings and the other has 4 siblings. The order of selection is unimportant as are the students (as long as one has 3 siblings and the other has 4 siblings). In Figure 8.4, the possible outcomes that would satisfy these requirements are shown. Notice that there are eight possible ways the two events could occur, because there are four students: two with 3 siblings and two with 4 siblings. To differentiate among these students, two students have been arbitrarily labeled in *italics* (*3* and *4*) and two in **boldface** (**3** and **4**). Also, the order of selection could vary, 3 selected first and then 4,

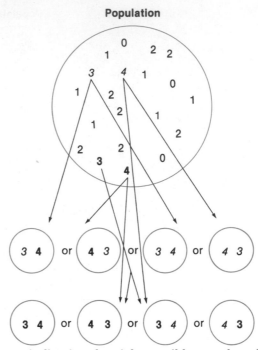

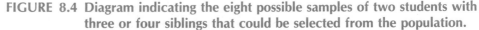

FIGURE 8.4 Diagram indicating the eight possible samples of two students with three or four siblings that could be selected from the population.

or 4 selected first and then 3. The probability of any one of the eight possible events' occurring is based on the multiplication rule. In each case the probability for each of the event's occurring is .05 $\times$ .05, or .0025. The probability of *one* of these eight event's occurring requires the use of the addition rule

$$p(3 \text{ and } 4) = p(3 \text{ then } \mathbf{4}) + p(\mathbf{4} \text{ then } 3) + p(3 \text{ then } \mathbf{4}) + p(\mathbf{4} \text{ then } 3)$$
$$+ p(\mathbf{3} \text{ then } \mathbf{4}) + p(\mathbf{4} \text{ then } \mathbf{3}) + p(\mathbf{3} \text{ then } \mathbf{4}) + p(\mathbf{4} \text{ then } \mathbf{3}).$$

This results in a probability equal to .0025 added eight times, or .02. In other words, there are two chances in one hundred of selecting two students from this population at random and have one with 3 siblings and the other with 4 siblings. As you can see working with samples larger than one involves the combined use of the addition and multiplication rules.

THE CONCEPT OF HYPOTHESIS TESTING

Given this brief introduction to probability theory, we will focus our attention on selecting samples from a population. With the exception of the last example combining the addition and multiplication rules, the examples from the fictitious population of 20 students have involved the probabilities of selecting *individual* values (the number of siblings associated with an individual student). However, the vast majority of research in the behavioral sciences involves samples of more than one value or observation.

For instance, although you can use Figure 8.1 to determine the likelihood that a student with no siblings came from that population (3/20, or .15), the diagram would be of little direct help in determining the probability of selecting two students from the population who have a mean of .5 siblings. The reason, of course, is that the diagram represents individual students and not samples of two people. There is no .5 represented in Figure 8.1. Yet, researchers are often faced with the task of determining the probability of a sample with more than one value being selected from a population. To determine these probabilities, researchers must rely on a type of distribution other than the population distribution.

THE ROLE OF THE SAMPLING DISTRIBUTION

An examination of the previous problem will help in describing this other distribution. Assume that another instructor comes to me and says that she has two students in her office. They have a mean number of .5 siblings. Obviously, one has no siblings and the other has one sibling. She asks me to determine the likelihood that they came from my population of 20 students. As we just saw, Figure 8.1 cannot be used to determine directly the probability for a sample of two students. That figure can be used only when determining the probability of selecting one student. What would be ideal is a diagram that consisted of all the possible combinations of two students from my population. Furthermore, each sample should be represented with the mean of the two sibling values in the sample. That way I could determine the probability of selecting a sample of two students with a mean of .5 siblings.

In Figure 8.5, the circle representing the population of values is presented. Below it are some of the samples of two values that could be selected from this population. For each sample, represented by a smaller circle, the values and the $\overline{X}$ are shown. Obviously, there is insufficient room in the figure to represent all samples. In fact, the total number of possible samples of $N = 2$ (two values in each sample) that can be selected from this population of 20 values is 20^2 or 400. This assumes that sampling with replacement is occurring. (The general formula is [Number of Values in Population]^N.)

In Figure 8.6, the diagram includes some of the samples of $N = 2$ rather than individual values. Each sample is represented by its $\overline{X}$. This diagram represents another type of distribution. This distribution is a **sampling distribution**—a distribution consisting of all samples of a particular size selected from a population distribution. In instances where the samples are represented by sample $\overline{X}$s, then this distribution is called the sampling distribution of the mean. We will examine this type of distribution in more detail in the next chapter.

The sampling distribution in Figure 8.6, if it were complete, would contain 400 circles, one for each sample of $N = 2$, and each circle would have

Population

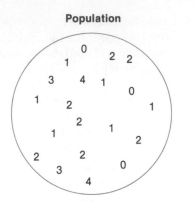

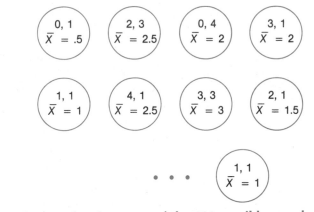

FIGURE 8.5 Diagram showing some of the 400 possible samples of $N = 2$ that could be selected from the population distribution.

its sample $\overline{X}$ inside. There would be 36 samples with a $\overline{X}$ of .5 siblings. There-fore, the probability of selecting a sample of two students at random from the population and the sample having a $\overline{X}$ of .5 siblings would be 36/400, or .09. There is a 9% chance of selecting this type of a sample at random.

It is necessary to use a sampling distribution when determining the prob-ability of selecting a particular *sample* from a population distribution. Al-though Figure 8.6 is appropriate for samples of $N = 2$, it would not be appro-priate in determining the probability of selecting samples of size $N = 3$ or $N = 4$. There is a family of sampling distributions that exist for a population distribution. The number of sampling distributions is limited only by the number of values in the population distribution. Each sampling distribution would represent samples of a particular size N. Figure 8.7 describes the sam-pling distributions of $N = 3$ and $N = 4$ for the population distribution we've been discussing.

Let's return to the reason for determining the probability of a sample of two students with a $\overline{X}$ of .5 siblings. Recall that I posed the situation of an-other instructor telling me that she has two students in her office with a $\overline{X}$

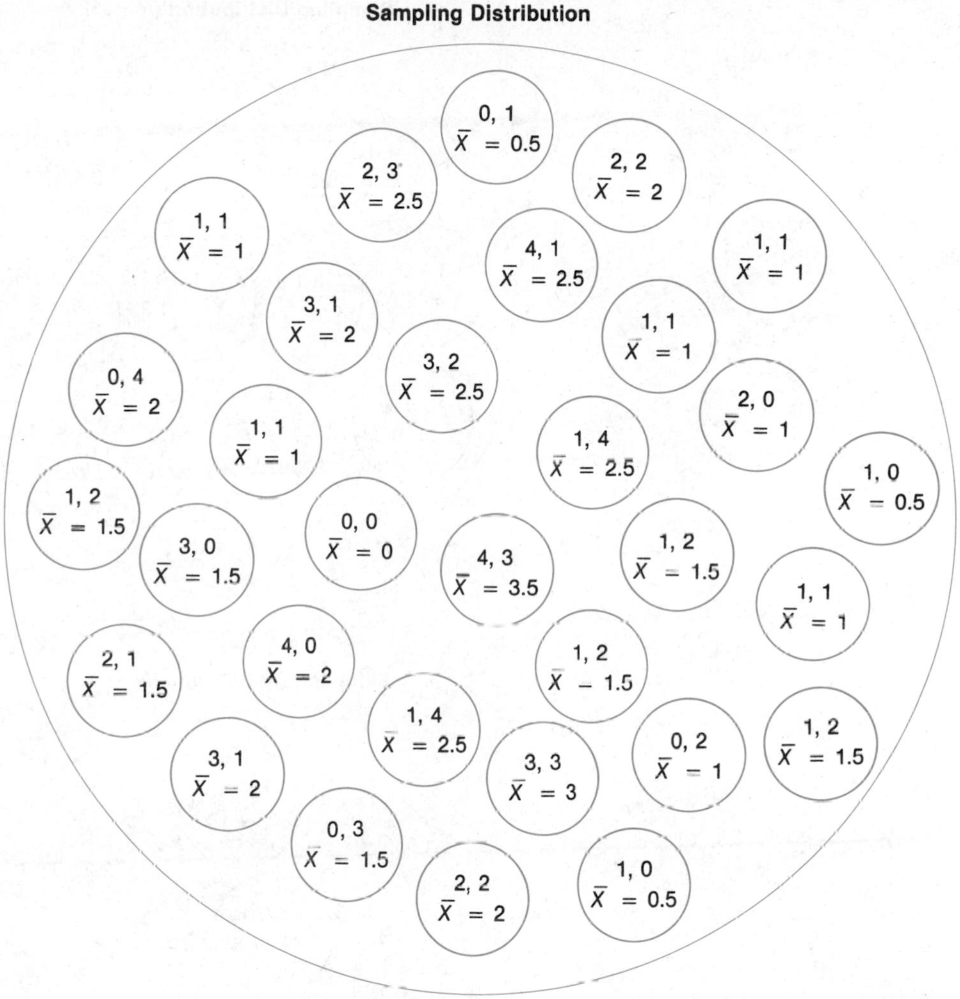

Sampling Distribution

FIGURE 8.6 Diagram of a sampling distribution with $N = 2$. Each circle
           represents a sample with two values selected from the population
           distribution. Sampling distribution would be based on 400 samples.

of .5 siblings. She asked me to determine the likelihood that they were randomly sampled from my population of 20 students. The probability is .09.
Therefore, I would conclude that it is not likely (less than a 10% chance). I
might be wrong, but the odds favor some other sample being taken from my
population of students. The probability of randomly selecting a sample of two
students and those students having a mean other than .5 siblings is .91
$(1 - p)$.

   If this other instructor asked me to make a yes or no decision I would
say no, the students are not from my class. As will be discussed in the next
section, a form of this type of decision-making process is used in inferential
statistics. However, often in behavioral science research a lower probability

Sampling Distribution (N = 3)

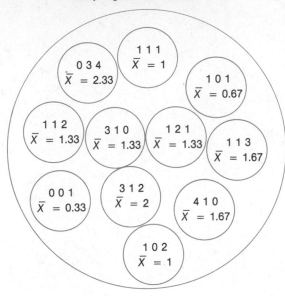

Sampling Distribution (N = 4)

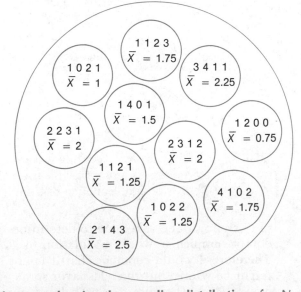

FIGURE 8.7 Diagrams showing the sampling distributions for N = 3 and
N = 4. Sampling distribution for N = 3 has 8,000 samples and
distribution for N = 4 has 160,000 samples.

value is needed before one can say no the sample did not come from a particular population distribution.

HYPOTHESIS TESTING

The example just discussed involved determining the probability of a sample being selected from a particular population. I could determine the probability of the sample coming from my population of students because I knew something about it. I had the values from that population. If the other instructor had asked me to determine the likelihood that the students came from her class, I would need to know or estimate information about her class or population before I could answer. The same kind of reasoning applies in using inferential statistics in the behavioral sciences.

In behavioral science research, descriptive statistics are used to describe the sample of data collected. And these statistics can be used to estimate parameters about the population from which the samples were taken. Yet, researchers often want to make statements or reach conclusions about the populations from which samples were selected. For example, in the Leary et al. (1986) study, the researchers have found rating differences in the $\overline{X}$s between their samples of boring and interesting targets. Yet, they wanted to extend their findings beyond these samples. They wanted to conclude that these differences between $\overline{X}$s reflected the fact that the samples were selected from two different populations of ratings. For instance, they might have hypothesized or predicted that the population distributions of ratings for "liking" look something like those shown in Figure 8.8.

Using the information in Table 8.1, we know that the students gave the boring target a $\overline{X}$ liking rating of 6.3, whereas the interesting target received a $\overline{X}$ rating of 7.1. The researchers would like to decide whether or not these two samples of ratings came from the same population distribution of ratings. If they did, then the difference in $\overline{X}$s is the result of chance and sampling and does not reflect a difference in the population distribution of ratings. If, on the other hand, the ratings do come from different population distributions of ratings, then the researchers certainly want to be able to reach that conclu-

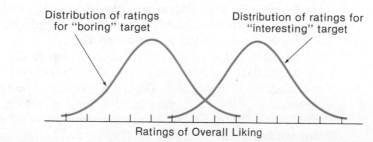

FIGURE 8.8 One possible representation of the population distributions for rating of overall liking from Leary et al. (1986) study.

sion. Therefore, they must decide if the two samples came from the same or a different population distribution of ratings. These are the only two possibilities.

As will be discussed in subsequent chapters, the possibility that both samples came from the same population distribution is easier to test statistically. If both samples came from the same population distribution, then we know that the population mean μ and population standard deviation σ are identical for both samples. If the samples came from different population distributions, then the number of different combinations of μs and σs is infinite. It's similar to the situation with my population of 20 students. I could determine the probability of a sample coming from my population, but not for all the other populations of students that could exist.

Therefore, statistically it is easier to determine the probability that the samples came from the same population distribution than determining the probabilities for all the possible combinations of different population distributions. If I test the likelihood that the samples came from the same population distribution and find that it is unlikely, then I would be left with the other possibility, the samples came from different population distributions. This line of reasoning involves the **concept of indirect proof**. By testing the assumption that the samples came from the same population distribution and finding that it is unlikely (based on probability theory), the researcher is left with the only other possible conclusion, the samples came from different population distributions.

Although this concept of indirect proof is critical to inferential statistics in the behavioral sciences, one must be aware of an important limitation. The concept has the word proof in it, yet because we rely on probability, we never know for certain whether our decision is correct or not. Therefore, proof in this case should not mean that a finding has been *proved*. There is an element of possible error in the decision. These *decision errors* will be discussed later.

These assumptions that samples come from the same or different population distributions are described as hypotheses in inferential statistics. The **null hypothesis (H_0)** most often describes the case in which the samples are selected from the same population distribution. The word *null* indicates "nothing" or "none." Therefore, the H_0 assumes that there is no difference among the samples in terms of the population distributions from which they were selected. The **alternative hypothesis (H_1)** describes the opposite case. The samples were selected from different population distributions. See Figure 8.9 for a representation of these hypotheses.

These hypotheses are statistical hypotheses and are based on assumptions about the data and the type of research design used. One of these hypotheses, the alternative hypothesis (H_1), is similar to the research hypothesis. Most research hypotheses in experiments predict a difference in behaviors across conditions. These behaviors differ depending on the independent variable in the study. In the Leary et al. (1986) study, the research hypothesis is that subjects' ratings will be different for boring and interesting individuals (who are called "targets" in the study). The research hypothesis is often stated in

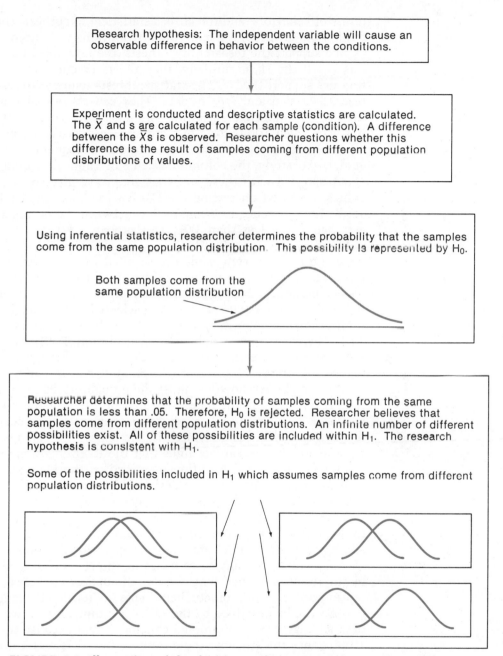

FIGURE 8.9 Illustration of the decision-making process in a two-condition experiment when a significant difference is found.

terms of behaviors, and the H_1 is a statistical hypothesis that translates these differences to different population distributions and, often, population means.

To support the research hypothesis, the researchers test the null hypothesis H_0. If the H_0 is unlikely, then the researchers can conclude that their findings support the H_1. The statistical tests required to test the H_0 vary with research design and type of data. They can also involve assumptions about the use of sampling distributions similar in character to those described earlier. The calculations for a test provide a statistic. The procedures for many of these calculations are the subject of the subsequent chapters. For the Leary et al. (1986) study, the column labeled F in Table 8.1 contains these statistics.

Associated with these statistics are probability values. These probability values are based on testing the H_0. For instance, in the Leary et al. (1986) study, the difference in liking ratings between the boring and interesting targets had a p of less than .001. This probability value can be interpreted in terms of the H_0. It is the likelihood that these samples or samples with even larger differences were randomly selected from the same population distribution of ratings. This is the case described by the H_0. It assumes both samples came from the same population distribution. The likelihood or probability that Leary et al. (1986) randomly selected two samples of ratings from the same population distribution *and* got the difference in $\overline{X}$s they did is less than .001. Therefore, they concluded that it is more likely that the samples were selected from different populations of ratings. They *rejected* the H_0 and concluded that the results *support* the H_1 and their research hypothesis.

You might ask how low must the probability be for a researcher to reject the H_0. That is, can the p be .10 or .25 and the researcher still reject H_0? The answer is no. A minimal standard has been generally accepted by those conducting and publishing research in the behavioral sciences. That minimal p value is .05. If a researcher finds that the likelihood his or her sample came from a population distribution described in the H_0 is .05 *or less*, then the researcher can reject the case described by the H_0. If the H_0 is rejected, then the only other available case is that described by H_1. When the probability of the sample being selected from a population distribution described by the null hypothesis is *greater than* .05, then the researcher must retain the possibility that the sample came from a population distribution described by the H_0. Obviously, in many cases retaining the H_0 indicates that differences may be the result of chance. This would not support the researcher's hypothesis.

A good example of not being able to reject H_0 using this standard of $p < .05$ can be described by the earlier example of the two students with a $\overline{X}$ of .5 siblings. In that example I concluded that because there was less than a 10% chance the students came from my class, it was unlikely that they did, in fact, come from my class. If the H_0 assumes that the sample of two students came from my population of students, and the H_1 assumes that it came from some other population distribution, then I would not be able to reject H_0 using a $p < .05$. Given that the probability of selecting a sample at random from my population is .09, it would not be sufficiently low for me to reject H_0. Therefore, if this example were a research study, I would be forced to retain H_0 and conclude that it is possible that the two students came from my population.

You may think that a probability level of .05 is too stringent for rejecting H_0. However, it is important to guard against concluding that a difference exists when, in fact, the difference found between samples is the result of sampling and chance and not differences in population distributions. This type of *decision* error is called a Type I error. A Type I error occurs when a researcher rejects H_0 when it is actually true. In terms of the Leary et al. study, a Type I error might occur if they conclude that the boring and interesting targets produced different ratings, when, in fact, they did not. Remember *different* here refers to different populations of rating values.

Not rejecting H_0 when it should be rejected produces a Type II error. This occurs when the samples have data that are similar enough that the researcher concludes that the samples could have come from the same population distribution, but in reality, they did not.

We will spend much more time on Type I and Type II errors in Chapter 12. It is important to remember, however, that these types of errors are decisions errors that cannot be totally eliminated because decision making in the behavioral sciences relies on probability. Anytime a decision is made using probability, there is a chance the wrong decision will be made. In Chapter 12 we will discuss steps that can be taken to minimize the probability of making these errors.

In the case of the Leary et al. (1986) study, there are a couple of instances in which the H_0 was retained. In these cases, the probability of the samples being selected from the same population distribution (the case described by the H_0) was greater than .05. In Table 8.1, the $\overline{X}$ ratings for competence were 4.3 for the boring target and 4.4 for the interesting target. The statistical test revealed that this difference of .1 was not large enough to rule out the possibility that these samples came from the same population distribution. That is, the probability of the two samples being selected at random from the same population distribution was greater than .05. Leary et al. reported this finding with the notation "ns" which means nonsignificant. Researchers often refer to situations in which the H_0 is retained as nonsignificant findings. When the H_0 is rejected, then the researchers refer to their findings as "significant." As you can see in Table 8.1, in most instances significant findings were reported. The probability values indicate the likelihood the samples came from the same population distribution (as described in H_0). These probabilities were low enough (less than .05) for Leary et al. to reject H_0 and to report support for their research hypothesis. The sample means were *significantly* different and the researchers were able to conclude that they came from different population distributions of ratings. In almost all instances, the ratings were significantly higher for the interesting target.

SUMMARY

Descriptive statistics are used to describe the data found in a sample. Inferential statistics are used to determine information about the populations from which the samples were selected. Much of inferential statistics relies on probability theory.

Classically, probability has been defined as the proportion of ways an event can occur relative to the total number of possible events. The addition rule of probability is used when determining the probability of one of a series of events occurring. The multiplication rule is used when the probability of a series of events occurring is desired.

Often, researchers are interested in determining the probability of a sample being selected from a population distribution. In these instances, the researcher must use a sampling distribution to determine the probability. A sampling distribution contains all the possible samples of a particular size N that could be selected from a population distribution. For each population distribution, a family of sampling distributions exist. Each sampling distribution corresponds to samples of a particular size N.

The statistical tests require two types of statistical hypotheses, the null hypothesis (H_0) and the alternative hypothesis (H_1). The null hypothesis often describes the case in which samples are selected from the same population distribution. The alternative hypothesis, which is the statistical hypothesis similar to the research hypothesis, describes the opposite case, the samples were selected from different population distributions.

Researchers use the concept of indirect proof in testing these hypotheses. The research determines the probability that the sample was selected from the case described by the H_0. If this probability is sufficiently low, less than .05, then the researcher *rejects* H_0. If H_0 is rejected, then the only other possible case is H_1, which is similar to the research hypothesis. Therefore, the researcher indirectly supports the research hypothesis, by rejecting the H_0. Because these decisions are based on probability, the researcher must realize that there is a possibility that these decisions are in error and, as a result, researchers refrain from stating that findings *prove* a research hypothesis, rather they state that the findings *support* the research hypothesis.

EXERCISES

1. In understanding and applying the findings of a study, is it necessary for the researcher to calculate both descriptive and inferential statistics? Explain.

2. Locate a research article in your area of study and identify any instances of the researchers using descriptive and inferential statistics.

3. Using the addition rule of probability, explain why the probability of a coin being flipped and coming up heads *or* tails must be 1.00.

4. Assuming two tests are independent of each other and your probability of getting an "A" on a test is .20, what is the probability that you will get "A"s on both tests? What is the probability you will not get an "A" on either test?

5. Using Figure 8.1, determine the probabilities for the following events:
   a. randomly selecting a student with 0 siblings
   b. randomly selecting either a student with 0 siblings or 5 siblings
   c. randomly selecting a student with 2 or fewer siblings
   d. randomly selecting a student with 2 or more siblings

6. Using Figure 8.1, what is the probability of randomly selecting all three students with 0 siblings on the first three picks? (Assume that a student is put back into the population after being selected.)

7. Using a combination of the addition and multiplication rules of probability, determine the probability of selecting a sample of two students from the population in Figure 8.1 and have the sample $\overline{X}$ equal 4.

8. Is there one sampling distribution that corresponds to a particular population distribution? Explain.

9. A researcher predicts that a new study guide will increase learning as measured on a comprehensive final exam. He randomly assigns one-half of his class to use the new study guide and the other half uses the old study guide. He reports that, "the new study guide resulted in significantly better performance (a mean test score of 83) than with the old study guide (a mean test score of 76), $t(34) = 3.62$, $p < .05$." Identify any *descriptive* statistics used in his report. What information is new to you?

10. In Exercise 9 state what you would assume are the null and alternative hypotheses. Which one is consistent with the research hypothesis?

11. Three fellow students interpret the "$p < .05$" differently. Student A reports that it means that only 5% in the population of the students did significantly better. Student B reports that the probability of getting the difference in test performance assuming the scores came from the same population distribution is less than .05. Student C reports that there is a 95% chance that the H_1 is correct. Which student is correct?

12. An instructor assumes that a sample of math test scores came from a class of fifth graders and not fourth graders. She has all the test scores for students in the fourth grade. How could she use the concept of indirect proof to support her assumption?

13. A psychologist reports that two groups do not significantly differ ($p > .05$) from each other on an interest survey. She has survey scores for each individual in each group. What does this mean with regard to the population distributions from which these samples have been selected?

14. You believe that men and women differ on a particular task. Would your H_0 assume that these people's scores on the task come from the same or different population distributions? Explain your answer.

15. Based on the information in Figure 8.4 and the calculations described in the text, we know that the probability of randomly selecting two students from my population distribution and these students having a mean of 3.5 siblings is .02. What would you conclude about the likelihood of selecting this type of sample? Why?

The *t* Test for One Sample

TERMS DISCUSSED

alpha level

sampling distribution of the mean

standard error of the mean, $s_{\bar{x}}$

Student's *t* distribution

degrees of freedom (df)

central limit theorem

nondirectional hypothesis

directional hypothesis

critical *t* value

obtained *t* value

point and interval estimation

PROCEDURES DESCRIBED

calculating $s_{\bar{x}}$

calculating the *t* for one sample

determining confidence intervals

testing for a significant linear
relationship

One aspect of human behavior that has received attention in newspapers involves highway driving speed. Numerous articles have addressed not only the effect of driving speed on accident rate and fatalities but also the attempts by government legislatures to change speed limits on highways and interstates. In traveling the highways, you have undoubtedly noticed that not everyone strictly observes the current speed limits. In fact, many people purchase radar detectors or CB radios in an effort to determine the location of police enforcing the speed limit, thereby hoping to ensure they can exceed the speed limit with impunity.

To better understand the driving behavior of college students, I asked my statistics class in psychology to indicate how fast they drive on the highway. Students were asked to indicate on a piece of paper how fast they drive relative to the posted speed limit on the highway. For example, students who felt that they drove an average of 3 mph under the speed limit recorded a −3 on the paper. On the other hand, students who consistently exceeded the speed limit by 7 mph recorded a +7. If the behavior of my students fits with my own observations on the highway, I would anticipate that most would have indicated that they drive over the posted speed limit. Their individual responses along with summary statistics are presented in Table 9.1.

This example will be used to demonstrate the combined use of descriptive and inferential statistics in the evaluation of data from a single sample. Prior to collecting the data, the researcher develops a research hypothesis. The research hypothesis for this example is based on the belief that students in the statistics class come from a population of individuals who do not drive at 55 mph. The researcher, in this case your author, intends to use the data from the sample to test this hypothesis. The first step is to describe the data in the sample.

DESCRIPTIVE STATISTICS: A MEASURE OF CENTRAL TENDENCY AND A MEASURE OF VARIABILITY

Presenting all the data in Table 9.1 would be too cumbersome in a research article and would require that the reader summarize the data in order to interpret the findings. Therefore, the descriptive procedures described in Chapter 3 should be used. Specifically, when working with data that correspond to an interval or ratio scale of measurement, the most frequently reported descriptive statistics are the mean and standard deviation. The data in this example correspond to a ratio scale of measurement (there is a "real" zero point and the possible values on the number line [. . . , −2, −1, 0, 1 , 2 , . . .] are equally spaced). The $\overline{X}$ is a measure of central tendency, and

TABLE 9.1	Listing of the Students' Estimates (in MPH) of the Difference between Their Average Driving Speed and the Speed Limit on Highways

Estimated Difference in Driving Speed from Speed Limit (in mph)
7
15
10
5
8
20
5
15
0
10
9
18
10
10
5
15
8
10
10
23
12
10
15
4
7
10
9
5
7
12
5
$\Sigma X = $ 309
$\Sigma X^2 = 3,819$
N = 31

the estimate of the population standard deviation serves as a measure of variability.

To calculate the $\overline{X}$, the sum of the values ΣX along with the number of values N for the sample are inserted into Formula 1

$$\overline{X} = \Sigma X/N. \tag{1}$$

Using the data from Table 9.1, the $\overline{X}$ is,

$$= 309/31$$
$$= 9.97 \text{ mph.}$$

The measure of variability to be calculated is s, which is the estimate of the population standard deviation. The calculations involve first determining SS, the sum of the squared deviations. Then the SS is divided by $N - 1$ to calculate an average of the squared deviations. The square root is then calculated so that the statistic is reported in the same units as the original values. These operations involve Formulas 3 through 5. The only additional information needed beyond that for calculating the $\overline{X}$ is ΣX^2. This sum is shown in Table 9.1. Remember that it is the sum of each squared value ΣX^2 not the sum squared $(\Sigma X)^2$. Using Formulas 3 through 5 provides s

$$SS = \Sigma X^2 - \frac{(\Sigma X)^2}{N} \tag{3}$$

$$= 3{,}819 - \frac{(309)^2}{31}$$

$$= 738.97,$$

and

$$s^2 = \frac{SS}{N - 1} \tag{4}$$

$$= \frac{738.97}{30}$$

$$= 24.63.$$

And

$$s = \sqrt{s^2} \tag{5}$$

$$= \sqrt{24.63}$$

$$= 4.96 \text{ mph}.$$

These calculations provide the two descriptive statistics necessary to summarize and describe the data in the sample. The $\overline{X}$ is 9.97 mph and s is 4.96 mph. Therefore, students in the sample appear to average about 10 miles over the speed limit and the standard deviation is just under 5 mph.

INFERENTIAL STATISTICS: HYPOTHESIS TESTING

Once the descriptive statistics have been calculated, they can be used in the procedures involving inferential statistics. Recall that these procedures allow the researcher to *infer* information about the population from which the sample was selected. Remember, I hypothesized that the sample came from a population of students who do not observe the posted speed limit. Inferential statistics will test that hypothesis.

If the sample comes from a population of individuals who do not observe the speed limit, then there are an infinite number of population distributions from which the sample could have been selected. That is, the sample may come from a population distribution of individuals who exceed the speed limit by an average (μ) of 4.00, 5.27, 7.93, or 11.31 mph, to list just a few possibilities. (It is also possible, although unlikely, that the sample could come from a population of individuals who drive slower than the speed limit [e.g., μs of -0.43, -6.17 mph].) If, however, the sample comes from a population distribution of individuals who observe the speed limit, then I know that the μ of that population distribution is 0.00. That is the mean of the population distribution of individuals who observe the speed limit.

The concept of indirect proof as described in the previous chapter will be used. In order to support my research hypothesis, it makes more sense to determine the probability of the sample coming from a population distribution of people who observe the speed limit, $\mu = 0.00$, rather than testing population distributions with μs other than 0.00. If I can show that it is unlikely that my sample came from this population distribution, then this distribution can be rejected and it can be assumed that the sample came from a distribution with a μ other than 0.00. The research hypothesis will be indirectly supported by ruling out the distribution with a μ of 0.00.

THE NULL AND ALTERNATIVE HYPOTHESES

The formal procedures for testing this hypothesis involves the use of the null H_0 and alternative H_1 hypotheses. The null hypothesis describes the case to be tested. In this example, the researcher is testing the likelihood that the sample came from a population distribution of individuals who observe the speed limit. Therefore, the H_0 assumes that $\mu = 0.00$ mph. The H_1 would describe all other possibilities, which would be all population distributions with a μ other than 0.00. Therefore, H_1 would be $\mu \neq 0.00$ mph. It is common to describe the H_0 and H_1 in terms of values for μ when testing one sample made up of interval or ratio data.

These two hypotheses describe all possible population distributions from which the sample could have been selected. Either H_0 or H_1 is true. Notice that the hypotheses differ only in terms of μ. One assumption of the test is that the standard deviations for all these population distributions, σs, are equal. That is, σ is the same whether the H_0 or H_1 is true. The only thing that differentiates these different population distributions is μ, the population mean.

THE ALPHA LEVEL

Reviewing the discussion from the previous chapter, it is necessary for the researcher to determine the probability of the sample being selected at random from the population distribution described by H_0. If the probability is .05 or less, then the researcher can reject H_0 and assume that H_1 is supported. If the probability of the sample being selected from the population distribution described by H_0 is greater than .05 then the researcher must retain the possibility that the sample did come from that distribution. This would not support the researcher's hypothesis.

The particular probability value to decide whether to retain or reject H_0

is called the **alpha level.** The alpha level is the probability value established by the researcher, *prior to collecting the data*, that will be used in determining whether to retain or reject H_0. In behavioral science research, the traditionally accepted alpha level is .05. That is, a researcher may decide that if the probability of a sample coming from a population distribution described by H_0 is .05 or less, then the researcher can reject H_0. Most scientific journals will not accept conclusions of researchers who reject H_0 if they have used an alpha level greater than .05.

As will be discussed in Chapter 12, there are occasions when researchers will want to use a more stringent alpha level. In some instances, researchers may set their alpha level to .01. In these cases, the researcher will reject H_0 only if the probability of the sample being selected from the population distribution described by H_0 is equal to or less than one out of one hundred. This more stringent alpha level is employed when researchers are concerned about avoiding a mistake in rejecting H_0 when it is true. An example is medical research in which researchers may want to be very confident inferring a treatment works (based on a sample of data). By using a more stringent alpha level, they are increasing the probability of retaining H_0 (the assumption a treatment has *no* effect) if it is true.

THE SAMPLING DISTRIBUTION OF THE MEAN

Given that an alpha level of .05 has been selected, it is necessary to determine the probability that the sample came from a population distribution with a μ of 0.00, the case described by H_0. As we saw in Chapter 8, the sample cannot be compared directly to the population distribution. The population distribution would be useful only if I wanted to determine the probability of selecting one individual from it, because it is comprised of individual values (speed estimates). Instead, what is needed is a distribution consisting of all the samples of $N = 31$ that can be selected from the population distribution with a μ of 0.00.

This distribution is a sampling distribution. Because each of the possible samples of $N = 31$ is represented by a single value, the sample mean $(\overline{X})$, the distribution is called the sampling distribution of the mean. The **sampling distribution of the mean** is a frequency distribution composed of all samples of a specific N that can be selected from a particular population distribution. The *x*-axis lists possible X values, but the *y*-axis represents the frequency or number of samples with a particular $\overline{X}$.

Properties of the Sampling Distribution of the Mean

There are a number of important properties about the sampling distribution of the mean that must be discussed. They involve the relationship between the sampling distribution and the other two distributions discussed so far—the population distribution and the sample distribution. In most studies, the researcher has data that result entirely from the sample distribution. From the sample distribution and the H_0, the researcher estimates information about the other two distributions—the population and sampling distributions.

For the chapter example, there are 31 values that constitute the sample distribution. From the statistics calculated from the sample distribution $\overline{X}$ and s, it is possible to estimate parameters for the population and sampling distribution. These estimates are possible because of the mathematical properties that exist among the three distributions.

For example, the X is an unbiased estimate of the population mean μ. For all sampling distributions selected from a population distribution, the mean of the sampling distribution $\mu_{\overline{x}}$ is equal to μ. That is, if one selects all possible samples of a specific N from a population distribution and then calculates the X for each sample, the mean of all the sample $\overline{X}$s, that is, $\mu_{\overline{x}}$ would equal μ, the mean of all the individual values in the population. The parameter $\mu_{\overline{x}}$ is used to identify the mean of a sampling distribution of the mean. The subscript $\overline{x}$ is used to indicate that the sampling distribution is a distribution of sample means. As will be discussed shortly, when testing the H_0 for one sample, the researcher uses the μ identified in the H_0 to determine $\mu_{\overline{x}}$ for hypothesis testing.

The measures of variability among the three distributions are also related. Recall that the population standard deviation is identified by the parameter σ. The standard deviation for the sampling distribution uses the parameter $\sigma_{\overline{x}}$. The relationship between σ and $\sigma_{\overline{x}}$ can be mathematically shown to be

$$\sigma_{\overline{x}} = \frac{\sigma}{\sqrt{N}}. \quad \text{(Def)}$$

The variability in the sampling distribution is directly related to the variability in the population distribution. However, for sampling distributions based on large samples (large Ns) the variability among the sample $\overline{X}$s will be less than the variability among the individual values in the population distribution. This should make intuitive sense. Consider the extreme case of samples of N = 1. In this case, the sampling distribution is based on samples of individual values. The sampling distribution and population distribution would be identical, $\mu = \mu_{\overline{x}}$ and $\sigma = \sigma_{\overline{x}}$. However, if each sample is composed of more than one value then it is less likely that the sample $\overline{X}$s would be as extreme as individual values because an extreme value in a large sample would be "diluted" by the other values in the sample. In a sample of N = 20, an extreme value has only 1/20th of an influence on the sample $\overline{X}$, whereas in a smaller sample N = 3, the influence of an extreme score is 1/3rd.

This concept is reflected in the formula for $\sigma_{\overline{x}}$. In fact, the mathematical relationship is defined in terms of the sample size for the sampling distribution. The variability in a sampling distribution based on samples of N = 25 will be 1/5th (1/N) of the variability in the population distribution. The fact that $\mu_{\overline{x}}$ is equal to μ and $\sigma_{\overline{x}}$ is equal to $\sigma/\sqrt{N}$ is demonstrated in Box 9.1 for a population of 4 values and samples of N = 3.

Researchers seldom know σ; therefore, an unbiased estimate must be derived from the sample distribution. That estimate is s, the estimate of the population standard deviation. You can use s to provide an estimate of the standard deviation for the sampling distribution of the mean. The relationship is the same as if σ were used. The formula for $s_{\bar{x}}$ is

$$s_{\bar{x}} = \frac{s}{\sqrt{N}}. \tag{15}$$

This statistic $s_{\bar{x}}$, which is an estimate of the standard deviation of the sampling distribution, is referred to as the **standard error of the mean.**

BOX 9.1   **An Example of a Population Distribution with Four Values and All the Possible Samples of $N = 3$ that Can Be Generated from That Population.**

POPULATION VALUES: 1   2   3   4 ($\Sigma X = 10$; $\Sigma X^2 = 30$; $N = 4$)
POPULATION MEAN, μ: 2.5
POPULATION STANDARD DEVIATION, σ: 1.12

A Listing of All 64 Samples (and Their $\overline{X}$) that Can Be Generated							
1	1	1	1	1	1	1	1
1	1	1	1	2	2	2	2
1	2	3	4	1	2	3	4
$\overline{X} = 1.00$	1.33	1.67	2.00	1.33	1.67	2.00	2.33
1	1	1	1	1	1	1	1
3	3	3	3	4	4	4	4
1	2	3	4	1	2	3	4
$\overline{X} = 1.67$	2.00	2.33	2.67	2.00	2.33	2.67	3.00
2	2	2	2	2	2	2	2
1	1	1	1	2	2	2	2
1	2	3	4	1	2	3	4
$\overline{X} = 1.33$	1.67	2.00	2.33	1.67	2.00	2.33	2.67
2	2	2	2	2	2	2	2
3	3	3	3	4	4	4	4
1	2	3	4	1	2	3	4
$\overline{X} = 2.00$	2.33	2.67	3.00	2.33	2.67	3.00	3.33
3	3	3	3	3	3	3	3
1	1	1	1	2	2	2	2
1	2	3	4	1	2	3	4
$\overline{X} = 1.67$	2.00	2.33	2.67	2.00	2.33	2.67	3.00

The lower variability for sampling distributions with larger N is an important property of the sampling distribution of the mean. The shapes of the sampling distributions based on $s_{\bar{x}}$ change with sample size. With small samples sizes, the sampling distribution may not be normal in shape. Yet, as the sample size (N) increases the shape of the sampling distributions begin to conform to that of the normal distribution. Figure 9.1 illustrates this graphically for sampling distributions of different N taken from the same population distribution.

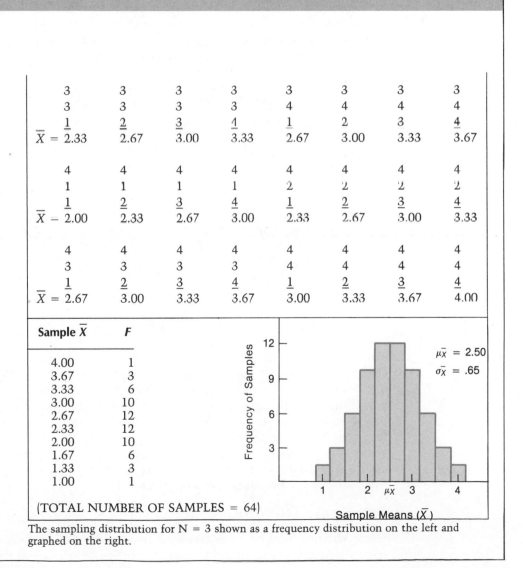

The sampling distribution for N = 3 shown as a frequency distribution on the left and graphed on the right.

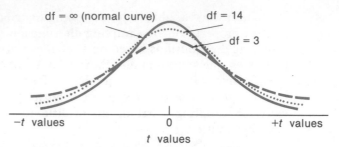

FIGURE 9.1 Sampling distributions for samples of different *N* taken from the same population distribution.

These different sampling distributions are known as the **Student's *t* distributions.** Student's *t* distributions, usually referred to simply as *t* distributions, are theoretical sampling distributions. They are named after a statistician named Gosset who published under the pen name Student. The different shapes are determined by a concept called **degrees of freedom (df).** Degrees of freedom is a complex statistical concept. For our purposes a simplified explanation will be offered. The number of degrees of freedom is equal to the number of values that can freely vary for a particular calculation. The number of degrees of freedom can be viewed as the number of values that can be *freely* assigned in a sample and still get a particular statistic. For example, if N = 5 and the $\overline{X}$ is 10, then the researcher knows that $\Sigma X = 50$. The researcher could pick any numbers for four of the values (e.g., 5, 20, 36, −7), but the fifth value (−4) would have to be one that would result in the sum of the values equalling 50. Therefore, with one sample of data the degrees of freedom is one less than the number of values in the sample, N − 1.

The *t* distributions are represented in terms of degrees of freedom as shown in Figure 9.1. Notice that with small N and low df, the sampling distributions have more variability or spread of $\overline{X}$s than the normal distribution. With increasing df, the variability decreases. The *t* distribution becomes normal only when the theoretical limit of N = ∞ is reached.

The last property of the sampling distribution to be discussed involves the relationship between the shape of the population distribution and the sampling distribution when the population distribution is not normal in shape. Regardless of the shape of the population distribution, the sampling distributions on which they are based are more normal in shape for sample distributions with increasing N. This is shown in Figure 9.2. This concept is based on the central limit theorem. The **central limit theorem** illustrates the fact that sampling distributions based on small N will retain some of the shape of the population distribution. However, as N increases the sampling distributions change shape and become more normal in shape regardless of the shape of the population distribution.

THE *t* TEST FOR ONE SAMPLE

Using the information just discussed, it is possible to introduce our first statistical test involving inferential statistics. The test is called the *t* test for one sample. It is used in determining the probability of one sample being selected

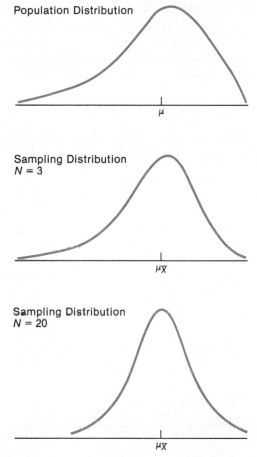

Population Distribution

μ

Sampling Distribution
$N = 3$

$\mu_{\overline{X}}$

Sampling Distribution
$N = 20$

$\mu_{\overline{X}}$

FIGURE 9.2 Graphic representation of the central-limit theorem. The population distribution at the top is skewed. The sampling distributions from this population become more normal in shape with larger *N*.

at random from a specific population distribution. It relies on the use of the $\overline{X}$ and the construction of the sampling distribution of the mean based on the H_0.

Returning to the chapter example, remember that the research hypothesis assumes that the sample comes from a population distribution of students who do not observe the posted speed limit. I hope to support that hypothesis by showing that it is unlikely that the sample comes from a population distribution of values based on students who observe the posted speed limit. Individuals who observe the posted speed limit would come from a population distribution with a $\mu = 0.00$ mph in terms of deviation from the posted speed limit. Statistically speaking, this situation is described by H_0. I need to know the probability that the sample of 31 students came from that population distribution. As was mentioned earlier, the alpha level has been set to a *p* value of .05. If the probability of the sample being randomly selected from the population distribution with a μ of 0.00 is .05 *or less* then H_0 will be rejected and it will be assumed that the sample came from a population distribution with a $\mu \neq 0.00$, which is the case described by H_1.

To determine this probability, it is necessary to construct the sampling distribution that assumes the sample came from a population distribution with a $\mu = 0.00$. Two values, $\mu_{\bar{x}}$ and $s_{\bar{x}}$, are necessary to construct the sampling distribution. Based on the properties associated with sampling distributions we know that $\mu_{\bar{x}}$ is equal to μ. Therefore, if the sample came from a population distribution with $\mu = 0.00$, then the sampling distribution must have a $\mu_{\bar{x}} = 0.00$. The value for $s_{\bar{x}}$ can be determined by using Formula 15

$$s_{\bar{x}} = \frac{s}{\sqrt{N}} \qquad (15)$$
$$= \frac{4.96}{\sqrt{31}}$$
$$= .89.$$

Based on these values, the sampling distribution for H_0 is shown at the top in Figure 9.3. Using the information discussed in Chapter 4 concerning z scores helps in interpreting this distribution and converting information into probabilities. Recall that the area under the curve represents the total proportion of samples that could be selected from the population distribution. This proportion equals 1.00. We have previously decided that if our sample has a p value of .05 or less of coming from this sampling distribution, then we would assume that it does not come from the population distribution on which this sampling distribution is based. Obviously, the deviant or low-probability samples would fall under the tails of the distribution in Figure 9.3 and not near the middle. That is, if our sample has a $\overline{X}$ of 0.12 mph, the sample would be near the middle of the sampling distribution and would have a fairly high probability of coming from the sampling distribution. On the other hand, the sample has a $\overline{X}$ of 9.97 mph, which should fall in the area under the right tail of the sampling distribution. The important question we must ask is whether it is in the extreme 5% (or .05 of the total proportion) of the distribution or not.

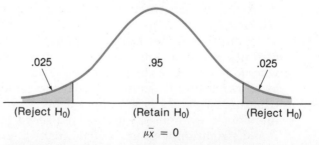

FIGURE 9.3 Sampling distribution for the chapter example. The distribution is based on H_0 and s_X. The shaded area represents the extreme .05 of the total area under the sampling distribution.

In Figure 9.3, the two shaded areas correspond to the extreme 5% of the total area under the curve. The 5% is split into two areas each equalling 2.5% of the total area. Remember the H_0 assumes $\mu = 0.00$ and H_1 assumes $\mu \neq 0.00$. Therefore, it is important to include the possibility that the students drive significantly *under* the speed limit, which is the area shaded under the left tail of the sampling distribution. Deviant samples in both directions away from $\mu_{\bar{x}}$ are to be considered.

The decision facing the researcher is to determine where the sample would fall under the sampling distribution at the bottom of Figure 9.3. If it falls in the middle 95% of the area, then the researcher must retain H_0 and conclude that it is possible that the sample came from a population distribution described by H_0. If, on the other hand, the sample falls in the extreme shaded areas, then the decision is to reject H_0. Then it can be assumed that the sample came from some other population distribution explained by H_1. To make that decision the researcher needs two important statistics. The first is the critical value that separates the middle area from the shaded area and the second is the statistic that determines the location of the sample.

Before describing the procedures needed to find those statistics, it is important to note that the example in Figure 9.3 involves the use of a nondirectional hypothesis. The **nondirectional hypothesis,** which is based on H_1, predicts a difference but not the direction of the difference. In this example, the H_1 describes the case in which the sample comes from a population distribution with a $\mu \neq 0.00$. It does not predict whether the sample comes from a population with a $\mu < 0.00$ or $\mu > 0.00$. All possible μs in either direction from 0.00 are assumed under H_1. The nondirectional hypothesis is used in the majority of behavioral science research. It results in half of the alpha level being located at each tail of the distribution described by H_0. The term "two-tailed test" was derived from the use of a nondirectional hypothesis.

Some researchers use a directional hypothesis. A **directional hypothesis,** which again is based on H_1, predicts a difference in a particular direction. Although we are using a nondirectional hypothesis to demonstrate the more common practice used in hypothesis testing, a directional hypothesis could have been used in this example. I could have predicted that the sample came from a population with a $\mu > 0.00$. If that had been my H_1, then H_0 would have to describe all other possibilities, $\mu \leq 0.00$. The H_0 would represent the cases in which the sample came from a population distribution with a μ of 0.00 or lower. The alpha level would have all been located at the upper tail of the distribution described by H_0. Hence, a "one-tailed test" would have been used. We will return to this distinction between nondirectional and directional hypotheses in more detail in the next three chapters.

The Critical *t* Value

If the sampling distribution was normally distributed, then the *z* scores in Table Z in Appendix E could be used to identify the value that separates the extreme 2.5% of the distribution at each tail of the distribution. Unfortunately, the sampling distribution would be normal only if N = ∞. The sampling distribution shown in Figure 9.3 is not a normal distribution but rather a t distribution with df (N − 1) of 30. Therefore, a different statistic is needed. That statistic is called the t because it is derived from the Student's t distribution.

The **critical t value** is derived from Student's t distribution and identifies the transition from the open area (retain H_0) to the shaded areas (reject H_0) in the sampling distribution. Like z scores, t values are expressed in terms of standard deviation units. A t value of 1.00 indicates a sample that is one standard deviation above the $\mu_{\bar{x}}$ in the sampling distribution. Because the variability is different depending on the df, the area under the t distributions is not the same for all t values.

Table 9.2 lists a portion of Table T which is printed in its entirety in Appendix E. Table T contains the critical t values for the alpha levels of .05 and .01. The first column lists df corresponding to the different sampling

TABLE 9.2   A Portion of Table T which Contains Critical t Values

	nondirectional hypothesis		directional hypothesis	
df	.05	.01	.05	.01
1	6.314	31.821	12.706	63.657
2	2.920	6.965	4.303	9.925
3	2.353	4.541	3.182	5.841
4	2.132	3.747	2.776	4.604
5	2.015	3.365	2.571	4.032
6	1.943	3.143	2.447	3.707
7	1.895	2.998	2.365	3.499
8	1.860	2.896	2.306	3.355
9	1.833	2.821	2.262	3.250
10	1.812	2.764	2.228	3.169
⋮				
30	1.697	2.457	2.042	2.750
40	1.684	2.423	2.021	2.704
60	1.671	2.390	2.000	2.660
120	1.658	2.358	1.980	2.617
∞ (z)	1.645	2.326	1.960	2.576

distributions. Each row lists different critical *t* values depending on the type of test conducted and the alpha level used.

The second and third columns list critical *t* values for directional hypotheses (one-tailed tests) while the fourth and fifth columns list values for nondirectional hypotheses (two-tailed *t* tests) like the one shown in Figure 9.3. Two alpha levels are shown, .05 and .01. In our example, the alpha level used is .05. This corresponds to the shaded area shown in Figure 9.3 and Figure 9.4.

To determine the critical *t* value for our test, we need the sampling distribution corresponding to df = 30 because for one sample df = N − 1 (in our example N − 31). Listed for the row with df = 30 and under the column for an alpha level of .05, two-tailed test, a critical *t* value of 2.042 is shown. This value indicates that samples which are 2.042 standard deviation units or more from $\mu_{\bar{x}}$ in the sampling distribution have a probability of .05 or less of being selected at random from the population distribution described by H_0. In Figure 9.4, the critical *t* values (both positive and negative) are inserted. If the sample has a *t* value equal to or greater than 2.042 (or equal to or less than −2.042), the researcher can reject H_0 and assume that the sample did not come from the population distribution described by H_0.

The Obtained *t* Value

The next step for the researcher is to determine where the sample falls in the sampling distribution. The procedure is similar to that for *z* scores in that the sample $\bar{X}$ is transformed into a *t* value that can then be compared with the critical *t* value. The formula for this conversion when testing for one sample is

$$t = \frac{\bar{X} - \mu_{\bar{x}}}{s_{\bar{x}}}. \tag{16}$$

This formula will convert the sample mean into a *t* value that corresponds to the scale shown in Figure 9.4. This *t* value is called the **obtained *t* value** because it is the value obtained for the sample being tested. For the example, the obtained *t* value would be

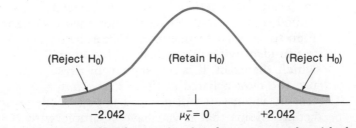

(Reject H_0)   (Retain H_0)   (Reject H_0)

−2.042 $\mu_{\bar{x}} = 0$ +2.042

FIGURE 9.4 **Sampling distribution for the chapter example with the critical *t* values included.**

$$t = \frac{\overline{X} - \mu_{\overline{X}}}{s_{\overline{x}}} \qquad (16)$$

$$= \frac{9.97 - 0.00}{.89}$$

$$= 11.20.$$

The value for $\mu_{\overline{x}}$ is based on the H_0. The sample has an obtained t value of 11.20. That is, it is 11.20 standard deviations beyond the $\mu_{\overline{x}}$ for the sampling distribution based on H_0. The sample falls within the shaded areas in Figure 9.4, which represent the alpha level for the test. Therefore, the decision is to reject H_0 and conclude that the sample comes from a population distribution with $\mu \neq 0.00$. This finding supports the research hypothesis.

The researcher concludes that, "The students come from a population of students who do not observe the posted speed limit, $\underline{t}(30) = 11.20, \underline{p} < .05$." When making a statement based on a statistical test, it is expected that the researcher will provide the necessary statistics to support the statement. For a t test this includes the df, shown in parentheses, the obtained t value, and the alpha level used. The t and p statistics are underlined in manuscripts because they indicate to the printer that these statistics should appear in italics when printed in a journal. In preparing scientific reports using the American Psychological Association's format, the accepted rule is for the author to underline statistics.

This concludes the example on hypothesis testing for one sample. Several points need to be reviewed. One is that the researcher should determine the H_0, H_1, and alpha level before collecting the data. In many instances when working with one sample the μ for H_0 may be some value *other than* 0.00. When testing if a sample came from a specific population distribution, the researcher may be provided with or assume a specific μ value. For example if an instructor tested the possibility that her class had a grade point average different from the college average of 2.43, she would assume that H_0 was $\mu = 2.43$ and that H_1 was $\mu \neq 2.43$. The specific value for μ in these instances is determined by the research hypothesis to be tested.

Once these are determined and the sample data are collected, it is necessary to calculate the $\overline{X}$ and s for the sample. In constructing the sampling distribution to test H_0 the researcher uses H_0 to determine $\mu_{\overline{x}}$ and s and N to calculate $s_{\overline{x}}$ (Formula 15). The critical t value as shown in Table T is needed to determine whether to retain or reject H_0. The obtained t value is determined from Formula 16. If the obtained t value is larger (in absolute value) than the critical t value, then H_0 can be rejected.

In identifying the critical t value from Table T, there may be instances in which the exact df is not shown. In those instances, the best practice is to use the closest listed df that is *less than* the one needed. This results in a test in which you will not exceed your predetermined alpha level. This procedure means that if you have a sample with N = 56, the critical t value corresponding to df = 40 should be used rather than df = 60.

INFERENTIAL STATISTICS: INTERVAL ESTIMATION

The previous section demonstrated hypothesis testing and determining the likelihood that a sample came from a specific population distribution. We know that it is unlikely that the sample came from a population with a μ of 0.00 mph. If someone were to ask you what your best estimate was for the population mean for this sample, you would probably reply with the $\overline{X}$ of 9.97 mph. That would be the correct answer because we know that the $\overline{X}$ is an unbiased estimate of μ.

Responding with a single value is an example of **point estimation.** Inferences about the population are based on a single point or estimate. It is possible, however, to make inferences using intervals. In **interval estimation** the researcher provides a range or interval of possible μ values from which the sample may have been selected. These intervals are often stated in terms of a specific confidence level and are called confidence intervals. The most commonly reported intervals correspond to the 95% and 99% confidence intervals.

Rather than providing a single or point estimate, the researcher provides a range of μ values. A 95% confidence interval indicates that the researcher is 95% confident that the sample came from a population distribution with a μ within the range listed. Obviously, to be 99% confident, the researcher would have to have a larger range of μ values.

The range for a confidence interval is fairly easy to determine. It is based on the $\overline{X}$, $s_{\overline{x}}$, and the critical t value for the sample size and confidence level. The formulas for the limits of a confidence interval for one sample are

$$\text{Upper Limit of } \mu = \overline{X} + (t_{\text{crit}(\alpha)} \cdot s_{\overline{x}}), \tag{17a}$$

and

$$\text{Lower Limit of } \mu = \overline{X} - (t_{\text{crit}(\alpha)} \cdot s_{\overline{x}}). \tag{17b}$$

The $t_{\text{crit}(\alpha)}$ is the critical t value found from Table T. It is based on the df in the sample $(N - 1)$ and the confidence interval used. If it is 95% then use the two-tailed test alpha level of .05. If the 99% confidence interval is desired then use the two-tailed alpha level of .01.

For the chapter example, the 95% confidence intervals would be

$$\begin{aligned}
\text{Upper Limit of } \mu &= \overline{X} + (t_{\text{crit}(\alpha)} \cdot s_{\overline{x}}) \tag{17a}\\
&= 9.97 + (2.042 \times .89)\\
&= 11.79,
\end{aligned}$$

and

$$\begin{aligned}
\text{Lower Limit of } \mu &= \overline{X} - (t_{\text{crit}(\alpha)} \cdot s_{\overline{x}}) \tag{17b}\\
&= 9.97 - (2.042 \times .89)\\
&= 8.15.
\end{aligned}$$

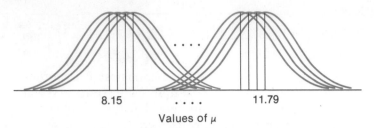

Values of μ

FIGURE 9.5 Population distributions encompassed within the 95% confidence interval for the chapter example.

Therefore, I am 95% confident that the sample came from a population distribution with a μ between 8.15 and 11.79 mph. Obviously, I am to conclude that my sample of students do not observe the posted speed limit. Based on the data, I am 95% confident that the students come from a population of students who exceed the speed limit by 8.15 to 11.79 mph. Figure 9.5 illustrates this graphically.

Interval estimation is useful when trying to identify the range of potential population distributions from which a sample may have been selected. Although hypothesis testing is used for testing a specific population distribution, interval estimation is used when determining likely population distributions from which the sample could be selected. It should be noted, that when using a 95% confidence interval, testing any μ outside the interval as H_0 would result in H_0 being rejected at the .05 level. If a μ is tested within the interval, then H_0 would be retained. The same relationship holds if one is using the 99% confidence interval and an alpha level of .01 for hypothesis testing.

INFERENTIAL STATISTICS: TESTING FOR A SIGNIFICANT LINEAR RELATIONSHIP

The last topic involves linear relationships and inferential statistics. Chapter 5 involved determining if a relationship existed for a sample of data. The determination of a linear relationship resulted in a Pearson r coefficient. Although the determination of an r indicated the strength of a linear relationship for a sample, it alone did not provide the researcher with the necessary information to determine if a linear relationship existed in the population from which the sample was selected.

It is possible with the use of the Student's t distribution to determine if a relationship found for a sample indicates a relationship in the population from which the sample was selected. Similar to hypothesis testing for one sample, it is necessary to construct an H_0 and H_1 to test for a relationship. The H_0 assumes the situation in which no linear relationship exists in the population. The Greek letter rho ρ is used to represent a linear relationship in a population. It is a parameter. H_0 assumes the case in which ρ = .00. The alternative hypothesis H_1 assumes the opposite; namely, that a relationship does exist in the population, $\rho \neq .00$. (Recall that relationships are indicated by two decimal values, the larger the absolute value the stronger the linear relationship.)

If the researcher is able to reject H_0, then the researcher can conclude that a relationship exists in the population. To test H_0 the researcher must convert the Pearson r calculated from Formula 9 into an obtained t value

$$t = \frac{r \sqrt{N-2}}{\sqrt{1-r^2}}. \tag{18}$$

The obtained t value found above is compared with the critical t value from Table T. In the case of testing for a significant relationship, the df is equal to $N - 2$, for which N is the number of subjects in the sample.

Using the first chapter example from Chapter 5, recall that 44 college students rated the attractiveness and potentiality as a date of another person. A Pearson r of $+.66$ was found for the sample. Assume that the researchers had determined prior to collecting the data that they would test H_0 $(\rho = .00)$ and had set an alpha level of .01. Using the statistics from the example and Formula 18 would result in

$$t = \frac{r \sqrt{N-2}}{\sqrt{1-r^2}} \tag{18}$$

$$= \frac{.66 \times \sqrt{44-2}}{\sqrt{1-.66^2}}$$

$$= \frac{4.28}{.75}$$

$$= 5.71.$$

The researchers would have an obtained t value of 5.71. Using Table T, with a nondirectional hypothesis and an alpha level of .01, the critical t value corresponding to df $= 40$ (which is the closest, smaller value to the one needed $[N - 2 = 44 - 2 = 42]$) is 2.704. The obtained t value exceeds the critical t value. Therefore, H_0 can be rejected because the probability is less than .01 that the sample was selected from a population distribution with no relationship between the two variables $(\rho = .00)$. Therefore, the researchers can conclude that, "their sample provides evidence of a significant relationship between ratings of attractiveness and potential as a date, $r(42) = .66$, $p \leq .01$." Again, as with the t test for one sample, researchers provide the necessary statistics when making a statement based on inferential statistics. In this case, the df are shown in parentheses and the Pearson r is reported along with the alpha level used.

It must be noted that this procedure is appropriate only when H_0 predicts that no relationship exists, $\rho = .00$. A similar procedure with a slightly modified formula exists for testing the H_0 for the Spearman r_s. However, tables with the critical values have been developed for both the Pearson r and Spearman r_s. The table with critical values for the Pearson r is based on procedures just described. Table R and Table Rs in Appendix E list the critical values for the Pearson r and Spearman r_s tests, respectively. If an obtained correlation coefficient equals or exceeds the critical value, then H_0 can be rejected. Values are listed for both nondirectional and directional hypotheses. In the case of a directional hypothesis, the researcher must predict the type of relationship, either positive or negative, prior to collecting the data. Then the obtained correlation coefficient must be consistent with the prediction and meet or exceed the listed critical value in order to reject H_0. For example, if the researcher predicts a negative relationship (H_1: $\rho < .00$) and has a sample with df = 10, then the researcher must have an $r \leq -.497$ to reject H_0 at the .05 alpha level. The value of .497 is found in Table R.

For a nondirectional hypothesis, the direction of the obtained relationship, either positive or negative, is not critical in determining whether to retain or reject H_0. The decision is based solely on the strength of the relationship.

SUMMARY

Descriptive and inferential statistics are often used in analyzing the data from one sample. A measure of central tendency and a measure of variability are commonly employed to describe the data. Researchers who are interested in *inferring* information about their sample often want to make statements about the population distribution from which the sample was selected.

Procedures involving inferential statistics allow the researcher to determine the probability that a sample was selected at random from a population distribution described by the H_0. These procedures include setting the alpha level. The alpha level is the probability level at which a researcher will reject H_0. It is based on the probability of a sample coming from the population distribution described by H_0. Commonly used alpha levels are .05 and .01.

When determining if a sample came from a particular population distribution or not, a t test for one sample is often used. This test is based on a theoretical sampling distribution called the Student's t distribution. The sampling distribution is a frequency distribution for all samples of a particular size N that are taken from a given population distribution.

The sampling distribution of the mean has several important properties. First, the mean of the sampling distribution $\mu_{\bar{x}}$ is equal to the population mean μ. Second, with larger sample sizes N, the sampling distributions have less variability. The variability is indicated by the standard deviation for the sampling distribution, called the standard error of the mean $s_{\bar{x}}$. With larger N, the $s_{\bar{x}}$ will decrease. Third, regardless of the shape of the population distribution from which a sample is taken, as the sample size increases, the sampling distribution becomes more normal in shape. This is called the central limit theorem.

The t test for one sample converts the sample $\bar{X}$ to an obtained t value. The t value is a statistic expressed in terms of standard deviation units and tells the researcher how far a sample $\bar{X}$ is from the mean of the sampling distribution for the H_0. If the distance or t is large, then the probability of the sample coming from a particular population is small.

The obtained t value is compared with a critical t value, which identifies the extreme portion of the sampling distribution. The critical t value is a function of the alpha level and the degrees of freedom (df) in the sample. The t distributions are based on df. With increasing df the t distribution approaches the normal curve.

If the obtained t value is equal to or larger than the critical t value (in terms of absolute value), then the researcher knows that the sample is in the extreme portion of the sampling distribution. This indicates that the probability of selecting this sample at random from the population distribution described by H_0 is equal to or less than the alpha level. Therefore, the H_0 is rejected and the researcher concludes that a significant result has been obtained. This indicates support for H_1 and the research hypothesis. If the obtained t value is less than the critical t value then the probability of the sample coming from the population distribution described by H_0 is greater than the alpha level and the researcher must retain H_0 and conclude that the research hypothesis has not been supported. In retaining H_0 the researcher is acknowledging the possibility that the sample was selected from the population distribution described by H_0.

Researchers may use another procedure involving inferential statistics when they want to provide a range of possible population distributions from which the sample was selected. This procedure involves interval estimation. The researcher establishes a specific confidence level for the interval. Commonly used confidence levels are 95% and 99%. The interval is based on the range population means μs from which the researcher is confident that a sample has been selected.

Lastly, the procedure for testing the existence of a linear relationship in a population was discussed. The test is based on the Pearson r which is the measure for a linear relationship in a sample. The r statistic along with the sample size is used to determine a t value. The H_0 assumes that no relationship exists in the population. When rejecting H_0, the researcher is supporting the hypothesis that a relationship exists in the population (which is described statistically by H_1).

SUMMARY FOR CALCULATING THE t FOR ONE SAMPLE

1. Determine the alpha level and state H_0 and H_1.

2. Calculate $\overline{X}$ and s using Formulas 1 and 3 through 5, respectively.

3. Calculate the standard error of the mean, $s_{\overline{x}}$, using

$$s_{\overline{x}} = \frac{s}{\sqrt{N}}. \tag{15}$$

4. Determine the obtained t value for one sample using

$$t = \frac{\overline{X} - \mu_{\overline{x}}}{s_{\overline{x}}}. \tag{16}$$

5. Determine the critical t value(s) using Table T (Appendix E) and your df $(N - 1)$. If the calculated t value in Step 4 is equal to or greater than the critical t value (in terms of absolute value), then reject H_0; otherwise, retain H_0.

6. The findings of the t test are often reported in sentence form with the following statistical information included: $\underline{t}$ (df) = obtained t, $\underline{p}$ < or > alpha level.

SUMMARY FOR INTERVAL ESTIMATION FOR ONE SAMPLE

1. Calculate $\overline{X}$ and s using Formulas 1 and 3 through 5, respectively.

2. Calculate the standard error of the mean, $s_{\overline{x}}$, using

$$s_{\overline{x}} = \frac{s}{\sqrt{N}}. \tag{15}$$

3. Determine the critical t value for Table T. The df equals $N - 1$ and the 95% confidence interval uses an alpha level of .05, whereas the 99% confidence interval uses the .01 alpha level.

4. Use Formulas 17a and 17b to establish the upper and lower limits

$$\textbf{Upper Limit of } \boldsymbol{\mu} = \overline{X} + (t_{\text{crit}(\alpha)} \cdot s_{\overline{x}}), \tag{17a}$$

and

$$\textbf{Lower limit of } \boldsymbol{\mu} = \overline{X} - (t_{\text{crit}(\alpha)} \cdot s_{\overline{x}}). \tag{17b}$$

5. State your findings in terms of being 95 or 99% confident that your sample was selected from a population distribution with a μ between the *lower limit of* μ and the *upper limit of* μ.

SUMMARY FOR TESTING FOR A SIGNIFICANT LINEAR RELATIONSHIP

1. Determine your alpha level. The null hypothesis H_0 assumes that no relationship exists in the population, $\rho = .00$. The alternative hypothesis H_1 assumes that a linear relationship does exist, $\rho \neq .00$.

2. Calculate the Pearson r for the two variables in the sample.

3. N equals the number of subjects in your sample. Calculate the obtained t value using

$$t = \frac{r\sqrt{N - 2}}{\sqrt{1 - r^2}}. \tag{18}$$

4. Determine the critical t value using Table T and your df $(N - 2)$. If the obtained t value in Step 4 is equal to or greater than the critical t value (in terms of absolute value), then assume that a linear relationship exists

in the population; otherwise, do not. Or, you may use Table R (for the Pearson r) or Table Rs (for the Spearman r_s) to compare the obtained coefficient directly with the critical value.

5. The findings are reported in sentence form with the following statistical information included: $\underline{r}$ (df) = Pearson r value, $\underline{p}$ < or > alpha level.

EXERCISES

1. In hypothesis testing for one sample, there are two statistical hypotheses. These hypotheses are often stated in terms of what population parameter?

2. Explain how the two statistical hypotheses H_0 and H_1 account for all possibilities of sampling from the family of population distributions.

3. If you were told that your basketball team was made up of individuals who were taller than the average student, what would you need to determine your null and alternative hypotheses? What statistical hypothesis would be more similar to your research hypothesis, which assumes that the basketball players are taller than the average student?

4. A student informs you that she has calculated a sampling distribution to have an $s_{\bar{x}}$ of 2.46. This is based on a sample of data you provided. Another student finds an $s_{\bar{x}}$ of 2.05. He contends that his sample (which is not identical to the other sample) came from the same population as the other sample. Why would the $s_{\bar{x}}$ statistics be different? Is there some mistake or is there a plausible explanation?

5. How does a sampling distribution differ from a sample distribution? Can there be more than one sampling distribution for a particular population distribution? Explain.

6. Define each of the following as a parameter or statistic and identify the type of distribution it represents:

   a. μ d. σ

   b. $s_{\bar{x}}$ e. $\overline{X}$

   c. $\mu_{\bar{x}}$ f. $\sigma_{\bar{x}}$

7. For the following 3 cases, estimate the population parameters:

A	B	C
$\overline{X}$ = 32	$\overline{X}$ = 48	$\overline{X}$ = 32
SS = 2,600	SS = 2,600	SS = 100,100
N = 26	N = 26	N = 1,001

8. Why is the sampling distribution used instead of the sample distribution in hypothesis testing?

9. For each situation below, determine the critical t value (always use a nondirectional hypothesis):

   a. $p = .05$; df $= 7$ **d.** $p = .01$; df $= 8$
   b. $p = .05$; N $= 376$ **e.** $p = .01$; N $= 18$
   c. $p = .05$; N $= 108$ **f.** $p = .01$; N $= 23$

10. A typing instructor estimates that previous students in her typing course make an average of 2 typing errors per page of a book report. She now provides a sample of 15 students with the opportunity to proofread each other's papers before submitting the final reports. She finds the following results in terms of typing errors in the book report:

    $\overline{X} = 1.56$ errors; s $= .67$; N $= 15$

    a. What are the H_0 and H_1?
    b. Determine the critical t value (use a nondirectional hypothesis, $p = .05$ alpha level) and calculate the t value.
    c. Is the H_0 retained or rejected?
    d. What conclusion should be drawn from the study?

11. For Exercise 10 calculate the 95% confidence interval and state it in words.

12. A clinical psychologist believes that a new smoking-reduction program is effective. As part of a pilot or preliminary study, she surveys 20 people who have participated in the program and records the number of cigarettes each person estimates he or she smokes per day 6 months after completing the program. She knows from previous research, that 6 months after other programs, the average person smokes 6.10 cigarettes per day. Her sample results are

    $\Sigma X = 116$; $\Sigma X^2 = 719$; N $= 20$

    a. What are the H_0 and H_1?
    b. Determine the critical t value (use a nondirectional hypothesis, $p = .05$ rejection region) and calculate the t value.
    c. Is the H_0 retained or rejected?
    d. What conclusion should be drawn from the study?

13. In Exercise 12 would the same conclusion have been made if an alpha level of .01 was used? Explain.

14. A political scientist samples the amount of money contributed to an incumbent in a state election. He knows that in the past, the mean contribution was $48.50. His sample provides the following data:

    $\overline{X} = \$37.25$; SS $= \$51,247.80$; N $= 45$

    a. What are the H_0 and H_1?
    b. Determine the critical t value (use a nondirectional hypothesis, $p = .05$ alpha level) and calculate the t value.
    c. Is the H_0 retained or rejected?
    d. What conclusion should be drawn from the study?

15. What is the 99% confidence interval for Exercise 14?

16. A sociologist tests the possibility that the number of serious crimes has dropped because of changes in a state's method of reporting such crimes. Prior to the new system, counties in this state reported an average of 2.06 crimes per 1,000 residents. Following the introduction of the new system, a random sampling of 11 counties provided the following statistics,

    $\overline{X} = 1.79$ crimes per 1,000 residents; s $= .65$

    a. What are the H_0 and H_1?
    b. Determine the critical t value (use nondirectional hypothesis, $p = .05$ alpha level) and calculate the t value.
    c. Is the H_0 retained or rejected?
    d. What conclusion should be drawn from the study?

17. A researcher calculates a t value of -1.93 for a sample of 23 values. Using a nondirectional hypothesis and a .05 alpha level, does she retain or reject H_0? Should she conclude that there is a good possibility that her sample came from the population distribution described by H_0? Explain.

18. A researcher rejects H_0 because his calculated t value is greater than the critical t value for a nondirectional hypothesis with a .05 alpha level. The critical value is 2.145. Can you determine either (a) the sample size or (b) the μ for H_0? Explain.

19. Complete the following incomplete statement as appropriate, "The sample (did, did not) differ significantly from the population distribution described by H_0, $t(24) = 2.09$, $p\ (\leq, \geq)\ .05$."

20. For the second chapter example in Chapter 5, determine if a significant relationship exists in the population. Use a nondirectional hypothesis and an alpha level of .01.

Interpreting Two-Condition Experiments with Interval or Ratio Data

OVERVIEW

The following three chapters begin the introduction of inferential statistics as they are used when testing a research hypothesis that predicts a difference. In the simplest of experiments and quasi experiments the independent variable involves only two levels or values. These levels are often referred to as conditions. Some experiments have only an experimental condition and a control condition. In Chapters 10 and 11, data from two-condition studies will be analyzed. The discussion will be limited to studies in which the data are based on variables from an interval or ratio scale of measurement.

In Chapter 10, the t test for independent samples will be introduced. It is the appropriate inferential statistical test when participants serve in only one of the two conditions in the experiment. Furthermore, the measure of behavior, the dependent variable, should be measured on an interval or ratio scale of measurement. That is, the researcher must assume that equal intervals exist between possible values for the dependent variable.

In Chapter 11, the t test for correlated samples will be discussed. It is often used in one of two types of experimental designs. The first design involves participants who serve in both conditions in a two-condition study. The other design depends on participants being *matched* in pairs, with one participant assigned to one condition and the other to the second condition. Again, this test assumes the data correspond to an interval or ratio scale of measurement.

In Chapter 12, the concept of statistical power will be discussed. Power involves the ability of the researcher to reject H_0 when it is false. That is, statistical power is the concept that deals with finding a significant difference if one truly exists in the population.

The *t* Test for Independent Samples

TERMS DISCUSSED

quasi experiment

quasi-independent variable

independent groups design

sampling distribution of the difference between the means

standard error of the mean difference $(s_{\bar{x}_1 - \bar{x}_2})$

parametric test

robust test

PROCEDURES DESCRIBED

calculating the standard error of the mean difference $(s_{\bar{x}_1 - \bar{x}_2})$

calculating the *t* value for the *t* test for independent samples

During the past 20 years, psychologists have studied a particular pattern of behavior labeled Type A. Individuals who show a Type A behavior pattern tend to be hard driving, competitive, and have a sense of urgency. For example, a person with a Type A behavior pattern might be one who works best under deadlines, whether imposed by the individual himself or someone else. Typical Type A behaviors might include quickened speech patterns, getting impatient while standing in lines or driving in heavy traffic, and the need to be early for appointments. On the other hand, a Type B behavior pattern would be the absence of these behaviors. A number of tests have been developed to identify individuals who show a Type A or Type B behavior pattern. As you might guess, most people tend to show a tendency toward one type or the other, but few are "pure" Type A or Type B. Some efforts have been made to determine if the Type A behavior pattern is related to stress and coronary heart disease. The results to date have been mixed. The example for this chapter is based on one of these studies.

Carver, Coleman, and Glass (1976) studied 20 male college students in a study on fatigue. Ten of these students were classified as showing Type A behaviors and the other 10 were classified as showing Type B behaviors. The students were instructed to wear running clothes to the experimental session. After recording a student's age, weight, height, and amount of body fat, the student was given five minutes of practice on a treadmill, which constituted a warm-up phase. Following that phase, the student was told that during the remainder of the session oxygen consumption on the treadmill would be measured. The student wore a mask which monitored the amount of oxygen consumed.

The student was also required to indicate his level of fatigue. The student used an 11-point scale that was printed on a board at the front of the room. An "11" was labeled "as fresh as I have ever been," and a "1" was labeled "as tired as I have ever been." Intermediate values were also labeled. For example a "9" was labeled "quite fresh" and a "5" was labeled "somewhat tired." Each student indicated his level of fatigue after the warm-up phase and every two minutes during the test phase.

During the test phase the treadmill was kept at a constant speed equivalent to a brisk walk and began with the treadmill surface in the horizontal plane. However, for every minute on the treadmill the grade was increased 1%. Oxygen consumption and fatigue were monitored during this test phase and the test phase continued until the student decided to stop.

The researchers' hypothesis was based on the assumption that students who show a Type A pattern are hard-driving and competitive. They believed that Type A students (1) would be more likely to suppress feelings of fatigue than Type B students and (2) would be more likely to exert more effort on the treadmill than Type B students. In order to eliminate other potential explanations for differences in performance between Type A and Type B students, Carver, Coleman, and Glass looked for initial differences between the two groups of students. They found no significant differences

TABLE 10.1	Fatigue Ratings at the End of the Treadmill Test for Students in the Chapter Example	
Type of Behavior Pattern		
Type A	*Type B*	
1	1	
2	2	
2	1	
3	2	
3	1	
2	1	
3	2	
1	2	
2	2	
$\underline{3}$	$\underline{1}$	
$\Sigma X_1 = 22$	$\Sigma X_2 = 15$	
$\Sigma X_1^2 = 54$	$\Sigma X_2^2 = 25$	
$N_1 = 10$	$N_2 = 10$	

in age, weight, height, aerobic capacity, or amount of body fat. The fatigue ratings at the end of the test phase along with summary statistics are shown in Table 10.1.

This example is based on a study on fatigue and begins the discussion of analysis of data from an experiment. In Chapter 9, a sample was tested against a particular population distribution. Now the emphasis is directed toward testing for differences between populations. As described earlier, an experiment is a research design that tests for differences among conditions. The research hypothesis is stated in terms of differences among conditions. The most basic experiment is one with two conditions.

ISSUES IN RESEARCH DESIGN

The conditions in an experiment represent values of the independent variable. In the chapter example the two conditions, Type A and Type B, are values of a variable that could be labeled "type of behavior pattern." If participants are randomly assigned to the conditions, then the design is a true experiment and the variable representing those values is the independent variable. If, however, participants come into the study already assigned to a condition, as is the case in the chapter example (they already show a Type A or Type B behavior pattern), then the design is a quasi experiment and the variable representing the conditions is a quasi-independent variable.

QUASI EXPERIMENTS

One common type of **quasi experiment** is one in which participants are not randomly assigned to conditions. Instead, the participants differ on some dimension of interest to the researcher. The **quasi-independent variable** is the variable or dimension of interest to the researcher for which the participant cannot be randomly assigned. (Examples of other quasi-independent variables include gender, age, and year in school.) These variables are also sometimes referred to as subject variables. The statistical procedures used in these cases are the same regardless of whether it is an experiment or a quasi experiment. The conclusions one makes, however, differ between an experiment and a quasi experiment.

In an experiment the researcher controls and manipulates the levels of the independent variable. In an experiment, the researcher can always assume that differences found in the participants' behaviors result from or are *caused* by changes in the independent variable. In a quasi experiment, the participants often *belong* to a particular level of the quasi-independent variable, such as male or female, when they participate in the study. The researcher does not *randomly assign* them to a sex. When a sex or gender difference is found, the researcher cannot conclude that it is the "maleness" or "femaleness" that causes the difference itself. It might be another variable related to sex, such as social development or society's expectations that influence and cause the behavior.

In the present example, the researchers hope to discover a difference in behavior between Type A and Type B individuals. If they do, they cannot assume that it is the type of behavior pattern that *caused* the difference. The difference could well be the result of another variable that is related to type of behavior pattern. Although the authors have controlled for other factors such as aerobic capacity and height, it is not possible to eliminate all variables that are related to behavior pattern. For instance, Type A individuals may have different experiences when working under stress than Type B people. If a difference is found, then the researchers know that type of behavior pattern is related to differences in perceived fatigue. Whether it is the result of the specific behavior pattern or another variable related to behavior pattern cannot be determined in this study. Further studies would need to be conducted which isolate and manipulate potential variables.

Quasi experiments are appropriate when an independent variable cannot be manipulated. For example, studies on gender differences provide important findings about behavioral differences between men and women. Quasi experiments are also helpful in the initial phases of a research project. For instance, the chapter example is appropriate as an initial study to determine if behavior type is related to differences in perceived fatigue.

INDEPENDENT GROUPS DESIGNS

A crucial concern in the statistical analysis is whether or not a participant serves in only one condition or in all the conditions in the experiment. Experimental and quasi-experimental designs in which a participant serves in only one condition are referred to as **independent groups designs**. In some texts, they may also be called between-groups designs. When participants are randomly assigned to conditions, the design may also be referred to as a random groups design. The essential feature is that a participant serves in only one condition of the independent variable. Obviously, in the chapter example a participant is in either the Type A condition or the Type B condition, but not both. Therefore, the design is an independent groups design.

THE RESEARCH HYPOTHESIS FOR THE CHAPTER EXAMPLE

Let's examine the research hypothesis. The research hypothesis for an experiment is stated in terms of a causal relationship. Some aspect of the environment (the independent variable) will have an effect on a behavior (the dependent variable). In this example one research hypothesis is that the behavior pattern of the participant is related to differences in fatigue ratings. It is believed that Type A individuals are more likely to suppress feelings of fatigue. Therefore, the fatigue ratings at the end of the test phase for the Type A individuals should be different from those for the Type B individuals. An alpha level of $p \leq .05$ will be used to test this hypothesis.

The dependent variable is the measure of behavior, which for this example is the rating of fatigue. The values for the dependent variable range from a possible low of 1 (extreme fatigue) to 11 (extreme freshness). The researchers assume that there are equal intervals between values; therefore, the scale of measurement is interval (notice that there is no 0 point on the scale).

It should be noted that rating scales are not always assumed to be on an interval scale. There is evidence that people do not use equal intervals in assigning ratings and that a rating scale may be on the ordinal scale of measurement. However, the researchers in this study (and the reviewers and editor of the journal in which it was published) accepted the position that the fatigue ratings did not violate assumptions of the statistical procedures described in this chapter.

DESCRIPTIVE STATISTICS: DESCRIBING THE SAMPLE DATA

The two sets of ratings in Table 10.1 represent samples of data. The first step is to calculate a measure of central tendency and a measure of variability for each sample. As is the case with most variables that have interval- or ratio-scale data, the $\overline{X}$ and s are the most frequently reported measures. Table 10.2 shows the procedure for calculating the $\overline{X}$ and s for each sample.

TABLE 10.2   Calculations for $\bar{x}$ and s for the Samples in the Example

Fatigue Ratings	
Type A	Type B
$\Sigma X_1 = 22$	$\Sigma X_2 = 15$
$\Sigma X_1^2 = 54$	$\Sigma X_2^2 = 25$
$N_1 = 10$	$N_2 = 10$

$$\text{Using Formula 1:}\quad \overline{X} = \Sigma X / N$$

$\overline{X}_1 = 22/10$	$\overline{X}_2 = 15/10$
$= 2.2$	$= 1.5$

$$\text{Using Formula 3:}\quad SS = \Sigma X^2 - \frac{(\Sigma X)^2}{N}$$

$SS_1 = 54 - \dfrac{22^2}{10}$	$SS_2 = 25 - \dfrac{15^2}{10}$
$= 5.6$	$= 2.5$

$$\text{Using Formula 4:}\quad s^2 = \frac{SS}{N-1}$$

$s_1^2 = \dfrac{5.6}{9}$	$s_2^2 = \dfrac{2.5}{9}$
$= .62$	$= .28$

$$\text{Using Formula 5:}\quad s = \sqrt{s^2}$$

$s_1 = \sqrt{.62}$	$s_2 = \sqrt{.28}$
$= .79$	$= .53$

Note that the subscripts 1 and 2 are used to differentiate between the two samples. Statistics with the subscript 1 refer to the data for Type A students, and the subscript 2 is used for data from Type B students. Although any subscript could be used, 1 and 2 are generally used in differentiating between two samples in a two-condition experiment.

The $\overline{X}$ fatigue rating for the Type A students is 2.2, which is higher than the $\overline{X}$ rating for Type B students, 1.5. Remember a high number indicates less fatigue. Therefore, it appears that the Type A students may be reporting a little less fatigue than Type B students. The s in both samples is small, .79 for Type A and .53 for Type B. This indicates that there is not a lot of variability in the ratings given by the students. When looking at the ratings in Table 10.1, note that Type A students gave ratings between 1 and 3, whereas Type B students gave ratings of only 1 or 2.

The descriptive statistics lead the researchers to believe that there is support for the research hypothesis. The $\overline{X}$ rating for Type A students is higher than that for Type B students. The Type A students are reporting less fatigue, on the average, than Type B students. However, it is necessary to conduct a statistical test to determine the probability that this difference between the samples results from chance factors or sampling error.

INFERENTIAL STATISTICS: TESTING FOR A DIFFERENCE

The statistical test that is used in determining if two samples differ significantly from each other requires the use of the null (H_0) and alternative (H_1) hypotheses. Therefore, as in Chapter 9, the discussion will center on population, sample, and sampling distributions. The sample distributions are based on the data in Table 10.1. If there is no statistical difference between the two samples, then it is assumed that the samples could have been selected from the same population distribution. The hypothesis that the samples were taken from the same population is described by H_0. It can be stated statistically in terms of the population means, μ_1 and μ_2. We use μ_1 to identify the mean of the population distribution for the first sample, Type A, and μ_2 represents the population mean for the other sample, Type B.

If the two samples were selected from the same population distribution of fatigue ratings, then the population means must be the same. Another way of stating this situation is to say that the difference between the two population means ($\mu_1 - \mu_2$) is 0. These two ways of stating the H_0 can be expressed symbolically as

$$H_0: \mu_1 = \mu_2,$$

or

$$H_0: \mu_1 - \mu_2 = 0.$$

These two expressions are mathematically equivalent. The H_0 assumes that any difference between sample $\overline{X}$s results from chance and random variation in the selection process.

The H_1 describes the case in which the samples are taken from different population distributions. Therefore, μ_1 and μ_2 are not equal to each other. Symbolically, this would be expressed either as

$$H_1: \mu_1 \neq \mu_2,$$

or as

$$H_1: \mu_1 - \mu_2 \neq 0.$$

The H_1 is the statistical hypothesis that corresponds to the research hypothesis. As was the case in Chapter 9, the statistical test to be used involves testing the H_0. If the probability of the samples coming from the same population distribution is low (equal to or less than the alpha level), then H_0 will be rejected and H_1 will be supported. This outcome would support the research hypothesis. A sampling distribution must be constructed to test H_0.

THE SAMPLING DISTRIBUTION OF THE DIFFERENCE BETWEEN THE MEANS

A sampling distribution based on the assumption that both samples are taken from the same population distribution is needed. This is different from the situation in Chapter 9. Then the sampling distribution was based on all possible samples of a particular size N being taken from a particular population distribution because we were testing a *single* sample. Instead in this chapter we are testing a *pair* of samples. Therefore, we need a sampling distribution based on all pairs of samples of particular sizes N_1 and N_2 being selected from the same population distribution (which is the case described by H_0).

This sampling distribution assumes that *all* possible pairs of samples (of size N_1 and N_2) are selected and the means for each pair of samples ($\overline{X}_1$ and $\overline{X}_2$) are compared. The differences between sample $\overline{X}$s are calculated. The **sampling distribution of the difference between the means** is a frequency distribution of these differences of sample means $\overline{X}_1 - \overline{X}_2$ for all *possible* pairs of samples of size N_1 and N_2. Each pair of samples is represented by a single value, the difference between the sample means. The frequencies refer to the number of pairs of samples with a particular mean difference.

Notice several important differences between this sampling distribution and the sampling distribution of the mean described in Chapter 9. First, this sampling distribution is based on pairs of samples. Second, rather than graphing sample $\overline{X}$s on the x-axis, this sampling distribution is based on the *difference* between pairs of sample $\overline{X}$s. Third, this sampling distribution is based on *two* sample sizes, N_1 and N_2. For any particular population distribution, a family of sampling distributions exists that is based on all possible combinations of N_1 and N_2.

It is possible to estimate the information needed to construct the sampling distribution of the difference between the means. The mean of the sampling distribution is defined in H_0. It is based on the difference between the population means $\mu_1 - \mu_2$. In the chapter example this difference is assumed to be 0. If both samples are drawn from the same population distribution, then the most frequently occurring mean difference should be 0. Sometimes $\overline{X}_1$ will be greater than $\overline{X}_2$ and sometimes it will be smaller, depending on random selection of the samples. However, the mean difference based on all pairs of samples will equal 0. Therefore, the mean of the sampling distribution is given in H_0 and it equals 0.

The standard deviation of the sampling distribution of the difference between the means is called **the standard error of the mean difference, $s_{\overline{x}_1 - \overline{x}_2}$**. It is based, in part, on the estimated population standard deviation s for each sample. It provides an estimate of the variability in the mean differences between samples selected from a particular population distribution. In calculating $s_{\overline{x}_1 - \overline{x}_2}$, it is necessary to take into account the possibility that N_1 is not equal to N_2. That is, calculating $s_{\bar{x}_1 - \bar{x}_2}$ is not as simple as taking the average of s for each sample. If one sample is larger than another ($N_1 \neq N_2$), then the s of the larger sample will contribute more to the standard error of the mean than the smaller sample. (See Question 18 in the exercises at the end of the chapter.)

The information needed in calculating $s_{\bar{x}_1 - \bar{x}_2}$ can be found in the descriptive statistics calculated earlier. The computational formula for the standard error of the mean difference is

$$s_{\bar{x}_1 - \bar{x}_2} = \sqrt{\left(\frac{SS_1 + SS_2}{N_1 + N_2 - 2}\right)\left(\frac{1}{N_1} + \frac{1}{N_2}\right)}. \tag{19}$$

This formula provides an unbiased estimate of the standard deviation for a sampling distribution of the difference between the means. The data needed for calculating the standard error of the mean are contained in the summary statistics for the samples. Using the statistics from Table 10.2, the standard error of the mean is

$$s_{\bar{x}_1 - \bar{x}_2} = \sqrt{\left(\frac{SS_1 + SS_2}{N_1 + N_2 - 2}\right)\left(\frac{1}{N_1} + \frac{1}{N_2}\right)} \tag{19}$$

$$= \sqrt{\left(\frac{5.6 + 2.5}{10 + 10 - 2}\right)\left(\frac{1}{10} + \frac{1}{10}\right)}$$

$$= \sqrt{\left(\frac{8.1}{18}\right)(.1 + .1)}$$

$$= \sqrt{(.45)(.20)}$$

$$= \sqrt{.09}$$

$$= .30.$$

In calculating $s_{\bar{x}_1 - \bar{x}_2}$ be careful to first work within each set of parentheses and to remember to take the square root as your last step.

The mean of the distribution is provided by H_0, and the standard deviation of the sampling distribution $s_{\bar{x}_1 - \bar{x}_2}$ is calculated from the sample statistics. The difference between the sample $\bar{X}$s in the example is 0.7 of a fatigue rating ($\bar{X}_1 - \bar{X}_2 = 2.2 - 1.5 = 0.7$). It is in the right portion of the sampling distribution. The question is whether it falls in the retain-H_0 or reject-H_0 regions of the distribution. The reject-H_0 regions equal .05 (the alpha level) of the total area under the sampling distribution. To answer that question, it is necessary to convert the difference between $\bar{X}$s to an obtained *t* value and to compare it with the critical *t* value for the alpha level used.

The *t* Test for Independent Samples

The *t* distribution is used by the researcher in transforming the difference between sample $\bar{X}$s into an obtained *t* value. The obtained *t* value measures the distance from the difference of the sample means ($\bar{X}_1 - \bar{X}_2$) to the mean of the sampling distribution $(\mu_1 - \mu_2)$ in standard deviation units (based on $s_{\overline{x}_1 - \overline{x}_2}$). The formula for calculating the t value is a bit more involved than that described in Chapter 9 because it involves a pair of samples. The formula is

$$t = \frac{(\overline{X}_1 - \overline{X}_2) - (\mu_1 - \mu_2)}{s_{\overline{x}_1 - \overline{x}_2}}. \tag{20}$$

Note the similarities between Formula 20 and Formula 16, which was used in Chapter 9

$$t = \frac{\overline{X} - \mu_{\overline{x}}}{s_{\overline{x}}}. \tag{16}$$

The numerator in both formulas is a calculation of the difference between a sample $\overline{X}$ (or the difference between the $\overline{X}$s) and the mean of the sampling distribution. The numerator is divided by the standard deviation of the sampling distribution, which results in an obtained t value. In instances in which the H_0 assumes no difference between the population means, the expression to the right in the numerator of Formula 20 $(\mu_1 - \mu_2)$ will equal 0.

To calculate the t value for the chapter example, use Formula 20

$$t = \frac{(\overline{X}_1 - \overline{X}_2) - (\mu_1 - \mu_2)}{s_{\overline{x}_1 - \overline{x}_2}} \tag{20}$$

$$= \frac{(2.2 - 1.5) - 0}{0.30}$$

$$= \frac{0.70}{0.30}$$

$$= 2.33.$$

The difference between the sample means is 2.33 standard deviation units beyond the mean of the sampling distribution. The question now is whether an obtained t value of 2.33 will be in the 'reject-H_0' region of the sampling distribution. Therefore, the critical t value is needed.

Table T in Appendix E lists the critical t values for all t tests. The two pieces of information needed are the probability value for the alpha level and the df. We will use a $p \leq .05$ for the alpha level and assume a nondirectional hypothesis (two-tailed test). The df are based on the number of free values that can be assigned. For each sample $\overline{X}$, one df is lost in estimation $(N - 1)$. Therefore, the total df is the addition of $N_1 - 1$ and $N_2 - 1$. For any t test for independent samples the total df can be simplified to

$$df = N_1 + N_2 - 2$$

In the chapter example the df is equal to

$$= 10 + 10 - 2$$
$$= 18$$

Using Table T with a $p = .05$ and a nondirectional hypothesis, a critical t value of 2.101 is found. Figure 10.1 shows the sampling distribution with

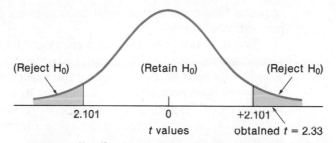

FIGURE 10.1 Sampling distribution for the chapter example with the critical *t*
values and calculated *t* value included.

the critical *t* values and the obtained *t* value for the example included. Note
that the obtained *t* value is in the shaded area. This indicates that there is
less than .05 chance that these two samples were selected from the same
population distribution. Therefore, H_0 is rejected and the research hypothesis
is supported.

The researchers' hypothesis was that Type A individuals suppress feelings of fatigue more than Type B individuals. The $\overline{X}$ rating of fatigue for Type
A individuals indicated less fatigue $\overline{X} - 2.2$ than for Type B individuals
$\overline{X} = 1.5$. The fact that the H_0 was rejected allows the researchers to state
that this difference in $\overline{X}$s is significant. The researchers can conclude that the
ratings of these two samples came from different population distributions. In
fact, the researchers could make a statement in their article to this effect,
"Type A individuals reported significantly less fatigue than Type B individu-
als, $\underline{t}(18) - 2.33$, $\underline{p} < .05$." As in the previous chapter, a statement about the
findings of a statistical test is followed with the *t*, df, obtained t value, and
the alpha level used.

The $\overline{X}$s provide the measure of difference between the samples. The *t* test
confirms that this difference is significant, that is, it is unlikely that these
samples came from the same population distribution. The use of descriptive
statistics and inferential statistics together enables the researchers to make
the claim that their research hypothesis is supported.

It is important that the researcher relate his or her findings from a statistical test to the descriptive statistics calculated earlier. Brief statements such
as, "A significant difference was found" do not provide enough information
about what the difference is, which group had a higher $\overline{X}$, and so forth. Always consider the findings of a statistical test in terms of the descriptive
statistics (often the $\overline{X}$) calculated earlier.

ASSUMPTIONS IN USING THE *t* TEST

The *t* test for independent samples is an example of a **parametric test** because
the statistical hypotheses H_0 and H_1 are stated in terms of population parameters, namely population means μ_1 and μ_2. The use of a parametric test often

requires that certain statistical assumptions are met. The t test has two important assumptions.

The first assumption is that the population distributions from which the samples were selected have equal population variances, σ^2. Since the discussion has focused on two samples, the assumption would be that each sample was taken from population distributions in which σ_1^2 equals σ_2^2. Even though the statistical hypotheses are stated in terms of either the same population mean $\mu_1 = \mu_2$ or different population means $\mu_1 \neq \mu_2$, both hypotheses assume $\sigma_1^2 = \sigma_2^2$. (See Box 10.1.)

The second assumption is that the samples are selected from population distributions that are normally distributed. With small sample sizes, the sampling distributions may not be normally distributed. This would make the use of the t distribution inappropriate.

Fortunately, a number of studies have been conducted using specific samples that violate these assumptions. The aim of these studies was to deter-

BOX 10.1   Testing for Homogeneity of Variance

Homogeneity of variance is the term used to describe the assumption that the samples were selected from population distributions with equal variances, $\sigma_1^2 = \sigma_2^2$. A test can be employed to determine if the population variances are significantly different from each other. The test involves a comparison of the estimates of the population variances for each sample s_1^2 and s_2^2.

The logic behind the test requires calculating the ratio of the two estimates. The larger estimate is divided by the lower estimate

$$s_{larger}^2 / s_{smaller}^2.$$

If the two estimates of the population variance are equal, then the ratio should be 1. When the ratio becomes large, then the researcher should be concerned that the samples come from population distributions with different variances.

The researcher can use this ratio to determine the probability that the samples come from population distributions with the same variance. The ratio calculated by the researcher can be compared with a critical F ratio found in Table F in Appendix E. The F ratio compares variances and will be discussed in greater detail in Chapters 13 through 15. At this point, it is important to know that if the calculated ratio meets or exceeds the critical F ratio (at a certain alpha level), then the researcher should conclude that the variances of the two population distributions are significantly different. Determining the critical F ratio is based on the df for the two samples. The df for the sample with the larger variance is represented by the

mine how closely the assumptions had to be met for the t test to be valid, that is, for it to give correct results. The findings of these studies indicate that the t test is a **robust test**. A robust test is one that provides correct interpretations even though the assumptions may not be entirely met. These studies have shown that some careful planning on the part of the researcher can reduce the need to meet these assumptions.

In practice, the assumptions of the t test are not as critical if the sample sizes are equal $N_1 = N_2$ and if the sample size is large. With equal sample sizes the contribution of each sample to the standard error of the mean $s_{\bar{x}_1 - \bar{x}_2}$ will be the similar. With a large sample, the shape of the sampling distribution will tend to be normally distributed regardless of the shape of the population distributions from which the samples are taken. This is the premise of the central limit theorem described in Chapter 9. In many cases, sample sizes of 15 or larger per condition or group enable the researcher to conclude that the sampling distribution is normally distributed. Therefore, as

columns in Table F and the df for the sample with the smaller variance is represented by the rows. If the exact df are not listed, then use the next lower value listed in Table F.

To illustrate this procedure, let's compare the variances for the samples in the first chapter example

$$s_A{}^2/s_B{}^2 = .79^2/.53^2 = 2.22.$$

The variance for the Type A sample was used in the denominator because it was larger. The estimate of the population variance for Type A students were 2.22 times larger than that for Type B students.

The df for each sample is 9. Using Table F, the critical F ratio with an alpha level of .05 is 3.18. The calculated ratio of 2.22 is less than this value. Therefore, the probability of these samples coming from population distributions with the same variance is greater than .05. The researchers cannot conclude that the variances are different.

If a significant difference had been found, the validity of the t test would not be questioned unless the sample sizes had been small. However, a significant difference would alert the researcher to examine the values within each sample carefully because a manipulation of the independent variable may be affecting behavior (the dependent variable) not only in terms of level as measured by the $\bar{X}$, but also in terms of the range of behavior. The sample with the larger variance will likely have a wider range of values on the dependent variable. This may indicate a further effect of the independent variable on behavior.

general guidelines in behavioral research, design experiments have an equal number of participants in each condition and try to test more than just a few participants in each condition. Adhering to these guidelines will make reliance on the assumptions of the t test less critical.

TESTING FOR A DIFFERENCE: A SECOND EXAMPLE

As was shown in the previous example, Carver et al. (1976) found support for the hypothesis that individuals displaying a Type A behavior pattern are more likely to suppress feelings of fatigue than Type B individuals. A second part of their hypothesis was that Type A individuals would exert more effort than Type B individuals. That is, although Type A individuals would report feeling less fatigued, they would exert more effort on the treadmill than Type B individuals. An analysis of the amount of time on the treadmill revealed no difference between the two groups of students. The researchers did record, however, the amount of oxygen consumed. Based on a series of tests and physiological measures, they were able to record the percentage of aerobic capacity each individual used during the test phase. The higher the percentage of aerobic capacity expended, the more effort the individual was putting into the task. For instance, a person with a percentage of 50 was using half of his physiological capacity for breathing. The percentage of aerobic capacity used during the test phase for each student is shown in Table 10.3.

Table 10.3 also includes the calculations for the $\overline{X}$ and s. Notice that Type A individuals used an average of 91.4% of their aerobic capacity, whereas Type B individuals used an average of 82.8%. The $\overline{X}$s tend to support the researchers' hypothesis. A t test for independent samples must be conducted, however, to determine if the difference is significant and not the result of random selection from the same population distribution.

Although the researchers in the example used a nondirectional hypothesis in that they tested for a difference in either direction, Type A < Type B or Type A > Type B, a directional hypothesis will be used in this second example to illustrate the differences between a nondirectional hypothesis (first example) and a directional hypothesis (this example).

The research prediction was that the Type A students would exert more effort than Type B students. Since H_1 is consistent with the research hypothesis, we can translate the research hypothesis into H_1, which states that the Type A students come from a population distribution with a higher mean (of aerobic capacity expended) than that for Type B students

$$H_1: \mu_1 > \mu_2.$$

TABLE 10.3	Calculations for $\bar{x}$ and s for Both Samples in the Second Example
Percent of Aerobic Capacity Used	
Type A	*Type B*
86	87
94	83
98	75
88	81
97	74
85	85
80	91
95	95
96	77
95	80
$\Sigma X_1 = 914$	$\Sigma X_2 = 828$
$\Sigma X_1^2 = 83{,}880$	$\Sigma X_2^2 = 68{,}980$
$N_1 = 10$	$N_2 = 10$

Using Formula 1: $\overline{X} = \Sigma X/N$

$\overline{X}_1 = 914/10 = 91.4$ $\overline{X}_2 = 828/10 = 82.8$

Using Formula 3: $SS = \Sigma X_2 - \dfrac{(\Sigma X)^2}{N}$

$SS_1 = 83{,}880 - \dfrac{914^2}{10} = 340.4$ $SS_2 = 68{,}980 - \dfrac{828^2}{10} = 421.6$

Using Formula 4: $s^2 = \dfrac{SS}{N-1}$

$s_1 = \dfrac{340.4}{9} = 37.82$ $s_2 = \dfrac{421.6}{9} = 46.84$

Using Formula 5: $s = \sqrt{s^2}$

$s_1 = \sqrt{37.82}$ $s_2 = \sqrt{46.84}$
$\quad = 6.15$ $\quad = 6.84$

The H_0 must account for all other possibilities which includes the samples coming from the same population distribution or Type A students coming from a population distribution with a μ less than that for Type B students

$$H_0: \mu_1 \leq \mu_2.$$

If H_0 is rejected, then the researchers can conclude that the Type A students exerted more effort. If H_0 is retained, then the researchers must retain the possibilities that (1) the Type A and Type B students did not differ in the amount of effort exerted and (2) the Type A students exerted less effort than Type B students. Because of the specific prediction made when using the directional hypothesis, the result of not rejecting H_0 prevents the researcher from separating the possibility of no difference from that of a difference in the opposite direction.

The procedures in calculating the t are identical to that when using a nondirectional hypothesis. The first step is to calculate the standard error of the mean difference $s_{\bar{x}_1 - \bar{x}_2}$ for the sampling distribution. Using Formula 19

$$s_{\bar{x}_1 - \bar{x}_2} = \sqrt{\left(\frac{SS_1 + SS_2}{N_1 + N_2 - 2}\right)\left(\frac{1}{N_1} + \frac{1}{N_2}\right)} \tag{19}$$

$$= \sqrt{\left(\frac{340.4 + 421.6}{10 + 10 - 2}\right)\left(\frac{1}{10} + \frac{1}{10}\right)}$$

$$= \sqrt{\left(\frac{762}{18}\right)(.1 + .1)}$$

$$= \sqrt{(42.33)(.20)}$$

$$= \sqrt{8.47}$$

$$= 2.91.$$

Once $s_{\bar{x}_1 - \bar{x}_2}$ is known, Formula 20 can be used to calculate the obtained t value

$$t = \frac{(\bar{X}_1 - \bar{X}_2) - (\mu_1 - \mu_2)}{s_{\bar{x}_1 - \bar{x}_2}} \tag{20}$$

$$= \frac{(91.4 - 82.8) - 0}{2.91}$$

$$= \frac{8.60}{2.91}$$

$$= 2.96.$$

The difference between the sample $\bar{X}$s results in an obtained t value of 2.96. To conclude whether H_0 should be rejected, the critical t value must be determined. As in the first example, the df $(N_1 + N_2 - 2)$ equals 18. The critical t value for a directional hypothesis with an alpha level of .05 is 1.734. As shown in Figure 10.2, the calculated t value of 2.96 exceeds the critical t value. Therefore, H_0 is rejected. A significant difference is found between the two groups of students. It can be concluded that individuals exhibiting a Type A behavior pattern exerted significantly more effort on the treadmill than individuals exhibiting a Type B behavior pattern, $\underline{t}(18) = 2.96$, $\underline{p} < .05$.

The findings of this study supported the research hypothesis proposed by

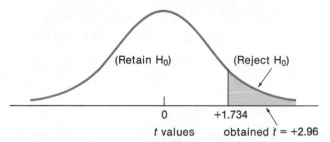

FIGURE 10.2 Sampling distribution for the second example. A directional hypothesis (one-tailed test) is used.

Carver et al. (1976). Type A individuals reported significantly less fatigue than Type B individuals. Yet, a measure of their physiological capacity revealed that these Type A students exerted significantly more effort than Type B students.

SUMMARY   In two-condition experiments involving an independent groups design, participants are assigned to one of the two conditions. To analyze the data of an independent groups design a *t* test for independent samples is used. The data must correspond to the interval or ratio scale of measurement.

The *t* test for independent samples is used in determining if both samples came from the same population distribution or not. The H_0 often describes the case in which both samples were selected from the same population distribution. To test this hypothesis a sampling distribution based on the differences between sample $\overline{X}$s is used. This sampling distribution is called the sampling distribution of the difference between the means. The mean of the distribution is the difference between population means μ_1 and μ_2, which is often 0. The standard deviation for this sampling distribution is called the standard error of the mean difference $s_{\overline{x}_1 - \overline{x}_2}$.

The *t* test for independent samples transforms the difference between the sample $\overline{X}$s and $(\mu_1 - \mu_2)$, the mean of the sampling distribution, into a *t* value that is based on $s_{\overline{x}_1 - \overline{x}_2}$ units. This value is then compared with the critical *t* value. The critical *t* value, which can be found in Table T is a function of the df $(N_1 + N_2 - 2)$ and the alpha level. If the H_0 is rejected, then the researcher concludes that the two samples came from different population distributions of values. The two groups are different and a significant difference is found.

The *t* test for independent samples is based on the assumptions that both samples were selected from normally distributed population distributions and that the variability in the population distributions, σ_1^2 and σ_2^2, are the same. Research has shown that these assumptions are less critical for accurate interpretation of the *t* test when samples are sufficiently large and the samples are of equal size.

SUMMARY FOR CALCULATING $s_{\overline{x}_1 - \overline{x}_2}$

After calculating the SS and N for each sample, use Formula 19

$$s_{\overline{x}_1 - \overline{x}_2} = \sqrt{\left(\frac{SS_1 + SS_2}{N_1 + N_2 - 2}\right)\left(\frac{1}{N_1} + \frac{1}{N_2}\right)}. \tag{19}$$

SUMMARY FOR USING THE t TEST
FOR INDEPENDENT SAMPLES

1. Develop the research hypothesis.
2. State the H_0 and H_1 and decide upon the alpha level, usually $p \leq .05$ or .01.
3. Calculate the descriptive statistics $\overline{X}$ and s for each sample. Use Formulas 1, 3, 4, and 5. Often one sample is given the subscript 1 and the other is given 2.
4. Calculate $s_{\overline{x}_1 - \overline{x}_2}$ using Formula 19.
5. Calculate the obtained t value for the difference between $\overline{X}$s using

$$t = \frac{(\overline{X}_1 - \overline{X}_2) - (\mu_1 - \mu_2)}{s_{\overline{x}_1 - \overline{x}_2}}. \tag{20}$$

(The difference between population means $\mu_1 - \mu_2$ is determined by H_0 and is usually 0.)
6. Determine the critical t value using Table T. The df $= N_1 + N_2 - 2$.
7. If the obtained t value is equal to or greater than the critical t (in absolute value), then reject H_0. The research hypothesis is supported and it can be assumed that the samples come from different population distributions. Otherwise, retain H_0 and assume that it is possible that the samples came from the same population distribution; the difference between $\overline{X}$s could result from random selection.
8. State your conclusions in sentence form and include the necessary t value information ($\underline{t}$ (df) = obtained t value, $\underline{p} \leq$ or $\geq$ alpha level).

EXERCISES

1. A researcher believes that one sample comes from a population with a $\mu = 6.57$ and $\sigma = 1.45$ and that another sample comes from a population with a $\mu = 8.32$ and $\sigma = 4.11$. Which assumption of the t test may be violated? Explain.
2. Which of the following variables would be considered to be quasi-independent variables in a research design:
   a. a person's gender in a study on sex differences,
   b. the presentation rate of symbols in a psychology experiment,
   c. the type of instructions given in a motivation study,

    d. the effect of a person's risk-taking behavior (high or low) on the type of problem a person chooses to solve?

3. For the second chapter example, graph the $\overline{X}$ values. Compare that graph with Figure 10.1.

4. Shown below are two population distributions. A researcher unknowingly samples from both. He takes three values from each ($N_1 = N_2 = 3$). What assumption of the *t* test is being violated?

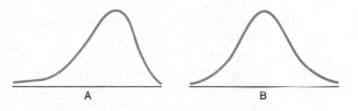

A   B

5. Another researcher samples from the same two population distributions in Exercise 4. What suggestions would you give the second researcher to enable her to avoid making the mistake the researcher made in Exercise 4?

6. To test whether or not student evaluations vary as a function of when the evaluation is given, a teacher gives one section of her introductory sociology course the evaluation prior to the last exam during the semester. She gives the same form to another section of the same course after returning the exam and the scores from the last exam. She compares the ratings she is given. The ratings are on a 5-point scale, with a high number indicating an excellent evaluation.

Before Exam	After Exam
$\Sigma X = 80$	$\Sigma X = 93$
$\Sigma X^2 = 293$	$\Sigma X^2 = 346$
$N = 22$	$N = 25$

    Determine if there is a significant ($p \leq .05$) difference in the ratings given.

7. In Exercise 6, are there any problems with the way students were assigned to conditions? How might that affect the conclusions of the study?

8. Determine the critical *t* values for each situation below:
    a. Each sample has 8 participants; use a nondirectional hypothesis, $p = .05$ for the alpha level.
    b. $N_1 = 15$ and $N_2 = 27$; use a directional hypothesis, $p = .01$ for the alpha level.
    c. $N_1 = 54$ and $N_2 = 88$; use a directional hypothesis, $p = .01$.

9. A psychology student gives 10 friends a questionnaire that measures sensation-seeking (the desire to do things such as "hang-gliding," etc.). Five of these students are men and five are women. Their scores on the questionnaire are shown below. The higher the score, the higher the person is in sensation-seeking. Determine if the men and women differ significantly ($p = .01$) in their sensation-seeking scores.

Female: 4, 5, 2, 11, 7
Male: 9, 10, 11, 4, 8

10. If a $p = .05$ rejection level had been used in Exercise 9, would the conclusion have been the same? Explain.

11. A computer company is interested in claiming that its computer is easier to learn to use. As a test, 30 secretaries are selected from a large firm, 15 are randomly assigned to learn to use the company's computer with a word-processing program. The other 15 use a competitor's computer with the same word-processing program. None of the secretaries had any previous computer experience. At the end of two weeks, each secretary was tested on the number of different functions that she could perform using the word-processing program. The statistics are shown below:

Computer company's computer: $\overline{X} = 21.64$, s = 3.10
Competitor's computer: $\overline{X} = 19.55$, s = 2.87

Determine if there is a significant difference between the computers. Use $p = .05$ and a nondirectional hypothesis.

12. In Exercise 11, is the design an experiment or a quasi experiment? Explain?

13. A fellow student provides you with the following information, $t = 2.08$, $N_1 = 18$, $N_2 = 19$. Is there a significant difference using a nondirectional hypothesis, $p = .05$ alpha level? What if the alpha level had been $p = .01$?

14. Another student tells you that she was able to reject H_0 using a $p = .01$ alpha level and a two-tailed test. The total number of participants she tested was 52. What do you know about her calculated t value?

15. A student is confused because he knows that the difference between two sample $\overline{X}$s (which is 12.03) should be significant. Yet, his calculations for $s_{\overline{x}_1 - \overline{x}_2}$ show that it is equal to 9.00. He provides you with the following information: $N_1 = 25$ and $N_2 = 25$, $s_1 = 11.00$ and $s_2 = 10.20$. Can you find his mistake? Once it has been corrected, is the difference significant ($p = .05$)?

16. You believe that students are happier early in the semester than late in the semester. You stop 20 students outside of the student union during the lunch hour of the first Friday of classes and ask each to rate his or her feelings of happiness on a 1-to-7 scale, with a high number indicating happiness. At the end of the semester, you again sample another 20 stu-

dents during the lunch hour of the last Friday of classes and ask for their ratings. You obtain the following information:

Early: $\overline{X}$ rating = 6.32, s = .95
Late: $\overline{X}$ rating = 5.30, s = 1.42

Would you conclude that your hypothesis has been supported? Use a directional hypothesis and a $p = .01$ alpha level.

17. Instructors often face a difficult decision in selecting a text for a course. At a large university, two texts are used in an introductory psychology course. Nine sections of the course use Text A, the other nine sections use Text B. At the end of the semester, the bookstore records the percentage of students from each section who sell the text back to the bookstore. The percentages are shown below:

Text A : 24, 30, 56, 44, 31, 37, 33, 28, 41
Text B : 43, 47, 52, 38, 29, 36, 42, 50, 45

Determine if the percentage of books sold back to the bookstore was different for the two texts. Use a nondirectional hypothesis, $p = .05$ alpha level.

18. For each of the two cases described below, calculate s_1 and s_2. Then calculate the standard error of the mean difference. Compare the results for each case. Discuss the reasons for any differences between cases.

Case A: $SS_1 = 437.76$, $N_1 = 20$; $SS_2 = 1,573.39$, $N_2 = 20$
Case B: $SS_1 = 207.36$, $N_2 = 10$; $SS_2 = 2,401.49$, $N_2 = 30$

19. In both cases shown in Exercise 18, the total number of participants is 40 and the df = 38. Would you feel equally confident in interpreting your findings in both cases? Explain.

20. A researcher provides one-half of her class with a computerized form of a student guide for an introductory psychology course. The other half of the class is assigned the standard student guide. At the end of the semester, the researcher determines if there is a difference between the two groups in course performance based on final grade average. She hypothesizes that the computerized version will increase student interest and should, therefore, improve grades. Test this hypothesis using a directional hypothesis and an alpha level of .05. The following statistics are provided:

	Computerized Form	Standardized Form
$\Sigma X =$	1,436	1,353
SS =	459.68	314.33
N =	18	18

CHALLENGE QUESTIONS

Beginning with this chapter and in subsequent chapters, two questions are presented that require the integration of the principles and procedures used in analyzing a research study. The answers to the first questions in each pair are included in Appendix D. For more information about the research, consult the parenthetical reference provided for the problem.

1. People who attended a course on "coping with depression" are given a questionnaire which measures their level of depression. Individuals are classified as "depressed" or "nondepressed." They are then given a questionnaire that measures their level of life satisfaction. The scale ranges from 0 to 100%. The higher the value, the greater the life satisfaction. The researcher is interested in determining if depressed and nondepressed individuals differ in their perception of life satisfaction. (Based on Sacco, P. (1985). Depression and expectations of satisfaction. *Psychological Reports, 57,* 99–102.)

Depressed	Nondepressed
62	95
55	100
50	87
67	80
80	90
40	95
25	90
50	80
65	75
60	95
	88
	93
	84

2. Some research indicates that people who change their views and attitudes frequently are evaluated negatively by other people. To further test that possibility, a researcher provided students with statements from fictitious political candidates. These statements consisted of the candidate's position on an issue. In one condition, the statements were consistent over time. In another condition, the statements indicated that the candidate had changed his position with the passage of time. Each of 30 students saw either the consistent or the inconsistent statements. Students rated the candidate's image on a 1-to-9 scale, with 9 being very positive. These ratings are shown below. Develop and test a reasonable directional hypothesis. (Based on Carlson, J. M., & Dolan, K. (1985). The waffle phenomenon and candidates' image. *Psychological Reports, 57,* 795–798.)

Type of Statements	
Consistent	Inconsistent
7	2
5	4
3	6
7	5
9	6
8	1
7	5
6	4
7	7
6	7
7	4
8	2
9	5
8	4
6	3

For Each Question Answer the Following:
a. What is a plausible research hypothesis?
b. What are the H_0 and H_1? (Assume a nondirectional hypothesis unless otherwise stated.)
c. Calculate the appropriate descriptive statistics.
d. Calculate the appropriate inferential statistic. Use an alpha level of .05 for Question 1 and .01 for Question 2.
e. State your findings in the proper format and provide a written conclusion about the findings (relating the inferential statistics to the descriptive statistics).

CHAPTER 11

The *t* Test for Correlated Samples

TERMS DISCUSSED

repeated measures design

block randomization

counterbalancing

matched groups design

PROCEDURES DESCRIBED

calculating the standard error of the mean difference for difference values $s_{\bar{d}}$

calculating the *t* value for the *t* test for correlated samples

One exciting area of research concerning human behavior has been the study of how the brain processes information. Research indicates that the two hemispheres of the human brain process different types of information. In most people, the left hemisphere is considered the "dominant" hemisphere because it is responsible for language processing. The right hemisphere plays an important role in processing spatial and nonverbal information.

Studies on brain processing have used a variety of different materials and tasks. In one study by Geffen, Bradshaw, and Wallace (1971) drawings of men's faces were used as the test stimuli. The researchers varied the hemisphere that saw the faces first and tested the participant's memory for the faces.

There were 15 college students in this study. Each student was given 10 minutes to study and memorize one of five faces. The particular face given to a student was varied so that each of the five faces was used as a "study" face for three different students. After studying the face, the student was told that a series of faces would be flashed on a screen. When a face was shown, the student was to push a button labeled "same" if the face was the same as the "study" face. Otherwise, the student was to push the button labeled "different."

The researchers varied the visual field in which the test faces were presented. For each of 80 trials, the student was instructed to focus on a small point in the middle of the screen. On half of the trials a face would then be presented for a little over a tenth of a second to the left of the point. This was the left visual field (LVF) condition. On the other half of the trials, the face was presented to the right of the point and this was the right visual field (RVF) condition. The field in which the face was presented was randomly determined on every trial. Therefore, on each trial the student did not know on which side of the point the face would be presented.

Because of the way the brain works, the information is first sent contralaterally, or to the hemisphere opposite of the visual field. That is, information presented in the LVF would be sent first to the right hemisphere. Information presented in the RVF would be sent first to the left hemisphere. (See Figure 11.1.) The researchers hypothesized that the memory for faces is stored in the right hemisphere because faces are nonverbal images. They predicted that the time it takes to push the "same" button when the "study" face was presented would be faster when it was presented in the LVF (and processed in the right hemisphere) than when it was presented in the RVF. When the face was presented to the RVF, the image would first be sent to the left hemisphere and then to the right hemisphere for processing. The extra time it takes to transfer the information from the left to the right hemisphere would be reflected in an increased response time. The mean of the "same" response times when the "study" face was presented was calculated for each student and these values are shown in Table 11.1.

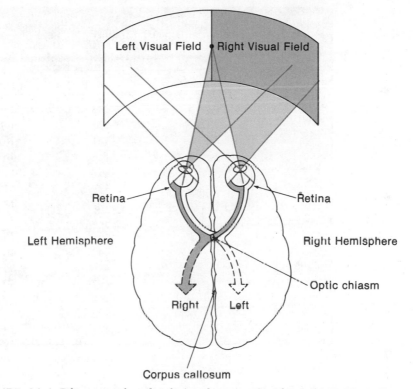

FIGURE 11.1 Diagram of path of visual processing for information presented in left (LVF) and right (RVF) visual fields. Information is sent directly to the hemisphere opposite that of the visual field.
Note. **(from** *Left Brain, Right Brain,* **revised edition (Fig. 2.4, p. 32) by Sally P. Springer and Georg Deutsch, 1981, San Francisco: W. H. Freeman and Co. Copyright © 1981. Reprinted with the permission of W. H. Freeman and Company.**

This study is an example of a true experiment. Similar to the example in Chapter 10, this experiment has two conditions, LVF and RVF. However, unlike the quasi experiment in Chapter 10, the independent variable was under the control and manipulation of the experimenters. A significant difference in the dependent variable can be causally attributed to the independent variable.

REPEATED MEASURES AND MATCHED GROUPS DESIGNS

Also, in the present example each participant serves in both conditions. This is an example of the repeated measures design. In a **repeated measures design** the participant serves in more than one condition. These studies are also

TABLE 11.1   Mean Times (in msec) for "Same" Responses for Each Participant in Chapter Example

	Visual Field of Presentation	
Student	Left (LVF)	Right (RVF)
a	373	336
b	473	468
c	451	467
d	416	468
e	397	411
f	381	413
g	407	437
h	428	512
i	360	356
j	442	462
k	496	556
l	467	505
m	469	513
n	444	463
o	431	443

called within-subjects designs. The independent variable is manipulated within each subject. In the chapter example, the two conditions, LVF and RVF, are the levels of the independent variable. The independent variable could be labeled "visual field of presentation."

BALANCING THE PRESENTATION ORDER OF CONDITIONS

There are two frequently used techniques in presenting conditions several times to each participant in a repeated measures design. One technique is to randomly order the conditions so that a participant does not *anticipate* the occurrence of a particular condition. If a number of conditions are used, then the experimenter may randomly order conditions in blocks. In **block randomization** each condition was represented once within a block of conditions and the order of conditions is randomly determined for every block of conditions. Block randomization is often used when three or more conditions are repeated several times for each participant. (See Box 11.1.)

The other technique involves a "balancing" procedure which is often used when each condition is presented only twice to each participant. In **counterbalancing** the conditions are presented in one order and then again in the reverse order. (See Box 11.1.)

When participants serve in each condition only once, then the researcher needs to ensure that the order of conditions vary across participants so that each condition occurs equally often at each stage of the study. For instance, if students were to participate in an experimental and control condition, the researcher would want half of the students to serve in the experimental condition first, then the control condition. The other half of the students would serve first in the control condition, then the experimental condition.

These controls for ordering prevent unwanted effects such as practice or fatigue from influencing one condition more than another. Since each condition occurs equally often at all stages of the experiment, effects of practice and fatigue should influence each condition equally.

MATCHED GROUPS DESIGN

In addition to the repeated measures design, the matched groups design also requires the statistical procedures described in this chapter. The matched groups design is different from both the independent groups and repeated measures designs. Unlike the repeated measures design, a participant serves in only one condition in the matched groups design. However, unlike in the independent groups design, participants are paired together, with one serving in one condition and the other serving in the second condition. In a **matched groups design,** participants are matched in pairs on a variable that is related to the dependent variable.

Two participants with similar or identical values on the matching variable are assigned with one member serving in one condition and the other serving in the other condition of the experiment. This matching variable is *not* the independent variable. For instance, in a study testing a new technique for teaching French, the researcher might match participants in terms of their past familiarity with French. The two people with the best scores on a French vocabulary test would be paired with one using the new technique and the other using the old technique. The two people with the next highest scores would also be paired, and so on. The dependent variable might be grades earned in the French course.

Sometimes the pairings occur somewhat naturally. In studying attitudes toward some topic at school, researchers might randomly assign one college roommate to one condition and the other roommate to a second condition. Or a husband and wife might each serve as a pair of participants in different conditions.

The important points in a matched groups design are (1) that each participant serves in one condition, (2) that participants are paired together, and (3) that when the pairing is done on the basis of a variable that is related to the dependent variable, the matching be done prior to assignment to conditions.

The last point is important. If the variable on which the matching is done is not related to the dependent variable, then matching serves no purpose. The matching is supposed to make the two conditions more alike in terms of the participants than if an independent groups design was used. And, the matching should be done before assignment to conditions. It is not acceptable for the researcher to record the data from the dependent variable and then determine which participants go together in pairs. Often a pretest using the matching variable is given, with participants being matched on the basis of their pretest scores.

BOX 11.1   Two Examples of Ordering Conditions in a Repeated Measures Design

When participants serve in more than one condition in a study it is important that the order of conditions be changed across participants. By changing the order, the researcher reduces the possibility that the order of presentation is influencing the findings in particular conditions. Although there are a number of different techniques used, two common techniques cited in the literature are block randomization and counterbalancing.

Block randomization

This technique requires that every condition must be presented before any individual condition can be repeated. Each condition is included within a *block*. The ordering of the conditions within a block is randomly determined. For example, assume that participants see pictures presented for varying times, 1, 3, or 5 sec. After seeing the pictures, the participant is asked to recognize the pictures from a large group of pictures including the ones just presented and some new pictures. Assume that a participant sees 5 pictures at each presentation time and that there are 15 pictures that must be shown. The order of presentation for the presentation times could be accomplished by using block randomization. The order of the times within a block is determined by the researcher, using a table of random numbers. Possible orderings of the presentation times for three participants might look like this:

Participant	Picture Being Shown														
	1	*2*	*3*	*4*	*5*	*6*	*7*	*8*	*9*	*10*	*11*	*12*	*13*	*14*	*15*
a	3	1	5	1	3	5	3	5	1	1	5	3	5	3	1
b	5	3	1	3	1	5	5	3	1	3	1	5	3	5	1
c	1	5	3	5	3	1	1	5	3	3	5	1	1	3	5

BENEFITS OF USING A REPEATED MEASURES OR MATCHED GROUPS DESIGN

The beauty of the repeated measures design is that individual differences are *reduced* between the two conditions. With the independent groups design, randomization controls for these differences but does not reduce them.

For each line, a new block begins after every third picture. A participant would see pictures exposed for times listed across the line. Obviously, the researcher would want to test a number of participants in the study and to give each of them their own order of presentation times.

Counterbalancing

This technique is often used when a participant serves in each condition twice. The order of presentation for the first time through each condition is randomly determined. The order of conditions is then reversed for the second time through the conditions. Assume students are asked to make judgments on three optical illusions, a, b, and c. The type of illusion is the independent variable. The judgment is the dependent variable. Each participant sees each illusion twice. The ordering of the illusions for six participants could be as follows:

Participant	Order of Presentation for Illusions					
	1	*2*	*3*	*4*	*5*	*6*
1	a	c	b	b	c	a
2	c	b	a	a	b	c
3	a	b	c	c	b	a
4	b	a	c	c	a	b
5	b	c	a	a	c	b
6	c	a	b	b	a	c

Notice that this ordering ensures that each illusion occurs equally often at each stage of presentation. Therefore, potential effects from practice should influence each illusion equally.

In the independent groups design, the researcher assumes that random assignment will result in the same mixture of different skills, motivational levels, and so forth in each condition. But, there is no easy way to extract these factors statistically from the values obtained. However, in the repeated measures design, these individual factors or individual differences are assumed to influence each condition equally. A participant brings the same skill, motivation level, and so on to both conditions. Therefore, these factors contribute equally to each condition and any difference in a participant's values between the two conditions results from the independent variable and not individual differences.

The same logic applies with a matched groups design. With this design the influence of the matching variable on the dependent variable is presumed to be similar in both conditions. If the matching variable is not related to the dependent variable, then nothing will be removed and the analysis will give the same result as the independent groups design.

THE DEPENDENT VARIABLE FOR THE CHAPTER EXAMPLE

The dependent variable in this example is the time it takes the student to push the button labeled "same" when the test face is the same as the face studied earlier. The response time is a measure of behavior. It is recorded in milliseconds (msec), which translates into thousandths of a second. Ten msec is equivalent to 0.01 (one-hundredth) of a second; 200 msec equals 0.200 (two-tenths) of a second.

Values for the dependent variable can range from 0 msec (no processing time) to 900 msec, the point at which the researchers considered a longer time as an error. This variable is on the ratio scale of measurement. There are equal intervals between the possible values and the 0 point reflects the absence of processing. It is a real 0 point, not an arbitrary one.

As in any experiment, the research hypothesis can be described as a cause and effect statement using both the independent and dependent variables. The researchers believe that the field in which the face is presented, the independent variable, will affect the response time, the dependent variable. Specifically, they expect the response time to be lower when the face is presented to the LVF. The reasoning is simple: information presented in the LVF is sent first to the right hemisphere, where the memory for the "study" face is presumed to be located.

DESCRIPTIVE STATISTICS: DESCRIBING THE SAMPLE DATA

Measures of central tendency and variability should be calculated for each sample. As is the case with most data that are on an interval or ratio scale, the $\overline{X}$ and s are the most commonly reported measures. Table 11.2 contains the necessary formulas (1, 3, 4 and 5) and the subsequent calculations. As

TABLE 11.2 Calculations for $\overline{X}$ and s for Both Samples in the Chapter Example

Visual Field of Presentation	
LVF	*RVF*
$\Sigma X_1 = 6{,}435$	$\Sigma X_2 = 6{,}810$
$\Sigma X_1^2 = 2{,}782{,}845$	$\Sigma X_2^2 = 3{,}139{,}764$
$N_1 = 15$	$N_2 = 15$

Using Formula 1: $\overline{X} = \Sigma X/N$

$\overline{X}_1 = 6{,}435/15$	$\overline{X}_2 = 6{,}810/15$
$= 429$	$= 454$

Using Formula 3: $SS = \Sigma X^2 - \dfrac{(\Sigma X)^2}{N}$

$SS_1 = 2{,}782{,}845 - \dfrac{(6{,}435)^2}{15}$	$SS_2 = 3{,}139{,}764 - \dfrac{6{,}810^2}{15}$
$= 22{,}230$	$= 48{,}024$

Using Formula 4: $s^2 = SS/N - 1$

$s_1^2 = 22{,}230/14$	$s_2^2 = 48{,}024/14$
$= 1{,}587.86$	$= 3{,}430.29$

Using Formula 5: $s = \sqrt{s^2}$

$s_1 = \sqrt{1{,}587.86}$	$s_2 = \sqrt{3{,}430.29}$
$= 39.84$	$= 58.57$

was predicted by the researchers, the $\overline{X}$ response time was lower when the "study" face was presented in the LVF, $\overline{X} = 429.0$ msec, than when it was shown in the RVF, $\overline{X} = 454.0$ msec. The responses were an average of 25 msec faster when the face was presented to the LVF. A bar graph of the $\overline{X}$ values is shown in Figure 11.2. The bar graph was used because the independent variable, visual field of presentation, corresponds to the nominal scale of measurement.

The estimate of the population standard deviation for the LVF condition is 39.84 msec, which is slightly less than that for the RVF condition, $s = 58.57$ msec. This indicates that there is slightly less variability in the response times for the LVF condition than for the RVF condition. In both conditions, however, it appears that the majority of the response times

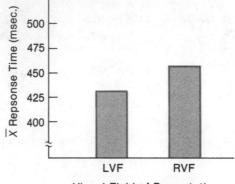

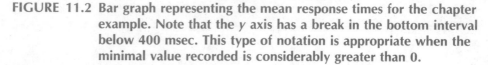

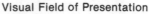

FIGURE 11.2 Bar graph representing the mean response times for the chapter
example. Note that the y axis has a break in the bottom interval
below 400 msec. This type of notation is appropriate when the
minimal value recorded is considerably greater than 0.

should be within approximately 100 msec of the $\overline{X}$. (Remember that approximately 95% of all values should fall within 2 s above and below the $\overline{X}$.)

The next step is to test the research hypothesis. This requires the use of inferential statistics and the calculation of an additional variable, a difference value. The difference value is found by subtracting the participant's value in one condition from the other condition.

Table 11.3 lists the difference value for each participant in the study. This is the difference between the response time in the LVF and RVF conditions. The letter d is used to denote this new variable. Also listed in Table 11.3 are the necessary calculations to determine the mean and estimated population standard deviation of the difference times. Notice that $\overline{X}_d$ is equal to $(\overline{X}_{lvf} - \overline{X}_{rvf})$. These new statistics $\overline{X}_d$ and s_d will be used in the calculations for the t test for correlated samples.

INFERENTIAL STATISTICS: TESTING FOR A DIFFERENCE

The statistical hypotheses to be used for the repeated measures design are similar to those used with the independent groups design. The null hypothesis H_0 assumes that the sample has paired values that were taken from the same population distribution

$$H_0: \mu_1 = \mu_2.$$

The alternative hypothesis H_1 assumes the opposite—that the values were taken from population distributions with different population means

$$H_1: \mu_1 \neq \mu_2.$$

TABLE 11.3   Calculation of the Difference Values for the Chapter Example

	Visual Field of Presentation		
Student	(LVF)	(RVF)	Difference Value (d)
a	373	336	37
b	473	468	5
c	451	467	−16
d	416	468	−52
e	397	411	−14
f	381	413	−32
g	407	437	−30
h	428	512	−84
i	360	356	4
j	442	462	−20
k	496	556	−60
l	467	505	−38
m	469	513	−44
n	444	463	−19
o	431	443	−12

$$\Sigma X_d = -375$$
$$\Sigma X_d^2 = 21{,}431$$
$$N_d = 15$$

Using Formula 1:

$$\overline{X} = \Sigma X/N$$

$$\overline{X}_d = -375/15$$
$$= -25$$

Using Formula 3:

$$SS = \Sigma X^2 - \frac{(\Sigma X)^2}{N}$$

$$SS_d = 21{,}431 - \frac{-375^2}{15}$$
$$= 12{,}056$$

Using Formula 4:

$$s^2 = SS/N - 1$$

$$s_d^2 = 12{,}056/14$$
$$= 861.14$$

Using Formula 5:

$$s = \sqrt{s^2}$$

$$s_d = \sqrt{861.14}$$
$$= 29.35$$

These hypotheses will take on a different form, however, because the type of design used, either repeated measures or matched groups, allows for the use of difference values. Because the researcher is working with difference values the hypotheses are

$$H_0: \mu_{\bar{d}} = 0$$

and

$$H_1: \mu_{\bar{d}} \neq 0.$$

The parameter $\mu_{\bar{d}}$ is the mean of the sampling distribution of the mean of the difference values. This sampling distribution is a frequency distribution with the mean of the difference values calculated for all samples of paired values of a particular size N. The samples are represented by the mean of their difference values $\bar{X}_d$. The sampling distribution, which is based on both samples being selected from the same population distribution, has a mean $\mu_{\bar{d}}$ of 0. Some samples selected from the same population would have an $\bar{X}_d$ greater than 0 and others would have an $\bar{X}_d$ less than 0. However, the overall mean of all the sample $\bar{X}_d$ would be 0. This sampling distribution is represented by the H_0.

If the values are selected from different population distributions, then the $\mu_{\bar{d}}$ would not be 0. An infinite number of sampling distributions exist that describe this situation. These sampling distributions are represented by H_1.

THE STANDARD ERROR OF THE MEAN DIFFERENCE FOR DIFFERENCE VALUES $s_{\bar{d}}$

The fact that variability resulting from individual differences is removed in the difference values is reflected in the standard error of the mean difference. The standard error of the difference between the means for the independent groups design is $s_{\bar{x}_1 - \bar{x}_2}$. You should recall from Formula 19 that it was based on a weighting of the sums of the squared deviations for each sample SS_1 and SS_2. The estimate of the standard deviation for the sampling distribution based on difference values is also referred to as the standard error of the mean difference. However, a different subscript is used to denote that it is based on difference values $\bar{d}$.

The formula for calculating the standard error of the mean difference when it is based on difference values is

$$s_{\bar{d}} = \frac{s_d}{\sqrt{N_d}}. \tag{21}$$

You should note the similarity between this formula and Formula 15, which provides the standard error for one sample

$$s_{\bar{x}} = \frac{s}{\sqrt{N}}. \tag{15}$$

The only difference is that Formula 21 is based on a sample of difference values, and Formula 15 is based on values of the dependent variable for one sample.

The necessary information for calculating s_d for the chapter example is in Table 11.3. Using Formula 21

$$s_{\bar{d}} = \frac{s_d}{\sqrt{N_d}} \tag{21}$$

$$= \frac{29.35}{\sqrt{15}}$$

$$= 7.58.$$

The distribution in Figure 11.3 shows the sampling distribution for the chapter example assuming H_0 is true. The mean is 0 and the standard deviation is 7.58. With the sampling distribution for H_0 complete, it is possible to calculate a t value for the sample of difference values.

THE t TEST FOR CORRELATED SAMPLES

The t test for correlated samples is used when testing the H_0 using difference values as is the case with repeated measures and matched groups designs. The calculated t value is based on the difference between $\overline{X}_d$ and $\mu_{\bar{d}}$ and is expressed in terms of units based on $s_{\bar{d}}$. The formula for calculating the t is

$$t = \frac{\overline{X}_d - \mu_{\bar{d}}}{s_{\bar{d}}}. \tag{22}$$

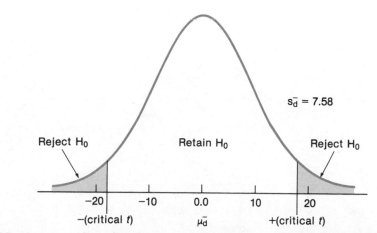

FIGURE 11.3 Sampling distribution for the chapter example. It is based on H_0 which assumes a mean of 0. Shaded area corresponds to the extreme .05 of the total area of the distribution.

Again you should note the similarity between this formula and that for the t test for one sample

$$t = \frac{\overline{X} - \mu_{\overline{x}}}{s_{\overline{x}}}. \qquad (16)$$

The difference is that Formula 22 is based on a sample of difference values, and Formula 16 is based on a sample of data from a dependent variable.

Using Formula 22 and substituting the necessary statistics from the chapter sample yields

$$t = \frac{\overline{X}_d - \mu_{\overline{d}}}{s_{\overline{d}}} \qquad (22)$$
$$= \frac{-25 - 0}{7.58}$$
$$= -3.30.$$

The obtained t value for the example is -3.30. The negative sign indicates that the $\overline{X}$ of the first sample, LVF, was less than that of the second sample, RVF. The fact that it is large indicates that it is in the tail of the sampling distribution for the H_0. The negative value indicates it is the left tail of the distribution. To determine if it is in the reject-H_0 region, it is necessary to determine the critical t value.

The critical t value for the direct difference t test is found in Table T in Appendix E. The df is based on the difference values and is equal to the number of difference values minus 1

$$df = N_d - 1.$$

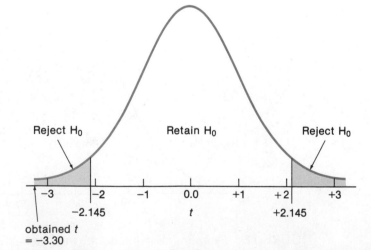

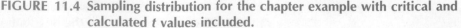

FIGURE 11.4 Sampling distribution for the chapter example with critical and calculated t values included.

For this example the df is 14 (15 − 1). As with other examples discussed earlier, we will use a nondirectional hypothesis and an alpha level of $p \leq .05$. A critical *t* value of 2.145 is listed in Table T. Therefore, a calculated *t* value less than −2.145 or greater than +2.145 will result in H_0 being rejected.

The calculated *t* value of −3.30 exceeds (in absolute value) this critical *t* value. Figure 11.4 shows the sampling distribution for the example with the calculated and critical *t*s included. The calculated *t* is in the reject-H_0 region. Because the probability is less than .05 of getting these difference values, *given* that they are based on samples selected from the same population distribution of values, Geffen et al. (1971) can reject H_0 and assume that H_1 is supported. They can conclude that a significant difference exists between the response times for faces presented in the LVF and RVF conditions. The response times came from different population distributions of values. The researchers could conclude that "response times were significantly faster when the 'study' face was presented to the left visual field than the right visual field, $\underline{t}(14) = -3.30, \underline{p} < .05$."

A COMPARISON OF THE *t* TEST FOR CORRELATED SAMPLES WITH THE *t* TEST FOR INDEPENDENT SAMPLES

Let's briefly compare how the findings of the *t* test for correlated samples differs from those that would have resulted had the *t* test for independent samples been used. Recall that earlier in this chapter the point was made that repeated measures designs reduce the variability resulting from individual differences. Because a participant serves in both conditions in a repeated measures design, individual capabilities and factors influence both conditions. In the independent groups design, participants are randomly assigned to conditions in order to *equalize* these effects across conditions. Variability resulting from individual differences is still included in the independent groups design; the researcher assumes that the random assignment equalizes this variability in each condition.

By using difference values in the repeated measures design, only *differences* in performance between conditions are analyzed and not actual levels of performance (behavior as measured by the dependent variable). Therefore, individual differences are eliminated from the analysis and only differences between conditions are analyzed. For example, Students "f" and "g" had similar difference values, −32 and −30 msec, respectively. (See Table 11.3.) Yet, Student "f" was faster at the task than Student "g." Student "f" had mean response times of 381 and 413 msec in the two conditions, whereas Student "g"'s times were 407 and 437 msec. Student "f" was 25 msec faster than Student "g" overall. However, the *t* test for correlated samples did not include this difference in individual performance. All that was analyzed was the difference *between* conditions, which was quite similar for both students.

This difference between tests is evident in the variability for the sampling distribution. When variability resulting from individual differences (or a matching variable in the case of a matched groups design) is removed, $s_{\bar{d}}$

will be less than $s_{\bar{x}_1 - \bar{x}_2}$. In the independent groups design, this variability cannot be removed because each participant provides only one value and it is impossible to determine how much of the behavior recorded is a function of individual differences.

Let's assume that the data in the chapter example were based on an independent groups design consisting of 30 students instead of the 15 students in a repeated measures design. It would be necessary to calculate $s_{\bar{x}_1 - \bar{x}_2}$ and to use the t test for independent samples. The data from Table 11.2 provide the necessary statistics to calculate the $s_{\bar{x}_1 - \bar{x}_2}$

$$s_{\bar{x}_1 - \bar{x}_2} = \sqrt{\left(\frac{SS_1 + SS_2}{N_1 + N_2 - 2}\right)\left(\frac{1}{N_1} + \frac{1}{N_2}\right)} \tag{19}$$

$$= \sqrt{\left(\frac{22,230 + 48,024}{15 + 15 - 2}\right)\left(\frac{1}{15} + \frac{1}{15}\right)}$$

$$= 18.29.$$

If one assumes independent samples, the variability in the sampling distribution (18.29) is considerably larger than if the same values are treated in a repeated measures design, ($s_{\bar{d}} = 7.58$). The two sampling distributions are shown in Figure 11.5. The only difference is reflected in the variability, the means of the sampling distributions (for H_0) are identical.

A sample mean difference of -25 msec is not as deviant or unexpected if the data are based on 30 individuals each providing one mean response time. In fact, if the analysis assuming an independent groups design is carried further, a t value could be calculated

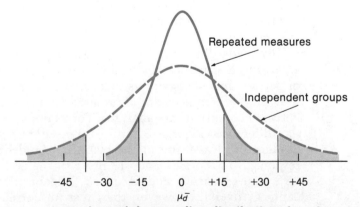

FIGURE 11.5 A comparison of the sampling distributions based on repeated measures design (solid line) and independent groups design (dashed line). Shaded areas represent .05 of the total area for each respective distribution. Note the greater variability in the sampling distribution for the independent groups design.

$$t = \frac{(\overline{X}_1 - \overline{X}_2) - (\mu_1 - \mu_2)}{s_{\overline{x}_1 - \overline{x}_2}} \qquad (20)$$

$$= \frac{(429 - 454) - 0}{18.29}$$

$$= -1.37.$$

This obtained t value of -1.37 would not exceed the critical t value (for 28 df) of ± 2.048. The researchers would *not* be able to reject H_0. Therefore, if these data had come from an independent groups design, the researchers would have had to conclude that the difference between conditions could result from chance. The difference is not significant.

The discussion in this section is designed only to show you that the repeated measures design reduces variability in the sampling distribution as compared with the independent groups design. Do *not* assume that researchers have the freedom to choose either of these tests to analyze the data. The t test to be used, whether it is for independent groups or correlated samples, depends on the type of design.

Although in studies such as this one, the researchers can choose to use either design, there are studies in which the repeated measures design cannot be used. The example in Chapter 10 illustrates this point. Type of behavior pattern, A and B, cannot be manipulated within a subject. A person cannot be both Type A and Type B. Or in some studies, the effect of participating in one condition may prohibit the person from serving in the other condition. For example, if an experimental condition involves a drug treatment it may be impossible to undo the effect in order for a person to then serve in the control condition. Therefore, there may be instances in which the researcher decides for theoretical or practical reasons to use the independent groups design.

In other situations, the researcher may have the option between designs. When the option is available, the researcher should be aware that a repeated measures design may be more appropriate from a *statistical* viewpoint. The use of a repeated measures design can reduce the variability in the sampling distribution that is based on H_0. It can also require the use of fewer participants than in an independent groups study. We will have more on this topic in the next chapter.

TESTING FOR A DIFFERENCE: A SECOND EXAMPLE

After completing the experiment on which the first example was based, Geffen et al. (1971) conducted several other experiments. In one of these studies, Geffen et al. changed not only the type of stimulus used from faces to digits, but also the type of response used from a button-pushing response to a digit-naming response. Rather than judging whether or not a face was the same as the "study" face, participants in this study were required to name a digit aloud which was presented to either the LVF or RVF.

Although the stimulus and type of response were different, the independent and dependent variables were identical to those in the first example. The independent variable was the field of visual presentation with two values or conditions, the left and right field. The dependent variable was the response time necessary to verbally identify or name the digit. Response times that exceeded 800 msec were considered incorrect. Therefore, the range of possible values could vary from 0 to 800 msec.

Each of ten participants, none of whom had participated in the other experiment, saw two blocks of 80 trials. Each trial consisted of one of four digits (1, 2, 4, or 5) being presented to either the LVF or RVF in a random order. The research hypothesis was different from the first example. Although a difference was predicted, it was that the response time for digits presented to the RVF would be less than that for digits presented to the LVF. The reasoning was quite straightforward. If the left hemisphere processed verbal information, then a digit that was presented to the RVF would be processed sooner in the left hemisphere than a digit presented to the LVF, which would be sent to the right hemisphere first and then transferred to the left hemisphere. The mean response times for each participant by visual field are shown in Table 11.4.

Table 11.4 also includes the calculation of the $\overline{X}$ and s for each visual field. Notice that the $\overline{X}$s for the two visual fields are in the predicted direction. The $\overline{X}$ for response times in the RVF (587 msec) is less than that for response times in the LVF (597 msec). This difference of 10 msec is not as large as that from the other study—a mean difference of 25 msec. The s for the LVF condition (53.19 msec) is similar to that for the RVF condition (50.04 msec). Based on an s of approximately 50 msec, one would predict that most, if not all, mean response times would be within 100 msec (2 s) of the $\overline{X}$.

Thus, the researchers found a mean difference of 10 msec between the two conditions. The use of the t test for correlated samples will enable them to determine the probability that this difference results from chance. Table 11.5 contains the necessary calculations for the difference scores, under the column labeled "Difference value." At the bottom of Table 11.5, the calculations of $\overline{X}_d$ and s_d are presented.

Again as in the previous chapter, in order to illustrate the difference between a nondirectional hypothesis and a directional hypothesis, this example will be analyzed using a directional hypothesis. (It should be noted that the researchers in the original study used a nondirectional hypothesis in analyzing their data.)

The researchers had predicted that response times would be faster for verbal material presented to the right visual field. To be consistent with the first example, the $\overline{X}$ for the RVF condition is subtracted from that for the LVF condition. Therefore, the researchers would predict a positive difference. Using a directional hypothesis, the alternate hypothesis is

$$H_1: \mu_{\bar{d}} > 0.$$

TABLE 11.4 Mean Response Times for Each Participant and Calculations for $\overline{X}$ and s for Both Samples in the Second Example

	Visual Field of Presentation	
Student	Left (LVF)	Right (RVF)
a	609	587
b	606	605
c	542	564
d	546	529
e	630	613
f	534	525
g	560	542
h	628	616
i	608	598
j	707	691
	$\Sigma X_1 = \quad 5,970$	$\Sigma X_2 = \quad 5,870$
	$\Sigma X_1^2 = 3,589,550$	$\Sigma X_2^2 = 3,468,230$
	$N_1 = \quad 10$	$N_2 = \quad 10$

Using Formula 1: $\quad \overline{X} = \Sigma X/N$

$\overline{X}_1 = 5,970/10$ $\qquad\qquad$ $\overline{X}_2 = 5,870/10$
$\quad = 597$ $\qquad\qquad\qquad$ $= 587$

Using Formula 3: $\quad SS = \Sigma X^2 - \dfrac{(\Sigma X)^2}{N}$

$SS_1 = 3,589,550 - \dfrac{5,970^2}{10}$ $\qquad$ $SS_2 = 3,468,230 - \dfrac{5,870^2}{10}$
$\quad = 25,460$ $\qquad\qquad\qquad\qquad$ $= 22,540$

Using Formula 4: $\quad s^2 = SS/N - 1$

$s_1^2 = 25,460/9$ $\qquad\qquad$ $s_2^2 = 22,540/9$
$\quad = 2,828.89$ $\qquad\qquad\quad$ $= 2,504.44$

Using Formula 5: $\quad s = \sqrt{s^2}$

$s_1 = \sqrt{2,828.89}$ $\qquad\qquad$ $s_2 = \sqrt{2,504.44}$
$\quad = 53.19$ $\qquad\qquad\qquad$ $= 50.04$

TABLE 11.5   Calculation of the Difference Values for the Second Example

Visual Field of Presentation			
Student	(LVF)	(RVF)	Difference Value (d)
a	609	587	22
b	606	605	1
c	542	564	−22
d	546	529	17
e	630	613	17
f	534	525	9
g	560	542	18
h	628	616	12
i	608	598	10
j	707	691	16

$$\Sigma X_d = 100$$
$$\Sigma X_d^2 = 2{,}452$$
$$N_d = 10$$

Using Formula 1:	$\overline{X} = \Sigma X/N$
	$\overline{X}_d = 100/10$
	$= 10$

Using Formula 3:	$SS = \Sigma X^2 - \dfrac{(\Sigma X)^2}{N}$
	$SS_d = 2{,}452 - \dfrac{100^2}{10}$
	$= 1{,}452$

Using Formula 4:	$s^2 = SS/N - 1$
	$s_d^2 = 1{,}452/9$
	$= 161.33$

Using Formula 5:	$s = \sqrt{s^2}$
	$s_d = \sqrt{161.33}$
	$= 12.70$

The H_0 must account for all other possibilities

$$H_0: \mu_{\overline{d}} \leq 0.$$

As in the first example an alpha level of $p \leq .05$ will be used. The next step is to calculate the necessary information for the sampling distribution of the difference between the means.

The mean of the sampling distribution is $\mu_{\overline{d}} = 0$. The standard error of the mean difference $s_{\bar{d}}$ can be determined by using Formula 21 and the statistics in Table 11.5

$$s_{\bar{d}} = \frac{s_d}{\sqrt{N_d}} \qquad (21)$$
$$= \frac{12.70}{\sqrt{10}}$$
$$= 4.02.$$

Once $s_{\bar{d}}$ is known, then the obtained t value for correlated samples can be determined by using Formula 22

$$t = \frac{\overline{X}_{\bar{d}} - \mu_{\bar{d}}}{s_{\bar{d}}} \qquad (22)$$
$$= \frac{10 - 0}{4.02}$$
$$= 2.49.$$

The calculated t value is 2.49. The critical t value can be found in Table T. The df are equal to the number of difference scores minus 1

$$df = N_d - 1.$$

Therefore, using a directional hypothesis (one-tailed test), an alpha level of $p \le .05$, and 9 df, the critical t value of 1.833 is found. The obtained t value 2.49 exceeds the critical t value, and we know that a sample with the mean difference of 10 msec would fall in the reject-H_0 region of the sampling distribution as shown in Figure 11.6. Therefore, it is unlikely that the sample

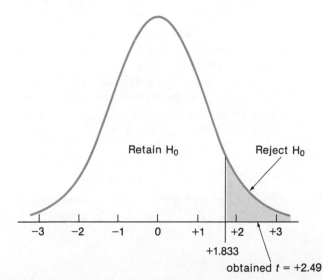

FIGURE 11.6 Sampling distribution for the second chapter example. A directional hypothesis (one-tailed test) was used.

has paired values that came from the same population distribution. The researchers conclude that their difference is significant, "The verbal response times in naming a digit are significantly faster when the digit is presented to the RVF rather than the LVF, $\underline{t}(9) = 2.49$, $\underline{p} < .05$."

The two examples in this chapter support the concept that different types of processing are performed in different hemispheres of the brain. With a non-verbal stimulus (a face), processing is faster when the face is presented in the left visual field and processed in the right hemisphere. With a verbal stimulus (a digit) and a verbal response, processing is faster when the digit is presented in the right visual field and processed in the left hemisphere.

SUMMARY

A repeated measures design is one in which the participant serves in more than one condition. A similar design is the matched groups design in which participants are matched in pairs. The matching is based on the participants' values on a variable that is related to the dependent variable. The t test for correlated samples is used in analyzing differences for both designs when there are two conditions or levels of the independent variable.

The t test for correlated samples is based on the same assumptions and procedures that are used for the t test for independent samples. The analysis, however, uses difference values. The H_0 assumes that both samples were drawn from the same population distribution. In terms of difference values, this would indicate that the mean of the population distribution of difference values μ_d would be zero.

The major difference between the t test for independent samples and the t test for correlated samples involves the standard error of the mean difference. The standard error of the mean difference for the t test for correlated samples $s_{\bar{d}}$ is less than that for the t test for independent samples $s_{\bar{x}_1 - \bar{x}_2}$. The difference values reflect a reduction in variability resulting from individual differences in the repeated measures design or the matching variable in the matched groups design.

The t test for correlated samples is used to calculate a t value that is based on the difference between the mean of the difference values and zero. This difference is expressed in $s_{\bar{d}}$ units. The critical t value is found in Table T and uses $N_d - 1$ as the df.

SUMMARY FOR CALCULATING $s_{\bar{d}}$

After calculating the difference values and s_d for the difference values (using Formulas 3 through 5), use Formula 21

$$s_{\bar{d}} = \frac{s_d}{\sqrt{N_d}}.$$

$$(21)$$

SUMMARY FOR USING THE *t* TEST FOR CORRELATED SAMPLES

1. Develop the research hypothesis.

2. State the H_0 and H_1 and decide on the alpha level (usually .05 or .01).

3. Calculate the descriptive statistics, $\overline{X}$ and s, for each condition using Formulas 1, 3, 4, and 5

4. Construct difference values for each individual or pair of values, then calculate $\overline{X}_d$ (using Formula 1) and s_d (using Formulas 3 through 5).

5. Calculate $s_{\overline{d}}$ using Formula 21.

6. Calculate the *t* value for *t* test for correlated samples using Formula 22

$$t = \frac{\overline{X}_d \quad \mu_{\overline{d}}}{s_{\overline{d}}}. \tag{22}$$

7. Determine the critical *t* value using Table T. The df $= N_d - 1$.

8. For a nondirectional hypothesis, if the obtained *t* value is equal to or greater than the critical *t* value (in terms of the absolute value), then reject H_0. The research hypothesis is supported and a significant difference is found. Otherwise, the H_0 is retained and it is assumed that the sample has paired values that could have come from the same population distribution. The difference between sample $\overline{X}$s could be the result of chance.

9. State your conclusion in sentence form and include the necessary *t* value information (t (df) = obtained t value, p < or > alpha level).

EXERCISES

1. Twenty students serve in each of two conditions in a problem-solving experiment. Everyone serves in Condition A first, which takes 45 min to complete. Following a 30-sec rest period, they each serve in Condition B, which also takes 45 min to complete. The researcher finds significantly better performance in Condition A than Condition B. What type of design is being used (independent groups, repeated measures, or matched groups)? Do you see any problems with this study? If so, how would you correct them?

2. A shoe company is interested in determining if their new type of running shoe is better than the leading competitor's shoe. This company selects 10 high-school track club members and randomly assigns 5 to wear their new shoe first and then to switch to the competitor's shoes. The other five use the shoes in the reverse order. Each student runs three 50-yard dashes with each pair of shoes, and the median time with each pair is recorded. What type of design is being used? What are the independent and dependent variables? Is the dependent variable on an interval or ratio scale of measurement? What are H_0 and H_1?

3. Another researcher wishes to replicate the study in Exercise 2 but wants to match the runners in pairs and use a longer distance—1,000 meters. He obtains the times of the 10 runners from a recent race. The times are listed below. Construct two matched groups, new shoe and competitor's shoe, with five runners serving in each condition.

Runner	Time
a	4:08
b	3:51
c	3:02
d	3:17
e	3:33
f	3:20
g	2:48
h	2:57
i	3:14
j	3:06

4. In Exercise 3, what effect should the matching have when compared with an independent groups design?

5. If the matching scheme in Exercise 3 is correct, then the $\overline{X}$ running time in the previous race should be approximately equal for the two groups you constructed. Is it?

6. Take the values in Table 11.4 (the second chapter example) and assume that each time represents a unique student, that is, assume that an independent groups design was used. Calculate the t test for independent samples. Is the difference significant?

7. In Exercise 6, what accounts for the difference in t values between the independent groups and repeated measures designs (the numerator or denominator in calculating the t)? Explain.

8. Graph the sample $\overline{X}$s for the second chapter example.

9. For each case, calculate the $s_{\overline{d}}$.
   a. $\overline{X}_d = -12.38$; $s_d = 16.43$; $N_d = 12$
   b. $\Sigma X_d = 261.30$; $\Sigma X_d^2 = 19865.70$; $N_d = 26$

10. Determine if you should retain H_0 (values were selected from the same population distribution) for each case in Exercise 9. List the critical t values, assuming an alpha level of .05 and a two-tailed test.

11. One common type of repeated measures design is one referred to as a "before-after" design. Participants are tested both before and after a "treatment" and the effect of the treatment is often inferred from the difference values. A psychology instructor has two forms of a test based on misconceptions about psychology. The two forms are equivalent in difficulty and

material. Each form contains true-false statements about psychology such as, "Schizophrenic individuals have multiple personalities"—Answer: False. The instructor administers one form on the first day of class and then administers the other form after the final exam. The number of misconceptions made concerning psychology were recorded for each of 13 students. The values are shown below:

Student	First Class	Final Exam
a	28	12
b	16	4
c	22	10
d	4	2
e	20	3
f	17	11
g	3	5
h	11	6
i	15	9
j	9	9
k	13	7
l	14	10
m	10	11

The instructor believes that the course will reduce the student's number of misconceptions. What are the H_0 and H_1? Using a .01 alpha level and a nondirectional hypothesis, determine if the instructor's hypothesis was supported.

12. A colleague of the instructor in Exercise 11 teaches an English literature course at the same time. In order to demonstrate that it is the psychology course itself and not the passage of time or a college course in general that makes the difference, she tests eight students in her course. They are given the same forms as the students from Exercise 11 on the first day and after the final exam. Their values are shown below:

Student	First Class	Final Exam
a	18	22
b	14	13
c	25	21
d	11	17
e	8	6
f	14	18
g	7	5
h	19	16

Using a .01 alpha level and a nondirectional hypothesis, determine if there is a significant difference. Did the English course result in a change in the students' misconceptions about psychology?

13. Dr. Smith is testing the taste preference of two dog foods, Brand 101 and Brand 444. Each of 20 dogs is given each of the brands on different days. Dr. Smith records the amount of food eaten. He reports a $\underline{t}(20) = -1.88$, $\underline{p} < .05$, and concludes that dogs prefer one brand over the other. Based on the information provided, determine if Dr. Smith analyzed the data correctly and reached the correct conclusions.

14. A graduate student studies the effect of lecturing about notetaking on subsequent behavior in a class of undergraduates. As part of a pilot study, she measures the number of pages of notes taken in a class of 16 students and then delivers a lecture about the importance of taking a sufficient amount of notes in class. She then measures the amount of notes taken in the same class a week later. She finds the following:

$$\overline{X}_{\text{before}} = 2.65 \text{ pages;} \quad \overline{X}_{\text{after}} = 3.10 \text{ pages;} \quad s_d = .30$$

She concludes that her lecture had a significant effect on the students' notetaking behavior. (She used a two-tailed test with an alpha level of .05.) Based on the information provided, determine if she analyzed the data correctly and reached the correct conclusions.

15. A researcher interested in (the study of) recreational behavior visits a video game arcade. He follows 10 different children and notes how long they are willing to wait to play a particularly popular game before moving on to a different game. He looks at the time they wait when there is only one person playing the game versus the situation when there is at least another person waiting in line in addition to the person playing the game. He finds the following:

$$\overline{X}_{\text{no one waiting}} = 10.56 \text{ minutes;} \quad \overline{X}_{\text{others waiting}} = 6.38 \text{ minutes;} \quad s_d = 6.32$$

He calculates his t statistic as 0.696 and concludes that whether there is a person waiting or not has no significant effect on how long the child will wait. Based on the information provided, determine if he analyzed the data correctly and reached the correct conclusions.

16. A researcher believes that a manipulation will result in higher performance scores in an experimental condition when compared with those from a control condition. Assuming that the experimental condition is designated as Condition 1 and the control condition as Condition 2, state appropriate H_0 and H_1 if a nondirectional hypothesis is used. What would the hypotheses be if a directional hypothesis is used?

17. For Exercise 16, determine the critical values using an alpha level of .05 for both the nondirectional and directional hypotheses. Assume that the same 25 students served in both conditions.

18. A fellow student decides to analyze data using the t test for correlated samples by matching subjects from two conditions in a study. He takes the subject with the highest value in one condition and matches to the

subject with the highest value in the other condition. He then repeats this procedure with the next highest value in each condition. Is he using the matching procedure correctly? Explain.

19. If you had only 12 students who could serve in a two-condition study and realistically could use either an independent groups design or a repeated measures design, which would you choose? Why? Assuming the use of a nondirectional hypothesis with an alpha level of .05, what would the critical *t* values be if you used (a) an independent groups design or (b) a repeated measures design.

20. If you are using a nondirectional hypothesis, does it matter which condition you designate as Condition 1 and Condition 2 in terms of calculating your *t* value? Is the same true if you are using a directional hypothesis? Explain your answer.

CHALLENGE QUESTIONS

1. Elementary school teachers were given two essays to grade. They were told that one was written by a "mainstream" student and the other by a "special education" student. In fact, both essays had been prepared by the researcher. The teachers were asked to read each essay and mark errors on the essay. The essays were matched for word length and number of errors. The order of essays was balanced across teachers and half of the teachers were told one essay was written by the mainstream student and the other half were told it was written by the special education student. The same was true for the other essay. Therefore, each essay was used equally often in each condition and for each type of student, and was given equally often as the first and second essay for grading. The researcher was interested in determining if the labeling of the student who wrote the essay would influence the grading. The number of errors found

	Type of Student	
Teacher	Special education	Mainstream
a	21	19
b	22	16
c	18	17
d	16	14
e	25	21
f	27	23
g	26	15
h	25	21
i	23	27
j	18	19
k	16	19

are shown below. Develop and test a directional hypothesis. (Based on Barowsky, E. I., 1986. Effects of stereotypic expectation on evaluation of written English attributed to handicapped and nonhandicapped students. *Psychological Reports, 59,* 1097–1098.)

2. Two groups of hospitalized patients were matched in pairs on the basis of age, sex, and clinical diagnosis (e.g., schizophrenia, substance abuse, and so forth.). One patient in each pair was allowed free access to caffeinated coffee, whereas the other patient had access only to decaffeinated coffee while in the hospital. Upon discharge the amount of minor tranquilizers taken while hospitalized was analyzed. The researchers were interested in determining if caffeine was related to differences in the amount of tranquilizers prescribed. The amount of tranquilizer in 1,000-mg units is shown below for each patient.

	Type of Coffee	
Patient pair	Caffeinated	Decaffeinated
a	.80	.60
b	1.20	1.40
c	3.40	2.00
d	4.10	3.80
e	3.00	3.60
f	.60	1.00
g	.00	.40
h	2.00	2.20
i	1.60	1.00
j	5.00	4.30

FOR EACH QUESTION ANSWER THE FOLLOWING:

a. What is a plausible research hypothesis?

b. What are the H_0 and H_1? (Assume a nondirectional hypothesis unless otherwise stated.)

c. Calculate the appropriate descriptive statistics.

d. Calculate the appropriate inferential statistic. Use an alpha level of .05 for Question 1 and .01 for Question 2.

e. State your findings in the proper format and provide a written conclusion about the findings (relating the inferential statistics to the descriptive statistics).

Statistical Decisions
and Power

TERMS DISCUSSED

Type I error
Type II error
statistical power
effect size
nondirectional hypothesis
directional hypothesis

PROCEDURES DESCRIBED

ways of increasing statistical power

During the late 1970s and early 1980s, researchers in human memory investigated the relationship between a person's mood and memory. Much of this work has focused on poorer memory performance for depressed or saddened individuals compared with that for normal or happy individuals. A considerable amount of this work has taken place in the laboratory with researchers inducing moods for college students who participated in memory studies.

Ellis, Thomas, and Rodriquez (1984) reported the findings of three studies focusing on mood and its relation to type of cognitive processing and cognitive effort. In the study on cognitive effort, 32 introductory psychology students were given a sentence completion task. The task required the student to complete a sentence by inserting a missing word. Some of the sentences were easy and required little effort (e.g., "The girl was awakened by her frightening _____."); while others were hard and required more effort (e.g., "The man was alarmed by the frightening _____."). (For both examples above the appropriate word is **dream**.) Each student completed 12 sentences of each type. Following the task, each student was given an unexpected free recall task and was asked to write as many of the words that he or she could remember.

Prior to the sentence completion task, half of the subjects were given a mood-inducement task. These students, who were in the depressed condition, read a series of 60 depressing statements such as "I just don't care about anything. Life just isn't any fun." The statements were ordered so that the more intensely depressing statements occurred later in the order. The other half of the students read 60 neutral statements such as "Oil candles are probably the oldest and simplest type of candle." These students served in the control condition. The condition students served in was randomly determined.

After the students finished the statements, they completed a depression adjective checklist. The list contained negative-mood (e.g., unhappy, hopeless) and positive-mood (e.g., good, lucky) adjectives. A mood score was determined by adding the negative items checked and the positive items not checked. The mood score for the depressed-condition students was different from that of the control-condition students. This indicated that the mood of the students was different before they participated in the sentence completion test.

Therefore, the study had four parts. The first involved reading 60 statements. This was followed by the mood checklist designed to measure that a mood change had occurred. Then the students did the sentence completion task, which had both low-effort and high-effort sentences. Lastly, the students were given an unexpected recall test and were asked to recall the words they had just generated.

The research hypothesis was that mood would influence recall of words from the different types of sentences. For the control-mood students, the mean percentage of words recalled from the high-effort sentences was 46% and from the low-effort sentences it was 27%. For the depressed-mood students, the values were 23% from high-effort sentences and 27% from *low-effort sentences. Significant differences, which we will discuss, were found in the recall of words as a function of mood and the amount of effort required in generating the words during the sentence-completion task.*

This chapter focuses on the decisions made by researchers when interpreting the findings and results of their statistical tests. The first topic involves decisions about whether to reject or retain H_0 and the types of decision error that may be involved. The chapter example provides the necessary findings to describe both types of errors.

DECISION ERRORS IN INFERENTIAL STATISTICS

The chapter example is based on a fairly complicated experiment. For the purposes of describing concepts in this chapter, the experiment will be treated as though two separate analyses were conducted. One analysis will be based on the data for the depressed students; the other will be based on the data for the control students. These analyses will be used to illustrate the concepts described in this chapter.

In any study involving hypothesis testing, either the null, H_0, or alternative, H_1, hypothesis is true. A researcher *never* knows for certain which state of the world is true, the one described by H_0 or the one described by H_1. Both cannot be true at the same time. For instance, when testing for a difference between two samples, either the values from the samples were selected from the same population distribution (described by H_0) or from different population distributions (described by H_1). Whether a researcher is correct or not in retaining or rejecting H_0 depends on the findings of the statistical test and whether H_0 describes the real world or not. Let us first examine the case when H_0 is in fact true.

DECISIONS WHEN THE H_0 IS TRUE

When testing for a difference among samples, if the H_0 is true, then the samples were selected from the same population of values. In this case, the sampling distribution shown in Figure 12.1 would accurately reflect the true state. The difference between sample $\overline{X}$s would be represented within that distribution.

As you should recall, in testing H_0 the researcher establishes an alpha level that defines the proportion of the distribution that will correspond to the reject-H_0 area. Figure 12.1 uses an alpha level of $p \leq .05$. The researcher has decided that if the difference between the $\overline{X}$s falls in the extreme 5% (2.5% at each tail of the distribution), then H_0 will be rejected. Otherwise, the researcher will retain H_0 as a possible description of the true state of

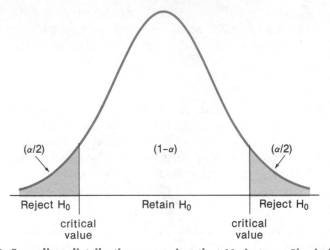

FIGURE 12.1 Sampling distribution assuming that H_0 is true. Shaded areas represent Type I error for pairs of samples represented in those areas.

affairs. If the samples were selected from the population distribution described by the sampling distribution, then there is a 95% chance of retaining H_0. Why? Because 95% of the difference in $\overline{X}$s between the samples would fall in the middle area of Figure 12.1. Only 5% would fall in the extreme reject-H_0 regions.

If the samples were selected from the same population distribution, then the correct decision is to retain H_0. Ninety-five percent of the pairs of samples selected would have a mean difference within the retain-H_0 region as shown in Figure 12.1. The proportion of the distribution in the retain-H_0 region is equal to 1 − alpha. With an alpha level of .05, if H_0 is true, then 95% of the time the researcher should retain H_0. There is a small probability, however, that the researcher will select samples, at random, from the population which will result in a large enough difference between the $\overline{X}$s to be in the reject-H_0 region. In this case, the researcher will conclude that a difference exists between samples, when in fact it results from chance. A Type I error will have been made.

A **Type I error** occurs when a researcher rejects H_0 when the H_0 describes the true state of affairs. The probability of making a Type I error, *given that H_0 is true*, is equal to alpha. If a researcher is using an alpha level of .05, then if the H_0 is rejected, the researcher knows that there is a slight risk that a decision error has been made. There is no way to eliminate the possibility of making a Type I error when a researcher rejects H_0. It is possible, however, to reduce the possibility.

If a researcher sets the alpha level to .01, then if the H_0 is in fact true, the researcher has a 99% (1 − alpha) chance of correctly retaining H_0. The probability of making a Type I error in this case is .01. In some cases, researchers will use the more stringent alpha level of .01 (and in some cases an alpha level of .001). This is true in some instances of medical research when a researcher needs to be confident that a difference found between a treatment group and a control group is not the result of chance. Statistically, that possibility is described by a Type I error. We don't always use an alpha level of .01 because it can increase the probability of another type of decision error we will discuss shortly.

On the other hand, you might correctly wonder why not set alpha to .15 or .20. Isn't a Type I error of .05 too stringent and shouldn't we be willing to accept a Type I error rate higher than .05? The answer is *no*. In the scientific community, a minimal Type I error rate has been established. For most behavioral science research it is $p \leq .05$. To conclude that you have a difference (that is, reject H_0) when the probability of making a Type I error rate is greater than .05, is unacceptable to most scientific journals and their reviewers. As you might conclude, the scientific community is quite cautious; it wants to maintain a low incidence of studies being published that report differences that are not real and that result from sampling error or chance.

DECISION ERRORS WHEN THE H_0 IS FALSE

When the H_0 does not describe the true state of affairs, the correct decision to be made is to reject H_0. If H_0 does not correctly describe the population distribution from which the samples were selected, then H_1 does. Therefore, we need to consider the possible statistical decisions that can be made when the samples are selected from a distribution other than the one described by H_0. In Figure 12.2 two sampling distributions are shown. The dotted-line distribution is based on H_0, which is always used by the researcher in establishing the 'retain-H_0' and 'reject-H_0' regions. The solid-line distribution to the right represents the true state of affairs.

Let us assume that the samples were selected from that sampling distribution described by H_1 (the difference between means is not 0). The proportion of area under this distribution that is in the retain-H_0 region is equal to

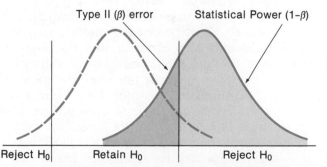

FIGURE 12.2 State of affairs when H_0 is false. Dotted line represents sampling distribution based on H_0, which is used to establish "retain H_0" and "reject H_0" regions. Solid line represents a sampling distribution based on H_1.

β. If one were to select samples from different population distributions and find that the difference between the $\overline{X}$s is so small that the difference falls in the retain-H_0 region, then a decision error would be made. The researcher would retain H_0 and conclude that it is possible that the samples came from the same population distribution, when in fact they did not. This error is a Type II error. A **Type II error** occurs when a researcher retains H_0 when H_0 is, in fact, false. The larger the proportion of area from the alternative distribution which is in the retain-H_0 region, the greater the probability of making a Type II error.

The proportion of area from the alternative distribution that falls in the reject-H_0 region represents a correct statistical decision. The researcher would reject H_0 when, in fact, it is false. The samples did come from a distribution different from the H_0. This proportion of area is equal to $1 - \beta$. The term "statistical power" is used to represent this area. **Statistical power** represents the probability of rejecting H_0 when it is false. The greater the proportion of area under the alternative distribution which is in the reject-H_0 region, the greater the statistical power of the test. When researchers refer to a test as being statistically powerful they are indicating that the test is likely to result in finding a significant difference if one exists, *that is H_0 is false.*

Obviously, statistical power and Type II error are related. The more powerful a statistical test is, the lower the probability is of making a Type II error.

POSSIBLE DECISION ERRORS IN THE CHAPTER EXAMPLE

It should be recognized that the researcher does not know at the time of analyzing the data in a study if a decision error has been made. Because much of the research reported in the literature is based on previous studies and theoretical predictions, the findings may support other research and the researchers may be confident in their conclusions.

In some cases being unable to replicate earlier findings of a significant difference may suggest that the original study involved a Type I error. In these instances, researchers may repeat the methodology in an earlier study and be unable to produce a significant difference. If they are repeatedly unable to do so, then the original findings may become suspect, and the scientific community may conclude that the original findings resulted from a Type I error. It is not a reflection on the ability of the original researchers or their methodology, because one does not know whether H_0 is true or false. There will be instances in which Type I errors will occur. One of the purposes of replicating earlier research is to confirm published findings and to determine that a Type I error was not made.

Type II errors are less critical in the scientific community because studies that do not produce significant differences are seldom printed in the literature. Remember a Type II error occurs when H_0 is mistakenly retained. This would describe the case when no difference is found. Editors of many journals do not accept studies with these findings unless they are direct replications of previous studies reporting a difference. If a Type II error is made, then it is likely that someone else (or the same researcher when repeating the study) will find a difference if it does exist and will then report the significant findings.

In the chapter example control-mood and depressed-mood students attempted to recall words from high-effort and low-effort sentences. At the left in Figure 12.3, note that performance for the control-mood students appears to be better for high-effort sentences than for low-effort sentences. The mean percentage of recall serves as the descriptive statistic for these two conditions. Since the same students participated in both the low-effort and high-effort sentences, the t test for correlated samples would be the appropriate t test. These data reveal a significant difference between conditions, $t(31) = 4.36, p < .05$.

Concluding that a significant difference was found in this case indicates that the researchers rejected H_0. Note that an alpha level of .05 was used. Because the researchers rejected H_0, we know they either (1) made a correct decision (if the true state of affairs is that recall of high-effort sentences is better than low-effort sentences) or (2) made a Type I error. The only way a Type I error could have been made in this case is if the recall values were selected from the same population of values, but because of chance, a difference occurred. This is unlikely, however, given that this result was consistent with their predictions based on previous research.

At the right in Figure 12.3, the statistics for the depressed-mood students are shown. A t test for correlated samples for these data would reveal that the recall was not significantly different between the two types of sentences, $t(31) = 1.02, p > .05$. Therefore, the researchers were unable to reject H_0. This indicates that they either (1) made a correct decision if the recall values for the two samples were selected from the same population distribution, or (2) they made a Type II error in that the recall values were selected from different distributions, but the statistical test was not powerful enough to detect the difference. Again, it is unlikely that this latter possibility is true,

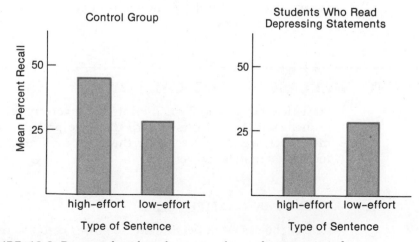

FIGURE 12.3 Bar graphs of performance from chapter example.

TABLE 12.1   Table Showing Possible Decisions That Can Be Made in
Interpreting Statistical Findings

	True State of Affairs	
Decision made	H_0 is true	H_0 is false
Retain H_0	Correct Decision $(1 - \alpha)$	Type II error (β)
Reject H_0	Type I error (α)	Correct Decision $(1 - \beta)$

Note. The true state of affairs is seldom known to researcher. Only one of the two states of affairs can be true.

given that the researchers were able to find a difference for the neutral-mood students.

In summary, researchers make a statistical decision when they complete an inferential statistical test. They can either retain H_0 or reject it. An alpha level is established prior to the test to aid in that decision. If the H_0 is retained, then the researcher may have made a correct decision or may have made a Type II error. This type of error occurs only if the samples were selected from different population distributions. If H_0 is rejected, then a correct decision may have been made or a Type I error may have occurred. The Type I error occurs if the samples were selected from the same population distribution, but appeared to be different because of chance or sampling error. These possibilities are summarized in Table 12.1.

It is impossible for researchers to be 100% sure that a correct decision has been made, because these statistical decisions are based on probability. Therefore, there always is some chance that the decision may be in error. A Type I error is controlled by the alpha level the researcher chooses. There are factors that can influence the probability of a Type II error. Let us examine some of them now.

WAYS TO INCREASE STATISTICAL POWER

Statistical power and Type II errors are inversely related. If statistical power is increased ($1 - \beta$ gets larger), then the probability of a Type II error (β) must decrease. As a researcher there are a number of things you can do to increase statistical power.

INCREASING SAMPLE SIZE

One of the easiest ways to increase power is to use more participants or subjects in your study. The effect of having more participants in your sample is a reduction in the variability in the sampling distribution. For example, $s_{\bar{x}}$,

$s_{\bar{d}}$ and $s_{\bar{x}_1 - \bar{x}_2}$ are influenced by sample size. As sample size increases the variability decreases. This can result in less overlap between the sampling distribution for the null distribution H_0 and the alternative distribution H_1.

For instance, assume that an experiment is conducted with an experimental and a control condition. Students wear special goggles in the experimental condition, but not in the control condition. The dependent variable is the amount of error made in adjusting a visual illusion. The H_0 describes the case of two samples selected from the same population distribution $\mu_{\bar{d}} = 0$. However, the samples were actually selected from population distributions that had a mean difference of 4 cm, $\mu_{exp.} - \mu_{control} = 4$. The population standard deviation (σ_d) for both samples is the same, 8 cm.

If the sample consisted of 10 students, then the standard deviation of the sampling distribution $(\sigma_{\bar{d}})$ would equal $(\sigma_d / \sqrt{N} = 8/3.16 =)$ 2.53. At the top in Figure 12.4, the sampling distribution for the H_0 is shown with the critical values (alpha level = .05) as well as the actual sampling distribution based on the parameters just given. Power is illustrated as the proportion of area that is shaded. It is the area under the real sampling distribution that falls in the reject-H_0 region.

At the bottom in Figure 12.4 is the same type of information, yet this example is based on a sample of 20 students instead of 10. The standard deviation of the sampling distribution would be smaller in this case because more students are in the sample $(\sigma_{\bar{d}} = 8/\sqrt{20} = 1.79)$. A greater proportion

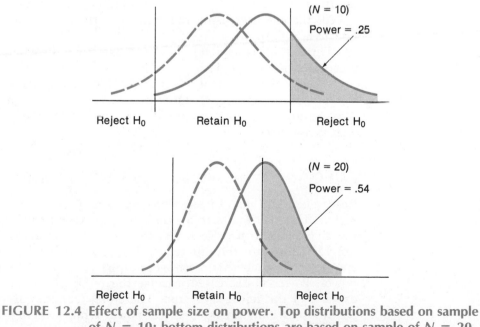

FIGURE 12.4 Effect of sample size on power. Top distributions based on sample of $N = 10$; bottom distributions are based on sample of $N = 20$. Distributions assume $\mu_{\bar{d}} = 4$ and $\sigma_{\bar{d}} = 8$. Dashed-line distribution is based on H_0.

of the area under the real sampling distribution would fall in the reject-H_0 region. Therefore, a significant difference would be more likely to be found in the case of a study with 20 students than in one of 10 students.

There is no "magical" number of participants for a study. The less the two distributions (the null and alternative) overlap, the less critical the sample size is. In many behavioral science studies, researchers have a minimum of at least 15 participants per condition. If the researcher believes that the effect of the independent variable is subtle or slight, then he would be advised to increase the number of participants in the study. Some advanced statistics texts list procedures for estimating the number of participants needed. Often, researchers use past studies as a guideline in determining the number of participants.

USING A REPEATED MEASURES DESIGN RATHER THAN AN INDEPENDENT GROUPS DESIGN

Another way of increasing statistical power is to use a repeated measures or within-subjects design in which each participant serves in all conditions of the study. As was shown in Chapter 11, the effect of using a repeated measures design is the reduction in variability in the sampling distribution. Variability resulting from individual differences can be removed or reduced when a repeated measures design is used. This has an effect similar to that described for increasing sample size. By reducing the variability in the sampling distribution, the overlap of the null and alternative distributions will be reduced, thereby increasing the area from the alternative distribution in the reject-H_0 region.

This option is available to the researcher only when it is feasible to use a repeated measures design. If the practical costs of conducting a repeated measures study are great, then an independent groups design may be preferred. And, of course, if the effects of participating in one condition may influence the behavior in another condition, then the repeated measures design is inappropriate.

USING AN ALPHA LEVEL OF .05 INSTEAD OF .01

Researchers can also increase power, by increasing the area of the reject-H_0 region. The maximal size for the reject-H_0 region can be obtained by setting the alpha level at $p \leq .05$ rather than .01. The sampling distributions in Figure 12.5 illustrate the difference. The relationship between the alpha level and power is such that a stringent alpha level (.01 instead of .05) decreases power. Power is decreased because the retain-H_0 region is increased at the expense of the reject-H_0 region. Therefore, using an alpha level of .05 gives the researcher maximal statistical power while keeping the Type I error rate at an acceptable level for the scientific community.

It should be noted that the probabilities for Type I errors and Type II errors influence each other inversely. If the researcher sets the probability for

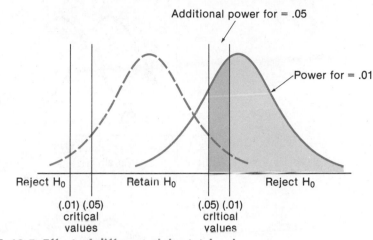

FIGURE 12.5 Effect of different alpha (α) levels on power.

a Type I error very low (such as .01 or .001) then statistical power will also be decreased, which increases the probability of a Type II error. The decision about what alpha to use is left to the researcher. If the major concern is to protect against concluding that a difference exists when it may not (a Type I error) then a low alpha level should be used. On the other hand, if the main concern is to find a difference if it exists, then the researcher is advised to set the alpha level at .05.

SIZE OF THE EFFECT

In designing a study, the researcher can increase statistical power by choosing levels of the independent variable that reasonably test the research hypothesis. The greater the differences in behavior among levels of the independent variable, the more likely it is that an effect will be found, if one exists.

Effect size refers to the difference between the means for population distributions in an experiment. The greater the difference between μs, the greater the effect size. In a two-condition independent groups experiment, the effect size is expressed in $\mu_{\bar{x}_1 - \bar{x}_2}$. The larger the value, the greater the effect size. If $\mu_{\bar{x}_1 - \bar{x}_2}$ is quite different from 0 (the mean for the sampling distribution for H_0), then the two distributions will have less overlap and the researcher will be more likely to obtain a significant difference. This is illustrated in Figure 12.6. At the top, the effect size is small. The bottom distributions show a greater effect size.

For example, assume that a social psychologist believes that impressions can be based on personal attributes used to describe a person. In a control condition, 20 neutral attributes (e.g., medium height) are given to describe a person. In a positive condition, one neutral attribute is replaced with a positive attribute (e.g., friendly). Participants are asked to rate the person using a 7-point judgment scale.

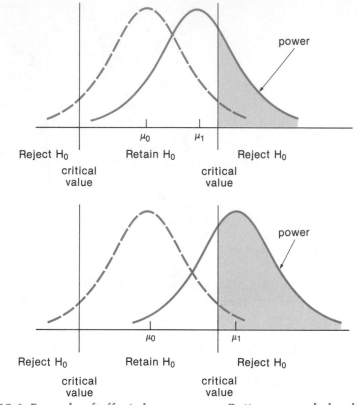

FIGURE 12.6 **Example of effect size on power. Bottom example has larger effect size (the difference between μs is greater).**

The effect of this change may be subtle given that only 1 attribute of 20 was changed. The judgments of participants in the positive condition may be slightly altered by this change, but not as much as if five attributes had been changed. Therefore, the researcher would be more likely to find a significant difference if five attributes had been changed rather than one. It is reasonable to expect that the effect size would be greater with five attributes changed rather than one.

As a researcher, you should carefully choose the levels of your independent variable. If the levels chosen produce small changes in behavior, then statistical power will be low. It may be difficult to produce a significant difference. On the other hand, choosing extreme levels may produce significant differences, but the practical implications may be slight and ethical considerations may influence their use. As a guideline, it is best to review previous research in selecting levels of the independent variable. If none exists, then preliminary testing with different levels may be appropriate before conducting the full experiment.

USING A DIRECTIONAL HYPOTHESIS INSTEAD OF A NONDIRECTIONAL HYPOTHESIS

It is also possible to enhance statistical power by placing the entire reject-H_0 region at one tail of the sampling distribution derived from H_0. Up to this point, we have been using the common practice of providing two reject-H_0 regions, one at each tail of the sampling distribution. Each region corresponded to one-half of the alpha level. For instance, if the alpha level is $p = .05$, then the extreme .025 proportion at each end of the sampling distribution was designated as the reject-H_0 region.

This procedure is based on the assumption of a nondirectional hypothesis for H_1. The **nondirectional hypothesis** is an alternative hypothesis stated in terms of a difference between population μs *without* a specific prediction as to which population μ will be larger

$$H_1: \mu_1 \neq \mu_2 \quad \text{or} \quad \mu_1 - \mu_2 \neq 0.$$

Using this type of hypothesis results in what some researchers refer to as a nondirectional or two-tailed test, because the hypothesis describes mean differences from population distributions at either end of the sampling distribution based on H_0.

It is possible to have an alternative hypothesis that is directional. A **directional hypothesis** is an alternative hypothesis that describes the case in which one sample was selected from a population distribution with a mean greater than that from which the other sample was selected. It normally takes one of two forms, either

$$H_1: \mu_1 < \mu_2$$

or

$$H_1: \mu_1 > \mu_2.$$

Since the designation of samples is left to the researcher, let's examine directional hypotheses by examining the top form. (The same logic applies for the bottom form, except that the differences are reversed.)

It is possible for a researcher to predict that behavior in one condition will differ in a particular fashion from another. For instance, a researcher might predict that performance in an experimental condition, Condition 2, will be better or higher than in a control condition, Condition 1. In this case, the alternative hypothesis would assume that values from the experimental condition come from a population distribution with a μ greater than those from the control condition

$$H_1: \mu_1 < \mu_2.$$

This is a directional hypothesis. The H_0 must account for all other possible outcomes including cases in which there is no difference between μs and when μ_1 is greater than μ_2

$$H_0: \mu_1 \geq \mu_2.$$

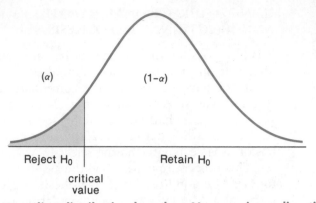

FIGURE 12.7 Sampling distribution based on H_0 assuming a directional hypothesis ($\mu_1 < \mu_2$).

The H_0 includes more than just the "no difference" case. Since H_0 must also include the possibility of μ_1 being greater than μ_2, the sampling distribution with the retain-H_0 and reject-H_0 regions look like that shown in Figure 12.7. Note that the entire alpha level (a proportion of .05) is placed at one tail of the distribution. Hence, this type of test is sometimes called a one-tailed or directional test.

If a difference is found in the direction predicted by H_1, then the use of a directional hypothesis results in more statistical power. This is illustrated in Figure 12.8. Note that having the entire alpha level represented at one end of the distribution puts more of the alternative distribution in the reject-H_0 region than if a nondirectional hypothesis is used. The use of a directional hypothesis can, therefore, increase statistical power. Yet, directional hypotheses are not often reported in the literature.

One reason that directional hypotheses are not used as often as you might expect results from potential differences in the direction opposite from what

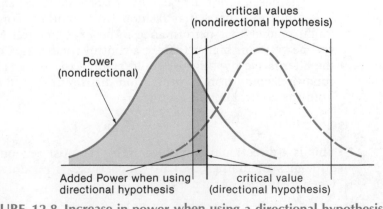

FIGURE 12.8 Increase in power when using a directional hypothesis and difference is in predicted direction.

is predicted, μ_1 is greater than μ_2. If this is found, then the researcher is unable to reject H_0 and the researcher must retain H_0 and assume that it is possible that no differences exist as well as the possibility that μ_1 is greater than μ_2. Therefore, although a directional hypothesis improves power if the difference is in the *predicted direction*, there is no statistical power for a difference in the *opposite* direction.

There are a few rules to follow in using a directional hypothesis. The decision must be made *before* the data are collected. The temptation exists to alter one's hypothesis *after* seeing the results. For one's research conclusion to be statistically and *ethically* correct, the decision to use a directional hypothesis must be made before data collection.

If a directional hypothesis is used, it should be based on sound theoretical assumptions. Editors of scientific journals must be satisfied that the decision to use a directional hypothesis is based on a convincing argument that does not depend on the data collected in the study. Some research journals do not look favorably on statistical tests involving directional hypotheses. They take a conservative view that a difference regardless of the way it is stated must be significant using a nondirectional hypothesis before it will be published. If the difference is significant using a directional hypothesis but not when using a nondirectional hypothesis, the importance of the findings may be called into question.

The examples used throughout this text assume the use of nondirectional hypotheses, even though one might make a case for using a directional hypothesis. This is admittedly a conservative view, but one in keeping with a number of scientific journals. Your instructor may require that you use directional hypotheses for some examples or for data collected in classroom demonstrations. In those instances, the critical values for various statistical tests are listed under the headings for directional tests.

It should be noted that these techniques for increasing statistical power do not influence the probability of a Type I error. If the H_0 is true, then the only factor influencing the probability of a Type I error is the alpha level. Techniques for increasing power are only effective if H_0 is false.

SOME FURTHER COMMENTS ABOUT HYPOTHESIS TESTING

There are two additional points to be made about hypothesis testing before concluding this chapter. The first involves interpreting statistical findings and the second involves applying them.

When H_0 is rejected, the researcher cannot say that the tests *prove* that a difference exists. Rather the tests *support* the view that a difference exists. The difference between *prove* and *support* is important. In a mathematical sense, the use of *prove* indicates that the statement has been shown to be true with no chance of it being false. Yet, as we have seen earlier in this chapter, the use of probability in our decision making allows for the possibility of error in our conclusions.

When H_0 is not rejected, we do not necessarily assume it is true. Rather, researchers talk of *retaining* the possibility that H_0 is true. Researchers seldom attempt to support the H_0. Rather they attempt to reject it as a possibility. When it is not rejected, the researcher concludes that the study did not provide the necessary evidence to reject it. Yet, that does not mean that the researcher is ready to embrace it as true. As we saw with statistical power, it may be that H_0 is in reality false, yet the experimental procedures and tests were not *statistically powerful enough* for the researcher to find a significant difference. Therefore, when making a decision concerning H_0, the two decisions are either to retain the possibility that H_0 is true or to reject it.

The second point involves applying the findings of a study. When a significant difference is found, the researcher should return to the descriptive statistics to decide what the difference means. A statistical difference means that when using a particular alpha level, the researcher was able to reject the statistical hypothesis known as H_0. Applying this knowledge in a meaningful fashion requires that the researcher examine the data to determine if it has any practical significance.

For example, a researcher may find that an educational program significantly increases the performance of students. Yet, upon closer examination of the mean values, one finds that the improvement is the difference of 1.2 months in terms of grade level (control group performs at an $\overline{X}$ of 5.2 years of education, whereas the experimental group performs at an $\overline{X}$ level of 5.3 years). The difference, although statistically significant, may not be sufficiently large to conclude that it is *practically* significant—especially if one is talking about implementing a costly program to improve performance slightly.

Researchers should examine the descriptive statistics once a statistical difference is found to interpret the findings. By combining descriptive and inferential statistics the researcher can more fully and completely interpret the findings of the research study.

SUMMARY

Statistical decision making involves the potential for decision errors because statistical tests are based on probabilistic decisions. A Type I error occurs when a researcher rejects H_0 when, in fact, it is true. The probability of this occurring, given that H_0 is true, is equal to the alpha level.

A Type II error occurs when H_0 is retained when it is false. Type II errors are inversely related to statistical power. Statistical power is equal to the probability of rejecting H_0 when it is false. It is expressed mathematically as $1 - \beta$.

Statistical power can be enhanced in a number of ways. Increasing sample size and using a repeated measures design reduce variability in the sampling distribution. Both have the effect of reducing the overlap between the sampling distribution described by H_0 and the true distribution described by H_1.

Choosing values of the independent variable that will increase the likelihood of influencing behavior (as measured by the dependent variable) can also increase statistical power.

Researchers can increase statistical power by making directional predictions and using a directional hypothesis. Although directional hypotheses are not reported often in the literature, they can increase power if the obtained difference is in the predicted direction.

EXERCISES

1. Does a Type I error indicate that the researcher made mistakes that could have been avoided if more care had been given to the design of the study? Explain.

2. A researcher is fearful that he made a Type II error. You find that he reports a significant difference with the following information, $t(25) = 3.89$, $p < .05$. What would you advise him?

3. According to the discussion in the text, when are replications of published studies more important, in detecting Type I or Type II errors? Explain.

4. In each case below, determine what type of decision error may have been made:
   a. $t(15) = 1.58$, $p > .05$
   b. $t(48) = 2.28$, $p < .05$
   c. $t(25) = 2.33$, $p > .01$
   d. $t(60) = 2.73$, $p < .01$

5. In each case listed in Exercise 4, describe a change the researcher could make that would reduce the probability of making the particular decision error listed.

6. A fellow student knows that by using an alpha level of .01, the probability of a Type I error is reduced as compared with an alpha level of .05. Yet, you know that this can increase the probability of a Type II error. How would you demonstrate this to your friend by using graphic depictions of the sampling distributions?

7. To reduce the probability of making a Type I error, a researcher increases the number of participants in a study from 10 to 30. Your comments?

8. A study is published which notes that a difference was found using a .01 alpha level. Would you conclude that the effect found is based on a statistically powerful test or the result of a powerful effect or both? Explain.

9. A student believes that the rate at which words are presented will influence memory recall. She presents a list of 30 words to students; some see the list at the rate of 1 word every second, others see the list at the rate of one word every 1.5 sec. She finds no significant difference after testing five students in each condition. She used an alpha level of .01. List at least three things she could do to increase the possibility of finding a significant difference if she were to conduct the study again.

10. In Exercise 9, what is the probability that the student made a Type I error? Why?

11. If in Exercise 9, the student had found a significant difference, with the slower presentation group recalling a mean of 16.60 words and the other group recalling a mean of 15.70, what would you conclude about the practical significance?

12. You read an article that claims that although the difference found is not statistically significant, it is practically significant. Does that make sense to you? Explain.

13. Two professors teach the same material in a particular course. One professor using Book A finds that his students do significantly poorer than students with the other professor who uses Book B. Assuming that the difference is, in fact, due to the different books, what should the professor consider before switching from Book A to Book B, especially since it will involve extensive restructuring of the course?

14. A study is published with results that are surprising given that they contradict current theoretical predictions. Several researchers are unable to replicate the significant differences reported in that study. What type of decision error might have been made in the original study? Why?

15. There are journals that publish studies that report nonsignificant findings. What do you believe is the goal of these journals? Describe your answer in terms of the topics discussed in this text.

16. A student tells you that he doesn't believe the significant findings reported in a study because only 10 students participated in the study. Does that make sense given what was discussed in this chapter?

17. Would you agree or disagree with the student in Exercise 16 if the study did not find a significant difference? Explain your answer.

18. Researchers sometimes refer to nonsignificant findings as "null results." Does that term make sense in terms of the discussion in the text?

19. A famous study on an effect in short-term memory known as "release from proactive interference (PI)" describes a series of empirical studies. A number of the studies did not find a significant effect and an effect was only found when several variables were carefully manipulated and many students were tested in each condition. What would you assume about the effect being studied by these researchers?

20. A student is unable to reject H_0 when using a nondirectional hypothesis and an alpha level of .01. After examining the data and reading most of this chapter, she decides to use a directional hypothesis and an alpha level of .05. Then a significant difference is found. What are your comments and suggestions to this student?

Analyzing Multiple-Condition Studies with Interval or Ratio Data

OVERVIEW

In contrast to the previous three chapters, which focused on experiments with two conditions, the next three chapters will deal with analyzing data from experiments with more than two conditions or groups. A different type of test, called the analysis of variance, is used in all three chapters. The statistical assumptions involved in using these tests are consistent with those described for the t test.

Chapters 13 and 14 deal with more complex studies using an independent groups design. In Chapter 13, experiments with one independent variable are discussed. Unlike Chapter 10, however, these experiments will have three or more conditions. Chapter 14 describes the analysis of experiments with two independent variables. Up until that point, all of the studies discussed have involved the analysis of one independent variable. The studies in Chapter 14 involve the combination of two independent variables in experiments called factorial designs.

The analysis of experiments with repeated measures is discussed in Chapter 15. Although Chapter 11 described studies with two conditions, the focus in Chapter 15 is on experiments with repeated measures involving three or more conditions.

The One-Way Analysis of Variance

TERMS DISCUSSED

experimentwise error rate

comparison error rate

systematic variability

error variability

F ratio

post hoc comparisons test

PROCEDURES DESCRIBED

conducting a one-way ANOVA

conducting the Tukey HSD test

Aggressive behavior has been one topic of study for social scientists. A number of investigators have attempted to elicit aggression in the laboratory setting. In 1972, Parke, Ewall, and Slaby studied the effect of verbal cues on aggressive behavior. They designed an experiment that consisted of two phases. In the first phase, 51 college men received verbal training. During this phase, each man saw a series of sets of three words. Each set contained an "aggressive" word (e.g., violent), a "neutral word" (e.g., plastic), and a "helpful" word (e.g., cooperation). Each student was instructed to pick the correct word from each set of three words. An equal number of men had either the aggressive words, the neutral words, or the helpful words as the correct words. When the student picked the correct word from the set, he was verbally reinforced by the experimenter saying "correct." The student continued to pick a word from each set until he correctly picked 20 consecutive words. It should be noted that the student was not told what type of word was correct for him. Presumably, through trial and error, the student learned what type of word was correct for him. Following this phase, the student participated in the aggression test phase.

In this second phase, the male student was told that another student was going to participate in the learning phase he had just completed. To determine the effect of electric shock on learning, he was asked to help the experimenter by shocking this other student when incorrect responses were made. Unknown to the subject, the other student was an assistant to the researchers and received no shocks. The subject was seated in front of a device with 10 buttons numbered 1 to 10, which indicated shock intensity and was given a sample of an electrical shock labeled 4.

When the other student made a mistake, indicated with a red light on the device, the subject pressed one of the 10 buttons to select a shock intensity and then pushed another button labeled "shock duration" to determine how long the shock lasted. The subject freely chose the intensity level and duration of the shock each time the other student made a mistake. Ten errors were made by this fictitious student who was seated in a room separate from the subject. The researchers recorded the intensity level chosen and the duration of shock on each of the error trials. The researchers summed the intensity levels chosen by the students for the 10 trials. These values are presented in Table 13.1.

Parke et al. (1972) hypothesized that students who had been verbally reinforced earlier for aggressive words would deliver more intense shocks than those who had been reinforced for neutral words. And, those students who had been reinforced for helpful words would deliver less intense shocks than the students who had been reinforced for aggressive or neutral words.

It should be mentioned that studies such as this one are reviewed by committees to ensure that ethical guidelines for research using human subjects are met. The benefit of learning more about human behavior must outweigh potential physical and psychological risks to the subjects. In studies such as this one, it is important to avoid psychological harm such

TABLE 13.1 Intensity Levels of Shock Selected by Students in the Chapter Example		
Type of Word Reinforced During Learning Phase		
Aggressive	Helpful	Neutral
67	17	44
57	23	25
51	36	48
35	39	53
28	35	50
66	42	33
29	31	36
58	10	43
32	11	61
35	10	37
55	28	52
40	10	47
69	49	49
51	15	31
39	36	37
70	34	38
45	21	30

as creating guilt feelings on the part of subjects who think they are administering harmful shocks to another person. Studies such as these are conducted only after careful review.

Parke et al. (1972) were interested in the effect of verbal reinforcement on subsequent behavior. Their study was partially based on the findings of an earlier study by Lovass (1961) who found that children reinforced for verbal hostility were more likely to play with an aggressive type of toy than children not reinforced for verbal hostility. In the present example, college students were used and aggression was measured in terms of electrically shocking another student.

The independent variable was the type of word reinforced during the learning phase. There were three values or conditions of this variable used in the study: aggressive, neutral, and helpful words. These conditions differ qualitatively not quantitatively; therefore, the independent variable corresponds to a nominal scale of measurement.

There were two dependent variables, or measures of behavior, in the study. One variable was the sum of all the shock intensities administered on the 10 error trials. Since the intensity of shock could vary from 1 to 10 on each error trial, the possible values for the sum of the intensities range from 10 to 100, with 10 representing an intensity of 1 on each of the 10 trials and a 100 representing an intensity of 10 on each of the 10 trials. This variable is quantitative and on an interval scale of measurement, because the possible values from 10 to 100 have equal intervals between them. (It is not on a ratio scale because a zero point was not defined.) The second dependent variable, which will not be analyzed further in this example, is the duration of the shock, which was measured and summed across all 10 error trials.

The research hypothesis is stated in terms of a causal effect. It is hypothesized that the type of word for which a person is reinforced will affect the intensity and duration of shocks administered in the subsequent aggression phase. The independent variable—the type of word reinforced—will influence the dependent variables—the intensity and duration of shocks given to another student.

This study is an example of a multiple-condition experiment because more than two conditions of the independent variable are used. Furthermore, the experiment uses an independent groups design in that each participant serves in one and only one condition. Each of the 51 male students was randomly assigned to one of the three conditions of the independent variable. Therefore, three groups or samples of 17 students participated in this study. As in all research studies, the first step is to summarize the data from each group using descriptive statistics.

DESCRIPTIVE STATISTICS: DESCRIBING THE SAMPLE DATA

The most appropriate measure of central tendency to report is the $\overline{X}$. Because the data are on an interval scale of measurement and because there is little evidence that the data in our sample are skewed, the $\overline{X}$ is the most appropriate measure. The estimate of the population standard deviation s is reported as the measure of variability. Table 13.2 provides the necessary summary statistics ΣX, ΣX^2, and N, along with the calculations for $\overline{X}$ and s for each of the three samples. The subscripts "a," "h," and "n" are used to differentiate among the three samples: "a" is used for the "aggressive" sample, "h" for the "helpful" sample, and "n" for the "neutral" sample.

The mean intensity level of shock for each sample is presented graphically in Figure 13.1. Note that the independent variable—the type of word used—is listed on the x-axis and the dependent variable—intensity level—is presented on the y-axis. A bar graph is used because the independent variable is qualitative. The mean results are in the direction predicted by the research hypothesis. The highest mean intensity level of shock was administered by the students who were earlier reinforced for "aggressive" words. And, the lowest mean intensity level was given by the students who were earlier reinforced for "helpful" words. Those students reinforced for "neutral" words ad-

TABLE 13.2 Summary Information and Descriptive Statistics for the Chapter Example

Type of Word Reinforced During the Learning Phase		
Aggressive	*Helpful*	*Neutral*
$\Sigma X_a = 827$	$\Sigma X_h = 447$	$\Sigma X_n = 714$
$\Sigma X_a{}^2 = 43{,}591$	$\Sigma X_h{}^2 = 14{,}309$	$\Sigma X_n{}^2 = 31{,}486$
$N_a = 17$	$N_h = 17$	$N_n = 17$

Using Formula 1: $\overline{X} = \Sigma X/N$

$\overline{X}_a = 827/17$	$\overline{X}_h = 447/17$	$\overline{X}_n = 714/17$
$= 48.65$	$= 26.29$	$= 42.00$

Using Formula 3: $SS = \Sigma X^2 - (\Sigma X)^2/N$

$SS_a = 43{,}591 - \dfrac{(827)^2}{17}$	$SS_h = 14{,}309 - \dfrac{(447)^2}{17}$	$SS_n = 31{,}486 - \dfrac{(714)^2}{17}$
$= 3{,}359.88$	$= 2{,}555.53$	$= 1{,}498.00$

Using Formula 4: $s^2 = SS/(N - 1)$

$s^2{}_a = 3{,}359.88/16$	$s^2{}_h = 2{,}555.53/16$	$s^2{}_n = 1{,}498.00/16$
$= 209.99$	$= 159.72$	$= 93.63$

Using Formula 5: $s = \sqrt{s^2}$

$s_a = \sqrt{209.99}$	$s_h = \sqrt{159.72}$	$s_n = \sqrt{93.63}$
$= 14.49$	$= 12.64$	$= 9.68$

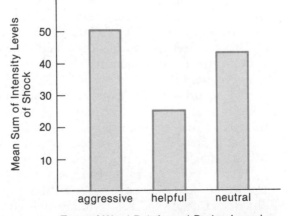

FIGURE 13.1 Bar graph for the chapter example.

ministered an intermediate level of shock. The goal of the procedures involving inferential statistics is to identify which, if any, of these differences among sample means is significant.

INFERENTIAL STATISTICS: TESTING FOR DIFFERENCES

There are three pairwise comparisons that can be made. The first involves the mean difference between the aggressive-word sample and the neutral-word sample. The second is based on the mean difference between the aggressive-word sample and the helpful-word sample. And the last comparison is based on the mean difference between the neutral-word sample and the helpful-word sample.

You might decide to do a series of t tests, one for each comparison. The decision to complete a series of t tests has two important limitations. The first involves time and effort. With 3 samples, 3 t tests are needed. However, as the number of samples or conditions in an experiment increase, the number of t tests that need to be conducted increases quickly. With 4 conditions, the number of t tests needed is 6. With 5 conditions, 10 t tests are needed. With 6 conditions, there are 15 t tests. As you can see, the number of pairwise comparisons increases quickly as the number of conditions increases. The number of possible pairwise comparisons for analyzing this type of study can be determined by using the following formula

$$\text{Number of comparisons} = \frac{(\text{Number of conditions}) \cdot (\text{Number of conditions} - 1)}{2}.$$

As the number of conditions increases, the number of t tests and necessary time and effort increase. The second limitation in conducting a series of t tests may not be as obvious but it is as important. As a researcher increases the number of statistical tests conducted, he increases the probability of making a decision error, specifically a Type I error.

If a researcher uses the .05 rejection level and conducts only one statistical test, then the probability of making a Type I error, that is, rejecting H_0 when it should have been retained, is .05. Since only one test was conducted in the experiment, the **experimentwise error rate**—the probability of making a Type I error in the *experiment*—is equal to the **comparison error rate**—the probability of making a Type I error in a *single statistical test*. (Although "experimentwise" may be a poor word choice, it is used more frequently than other terms, such as "per experiment error rate.")

However, if several tests are conducted within a single experiment, then the experimentwise error rate will be greater than .05. For example, in the chapter example three t tests are needed. The rejection level for a single t test, the comparison error rate, could be set at .05. Because three t tests are being conducted, a Type I error might be made in the first, the second, or the third t test. The experimentwise error rate reflects the fact that in the *experiment overall*, the probability of making a Type I error rate is greater than .05. The experimentwise error rate can be estimated by multiplying the number of tests by the comparison error rate. In this example, the experimentwise error rate would be approximately .15 (i.e., 3 tests × .05).

It should make sense that as a researcher increases the number of tests in an experiment, the probability of making a decision error, specifically a Type I error, increases. This increase is reflected in the experimentwise error rate. If a researcher conducts six independent tests at the .05 level in one experiment, then the experimentwise error rate would be approximately .30 (6 tests × .05). Notice that even though each test uses a .05 level, there is a .30 chance ($p = .30$), that the researcher may falsely conclude that a significant difference exists based on one of the five tests conducted. To avoid this increase in the experimentwise error rate, the analysis of variance is used. It is a single test that allows for many comparisons and keeps the probability of an experimentwise error equal to that of the comparison error, whether it be .05 or .01.

ANALYSIS OF VARIANCE: A CONCEPTUAL APPROACH

The analysis of variance, or as it is abbreviated ANOVA, is a statistical test that allows for the comparisons of two or more samples in a single test. The null hypothesis assumes that all samples were taken from the same population distribution. It can be expressed symbolically as

$$H_0: \mu_1 = \mu_2 = \cdots = \mu_k.$$

The symbol k is used to indicate the number of different samples or conditions in the experiment.

The alternative hypothesis assumes that at least one sample comes from a population distribution with a μ different from those of the population distributions for the other samples. There is no easy way to express H_1 symbolically. Notice that H_1 assumes that at least one difference exists, but does not preclude the possibility that more than one difference exists. The H_1 for the ANOVA consists of a series of possibilities describing all possible combinations of differences among population distributions.

In the chapter example with three conditions, there are four different possibilities that are described by H_1:

$$\mu_1 = \mu_2 \neq \mu_3,$$
$$\mu_1 \neq \mu_2 = \mu_3,$$
$$\mu_1 = \mu_3 \neq \mu_2,$$

and

$$\mu_1 \neq \mu_2 \neq \mu_3.$$

Obviously, as the number of samples increases, the number of possibilities increases. Therefore, the H_1 can be stated in words rather than in symbols for the ANOVA:

H_1:   At least one sample comes from a population distribution with a mean (μ) different from that of the other samples.

The ANOVA test itself deals with the variance found in the data, hence the term "analysis of variance." In fact, the one-way ANOVA divides the total variability found in the data into two segments. (It is called a one-way ANOVA because there is only one independent variable.) One segment of the variability is based on differences among the sample means. The other portion is based on variability within each sample. An example may help.

Table 13.3 contains fictitious data for three samples along with the $\overline{X}$ for each sample and the overall $\overline{X}$ for all values. The three $\overline{X}$s differ quite a bit among each other. There is variability among the different $\overline{X}$s. Notice also that in each sample there is some variability among the values; the values within each sample are not all the same. The differences within the samples, however, are not as great as the differences across the samples.

The ANOVA assumes that every value in the sample is influenced by two things: the particular sample the value happens to be in and the variability within that sample. For example, let's say a participant in this example produced a value of 4, the lowest value in the set. This person has a value that is 11 points below the overall mean $\overline{X}_{tot}$, which is 15. The $\overline{X}_{tot}$ is the mean of all the values in the study. Part of the difference (9 points) can be explained by noting that the person is in the sample with the lowest sample $\overline{X}$, which is 6

$$(\overline{X}_1 - \overline{X}_{tot}) = (6 - 15) = -9.$$

The fact that the person is 2 points lower than the sample $\overline{X}$ is the result of variability within the sample

$$(X - \overline{X}_1) = (4 - 6) = -2.$$

TABLE 13.3   Fictitious Data for Three Samples (N = 6 per Sample)

	Sample		
1	*2*	*3*	*Overall*
4	11	24	
5	12	24	
6	13	25	
6	15	25	
7	16	25	
8	17	27	
$\Sigma X_1 = 36$	$\Sigma X_2 = 84$	$\Sigma X_3 = 150$	$\Sigma X_{tot} = 270$
$N_1 = 6$	$N_2 = 6$	$N_3 = 6$	$N_{tot} = 18$
$\overline{X}_1 = 6$	$\overline{X}_2 = 14$	$\overline{X}_3 = 25$	$\overline{X}_{tot} = 15$

The difference of 11 points can be divided into two portions, one accounting for 9 points and the other for 2 points. This process of segmenting the difference or deviation between a value and the $\overline{X}_{tot}$ can be expressed symbolically

$$X - \overline{X}_{tot} = (\overline{X}_k - \overline{X}_{tot}) + (X - \overline{X}_k)$$

Deviation from $\overline{X}_{tot}$ = Variability among Samples

+ Variability within Sample.

For each value, the deviation between the value and the overall mean can be partitioned into these two components. This process of partitioning the deviation is shown graphically in Figure 13.2 for three values including the value of 4, from the chapter example.

The analysis of variance involves partitioning the squared deviations. Recall that it was demonstrated in Chapter 3 that in order to avoid having the sum of the deviations equal 0, $(\Sigma(X - \overline{X}) = 0)$, it is necessary to square the deviations. In fact, the one-way ANOVA calculates three sums of squared deviations (SS). Each of these sums accounts for one component of the differences which was just demonstrated with individual values.

The sum of the squared deviations of each value from the overall mean $\overline{X}_{tot}$ is represented by SS_{tot}. This sum should be taken as a measure of the total variability in the experiment

$$SS_{tot} = \Sigma(X - \overline{X}_{tot})^2. \tag{Def}$$

A portion of this total variability is the result of differences among the groups. That is, this term not only includes variability within the groups but also the effect of the experimenter's manipulation.

An individual's score is influenced by the individual's condition or group. For instance, in the chapter example the sum of the shock intensity may be influenced by the type of word the individual had received reinforcement for earlier—either aggressive, helpful, or neutral. This portion of the variability is found in the SS_a, which describes the sum of the squared deviations among the groups

$$SS_a = \Sigma(\overline{X}_k - \overline{X}_{tot})^2. \tag{Def}$$

(You may also see SS_a described as SS_b, which stands for the sum of the squared deviations "between" groups. "Among" is used rather than "between" because the comparisons often involve more than two groups.) For each value in the data set, the squared deviation between the group $\overline{X}$ for that value and the $\overline{X}_{tot}$ is calculated. The squared deviations are then summed.

The last sum involves only the variability that is found within each group. It is based on the deviation of each value from the group $\overline{X}$. This variability is not the result of anything that the experimenter did. It can be considered to be "error variability." This variability may result from individual differences (how the participant felt that day, individual skills, motivation, etc.) and chance factors. This variability is depicted in the different values within each column of data in Table 13.1. If all the values *within* a column were the same, there would be no error variability. However, that seldom, if

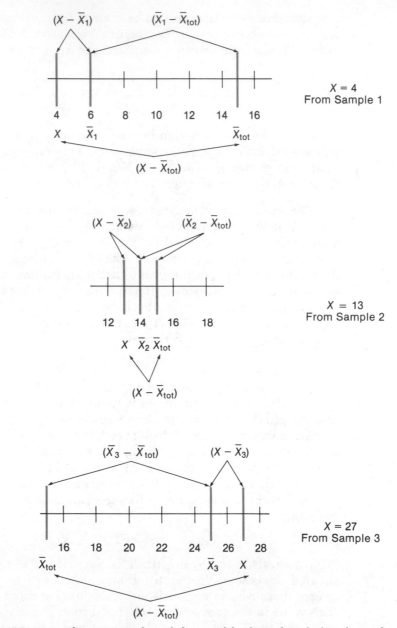

FIGURE 13.2 Three examples of the partitioning of variation from the sample data in Table 13.3

ever, occurs. This sum SS_w is called the sum of the squared deviations within groups

$$SS_w = \Sigma(X - \overline{X}_k)^2. \qquad \text{(Def)}$$

These three sums are related in the following fashion:

$$SS_{tot} = SS_a + SS_w.$$

TABLE 13.4 Calculation of the Sums of the Squared Deviations for the Fictitious Data

X	$\bar{X}_k$	$\bar{X}_{tot}$	$(X - \bar{X}_{tot})^2$	$(\bar{X}_k - \bar{X}_{tot})^2$	$(X - \bar{X}_k)^2$
4	6	15	$(4 - 15)^2 =$ 121	$(6 - 15)^2 =$ 81	$(4 - 6)^2 =$ 4
5	6	15	$(5 - 15)^2 =$ 100	$(6 - 15)^2 =$ 81	$(5 - 6)^2 =$ 1
6	6	15	$(6 - 15)^2 =$ 81	$(6 - 15)^2 =$ 81	$(6 - 6)^2 =$ 0
6	6	15	$(6 - 15)^2 =$ 81	$(6 - 15)^2 =$ 81	$(6 - 6)^2 =$ 0
7	6	15	$(7 - 15)^2 =$ 64	$(6 - 15)^2 =$ 81	$(7 - 6)^2 =$ 1
8	6	15	$(8 - 15)^2 =$ 49	$(6 - 15)^2 =$ 81	$(8 - 6)^2 =$ 4
11	14	15	$(11 - 15)^2 =$ 16	$(14 - 15)^2 =$ 1	$(11 - 14)^2 =$ 9
12	14	15	$(12 - 15)^2 =$ 9	$(14 - 15)^2 =$ 1	$(12 - 14)^2 =$ 4
13	14	15	$(13 - 15)^2 =$ 4	$(14 - 15)^2 =$ 1	$(13 - 14)^2 =$ 1
15	14	15	$(15 - 15)^2 =$ 0	$(14 - 15)^2 =$ 1	$(15 - 14)^2 =$ 1
16	14	15	$(16 - 15)^2 =$ 1	$(14 - 15)^2 =$ 1	$(16 - 14)^2 =$ 4
17	14	15	$(17 - 15)^2 =$ 4	$(14 - 15)^2 =$ 1	$(17 - 14)^2 =$ 9
24	25	15	$(24 - 15)^2 =$ 81	$(25 - 15)^2 =$ 100	$(24 - 25)^2 =$ 1
24	25	15	$(24 - 15)^2 =$ 81	$(25 - 15)^2 =$ 100	$(24 - 25)^2 =$ 1
25	25	25	$(25 - 15)^2 =$ 100	$(25 - 15)^2 =$ 100	$(25 - 25)^2 =$ 0
25	25	25	$(25 - 15)^2 =$ 100	$(25 - 15)^2 =$ 100	$(25 - 25)^2 =$ 0
25	25	25	$(25 - 15)^2 =$ 100	$(25 - 15)^2 =$ 100	$(25 - 25)^2 =$ 0
27	25	25	$(27 - 15)^2 =$ 144	$(25 - 15)^2 =$ 100	$(27 - 25)^2 =$ 4
			$SS_{tot} = 1,136$	$SS_a = 1,092$	$SS_w = 44$

In Table 13.4, the three sums were calculated for the fictitious example. Notice that when SS_a is added to SS_w, the sum is SS_{tot}. In addition, note the relationship between SS_a and SS_w. The sum of the squared deviations among (SS_a) is considerably larger than that within (SS_w) the groups. Although ANOVA involves the comparison of the mean of these squared deviations, it is helpful to compare these two sums. The values of SS_a and SS_w will be used in determining the effect of the experimenter's manipulation.

The data were arranged in Table 13.3 so that it was obvious that the groups differed from each other. For comparison purposes, the same data are presented again in Table 13.5. However, the values were randomly assigned to one of the three groups. At the bottom of Table 13.5 the SS_{tot}, SS_a, and SS_w are shown. Notice that the SS_{tot} is the same as in Table 13.4. The total variability has not changed. However, the relative values of SS_a and SS_w have changed considerably. Now the variability resulting from the group $\bar{X}$s (SS_a) is substantially less than in Table 13.4. And SS_w, which measures only individual and chance variation, is much larger. In this case, it is unlikely that the researcher's manipulation had much of an effect.

Obviously, the researcher wants to reject H_0 and conclude that a difference exists. Therefore, it is necessary to demonstrate that the variability re-

TABLE 13.5   The Fictitious Data Rearranged (N = 6 per Sample)

	Sample			
	1	*2*	*3*	*overall*
	25	6	16	
	5	8	4	
	17	24	7	
	15	13	25	
	12	6	24	
	<u>27</u>	<u>25</u>	<u>11</u>	
	$\Sigma X_1 = 101$	$\Sigma X_2 = 82$	$\Sigma X_3 = 87$	$\Sigma X_{tot} = 270$
	$N_1 = 6$	$N_2 = 6$	$N_3 = 6$	$N_{tot} = 18$
	$\overline{X}_1 = 16.83$	$\overline{X}_2 = 13.67$	$\overline{X}_3 = 14.50$	$\overline{X}_{tot} = 15$

$SS_{tot} = \Sigma(X - \overline{X}_{tot})^2 = (25 - 15)^2 + (5 - 15)^2 + \cdots + (11 - 15)^2 = 1{,}136.$

$SS_a = \Sigma(\overline{X}_k - \overline{X}_{tot})^2 = (16.83 - 15)^2 + (16.83 - 15)^2 + \cdots + (14.5 - 15)^2 = 32.33$

$SS_w = \Sigma(X - \overline{X}_k)^2 = (25 - 16.83)^2 + (5 - 16.83)^2 + \cdots + (11 - 14.5)^2 = 1{,}103.67$

sulting from the researcher's manipulation (the independent variable) is greater than that from individual and chance factors (the error variability). Before the discussion on how this comparison is made, let us look at the computational formulas for calculating the three *SS*s just described.

THE COMPUTATIONAL FORMULAS FOR THE ANOVA

The secret to using the computational formulas is organization. If the data are organized in a clear fashion, the computations are straightforward. The summary statistics calculated for the chapter example that are shown in Table 13.2 are presented again in Table 13.6. The only new information is the last column labeled "Total." This column is the addition of the information in each row. All of the necessary calculations can be made using these values.

The first step is the calculation of SS_{tot}. The computational formula is

$$SS_{tot} = \Sigma X_{tot}^2 - \frac{(\Sigma X_{tot})^2}{N_{tot}}. \tag{23}$$

TABLE 13.6   Summary Information for the Chapter Example

Type of Word Reinforced During Learning Phase			
Aggressive	*Helpful*	*Neutral*	*Total*
$\Sigma X_a = 827$	$\Sigma X_h = 447$	$\Sigma X_n = 714$	$\Sigma X_{tot} = 1{,}988$
$\Sigma X_a^2 = 43{,}591$	$\Sigma X_h^2 = 14{,}309$	$\Sigma X_n^2 = 31{,}486$	$\Sigma X_{tot}^2 = 89{,}386$
$N_a = 17$	$N_h = 17$	$N_n = 17$	$N_{tot} = 51$

Using the information in the last column of Table 13.6 provides

$$SS_{tot} = \Sigma X_{tot}^2 - \frac{(\Sigma X_{tot})^2}{N_{tot}}$$ (23)

$$= 89,386 - \frac{(1,988)^2}{51}$$

$$= 89,386 - 77,493.02$$

$$= 11,892.98.$$

The calculation of SS_a involves the sums of each group. The computational formula is

$$SS_a = \frac{(\Sigma X_1)^2}{N_1} + \frac{(\Sigma X_2)^2}{N_2} + \cdots + \frac{(\Sigma X_k)^2}{N_k} - \frac{(\Sigma X_{tot})^2}{N_{tot}}.$$ (24)

Again, remember that k refers to the number of groups in the experiment. There are three groups in the example. Using the information in Table 13.6, the calculation of S_a would provide the following:

$$SS_a = \frac{(\Sigma X_1)^2}{N_1} + \frac{(\Sigma X_2)^2}{N_2} + \cdots + \frac{(\Sigma X_k)^2}{N_k} - \frac{(\Sigma X_{tot})^2}{N_{tot}}$$ (24)

$$= \frac{(827)^2}{17} + \frac{(447)^2}{17} + \frac{(714)^2}{17} - \frac{(1,988)^2}{51}$$

$$= 40,231.12 + 11,753.47 + 29,988.00 - 77,493.02$$

$$= 81,972.59 - 77,493.02$$

$$= 4,479.57.$$

The last sum to be calculated is SS_w. It involves the variability within each group and is the sum of the individual SS for each sample. The computational formula is

$$SS_w = SS_1 + SS_2 + \cdots + SS_k.$$ (25)

The calculation of SS_w for the example involves only three groups. Substituting values from Table 13.2 into Formula 25 provides the following:

$$SS_w = SS_1 + SS_2 + \cdots + SS_k$$ (25)

$$= 3,359.88 + 2,555.53 + 1,498.$$

$$= 7,413.41.$$

When the calculations have been completed, add SS_a to SS_w to check that the sum equals SS_{tot},

$$SS_{tot} = SS_a + SS_w$$

$$11,892.98 = 4,479.57 + 7,413.41.$$

This procedure serves as an excellent check that the calculations in Formulas 23, 24, and 25 were completed correctly. No negative SS values are possible. If the calculation of an SS results in a negative value, then often either a value was substituted incorrectly or a mistake was made in the calculations. Now that the SS values have been determined, let us proceed to the next step.

CONSTRUCTING THE SUMMARY TABLE AND CALCULATING THE *F* RATIO

The critical comparison in the ANOVA occurs between the variability among the groups and the variability within the groups. The SS_a and SS_w, however, are sums and are influenced by the number of groups and values within each group. The more groups or more values included per group, the larger the *SSs* will be. Therefore, a mean variability statistic is needed. The variance is the statistic that will be used. In an ANOVA it is often called "the mean squared," abbreviated as MS.

Similar to estimating of the population variance and standard deviation from a sample, it involves dividing SS by degrees of freedom (recall $s^2 = SS/N - 1$). In ANOVA, each SS is divided by the appropriate degrees of freedom to get the MS

$$MS = SS/df. \qquad (26)$$

The total df is based on the total number of values minus 1: $df_{tot} = N_{tot} - 1$. For the chapter example, df_{tot} is $51 - 1$ or 50. As shown in Figure 13.3, the df_{tot} is partitioned in a fashion similar to that for the SS_{tot}. Notice that in each diagram, the values on the right branches must equal the total value on the left.

In the case of SS_a the degrees of freedom among groups df_a, is $k - 1$, where k is the number of groups in the experiment. In the chapter example there are three groups, therefore the df_a is 2. For SS_w, the degrees of freedom within

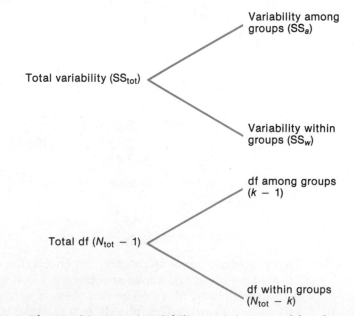

FIGURE 13.3 The partitioning of variability and degrees of freedom (df) for the one-way ANOVA.

df_w is $N_{tot} - k$, which is the same as adding the $(N - 1)$ together for each group. The N_{tot} is 51 and subtracting 3, the number of groups k, results in df_w equalling 48. As a check, df_a plus df_w must equal df_{tot} $(2 + 48 = 50)$.

A summary table is usually constructed to help present this information in an organized fashion. The general form of a summary table for the one-way ANOVA is presented at the top in Table 13.7. Note that the first column lists the sources of variation, among groups and within groups, which together equal the total variability. The second column lists the SS values that can be found using Formulas 23 through 25. The df are shown in the third column, and the SS is then divided by the appropriate df to get the MS, which is shown in the fourth column. A statistic called the F ratio can be calculated by dividing MS_a by MS_w. The importance of the F ratio will be discussed in the next section.

At the bottom in Table 13.7, the SS and df are shown for the chapter example along with the MS_a and MS_w and F ratio. Note that SS_{tot} and df_{tot} are equal to the sum of the respective SSs and dfs.

To determine whether or not to retain H_0, a comparison must be made between MS_a and MS_w. The variability among the groups as measured by MS_a contains variability resulting from two sources. One source is the experimenter's manipulation of the independent variable, which is called **systematic variability.** The other source of variability is the unexplained variability that occurs within the groups. This variability is called **error variability** and, as was mentioned earlier, it contains variability from individual differences and chance factors. Both are included because the difference among $\overline{X}$s is a function of both sources of variability.

On the other hand, error variability is the only source of variability in the MS_w. Differences within a group or sample can only be accounted for by individual differences and chance factors. If the values vary considerably

TABLE 13.7 Summary Table for the One-Way ANOVA (Top) and Summary Table for Chapter Example (Bottom)

Source	SS	df	MS	F
Among groups	(Formula 24)	$k - 1$	SS_a/df_a	MS_a/MS_w
Within groups	(Formula 25)	$N_{tot} - k$	SS_w/df_w	
Total variability	(Formula 23)	$N_{tot} - 1$		

Source	SS	df	MS	F
Among groups	4,479.57	2	2,239.78	14.50
Within groups	7,413.41	48	154.45	
Total variability	11,892.98	50		

within each group or condition, then MS_w will be higher than if the values within each group were quite similar.

Calculating the F Ratio

The ANOVA involves a comparison of MS_a and MS_w. The comparison involves dividing MS_a by MS_w. This procedure produces a ratio statistic called the F ratio. The **F ratio** is a statistic resulting from the division of MS_a by MS_w

$$F = \frac{\text{Systematic variability} + \text{Error variability}}{\text{Error variability}} = \frac{MS_a}{MS_w}. \quad (27)$$

To understand the F ratio, examine what happens if the independent variable is ineffective. If it is, then there will be no systematic variability because systematic variability is a reflection of the effect of being in a particular group or sample. Looking at the formula above, if systematic variability is zero, then the F ratio should equal 1 because you have error variability being divided by error variability. On the other hand, if the independent variable is effective, then the numerator (MS_a) should be larger than the denominator (MS_w) and as a result the F should be greater than 1.

A negative F ratio is not possible. All F ratios must be positive because it is based on two MS statistics, both of which are positive. If the H_0 is true, then in most instances the F should be close to 1. If, however, H_0 is false and the independent variable has an effect, the F should be greater than 1. The larger the F ratio, the greater the effect of the independent variable is relative to the error variability.

When computed for a study with two groups, the F ratio is related to the t value. When the one-way analysis of variance is substituted for the t test for independent samples, the F ratio will equal t^2.

Let us calculate the F ratio for the chapter example. The necessary information is shown in the summary table in Table 13.7. The MS_a ($= 2239.78$) is larger than the MS_w ($= 154.45$). This indicates that there was systematic variability in this study. In fact, an F ratio of 14.50 was obtained

$$F = \frac{MS_a}{MS_w} \quad (27)$$

$$= \frac{2239.78}{154.45}$$

$$= 14.50.$$

The question is whether this F ratio should lead the researchers to reject H_0 or not.

Finding the Critical F Ratio

As was the case with t tests, a critical F ratio must be found. Distributions of F ratios exist. They are a function of the df_a and df_w. If H_0 is true, then the distribution of F ratios would look something like that shown in Figure 13.4

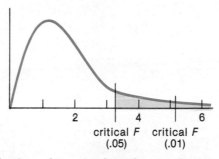

FIGURE 13.4 A distribution of F ratios based on H_0 being true. The shaded area represents .05 of the total area.

The distribution is not symmetric as in the case of sampling distributions discussed earlier. Rather it is positively skewed with a mean near 1.00, the most likely F ratio if the systematic variability is zero (which describes the situation in which all groups come from the same population).

The reject-H_0 region is located in the right tail of the distribution. If H_0 is false, then at least one sample came from a population distribution with a different μ than the other samples. In terms of the F ratio, this would indicate that there was a considerable amount of systematic variability (relative to error variability). Critical F ratios for both the .05 and .01 alpha levels are shown for the chapter example.

The extreme 5% of this distribution is shaded. If the calculated F ratio exceeds the critical F ratio, then there are less than 5 chances out of 100 ($p < .05$) that the groups in the study have values all selected from the same population distribution. Obviously, a researcher wants to find an F ratio larger than the critical F ratio in order to reject H_0 and conclude that a significant difference exists among the groups.

The critical F ratios are shown in Table F in Appendix E. A portion of that table is shown in Table 13.8. To locate a critical F ratio, one needs both the df_a and df_w since they determine the shape of particular F distribution used. The df_a are represented across the top of Table F, and df_w are represented in the rows. Since the chapter example has df_a equal to 2, the second column of F ratios will be used. The row with df_w of 48 would be used. Two critical F ratios are listed, 3.19 and 5.08. The regular-print F ratio (3.19) represents the critical F ratio using the .05 alpha level, whereas the boldfaced F ratio (5.08) represents the critical F ratio for the .01 alpha level. (Remember the alpha level to be used, either .05 or .01, should be chosen before the data are collected.)

Since the .05 level is used in this example, the critical F ratio is 3.19. The calculated F ratio of 14.50 is greater than the critical F ratio and is in the reject-H_0 region of the distribution (see Figure 13.4). Therefore, the researchers can conclude that all three groups did not come from the same population distribution of shock intensity values. Box 13.1 shows the summary tables for the fictitious examples described earlier in the chapter.

Traditionally, the calculated F ratio is reported along with the df_a, df_w,

TABLE 13.8   A Portion of Table F Which Lists the Critical F Ratios

Degrees of Freedom: Denominator	Degrees of Freedom: Numerator														
	1	2	3	4	5	6	7	8	9	10	11	12	14	16	20
1	161 / 4,052	200 / 4,999	216 / 5,403	225 / 5,625	230 / 5,764	234 / 5,859	237 / 5,928	239 / 5,981	241 / 6,022	242 / 6,056	243 / 6,082	244 / 6,106	245 / 6,142	246 / 6,169	248 / 6,208
2	18.51 / 98.49	19.00 / 99.00	19.16 / 99.17	19.25 / 99.25	19.30 / 99.30	19.33 / 99.33	19.36 / 99.34	19.37 / 99.36	19.38 / 99.38	19.39 / 99.40	19.40 / 99.41	19.41 / 99.42	19.42 / 99.43	19.43 / 99.44	19.44 / 99.45
3	10.13 / 34.12	9.55 / 30.82	9.28 / 29.46	9.12 / 28.71	9.01 / 28.24	8.94 / 27.91	8.88 / 27.67	8.84 / 27.49	8.81 / 27.34	8.78 / 27.23	8.76 / 27.13	8.74 / 27.05	8.71 / 26.92	8.69 / 26.83	8.66 / 26.69
⋯				⋯	⋯	⋯					⋯	⋯	⋯		
46	4.05 / 7.21	3.20 / 5.10	2.81 / 4.24	2.57 / 3.76	2.42 / 3.44	2.30 / 3.22	2.22 / 3.05	2.14 / 2.92	2.09 / 2.82	2.04 / 2.73	2.00 / 2.66	1.97 / 2.60	1.91 / 2.50	1.87 / 2.42	1.80 / 2.30
48	4.04 / 7.19	3.19 / 5.08	2.80 / 4.22	2.56 / 3.74	2.41 / 3.42	2.30 / 3.20	2.21 / 3.04	2.14 / 2.90	2.08 / 2.80	2.03 / 2.71	1.99 / 2.64	1.96 / 2.58	1.90 / 2.48	1.86 / 2.40	1.79 / 2.28
50	4.03 / 7.17	3.18 / 5.06	2.79 / 4.20	2.56 / 3.72	2.40 / 3.41	2.29 / 3.18	2.20 / 3.02	2.13 / 2.88	2.07 / 2.78	2.02 / 2.70	1.98 / 2.62	1.95 / 2.56	1.90 / 2.46	1.85 / 2.39	1.78 / 2.26
⋯				⋯	⋯	⋯					⋯	⋯	⋯		
1,000	3.85 / 6.66	3.00 / 4.62	2.61 / 3.80	2.38 / 3.34	2.22 / 3.04	2.10 / 2.82	2.02 / 2.66	1.95 / 2.53	1.89 / 2.43	1.84 / 2.34	1.80 / 2.26	1.76 / 2.20	1.70 / 2.09	1.65 / 2.01	1.58 / 1.89
∞	3.84 / 6.64	2.99 / 4.60	2.60 / 3.78	2.37 / 3.32	2.21 / 3.02	2.09 / 2.80	2.01 / 2.64	1.94 / 2.51	1.88 / 2.41	1.83 / 2.32	1.79 / 2.24	1.75 / 2.18	1.69 / 2.07	1.64 / 1.99	1.57 / 1.87

and the alpha level used. The form is $\underline{F}(df_a, df_w) =$ 'calculated F', $\underline{p} \leq$ (or $\geq$) level. For the chapter example, the researchers might state their findings as, "A significant difference was found in the shock-intensity levels administered among the three groups of college students, $\underline{F}$ (2, 48) = 14.50, $\underline{p} < .05$."

Some journals now require that the researcher substitute the MS_w for the p value. These journals suggest that authors state an alpha level early in their results and use that level for all tests. Any time a finding is described as "significant," the reader knows the particular alpha level used.

By reporting the MS_w, the authors provide the reader with information

---

BOX 13.1 **A Comparison of the Summary Tables for the Two Examples with Fictitious Data**

Earlier in the chapter, data from three samples with six values in each sample were used to demonstrate the partitioning of variability. Listed below are the summary tables for the two examples in this chapter. The top summary table is based on the data from Tables 13.3 and 13.4. These data result in a significant difference.

Source	SS	df	MS	F
Among groups	1,092.00	2	546.00	186.35*
Within groups	44.00	15	2.93	
Total variability	1,136.00	17		

*$p \leq .05$

The summary table below is based on the data "rearranged" in a random order. These data are shown in Table 13.5. No significant difference was found among the samples.

Source	SS	df	MS	F
Among groups	32.33	2	16.16	.22
Within groups	1,103.67	15	73.58	
Total variability	1,136.00	17		

Note. The only identical statistics in both summary tables are SS_{tot} and df. The random ordering of values in the second data set resulted in less variability among groups (reduced systematic variability) and greater variability within groups (increased error variability).

concerning error variability much like researchers who provide the s for samples when reporting descriptive statistics. Using this approach, the authors might state their results as, "A significance level of $\underline{p} \leq .05$ was used for all tests. A one-way analysis of variance revealed a significant difference in the shock-intensity levels administered among the three groups of students, $\underline{F}$ (2, 48) = 14.50, $\underline{MS}_w$ = 154.45."

The researchers still have an additional analysis to complete when a significant difference is found among more than two groups. That analysis will identify which group or groups come from different population distributions. The F ratio tells the researcher that at least one group comes from a population distribution different from the other groups. However, it does not provide the necessary information to know how many or which groups are different.

THE POST HOC COMPARISONS TEST: THE TUKEY HSD TEST

Once it has been determined that the calculated F ratio is significant and the H_0 has been rejected, the researcher can use a post hoc comparisons test to determine which samples or groups are significantly different from each other. Post hoc translates as "after the fact." A post hoc comparisons test can be used only when a significant F ratio has been obtained. A **post hoc comparisons test** involves comparisons of pairs of sample means to determine which samples came from different population distributions. There are several different types of post hoc comparisons tests to choose from including the Duncan, the Newman-Keuls, the Scheffé, and Tukey tests. They all share one common feature—they are designed to maintain the experimentwise error rate at a particular alpha level, often .05 or .01, regardless of the number of samples or comparisons made. They differ in that some are more conservative (have a slightly lower alpha level) than others. The test described in this chapter is referred to as the Tukey HSD (for "honestly significant difference") test.

Once it has been determined that a significant difference exists among the samples, the researcher needs to determine the minimum difference between $\overline{X}$s that is necessary for the researcher to conclude that two samples came from different population distributions. This difference is called the HSD and requires three pieces of information that are used in the following formula:

$$\text{HSD} = q \sqrt{\frac{\text{MS}_w}{\text{N}_k}}. \tag{28}$$

The first is the MS_w used in the calculation of the significant F ratio. From the summary table (Table 13.7), MS_w is 154.45. The second is N_k, the number of values *per* sample if the number of participants is the same for all conditions. This is referred to as an equal-N study. In the chapter example N_k is 17.

If the number of participants is not the same in each condition, an unequal-N study, then the harmonic mean for $\tilde{\text{N}}_k$ must be calculated. The notation $\tilde{N}_k$ will be used as the symbol for the harmonic mean. The calculation of the $\tilde{N}_k$ when there are different N values is

$$\tilde{N}_k = \frac{k}{1/N_1 + 1/N_2 + \cdots + 1/N_k}. \tag{28a}$$

You should note that the calculation of $\tilde{N}_k$ applies only for the Tukey HSD test. It is not necessary to make any adjustments in the calculations for the one-way ANOVA. Those formulas and procedures are identical for equal-N and unequal-N studies.

The last value needed for Formula 28 is the Studentized range statistic. It is referred to as q and is a function of the rejection level being used, the number of samples in the study, and the df_w. The q value is the value that maintains the experimentwise error rate at the level determined by the researcher. These q values are found in Table Q in Appendix E. Table 13.9

TABLE 13.9 A Portion of Table Q Which Lists q, the Studentized Range Statistic

df in Error term	Number of Means to Be Compared										
	2	3	4	5	6	7	8	9	10	11	12
5	3.64	4.60	5.22	5.67	6.03	6.33	6.58	6.80	6.99	7.17	7.32
	5.70	6.98	7.80	8.42	8.91	9.32	9.67	9.97	10.24	10.48	10.70
6	3.46	4.34	4.90	5.30	5.63	5.90	6.12	6.32	6.49	6.65	6.79
	5.24	6.33	7.03	7.56	7.97	8.32	8.61	8.87	9.10	9.30	9.48
7	3.34	4.16	4.68	5.06	5.36	5.61	5.82	6.00	6.16	6.30	6.43
	4.95	5.92	6.54	7.01	7.37	7.68	7.94	8.17	8.37	8.55	8.71
⋮				⋮				⋮			
40	2.86	3.44	3.79	4.04	4.23	4.39	4.52	4.63	4.73	4.82	4.90
	3.82	4.37	4.70	4.93	5.11	5.26	5.39	5.50	5.60	5.69	5.76
60	2.83	3.40	3.74	3.98	4.16	4.31	4.44	4.55	4.65	4.73	4.81
	3.76	4.28	4.59	4.82	4.99	5.13	5.25	5.36	5.45	5.53	5.60
120	2.80	3.36	3.68	3.92	4.10	4.24	4.36	4.47	4.56	4.64	4.71
	3.70	4.20	4.50	4.71	4.87	5.01	5.12	5.21	5.30	5.37	5.44
∞	2.77	3.31	3.63	3.86	4.03	4.17	4.29	4.39	4.47	4.55	4.62
	3.64	4.12	4.40	4.60	4.76	4.88	4.99	5.08	5.16	5.23	5.29

contains a portion of that table. As in Table F, the regular-print values are used for the .05 rejection level and the boldfaced values are used for the .01 level. The columns represent the number of samples to be compared, and df_w is represented along the rows. The same rejection region used for the F ratio should be used for the Tukey HSD test. Since the chapter example has three samples and the closest entry to the example's df_w of 48 is 40, the q for the test is 3.44.

Using this information in Formula 28 provides the following:

$$\mathbf{HSD} = q \sqrt{\frac{MS_w}{N_k}} \tag{28}$$

$$= 3.44 \sqrt{\frac{154.45}{17}}$$
$$= 3.44 \times 3.01$$
$$= 10.35.$$

Any two samples that have a difference between $\overline{X}$s equal to or greater than 10.35 shock intensity values will be presumed to be from different population distributions.

The next step is to compare the $\overline{X}$s of the samples. There are three sample $\overline{X}$s in the chapter example, with the aggressive sample having a $\overline{X}$ shock intensity level of 48.65, followed by the neutral sample with a $\overline{X}$ of 42.00 and the helpful sample with a $\overline{X}$ of 26.29. The differences between $\overline{X}$s should then be calculated.

The difference between the $\overline{X}$ of the aggressive sample and the $\overline{X}$ of the helpful sample is 22.36 shock-intensity values. This difference of 22.36 is greater than the HSD of 10.35. Therefore, the aggressive sample and the helpful sample come from population distributions with different μs. The students in the aggressive sample gave significantly higher levels of shock than the students in the helpful sample.

The next comparison involves the aggressive and neutral samples. This difference in $\overline{X}$s is 6.65 and is less than the HSD of 10.35. Therefore, the probability that these two samples came from the same population distribution is greater than .05. The researchers would conclude that there is no significant difference in the shock intensity levels between the aggressive and neutral samples.

The last comparison involves the neutral sample and the helpful sample. This difference of 15.71 is greater than the HSD of 10.35. Therefore, these two samples are significantly different and we conclude that they came from different population distributions.

The job of the researcher is to interpret the findings of the Tukey HSD test. The findings indicate that the helpful sample is significantly different from the other two samples, which do not differ from each other. The researchers might follow their statement about obtaining a significant difference among conditions (significant F ratio) with the following:

The Tukey HSD test was conducted to identify differences among the conditions. The comparisons revealed that the students in the helpful-word condition administered significantly lower levels of shock than students in the other two conditions. The students in the neutral-word and aggressive-word conditions did not differ significantly in the levels of shock administered.

The researchers' hypothesis has been only partially confirmed. It was predicted that reinforcement of aggressive words would lead to more aggressive behavior. This was not found when the aggressive sample was compared to the neutral sample. However, the hypothesis was confirmed with regard to the reinforcement of helpful words. Students who were reinforced for helpful words significantly reduced their intensity level of shock when compared with students in the neutral sample. The Tukey HSD test identified the significant differences among the samples and completed the procedure used in inferential statistics, which began with the finding of a significant F ratio from the one-way analysis of variance. Let us look at a second example which comes from the area of cognitive psychology.

A SECOND EXAMPLE

Since the early 1970s, considerable time has been devoted to the study of comprehending and understanding textual material. One area of interest has been the importance of context in the comprehension of textual material. It has been assumed that knowing the topic before reading an article would help the reader in understanding and remembering information in an article. In 1972, Bransford and Johnson reported the results of a study in which information about an ambiguous passage was manipulated. Here is the passage they used:

If the balloons popped, the sound wouldn't be able to carry since everything would be too far away from the correct floor. A closed window would also prevent the sound from carrying, since most buildings tend to be well insulated. Since the whole operation depends on a steady flow of electricity, a break in the middle of the wire would also cause problems. Of course, the fellow could shout, but the human voice is not loud enough to carry that far. An additional problem is that a string could break on the instrument. Then there could be no accompaniment to the message. It is clear that the best situation would involve less distance. Then there would be fewer potential problems. With face to face contact, the least number of things could go wrong. (p. 719)

A total of 50 college students heard this passage in groups of 10 students each. One group of students, the no context (1) group, heard the passage once. Another group, the no context (2) group, heard the passage twice. A third group, the partial context group, was shown a picture illustrating part of the passage 30 seconds before the passage was presented. This picture is shown on the right in Figure 13.5. A fourth group, the context before group, was shown a more complete picture 30 seconds before the passage was presented. This picture is shown on the left in Figure 13.5. The fifth group,

FIGURE 13.5 Pictures used in the Bransford and Johnson study (second chapter example). Picture on right was used in the partial-context condition and the picture on the left was used in the context-before and context-after conditions. *Note.* "Contextual Prerequisites for Understanding: Some Investigations of Comprehension and Recall" by J. D. Bransford and M. K. Johnson, 1972, *Journal of Verbal Learning and Verbal Behavior, II,* Figs. 1 and 2, pp. 718–719. Copyright 1972 by the 'Academic Press', Inc. Reprinted by permission.

the context after group, was shown the complete picture for 30 seconds after the passage was presented.

The independent variable is the type of information presented. There are five conditions, two involving no information and three involving the presentation of a picture. The researchers believed that this manipulation would affect the number of ideas the students could recall after hearing the passage. The number of ideas recalled was the dependent variable. Based on previous research, Bransford and Johnson (1972) believed that presenting a picture (topical information) before the passage would help the student comprehend the passage and improve recall. The other conditions served as various types of control groups. The number of ideas each student recalled by condition is shown in Table 13.10.

TABLE 13.10	Number of Ideas Each Student Recalled for the Chapter's Second Example			
Condition				
No context (1)	No context (2)	Partial context	Context before	Context after
4	4	3	8	4
4	4	5	8	3
3	5	4	7	5
4	3	4	8	3
4	3	4	8	3
3	4	5	8	3
3	3	4	8	3
3	3	4	8	4
5	4	4	8	3
3	5	3	9	5

The first step is to summarize and describe the data for each condition. Table 13.11 contains the necessary summary statistics and the $\overline{X}$ and s for each of the five conditions. In Figure 13.6, the graph of the mean number of ideas recalled by condition is shown. A bar graph was used because the independent variable is qualitative. The different conditions cannot be ordered in any definitive sequence. Notice that the $\overline{X}$ number of ideas recalled in the context before condition appears to be greater than in any other condition. To determine if this difference is significant, the researchers can conduct a one-way ANOVA. And, for the sake of example, let us assume that the researchers decided to use an alpha level of $p \leq .01$ for this study.

TESTING FOR DIFFERENCES: ONE-WAY ANOVA

The researchers need to state their statistical hypotheses, H_0 and H_1. The null hypothesis describes the possibility that all five samples come from the same population distribution; that is, the population mean μ is identical for all five samples

$$H_0: \quad \mu_1 = \mu_2 = \mu_3 = \mu_4 = \mu_5.$$

The alternate hypothesis describes the situation in which *at least* one sample comes from a population distribution with a μ different from those for the other samples. Obviously, this hypothesis that describes a difference is more similar to the researchers' hypothesis. Therefore, the researchers want to reject H_0 which would allow them to conclude that H_1 and their research hypothesis were supported.

Figure 13.7 is a diagram of how the total variability can be divided between the variability among groups and the variability within groups. The values in parentheses are the df. Below the diagram is the summary table for

TABLE 13.11   The Summary and Descriptive Statistics for the 5 Conditions in the Second Example

	Condition				
	No context (1)	No context (2)	Partial context	Context before	Context after
$\Sigma X =$	36	38	40	80	36
$\Sigma X^2 =$	134	150	164	642	136
N =	10	10	10	10	10
Using Formula 1: $\overline{X} = \Sigma X/N$					
$\overline{X} =$	3.60	3.80	4.00	8.00	3.60
Using Formula 3: $SS = \Sigma X^2 - (\Sigma X)^2/N$					
SS =	4.40	5.60	4.00	2.00	6.40
Using Formula 4: $s^2 = SS/(N-1)$					
$s^2 =$	.49	.62	.44	.22	.71
Using Formula 5: $s = \sqrt{s^2}$					
s =	.70	.79	.67	.47	.84

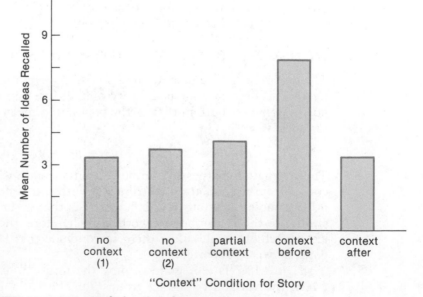

FIGURE 13.6 Bar graph for the chapter example.

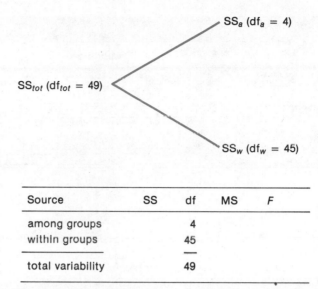

Source	SS	df	MS	F
among groups		4		
within groups		45		
total variability		49		

FIGURE 13.7 Diagram of the partitioning of variability and a partially completed summary table for the second chapter example.

this example, with the df entered into their appropriate places. Table 13.12 contains the necessary information and steps needed to calculate the sum of the squared deviations for each source of variability SS_{tot}, SS_a, and SS_w. Once these values are known then the appropriate mean squared deviations can be calculated by dividing the SS by the appropriate df

$$MS = SS / df. \tag{26}$$

This information is included in the completed summary table shown in Table 13.13. Notice that an F has been calculated by using Formula 27

$$F = \frac{MS_a}{MS_w} \tag{27}$$
$$= \frac{36.40}{0.50}$$
$$= 72.80.$$

To determine if this F ratio is large enough for the researchers to reject H_0, it is necessary to compare it with the critical F ratio from Table F. To use this table we need to know the alpha level and the df_a and df_w. Recall that an alpha level of $p \leq .01$ is being used. The df_a is 4 (for the correct column in Table F) and the df_w is 45 ($df_w = 44$ is used since it is the closest value listed which is less than 45). The critical F ratio is 3.78. The calculated F ratio 72.80 is larger than the critical F ratio. Therefore, the researchers can reject H_0; at least one sample did come from a different population distribution. The Tukey HSD test would be used to identify the differences among the conditions.

TABLE 13.12	Calculation of the Sums of the Squares (SS) for the Second Example					
	Condition					
	No context (1)	No context (2)	Partial context	Context before	Context after	Total
$\Sigma X =$	36	38	40	80	36	230
$\Sigma X^2 =$	134	150	164	642	136	1,226
$N =$	10	10	10	10	10	50

$$\text{Using Formula 23:} \quad SS_{tot} = \Sigma X_{tot}^2 - \frac{(\Sigma X_{tot}^2)}{N_{tot}}$$

$$SS_{tot} = 1{,}226 - \frac{(230)^2}{50}$$

$$= 168$$

$$\text{Using Formula 24:} \quad SS_a = \frac{(\Sigma X_1^2)}{N_1} + \frac{(\Sigma X_2^2)}{N_2} + \cdots + \frac{(\Sigma X_k^2)}{N_k} - \frac{(\Sigma X_{tot}^2)^2}{N_{tot}}$$

$$SS_a = \frac{(36)^2}{10} + \frac{(38)^2}{10} + \frac{(40)^2}{10} + \frac{(80)^2}{10} + \frac{(36)^2}{10} - \frac{(230)^2}{50}$$

$$= 145.6$$

$$\text{Using Formula 25:} \quad SS_w = SS_1 + SS_2 + SS_3 + SS_4 + SS_5$$

$$SS_w = 4.00 + 5.60 + 4.00 + 2.00 + 6.40$$

$$= 22.4$$

IDENTIFYING THE DIFFERENCES: TUKEY HSD TEST

The Tukey HSD test, which is used only when a significant F ratio is obtained, allows the researcher to determine which samples differ from each other. The first step is to determine the minimum mean difference which would allow the researchers to conclude that the two samples came from different population distributions. This difference is called HSD and can be found by using Formula 28

$$\textbf{HSD} = q\sqrt{\frac{MS_w}{N_k}}. \tag{28}$$

The value q can be found in Table Q in Appendix E. The number of conditions determines the appropriate column to use, which in this example is 5. The row is determined by the df_w, which is 45. Because 45 is not listed, we use the closest value less than 45 which is 40. With an alpha level of .01, the same level used for the F ratio, the q value is 4.93. The MS_w can be found in

TABLE 13.13	The Completed ANOVA Summary Table for the Second Example				
Source	**SS**	**df**	**MS**	**F**	
Among groups	145.6	4	36.40	72.80	
Within groups	22.4	45	0.50		
Total variability	168.0	49			

Table 13.13. The number of values *per* sample is represented by N_k, which is 10. Using this information in Formula 28 provides the following:

$$\text{HSD} = q\sqrt{\frac{\text{MS}_w}{\text{N}_k}}$$

$$= 4.93\sqrt{\frac{.50}{10}} \tag{28}$$

$$= 1.10.$$

Once HSD is known, the differences between sample $\overline{X}$s should be calculated. The $\overline{X}$s are shown in Table 13.11. The largest difference, between the no context (1) and the context before groups, is 4.40 and exceeds HSD. Therefore, the two groups are significantly different. In fact the differences in $\overline{X}$s between the context before group and all other groups are greater than the HSD. Therefore, the context before group is significantly different from all other groups. The differences between all other pairs of $\overline{X}$s are less than the HSD. None of these groups are significantly different from one another.

Therefore, the researchers can conclude that the context before group recalled significantly more ideas than the other groups. They might state their conclusion in the following fashion:

A significant difference was found among the five conditions, $\underline{F}(4, 45) = 72.80$, $\underline{p} < .01$. A Tukey HSD test revealed that the context before group recalled significantly more ideas than the other groups. Providing the complete picture before the passage was read significantly aided comprehension and recall relative to presenting no picture, a partial picture, or the complete picture after the passage had been presented. For a picture to aid comprehension it must be complete and be presented before the passage.

SUMMARY Experiments are often designed that involve more than two conditions or levels of the independent variable. In those instances, it is inappropriate to conduct a series of *t* tests comparing all possible pairs of conditions. A series of *t* tests inflates the researcher's alpha level beyond an acceptable value. Instead an analysis of variance, abbreviated ANOVA, is used.

The ANOVA is a test that divides the total variability of all values in the study into two components. One component is based on variability among the different groups. This component is measured by the sum of the squares among groups SS_a and the corresponding mean squared deviation among groups MS_a. The other component represents the variability within the groups. The sum of the squares within groups SS_w and the mean squared deviation within groups MS_w estimate this component of the total variability. The MS_a consists of the systematic variability resulting from the experimenter's manipulation of the independent variable and error variability. The MS_w consists solely of error variability.

A statistic, called the F ratio, compares MS_a to MS_w. The larger the F ratio, the greater the amount of systematic variability in the experiment relative to the error variability. If the calculated F ratio exceeds the critical F ratio, then the researcher can reject H_0, which assumes that all samples were taken from the same population of values. A significant F ratio indicates that the researcher's manipulation of the independent variable had a greater effect on the total variability than the error variability found within the groups.

Once the H_0 is rejected, the researcher should determine which of the samples comes from different populations. The ANOVA establishes that a difference among samples exists, but it does not identify the difference. The Tukey HSD test, is a post hoc comparisons test, that allows the researcher to determine the location of differences among the samples. It is used only when a significant F ratio has already been found.

SUMMARY FOR USING THE ONE-WAY ANOVA

1. Develop the research hypothesis.
2. State the H_0 and H_1, and decide on the alpha level (usually $p \leq .05$ or $p \leq .01$).
3. Calculate the appropriate descriptive statistics, usually $\overline{X}$ and s, for each condition.
4. Organize the necessary summary statistics, ΣX, ΣX^2, and N, for each condition and for the total (the sum of each statistic across conditions).
5. Calculate the three sums of squared deviations, SS_{tot}, SS_a, and SS_w, by using the appropriate formulas

$$\mathbf{SS_{tot}} = \Sigma X_{tot}{}^2 - \frac{(\Sigma X_{tot})^2}{N_{tot}}, \tag{23}$$

$$\mathbf{SS_a} = \frac{(\Sigma X_1)^2}{N_1} + \frac{(\Sigma X_2)^2}{N_2} + \ldots + \frac{(\Sigma X_k)^2}{N_k} - \frac{(\Sigma X_{tot})^2}{N_{tot}}, \tag{24}$$

and

$$\mathbf{SS_w} = SS_1 + SS_2 + \ldots + SS_k. \tag{25}$$

6. Construct a summary table for a one-way ANOVA similar to that shown in Table 13.7. The df_a is equal to $k - 1$ where k is the number of conditions. The df_w equals $N_{tot} - k$. The df_{tot} is equal to $N_{tot} - 1$.

7. Calculate the MS_a by dividing SS_a by df_a, and calculate the MS_w by dividing SS_w by df_w. An F ratio can then be determined by using the following formula:

$$F = \frac{MS_a}{MS_w}.$$ (27)

8. The critical F ratio can be found in Table F. If the F ratio calculated in Formula 27 is equal to or greater than the critical F ratio found in Table F, then the researcher should reject H_0, conclude that at least one sample came from a population distribution different from the other samples, and complete the Tukey HSD test. If the H_0 is not rejected, then the researcher must conclude that the samples could have come from the same population distribution and that the experimental manipulation of the independent variable had no effect on behavior.

9. State your conclusion in sentence form and include the necessary statistical information ($\underline{F}(df_a, df_w)$ = calculated F ratio, $\underline{p} \leq$ or $\geq$ alpha level or $F(df_a, df_w)$ = calculated F ratio, $\underline{MS}_w$ = calculated MS_w).

SUMMARY FOR USING THE TUKEY HSD TEST

1. Use only if a significant F ratio has been found.
2. Order the sample $\overline{X}$s from lowest value to highest value.
3. Calculate the mimimum difference between sample $\overline{X}$s necessary to conclude that the samples come from different populations. This difference is called the HSD and can be determined by using the following formula:

$$HSD = q\sqrt{\frac{MS_w}{N_k}}.$$ (28)

The Studentized range statistic q is found in Table Q (use the same alpha level as was used in the ANOVA). The MS_w can be found from the summary table for the ANOVA. It is the value in the denominator when calculating the F ratio. The number of values in a sample is represented by N_k. If N is not the same in each condition, then calculate the harmonic mean for N, $\tilde{N}_k$

$$\tilde{N}_k = \frac{k}{1/N_1 + 1/N_2 + \cdot\cdot\cdot + 1/N_k}.$$ (28a)

4. Beginning with the two most different sample $\overline{X}$s and then progressing "inward" make all necessary pairwise comparisons of sample $\overline{X}$s. If the difference between $\overline{X}$s is equal to or greater than HSD, then the samples came from different populations.

5. State your conclusions in sentence form. Indicate which samples are significantly different from one another.

EXERCISES

1. A researcher studies the behavior of rats in five different settings. She records the amount of time it takes the rat to locate the food in the particular setting. If she decides, incorrectly, to do a series of t tests, how many will she need to do to make all possible pairwise comparisons? If she uses an alpha level of .01 for rejecting H_0, what is her approximate experimentwise error rate?

2. When conducting a single t test and using a rejection level of $p \leq .05$, (a) what is the experimentwise error rate? the comparison error rate? (b) If six t tests are conducted in the same experiment, what is the approximate experimentwise error rate? the comparison error rate?

3. A fellow student knows that the H_0 in a one-way ANOVA describes the possibility that all samples come from the same population distribution. He reasons, therefore, that the H_1 is all samples that come from different population distributions. Do you agree with his reasoning? Explain.

4. A clinical researcher investigates the effectiveness of four different therapies in treating mood disorders: behavior modification, psychotherapy, group therapy, and drug therapy. He has 20 patients randomly assigned to each of the four conditions ($N_{tot} = 80$). Following four months of therapy, each patient is evaluated by a panel of psychologists who do not know the conditions each patient was in. A rating from 1 to 15 is given, with a high value indicating the presence of the mood disorder. What are the H_0 and H_1 for this study? Which statistical hypothesis would you suspect is consistent with the researcher's hypothesis?

5. In Exercise 4, what are the independent and dependent variables?

6. From the information in Exercise 4, set up the summary table with the information that is available.

7. In theory, it is possible for a researcher to have an SS_{tot} that equals zero. How could that occur? How would it be possible for the SS_a to equal zero? Under what circumstances could the SS_w equal zero?

8. The following statistical information is provided: $F(5, 114) = 2.76$. How many conditions or groups (k) are there in the study? Assuming that each condition has the same number of participants, what is the N per condition?

9. In Exercise 8, should the researcher reject H_0 at the .05 level? at the .01 level? In which situation, if either, would the Tukey HSD be appropriate? If the Tukey is appropriate, then what value(s) would you still have to ask the researcher for in order to determine the HSD?

10. A student tells you that his research hypothesis is that his manipulation will affect behavior differently in the four conditions of his study. Since he is concerned about where the differences are and not whether a difference exists or not, he decides to skip calculating the F ratio and immediately does the Tukey HSD test, once he has the necessary statistics. What are your comments to him?

11. Another student is having trouble with his ANOVA and shows you the following:

	Cond. A	Cond. B	Cond. C	Total
$\Sigma X =$	200	250	180	630
$\Sigma X^2 =$	3700	6325	3300	13325
$N =$	10	10	10	30

He tells you that his $SS_{tot} = 95$ and $SS_a = 260$ and $SS_w = -165$. He knows that it is impossible to get a negative SS, yet $SS_a + SS_w = SS_{tot}$. Can you find the student's error and tell him what he needs to recalculate?

12. A developmental psychologist investigates the number of different toys that children of different ages play with during a 30-minute period alone. There are eight children each in each of the following age groups, 3-year-olds, 5-year-olds, 8-year-olds, and 10-year-olds. She hypothesizes that the older children will be more likely to play with more toys because they will lose interest in each toy sooner than younger children. Draw a diagram similar to that shown in Figure 13.7 that shows the distribution of df and the summary table for this example.

13. In Exercise 12, what are the independent and dependent variables? If the following sample $\overline{X}$s were given, draw the appropriate graph.

	3-year-olds	5-year-olds	8-year-olds	10-year-olds
$\overline{X} =$	9.34	8.65	11.47	13.00

14. Given the information in Exercise 12 and 13 and that $MS_w = 1.80$ and a significant $(p \leq .05)$ F ratio was found, determine the HSD. Conduct the appropriate comparisons and state your conclusion in words with regard to the researcher's hypothesis and what was found.

15. To demonstrate the fact that one can create a summary table from a limited amount of information, complete the entire summary table for a one-way ANOVA with the following: The experiment has five groups with 20 subjects each. The F ratio is 3.18 and $MS_w = 0.95$.

16. A teacher randomly divides his class into three groups of four students each. Each student is asked to write an essay on a particular current issue. One group is provided background information from an encyclopedia. Another group is given information from a recent news magazine.

The third group watches a videotaped presentation on the topic. Each student's essay is graded by another teacher in terms of the number of ideas incorporated within the essay. The following data are obtained:

Encyclopedia	News Magazine	Videotaped Presentation
2	4	2
3	3	2
3	6	1
4	6	3

Determine if a signficant difference exists among the three conditions. Use the $p < .05$ rejection level. If a significant difference is found, what type of decision error might you be making? If appropriate, conduct a Tukey HSD test.

17. A psychologist finds a significant difference among conditions, $F(4, 50) = 2.63$, $p < .05$. The conditions differ in terms of the temperature at which workers complete a manual task. The amount of time (in minutes) to complete the task is the dependent variable. Knowing that $MS_w = 20.17$ and that an equal number of workers participated in each condition, what is the minimum difference in $\overline{X}$s needed between any two samples to conclude that the samples come from different populations? Using the information shown below, describe any significant differences:

	30°	50°	70°	90°	110°
$\overline{X} =$	43.45	30.21	28.75	36.11	44.77

18. Given the information below in each case, complete the necessary information:
   a. $df_w = 60$, $k = 5$, $N_{tot} = ?$, $df_{tot} = ?$
   b. $F = 3.55$, $SS_a = 7.83$, $k = 4$, $N_{tot} = 110$, $MS_w = ?$, $SS_{tot} = ?$

19. An F ratio of 1.00 is found. Is that unexpected if the H_0 is really true? What does an F ratio indicate about the relative values of the systematic and error variability?

20. A researcher has an experiment with two conditions, an experimental condition and a control condition. Instead of doing a t test for independent samples, the researcher conducts a one-way ANOVA. A significant F ratio is obtained. Should the researcher conduct a Tukey HSD test? Explain.

CHALLENGE QUESTIONS

1. A researcher was interested in testing the possibility of reducing stress in women who were recently diagnosed as having breast cancer. Seven of the women were assigned to a biofeedback group, five to a cognitive therapy group, and seven to a no-treatment control group. Following treatment in the group, each woman completed a questionnaire to measure her level of anxiety. The scores are reported below. A high score indicates a high level of stress and anxiety. (Based on Davis, H., IV. (1986). Effects of biofeedback and cognitive therapy on stress in patients with breast cancer. *Psychological Reports, 59*, 967–974).

Type of Treatment		
Biofeedback	*Cognitive therapy*	*No treatment*
29	35	32
32	32	40
35	29	24
26	27	26
24	37	38
30		35
27		28

2. It has been suggested numerous times that the moon influences behavior especially on nights when it is full. To determine the level of belief in this "lunar effect," researchers sampled three types of individuals concerning their belief in lunar effects. Police officers, psychiatric personnel, and pedestrians in a park were interviewed. Each person completed a questionnaire which contained a series of statements with which a person indicated agreement or disagreement. The higher the score the greater the belief in the lunar effect. The scores are shown below. (Based on Rotton, J., Kelly, I. W., & Elortegui, P. (1986). Assessing belief in lunar effects: Known-groups validation. *Psychological Reports, 59*, 171–174.)

Group		
Pedestrian	Psychiatric personnel	Police
12	9	20
4	10	18
7	8	15
8	11	13
7	7	10
9	8	12
11	16	11
15	4	6
8	11	13
0	13	14
8	4	7
9	12	10
12	6	13
13	15	8
12	10	7

For Each Question Answer the Following:

   a.   What is a plausible research hypothesis?

   b.   What are the H_0 and H_1?

   c.   Calculate the appropriate descriptive statistics and graph the means.

   d.   Calculate the appropriate inferential statistic. Use an alpha level of .05 for Question 1 and .01 for Question 2.

   e.   State your findings in the proper format and provide a written conclusion about the findings (relating the inferential statistics to the descriptive statistics).

The Factorial Analysis
of Variance

TERMS DISCUSSED

factorial experiment

main effects

interaction effects

cell means

PROCEDURES DESCRIBED

graphing and interpreting an
interaction

calculating the F ratio for the factorial
ANOVA

Since the 1960s, psychologists have been interested in identifying the effect of the environment on eating behavior. Schachter (1971) conducted a number of studies looking at the effects of various environmental cues on eating behavior of normal and obese individuals. His primary hypothesis was that obese individuals were more likely to be influenced by environmental cues than individuals of normal weight. Normal individuals, on the other hand, would be more likely to attend to internal body cues signalling hunger.

In one study on eating behavior, Schachter and Gross asked male students to participate in a study on "the relation between physiological reactions and psychological characteristics" (1968, p. 99). The students were tested individually in a small windowless room. The students were either of normal weight or obese (more than 15% over normal weight for their age and build). During the first five minutes of the study, the researcher attached wires to the student to record physiological information. For 30 minutes the student was left alone and watched a record of his heart rate and galvanic skin response (GSR) on a recording machine. The only other thing the student could do during this time was think and watch a clock on the wall.

Schachter and Gross (1968) manipulated the speed of the clock. For half of the students the clock was moving at twice the normal speed. Even though only 30 minutes had passed, the clock showed that 60 minutes had passed. For the remainder of the students, the clock moved at half the normal speed. The clock showed that 15 minutes had passed, when actually 30 minutes had passed.

After the actual passage of 30 minutes, the experimenter returned and asked the student to complete a psychological test. The experimenter also brought a box of crackers for the student to eat if he so desired. The experimenter left the student alone for an additional 10 minutes, during which time the clock either ran fast or slow again. Then the experimenter returned, removed the crackers, and asked the student to fill out several questionnaires. The experiment always began at 5:00 P.M. and ended at 5:50 P.M. in real time. For students in the fast condition, the clock ran fast and showed 6:20 P.M. at the end of the study. For students in the slow condition, the clock showed 5:35 P.M.

Schachter and Gross (1968) believed that the obese individuals would be influenced by the environmental cue—the time on the clock. Because the clock in the fast condition, showed that the study was carrying over into the dinner hour, they would be more likely to eat than the obese individuals who saw the clock move slowly. Schachter and Gross believed that the individuals of normal weight would be unaffected by the change in time, because they pay more attention to internal body signals than to external cues such as time. The way Schachter and Gross measured eating behavior, was quite ingenious. They measured the weight of the crackers each student ate. The weight of the crackers was measured in grams for each student. The data are shown in Table 14.1.

TABLE 14.1 The Amount of Crackers Eaten (in Grams) for Each Student in the Chapter Example

Weight of Student			
Normal		Obese	
Slow clock	Fast clock	Slow clock	Fast clock
37	34	9	18
19	0	11	61
62	0	3	25
58	34	8	33
23	0	42	53
61	0	49	8
24	8	12	44
42	22	9	23
62	4	8	47
14	37	23	48
55	37	45	53

In this study, the researchers have two independent variables. The first is the manipulation of time, the clock either ran fast or slow. These two time conditions, fast and slow, are the levels of this independent variable. The second independent variable is technically a quasi-independent variable because the researchers could not randomly assign students to the conditions. This variable was the weight of the students who served in the study. The students were either normal in weight or obese. Normal and obese are the levels of the second independent variable. The dependent variable was the weight of the crackers eaten by the students.

This study is different from previous studies because there are two independent variables that are combined to produce four conditions. Two of the conditions involved students of normal weight who saw the clock either move slowly or quickly. The other two conditions had obese individuals who saw a fast or slow clock. Schachter and Gross (1968) combined the two levels of each independent variable, which resulted in a study with four conditions. Combining independent variables in a study like this results in a factorial experiment.

In a **factorial experiment** each level of an independent variable is combined with every level of another independent variable to create the conditions in the experiment. This procedure of combining levels of the independent variables results in a matrix of conditions. The number of conditions that one gets can be determined by multiplying the levels of each independent variable together. For instance, in the chapter example each independent variable has two levels. Therefore, this study has four conditions (2 levels × 2 levels = 4 conditions).

In Box 14.1, the matrix of conditions for this study and for two other example studies are shown. Factorial experiments are often described in terms of the levels of the independent variables. The chapter example is described as a 2×2, or two-by-two factorial experiment. The middle example in Box 14.1 is a 2×4 factorial experiment and the bottom example is a 3×3 experiment.

The number of integers indicates the number of independent variables. Each example in Box 14.1 has two independent variables. A $2 \times 2 \times 2$ factorial experiment describes a study with three independent variables. The values of the integers indicate the levels of each independent variable. For the $2 \times 2 \times 2$ experiment, each independent variable has two levels. The total number of conditions in the study would be eight ($2 \times 2 \times 2 = 8$).

A factorial experiment allows the researcher to determine the effect of each independent variable on the dependent variable. The effect of an independent variable on the dependent variable is referred to as a **main effect**.

Box 14.1   Three Examples of Factorial Experiments

2×2 EXPERIMENT—THE CHAPTER EXAMPLE

independent variables: weight of the subjects (quasi-independent) speed of the clock

dependent variable: amount of crackers eaten

		Speed of the Clock	
		Slow	*Fast*
Subject's weight	Normal		
	Obese		

2×4 EXPERIMENT—STUDENTS WRITE AN ESSAY ABOUT A RANDOMLY ASSIGNED TOPIC

independent variables: Sex of the student (quasi-independent) topic of the assigned paper

dependent variable: length of the essay

The chapter example has two potential main effects—the effect of the weight of the student and the effect of time on eating behavior.

The factorial experiment also permits the researcher to investigate the effect of combining independent variables. The effect of the independent variables together on the dependent variable is called the **interaction effect.** An interaction effect indicates that the effect of one independent variable (on the dependent variable) depends on the level of the other independent variable.

For instance, in this study the researchers' hypothesis predicts an interaction effect. Schachter and Gross (1968) believe that the speed of the clock (one independent variable) will have an effect on the eating behavior of obese individuals (one level of the other independent variable), but not on the eating behavior of individuals of normal weight (the other level of the second independent variable).

Factorial experiments often more accurately represent real life because more than one aspect of the situation is changing. In real life our behavior is

		Topic assigned to the student			
		Gun Control	Abortion	Economy	Death Penalty
Student's sex	Female				
	Male				

3 × 3 EXPERIMENT—STUDY ON THE EFFECTIVENESS OF DIFFERENT THERAPIES FOR DIFFERENT PHOBIAS

independent variables: type of phobia (Quasi-independent) type of therapy
dependent variable: rated cure by independent therapist

		Type of Therapy		
		Implosive	Desensitization	Group
Phobia	Acrophobia			
	Fear of snakes			
	Claustrophobia			

often determined by several factors, not just one. A factorial experiment is more complicated to conduct but it provides the researcher with information about how variables combine to influence behavior. More time will be spent on interactions once we've calculated the necessary descriptive statistics.

DESCRIPTIVE STATISTICS: DESCRIBING THE SAMPLE DATA

As in previous chapters, the first thing for the researcher to do is calculate an appropriate measure of central tendency and a measure of variability. Table 14.2 provides the necessary summary statistics along with the calculations for the $\overline{X}$ and s.

Rather than presenting the statistics in a graph, which would also be appropriate in this example, the statistics are presented in a table. Table 14.3 demonstrates how descriptive statistics are presented in a manuscript under

TABLE 14.2   Summary Information and Descriptive Statistics for the Chapter Example

Type of Student			
Normal		Obese	
Slow clock	Fast clock	Slow clock	Fast clock
$\Sigma X = 457$ $\Sigma X^2 = 22{,}593$ $N = 11$	$\Sigma X = 176$ $\Sigma X^2 = 5{,}614$ $N = 11$	$\Sigma X = 219$ $\Sigma X^2 = 7{,}283$ $N = 11$	$\Sigma X = 413$ $\Sigma X^2 = 18{,}419$ $N = 11$
Using Formula 1: $\overline{X} = \Sigma X/N$			
$\overline{X} = 41.55$	$\overline{X} = 16.00$	$\overline{X} = 19.91$	$\overline{X} = 37.55$
Using Formula 3: $SS = \Sigma X^2 - (\Sigma X)^2/N$			
$SS = 3{,}606.73$	$SS = 2{,}798.$	$SS = 2{,}922.91$	$SS = 2{,}912.73$
Using Formula 4: $s^2 = SS/(N - 1)$			
$s^2 = 360.67$	$s^2 = 279.80$	$s^2 = 292.29$	$s^2 = 291.27$
Using Formula 5: $s = \sqrt{s^2}$			
$s = 18.99$	$s = 16.73$	$s = 17.10$	$s = 17.07$

TABLE 14.3 Example of a Table Prepared for a Scientific Journal

TABLE 1 Mean Weight (in grams) of Crackers Consumed by Students

		Speed of the Clock		
Student's wgt.	Statistic	Slow	Fast	Wgt. overall
Normal	$\overline{X}$	41.55	16.00	28.77
	s	18.99	16.73	21.81
	N	11	11	22
Obese	$\overline{X}$	19.91	37.55	28.73
	s	17.10	17.07	18.96
	N	11	11	22
Time Overall	$\overline{X}$	30.73	26.77	
	s	20.82	19.84	
	N	22	22	

review for many scientific journals. Researchers often prepare tables for presenting descriptive information in research articles. The title of the table should provide information about the dependent variable of the study. The rows and columns describe the levels of the independent variables in a factorial experiment. Researchers list, at the minimum, the measure of central tendency for each condition. And, often a measure of variability will be included as is the case in Table 14.3. Notice that overall, obese and normal individuals ate approximately the same amount of crackers (shown in the last column of Table 14.3). These two $\overline{X}$ values of 28.77 and 28.73 indicate *overall* that normal-weight and obese students ate approximately the same amount of crackers. The last row of Table 14.3 provides an estimate of the effect of time overall. Students in the slow condition ate slightly more crackers, $\overline{X} =$ 30.73 gm, than those in the fast condition, $\overline{X} = 26.77$ gm.

Both of these comparisons involve the main effects of the independent variables. By looking at the margin means, those means in the margins on the right and on the bottom, the researcher can note the main effect of each independent variable. To determine if an interaction may be present, the researcher is best advised to graph the means of each condition. In all cases, an ANOVA is then conducted to determine if the differences observed are significant.

GRAPHING AN INTERACTION FOR DESCRIPTIVE PURPOSES

An easy way to represent an interaction is to graph the means of each condition. The means of each condition are often referred to as **cell means.** A cell represents a condition. In the chapter example, there are four conditions or cells. When a factorial experiment is represented in a matrix form, each condition represents a cell.

When graphing an interaction, the dependent variable is always on the *y*-axis. As a general rule, the independent variable with the greater number of levels is put on the *x*-axis or if one independent variable is on a nominal scale of measurement, then the nominal variable is put on the *x*-axis. In some instances, the researcher may feel that it makes more intuitive sense to violate this rule. It is ultimately up to the researcher, because the graph is primarily an aid to help him to interpret the interaction and is often not reported graphically in the final research report. The second independent variable is represented by separate lines in the graph. A separate line is used to represent each level of this independent variable.

For the chapter example, the amount of crackers eaten, the dependent variable is represented on the *y*-axis. Since both independent variables have two levels, but the speed of the clock is quantitative, speed of the clock is placed on the *x*-axis. The other independent variable, the weight of the student, is represented as two separate lines, one for normal-weight students and one for obese students. In Figure 14.1, the interaction for the chapter example is shown. Notice that the two lines cross. They are not parallel. An interaction exists when the lines in the graph are not parallel, although they need not cross.

These data in Figure 14.1 appear to partially support the researchers' hypothesis. Obese individuals appear to eat more crackers when the clock is fast, seeming to run into the dinner hour, than when the clock is slow. Normal-weight individuals appear to behave in the opposite fashion, eating fewer crackers when the clock is fast. This second finding was not predicted by the researchers, but may be explained by the fact that several of the normal-

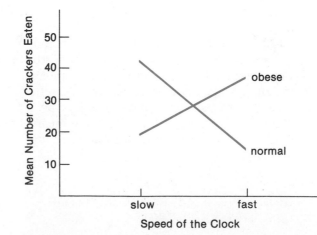

FIGURE 14.1 **Line graph of the mean number of crackers eaten in the chapter example.**

weight individuals in the fast condition of the Schachter and Gross (1968) study mentioned that they did not want to eat any crackers because the crackers might spoil their appetites for dinner.

Figure 14.2 contains three additional graphs of factorial experiments. Notice that in the top two graphs, no interaction is indicated because the lines are parallel. In the top example, the independent variables are the student's sex and the word list used. There seems to be a main effect for the variable on the *x*-axis, the word list used, because the slope of the lines is not zero.

Example A—Effect of the student's sex and word list on recall

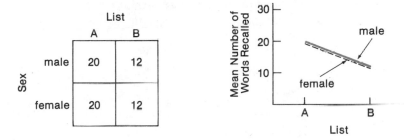

Example B—Effect of type of class and time of class on test scores

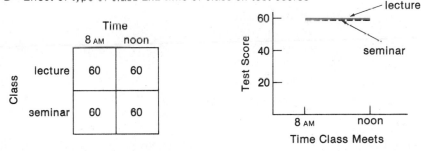

Example C—Effect of the attractiveness of the student and the attractiveness of the date on a student's willingness to date

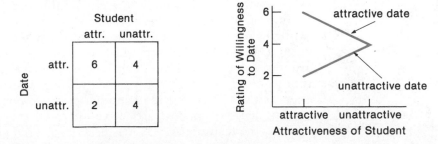

FIGURE 14.2 Three examples of factorial experiments.

The margin means for the columns are different: List A was easier than List B. The fact that the two lines are close to each other indicates no main effect for the other independent variable, the sex of the student. The margin means for the rows are the same.

In the middle example, the independent variables are the time a class meets and the type of class. The researcher is interested in determining if either variable is related to test scores. There are no main effects present. The marginal means are identical. And, because the lines are parallel, there is no interaction effect.

The bottom example is a study in which the attractiveness of the student in the study and the attractiveness of a potential date are the independent variables. Students are rated in terms of their own attractiveness, a quasi-independent variable, and then are shown the picture of either an attractive or unattractive person of the opposite sex. The students then individually rate their willingness to ask this other person out on a date using a 1-to-8 scale with 8 representing "very willing."

The graph in Figure 14.2 shows a potential interaction effect along with a possible main effect for the independent variable represented by the lines, the attractiveness of the date. This effect is demonstrated by the finding that the "attractive" line is above the "unattractive" line. Photos of the attractive date were given a $\overline{X}$ rating of 5, the marginal mean for the top row of the matrix, whereas those of the unattractive date received a $\overline{X}$ rating of 3, the marginal mean of the bottom row.

In terms of describing the interaction, students who perceived themselves as being attractive were more willing to date an attractive person than an unattractive one. On the other hand, students who perceived themselves as being unattractive showed no difference in their preferences.

In a factorial experiment, main effects and interaction effects are independent of each other. It is possible to get any combination of main and interaction effects. The main effects indicate overall effects of the independent variables. The interaction describes the combined effects of the independent variables.

In most instances, the presence of an interaction effect is the more interesting finding for the researcher. An interaction effect means that the researcher must discuss the combined effect of both variables in order to describe the behavior. For instance, in the chapter example, the researchers must report that the time of the clock influences eating behavior *differently* for normal-weight and obese students. A fast clock increases obese students' eating behavior and decreases normal-weight students' eating behavior. Likewise, in the bottom example of Figure 14.2 it is necessary to talk about the attractiveness of the subject and the attractiveness of the person in the picture in order to describe a person's willingness to date another person. The effect of the attractiveness of another person on one's willingness to date that person, depends on how attractive one perceives oneself to be. In the next section, the factorial ANOVA is described. This is used in determining if an interaction effect and the main effects are significant.

INFERENTIAL STATISTICS: TESTING FOR MAIN AND INTERACTION EFFECTS

As was the case in Chapter 13, when the researcher has interval or ratio data and more than two conditions, an ANOVA is the appropriate test to conduct. Because there is more than one independent variable, the one-way ANOVA is inappropriate. The test in this case is a factorial ANOVA. The principles and rationale behind the test are the same as those for the one-way ANOVA. In the factorial ANOVA, the total variability is divided into variability among the conditions and variability within the conditions. However, because the variability among groups results from more than one independent variable, it is necessary to further differentiate the variability among groups.

PARTITIONING THE VARIABILITY

The variability in a factorial ANOVA can be divided into the variability resulting from the researcher's manipulation, the independent variables, and error variability, which is measured by the variability within groups. In the top diagram of Figure 14.3, the total variability as measured by SS_{tot} is partitioned into the variability among groups SS_a and the variability within groups SS_w. For a factorial experiment with two independent variables, the SS_a is further partitioned into SS_{rows}, SS_{col}, and $SS_{r \times c}$. The variability explained by the independent variable shown in the rows of a factorial matrix is represented by SS_{rows}. Likewise, SS_{col} represents the variability resulting from the independent variable in the columns of the factorial matrix. The systematic variability resulting from the main effects of the two respective independent variables is accounted for by SS_{rows} and SS_{col}. The systematic variability resulting from the combination of the two independent variables, which is the interaction effect, is represented by $SS_{r \times c}$. Therefore, in a factorial experiment the variability among groups is divided into variability resulting from main effects of the independent variables and interaction effects.

In the bottom diagram of Figure 14.3, the variability for the chapter example is divided into the appropriate components. The assignment of the independent variables to rows and columns is based on the matrix in Box 14.1 and Table 14.3; the rows representing the weight of the subjects and the columns representing the speed of the clock.

STATING THE H_0 AND H_1 FOR THE FACTORIAL ANOVA

Since the factorial ANOVA for two independent variables involves an analysis of the main effects of two independent variables and an interaction effect, there are three sets of H_0 and H_1. Two sets of the hypotheses deal with the main effects and the third deals with the interaction.

The description of the H_0 and H_1 for the main effects is the same as for

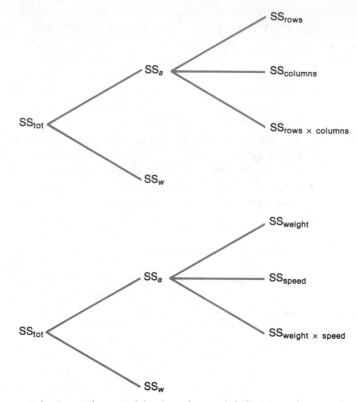

FIGURE 14.3 Diagrams for partitioning the variability in a factorial experiment. The top diagram describes the general model and the bottom diagram describes the chapter example.

the effect of the independent variable in the one-way ANOVA, except that it is stated in specific terms for each of the independent variables. For instance, the H_0 for the main effect of the independent variable represented in the rows would be that the values represented in each *entire* row of the matrix were all selected from the same population distribution

$$H_0: \mu_{row(1)} = \mu_{row(2)} = \cdots = \mu_{row(i)}.$$

The subscript i represents the number of rows, which is the levels of the independent variable described by the rows. For the chapter example, the H_0 for rows could be stated as

$$H_0: \mu_{normal} = \mu_{obese}.$$

Similarly, the H_0 for the independent variable described by the columns would be

$$H_0: \mu_{column(1)} = \mu_{column(2)} = \cdots = \mu_{column(j)}.$$

The j refers to the number of columns in the matrix. For the chapter example, H_0 for columns is

$$H_0 : \mu_{slow} = \mu_{fast}.$$

For both main effects, the H_1 assumes that at least one sample in the respective rows or columns came from a different population distribution,

H_1 for rows: At least one sample represented by the rows came from a different population distribution.

H_1 for columns: At least one sample represented by the columns came from a different population distribution.

The H_0 and H_1 for the interaction effect are best described in words. If you recall from the previous discussion on interaction, an interaction occurs when the lines in the graph are not parallel. This indicates that the pattern of results differs depending on the levels of the independent variables. If no interaction occurs, then the pattern of differences that occur at one level of an independent variable will be the same as for all other levels of the independent variable. Notice that this statement does not imply that there are no differences. Rather, it indicates that the *pattern* of differences found for one independent variable will be the same for each level of the other independent variable. For instance, if there is a difference in the μs for normal students between the fast and slow conditions, then the same difference in μs will be found for obese students

$$\mu_{normal,\ fast} - \mu_{normal,\ slow} = \mu_{obese,\ fast} - \mu_{obese,\ slow}.$$

The general form of the statistical hypotheses in terms of population distributions is,

H_0 : The pattern of μ differences found for one independent variable at one level of the second independent variable will be the same as the pattern of differences for all other levels of the second independent variable.

H_1 : The patterns of μ differences for one independent variable will differ depending on the level of the second independent variable.

The H_1 for the interaction from the chapter example could be described as

$$\mu_{normal,\ fast} - \mu_{normal,\ slow} \neq \mu_{obese,\ fast} - \mu_{obese,\ slow}.$$

Therefore, in a factorial experiment with two independent variables there are three statistical hypotheses to test—two for potential main effects (one for each independent variable) and one for a possible interaction effect.

PARTITIONING THE SUM OF THE SQUARED DEVIATIONS (SS)

The testing of each statistical hypothesis involves the calculation of an F ratio. For the testing of all hypotheses, the appropriate error term (the denominator in calculating the F ratio) is MS_w, the mean squared deviations within groups. As described in Chapter 13, the MS_w contains only error variability. It is based on the variability within each group and will be the same for the tests of the main effects and the interaction effect.

Different MS values must be calculated for the main effects and the interaction. In each case, the appropriate MS will contain systematic variability related to the particular effect (either main or interaction) and error variability. If the F ratio formed by dividing this MS by MS_w is significant, then the researcher can conclude that the manipulation had an effect on behavior and the relevant H_0 can be rejected.

The Summary Table for a Factorial ANOVA

Organization is again critical in calculating the needed inferential statistics. Figure 14.4 contains the general diagram for the factorial ANOVA. Below it is the summary table that must be completed. In addition to SS_{tot}, the table contains all sources of variability based on the rightmost branching of the diagram. Note that there are two main effects and the interaction effect, in addition to the variability within groups. The most difficult part of completing the summary table involves the calculation of the various SS components. The best approach is to begin calculating SS components at the left of the diagram in Figure 14.4 and work your way to the right.

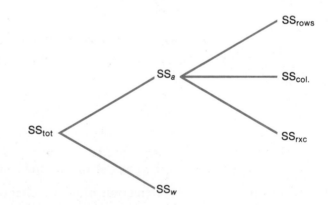

Source	SS	df	MS	F
row (R) effect	(Formula 30)	Rows − 1	SS_{rows}/df_{rows}	MS_{rows}/MS_w
column (C) effect	(Formula 31)	Cols. − 1	$SS_{col.}/df_{col.}$	$MS_{col.}/MS_w$
R X C effect	(Formula 32)	df_{rows}X $df_{col.}$	SS_{rxc}/df_{rxc}	MS_{rxc}/MS_w
within groups	(Formula 25)	$N_{tot} − k$	SS_w/df_w	
total variability	(Formula 23)	$N_{tot} − 1$		

FIGURE 14.4 Diagram and summary table for the factorial ANOVA.

Calculating the Appropriate SS Values

Table 14.4 contains the necessary summary statistics for completing a factorial ANOVA with two independent variables. The values inside the four cells represent summary information already calculated for the descriptive statistics (see Table 14.2). The values in the row and column margins are the sums across each respective row and column. The values in the lower right-hand corner are the summary statistics for the total variability. The values in the row margins, as well as those in the column margins, should sum to equal the total variability. It is a good practice to verify that the values and sums are correct before proceeding any further. To make the calculations more manageable, it is assumed that all cells have the same number of values N_k. Having cells with equal Ns also helps the researcher to meet the assumptions of the ANOVA, which are discussed later in this chapter. There are other sources (see Keppel, 1973) to help analyze studies with unequal-n studies.

You will notice that some of the calculations are quite similar to those used in Chapter 13. The first step is to calculate the SS_{tot}, which involves the use of Formula 23

$$SS_{tot} = \Sigma X_{tot}^2 - \frac{(\Sigma X_{tot})^2}{N_{tot}}. \tag{23}$$

Using the data from Table 14.4 for the chapter example provides the following:

$$SS_{tot} = 53,909 - \frac{1,265^2}{44}$$
$$= 17,540.25.$$

The calculation of the SS_a involves the use of Formula 29. The only difference between Formula 24 used in Chapter 13 is that Formula 29 takes advantage of the common denominator n (because each cell has the same number of values). The number of "cells" in the matrix is represented by k. For the chapter example $k = 4$. Formula 29 is

$$SS_a = \frac{(\Sigma X_1)^2 + (\Sigma X_2)^2 + \cdots + (\Sigma X_k)^2}{N_k} - \frac{(\Sigma X_{tot})^2}{N_{tot}}. \tag{29}$$

Using the data from Table 14.5 for the chapter example provides the following:

$$SS_a = \frac{457^2 + 176^2 + 219^2 + 413^2}{11} - \frac{1,265^2}{44}$$
$$= 41,668.64 - 36,368.75$$
$$= 5,299.89.$$

The calculation of the variability within groups is identical to that used in the one-way ANOVA and involves the use of Formula 25

$$SS_w = SS_1 + SS_2 + \cdots + SS_k \tag{25}$$
$$= 3,606.73 + 2,798.00 + 2,922.91 + 2,912.72$$
$$= 12,240.36.$$

TABLE 14.4   The Summary Statistics for the Chapter Example (Cell Values Are in Bold Print)

		Speed of the Clock		
		Slow	Fast	Wgt overall
Normal	ΣX	**457**	**176**	$\Sigma X_{row\ 1} = 633$
	ΣX^2	**22,593**	**5,614**	$\Sigma X_{row\ 1}{}^2 = 28,207$
	SS	**3,606.73**	**2,798.00**	
	N_k	**11**	**11**	$N_{row\ 1} = 22$
STUDENT'S WEIGHT				
Obese	ΣX	**219**	**413**	$\Sigma X_{row\ 2} = 632$
	ΣX^2	**7,283**	**18,419**	$\Sigma X_{row\ 2}{}^2 = 25,702$
	SS	**2,922.91**	**2,912.72**	
	N_k	**11**	**11**	$N_{row\ 2} = 22$
Time Overall		$\Sigma X_{col\ 1} = 676$	$\Sigma X_{col\ 2} = 589$	$\Sigma X_{tot} = 1,265$
		$\Sigma X_{col\ 1}{}^2 = 29,876$	$\Sigma X_{col\ 2}{}^2 = 24,033$	$\Sigma X_{tot}{}^2 = 53,909$
		$N_{col\ 1} = 22$	$N_{col\ 2} = 22$	$N_{tot} = 44$

As the first check in our calculation of the SSs, the following should be true:

$$\mathbf{SS_{tot}} = SS_a + SS_w$$
$$17,540.25 = 5,299.89 + 12,240.36.$$

The procedures in this chapter involve partitioning SS_a into the SSs for the two main effects and the interaction effect.

Determining the three SSs for the rightmost branching in the diagram of Figure 14.4 is fairly easy. Calculating the SS for each main effect involves the use of the totals in the margins. The interaction is determined by subtraction. Let us look at the SS for the independent variable described by the rows.

To calculate the SS for the "row" main effect, the totals in the rightmost column are used. Formula 30 is used

$$SS_{rows} = \frac{(\Sigma X_{row\ 1})^2 + (\Sigma X_{row\ 2})^2 + \cdots + (\Sigma X_{row\ i})^2}{N\ (per\ row)} - \frac{(\Sigma X_{tot})^2}{N_{tot}}. \quad (30)$$

The rows for the chapter example represent the independent variable of weight of the student. There are two values—normal and obese. Using Formula 30 for the chapter example results in

$$SS_{rows} = \frac{633^2 + 632^2}{22} - \frac{1,265^2}{44}$$
$$= 36,368.77 - 36,368.75$$
$$= .02.$$

The calculation of the SS for the columns follows the same procedure, except that the column totals rather than the row totals are used. Formula 31 provides the SS for the independent variable represented in the columns

$$SS_{col} = \frac{(\Sigma X_{col\ 1})^2 + (\Sigma X_{col\ 2})^2 + \cdots + (\Sigma X_{col\ j})^2}{N\ (per\ column)} - \frac{(\Sigma X_{tot})^2}{N_{tot}}. \qquad (31)$$

The columns represent the levels of the second independent variable—the speed of the clock. Using the summary statistics from Table 14.4 in Formula 31 provides

$$SS_{col} = \frac{676^2 + 589^2}{22} - \frac{1{,}265^2}{44}$$
$$= 36{,}540.77 - 36{,}368.75$$
$$= 172.02.$$

To calculate the $SS_{r \times c}$, the sum of the squared deviations for the interaction, one can subtract the SSs for the rows and columns from the SS_a. As can be seen in the diagram in Figure 14.4, the SSs for the main effects and interaction effect must sum to equal the SS_a. The SS for the interaction contains variability that cannot be explained by either main effect. The formula for calculating $SS_{r \times c}$ is

$$SS_{r \times c} = SS_a - SS_{rows} - SS_{col}. \qquad (32)$$

In the chapter example, this formula results in

$$SS_{r \times c} = 5{,}299.89 - 0.02 - 172.02$$
$$= 5{,}127.85.$$

Calculating the F Ratios

Once the $SS_{r \times c}$ has been calculated, all of the variability components will have been determined. The next step is to calculate the MS for each component. Figure 14.4 shows the necessary calculations. In each case the SS is divided by the appropriate df. The df_{rows} is equal to the number of rows minus 1. Similarly, df_{col} equals the number of columns minus 1. In each case, the df for the main effect of an independent variable is equal to the number of levels

TABLE 14.5	The Completed ANOVA Summary Table for the Chapter Example			
Source	**SS**	**df**	**MS**	**F**
Student's weight	.02	1	.02	.00
Speed of clock	172.02	1	172.02	.56
Weight × speed	5,127.85	1	5,127.85	16.76
Within groups	12,240.36	40	306.01	
Total variability	17,540.25	43		

of that variable minus 1. The $df_{r \times c}$ is found by multiplying the dfs for the two main effects. Therefore,

$$df_{r \times c} = df_{rows} \times df_{col}.$$

The F ratios for each main effect and the interaction effect can be determined by dividing the appropriate MS by the MS_w, which serves as the error

---

BOX 14.2   **A Comparison of the Summary Tables for the One-Way and Factorial ANOVAS**

To illustrate the differences between a one-way ANOVA and a factorial ANOVA, assume that a problem-solving experiment with six groups is conducted. The groups result from the factorial combination of the information provided (none, or the algebraic rule for solving the problem, or an example of a similar problem that has been solved) and the imposition of a speed instruction (no instruction, or subjects are told that speed in completing the problem is important). The time in minutes it takes to solve the problem is the dependent variable. Three students serve in each condition and the following table shows the data:

Speed Instruction	Information Provided			
	None	Rule	Example	Row $\overline{X}$
Yes	10, 9, 14 $\overline{X} = 11$	3, 2, 4 $\overline{X} = 3$	3, 1, 5 $\overline{X} = 3$	$\overline{X} = 5.67$
No	6, 7, 14 $\overline{X} = 9$	13, 13, 10 $\overline{X} = 12$	8, 13, 9 $\overline{X} = 10$	$\overline{X} = 10.33$
COLUMN $\overline{X}$	$\overline{X} = 10$	$\overline{X} = 7.50$	$\overline{X} = 6.50$	

If one assumes that the six groups are levels of only one independent variable, perhaps type of condition, and then conducts a one-way ANOVA, the summary table would be,

Source	SS	df	MS	F
Among groups	240.00	5	48.00	7.02*
Within groups	82.00	12	6.83	
Total variability	322.00	17		

*$p \leq .05$

term for each F ratio. The results of these calculations for the chapter example are shown in the completed summary table in Table 14.5. (Also see Box 14.2.)

There are three effects, two main effects and an interaction, which are tested in this example. To determine which effects are significant, it is necessary to compare the calculated F ratios in Table 14.5 with the critical F

A significant difference would be found among the conditions and then the researcher would conduct the appropriate Tukey HSD test to determine which conditions differ.

If, on the other hand, the researcher correctly treats the experiment as a 2×3 factorial and conducts a factorial ANOVA, the summary table would be,

Source	SS	df	MS	F
Speed instruction	98.00	1	98.00	14.35*
Information	39.00	2	19.50	2.86
Speed × instruct.	103.00	2	51.50	7.54*
Within groups	82.00	12	6.83	
Total variability	322.00	17		

*$p \leq .05$

In terms of the summary tables, note that the total and within groups variability are identical. The only difference is that the factorial ANOVA divides the SS_a from the one-way ANOVA (240.00) into the variability attributable to each independent variable and interaction term.

The factorial ANOVA indicates that the speed variable and the interaction of speed and information were significant. The main effect of information was not significant. However, the interaction best describes the findings from this example. While the main effect of information was not significant, the interaction reveals that is true only for those students not given the speed instruction. For those given the speed instruction, students completed the problem significantly faster in the rule and example conditions as compared to the No information condition (based on a post hoc Tukey HSD test).

ratios found in Table F in Appendix. The critical F ratio for all three effects is the same since the df in the numerator of the F ratios is 1 and the df in the denominator of the F ratios is 40. Using an alpha level of $p \leq .05$, the critical F ratio found in Table F is 4.08.

Comparing the critical F ratio of 4.08 to the F ratios calculated in Table 14.5 reveals that only one F ratio, that for the interaction effect, is greater than 4.08. Therefore, the example reveals only one significant effect. The main effects of the students' weight and the speed of the clock were not significant. The fact that a significant interaction was obtained indicates that the two independent variables combine to effect eating behavior.

In returning to the statistics in Figure 14.1 or Table 14.2, a description of this interaction is fairly straightforward. The researchers would conclude that, " . . . a significant interaction between the students' weight and speed of the clock was found, $\underline{F}(1, 40) = 16.76$, $\underline{p} < .05$. Obese students ate more crackers when the clock was fast than when it was slow. Normal-weight students, on the other hand, ate fewer crackers when the clock was fast than when it was slow." The research hypothesis was supported with regard to obese students.

This description describes the complex nature of an interaction. In this example it was fairly easy because there were only two levels of each independent variable. Any time a significant interaction is obtained, it indicates that the effect of one of the independent variables is different at one level of the other independent variable than it is for other levels of that variable. Graph the interaction to determine visually where the difference occurs. Researchers often then rely on post hoc comparisons, such as the Tukey HSD test, to confirm that differences apparent in the graph are significant.

When detailing the findings of a factorial ANOVA, researchers often describe a significant interaction before reporting and interpreting main effects. Because a significant interaction indicates the existence of a complex relationship between the independent and dependent variables, this interaction often presents a more complete picture of this relationship. After describing the interaction, researchers may interpret and describe any significant main effects that add to the understanding of the relationship. Before looking at a second example, let us briefly touch on some of the underlying assumptions of the ANOVA.

ASSUMPTIONS UNDERLYING THE USE OF THE ANALYSIS OF VARIANCE

The assumptions for the one-way and factorial ANOVA are similar to those for the t test. The first assumes that the population variability σ^2 for each cell or condition is equal. This assumption is known as homogeneity of variance. A second assumption is that the population distribution from which each sample cell is drawn is normal in shape. If the population distributions from which the samples were taken are not normal in shape, then one needs to be careful, especially if N is small.

A third assumption for the one-way ANOVA and factorial ANOVA is that of independence for each observation. Independence means that the value in a particular cell or condition does not influence other values obtained in that cell or in other cells or conditions. In behavioral research this assumption implies that participants in independent groups designs should be assigned to one and only one condition or cell in the experiment and that one participant's performance cannot influence that of another. Violations of this assumption can invalidate the statistical conclusions from the ANOVA.

As was the case with the t tests, the ANOVA is a fairly robust test. This means that with moderate to large sample sizes, the assumptions concerning the homogeneity of the population variance and the normality of the shape of the population distribution may be violated and the ANOVA will still provide accurate conclusions. In many studies, sample sizes of N = 15 or larger per cell should be sufficient to minimize the need to fulfill the assumptions of homogeneity and normality. If the assumptions of random assignment and independence are not met, then the one-way or factorial ANOVA may be an inappropriate choice as a statistical test. In the next chapter, the repeated measures ANOVA will be discussed. This test is appropriate when the same subject serves in more than one condition and the values in each condition are not independent.

The use of factorial experiments has become quite popular in the behavioral sciences because they allow the researcher to combine independent variables in the same study. The examples in this study have been limited to factorial experiments with two independent variables. However, it is possible to design studies with three or more independent variables. In those studies, a larger number of interactions can be studied including two-way interactions (those involving the effect of combining two independent variables), three-way interactions (which involve the effect of combining three independent variables together), and so on. Obviously, analysis of these designs is beyond the scope of this text, but the principles and assumptions are similar to those illustrated here. Sources describing procedures for analyzing more complicated factorial experiments are listed in Keppel (1973).

A SECOND EXAMPLE

This second example also deals with eating behavior. Schachter (1971) discussed a finding that obese rats will not work for food if it is not easily available. Johnson (1970) tested this finding with humans. The data in this study were based on Johnson's study. Normal and obese humans had to use their index fingers to pull on a ring that was attached to a seven-pound weight. After an average of 50 pulls, the student was rewarded with a quarter of a sandwich. The number of "pulls" on the ring was the dependent variable. One of the independent variables was the weight of the subject with two levels, normal and obese.

The other independent variable involved the manipulation of the availability of the food. Johnson (1970) manipulated the prominence of the display of the food. For one-third of the students, when the sandwich was "earned" by making the appropriate number of pulls, the quarter of a sandwich was placed before the student wrapped in waxed paper. The cue of food was "invisible" in this condition. For another third, the sandwich was wrapped in transparent sandwich wrap for the subject to see. In this condition, one food cue, the sight of the food was present. For the last third of the subjects, the food was wrapped in the transparent wrap and the subject tasted and ate a quarter of the sandwich before the start of the experiment. These subjects had two cues, the sight of the sandwich and the memory of the taste of the sandwich. (The other subjects ate an equivalent amount of white bread before starting the experiment, as a control.) Subjects were not allowed to eat any of the sandwiches they earned until a 12-minute test period had ended. The number of pulls made by each student is shown in Table 14.6. For this example, an alpha level of $p \le .01$ was used.

This study is an example of a factorial experiment with the student's weight and the number of food cues present during the test as the independent variables (the first of which, weight, is actually a quasi-independent variable). There are two levels for the weight of the subject, normal and obese. There are three levels for the number of food cues, zero, one and two cues. Therefore, this study is a 2×3 factorial experiment with six conditions. The

TABLE 14.6   The Number of Pulls Made by Each Subject in the Second Example

Weight of Student					
Normal			Obese		
0 Cues	1 Cue	2 Cues	0 Cues	1 Cue	2 Cues
346	463	462	333	396	675
530	336	302	382	594	524
496	331	463	340	473	587
437	425	313	379	521	708
502	482	394	298	422	489
360	360	296	387	612	518
504	451	290	301	503	522
367	328	457	383	554	697

dependent variable is the number of pulls made during the 12-minute test period. This variable corresponds to a ratio scale of measurement.

The research hypothesis is based on the findings with obese rats. As the number of food cues increase, the obese student should be more likely to work harder because food is more apparent and available. Normal-weight students, on the other hand, should not be affected by the number of food cues, especially if their eating behavior is dictated primarily by internal body signals. Therefore, an interaction effect is predicted. The effect of the cues will be different for obese and normal-weight students.

DESCRIBING THE DATA

The data from Table 14.6 were summarized into the appropriate statistics shown in Table 14.7. Note that there are six cells in this study. The statistics in the row and column margins provide the necessary information for partitioning the variability for the main effects. In Figure 14.5, the $\overline{X}$ for each cell is shown. Note that the data do seem to support the research hypothesis. As the number of cues increase, the obese students make more pulls on the ring. Normal-weight students seem to be unaffected by the food cues.

TESTING FOR MAIN AND INTERACTION EFFECTS

To test the effects of the variables in this example, a factorial ANOVA must be conducted. In Figure 14.6, the diagram for partitioning the variability is shown along with the necessary calculations for the SS for each component. These calculations are based on the statistics in Table 14.8. Once the SS components have been determined, the researcher can complete the summary table for the factorial ANOVA and calculate the needed MS values and F ratios. Recall that the MS values are determined by dividing the SS by the appropriate df. The resulting F ratios are based on the MS for each effect (both mains and the interaction) divided by the MS_w, which contains only error variability. Table 14.8 contains the completed summary table for this example.

Because the df vary for the different effects, it is necessary to determine two critical F ratios—one for the effect of the student's weight and one for both the effect of the number of food cues and the interaction effect. The critical F ratio, using a .01 alpha level, for the effect of weight is based on 1 df in the numerator and 42 in the denominator. It is 7.27. Since the calculated F ratio of 14.23 exceeds this value, the researcher concludes that a significant difference exists in the number of pulls between obese and normal-weight students.

For the other two effects, the critical F ratio based on 2 df in the numerator and 42 df in the denominator is equal to 5.15. Both calculated F ratios—the one for the effect of food cues and the other for the interaction—exceed the critical F ratio. Therefore, there is a significant main effect for the num-

TABLE 14.7 The Summary Statistics for the Second Example

		Number of Food Cues			
		Zero	One	Two	Wgt overall
STUDENT'S WEIGHT	Normal				
	ΣX	3,542	3,176	2,977	$\Sigma X_{row\,1} =$ 9,695
	ΣX^2	1,607,910	1,290,360	1,152,787	$\Sigma X_{row\,1}^2 =$ 4,051,057
	SS	39,689.50	29,488.00	44,970.88	
	N_k	8	8	8	$N_{row\,1} =$ 24
	Obese				
	ΣX	2,803	4,075	4,720	$\Sigma X_{row\,2} =$ 11,598
	ΣX^2	991,917	2,117,375	2,841,772	$\Sigma X_{row\,2}^2 =$ 5,951,064
	SS	9,815.88	41,671.88	56,972.00	
	N_k	8	8	8	$N_{row\,2} =$ 24
Food Cues		$\Sigma X_{col\,1} =$ 6,345	$\Sigma X_{col\,2} =$ 7,251	$\Sigma X_{col\,3} =$ 7,697	$\Sigma X_{tot} =$ 21,293
Overall		$\Sigma X_{col\,1}^2 =$ 2,599,827	$\Sigma X_{col\,2}^2 =$ 3,407,735	$\Sigma X_{col\,3}^2 =$ 3,994,559	$\Sigma X_{tot}^2 =$ 10,002,121
		$N_{col\,1} =$ 16	$N_{col\,2} =$ 16	$N_{col\,2} =$ 16	$N_{tot} =$ 48

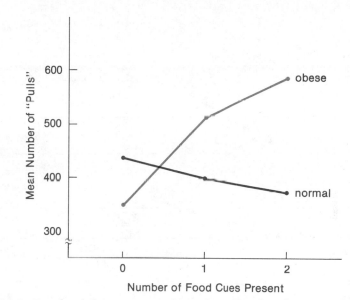

FIGURE 14.5 Graph of the mean number of "pulls" for the second example

ber of food cues and the interaction of the student's weight and the number of cues.

When researchers find significant main effects and a significant interaction, they often discuss only the interaction in detail. Because the interaction provides a description of how the two independent variables combine and interact to influence behavior, the interaction often is of greater practical importance. Many times researchers will analyze what are called the "simple main effects" in an interaction. This involves considering each level of one independent variable separately and testing for differences resulting from the other independent variable. For instance, in this second example, it would make sense for the researcher to look at normal and obese students separately and to test for the effect of the number of food cues on the number of pulls.

Looking at Figure 14.5, it appears that obese students made more response pulls as the number of food cues increased, whereas normal-weight students were not affected by the number of food cues. Testing for these effects in order to explain interactions is outside the scope of this text. Additional sources on the topic are provided in Keppel (1973).

At this level of presentation, knowing what a significant interaction means and being able to describe it in words based on seeing a graph of the interaction will suffice. The researcher in this second example could conclude that

A significant main effect for the weight of the student was found, $\underline{F}(1, 42) = 14.23$, $\underline{p} < .01$. Also, the number of food cues present significantly influenced the number of response pulls made, $\underline{F}(2, 42) = 5.60$, $\underline{p} < .01$. Lastly, a significant interaction was found, $\underline{F}(2, 42) = 18.78$, $\underline{p} < .01$. An inspection of the $\overline{X}$ for each condition reveals that obese individuals made more pulls when more food cues were present.

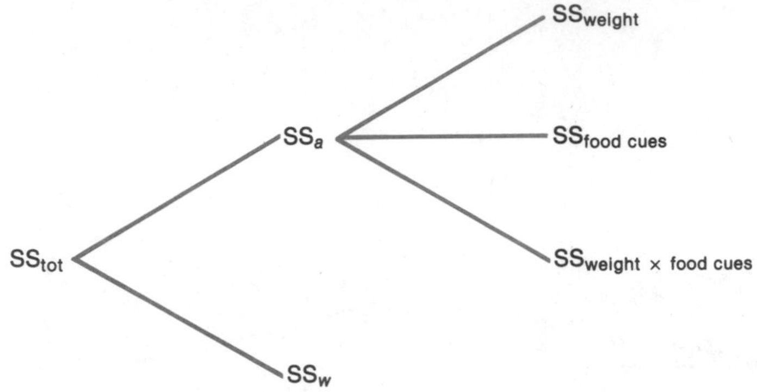

$$SS_{tot} = \Sigma X_{tot}^2 - \frac{(\Sigma X_{tot})^2}{N_{tot}} \tag{23}$$

$$= 10{,}002{,}121 - \frac{(21{,}293)^2}{48} = 556{,}457.48$$

$$SS_a = \frac{(\Sigma X_1)^2 + \Sigma X_2)^2 + \cdots + (\Sigma X_k)^2}{N_k} - \frac{(\Sigma X_{tot})^2}{N_{tot}}, \tag{29}$$

$$= \frac{3{,}542^2 + 3{,}176^2 + 2{,}977^2 + 2{,}803^2 + 4{,}075^2 + 4{,}720^2}{8} - \frac{21{,}293^2}{48} = 333{,}849.35$$

$$SS_w = SS_1 + SS_2 + SS_3 + \ldots + SS_k \tag{25}$$

$$= 39{,}689.50 + 29{,}488.00 + 44{,}970.88 + 9{,}815.88 + 41{,}671.87 + 56{,}972.00 = 222{,}608.13$$

$$SS_{rows} = \frac{(\Sigma X_{row\ 1})^2 + (\Sigma X_{row\ 2})^2 + \cdots + (\Sigma X_{row\ i})^2}{N_i} - \frac{(\Sigma X_{tot})^2}{N_{tot}}, \tag{30}$$

$$= \frac{9{,}695^2 + 11{,}598^2}{24} - \frac{21{,}293^2}{48} = 75{,}446.02$$

$$SS_{col} = \frac{(\Sigma X_{col\ 1})^2 + (\Sigma X_{col\ 2})^2 + \cdots + (\Sigma X_{col\ j})^2}{N\ (per\ column)} - \frac{(\Sigma X_{tot})^2}{N_{tot}}, \tag{31}$$

$$= \frac{6{,}345^2 + 7{,}251^2 + 7{,}697^2}{16} - \frac{21{,}293^2}{24} = 59{,}326.17$$

$$SS_{r \times c} = SS_a - SS_{rows} - SS_{col} \tag{32}$$

$$= 333{,}849.35 - 75{,}446.02 - 59{,}326.17 = 199{,}077.16$$

FIGURE 14.6 Diagram of partitioned variance for the second chapter example and the calculation of the SS components.

Normal-weight individuals did not show an increase in the number of pulls as the number of food cues increased. Therefore, it appears that, unlike normal-weight students, obese students will work harder, that is make more pulls, when the food is more readily observable and apparent. The research hypothesis was supported.

In those instances in which a significant interaction is not obtained, but significant main effects are found, the researcher can perform Tukey HSD

Source	SS	df	MS	F
TABLE 14.8 The Completed ANOVA Summary Table for the Second Example				
Student's weight	75,446.02	1	75,446.02	14.23
Number of food cues	59,326.17	2	29,663.09	5.60
Weight × cues	199,077.16	2	99,538.58	18.78
Within groups	222,608.13	42	5,300.19	
Total variability	556,457.48	47		

tests for the main effects. If a significant main effect is found, then the researcher may conduct a Tukey HSD test using the appropriate margin $\overline{X}$s—either the row means or the column means. The formula for the Tukey HSD is

$$\text{HSD} = q\sqrt{\frac{\text{MS}_w}{\text{N}_k}}. \qquad (28)$$

In determining the appropriate q statistic, k would equal the number of rows or columns, depending on which effect is being tested. The number of values per row would be represented by N_k, provided you are testing for differences among rows or the number of values per column and provided you are testing for differences among columns. Remember a Tukey HSD test requires that a significant main effect be found and should be performed only when there are more than two levels of the independent variable. (When there are only two levels and a difference is found, the researcher knows that the two rows or columns are significantly different.)

SUMMARY

Experiments can involve more than one independent variable. A factorial experiment is a study that combines two or more independent variables. Factorial experiments are described in terms of the levels for each independent variable. For instance, a $2 \times 3 \times 3$ study is a factorial experiment with three independent variables. One independent variable has 2 levels and the other two have 3 levels each. A 3×4 study has two independent variables, one with 3 levels and the other with 4 levels. The total number of conditions, or cells, in the study can be determined by multiplying the levels together (e.g., 18 in the first case and 12 in the second).

A factorial ANOVA is used in analyzing the effects of the independent variables. Each independent variable can influence behavior separately, as measured by the dependent variable. This influence would be called a main effect. It is also possible for behavior to be affected by the combination of the independent variables. This effect is called an interaction. An interaction can be visualized by graphing the cell $\overline{X}$s. One independent variable is represented on the x-axis, and levels of the other independent variable are represented as separate lines in the graph. If the lines are not parallel statistically, then an interaction is present. It is necessary to describe an interaction in terms of both independent variables.

The factorial ANOVA involves partitioning the variability among groups SS_a into variability components for each main effect SS_{rows} and SS_{col} and the interaction $SS_{r \times c}$. Separate F ratios are calculated for each effect by dividing the appropriate MS by MS_w, the error term. A significant F ratio indicates that systematic variability resulting from the particular effect was present.

The assumptions of the one-way and factorial ANOVAs are similar to those for the t test. It is assumed that the population distributions are homogeneous in variability $(\sigma_1^2 = \sigma_2^2 = \ldots = \sigma_k^2)$ and normal in shape. It is also assumed that the values within each cell are independent of values within that cell and other cells.

SUMMARY FOR USING THE FACTORIAL ANOVA

1. Identify the independent variables and the dependent variable. Develop the research hypothesis.

2. State the H_0 and H_1 for each effect and decide on the alpha level (usually .05 or .01).

3. Calculate the appropriate descriptive statistics, usually $\overline{X}$ and s. Graph the cell $\overline{X}$s to determine visually if an interaction effect is present.

4. Organize the necessary summary statistics ΣX, ΣX^2, and N for each cell, row margin, column margin, and total.

5. Construct a diagram for partitioning the variability and a summary table for the factorial ANOVA similar to that shown in Figure 14.4.

6. Calculate the appropriate SS to complete the summary table. The formulas include

$$SS_{tot} = \Sigma X_{tot}^2 - \frac{(\Sigma X_{tot})^2}{N_{tot}}, \tag{23}$$

$$SS_a = \frac{(\Sigma X_1)^2 + (\Sigma X_2)^2 + \cdots + (\Sigma X_k)^2}{N_k} - \frac{(\Sigma X_{tot})^2}{N_{tot}}, \tag{29}$$

$$SS_w = SS_1 + SS_2 + \cdots + SS_k, \tag{25}$$

$$SS_{rows} = \frac{(\Sigma X_{row\ 1})^2 + (\Sigma X_{row\ 2})^2 + \cdots + (\Sigma X_{row\ i})^2}{N\ (per\ row)} - \frac{(\Sigma X_{tot})^2}{N_{tot}}, \tag{30}$$

$$SS_{col} = \frac{(\Sigma X_{col\ 1})^2 + (\Sigma X_{col\ 2})^2 + \cdots + (\Sigma X_{col\ j})^2}{N\ (per\ column)} - \frac{(\Sigma X_{tot})^2}{N_{tot})}, \tag{31}$$

and

$$SS_{r \times c} = SS_a - SS_{rows} - SS_{col}. \tag{32}$$

7. Once the various SS components have been calculated, the summary table can be completed. The MS for each effect is determined by dividing the SS

by the appropriate df. The F ratios for each main effect and the interaction effect are calculated by dividing the appropriate MS by MS_w.

8. The critical F ratio(s) are found in Table F, Appendix E. If the calculated F ratio is equal to or greater than the critical F ratio found in Table F for a main effect, then the researcher should reject H_0, conclude that a difference does exist, and perform the Tukey HSD test if necessary (more than two levels of the independent variable). If a significant interaction is obtained, then the researcher may describe the interaction in terms of the graph of the interaction or perform additional tests by consulting Keppel (1973).

9. State your conclusions in sentence form and include the necessary statistical information ($\underline{F}(df_{effect}, df_w)$ = calculated F ratio, $\underline{p}$ < or > alpha level or $\underline{F}(df_{effect}, df_w)$ = calculated F ratio, $\underline{MS}_w$ = calculated MS_w).

EXERCISES

1. An educator wishes to investigate the effect testing has on performance in a college education course. It is hypothesized that frequent testing during a course encourages the students to stay current with course material. The course is either taught in a lecture format or in a discussion format. Three classes from each format are selected. For one class in each format only a midterm and final exam are given. For another class in each format there are three tests given during the term, one every five weeks. For the remaining class in each format, weekly tests are given. At the end of the semester performance is measured by a standardized exam.
   a. What are the two independent variables (and the levels of each) in this study?
   b. What is the dependent variable?

2. Factorial experiments can be described with integers such as a "2×2 experiment," indicating that the experiment had two independent variables, each with two levels. How would you describe the experiment described in Exercise 1?

3. Use the description of the study in Exercise 1 to answer each of the following problems:
   a. Describe the educator's conclusions if he only finds a significant main effect for class format, discussion classes outperform lecture classes. What would he conclude about the number of tests and the interaction of tests and format?
   b. Describe the educator's conclusions if he finds a significant interaction between format and number of tests. What conclusions could he make about the effectiveness of testing? Would he need to be careful in making generalizations? Explain.

4. How does an interaction effect differ from a main effect?

5. For each of the experiments described below, list the number of indepen-

dent variables, the number of levels for each independent variable, and the total number of conditions in the study.

   a. 2 × 3 experiment

   b. 3 × 4 experiment

   c. 2 × 2 × 3 experiment

6. In terms of descriptive statistics, what is the easiest way to determine if an interaction may exist in a factorial experiment?

7. A fellow student argues that it is impossible to get a significant interaction without getting at least one significant main effect. You know that he is wrong. To prove your point, create four cell $\overline{X}$s for the example below so that no main effects exist, but a significant interaction does.

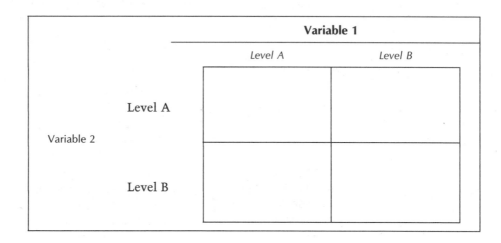

8. Another student tells you that the marginal $\overline{X}$s are needed in understanding main effects but that cell $\overline{X}$s are critical for interaction effects. Do you agree with her? Explain.

9. Sixty female students, 30 freshmen and 30 seniors, serve in a social psychology experiment. Each student is placed in a room alone and told that she is working on a problem with several other students and must communicate with them over a telephone. The number of other students working on the problem is manipulated by the experimenter. An equal number of the female students work with either one, three, or five students. Unknown to the female students, these other students are actually working for the experimenter. During the problem-solving session, one of these other students feigns an emergency and asks for help. The experimenter records the amount of time the female student takes before seeking help by either leaving the room and looking for help or by calling for help on the phone. What are the independent variables in this study? How would you describe this factorial experiment (e.g., 2 × 2, etc.)?

10. Construct a summary ANOVA table for the experiment in Exercise 9.

List the sources of variation and include the appropriate degrees of freedom for each.

11. The data listed below are the $\overline{X}$ response times for each cell $\overline{X}$ from Exercise 9. Any $\overline{X}$ difference greater than 35 seconds should be considered significant. Determine if any main effects or interaction effect are significant. If so describe the effect.

	Number of Other Students		
	1	3	5
Freshmen	28 sec	118 sec	140 sec
Seniors	20 sec	95 sec	110 sec

12. Graph the cell $\overline{X}$s in Exercise 11 in order to describe the interaction of the two variables. Label the axes appropriately. Do the lines appear to be parallel? Does this indicate that an interaction effect exists?

13. A 3 × 5 experiment with 10 students per cell or condition is conducted. Construct the summary ANOVA table listing the sources of variation and the appropriate degrees of freedom.

14. For each of the three graphs shown below, determine which indicates (a) one significant main effect and no interaction effect; (b) two significant main effects and no interaction; and (c) two significant main effects and a significant interaction effect.

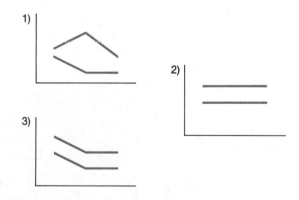

15. Is it possible to find differences among conditions in a factorial experiment and yet not have a significant interaction effect? Explain your answer in terms of the H_0 for the interaction effect.

16. Does the SS_w differ between the one-way ANOVA and the factorial ANOVA in terms of how it is calculated and what it represents? Explain.

17. A researcher has 10 men and 10 women serving in each of four conditions. The order in which the subjects participate in the conditions is varied across the subjects. The researcher has a 2 × 4 experiment. Why would the procedures outlined in this chapter be inappropriate for this study? What assumption(s) of the factorial ANOVA is being violated?

18. In terms of partitioning variability, how does the one-way ANOVA differ from the factorial ANOVA?

19. From a practical viewpoint, what is the benefit of conducting a factorial experiment over a single-variable experiment?

20. A developmental psychologist obtains the following data on mean performance of 8-year-, 10-year-, and 12-year-old children on each of three tasks. Each value represents the percentage correct on the test. An $\overline{X}$ difference of 10% or greater is significant. Describe the interaction in practical terms.

Percentage Correctly Answered on Each Task			
	Verbal task	Spatial task	Logic task
8-year-olds	65%	60%	30%
10-year-olds	70%	80%	50%
12-year-olds	80%	80%	75%

CHALLENGE QUESTIONS

1. Kindergarten and first-grade children were given a test in which they were asked to think of ideas and uses for objects typically used by members of their same sex or the opposite sex. The number of ideas generated

Sex of the Child			
Boy		Girl	
Role adopted		Role adopted	
Boy	Girl	Boy	Girl
3	1	4	5
5	4	7	7
6	2	6	8
8	3	5	6
7	0	5	9
2	2	5	8
3	1	6	7

were analyzed for differences as they related to the sex of the child (boy or girl) and the role the child was to assume (either boy or girl). The number of ideas are shown. (Based on Lewis, C. D., & Houtz, J. C., (1986). Sex-role stereotyping and young children's divergent thinking. *Psychological Reports, 59*, 1027–1033.)

2. A study was conducted on students' ratings of an interviewer. The students heard a tape of either a good interviewer or a poor interviewer. The content of the interview was staged and under the control of the researcher. More than two months later the students were given a memory test on the interview. The students were classified as either having above-average or below-average memory. The students also rated the interviewer in terms of performance on a 1-to-8 scale. These ratings are shown below. It was assumed that students with good memories would more accurately rate the performance of the interviewers. (Based on Larson, J. R., Jr. (1985). Role of memory in the performance-evaluation process: With special reference to diary-keeping. *Psychological Reports, 57*, 775–782.)

Type of Interviewer			
Good		Poor	
Memory performance		Memory performance	
Above average	Below average	Above average	Below average
4	6	2	7
6	4	3	5
5	8	5	3
3	5	4	8
3	7	3	6
6	4	4	7
5	8	1	8
4	4	5	7
2	6	1	5
2	8	8	4

For each question answer the following:

a. What is a plausible research hypothesis? Describe the research design (i.e., 2 × 3, 2 × 2, etc.).

b. What are the H_0 and H_1?

c. Calculate the appropriate descriptive statistics and graph the means.

d. Calculate the appropriate inferential statistic. Use an alpha level of .05 for Question 1 and .01 for Question 2.

e. State your findings in the proper format and provide a written conclusion about the findings (relating the inferential statistics to the descriptive statistics).

The Analysis of Variance
for Repeated Measures

PROCEDURES DESCRIBED

calculating the F ratio for the
ANOVA for repeated measures

In 1972, Craik and Lockhart proposed a new model for human memory. The model was based on the assumption that the type of mental processing that occurred at the time of learning for an item or event affected a person's ability to remember the item or event later. If an item or event was processed at a "shallow" level, then memory for the item or event would not be as good as if it had been processed at a "deeper" level. "Shallow" and "deep" referred to the quality of the processing. The more a person attaches meaning to an item, the deeper the processing. For instance, deciding that the word dog *starts with the letter* d *is shallower processing than knowing that* dog *is an animal and that it fits in the sentence "The _____ was the family pet."*

Research in the 1970s tested this model using an "incidental learning" task. The procedure used a task that did not require any memorization of information. Once the task was completed, however, the subject was given an unexpected memory test. Any information recalled was presumed to have been learned incidentally *because the subject was not intentionally trying to memorize information. For example, sometimes after reading a novel for enjoyment you may find yourself remembering interesting or funny events in the novel. These events were learned incidentally because you were not consciously trying to learn or memorize the events in the novel.*

In 1975, Craik and Tulving reported a series of experiments using an incidental learning task. The task varied in terms of the type of mental processing college students were required to perform. In the first experiment, 20 students were asked questions about common English words. There were 40 words used in the task. Before each word was shown, a question was presented. Then the word was shown for one-fifth of a second. The student had to respond yes or no with regard to the question asked and the word presented. The type of question asked required different levels of mental processing. The type of question was manipulated by the researchers and they used five different types. At the shallowest level of processing was the question "Is there a word present?" If a word was presented the student responded yes. At the next level called structural the student was asked "Is the word in capital letters?" A student would respond yes to table *but no to* office. *At a deeper level, the phonemic level, the question involved rhyming. A student would answer yes to the question "Does the word rhyme with great?" when the word* crate *was presented. At the fourth level of processing the semantic category of the word was tested. A student would respond yes when the question "Is the word a type of fish?" was asked for the word* shark, *but no if the question was "Is the word a piece of furniture?" The deepest level of processing dealt with the word fitting into a sentence. For instance, when shown the question "Would the word fit in the sentence: He met a _____ in the street?" and the word* friend *was shown, a student would respond yes.*

Each of these five types of questions was asked equally often. Half of the correct responses were yes and the other half were no responses. The students were tested separately and were instructed to respond as quickly as possible to each question. It took about 10 seconds to test a word. After seeing all 40 words, the student was given a sheet of paper listing the 40 words along with 40 words the student had not seen. The words were randomly ordered on the sheet and the student had to place a check in front of each word he had seen earlier. This memory test was unexpected because the student was not told earlier about it.

This memory test was crucial to the study. Remember, the memory model being tested assumed that memory is a function of the type of processing that occurs for each of the words. Therefore, the incidental learning task was useful in that it forced the students to process words to a particular level in order to answer the questions. The memory test was designed to measure the effect of the processing on later memory.

The hypothesis that Craik and Tulving (1975) were using predicted that words that had been processed to a deeper level in the incidental learning task would be better remembered than those that had not. To make the analysis for this example easier only the yes words will be used. It is presumed that yes words must get the full amount of processing in order for a student to say yes and these words are the critical words to test the model and the researchers' hypothesis. In Table 15.1 the number of yes words recognized by the students during the memory test is shown. There were four yes words for each type of question. The words are listed by the type of question that was asked on the incidental learning task.

This study is an experiment with one independent variable, the type of question asked. Five different types of questions were used. These questions are the levels of the independent variable. Since the types of questions refer to different levels of processing, one could argue that they can be ordered on a dimension from shallow to deep processing. That is, there is a theoretical ordering for the questions with the question "Is there a word present" at one end and the sentence question at the other. However, this dimension is not continuous nor are the levels equally spaced. Therefore, the variable corresponds to the ordinal scale of measurement.

The dependent variable is the number of words that are recognized (and checked by the student) on the memory test. Integer values between 0 and 4 were possible for each type of question. This variable corresponds to a ratio scale of measurement.

This study differs from those in the two previous chapters in that each subject participated in all conditions rather than just one condition. The study in this example is a repeated measures design. It is similar to those described in Chapter 11, which had subjects participating in two conditions. However, since the present example has five conditions and not two, the *t* test for correlated samples is inappropriate. At the same time, the ANOVAs discussed in the previous chapters are also inappropriate because they assume independence between conditions (subjects can serve in only one condition). There is, however, an analysis of variance appropriate for repeated measures

TABLE 15.1   The Number of Yes Words Recognized on the Memory Test in the Chapter Example

Subject	Type of Question Asked on the Incidental-Learning Task				
	Word-present	Structural	Phonemic	Category	Sentence
A	1	1	3	4	3
B	1	1	3	4	4
C	0	0	2	2	4
D	1	2	4	4	4
E	1	0	3	3	4
F	0	0	4	4	4
G	0	0	2	3	4
H	2	2	3	4	4
I	0	0	2	4	3
J	1	1	3	4	4
K	1	0	3	3	4
L	1	1	4	4	4
M	2	2	4	4	4
N	0	0	2	3	4
O	1	1	4	4	4
P	1	0	3	4	3
Q	1	1	4	4	4
R	1	0	2	4	4
S	1	1	3	4	4
T	1	1	4	4	4

designs. But before discussing it, let us calculate the appropriate descriptive statistics for this example.

DESCRIPTIVE STATISTICS: DESCRIBING THE SAMPLE DATA

The appropriate descriptive statistics to calculate for each condition in this example are the $\overline{X}$ and s. The summary statistics for each condition along with the $\overline{X}$ and s are shown in Table 15.2. Since the independent variable is on an ordinal scale, a bar graph is the appropriate type of graph to use. Figure 15.1 shows the $\overline{X}$ number of words recognized by the type of question asked. Notice that the general pattern of results fits the research hypothesis. As the level of processing gets deeper, that is as it involves the meaning of the word, the memory for the word improves. There is an increase in recognition when the phonemic question is asked and then when either a category or sentence question is asked. The analysis of variance will enable the researchers to determine which of the questions resulted in significant differences in memory.

TABLE 15.2 Summary Information and Descriptive Statistics for the Chapter Example

	Type of Question Asked on the Incidental Learning Task				
	Word-present	Structural	Phonemic	Category	Sentence
$\Sigma X=$	17	14	62	74	77
$\Sigma X^2 =$	21	20	204	280	299
N =	20	20	20	20	20
Using Formula 1: $\overline{X} = \Sigma X/N$					
$\overline{X} =$	0.85	0.70	3.10	3.70	3.85
Using Formula 3: $SS = \Sigma X^2 - (\Sigma X)^2/N$					
SS =	6.55	10.20	11.80	6.20	2.55
Using Formula 4: $s^2 = SS/(N-1)$					
$s^2 =$	.34	.54	.62	.33	.13
Using Formula 5: $s = \sqrt{s^2}$					
s =	.59	.73	.79	.57	.36

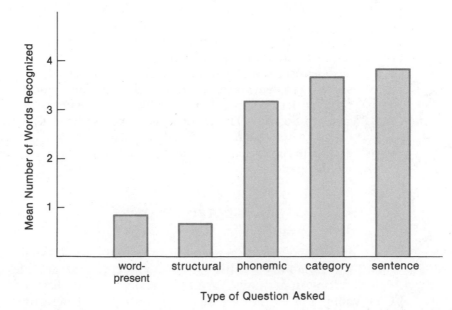

FIGURE 15.1 Bar graph for the chapter example.

INFERENTIAL STATISTICS: TESTING FOR A DIFFERENCE

The research hypothesis is based on the independent and dependent variables in the chapter example. The researchers predict that the type of processing in the incidental learning task (the independent variable) will affect memory performance and word recognition, (the dependent variable). A difference is being predicted. The research hypothesis is similar to the statistical hypothesis called the alternative hypothesis, H_1.

The two statistical hypotheses, the null and alternative hypotheses, are identical to those used in Chapter 13. The null hypothesis assumes that all conditions or levels of the independent variable are samples that came from the same population distribution

$$H_0: \quad \mu_1 = \mu_2 = \mu_3 = \cdots = \mu_k \quad (k = \text{number of conditions}).$$

For this example H_0 could be stated as

$$H_0: \quad \mu_{word} = \mu_{struct} = \mu_{phon} = \mu_{categ} = \mu_{sent}.$$

The alternative hypothesis assumes that at least one sample comes from a population distribution with a μ different from those for the other samples. Since this hypothesis incorporates a number of different possibilities (i.e., one sample different; two samples different, etc.) H_1 is best expressed in words rather than parameters,

H_1:   At least one sample comes from a population distribution with a μ different from the other samples.

The analysis of variance for repeated measures is different from the one-way ANOVA and the factorial ANOVA in that each participant provides a value for each of the conditions in the experiment. In the one-way and factorial ANOVAs, each participant provides only one value—for the single condition in which the subject participated. The fact that the repeated measures design results in a value for each subject for each condition allows the researcher to control the effect of individual differences among the subjects. In the chapter example, not all subjects had equally good memories or incentives to do well. Therefore, it is to be expected that some students will do better overall than other students. The ANOVA for repeated measures enables the researcher to isolate the variability that results from these individual differences.

ANOVA FOR REPEATED MEASURES: PARTITIONING THE VARIABILITY

In an ANOVA for repeated measures the total variability is divided into (1) the variability resulting from the independent variable; (2) the variability resulting from individual differences, which is measured by the "subject" variable; and (3) the "residual" variability resulting from random error. A measure of variability SS will be calculated for each of these three sources.

The ANOVA for the repeated measures design differs from the one-way ANOVA in terms of these last two components of variability. As you can see in the top diagram of Figure 15.2, there are two sources of variability in the one-way ANOVA, SS_a and SS_w. The within-group variability SS_w, contains all variability that cannot be attributed to the independent variable. We referred to this as error variability.

The within-group variability includes variability resulting from individual differences, such as motivational and intellectual differences and chance error. Because the one-way ANOVA is based on an independent groups design with each participant providing one value on the dependent variable, it is not possible to measure any individual differences. A participant's data point may be influenced by the independent variable, individual abilities, and chance factors. Except for using the group $\overline{X}$ as a measure of the effect of the independent variable, which is the basis for SS_a, there is no way of separating these components from each other.

On the other hand, with a repeated measures design, each participant provides a value for each level of the independent variable. It is therefore possible to measure the variability resulting from individual differences. By recording a participant's overall behavior (adding together a participant's val-

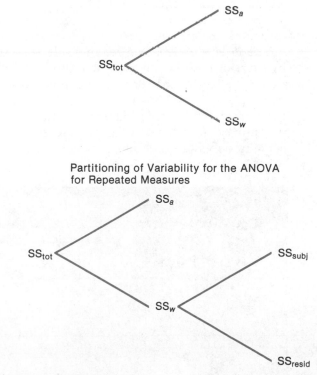

Partitioning of Variability for the One–Way ANOVA

SS_a

SS_{tot}

SS_w

Partitioning of Variability for the ANOVA
for Repeated Measures

SS_a

SS_{tot}

SS_{subj}

SS_w

SS_{resid}

FIGURE 15.2 Diagrams for partitioning of variability. ANOVA for repeated measures divides SS_W into SS_{subj} and SS_{resid}.

ues from all conditions), it is possible to measure differences among individuals. The bottom diagram in Figure 15.2 shows the three variability components in an ANOVA for repeated measures.

Note that the SS_w is divided into two components. The first, SS_{subj} (sum of the squared deviations for subjects), reflects variability resulting from individual differences. The other, SS_{resid} (sum of the squared deviations for residuals), contains the variability resulting from chance and random factors. This latter term SS_{resid} will be the error term used in the ANOVA for repeated measures.

COMPARING THE ONE-WAY ANOVA AND THE ANOVA FOR REPEATED MEASURES WITH AN EXAMPLE

Let us illustrate the difference between the two ANOVAs with an example. Table 15.3 contains fictitious data for an experiment with three conditions, labeled high, medium, and low. Let us assume that these conditions represent levels of a bothersome sound rats are exposed to while running a maze. The dependent variable is the number of errors each rat makes.

If the data are treated as an independent groups design, that is, there are 15 rats, each randomly assigned to one level of sound, then the two variability components would be SS_a and SS_w. Based on the procedures for a one-way ANOVA, these values are shown in Figure 15.3. The resulting F ratio of 2.64 would be nonsignificant, $p > .05$.

On the other hand, let us assume that the experiment was a repeated measures design with each rat serving in each of the three conditions on different days. As you can see in Table 15.3, the total number of errors made by each rat is shown in the last column. These values are used for determining SS_{subj}. Notice that Rat 2 made more errors than the others and that Rat 5 made the fewest. Rats 1 and 3 made the identical number of errors. This information concerning individual differences can be obtained in a repeated measures design but not in an independent groups design, where subjects serve in only one condition.

TABLE 15.3 Fictitious Data for Comparison of One-Way ANOVA and ANOVA for Repeated Measures

| | Level of Bothersome Noise | | | |
Rat	Low	Medium	High	Total
1	4	3	5	12
2	4	7	8	19
3	3	3	6	12
4	4	3	6	13
5	3	1	3	7
$\overline{X} =$	3.6	3.4	5.6	12.6

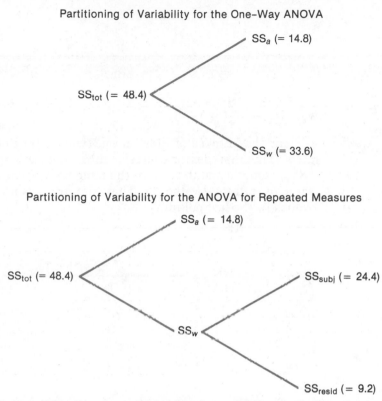

Partitioning of Variability for the One-Way ANOVA

SS_a (= 14.8)

SS_{tot} (= 48.4)

SS_w (= 33.6)

Partitioning of Variability for the ANOVA for Repeated Measures

SS_a (= 14.8)

SS_{tot} (= 48.4)

SS_{subj} (= 24.4)

SS_w

SS_{resid} (= 9.2)

FIGURE 15.3 Diagrams for partitioning the variability with the values of the components included from the fictitious example.

The values of the various SS components are shown at the bottom in Figure 15.3. What was formerly SS_w in the top example has been divided into two components, SS_{subj} and SS_{resid}. The second component SS_{resid} contains the error variability. It is less than SS_w because of the removal of variability resulting from individual differences.

You can see an example of the error variability contained in the SS_{resid} by looking at the data for Rats 1 and 3 in Table 15.3. They both performed the same overall in that each rat made 12 errors. However, their errors are not identical across conditions. Rat 1 when compared with Rat 5 made one more error in the Low condition and one fewer error in the High condition. This difference cannot be explained by individual differences nor the experimental manipulation. Therefore, this variability is found in the SS_{resid}. See Box 15.1 for further examples.

Because SS_{resid} is smaller than SS_w (and MS_{resid} is less than MS_w), the F ratio will be different for the repeated measures design. In fact, if the data were treated as coming from a repeated measures design, a significant F ratio (MS_a/MS_{resid}) would have been found, $F (2, 8) = 6.43$, $p < .05$. By removing variability from individual differences, the ANOVA for repeated measures is

BOX 15.1   **Examples Involving (1) No Variability among Subjects and (2) No Residual Variability**

For the purpose of illustration, two sets of fictitious data were generated. The first demonstrates a difference among conditions. However, SS_{subj} would equal 0. Note in the table below that each participant has the same overall total value, 19. Therefore, there is no variability based on the values in the last column.

	Condition				
Participant	A	B	C	D	Total
m	4	7	2	6	19
n	3	8	0	8	19
o	2	4	4	9	19
p	4	8	1	7	19

In the next example, SS_{resid} would be 0. There are individual differences among the individuals as shown in the last column of the table below. Therefore SS_{subj} would not be 0. These individual differences account for or explain all the variability within each condition. Therefore, variability within conditions is the result of SS_{subj} and there would be no residual error. This is an extremely unlikely event in a real study. If it were to occur, the F ratio would be undefined because MS for the denominator would be 0.

	Condition				
Participant	A	B	C	D	Total
m	0	4	2	5	11
n	1	5	3	6	15
o	2	6	4	7	19
p	3	7	5	8	23

statistically more powerful. Let us turn to the computational formulas for these variability components and use the data from the chapter example.

CALCULATING THE VARIABILITY COMPONENTS

The necessary summary statistics for calculating the SS values are shown in Table 15.4. Notice that the ΣX and ΣX^2 are calculated for each type of question in the study. The ΣX_{tot} and ΣX_{tot}^2 at the bottom in Table 15.4 represent the sum of the group statistics. The last column is the sum of the individual values for each participant. High values represent individuals who performed better on the memory test than those who did not. These values in the last column represent subject or individual differences.

TABLE 15.4 The Data and Summary Statistics for the Chapter Example

Subj.	Word-present	Structural	Phonemic	Category	Sentence		Subject total
			Type of Question Asked				
A	1	1	3	4	3		12
B	1	1	3	4	4		13
C	0	0	2	2	4		8
D	1	2	4	4	4		15
E	1	0	3	3	4		11
F	0	0	4	4	4		12
G	0	0	2	3	4		9
H	2	2	3	4	4		15
I	0	0	2	4	3		9
J	1	1	3	4	4		13
K	1	0	3	3	4		11
L	1	1	4	4	4		14
M	2	2	4	4	4		16
N	0	0	2	3	4		9
O	1	1	4	4	4		14
P	1	0	3	4	3		11
Q	1	1	4	4	4		14
R	1	0	2	4	4		11
S	1	1	3	4	4		13
T	1	1	4	4	4		14
						TOTAL	
$\Sigma X =$ 17	14	62	74	77	**244**	$\Sigma X_{subj} =$	244
$\Sigma X^2 =$ 21	20	204	280	299	**824**	$\Sigma X_{subj}^2 =$	3,076
N = 20	20	20	20	20	**100**		

$(k$ = number of conditions = 5)

The summary statistics for this column ΣX_{subj} and ΣX_{subj}^2 will be used in calculating SS_{subj}. Notice that ΣX_{tot} equals ΣX_{subj}. This serves as a check for your calculation of the sums. The sum of the group statistics squared ΣX_{tot}^2 will not equal ΣX_{subj}^2, however, because these sums are based on the squaring of different values.

The first variability component to be calculated is SS_{tot}, which is the same as in the previous chapters. Formula 23 provides the following:

$$SS_{tot} = \Sigma X_{tot}^2 - \frac{(\Sigma X_{tot})^2}{N_{tot}}. \tag{23}$$

Substituting the values from Table 15.3 into Formula 23 results in

$$= 824 - 595.36$$
$$= 228.64.$$

The calculation of the SS_a is identical to that used for the factorial ANOVA because N is the same for each condition. Using Formula 29 results in the following:

$$\mathbf{SS_a} = \frac{(\Sigma X_1)^2 + (\Sigma X_2)^2 + \cdots + (\Sigma X_k)^2}{N_k} - \frac{(\Sigma X_{tot})^2}{N_{tot}} \tag{29}$$
$$= \frac{17^2 + 14^2 + 62^2 + 74^2 + 77^2}{20} - \frac{244^2}{100}$$
$$= 786.70 - 595.36$$
$$= 191.34.$$

To calculate the variability that results from differences among the subjects, SS_{subj} is needed. The theoretical formula for SS_{subj} is based on the sum of the squared deviations for each subject's own mean value from the overall mean

$$SS_{subj} = \Sigma(\overline{X}_{subj} - \overline{X}_{tot})^2. \tag{Def}$$

This formula measures the deviations among the subjects. If there are no overall individual differences then SS_{subj} will equal zero because each subject will have the same total value (see Box 15.1). In almost all behavioral science research, individual differences are expected and SS_{subj} should be greater than zero.

The computational formula for SS_{subj} is given in Formula 33. The statistics in the last two columns of Table 15.3 are used in Formula 33 to calculate SS_{subj}

$$SS_{subj} = \frac{\Sigma X_{subj}^2}{k} - \frac{(\Sigma X_{tot})^2}{N_{tot}}. \tag{33}$$

This formula first takes the sum of all the squared subject totals and divides them by the number of conditions k. This value k is the number of values each subject provides in the study. Then the overall total squared is divided by the number of observations. This latter value is then subtracted from the first value. For the chapter example, Formula 33 results in

$$SS_{subj} = \frac{\Sigma X_{subj}^2}{k} - \frac{(\Sigma X_{tot})^2}{N_{tot}} \tag{33}$$

$$- \frac{3076}{5} - \frac{244^2}{100}$$

$$= 615.20 - 595.36$$

$$= 19.84.$$

Once SS_a and SS_{resid} have been calculated, the remaining variability SS_{resid} is found through subtraction

$$SS_{resid} = SS_{tot} - SS_{subj} - SS_a \tag{34}$$

$$- 233.64 - 19.84 - 191.34$$

$$= 22.46.$$

These three components of variability, SS_{subj}, SS_a, and SS_{resid}, must equal SS_{tot}. This was shown earlier in the bottom diagram in Figure 15.2. Let us now look at completing the summary table and calculating the F ratio for the ANOVA for repeated measures.

THE SUMMARY TABLE FOR THE ANOVA
FOR REPEATED MEASURES

The summary table for the ANOVA for repeated measures is similar to those constructed in the previous two chapters. The general form of the summary table is shown at the top in Table 15.5. Notice that the sources of variability correspond to those calculated in the previous section. The subject variability SS_{subj} is normally listed first. The formulas for the various df are also shown. The only new df are for SS_{subj}, which is equal to the number of subjects minus 1, and SS_{resid}, which can be found by multiplying df_{subj} with df_a. Note that the df for the various components must equal df_{tot}.

Usually only one F ratio is calculated in the ANOVA for repeated measures. That F ratio is based on the MS_a and MS_{resid}. These two values allow the researcher to determine the contribution of the independent variable by comparing systematic variability (resulting from the independent variable) with error variability. The ratio formed is based on the following effects:

$$F = \frac{MS_a}{MS_{resid}} = \frac{\text{Systematic Variability} + \text{Error Variability}}{\text{Error Variability}}. \tag{35}$$

This error variability is composed of error that cannot be attributed to individual differences. This includes, but is not limited to, differences that result when two individuals with the same overall performance differ in their performance across conditions. Subjects P and R in Table 15.4 are good examples. Notice that they both have the same overall performance, 11 words recognized. Yet, their performance in the individual conditions was different.

TABLE 15.5   The General Form for the Summary Table for the ANOVA for Repeated Measures and the Completed Summary Table for the Chapter Example

General Form of the Summary Table for the ANOVA for Repeated Measures

Source	SS	df	MS	F
Subjects (subj)	(Formula 33)	(Number of subj) $-$ 1	SS_{subj}/df_{subj}	———
Among groups (a)	(Formula 29)	$k - 1$	SS_a/df_a	MS_a/MS_{resid}
Residual (resid)	(Formula 34)	$(df_{subj})(df_a)$	SS_{resid}/df_{resid}	
Total variability	(Formula 23)	$N_{tot} - 1$		

Completed Summary Table for the Chapter Example

Source	SS	df	MS	F
Subjects (subj)	19.84	19	1.04	———
Type of processing	191.34	4	47.84	208.00
Subj $\times$ processing	17.46	76	0.23	
Total variability	228.64	99		

This variability is included as error variability because it cannot be explained solely by the manipulation of the independent variable.

As we have seen in Chapters 13 and 14, a large F ratio indicates that the proportion of systematic variability in the study outweighs that of error variability. If the F ratio is large enough for the researcher to reject H_0, then the researcher can conclude that a significant difference exists among the conditions of the independent variable.

The completed summary table for the chapter example is shown at the bottom in Table 15.5. Only the F ratio for the independent variable is tested because the researchers are hypothesizing differences among the types of conditions. There is seldom a theoretical interest in determining if the individual differences are significant. Therefore, the F ratio for the subjects variability is not calculated.

To determine if the calculated F ratio of 208.00 is significant, the critical F ratio must be found in Table F. In using Table F the df_a should be used for the columns and df_{resid} should be used for the rows. Using an alpha level of .05, the critical F ratio listed under the column, with df = 4 and under the row, with df = 70 (closest df to 76 that is less than 76) is 2.50. The calculated F ratio exceeds the critical F ratio. Therefore, the researchers should reject H_0 and conclude that a difference in memory performance exists based on the type of question asked. As was the case in the previous chapters, when a significant difference is found and there are more than two conditions, the Tukey HSD test should be performed.

THE TUKEY HSD TEST: DETERMINING
WHICH CONDITIONS DIFFER

Once a significant difference has been found and the H_0 has been rejected, the researcher may use the Tukey HSD test. The procedure is identical to that described earlier except that MS_{resid} is substituted for MS_w in the formula

$$HSD = q\sqrt{\frac{MS_{resid}}{N}}. \tag{36}$$

The Studentized range statistic q can be found in Table Q in Appendix E. Column 5 should be used because the example has five conditions. The row with df = 60 should be used, again because it is the closest value to 76 (df_{resid}) without exceeding it. Using the .05 rejection region, the q value is 3.98. Substituting this value along with the necessary MS values from Table 15.5 results in

$$HSD = q\sqrt{\frac{MS_{resid}}{N}} \tag{36}$$

$$= 3.98\sqrt{\frac{.23}{20}}$$

$$= 3.98 \times .11$$

$$= .44.$$

Therefore, any difference greater than or equal to 0.44 between a pair of sample $\overline{X}$s will indicate that the two samples came from different population distributions. In Figure 15.4, the five $\overline{X}$s are listed in ascending order. Then the possible pairwise comparisons are made. With two exceptions, the difference between the structural and word-present $\overline{X}$s and the difference between the category and sentence $\overline{X}$s, all differences between sample $\overline{X}$s are greater than the HSD. Therefore, all samples come from population distributions with different μs, except for the structural and word-present samples and the category and sentence samples. In those two cases, the samples could have come from population distributions with the same respective μs.

The data support the researchers hypothesis in that deeper processing during the question phase of the study does seem to lead to better memory performance later. In fact, an appropriate conclusion to this example might be,

A significant difference was found in the number of words recognized as a function of the type of question asked earlier, $\underline{F}(4, 76) = 208.00$, $\underline{p} < .05$. A Tukey HSD

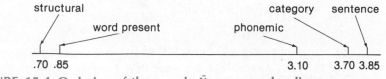

FIGURE 15.4 Ordering of the sample $\overline{X}$s on a number line.

test revealed that more words were recognized from the sentence and category questions than any other questions. The sentence and category questions did not differ significantly from each other. Furthermore, the phonemic question led to more words being recognized than in either of the structural or word-present questions. These last two conditions were not significantly different from each other.

A SECOND EXAMPLE

The second chapter example also comes from the Craik and Tulving (1975) study described in the first example. In addition to recording the number of words correctly recognized on the memory test, Craik and Tulving recorded the amount of time it took the subjects to answer each of the questions on the incidental-learning task. The assumption was that differences in depth of processing may result in differences in the time it takes to process the words. That is, as deeper processing is required to answer a question, the time it takes to give an answer will increase. One would expect, therefore, that the time it takes to answer whether or not a word was present would be less than the time it takes to answer whether a word fits in a sentence or not.

To eliminate the possibility that reading the question influenced response time, Craik and Tulving (1975) showed the question first and then the word two seconds later. The time it took from when the word was shown to when the subject said yes or no was recorded.

For the yes responses, the median response time was calculated. Often when dealing with response times, researchers will use the median rather than the mean as the dependent measure. This is done because the distribution of response times is often skewed. It is not unusual to find an extremely long (or short) response time among the times recorded for a subject in a particular condition of the study. If the mean were used to calculate an "average" time for the subject, then this extreme response time will exaggerate the average time. This is especially critical when so few responses are being recorded.

In the present example, there were only four times for the yes responses for each question. If a subject had the following times, 0.43, 0.46, 0.48, and 0.71, then the mean would be 0.52 seconds. Obviously, the last response time is exaggerating the true "average" time. In this case, the median, the "middle" value, is a better estimate of the average response time. In this example, the median would be the average of the two middle times, 0.46 and 0.48, resulting in a median response time of 0.47 seconds. The median response time to the yes answers for each type of question is shown in Table 15.6. The times is shown in hundredths of a second without the decimal point included.

This example contains additional data from the same study described in the first example. Consequently, the independent variable—the type of ques-

TABLE 15.6	The Median Response Time (in Hundredths of a Sec) for Answering the Questions in the Second Example				
	Type of Question Asked on the Incidental-Learning Task				
Subject	Word-present	Structural	Phonemic	Category	Sentence
A	45	52	54	61	57
B	42	33	53	47	51
C	52	50	47	52	66
D	58	55	59	56	66
E	59	56	70	65	68
F	60	68	70	68	80
G	64	66	74	79	75
H	66	66	75	83	93
I	64	78	98	85	81
J	81	80	99	94	99
K	42	50	39	45	50
L	46	37	49	53	55
M	55	50	78	75	60
N	57	53	59	56	65
O	60	65	65	70	78
P	60	70	71	80	85
Q	68	71	79	80	90
R	70	76	76	83	89
S	72	83	92	89	91
T	61	55	70	66	91

tion asked—is the same. The dependent variable is different, however. The dependent variable is the time it took a subject to answer the question. Since the research design is identical to that in the first example, the same statistical procedures will be followed.

DESCRIBING THE DATA

The $\overline{X}$ of the median response time for each question is shown in Figure 15.5. Notice that there is a general trend: as the depth of processing increased, the response time increased. This would support the hypothesis that depth of processing is related to the amount of processing time needed to answer a question.

The s for the word-present question (10.19 seconds) was slightly lower than for the other four questions. For the structural question the s was 13.80 seconds, and for the phonemic question it was 16.30 seconds. For the two questions dealing with semantic (word meaning) processing, the s was 14.66 seconds in the category question and 15.32 seconds in the sentence question. These statistics indicate that generally the variability in response times among subjects was similar for the different questions.

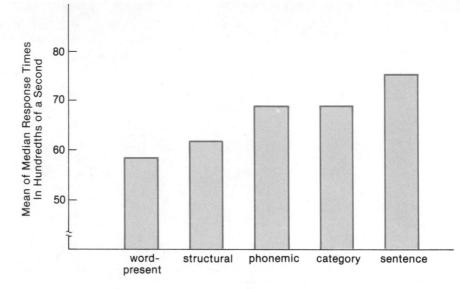

FIGURE 15.5 Bar graph for the second example.

TESTING FOR DIFFERENCES: ANOVA FOR REPEATED MEASURES

As in the first example, it is necessary to identify the various sources of variability in the design and then to calculate the SS values. The diagram in Figure 15.6 shows the partitioning of the variability for this example. The necessary summary statistics and the calculation of the SS values are shown in Table 15.7.

Once the various SS values have been calculated, the summary table can be completed. In Table 15.8, the summary table for this example is shown. The df_{subj} is 19 (number of subjects minus 1). The df_a is 4 (k, the number of conditions, minus 1) and df_{resid} is 76 (df_{subj} multiplied by df_a).

An F ratio of 25.70 was obtained. From Table F the critical F ratio, using the .05 level with df = 4 for the columns and df = 70 for the rows, is 2.50.

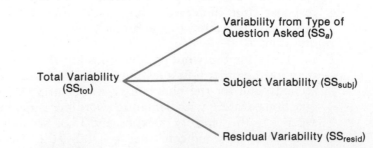

FIGURE 15.6 Partitioning of the variability for the chapter example.

TABLE 15.7 Calculation of the SS Values for the Second Example

	Type of Question Asked						
	Word-present	Structural	Phonemic	Category	Sentence	Total	Subject total
$\Sigma X =$	1,182	1,214	1,377	1,387	1,490	6,650	$\Sigma X_{subj} =$ 6,650
$\Sigma X^2 =$	71,830	77,308	99,855	100,271	115,464	464,728	$\Sigma X_{subj}^2 =$ 2,294,758
$N =$	20	20	20	20	20	100	

(k = number of conditions = 5)

$$SS_{tot} = \Sigma X_{tot}^{\,2} - \frac{(\Sigma X_{tot})^2}{N_{tot}}$$
$$= 464,728 - \frac{(6,650)^2}{100}$$
$$= \mathbf{22,503.0} \tag{23}$$

$$SS_{subj} = \frac{\Sigma X_{subj}^{\,2}}{k} - \frac{(\Sigma X_{tot})^2}{N_{tot}}$$
$$= \frac{2,294,758}{5} - \frac{(6,650)^2}{100}$$
$$= \mathbf{16,726.6} \tag{33}$$

$$SS_a = \frac{(\Sigma X_1)^2 + (\Sigma X_2)^2 + \cdots + (\Sigma X_k)^2}{N_k} - \frac{(\Sigma X_{tot})^2}{N_{tot}}$$
$$= \frac{(1,182)^2 + (1,214)^2 + (1,377)^2 + (1,387)^2 + (1,490)^2}{20} - \frac{(6,650)^2}{100}$$
$$= \mathbf{3,320.9} \tag{29}$$

$$SS_{resid} = SS_{tot} - SS_{subj} - SS_a$$
$$= 22,503.0 - 16,726.6 - 3,320.9$$
$$= \mathbf{2,455.5} \tag{34}$$

TABLE 15.8 The Completed Summary Table for the Second Example				
Source	**SS**	**df**	**MS**	**F**
Subjects (subj)	16,726.6	19	880.35	————
Type of processing	3,320.9	4	830.23	25.70
Residual	2,455.5	76	32.31	
Total variability	22,503.0	99		

Therefore, the H_0 can be rejected. The samples do not come from the same population distribution of response times. At least one sample comes from a different population distribution. The Tukey HSD test should be used to determine which conditions or samples are different.

Using Formula 36, the HSD value can be calculated

$$\textbf{HSD} = q\sqrt{\frac{MS_{resid}}{N}} \tag{36}$$

$$= 3.98\sqrt{\frac{32.31}{20}}$$

$$= 3.98 \times 1.27$$

$$= 5.05.$$

The Studentized range statistic q of 3.98 was obtained from Table Q (see Appendix E). The statistics under the square root are found in Table 15.8. Any two conditions with a $\overline{X}$ difference of 5.05 seconds or more will be considered to be from different population distributions.

The $\overline{X}$s for the five questions are shown in Table 15.9. The first comparison involves the two questions with the greatest $\overline{X}$ difference, the sentence and word-present conditions. Then the sentence question is compared to each of the other questions. Notice that the response time is significantly longer for the sentence question than any other question. Further comparisons reveal significant differences among the other questions except for that between the word-present and structural questions and that between the phonemic and category questions. The researchers could conclude that,

A significant difference was found in response time among the different types of questions, $\underline{F}(4, 76) = 25.70$, $\underline{p} < .05$. A Tukey HSD test revealed that the response time was longest for the sentence question. The response times for the phonemic and category questions were significantly longer than those for the word-present and structural questions. No other differences were significant.

TABLE 15.9 Conditions Ordered by $\overline{X}$ Time for Second Example				
	Word-Present	**Structural**	**Phonemic**	**Category**	**Sentence**
$\overline{X}$	59.10	60.70	68.85	69.35	74.50

It should be noted that although differences in response time were found in this study, subsequent studies by Craik and Tulving (1975) and others have shown that the processing time itself cannot account for differences in memory performance. That is, it is not the quantity (or time) of processing but rather the quality of processing that influences memory performance. The more processing involving the meaning of the words, the better the memory performance.

SUMMARY

The ANOVA for repeated measures is the appropriate statistical test to use when analyzing data from experiments in which there is one independent variable and participants serve in all levels or conditions of that variable. Unlike the ANOVAs discussed previously, the ANOVA for repeated measures does not assume that a participant served in only one condition in the experiment.

The ANOVA for repeated measures partitions the total variability in the study into three components. One component SS_a results from the researcher's manipulation of the independent variable. This component contains both systematic variability and error variability. Another component SS_{subj} is based on variability among the participants. This variability is derived from differences in the overall data values among subjects and reflects individual differences among participants. The third component of variability SS_{resid} is the remaining variability and contains error variability and is used in determining the error term for the F ratio, MS_{resid}. Usually only the independent variable is tested for a significant difference.

The F ratio is formed by dividing MS_a by MS_{resid}. If a significant difference is found, then the researcher is permitted to conduct the Tukey HSD test to determine which condition(s) or sample(s) are different from one another.

SUMMARY FOR USING THE ANOVA FOR REPEATED MEASURES

1. Develop the research hypothesis.

2. State the H_0 and H_1; decide on the alpha level (usually $p \leq .05$ or $p \leq .01$).

3. Calculate the appropriate descriptive statistics, including a measure of central tendency (often the $\overline{X}$), and a measure of variability (often the s). If necessary, present the measure of central tendency for each condition in a table or graph.

4. Calculate and organize the necessary summary statistics for the ANOVA for repeated measures. These statistics include the ΣX and ΣX^2 for each condition, along with the number of values in each condition N_k. Also calculate the ΣX_{tot}, ΣX_{tot}^2, and N_{tot}, which are based on the sum of all of the conditions ΣX, ΣX^2, and N_k, respectively. Lastly, construct a new col-

umn of values that are the sum of all values for each subject. From this column calculate ΣX_{subj} and ΣX_{subj}^2.

5. Calculate the necessary SS values using the formulas listed below:

$$SS_{tot} = \Sigma X_{tot}^2 - \frac{(\Sigma X_{tot})^2}{N_{tot}} \tag{23}$$

$$SS_{subj} = \frac{\Sigma X_{subj}^2}{k} - \frac{(\Sigma X_{tot})^2}{N_{tot}} \tag{33}$$

where k = number of conditions.

$$SS_a = \frac{(\Sigma X_1)^2 + (\Sigma X_2)^2 + \cdots + (\Sigma X_k)^2}{N_k} - \frac{(\Sigma X_{tot})^2}{N_{tot}} \tag{29}$$

$$SS_{resid} = SS_{tot} - SS_{subj} - SS_a. \tag{34}$$

6. Construct a summary table for the ANOVA for repeated measures similar to that shown in Table 15.5. The df_{subj} is equal to the number of subjects minus 1. The df_a is equal to the number of conditions k minus 1. And the df_{resid} is determined by multiplying df_{subj} with df_a.

7. Calculate each MS value by dividing each SS by the appropriate df. The calculated F ratio is found by dividing MS_a by MS_{resid}

$$F = \frac{MS_a}{MS_{resid}}. \tag{35}$$

The critical F ratio is found in Table F. The column entry in Table F is represented by df_a, and df_{resid} is used for the row entry.

8. If the H_0 is rejected (calculated F ratio is equal to or larger than the critical F ratio), then the researcher should reject H_0 and perform a Tukey HSD test. The HSD value is found by using the following formula:

$$HSD = q\sqrt{\frac{MS_{resid}}{N}}. \tag{36}$$

The Studentized range statistic q is found in Table Q; the other values can be found in the summary table. Comparisons are then made between every pair of sample $\overline{X}$s. Any difference between $\overline{X}$s equal to or greater than HSD indicates that the two samples came from different populations.

9. State your conclusions in sentence form and include the necessary statistical information ($\underline{F}(df_a, df_{resid})$ = calculated F ratio, $\underline{p}$ < or > alpha level).

EXERCISES

1. A developmental psychologist is interested in studying differences in play behavior among 4-year-old boys. Each of 12 boys is left alone in a playroom on three separate occasions. On one occasion the room contains only toys that society would label male oriented such as trucks, toy guns, and so forth. On another occasion the room contains toys that society

would label female oriented—toy cooking utensils, dolls, and so forth. On a third occasion the room contains neutral toys such as coloring books and blocks. The order in which the children see the three types of toys is varied across children. The child is left alone for 30 minutes on each occasion. The amount of time the child plays with the toys is recorded.
a. What are the independent and dependent variables?
b. What do you believe the researcher's hypothesis is?

2. In Exercise 1 the researcher decides to use a one-way ANOVA. Do you agree? Why or why not? If the researcher decides to use a series of *t* tests for correlated samples (e.g., compare male toys with female toys, male toys with neutral toys, etc.) what would be your comment?

3. Construct a diagram of the partitioning of variability for Exercise 1. Construct a summary table and complete it as much as you can with the information in that exercise.

4. A political scientist is studying attitudes toward terrorism by providing three different scenarios to people in 10 different counties in a particular state. The scenarios differ in terms of who the victims are. She samples 15 people in each county and then gets a mean attitude toward each scenario for the county. Therefore, she has 30 values—10 for each of the three scenarios. Each of the 10 values represents a different county. There are three variables in this study, the scenario, the county tested, and the attitude expressed. Set up the ANOVA summary table with as much information as you can from this example.

5. Usually, the "subjects" variable is not tested for a significant difference. Would it make sense to test this type of variable in Exercise 4? Explain.

6. Eight college students are shown a list of 20 common words in class one day. Five words are nouns, five are verbs, five are adverbs, and five are adjectives. The words are presented one at a time in a random order. Each word is shown on a screen for two seconds. The following day the students are asked to recall as many words as possible in two minutes. The number of words recalled is shown below:

Subject	Noun	Verb	Adjective	Adverb
a	3	1	2	2
b	2	2	1	2
c	1	1	0	0
d	4	3	3	1
e	2	1	2	3
f	3	3	4	1
g	1	1	2	1
h	2	2	0	3

   a. What are the independent and dependent variables?
   b. Test H_0; use an alpha level of .01.

7. In a perception experiment, words are presented briefly on a screen to students. The student is supposed to identify the word as quickly as possible. The background of the screen varies. In one instance, it is clear. In another, it contains the faint outline of parts of letters. In another, there is a faint outline of complete letters. And in a fourth condition, the background contains the outline of three-letter words. The researcher hypothesizes that the more similar the background is to the words, the more difficult it will be to identify the words. Each student sees 10 words from each background. The order in which the backgrounds are shown is varied across students. The researcher records the number of words identified in each condition. Identify the independent and dependent variables. State the H_0 and H_1.

8. The data from Exercise 7 are as follows:

| Subject | Type of Background | | | |
	Clear	Part letters	Full letters	Words
a	9	7	7	6
b	8	8	5	5
c	8	6	6	4
d	9	6	7	2
e	9	9	8	5
f	7	4	4	2
g	9	7	7	6

   a. Graph the $\overline{X}$s for each condition.
   b. Calculate the F ratio for this example (use an alpha level of .05), conduct a Tukey HSD test if necessary, and state your conclusion in words.

9. If the researcher in Exercise 7 had shown all words from the Clear condition first, then from the Part-Letter condition, followed by the Full-Letter and Word conditions, would you accept the conclusion that the background *alone* could account for differences in word recognition? Explain.

10. A taste test is conducted at a local supermarket. Three brands of cookies are given to shoppers. Each shopper rates each cookie on a 1-to-7 scale, with 7 indicating high preference. The following ratings were obtained:

Subject	Brand A	Brand B	Brand C
a	5	4	6
b	6	6	5
c	4	4	7
d	5	5	7
e	3	3	4
f	6	6	3
g	5	4	2
h	1	1	1
i	6	3	3
j	5	5	4

a. Conduct the appropriate tests using an alpha level of .01 and state your conclusion in words.

b. Graph the Xs for the three conditions.

11. Since most introductory psychology courses survey a number of different areas of psychology, a psychologist decides to measure student interest in each of the areas prior to the beginning of the first lecture. At the first class meeting, she randomly samples 5 students from her class of 40 students and asks each to rate (on a 1-to-5 scale) his or her interest in each topic area. The higher the rating, the greater the interest. The ratings are as follows:

	Area of Psychology				
Student	Physiology	Learning	Developmental	Abnormal	Social
a	2	2	3	3	1
b	3	2	5	5	4
c	1	3	3	3	1
d	3	4	4	5	4
e	4	4	5	5	4

a. State the H_0 and H_1.

b. Graph the $\overline{X}$ for each area of psychology.

c. Conduct the appropriate tests, using an alpha level of .05, complete the summary table, and state your conclusions in words.

12. Someone might argue that there is very little difference in the interest level of students in the introductory psychology course described in Exercise 11. Is there any evidence in the summary table (or in the interest levels recorded in the data) to support that assumption? Explain.

13. To demonstrate the relationship between the ANOVA for repeated measures and the t test for correlated samples, using the ANOVA for repeated

measures reanalyze the data from the first chapter example in Chapter 11. Take the square root of the F ratio obtained and compare it with the t value obtained in Chapter 11. Are they the same?

14. Based on what you found in Exercise 13, could you use the ANOVA for repeated measures in place of the t test for correlated samples when you have only two conditions? Would you reach the same conclusion with regard to retaining or rejecting H_0 in terms of the procedures used in Exercise 13 and those in Chapter 11?

15. A reseacher has 15 subjects who each serve in five conditions. Therefore there are 75 data values obtained. Construct a partial summary ANOVA table, including the df. What would be the critical F value if the researcher uses an alpha level of .01?

16. To emphasize the relationship between the ANOVA for repeated measures and the one-way ANOVA, reanalyze the data from Table 13.1, which were used in the first chapter example in Chapter 13. Assume that the study consisted of 17 students who each served in all three conditions. Each line of data represents a different student. Compare the SS values obtained in the reanalysis, which is based on the ANOVA for repeated measures, with that found in the original example as described in Chapter 13. Identify values that are identical or are based on combinations of other SS values.

17. Construct a summary table for the ANOVA for repeated measures conducted in Exercise 16. Does the obtained F ratio result in the same statistical decision as that found in Chapter 13?

18. Conduct an ANOVA for repeated measures using the data listed below. Use an alpha level of .05.

			Condition	
Subject	A	B	C	D
a	3	7	5	2
b	1	10	6	0
c	4	8	6	-1
d	5	7	3	2
e	2	9	3	3
f	0	10	4	3

19. Is there anything unusual about the SS values obtained in Exercise 18? If so, explain what is unusual and how it occurred.

20. In Exercise 18 if the design were treated as an independent groups design, would the SS_w be the same as the SS_{resid}? Would the MS_w be the same as the MS_{resid}? Explain your answer in each case.

CHALLENGE QUESTIONS:

1. A person's name is an important part of her self-identity. Female students were asked to rate the first, middle, and last names on a 7-point scale, indicating how much they liked each name. Eighteen students provided the ratings for each name. Their ratings are shown below. (Based on Joubert, C. E. (1985). Factors related to individuals' attitudes toward their names. *Psychological Reports, 57,* 983–986.)

	Name		
Woman	First	Middle	Last
a	6	5	5
b	7	6	6
c	4	5	6
d	7	6	7
e	6	5	5
f	7	6	6
g	4	3	4
h	4	7	6
i	5	4	4
j	5	5	6
k	6	5	4
l	7	3	6
m	6	6	7
n	7	6	5
o	4	5	3
p	5	6	5
q	6	5	4
r	7	6	7

2. Students who scored high on a trait-anxiety scale were given each of three different relaxation therapies. The therapies involved biofeedback, progressive muscle relaxation, and self-relaxation. The order of therapies was balanced across students. Each therapy following instructions lasted 24 minutes. The reduction in muscle tension was recorded for each therapy. The values are shown on the following page. (Based on Rawson, J. R., Bhatnagar, N. S., & Schneider, H. G. (1985). Initial relaxation response: Personality and treatment factors. *Psychological Reports, 57,* 827–830.)

	Type of Therapy		
Student	Biofeedback	Muscle relax.	Self-relaxation
a	2.1	1.1	0.2
b	1.7	0.9	0.4
c	1.8	1.5	0.4
d	2.2	1.0	0.1
e	1.8	0.9	0.3
f	1.7	1.1	0.2
g	1.2	0.6	0.5
h	1.3	1.2	0.4
i	2.6	2.1	0.2
j	2.3	1.9	0.3
k	1.8	1.9	0.6
l	1.5	1.5	0.0

For each question answer the following:
a. What is a plausible research hypothesis?
b. What are the H_0 and H_1?
c. Calculate the appropriate descriptive statistics and graph the means.
d. Calculate the appropriate inferential statistic. Use an alpha level of .05 for Question 1 and .01 for Question 2.
e. State your findings in the proper format and provide a written conclusion about the findings (relating the inferential statistics to the descriptive statistics).

Analyzing Nominal or Ordinal Measurement

OVERVIEW

The previous chapters on inferential statistics have described tests that are used in analyzing data from an interval or ratio scale of measurement. The next four chapters describe statistical procedures that are used when the type of data obtained in a study are (1) on the nominal or ordinal scale of measurement or (2) violate assumptions of the t test or analysis of variance.

In Chapter 16, the chi-squared tests are described. These tests are used most frequently for behavioral data that conform to the nominal scale of measurement. Variables on the nominal scale of measurement have values that cannot be ordered. Gender, color, most appealing candidate in an election, are all examples of nominal-scale variables. The values, whether they be male or female, red or blue, Mr. Jones or Ms. Smith, cannot be quantifiably ordered.

Chapters 17 and 18 describe tests that are used in two-condition studies when the t test cannot or should not be used. The Mann-Whitney U test is used in place of the t test for independent samples, and the Wilcoxon matched-pairs test is an alternative to the t test for correlated samples. Chapter 19 describes two tests that are alternative tests for multiple-condition experiments. The Kruskal-Wallis test is an alternative to the one-way ANOVA, and the Friedman test is an alternative to the ANOVA for repeated measures.

The tests in these three chapters are used when the data conform to an ordinal scale of measurement. Variables on the ordinal scale of measurement have values that are ordered but may not have equal intervals between the values. For instance, football rankings seldom indicate that the differences between teams are equal. A common type of ordinal variable in behavioral science research is ranking.

These tests are also used when the data do not meet the assumptions of the t test or ANOVA. The assumption that the population distributions have equal variability, that is, $\sigma_1^2 = \sigma_2^2 = \sigma_3^2 \cdots$, may not be met or the shape of population distributions may not be normal. With small or unequal N, violations of these assumptions may invalidate the findings of a t test or ANOVA. Therefore, the researcher may use the appropriate test described in the following chapters.

The Chi-Square (χ^2) Test

TERMS DISCUSSED

nominal scale of measurement

frequency observed (f_o)

frequency expected (f_e)

contingency table

inflated N

PROCEDURES DESCRIBED

calculating the χ^2 test for goodness of fit

calculating the f_e for the χ^2 test of independence

calculating the χ^2 test of independence

A number of undergraduate curricula in the behavioral sciences include the possibility for students to enroll in independent-study courses. As the number of independent-study projects increases, the number of individuals needed to supervise the projects increases. Carsrud (1984) reported the findings of a study conducted at the University of Texas at Austin that involved graduate students in psychology supervising undergraduate independent-study projects. Carsrud was interested in the effect of graduate supervision of undergraduate projects on both graduate and undergraduate education.

Twenty-five undergraduates and 25 graduate students participated in this research apprenticeship program. All of the graduate students were in their third year or beyond of graduate study and each graduate student supervised one undergraduate. Each graduate student submitted a proposal for a joint research project involving himself and an undergraduate. All of the undergraduates had grade point averages of 3.5 or better (on a 4-point scale) and had participated in an independent project previously that was directed by a faculty member. The graduate student and undergraduate student met an average of 4-to-8 hours a week on the project.

At the end of the semester each student was asked to evaluate the program on a number of different variables. Of interest in this example are the responses of the graduate students to the question "Did the program increase your research productivity?" Among the many questions Carsrud (1984) wanted to answer was whether or not participation in this type of program was of benefit to graduate students in terms of improving their research skills and productivity. Carsrud assumed that the program would be beneficial to the students. He decided to test his hypothesis using an alpha level of .05. Of the 25 graduate students in the study, 15 answered yes, the program had improved their research productivity, 10 were unsure, and none responded no.

This example is different from previous examples for a number of reasons. First, the type of response is different. The possible responses are yes, no, or not sure. These responses, which cannot be easily ordered on a quantitative dimension are values for a variable that might be called "student's opinion."

A variable that has values that cannot be ordered along a quantitative dimension is on a **nominal scale of measurement.** It might be helpful to think of *nominal* as describing a variable that is a dimension in "name only." There is no underlying ordered dimension for a nominal variable. Values for a nominal-scale variable are often categorical in nature. That is, the values represent distinct categories. For instance, the values yes, no, and not sure describe distinct categories of responses. Nominal-scale variables are often referred to as "categorical variables" in behavioral science research because the values represent different categories.

The other different feature of this example is that it is not an experiment or a correlational study. There is only one variable in this study, perceived effect on research productivity. There are no independent and dependent variables. It is not possible to talk about causal relationships in this example. In fact, because there is only one variable it is inappropriate to discuss relationships at all. For a relationship to exist, there must be at least two variables. Later examples in this chapter will include studies with two variables, but the appropriate beginning point now is a study with only one variable.

DESCRIPTIVE STATISTICS: DESCRIBING THE SAMPLE DATA

In summarizing data from a nominal variable, researchers often report the frequency or number of times each value was given in the sample. In the chapter example the researcher would report that 15 students said yes, 10 said not sure, and no one said no. Because the variable is on a nominal scale, the only measure of central tendency that can be reported is the mode. In this example, the researcher could report that the most frequent response was yes.

There is no appropriate measure of variability to report because the values do not exist on a quantifiable dimension. Remember the measure of variability describes the spread of values on a number line. In graphing the data from a nominal variable, researchers report values of the variable on the x-axis and frequency on the y-axis. In Figure 16.1, the data from the chapter example are shown. A bar graph is used because the variable on the x-axis is nominal. Often, researchers use a "common-sense" approach in ordering the

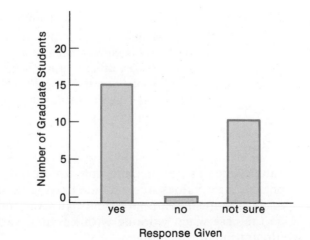

FIGURE 16.1 Bar graph of the data for the first chapter example.

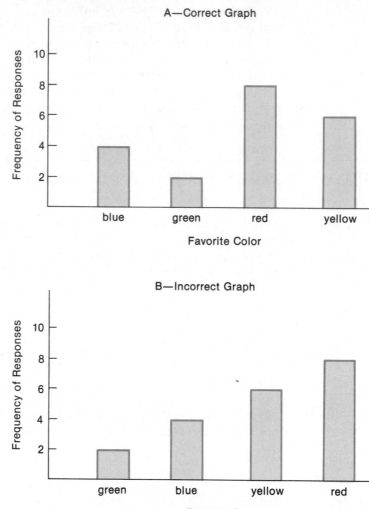

FIGURE 16.2 Two examples of bar graphs for a nominal-scale variable (color).
Top graph is correct because the values are ordered alphabetically
on the x-axis. Bottom graph is incorrect because values are
ordered solely on the basis of frequency of responses. Bottom
graph may give the reader the false impression that a trend exists
across values of color.

values, such as yes, no, and not sure or order the values alphabetically. Do
not order the values *solely* on the basis of their frequencies. This can give the
reader the mistaken impression that some sort of trend exists, which cannot
be the case when working with nominal variables. Figure 16.2 provides an
illustration of this problem.

INFERENTIAL STATISTICS: TESTING FOR A DIFFERENCE

The research hypothesis is fairly straightforward. The hypothesis is that a difference exists among the three types of responses (the values of the nominal variable). The statistical hypotheses H_0 and H_1 are slightly more complicated.

The null hypothesis H_0 assumes that the sample was taken from a population with a particular frequency distribution. In many cases, including the chapter example, this distribution assumes that all values have the same or equal frequencies. That is, if there is no difference among the values given, then the frequencies for all values should be the same. The alternative hypothesis H_1 assumes that the population is described by a different type of frequency distribution, one in which the frequencies for each value are not the same. This statistical hypothesis, of course, is more similar to the research hypothesis than is H_0. Therefore, the researcher in this example wants to reject H_0 and thereby support the research hypothesis.

THE CHI-SQUARE (χ^2) TEST FOR GOODNESS OF FIT

The appropriate nonparametric test to use is called the chi-square test for goodness of fit. The term "goodness of fit" is used because the test measures how well a sample of frequency values "fits" with a population distribution described by H_0. The test is also sometimes referred to as the chi-square test for one sample because only one sample is used and being compared with the population distribution.

The test provides the researcher with a statistic called chi-square χ^2 (the Greek letter chi, pronounced ki). It is based on the probability of obtaining a sample distribution with different frequencies or occurences of values, given that it came from the population distribution described by H_0. The test and the statistical hypotheses make no assumptions about population parameters nor do they assume that the shape of the population distribution is normal; therefore, the test is nonparametric.

The statistic χ^2 is based on the discrepancy or difference between the actual observed frequencies and the frequencies expected if the H_0 is true. If H_0 is true, then one might expect the discrepancy to be small and χ^2 will be small. If H_0 is false, then the discrepancy between the observed and expected frequencies will be large and χ^2 will be large.

Notice that the χ^2 statistic is squared. This indicates that negative values are not possible. It is based on the squared deviations of what was observed in the sample and what was expected based on H_0. For each categorical value, the discrepancy in frequencies between what was observed and what was expected is squared and then divided by the frequency expected.

The range of χ^2 values is from 0 to ∞ (infinity). The larger the value, the greater the discrepancy between the observed and expected frequencies. Obviously, if there is no discrepancy between what was observed and what was predicted by H_0, then the squared deviations will be 0 or quite small. This would indicate "good fit" between the sample and the population distribution described by H_0. With larger values of χ^2, the deviations between what is observed and what is expected are larger and the fit between the sample distribution and population distribution described by H_0 is not good. Since most researchers want to reject H_0 in order to support their research hypothesis, researchers hope that the fit is not good. Let us now see how to calculate the χ^2 statistic.

CALCULATING χ^2 STATISTIC

The procedure for calculating χ^2 is easy and straightforward. For each category, the researcher must know the frequency observed f_o and the frequency expected f_e if H_0 is true. In the chapter example there are three categories or response values, yes, no, and not sure. The f_o for each respective category is 15, 0, and 10. The **frequency observed f_o** is based on the actual frequencies observed in the sample. The frequency expected f_e is based on the expected frequencies, given that the H_0 is true. To determine f_e it is necessary to use H_0 to calculate the proportion of the population distribution corresponding to each category value. Once the proportions are determined, the f_e for each value is calculated by multiplying the proportion by the sample size N

$$f_e = \text{Proportion of Distribution} \times N. \tag{37}$$

In the chapter example, H_0 assumes that the proportion of responses among the categories are equal to one another. Since there are three categories, the proportion of the distribution for each response is .33 (1/number of categories, 3). Using Formula 37 in the chapter example results in

$$\begin{aligned} f_e &= \text{Proportion of Distribution} \times N \\ &= .33 \times 25 \\ &= 8.33. \end{aligned} \tag{37}$$

The f_e is identical for each category because the H_0 describes the situation in which each response category has the same frequency. If there is no difference among the three different responses, then 8.33 graduate students should have given each response in the sample of 25 students. (Obviously it is not possible to have 0.33 students, but in calculating the f_e it is common practice to round off at two decimal places.)

Therefore, f_o is based on the sample data and f_e is based on H_0. The f_o and f_e for each response category for the chapter example are shown at the top in Table 16.1. To determine if the difference is large enough to reject H_0, it is necessary to calculate χ^2. The formula for χ^2 is

$$\chi^2 = \Sigma \frac{(f_o - f_e)^2}{f_e}. \tag{38}$$

TABLE 16.1   Procedure for Calculating the χ^2 Statistic for the Chapter Example

	Type of Response		
	Yes	No	Not sure
f_o	15	0	10
f_e	8.33	8.33	8.33

Using Formula 38: $\chi^2 = \Sigma \dfrac{(f_o - f_e)^2}{f_e}$

$$\chi^2 = \frac{(15 - 8.33)^2}{8.33} + \frac{(0 - 8.33)^2}{8.33} + \frac{(10 - 8.33)^2}{8.33}$$

$$= \frac{44.49}{8.33} + \frac{69.39}{8.33} + \frac{2.79}{8.33}$$

$$= 5.34 + 8.33 + 0.33$$

$$= 14.00$$

The procedure involved in Formula 38 requires that *for each response cate-gory* the difference between f_o and f_e is calculated and squared and that this squared difference is then divided by f_e for that category. The resulting values for each response category are then added together to give the χ^2 statistic. It is important to note that the summation refers to adding the values for each category. In some studies, discrepancies between the observed and expected frequencies may occur in only a few of the response categories. The procedure is shown in Table 16.1 for the chapter example.

If H_0 is true, then the differences between f_o and f_e should be small and the χ^2 statistic will be small. If the differences are large, then the fit between what is observed and what is expected is not good and the χ^2 statistic will be large.

Common mistakes made in calculating the χ^2 statistic include not squar-ing the difference between f_o and f_e, forgetting to divide by f_e, and failing to sum the values for all the response categories. As a good operating rule look at the difference between f_o and f_e and anticipate whether χ^2 will be large or small. Remember it can never be less than 0.

DETERMINING WHETHER TO RETAIN OR REJECT H_0

Once the χ^2 statistic has been calculated it can be compared to a critical χ^2 value. If H_0 is true, then the χ^2 values are distributed in a positively skewed fashion. This distribution is known as the χ^2 distribution. Briefly, it is a frequency distribution that describes the distribution of standard (z) scores that are squared (or sums of squared z scores). Obviously, if z scores are squared, then negative values are not possible, and as you might suspect, the greatest frequency of squared values would be between 0 and 1, since approximately two-thirds of all z scores in a normal distribution fall between z scores of -1

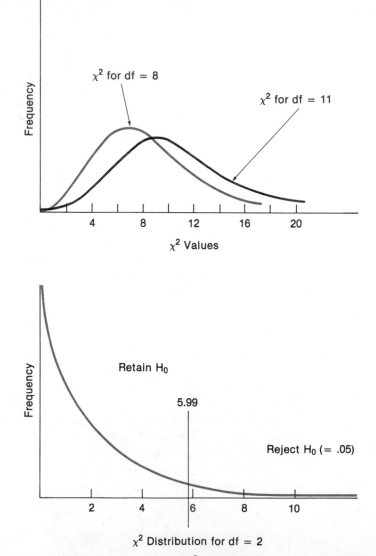

FIGURE 16.3 Examples of chi-square (χ^2) distributions. The top diagram illustrates two distributions; the bottom diagram shows the distribution for the chapter example.

and $+1$. Deviant z scores would have large positive values because both the extreme negative and positive z scores would be squared.

Although discussion of the nature of χ^2 distributions is outside the scope of this text, it is important to note two properties. The first is that it is positively skewed. The second is that a family of distributions exists that is defined by one value, the degrees of freedom. However, as the number of response categories increase (and df increases), the shape becomes less skewed. Two of these distributions are shown at the top in Figure 16.3.

The bottom distribution in Figure 16.3 is the χ^2 distribution for this example. It is based on 2 degrees of freedom. The df for the χ^2 test for goodness of fit is equal to the number of categories minus 1

$$df = \text{Number of Categories} - 1.$$

In the chapter example the df equals 2 (3 categories $-$ 1). Using Table X in Appendix E and an alpha (rejection) level of .05, the critical χ^2 is 5.99. The calculated χ^2 value from Table 16.1 is 14.00. Clearly, this value is in the reject-H_0 region. Therefore, H_0 would be rejected, and the researcher would conclude that all of the responses were not equally likely. In fact Carsrud (1984) could state that, "the graduate students felt the program increased their research productivity, $\chi^2(2) = 14.00$, $\underline{p} < .05$."

This conclusion is based on the statistical result and a visual inspection of the frequency data. Because the majority of the students responded yes and none responded no, it is obvious that the difference in the example is in the direction of the students feeling that the program was beneficial. In reporting the calculated χ^2 statistic the df are reported in parentheses and the alpha level should also be included.

A SECOND EXAMPLE OF THE χ^2 TEST FOR GOODNESS OF FIT

Let us consider another example for one variable before moving on to more complicated examples. An instructor has the reputation of being a hard grader. That is, she does not give as many high grades, "A"s and "B"s, as other instructors. She tells you that in the most recent semester, 5 students in her class earned "A"s, 10 students earned "B"s, 27 students earned "C"s, 7 students earned "D"s, and 1 received an "F." She also tells you that in the college, generally 20% of the grades awarded were "A"s, 30% were "B"s, 40% were "C"s, 8% were "D"s, and 2% were "F"s. You would like to determine if her distribution of grades, that is, the number of students getting different grades, is different from that in the college. In this example, let us use an alpha level of .05.

This example has one variable, the grade in the course. There are five values or categories possible, "A," "B," "C," "D," and "F." Her sample size N is 50, and the f_o for each of the respective categories is shown at the top in Table 16.2. The H_0 is needed in order to determine the f_e.

TABLE 16.2   Data and Calculation of χ^2 for the Second Example

	Grade Received				
	"A"	"B"	"C"	"D"	"F"
f_o (number of students)	5	10	27	7	1

Using Formula 37: f_e = Proportion of Distribution × N

$$= \quad \begin{matrix} (.20 \times 50) \\ 10, \end{matrix} \quad \begin{matrix} (.30 \times 50) \\ 15, \end{matrix} \quad \begin{matrix} (.40 \times 50) \\ 20, \end{matrix} \quad \begin{matrix} (.08 \times 50) \\ 4, \end{matrix} \quad \begin{matrix} (.02 \times 50) \\ 1 \end{matrix}$$

Using Formula 38: $\chi^2 = \Sigma \dfrac{(f_o - f_e)^2}{f_e}$

$$= \frac{(5-10)^2}{10} + \frac{(10-15)^2}{15} + \frac{(27-20)^2}{20} + \frac{(7-4)^2}{4} + \frac{(1-1)^2}{1}$$

$$= \frac{25}{10} + \frac{25}{15} + \frac{49}{20} + \frac{9}{4} + \frac{0}{1}$$

$$= 2.50 + 1.67 + 2.45 + 2.25 + 0.00$$

$$= \mathbf{8.87.}$$

Unlike the previous example, H_0 does not assume that each category should have the same frequency. Rather, the H_0 we are testing is that her sample of grades came from a population described by the college distribution of grades. And in that population the grades are *not* equally distributed. The proportion of grades differs for each grade category. The H_1 assumes that her distribution of grades came from a different population distribution.

The calculation of f_e for each response category depends on the proportion for that category in the population. These proportions are expressed as the percentage of students receiving a particular grade at the college. Formula 37 can be used to provide the necessary f_e

$$f_e = \text{Proportion of Distribution} \times N. \tag{37}$$

In Table 16.2 the calculations for each f_e are shown. The sample size is 50.

Once f_o and f_e have been determined for each category, then Formula 38 can be used to calculate χ^2. The calculations are shown in Table 16.2. A χ^2 of 8.87 was calculated. To determine if H_0 should be rejected, it is necessary to find the critical χ^2 value. There are five response categories in this example. Therefore, the df = 4 (number of categories [5] − 1). The critical χ^2 value in Table X with a rejection region of .05 and 4 df is 9.48. The calculated χ^2 is less than this value. Therefore, H_0 should be retained. The grading distribution of this instructor does not differ significantly from that of the college in general, $\underline{\chi}^2(4) = 8.87$, $\underline{p} > .05$.

THE χ^2 TEST OF INDEPENDENCE

Darley and Latané (1968) reported a study on bystander apathy, that is, whether an individual helps another person in an emergency. Briefly, bystander apathy is related to the finding that people in groups are less likely to help in an emergency situation than when they are alone. College students participated in a study in which the cover story was that the study concerned personal problems faced by students in a college environment. To avoid possible embarrassment and assure anonymity, the students were placed in separate rooms and interacted over an intercom. The students were told that the experimenter would not be present to listen to the conversation and that only one microphone would be active at a time. During the study, one of the subjects, a confederate cooperating with the experimenter, feigned an epileptic seizure and asked for help. Darley and Latané were interested in whether or not the student left the room to seek help. Darley and Latané manipulated the number of people who were supposedly involved in the conversation. In some cases, only the subject and the confederate were involved, a 2-person group. In other cases, the subject was led to believe there were two other people, a 3-person group; or five other people, a 6-person group. A student served as a subject in only one group. Darley and Latané hypothesized that as the size of the group increased, helping behavior would decrease. The number of students who sought help and did not seek help is shown in Table 16.3.

This example is more involved than the previous two in that there are two variables of interest. The first variable is the independent variable, the size of the group. There are three values: 2, 3, and 6. This variable is on the ratio scale of measurement. (The values can be placed on a number line with equal intervals and there is a real zero point.)

The other variable, the dependent variable, is the student's helping response. There are two possible values, sought help or did not help. This variable is on the nominal scale of measurement. The values cannot be ordered. Only the number or frequency of responses can be tabulated. Because the

TABLE 16.3 The Number of Students Who Helped or Did Not Help in the Third Chapter Example

	Size of Group		
	2 People	*3 People*	*6 People*
Helped	11	16	4
Did Not Help	2	10	9

variable being analyzed is nominal, a χ^2 test will be used. Unlike the previous examples, which had only one variable, this example has two and therefore the χ^2 test for goodness of fit is inappropriate.

In this example the researchers want to determine if group size (the independent variable) influenced helping behavior (the dependent variable). They want to determine if a relationship exists between the two variables. They assume from previous research and observation, that it does. The test to use in this case is the χ^2 test of independence. This test is used when there are two variables, one of which is on a nominal scale, and the researcher is interested in determining if a relationship exists between the variables.

DESCRIBING THE DATA

As was shown earlier, the researcher can only tabulate the number or frequency of responses for each category. Using the data from Table 16.3, a graph of the responses by group size is shown in Figure 16.4. The independent variable is graphed on the x-axis, and frequency is reported on the y-axis. The two different response categories are represented by different shaded bars. A bar graph was used instead of a line graph because the independent variable, although quantitative, is noncontinuous (it is not possible to have groups with fractions of people). Notice that the data tend to support the researchers' hypothesis. As group size increases, the proportion of students who seek help decreases.

TESTING FOR A DIFFERENCE

Because two variables are involved, it is necessary to use the χ^2 test of independence. The null hypothesis H_0 for this test assumes that the two variables are unrelated and independent of each other. This hypothesis describes the

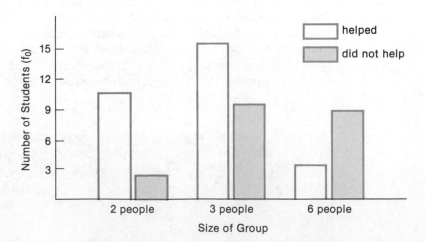

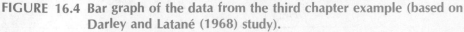

FIGURE 16.4 Bar graph of the data from the third chapter example (based on Darley and Latané (1968) study).

situation in which the population proportions (or frequencies) for any level or value of one variable are the same at all levels of the other variable. In the example, this means that the proportion who help is the same for each group size.

The alternative hypothesis H_1 assumes that the variables are related to each other. This describes the situation in which the population proportions at a particular level of variable depend on the level or value of the second variable. Using the example, this describes the case in which the proportion who help depends on the size of the group. Obviously, the H_1 is more similar to the research hypothesis. Therefore, the researchers test the H_0 and hope to reject it as a plausible hypothesis. For this example, an alpha level of .05 will be used.

To compute χ^2 for this example Formula 38 will again be used

$$\chi^2 = \Sigma \frac{(f_o - f_e)^2}{f_e}. \tag{38}$$

The f_o are shown at the top in Table 16.4 and are identical to those from Table 16.3. There are six categories or cells in this study. They are displayed in a contingency table. A **contingency table** displays the frequencies observed in a study involving two variables. The categories result from combining the levels of each variable—two possible responses and three group sizes. This table can be referred to as a 2×3 contingency table. The numbers refer to the number of rows and columns (the levels of each variable).

In a χ^2 test of independence the number of levels of the two variables are multiplied to identify the number of categories or cells. Each cell will have its own f_o. It is also necessary to calculate an f_e for each cell. This is more complicated because the f_e is based on the H_0, which assumes that the two variables are independent of each other.

To determine the f_e for each cell, the researcher needs the row and column totals along with N, the sample size. In the contingency tables in Table 16.4, the row and column margins are shown. If H_0 is true, then the two variables are unrelated. The contingency table in the middle of Table 16.4 describes this situation. The frequencies in this contingency table are based on the assumption that the two variables are independent of each other.

If the variables are independent of each other, then the overall proportion of observations for a given row should be the expected proportion for each column entry in that row—for example, 31 of the 52 students helped in the example. The proportion that helped is 31/52 or .596. Given that there were 13 students in the 2-people condition, it would be expected that .596 of those students would help. Likewise, .596 of those in the 3-people and 6-people conditions would help. This assumes, of course, that the two variable sizes of the group and helping behavior are independent.

It is possible to calculate the f_e by first calculating the overall proportion for each row and then multiplying the proportion by the overall N for each column. For example, for the 2-people group, the f_e could be determined by multiplying the row proportion (31/52) by the column N, 13. The resulting value is 7.75. This same procedure could be followed for each cell.

TABLE 16.4   Calculation of f_e and χ^2 for the Third Chapter Example

	Size of Group			
Response	2 People	3 People	6 People	Row tot.
Helped	11	16	4	31
Did Not Help	2	10	9	21
Column Tot.	13	26	13	N = 52

$$\text{Using Formula 39:}\quad f_e = \frac{\text{Row Total} \times \text{Column Total}}{N}$$

	Size of Group			
Response	2 People	3 People	6 People	Row tot.
Helped	$\frac{31 \times 13}{52} = 7.75$	$\frac{31 \times 26}{52} = 15.50$	$\frac{31 \times 13}{52} = 7.75$	31
Did Not Help	$\frac{21 \times 13}{52} = 5.25$	$\frac{21 \times 26}{52} = 10.50$	$\frac{21 \times 13}{52} = 5.25$	21
Column Tot.	13	26	13	N = 52

$$\text{Using Formula 38:}\quad \chi^2 = \Sigma \frac{(f_o - f_e)^2}{f_e}$$

$$\chi^2 = \frac{(11 - 7.75)^2}{7.75} + \frac{(16 - 15.50)^2}{15.50} + \frac{(4 - 7.75)^2}{7.75} + \frac{(2 - 5.25)^2}{5.25} + \frac{(10 - 10.50)^2}{10.50} + \frac{(9 - 5.25)^2}{5.25}$$

$$= \frac{10.56}{7.75} + \frac{0.25}{15.50} + \frac{14.06}{7.75} + \frac{10.56}{5.25} + \frac{0.25}{10.50} + \frac{14.06}{5.25}$$

$$= 1.36 + 0.02 + 1.81 + 2.01 + 0.02 + 2.68$$

$$= 7.90$$

Formula 39 combines these two steps into one

$$f_e = \frac{\text{Row Total} \times \text{Column Total}}{N}. \tag{39}$$

This procedure was followed for all six cells in the example. Note that the f_e for the cells in a column or row must equal the column or row totals.

The two contingency tables in Table 16.4 provide the researcher with the necessary information to calculate χ^2. The top contingency table, containing the f_o, is based on the actual sample data. The other contingency table, containing the f_e, lists the way the sample data would be distributed if the H_0 was true and the two variables were independent of each other.

Notice that the f_e is not identical in each cell. The only way that would occur is if all row and column totals were the same. By inspecting the tables in Table 16.4, you can see that twice as many students participated in the 3-

group condition than in the other conditions. You would expect, therefore, more students to help in this condition, which is what f_e shows.

The χ^2 test of independence allows the researcher to determine if the contingency table based on observed frequencies is different enough from the contingency table based on H_0 to conclude that the frequencies came from different population distributions. To calculate χ^2, the same formula used earlier is needed

$$\chi^2 = \Sigma \, \frac{(f_o - f_e)^2}{f_e}. \tag{38}$$

The squared difference between f_o and f_e is divided by f_e for each *cell*. These values are then added together. The procedure for the example is shown at the bottom in Table 16.4.

A χ^2 of 7.90 was calculated. To determine the critical χ^2 from Table X it

---

BOX 16.1   **Measuring the Association between Two Variables Using Frequency Data**

Like the Pearson r coefficient, which measures the strength of a linear relationship between two variables, Cramer's ϕ coefficient measures the strength of a relationship between two variables using frequency data. The range of the coefficient is from 0 (no relationship) to 1 (a perfect relationship). The calculation of the coefficient is very easy

$$\phi = \sqrt{\frac{\chi^2}{N(k-1)}}.$$

The χ^2 value is that obtained from Formula 38; N is the sample size; and, k is the smaller value of the number of columns or number of rows. For the example based on the Darley and Latané (1968) study, the following coefficient would be obtained:

$$\phi = \sqrt{\frac{7.90}{52(1)}}$$

$$\phi = .39.$$

Although a significant relationship exists between the size of the group and helping behavior, the ϕ coefficient of .39 reveals that the relationship is on the weak side. Assuming that a coefficient between .40 and .60 would be moderate, we can see that in this study the size of the group accounts for a small portion of the variability in helping behavior.

is necessary to calculate the appropriate df. For the χ^2 test of independence the df are based on the number of rows and columns in the contingency table

$$df = (\text{Number of Rows} - 1)(\text{Number of Columns} - 1). \qquad (40)$$

In this example the df are

$$df = (2 - 1)(3 - 1)$$
$$= 2.$$

Using a rejection level of .05 and df of 2, the critical χ^2 in Table X is 5.99. The calculated χ^2 is greater than the critical χ^2. Therefore, H_0 is rejected. Darley and Latané can conclude "that as group size increased, fewer students sought help, $\chi^2(2) = 7.90, p < .05.$"

As was mentioned in Chapter 5, the χ^2 test of independence can also be used to determine the strength of the relationship between two variables, when one or both of the variables are on the nominal scale of measurement. This procedure is described in Box 16.1.

ANOTHER EXAMPLE OF THE χ^2 TEST OF INDEPENDENCE

Stanley Milgram was well known for his work on obedience to authority. In the 1960s, he conducted a number of studies in which individuals were asked to shock another person as part of a learning experiment. Although the individuals did not know it then, the other person was never shocked. Milgram was particularly interested in how long an individual would obey his commands to keep increasing the shock intensity that the other person was supposedly getting. Milgram (1965) reported one study in which he manipulated the distance between the person giving the shock and the person receiving it. In a remote condition, the person receiving the shock was in another room and the individual administering the shock could not hear or see the other person. In the voice-feedback condition, the person receiving the shock was in another room but the door was left ajar so that the individual could hear the complaints of the person being shocked. In the proximity condition, the two individuals sat 1 1/2 feet apart so that both voice and visual information was available. In the touch proximity condition, the person being shocked refused to place his hand on a shock plate, so the individual administering the shock actually had to have physical contact with the person by placing the person's hand on the shock plate when the shock was over 150 volts. There were 40 participants in each of these four conditions.

Milgram (1965) believed that the closer a person was to the person being shocked, the less likely he would be to continue to harm the person and obey the authority figure who was ordering more intense electrical shocks. Milgram recorded the number of individuals in each condition who obeyed his orders to continue the shocks until reaching the maximal level and the number of individuals who defied his orders. These frequencies are shown in Table 16.5. In testing his hypothesis an alpha level of .01 will be used.

TABLE 16.5	The Number of Subjects Who Obeyed or Disobeyed in the Fourth Chapter Example			
	Proximity of the Subject and Victim			
Response	Remote	Voice feedback	Proximity	Touch proximity
Obeyed	26	25	16	12
Disobeyed	14	15	24	28

This example like the last is an experiment with two variables. The independent variable is the proximity of the subject and the victim. There are four levels or values of this variable, remote, voice feedback, proximity, and touch proximity. This is an ordinal variable. The dependent variable is a nominal variable. It is the obedience of the subject. The subject either obeys or disobeys the authority figure in giving the shock. The research hypothesis is that the proximity of the subject and victim will influence the subject's obedience. The closer the two are, the less likely the subject is to obey.

A bar graph of the number of subjects who obeyed and disobeyed in each condition is shown in Figure 16.5. The independent variable is represented on the x-axis, frequencies on the y-axis, and the two possible responses as

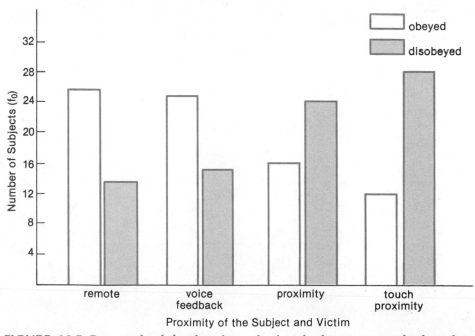

FIGURE 16.5 Bar graph of the data from the fourth chapter example (based on Milgram (1965) study).

differently shaded bars. Notice that the data tend to support Milgram's hypothesis. In fact, the condition with the largest number of obedient subjects is the remote condition.

The H_0 assumes that the two variables are unrelated to each other. The H_1 assumes the opposite; namely, that obedience is related to proximity. The research hypothesis is more similar to the H_1. To test the H_0, it is necessary to determine the f_o and f_e for each cell or category.

In Table 16.6, the 2×4 contingency table for the observed frequencies f_o is shown at the top. Below it is the contingency table showing the f_e for each cell. These values were calculated using Formula 39. This table reflects

TABLE 16.6   Calculation of f_e and χ^2 for the Fourth Chapter Example

| | \multicolumn{4}{c}{Proximity of the Subject and Victim} | |
	Remote	Voice feedback	Proximity	Touch proximity	Row tot.
Obeyed	26	25	16	12	79
Disobeyed	14	15	24	28	81
Column Tot.	40	40	40	40	N = 160

$$\text{Using Formula 39:} \quad f_e = \frac{\text{Row Total} \times \text{Column Total}}{N}$$

| | \multicolumn{4}{c}{Proximity of the Subject and Victim} | |
Response	Remote	Voice feedback	Proximity	Touch proximity	Row tot.
Obeyed	$\frac{79 \times 40}{160} = 19.75$	$\frac{79 \times 40}{160} = 19.75$	$\frac{79 \times 40}{160} = 19.75$	$\frac{79 \times 40}{160} = 19.75$	79
Disobeyed	$\frac{81 \times 40}{160} = 20.25$	$\frac{81 \times 40}{160} = 20.25$	$\frac{81 \times 40}{160} = 20.25$	$\frac{81 \times 40}{160} = 20.25$	81
Column Tot.	40	40	40	40	N = 160

$$\text{Using Formula 38:} \quad \chi^2 = \Sigma \frac{(f_o - f_e)^2}{f_e}$$

$$\chi^2 = \frac{(26 - 19.75)^2}{19.75} + \frac{(25 - 19.75)^2}{19.75} + \frac{(16 - 19.75)^2}{19.75} + \frac{(12 - 19.75)^2}{19.75} +$$
$$\frac{(14 - 20.25)^2}{20.25} + \frac{(15 - 20.25)^2}{20.25} + \frac{(24 - 20.25)^2}{20.25} + \frac{(28 - 20.25)^2}{20.25}$$
$$= \frac{39.06}{19.75} + \frac{27.56}{19.75} + \frac{14.06}{19.75} + \frac{60.06}{19.75} + \frac{39.06}{20.25} + \frac{27.56}{20.25} + \frac{14.06}{20.25} + \frac{60.06}{20.25}$$
$$= 1.98 + 1.40 + 0.71 + 3.04 + 1.93 + 1.36 + 0.69 + 2.97$$
$$= \mathbf{14.08}$$

what should have been found if H_0 were true and the two variables were independent of each other. Notice that since the column totals are all the same (40), the f_e across each row is the same. At the bottom of Table 16.6, the calculations of χ^2 are shown. A χ^2 of 14.08 was calculated.

To determine the critical χ^2, it is necessary to determine the df

$$\begin{aligned} df &- \text{(Number of Rows} - 1)\text{(Number of Columns} - 1)(40) \qquad (40) \\ &= (2 - 1)(4 - 1) \\ &= 3. \end{aligned}$$

Using an alpha level of .01, the critical χ^2 is 11.34. The calculated χ^2 is greater than the critical χ^2; therefore, H_0 can be rejected. Milgram can conclude "that subjects were less likely to obey an authority figure and shock another person if they were physically close to the victim, $\chi^2(3) - 14.08$, $p < .01$."

It should be mentioned that both the Darley and Latané (1968) and Milgram (1965) studies are famous studies cited often in the literature. Both raised a number of ethical questions with regard to the treatment of human subjects, primarily in terms of potential psychological risk to the subject. Although they were of considerable benefit to the field of psychology at the time they were conducted, exact replications of these studies would be nearly impossible today. The benefits to our understanding of human behavior would probably not outweigh the potential risks to the participants and therefore repeating the studies would be difficult to justify.

ASSUMPTIONS AND LIMITATIONS IN USING THE CHI-SQUARE TESTS

There are a number of important issues that a researcher needs to be aware of in using the χ^2 test. The first is that it is a nonparametric test. The statistical hypotheses involved in the χ^2 test make no assumptions about parameters, about the equal variability in the population distributions, or about the shape of the population distribution being normal.

Another point is that the test assumes the researcher is analyzing frequencies. The researcher must be using number of respondents or frequency information. The χ^2 test cannot be used with percentages or proportions. If the data are in the form of percentages, then multiply the percentages by N to transform them into frequencies.

Another assumption is that the frequencies are independent of each other. This means, among other things, that the research design must be an independent groups design. A participant cannot give a response that fits in more than one category. This problem is referred to as an inflated N. An **inflated N** occurs when participants are allowed to give more than one response resulting in an N larger than the number of participants. Furthermore, the response of any one participant must be independent or unrelated to the responses of other participants. For instance, if one participant responds yes, then that cannot influence any other respondent to either say yes or no.

An additional assumption is that all respondents are included in the frequency information. All response levels must be included in the analysis. For example, if a researcher were investigating consumer preference for soft drinks and asked individuals if they liked a particular soft drink, she could not just analyze the yes responses. The researcher would need to include both the yes and no frequencies for each type of soft drink. To check that this assumption is being met, the researcher should be sure that the sample size N is the same as the sum of all the observed frequencies f_o.

The last issue deals with sample size N. As the sample size increases, the probability of getting a significant finding increases. Since f_o and f_e are based on N, an increase in N makes it more likely that significant differences will be found. Significant differences are more likely with larger sample sizes. Therefore, the researcher must be aware of the distinction between a significant difference and a difference big enough to be meaningful when the sample size is large. Conversely, with small sample sizes, a difference may appear to be large yet not reach a signficance level needed for rejecting H_0. With a small sample size, the χ^2 may not be very powerful statistically.

Related to this issue of sample size is a problem when the f_e is small in a cell or category. The χ^2 test may not accurately test the H_0 when df = 1 (for instance, a 2 × 2 contingency table) and there are cells with f_e less than 5. Some people suggest that a correction factor be used, others suggest that a correction factor is not necessary. The reader is referred to Camilli and Hopkins (1978), who suggest that no correction factor is needed when the sample size is 20 or larger.

SUMMARY

When a study involves data that correspond to a nominal scale of measurement, the χ^2 test is appropriate to use. A variable that is on the nominal scale of measurement will have values that are qualitatively different and cannot be ordered on a quantitative (numerical) dimension. These variables are often called "categorical" variables. The only measure of central tendency that can be reported is the mode. No measure of variability is really appropriate for a nominal variable.

When looking for differences in the frequency of behavior for one variable, the χ^2 test for goodness of fit is the appropriate test to use. The H_0 assumes that the observed frequencies of behavior f_o for the various levels of the variable will be based on a particular population frequency distribution. The H_1 assumes that the sample data came from a different population distribution.

If the reseacher is analyzing a study in which the variable measuring behavior is a nominal variable, then the χ^2 test of independence should be used. The H_0 describes the situation in which the research variables are unrelated to or independent of each other. The H_1 describes the situation in which the variables are related. Since most research hypotheses assume that the variables of study are related, the research hypothesis is more similar to the H_1.

For both χ^2 tests, the χ^2 statistic involves calculating the squared difference between the frequencies observed f_o and the frequencies expected f_e if the H_0 is true. The larger the differences between these frequencies, the larger the χ^2 statistic. The calculated χ^2 is compared with the critical χ^2 value, which is based on a χ^2 distribution for the H_0. If the calculated χ^2 equals or exceeds the critical χ^2, then the H_0 is rejected and the research hypothesis is supported.

Assumptions of the χ^2 test include that (1) the sample is randomly selected from the population, (2) the analysis is based on frequencies, (3) the frequencies are independent of each other, and (4) all frequencies observed are included in the analysis. When large sample sizes are used, it is possible to get a significant difference that may have little practical significance. Likewise, with small sample sizes the χ^2 test may not be statistically powerful enough for the researcher to reject a false H_0.

SUMMARY FOR USING THE χ^2 TEST FOR GOODNESS OF FIT

1. Develop the research hypothesis and determine the alpha level, usually .05 or .01.

2. State H_0 and H_1. Based on H_0, determine f_e for each category or level of the variable using Formula 37

$$f_e = \text{Proportion of Distribution} \times N. \tag{37}$$

3. Using the frequency observed, f_o, and f_e for each level of the variable, calculate χ^2 with Formula 38

$$\chi^2 = \Sigma \frac{(f_o - f_e)^2}{f_e}. \tag{38}$$

4. Find the critical χ^2 from Table X in Appendix. The degrees of freedom is one less than the number of levels or categories of the variable

$$df = \text{Number of Categories} - 1.$$

5. If the calculated χ^2 is equal to or greater than the critical χ^2, then reject H_0; otherwise, retain H_0. State your conclusion in words and include the necessary statistics, $\underline{\chi}^2(df) = $ calculated χ^2, $\underline{p} < $ or $>$ rejection level used.

SUMMARY FOR USING THE χ^2 TEST OF INDEPENDENCE

1. Develop the research hypothesis and determine the alpha level, usually .05 or .01. The research hypothesis usually is stated in terms of a relationship existing between the variables.

2. State H_0 and H_1. The null hypothesis H_0 assumes that the two variables are independent of or unrelated to each other. The alternative hypothesis H_1 assumes that a relationship exists between the two variables.

3. Construct a contingency table, with the levels of one variable represented in columns and the levels of the other variable in rows. The f_o for each

category or cell should be listed. Calculate the margin totals for each row and column.

4. Use Formula 39 to find the f_e for each cell

$$f_e = \frac{\text{Row total} \times \text{Column Total}}{N}.$$ (39)

5. Using the frequency observed f_o and f_e for each level of the variable, calculate χ^2 with Formula 38

$$\chi^2 = \Sigma \frac{(f_o - f_e)^2}{f_e}$$ (38)

6. Find the critical χ^2 from Table X. The degrees of freedom are based on the number of rows and columns

$$\text{df} = (\text{Number of Rows} - 1)(\text{Number of Columns} - 1).$$ (40)

7. If the calculated χ^2 is equal to or greater than the critical χ^2, then reject H_0; otherwise, retain H_0. State your conclusion in words and include the necessary statistics, $\underline{\chi}^2(\text{df}) = \text{calculated } \chi^2$, $\underline{p} <$ or $>$ rejection level used.

EXERCISES

1. How does a nominal-scale variable differ from an ordinal-scale variable? From an interval- or ratio-scaled variable? Give an example of each.

2. An advertising agency asks 50 people to taste each of three soft drinks. One is a regular drink, another is the diet version, and the third is the caffeine-free version. After testing each drink, the people state whether they like it or not. They find that 40 like the regular drink and 10 dislike it, 15 say they like the diet drink and 35 do not, and 45 like the caffeine-free drink and 5 do not. What are the two variables in this study? If you set up a contingency table, what would it look like? On what scale of measurement is each variable?

3. What assumption of the χ^2 test is being violated in Exercise 2?

4. A political survey is taken two weeks before an election. Five hundred people are asked their preference from among three candidates. What type of χ^2 test would be appropriate? What is the f_e? (Assume people express an opinion for only one of the three candidates.)

5. In Exercise 4, the following f_o are obtained: Candidate A has 180 favorable responses, Candidate B has 140, and Candidate C has 140. Using an alpha level of .05, what should be the conclusion of the survey?

6. Students often ask if instructors will grade on the normal curve. Assuming a normal curve, 4% of the class should get an "F" and 4% an "A," 12% should get "D"s and 12% should get "B"s, with the remaining students getting "C"s. Take the data from the second example in the chapter

with the instructor's distribution of grades and determine if her distribution differs significantly from the normal curve. Use an alpha level of .05.

7. Construct a graph of the f_o for the data from the second chapter example.

8. A researcher tries to replicate a study using nominal data. The original study was based on a sample of 400 and reported a significant difference with an alpha level of .05. In the replication, the researcher uses 50 college students and does not find a difference, although the proportions are almost identical to those in the original study. What could statistically explain this inability to replicate the original study's finding?

9. A fellow student tells you that he has conducted a survey on the desirability of coed dorms. He reports that 86 men and 33 women were in favor of coed dorms. He uses a χ^2 test for goodness of fit, with gender as that variable and finds a significant difference. What comments do you have for him with regard to this test?

10. A researcher has a 4×3 contingency table. What are the df and the critical χ^2 for an alpha level of .01? If only the margin totals were provided to you, what other information would you need to calculate the f_e for each category? Explain.

11. A hospital is interested in determining the staffing needs for the hospital for the next year. They look at the list of all patients from the previous year and find that there were 15,292 people admitted during the previous year. They categorize the patients by the month they were first admitted and report the following:

    January—1400; February—1603; March—992; April—855; May—1012; June—1275; July—1324; August—1020; September—1453; October—1387; November—1529; December 1442.

    Using an alpha level of .01, determine if there is a significant difference in hospital admissions across the different months.

12. Assuming that winter consists of December, January, and February; spring of the next three months; summer the next three; and fall of September, October, and November, use the data from Exercise 11 and determine if there is a seasonal difference in hospital admissions (use an alpha level of .01).

13. What limitation of the χ^2 test should the researcher be aware of in Exercises 11 and 12?

14. People trying to stop smoking are randomly assigned to one of three therapies or to a control group. In one therapy, behavior modification is used; in another, aversive training; in the third, hypnosis. In the control group, people are told that they will begin therapy in three months. At the end of three months each person reports on whether he or she is smoking more, less, or the same as at the start of the program. The number who respond in each category is shown below. Using an alpha level of .05,

determine if there is a significant difference among the groups. If so, describe it in your own words.

	Behavior Modification	Aversive	Hypnosis	Control
Smoke more	2	10	3	26
Smoke same	8	14	5	30
Smoke less	32	18	32	4

15. In constructing a graph of the data from Exercise 14, it might be confusing to report frequencies for all groups and responses. Instead determine the percentage of individuals in each group who smoke less and graph it (instead of frequencies) by group. Does it help in the interpretation of the results from Exercise 14?

16. Eighty introductory psychology instructors are asked to indicate what the most important feature is for them in selecting a textbook. They answer in the following manner:

Reputation of author(s)—12
Readability of the book—21
Orientation of the book (research, clinical, etc.)—38
Other—9

Determine if one factor is significantly more important than the others (use an alpha level of .05).

17. You also learn that of these 80 instructors in Exercise 16, 40 are men and 40 are women. The breakdown of responses by gender is as follows:

	Author Reputation	Readability	Orientation	Other
Women	8	8	20	4
Men	4	13	18	5

Determine if gender is related to the type of response (use an alpha level of .05).

18. In Exercises 16 and 17, the researchers should get different findings; in one case there is a significant finding, in the other there is no significant difference. How would you explain that to another student? Aren't Exercises 16 and 17 asking the same question?

19. Business executives and school principals are asked which type of microcomputer they prefer. They respond in the following fashion:

	Computer A	Computer B	Computer C	Computer D
Business Executives	65	37	12	18
Principals	20	11	6	74

Determine if these two types of people differ in terms of computer preference (use an alpha level of .01).

20. Families of different sizes (number of children) are asked to indicate their preference for different types of dwellings. Determine if family size is related to dwelling preference (use an alpha level of .05).

	Ranch Style	Split-Level	Two-Story
0 children	5	23	18
1 child	8	17	21
2 children	14	12	11
3 children	23	9	24
4 or more children	29	3	15

CHALLENGE QUESTIONS

1. College women and men were asked to indicate their first preference for a boy's name. The researcher was interested in determining if sex of the respondent was related to the type of name generated, either common, unusual, recently popular, or dated. The classification of names was determined by consulting lists of names of recent graduates at the university. The frequency of names offered are shown below. Determine if a relationship exists. (Based on Joubert, C. E. (1985). Sex differences in given name preference. *Psychological Reports, 57*, 49–50.

	Type of Name Preferred			
Respondent	Common	Unusual	Recently popular	Dated
Men	40	24	31	5
Women	30	22	47	1

2. It has been suggested that the motivation for playing video games may differ among individuals. A survey of frequent video game players (play

1–5 times per week) and infrequent game players (do not play weekly, but have played 2–9 different games in the past year) measured a number of different attitudes and behaviors. One dealt with the switching of games. The players were asked whether they agreed, disagreed, or were neutral with regard to the statement, "I switch games if my scores stop improving." Determine if the responses are related to the type of player. (Based on Morlock, H., Yando, T., & Nigolean, K. (1985). Motivation of video game players. *Psychological Reports, 57,* 247–250.)

	Type of Response		
Type of player	Agree	Neutral	Disagree
Frequent	11	19	31
Infrequent	4	28	8

For each question answer the following:
a. What is a plausible research hypothesis?
b. What are the H_0 and H_1?
c. Graph the frequency values.
d. Calculate the appropriate inferential statistic. Use an alpha level of .05 for Question 1 and .01 for Question 2.
e. State your findings in the proper format and provide a written conclusion about the findings (relating the inferential statistics to the descriptive statistics).

The Mann-Whitney U Test

TERMS DISCUSSED

parametric tests
nonparametric tests

PROCEDURES DESCRIBED

calculating U_1 and U_2 for the Mann-Whitney U test
assigning ranks

The interaction of people in their environment has been the focus of research in the discipline known as environmental psychology. Environmental psyhologists have studied how the environment affects people's behavior and their activities. A study by van Wagenberg, Krasner, and Krasner (1981) investigated the training of 8- and 9-year-old children in environmental design. The hypothesis was that children at this early of an age could be taught some of the basic principles in environmental design.

Six children were formed into three pairs of "fellow architects." Each pair was instructed by an architect, van Wagenberg, in some of the principles used in designing an "ideal" classroom. These students participated in weekly sessions for one semester. Each session lasted approximately 1 1/2 hours and was devoted to building models of the ideal classroom and analyzing the environment in terms of the activities that took place in the classroom. At the final meeting of the semester each of the students in the class, the 6 who had been meeting with the architect (the trained group) and 18 who had not (the control group), made a floor plan of their "ideal" room at home in which they would live and sleep. Students were given 1 1/2 hours to complete this task.

Following this task, two architects who did not know the groups in which the children had participated ranked the designs from 1 (poorest) to 24 (best). The rankings were done separately by each architect and the final rankings were very similar to each other. The rankings of one of the architects, Architect A, will be discussed. These rankings are presented in Table 17.1.

This study is an example of a two-condition experiment. There is one independent variable, training in environmental design, with two levels. These levels are represented by the different experimental groups. In one group, the trained group, meetings were held with the architect. In the other group, the control group, no training was given. Since the children participated in one and only one condition, an independent groups design was used.

The dependent variable was the quality of the design of each child's "ideal" room. This variable was measured by the rankings of outside architects. As described in the Overview for Chapters 16 through 19, ranks are on an ordinal scale of measurement. That is, although the ranks can be ordered we cannot assume equal intervals between the ranks. They also violate the assumption of independence described earlier for t tests and ANOVA in that the rank assigned to an individual cannot be independent of ranks assigned to other individuals. Therefore, the statistical procedures described for those tests would be inappropriate for this example.

The researchers' hypothesis is that training will result in improved designs. This means that the designs by the children in the trained group should have higher rankings than those by the children in the control group.

TABLE 17.1	Architect A's Rankings of the Children's Designs of Their "Ideal" Room for the Chapter Example. The Designs are Ordered and Ranked from Poorest (Rank = 1) to Best (Rank = 24).

Group in which Children Participated	
Training	Control
14	1
16	2
17	3
20	4
22	5
24	6
	7
	8
	9
	10
	11
	12
	13
	15
	18
	19
	21
	23

DESCRIPTIVE STATISTICS: DESCRIBING THE SAMPLE DATA

Because the data in Table 17.1 are ranks and it cannot be assumed that the ranks are equally spaced (interval scale of measurement), the median is the appropriate measure of central tendency. The median provides the middle, or 50th percentile, rank for each group.

For the trained group which has 6 ranks, the median would be the average of the third and fourth ranks—the two middle ranks. The two middle ranks are 17 and 20. Therefore, the median rank is 18.5. For the control group, which had 18 students, the middle rank corresponds to the average of the 9th and 10th ranks—the two middle ranks. Table 17.1 shows these two ranks as 9 and 10. Therefore, the median rank for the control group is 9.5. Clearly, the training group has a higher median rank than the control group, lending support to the research hypothesis.

Because no $\overline{X}$ rank is calculated, it would be inappropriate to calculate a standard deviation, which is based on deviations from the $\overline{X}$. Instead, the range of ranks should be determined for each group as a measure of variability. In the trained group, the range is 10 ranks (high rank of 24 minus the low rank of 14). For the control group, the range is 22 ranks (high rank of 23 minus the low rank of 1). This measure of variability indicates that there was more variability in the quality of the designs among the children in the control group than in the trained group.

INFERENTIAL STATISTICS: TESTING FOR A DIFFERENCE

In testing the researchers' hypothesis that the trained group had better designs than the control group, it is necessary to develop the appropriate statistical hypotheses, H_0 and H_1. Inferential statistical tests such as the t tests and ANOVA used the population means μs in stating statistical hypotheses. These tests are referred to as **parametric tests** because the statistical hypotheses and assumptions include parameters such as μ and σ. For instance, these tests assume that the population distributions are normally distributed and have the same variability σ^2.

Because we cannot meet these assumptions in this example, the statistical hypotheses cannot be stated in terms of parameters such as the population mean μ. There is no mean population rank assumed for this example. Therefore a different class of statistical tests is used. These tests are called **nonparametric tests.** They are based on statistical hypotheses that do not contain parameters and that do not make assumptions about the shape of the population distributions. These tests are also referred to as distribution-free tests. The tests do not depend on any assumptions about the shape of the distribution (normality) or the variability in the population distributions (homogeneity).

Nonparametric tests are appropriate when the data do not correspond to at least an interval scale of measurement (you cannot assume equal intervals between values) or when the assumptions of a parametric test cannot be met. For instance, it appears that the assumption of equal variability in the population distributions is being violated.

The null hypothesis for a two-condition experiment involving a nonparametric test can be stated as follows:

H_0: the samples were taken from the same population distribution.

The alternative hypothesis describes the opposite situation,

H_1: the samples were taken from different population distributions.

These hypotheses are similar to those for the t test for independent samples, except they make no statement about μs and do not assume anything about the variability in the population distributions. As will be discussed later in this chapter, the nonparametric test is usually less powerful when a parametric test can be used.

As is usually the case, the research hypothesis is more similar to the alternative hypothesis. Therefore, the same statistical reasoning (concept of indirect proof) applies for nonparametric tests as for parametric tests. The researcher wants to support the research hypothesis by finding statistical support for the H_1. If the researcher is able to reject H_0, she has supported H_1 and the research hypothesis.

THE MANN-WHITNEY *U* TEST

The appropriate nonparametric test for a two-condition independent groups experiment is the Mann-Whitney *U* test. The test requires that the data for both groups consist of ranks or be converted to ranks. Furthermore, the ranks should not be made for each group separately. Instead, the ranks should be based on the ordering of all values overall. The data in Table 17.1 meet this requirement.

The test assumes that if both samples were drawn from the same populations, then the weighted sum of the ranks in each group would be the same. The word *weighted* is used to account for experiments in which the N for the two groups are not equal. If the two samples were drawn from the same population, then the sum of the ranks should be nearly identical. However, if the samples were taken from different populations, then the sums of the ranks would be different.

In order to test for a difference between the two samples, a statistic called *U* is calculated for each sample. This statistic is based on weighting the sums of the ranks. If H_0 is true, then the *U* values, or weighted sum of the ranks, for each sample will be similar to each other. Assuming H_0 is true, then the ranks will have been selected at random from the same population of ranks and it would be expected that the only difference between the weighted sums of the ranks would be the result of random selection. However, if H_0 is false and the two samples of ranks did not come from the same population of ranks, then the *U* values may be quite different. The research hypothesis is based on the assumption that H_0 is false.

The first step in determining the *U* value for each sample is to calculate the sum of the ranks for each group, ΣR. Using the data from Table 17.1 the ΣR for the trained group equals 113 and the ΣR for the control group equals 187.

To distinguish between the *U* values for the two samples, a common practice is to assign U_1 to the group with the smaller sum of the ranks and designate it as Group 1, with ΣR_1 as the sum and to assign U_2 to the group with the larger sum of the ranks and designate it as Group 2, with the sum as ΣR_2. The following formula provides U_1:

$$U_1 = (N_1 \times N_2) + \frac{N_1(N_1 + 1)}{2} - \Sigma R_1. \qquad (41)$$

The formula for U_2 is nearly identical except that it uses the N and ΣR values from the second group

$$U_2 = (N_1 \times N_2) + \frac{N_2(N_2 + 1)}{2} - \Sigma R_2. \tag{42}$$

The number of values N_1 for the trained group is 6, and ΣR_1 is 113. The number of values N_2 for the control group is 18, and ΣR_2 is 187. Substituting the appropriate values into Formula 41 provides

$$U_1 = (N_1 \times N_2) + \frac{N_1(N_1 + 1)}{2} - \Sigma R_1 \tag{41}$$

$$= (6 \times 18) + \frac{6 \times 7}{2} - 113$$

$$= 108 + 21 - 113$$

$$= \mathbf{16.}$$

Using Formula 42 and the appropriate values from the control group results in the following for U_2:

$$U_2 = (N_1 \times N_2) + \frac{N_2(N_2 + 1)}{2} - \Sigma R_2 \tag{42}$$

$$= (6 \times 18) + \frac{18 \times 19}{2} - 187$$

$$= 108 + 171 - 187$$

$$= \mathbf{92.}$$

As a check of your calculations, the sum of the two values U_1 and U_2 should equal the product of N_1 and N_2

$$U_1 + U_2 = N_1 \times N_2$$
$$16 + 92 = 6 \times 18$$
$$108 = 108.$$

The two calculated values U_1 and U_2 are quite different from each other. This would suggest that the samples come from different populations. However, in order to determine that this difference between U_1 and U_2 is not the result of chance or sampling error, it is necessary determine the critical limits for U_1 and U_2.

REJECTING H_0 WHEN USING THE MANN-WHITNEY U TEST

With samples of 20 or fewer ranks per group, Table U (see Appendix E) lists the critical U values. Table U is arranged according to the sample sizes for each group. Determine the alpha level and if a directional or nondirectional hypothesis is being used. In this example, we will assume a $p \leq .05$ alpha level and a nondirectional hypothesis (H_1 hypothesizes a difference without specifying which population has larger ranks).

Using Table U, locate the appropriate critical U_1 and U_2 values by locating one sample size N_1 in the column entries and the other sample size N_2 in the row entries. To be able to reject H_0, that is, to assume that the samples came from different population distributions, the calculated U_1 and U_2 values must be equal to or outside the range of U_1 and U_2 values in the table.

For the chapter example with samples of $N_1 = 6$ and $N_2 = 18$, the critical U_1 and U_2 values are 24 and 84. To reject H_0, the calculated U_1 must be 24 or less and U_2 must be 84 or larger. In Figure 17.1, the decision process is shown on a number line with the critical values and calculated values for the example shown. The most discrepant U values that could be obtained with the sample sizes in this example are 0 and 108. If the two values are identical for samples of this size, then the U values would be 54. Remember the sum of the U values must equal the product of the two samples sizes.

If U_1 and U_2 are within 24 and 84, then it is possible that the two samples came from the same population distribution. If H_0 is true, then 95% of the pairs of samples (of $N_1 = 6$ and $N_2 = 18$) selected from the same population will have U values between 24 and 84.

If the values are outside the region, then H_0 is rejected because the likelihood of getting this result given that H_0 is true is less than .05. It should be mentioned that it is not possible for one calculated value, either U_1 or U_2, to be within the region and the other value outside. Either both will be within the retain-H_0 region or both will be in the reject-H_0 region.

The critical values of U_1 and U_2 vary with sample size because they are a weighted sum of the ranks and the values of the ranks are directly related to sample size (e.g., it's not possible to have a rank of 25 without $N_1 + N_2 \geq 25$). Since H_0 would predict equal or similar values of U_1 and U_2, the critical U values in Table U define the maximum difference between the values that would be allowed given a particular alpha level.

For the chapter example, the calculated U_1 and U_2 values are in the reject-H_0 region; therefore, the researchers can conclude that the samples came from different population distributions. The researchers could conclude that, "The children with training in environmental design constructed better designs of their 'ideal' room than children with no training, $\underline{U} = 16$, $\underline{p} < .05$."

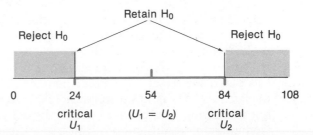

FIGURE 17.1 Diagram illustrating the role of critical U values in deciding whether to retain or reject H_0 for the chapter example. A nondirectional hypothesis and α level of .05 is used.

Although you should calculate both U_1 and U_2, researchers often report only the lower value as U.

When either sample has an N greater than 20, the U statistic is normally distributed and the researcher can calculate a z score. Recall from Chapter 4 that z scores are standard scores that reflect the discrepancy of a value from the mean of a distribution. When either sample has an N greater than 20, a normal distribution of U values can be approximated for cases when H_0 is true. The formula for obtaining a z score in these cases is

$$z = \frac{U - (N_1 \times N_2)/2}{\sqrt{[(N_1 \times N_2)(N_1 + N_2 + 1)]/12}}. \tag{43}$$

If a directional test is being used, then the critical z score at the .05 level is 1.65, and at the .01 level, it is 2.33. If a nondirectional test is being used, then the critical value at the .05 level is 1.96, and at the .01 level it is 2.58. If the absolute value of the z score equals or exceeds the critical z score, then the researcher should reject H_0 and assume that a significant difference exists between the two conditions.

ASSUMPTIONS CONCERNING THE MANN-WHITNEY U TEST

The Mann-Whitney U test has relatively few assumptions. The major ones are (1) that the two groups are independent of each other (different participants in each group), (2) that the samples are randomly selected from the population, and (3) that the U statistics are based on ranks. As will be shown in the second chapter example, it is sometimes necessary to take the data and rank the values in order to use the Mann-Whitney U test. The test makes no assumptions about the shape of the population distribution nor about homogeneity of population variances σ^2. Therefore, this test is preferred when the t test for independent samples cannot be used. In the behavior sciences, the Mann-Whitney U test is used (1) when the data are in the form of ranks or (2) when the assumptions underlying the t test are violated and the sample size is small.

The procedures outlined in the previous section assume no tied ranks exist. Notice that in Table 17.1 all of the designs had different ranks, no ties existed. If ties exist across groups, then the procedures outlined previously tend to result in a conservative statistical conclusion. That is, when tied ranks exist across groups, the rejection region is slightly smaller than that shown in Table U. For instance, instead of a rejection region of .05 when no ties exist, the rejection region might be .047 when ties in rankings exist. In most cases, this is not a major concern in decision making because you are not increasing your chances of making a Type I error. In fact, you are making it slightly more difficult to find a significant difference, reducing statistical power. Unless, a number of ties exist and the calculated U_1 and U_2 values are close to the critical U_1 and U_2 values, no correction is needed to the procedures outlined previously. If, however, the calculated values are close to the critical values, then you may want to correct for ties, by using the procedure outlined in Siegel (1956).

A SECOND EXAMPLE

The ranking of the designs by two architects was one of two dependent variables in the study by van Wagenberg et al. (1981). The ranking was a subjective measure that depended on the experienced judgments of the architects. Van Wagenberg et al. included an objective measure of performance in the original study. They hypothesized that children trained in environmental design would include more basic elements in the design of their "ideal" room than children with no training. They defined basic elements as items such as "walls, windows, entrance, chairs or bench, bed, desk or table, closet, light fixture, and a bathroom or washstand" (1981, p. 358). Therefore, a design could contain anywhere from 0 to 9 basic elements. Each design was scored for the number of basic elements it contained. The number of basic elements for each design by group is shown in Table 17.2.

TABLE 17.2 Number of Basic Elements Included in the Designs of the Children for the Second Example

Group in which Children Participated	
Training	Control
5	0
5	1
6	1
6	1
8	2
9	2
	2
	2
	2
	2
	2
	2
	3
	3
	4
	6
	7
	9

The independent variable in this second example is the same as in the first example, namely, training in environmental design. The dependent variable is different, however. Rather than the rankings of an architect, this example has the number of basic elements within the design as the dependent variable. This variable is on the ratio scale of measurement because there are equal intervals between the possible values of 0 and 9 and because the 0 is a "real" zero point, indicating the absence of basic elements in the design. However, the researchers did not use a t test for independent samples to analyze these data. Notice in Table 17.2 that the distributions of values are not similar for the two groups. The distribution for the control group appears to be positively skewed (many low values and few high values), but the training group is not skewed.

The researchers cannot assume that the two samples were taken from population distributions that are normal in shape and have equal variability, $\sigma_1^2 = \sigma_2^2$. These are statistical assumptions for using the t test for independent samples. Violating these assumptions would not be a serious problem if the sample sizes were larger and equal to each other. However, because the training group has only 6 values and the control group has 18 values, it is possible that the use of the t test would provide erroneous findings. Therefore, the Mann-Whitney U test was used by the researchers.

DESCRIBING THE DATA

The data in Table 17.2 were used in calculating the median number of elements incorporated in designs for each group. Because the data for the control group are skewed, the median is a more appropriate measure of central tendency to report than the $\overline{X}$. For the training group, the median number of elements is 6. For the control group, the median number of elements is 2. In each group, the median was found by finding the 50th percentile or middle value for the group. The descriptive statistics indicate that the children in the training group included more basic elements in their designs than the children in the control group. The Mann-Whitney U test will determine if this difference is significant.

TESTING FOR A DIFFERENCE

As was the case with the first example, H_0 hypothesizes that both samples came from the same population distribution. The alternative hypothesis H_1 hypothesizes that the samples came from different population distributions. As is usually the case, the research hypothesis is similar to the H_1 in that the researchers assume that the training group included more basic elements in their designs than the control group.

Because the Mann-Whitney U test analyzes ranks, the researcher needs first to rank the data from this example. To rank the data, it is necessary to assign ranks without regard to the group from which the values were obtained. The number of basic elements shown in each design is listed in Table

TABLE 17.3   The Ranking of the Designs Based on the Number of Basic Elements Contained in the Designs

| | | Location In | | Ranks | |
| | | *Number of* | | | |
Design	Group	elements	Ordering	R_1	R_2
A	CONTROL	0	(1)		1
B	CONTROL	1	(2)		3
C	CONTROL	1	(3) Avg. = 3		3
D	CONTROL	1	(4)		3
E	CONTROL	2	(5)		8.5
F	CONTROL	2	(6)		8.5
G	CONTROL	2	(7)		8.5
H	CONTROL	2	(8)		8.5
I	CONTROL	2	(9) Avg. = 8.5		8.5
J	CONTROL	2	(10)		8.5
K	CONTROL	2	(11)		8.5
L	CONTROL	2	(12)		8.5
M	CONTROL	3	(13) Avg. = 13.5		13.5
N	CONTROL	3	(14)		13.5
O	CONTROL	4	(15)		15
P	TRAINING	5	(16) Avg. = 16.5	16.5	
Q	TRAINING	5	(17)	16.5	
R	TRAINING	6	(18)	19	
S	CONTROL	6	(19) Avg. = 19		19
T	TRAINING	6	(20)	19	
U	CONTROL	7	(21)		21
V	TRAINING	8	(22)	22	
W	CONTROL	9	(23) Avg. = 23.5		23.5
X	TRAINING	9	(24)	23.5	
				$\Sigma R = $ **116.5**	**183.5**

17.3. These data in the third column of Table 17.3 are the same as those shown in Table 17.2. However, for the purpose of ranking, all values are listed together. The lowest value of all values is assigned a rank of 1. Increasing values are assigned higher ranks. In the case of ties, an average rank is assigned to each of the tied values

Average Rank = Sum of Ranks for Tied Values/Number of Tied Values.

For example, the second, third, and fourth designs each had one basic element. They were assigned the average of Ranks 2, 3, and 4, which is a rank of 3. There were 8 designs with two basic elements. These designs ranked from fifth to twelfth overall. The sum of Ranks 5 through 12 is 69. When 69 is divided by 8, the number of designs, the average rank assigned to each of the designs with two elements is 8.5.

When only two values are tied, the average rank is the midpoint between the two ranks. There are two designs with three elements. These two designs are the 13th and 14th in the series of designs. Therefore, the average rank for each design is 13.5. Following this procedure it is possible to assign a rank to each value. This example is more complicated than many you will face in assigning ranks because of the number of instances of tied values.

Once the ranks have been established, the sum of the ranks ΣR for each group should be determined as shown in the last two columns of Table 17.3. Then U_1 and U_2 can be calculated by using Formulas 41 and 42

$$U_1 = (N_1 \times N_2) + \frac{N_1(N_1 + 1)}{2} - \Sigma R_1 \qquad (41)$$

$$= (6 \times 18) + \frac{6 \times 7}{2} - 116.5$$

$$= 108 + 21 - 116.5$$

$$= \mathbf{12.5.}$$

Using Formula 42 and the appropriate values from the control group results in the following for U_2,

$$U_2 = (N_1 \times N_2) + \frac{N_2(N_2 + 1)}{2} - \Sigma R_2 \qquad (42)$$

$$= (6 \times 18) + \frac{18 \times 19}{2} - 183.5$$

$$= 108 + 171 - 183.5$$

$$= \mathbf{95.5.}$$

As a check of your calculations, the sum of the two values U_1 and U_2 should equal the product of N_1 multiplied by N_2,

$$U_1 + U_2 = N_1 \times N_2$$
$$12.5 + 95.5 = 6 \times 18$$
$$108 = 108.$$

These two values, 12.5 and 95.5, are quite dissimilar. Using a nondirectional hypothesis with a .05 rejection region, one can find the critical U_1 and U_2 values in Table U (Appendix E). These values are 24 and 84. The calculated values lie outside the region within these two critical values. Therefore, H_0 can be rejected. The alternative hypothesis and the research hypothesis are supported. The researchers can conclude that, "Children in the training group included significantly more basic elements in their designs than children in the control group, $\underline{U} = 12.5$, $\underline{p} < .05$." In both of these examples, the children in the training group outperformed the children in the control group. This was interpreted by van Wagenberg et al. (1981) as evidence that children can be taught principles in the design of their own environment.

It should be noted that the most troublesome task faced by researchers using the Mann-Whitney U test is assigning ranks. One needs to be careful to assign ranks to values without regard to group membership. And, when ties exist, care must be taken to ensure that the average rank is assigned properly. The calculation of U_1 and U_2 cannot proceed until the ranks are assigned and summed.

Lastly, when using a directional hypothesis, the differences in U_1 and U_2 must be in the appropriate direction. For instance, if the prediction is that the first sample will have lower ranks, then if U_1 and U_2 fall in the reject-H_0 region, you need to examine the median rank for each sample. The median rank for the first sample must be less than that for the second sample to reject H_0. Otherwise H_0 must be retained.

For example, let's assume that a researcher predicts that an experimental group will have lower rankings than a control group. For a significant difference to occur, not only must the U statistics be in the reject-H_0 region but the median ranking for the experimental group must be less than that of the control group. If it is higher, then the difference is not in the predicted direction and H_0 must be retained. Therefore, for a significant difference when using a directional test, the calculated values of U_1 and U_2 must be less and greater than their respective critical values, and the median ranks for the samples must be in the predicted direction.

STATISTICAL POWER OF NONPARAMETRIC TESTS

In this and the next two chapters, experiments are described that *required* the use of a nonparametric test. However, as a student of statistics you will have noticed that the calculations for nonparametric tests are easier than for the parametric tests. This might lead to the question of why researchers don't use nonparametric tests in place of parametric tests when they have a choice. The answer has to do with statistical power.

Remember that statistical power is the ability to reject H_0 when it is false. That is, power refers to the researcher's ability to find a significant difference when a difference exists in the population. In comparing types of tests, the parametric test is more powerful than its comparable nonparametric test. For instance, if one has data that meet the assumptions of the t test, then the t test will be more likely to find a significant difference (if it actually exists) than if a nonparametric test such as the Mann-Whitney U or Wilcoxon matched-pairs tests is used.

The nonparametric tests make no assumptions about population parameters and their calculations do not involve the precision found in the t tests. This is especially true when values are converted to ranks as in the second chapter example and as will be the case in the next chapter. Information is lost when transforming values into ranks.

A nonparametric test is easier to complete but may not provide the statistical power found in a parametric test. Therefore, if a researcher can meet the assumptions of a parametric test or the sample size is large enough to overcome violating the assumptions of the test, the parametric test should be used. It will increase the chances that the researcher can reject H_0 if it is really false. If, however, the data are not on at least an interval scale of measurement, or if the assumptions for a parametric test are not met and the sample size is small, then the researcher must use a nonparametric test.

SUMMARY

In a two-condition, independent groups experiment the Mann-Whitney U test serves as the appropriate nonparametric test when the t test for independent samples cannot be used. The Mann-Whitney test should be used when the data are ranks or on the ordinal scale of measurement (equal intervals between values cannot be assumed). And, the Mann-Whitney U test is appropriate when interval or ratio data do not meet the assumptions of the t test (normality and homogeneity of variance in the population distributions) and the two sample sizes are unequal with at least one sample having a small N.

The H_0 for the Mann-Whitney U test assumes that both samples were drawn from the same population distribution, whereas the H_1 assumes that the samples were drawn from different populations. The median often is reported as the measure of central tendency for each sample and the range is reported as the measure of variability.

The Mann-Whitney U test assumes that the data to be analyzed are in the form of ranks. If the data are not in the form of ranks, then the values must be ranked before the U_1 and U_2 statistics can be calculated. The U_1 and U_2 are based on the weighted sum of the ranks for each condition. The null hypothesis assumes that U_1 is equal to U_2. If U_1 and U_2 are significantly different from each other, then the assumption is that the samples were selected from different populations and H_0 is rejected. For samples of N $\leq$ 20, Table U provides the critical U_1 and U_2 values. For larger samples, a z score based on Formula 43 is used.

The three basic assumptions for using the Mann-Whitney U test are that (1) the samples are independent of each other, (2) the samples were randomly selected from the population distribution, and (3) the data are in the form of ranks, with the ranks assigned without regard to group membership.

The power of nonparametric tests is lower than that for parametric tests. If a researcher has the option of using either type of test, the parametric test should be used because of the increase in statistical power—the ability to reject a false H_0.

SUMMARY FOR USING THE MANN-WHITNEY U TEST

1. Develop the research hypothesis.
2. State the H_0 and H_1 and decide upon the alpha level, usually .05 or .01.
3. Calculate the median and range as the appropriate measures of central tendency and variability for each sample.
4. If the data are not in the form of ranks or if ranking was done separately for each group, then assign ranks to the values without regard to group

membership. In the case of tied values an average rank can be computed using

Average Rank = Sum of Ranks for Tied Values/Number of Tied Values.

5. Calculate the sum of the ranks ΣR for each group.

6. Using the sample sizes and ΣR for each group, compute U_1 and U_2 using Formulas 41 and 42

$$U_1 = (N_1 \times N_2) + \frac{N_1(N_1 + 1)}{2} - \Sigma R_1 \tag{41}$$

$$U_2 = (N_1 \times N_2) + \frac{N_2(N_2 + 1)}{2} - \Sigma R_2. \tag{42}$$

7. Check your calculations. The following must be true,

$$U_1 + U_2 = N_1 \times N_2.$$

8. If both samples have $N \leq 20$, then find the critical U_1 and U_2 values in Table U. If the obtained U_1 and U_2 values are equal to or outside the range of the critical U and U' values, then reject H_0 and assume that a difference exists between the two samples. (For directional hypotheses, confirm that the median ranks of the samples are in the predicted direction.) If either sample has an $N > 20$, then calculate a z score using

$$z = \frac{U - (N_1 \times N_2)/2}{\sqrt{[(N_1 \times N_2)(N_1 + N_2 + 1)]/12}}. \tag{43}$$

If a directional hypothesis is used, then the critical z score at the .05 level is 1.65, and at the .01 level it is 2.33. If a nondirectional hypothesis is used, then the critical value at the .05 level is 1.96, and at the .01 level it is 2.58. If the absolute value of the z score equals or exceeds the critical z score, then the researcher should reject H_0 and assume that a significant difference exists between the two conditions.

9. State your conclusion in sentence form and include the necessary statistics, $\underline{U}$ = calculated U value, $\underline{p}$ < or > alpha level used.

EXERCISES

1. A researcher has a two-condition experiment with independent groups. There are 4 values in one condition and 15 in the other. The sample distributions do not appear to be similar in shape. He plans to use a *t* test for independent samples because the data are on an interval scale of measurement. What would you suggest to him? If each of his samples had 30 values each, what would be your suggestion?

2. How do the H_0 and H_1 differ between a parametric test such as the *t* test for independent samples and a nonparametric test such as the Mann-Whitney *U* test? Consult Chapter 10 if necessary.

3. If the H_0 for the Mann-Whitney *U* test assumes that the ranks are randomly distributed between the two groups, why can't the researcher just

compare the ΣR for the two groups? Why is it necessary to calculate the U_1 and U_2 statistics?

4. What is specifically meant when a test is called nonparametric?

5. In the second chapter example, the data are on a ratio scale of measurement, yet the Mann-Whitney U test was used because of serious questions with regard to the shape of the two sample distributions. Calculate the $\overline{X}$ for each sample and compare it with the medians reported in the chapter. And, construct a frequency distribution for each sample. Does it appear that either of the samples are skewed?

6. Although a researcher may not know σ^2, the population variance, it is possible to estimate it by calculating s^2. Calculate s^2 for each sample in Table 17.2. If $s_{training}^2$ is different from $s_{control}^2$, then have any of the assumptions of the t test for independent samples been violated? If so, which one(s)?

7. A teacher ranks male and female students with regard to their performance on a spatial task. He ranks the men among themselves and the women among themselves and gets the following rankings:

Male	Female
2	4
1	3
5	2
4	1
3	5

Would the Mann-Whitney U test be appropriate with these ranks? Explain.

8. A psychologist has two samples with $N_1 = 15$ and $N_2 = 14$. What will be the sum of U_1 and U_2? Assume that both samples were taken from the same population distribution? Would a possible outcome be that $U_1 = U_2$? If so, what should they equal?

9. As a test of the importance of note taking in class, the notes from the eight best and eight worst students in an educational psychology course are collected. An instructor who does not know the students or which students wrote the notes, ranks the quality of the notes. The rankings are listed below:

A & B Students	D & F Students
13	6
7	1
15	5
12	10
9	2
8	4
16	3
14	11

Calculate the median rank and range for each group. Using a nondirectional hypothesis and an alpha level of $p < .01$, determine if there is a significant difference in the rankings between the two groups. State your conclusion in words.

10. A researcher believed that an experimental group would perform better than a control group. Ten students were randomly assigned to either the experimental or control group. The students were ranked in terms of their performance (1 = best, 10 = worst). Determine if there is a significant difference between the groups. Use a directional hypothesis and an alpha level of .05.

Experimental	Control
1	5
2	6
3	7
4	9
8	10

11. In Exercise 10, if you had used a nondirectional hypothesis with an alpha level of .05, would your conclusion had been the same? Explain.

12. Another researcher hearing about the study described in Exercise 9 decides to investigate the amount of notes that men and women in her class take before a test. She collects the notes taken over a one-week period and calculates the length of notes in pages for each student. She obtains the following data for the men and women in her class:

Number of Pages of Notes	
Women	Men
19	7
14	6
10	6
8	6
7	5
6	
6	
6	
5	
5	
4	

Calculate the mean and median for each sample. Which test would be appropriate to use to test the research hypothesis that men and women differ in the amount of notes they take? Why?

13. Complete the appropriate test for Exercise 12, using a nondirectional hypothesis with a .05 alpha level. State your conclusion words.

14. A fellow student brings you the results of his Mann-Whitney U test and wants to know if he should reject or retain H_0. His data are $N_1 = 12$, $N_2 = 15$, $U_1 = 35$, $U_2 = 145$. Using a nondirectional hypothesis with a .05 alpha level, what should he conclude?

15. Having given the student in Exercise 14 the correct advice, another student seeks your help. She cannot find the critical U_1 and U_2 values for her data in Table U. Her data are $N_1 = 15$, $N_2 = 25$, $U_1 = 115$ and $U_2 = 260$. Help her determine if she should reject H_0 using a nondirectional test with a $p < .05$.

16. Minutes before a homework assignment is due, you find that your U_1 statistic is in the reject-H_0 range but your U_2 statistic is not. The data are $N_1 = 10$, $N_2 = 16$, $U_1 = 15$, and $U_2 = 90$. What do you suspect happened? Can you reach a conclusion based on these data?

17. With the following information determine whether to retain or reject H_0:
    a. $N_1 = 21$, $N_2 = 23$, $U_1 = 189$, $U_2 = 294$, nondirectional hypothesis, $p < .01$
    b. $N_1 = 11$, $N_2 = 11$, $U_1 = 24$, $U_2 = 97$, directional hypothesis (Group 1 was predicted to have lower rankings than Group 2), $p < .01$
    c. $N_1 = 8$, $N_2 = 17$, $U_1 = 31$, $U_2 = 105$, nondirectional hypothesis, $p < .05$
    d. $N_1 = 31$, $N_2 = 20$, $U_1 = 258$, $U_2 = 362$, nondirectional hypothesis, $p < .05$

18. You complete a Mann-Whitney U test and find that $U_1 = 24$ and $U_2 = 24$. Is it necessary to know N_1 and N_2 in order to determine whether to retain or reject H_0? Explain.

19. An administrator at a small college is interested in student popularity for courses taught at different times during the day. She circulates a survey asking students to rate (on a 0-to-5 scale) their preference for courses at different times during the day. She calculates the average rating for each time period. The higher the value the more preferred the time is. The data are as follows:

Time	Rating
7 A.M.	1.60
8 A.M.	3.23
9 A.M.	4.58
10 A.M.	4.67
11 A.M.	4.60
noon	3.20
1 P.M.	4.06
2 P.M.	3.11
3 P.M.	2.22
4 P.M.	0.93
5 P.M.	0.79

The administrator decides to use a nonparametric test to determine if courses at noon or later are more or less preferred than morning courses. Conduct the appropriate test and state your conclusions (use a nondirectional hypothesis, $p < .05$).

20. In a taste test, a student rates regular and diet soft drinks. Seven popular drinks of each type are presented to the student in a random order. The student is blindfolded to prevent her from identifying the drink by sight. She rates each drink on a 1-to-6 scale, with 6 representing the best taste. Her ratings are shown below:

Regular	Diet
6	3
2	1
3	4
6	5
5	3
4	2
5	2

With these small sample sizes and the possibility that the samples come from population distributions of ratings with different variances, it is appropriate to use a nonparametric test. Determine the median rating for each type of soft drink, complete the appropriate test (nondirectional hypothesis, $p < .05$), and state your conclusion in words.

CHALLENGE QUESTIONS

1. Attorneys were given fictitional transcripts of an interview with a client. Half of the transcripts described the defendant to be a "lower class defendant." The other half described the defendant as a "middle class defendant." The researchers were interested in determining if this information would bias the ratings of the attorneys with regard to their opinions concerning the ease in representing the defendant. The overall ratings are shown below. A high rating indicates a negative evaluation. Because of the small N and the distribution of ratings, use a Mann-Whitney U test. (Based on Gordon, R. H., & Bauer, G. (1985). Social class biases of practicing attorneys. *Psychological Reports, 57*, 931–935.)

Type of Defendant	
Lower class	*Middle class*
1.07	1.68
3.65	4.87
1.53	1.23
4.67	2.95
2.08	5.00
4.38	4.87
3.97	2.33

2. Sex differences in spatial processing have been studied in recent years. A spatial task was used requiring the participant to press a key when two identical stimuli were presented. The orientation of the stimuli was varied. One of the dependent variables was the number of errors (indicating the stimuli matched when they did not or vice versa) made across 144 trials. These values are shown below. Because of the distribution of errors and the number of participants in each condition, the researchers used a Mann-Whitney U test. (Based on Galluscio, E. H., Kuehner, K. V., & VanBuskirk, A. W. (1984). Multiple resources and brain laterality. *Perceptual and Motor Skills, 59*, 815–824.)

Gender of Participant	
Men	Women
18	27
23	84
10	117
6	93
2	16
0	35
31	126
36	47
5	78
23	10

For each question answer the following:

a. What is a plausible research hypothesis?

b. What are the H_0 and H_1?

c. Calculate the appropriate descriptive statistic for each condition.

d. Calculate the appropriate inferential statistic. Use an alpha level of .05 for Question 1 and .01 for Question 2.

e. State your findings in the proper format and provide a written conclusion about the findings (relating the inferential statistics to the descriptive statistics).

The Wilcoxon Matched-Pairs Test

TERMS DISCUSSED

statistical power for parametric versus
nonparametric tests

PROCEDURES DESCRIBED

calculating W for the Wilcoxon
matched-pairs test

Developmental psychologists have investigated differences in memory ability among young children. DeLoache and Brown (1984) studied the ability of children between 1 1/2 and 2 1/2 years of age to use their memories to find a hidden object. Past research has shown that when an object is missing in a normal environmental setting, young children will search the immediate area for the object. If the object is not found, then the children may rely on their memory to help them recall where the object was.

In the present study, Deloache and Brown (1984) had 24 boys and girls play a version of hide-and-seek in their homes on two successive days. Each child watched while the experimenter hid a stuffed toy somewhere in the home, such as under a couch or behind a door. Then the child was given a time delay between one and five minutes during which the child could do anything except retrieve the toy. After the delay passed the child was allowed to search for the toy. On each day of testing, this game was played five times. On the second day, there were two times when the experimenter moved the toy to a new spot when the child was not looking. These were called "surprise trials" because the toy was not in the spot where it had been placed when the child was watching. The behaviors of the children on these surprise trials were of interest because the child had to engage in a search strategy for up to one minute in order to find the missing toy. If a child used his memory and remembered that the toy was left in a particular location, then he might search in that specific area. For instance, if the toy had been hidden under a sofa cushion, then the child might check the other cushions. This behavior of searching in an area related to the original location was called a "related search." On the other hand, if the child did not rely on her memory, then she might engage in search unrelated to the original location. For instance, searching under a desk rather than the sofa cushions.

The search strategies on these two "surprise" trials were compared with the search strategies on "error" trials. Error trials were those trials in which the child looked in the wrong place when the toy had not been moved. These trials served the function of control trials—the observation of behavior when the researchers did not change anything. Presumably, the child's memory on an error trial was faulty because the child searches in the wrong location initially. Error trials were infrequent, because on 75% of the trials in which the toy was not moved by the experimenter, the child immediately located the toy in its correct location. In fact, 6 of the 24 children never had an error trial.

DeLoache and Brown (1984) hypothesized that the behavior of young children (18 to 23 months of age) would be different from older children (25 to 30 months of age) on these surprise and error trials. They predicted that young children would not use their memory to aid them in their searches. Therefore, the number of related searches should not differ when the experimenter moved the toy (the surprise trials) from when the child made a mistake on his or her own (the error trials).

On the other hand, they predicted that older children would use their memories. They would be more likely to make more related searches on surprise trials than on error trials. On surprise trials, the child would be more likely to conclude that the toy must be nearby somewhere because of their memory recall. On error trials, the child would be likely to realize his or her mistake and search in the correct location, which is unrelated to the original location searched. These two predictions are tested separately. The first example looked at the behavior of the young children, and the second example looked at the behavior of the older children. Table 18.1 contains the number of related searches made by the young children on the two types of trials. The data from 2 of the original 12 young children are not included because they never had an error trial during the two days of testing.

This study is an example of a repeated measures design because each child is providing two data values, one for each condition in the study. It differs from the example in the previous chapter which involved an independent groups design. The conditions are the surprise and error trials. These two trials make up the independent variable which is the type of trial.

The dependent variable is the number of related searches made. This variable is quantitative and on a ratio scale of measurement because a real zero point exists and the interval differences between possible number of searches (for example, 1 and 2, or 2 and 3) are equal.

Based on this information a researcher might be tempted to use the *t* test for correlated samples discussed in Chapter 11. However, the data in Table 18.1 led DeLoache and Brown (1984) to believe that if they used this test they

TABLE 18.1	The Number of Related Searches Made by the Younger Children on the Surprise and Error Trials in the Chapter Example		
		Type of Trial	
	Child	*Surprise*	*Error*
	A	1	0
	B	2	1
	C	2	0
	D	1	1
	E	1	0
	F	1	0
	G	0	1
	H	0	0
	I	0	1
	J	0	0

might be violating an assumption of the t test. Note in Table 18.1 that most of the values are either 0 or 1. If these samples are representative of the population distributions from which they were selected, it is unlikely that the population distributions are normally distributed and with a small sample size: the t test for correlated samples may provide incorrect results. Therefore, the nonparametric equivalent of this test was used. This test is called the Wilcoxon matched-pairs signed-ranks test. We will call it the Wilcoxon matched-pairs test, although you may find it also referred to as the Wilcoxon signed-ranks test or the Wilcoxon test.

The Wilcoxon matched-pairs test is appropriate when the dependent variables are on an ordinal scale of measurement. This can occur when the data are ranks. It can also be used when the assumptions of the t test for correlated samples cannot be met *and* the sample size is small. The data in the chapter example correspond to this second case.

Researchers in the behavioral sciences often use the Wilcoxon matched-pairs test when the data are limited to a small range of values. In the chapter example, the range is from 0 to 2, a range of only three values. When the range of values is small, the sample distributions are rarely normal in shape. And, since the sample distributions are used to generate estimates of the population distribution s, these estimates often indicate that the samples were selected from population distributions with unequal variability. Therefore, the assumptions of the t test have been violated. With larger samples this is not a major concern to the researcher because the t test is a robust test. However, with a sample of N = 10, the Wilcoxon matched-pairs test is the appropriate test to use. Before using the test, let us calculate the appropriate descriptive statistics.

DESCRIPTIVE STATISTICS: DESCRIBING THE SAMPLE DATA

Because of the limited range of the data, relying on the $\overline{X}$ as the sole measure of central tendency might be inappropriate. When a researcher has questions about the shape of the sample distributions, it is a good practice to calculate more than one measure of central tendency. Therefore, both the $\overline{X}$ and the median have been calculated for each type of trial. On the surprise trials the $\overline{X}$ and median are similar, the $\overline{X}$ is .8 and the median is 1 relevant search. On the error trials, the $\overline{X}$ is .4 relevant searches and the median is 0 searches.

For both measures, the number of related searches is slightly higher on the surprise trials. These values are shown in Figure 18.1. The $\overline{X}$s are shown in the left panel and the medians in the right panel. In both cases a bar graph was used because the independent variable, type of trial, corresponds to a nominal scale of measurement.

The s was calculated for each sample using Formulas 3 through 5. The s for the surprise trials is .79 relevant searches and the s for the error trials is

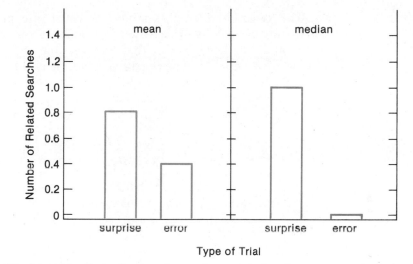

FIGURE 18.1 Number of related searches made by the younger children in the chapter example.

.52. The fact that the s is slightly higher for the surprise trials results from the two individuals who had two relevant searches on the surprise trials.

INFERENTIAL STATISTICS: TESTING FOR A DIFFERENCE

The statistical hypotheses for the Wilcoxon matched-pairs test are the same as for the Mann-Whitney U test. The null hypothesis H_0 assumes that the samples were taken from the same population distribution. The alternative hypothesis H_1 assumes that the samples came from different population distributions. Neither hypothesis includes population parameters and the test makes no assumptions about the shapes of the population distributions.

The assumptions of the Wilcoxon matched-pairs test are (1) that the samples have been randomly selected from the population distributions, (2) that the samples are related, either the same subjects in both samples or subjects have been matched in pairs, and (3) that the values are at least from the ordinal scale of measurement.

DeLoache and Brown (1984) have two specific hypotheses. They predict no difference in performance for the young children but are predicting a difference for older children. Because this first example involves only the young children, DeLoache and Brown hope that the H_0 is not rejected.

It should be noted that attempting to support the H_0 is seldom the goal of a research study. By retaining H_0 a researcher is concluding that there is insufficient evidence to reject it. That does not mean that the researcher can conclude that no difference exists.

The researchers in this study, however, are predicting an interaction. This study has a quasi-independent variable, age of the child, with two levels, young and old. They predict that this variable will interact with their other independent variable, type of trial. For young children, they predict no difference as a function of trial. For older children, they predict a difference. If they are successful in finding a difference for older children but not for younger children, they can conclude that age interacts with the type of trial.

COMPLETING THE WILCOXON MATCHED-PAIRS TEST

The first step in conducting the Wilcoxon matched-pairs test is to calculate a difference value for each pair of values. In Table 18.2, the difference values are shown in the fourth column, labeled "Difference value." The absolute values of these difference scores are then ranked. Differences of 0 are ignored in the Wilcoxon matched-pairs test. Ranks begin with the lowest difference value and increase until the highest difference value is given the largest rank. In the chapter example there are six difference values with an absolute value of 1. Each would be assigned the average of the ranks from 1 to 6

$$\text{Average Rank} = \text{Sum of Ranks for Tied Values/Number of Tied Values}$$
$$3.5 = (1 + 2 + 3 + 4 + 5 + 6)/6.$$

Child C who has a difference value of two would be assigned the rank of 7. These ranks are shown in the last column of Table 18.2. Before each value

TABLE 18.2 Calculation of the Difference Values and the Ranks for the Number of Related Searches Made by the Younger Children in the Chapter Example

| Child | Type of Trial | | Difference value | Rank |
	Surprise	Error		
A	1	0	+1	(+) 3.5
B	2	1	+1	(+) 3.5
C	2	0	2	(+) 7
D	1	1	0	—
E	1	0	+1	(+) 3.5
F	1	0	+1	(+) 3.5
G	0	1	−1	(−) 3.5
H	0	0	0	—
I	0	1	−1	(−) 3.5
J	0	0	0	—

$$\Sigma R_- = 7.0$$
$$\Sigma R_+ = 21.0$$

either a + or − sign indicates the direction of the original difference value. It is not of importance in the assigning of ranks since the ranking is based on the absolute values of the difference values. The sign is important, however, in the next step of the Wilcoxon matched-pairs test.

The Wilcoxon matched-pairs test assumes that if both samples were drawn from the same population distribution, then the sum of the ranks for positive differences ΣR_+ should equal the sum of the ranks for negative differences ΣR_-. If, however, the H_0 is false, then the sum of the ranks for one of the signs should be greater than the other. This would indicate that the values in one sample were significantly different from those in the other.

At the bottom of the last column in Table 18.2 the sum of the ranks for the positive difference values ΣR_+ and the sum of the ranks for the negative difference values ΣR_- are shown. The ΣR_- is smaller than ΣR_+, which indicates that there were slightly more relevant searches on the surprise searches. This finding is evident in Figure 18.1 and from our descriptive statistics. However, the Wilcoxon matched-pairs test enables the researchers to determine if this difference is significant.

Once the ΣR_+ and ΣR_- have been calculated, the statistic W (for Wilcoxon) is assigned the smaller of the two values. In the chapter example $W = 7$. This value must be compared with the critical W value which can be found in Table W (see Appendix E).

As in previous tests, the researcher should have already determined the alpha level and whether a directional or nondirectional hypothesis is being used. In this example assume that the alpha level is $p < .05$, with a nondirectional hypothesis. To find the critical W value, the researcher needs to know the number of values ranked. In this case, it is seven. Notice that the number of values ranked may differ from the sample size because the Wilcoxon matched-pairs test does not include any differences of 0.

In Table W, the critical W value for a nondirectional hypothesis with a rejection level of .05 and seven ranked values is 2. In order to reject H_0, the obtained W must be equal to or less than 2. Otherwise, H_0 should be retained as in this example.

Recall that this test is based on the assumption that if H_0 is true, then the ΣR_+ and ΣR_- will be similar. Rather than providing two critical values as was the case with the Mann-Whitney U test, the common practice with the Wilcoxon is to compare only the lower value W with the critical value in the table. In the case of a directional hypothesis, the researcher must predict before collecting the data whether ΣR_+ or ΣR_- will be smaller and then use that value in the comparison. For a nondirectional hypothesis, the researcher is free to use whichever one is smaller.

Although slightly more relevant searches were made in the surprise trials, the difference between the surprise and error trials could be the result of random variation. The researchers should conclude that, "Young children did not differ in the number of relevant searches made on surprise and error trials, $\underline{W} = 7$, $\underline{p} > .05$." The first part of DeLoache and Brown's (1984) research hypothesis has been supported. The second example will test the other part of the hypothesis.

A SECOND EXAMPLE

The second example is based on the number of related searches made by the older children. The number of related searches made on the surprise and error trials are shown for each older child in the second and third columns of Table 18.3. These children were between 25- and 30-months-old. Although there were 12 children who participated, only 8 had error trials, so this analysis is limited to those 8 children.

The independent and dependent variables are the same as in the first example. The research hypothesis is different, however. DeLoache and Brown (1984) believed that these older children would use their memory to aid them in searching for the toy. Therefore, on the surprise trials a child believed that the toy must be nearby and would search for it in related locations. On the error trials, however, the child realized his or her mistake and searched in a new place unrelated to the original location searched. The research hypothesis was that the type of trial, the independent variable, would result in differences in the number of related searches, the dependent variable.

DESCRIBING THE DATA

The $\overline{X}$ and median for each type of trial are shown at the bottom of the second and third columns in Table 18.3. Notice that for both measures of central tendency, the number of related searches is greater on the surprise

TABLE 18.3 Calculation of the Difference Values and the Ranks for the Number of Related Searches Made by the Older Children in the Second Example

| Child | Type of Trial | | Difference value | Rank |
	Surprise	Error		
A	2	1	+1	(+) 1.5
B	3	0	+3	(+) 6
C	4	0	+4	(+) 7
D	1	1	0	—
E	3	1	+2	(+) 4
F	2	0	+2	(+) 4
G	1	2	−1	(−) 1.5
H	2	0	+2	(+) 4
	$\overline{X} = 2.25$	$\overline{X} = 0.63$		$\Sigma R_- = 1.5$
				$\Sigma R_+ = 26.5$
	Median = 2	Median = 0.5		$W = 1.5$

trials. This finding is consistent with the prediction made in the research hypothesis.

The estimate of the population standard deviation was computed for each type of trial using Formulas 3 through 5. The s for the surprise trials is 1.04 related searches and for the error trials it is 0.74 related searches. The variability in the two conditions are similar.

TESTING FOR A DIFFERENCE

The research hypothesis predicts a difference in the number of relevant searches between the two types of trials. This hypothesis is similar to H_1 in that it describes the case in which the two samples are taken from different population distributions. The H_0 describes the situation in which the two samples are taken from the same population distribution. As in the previous test, a nondirectional hypothesis with an alpha level of .05 will be used.

To conduct the Wilcoxon matched-pairs test, difference values must be calculated. These are shown in the fourth column of Table 18.3. Note that one of the eight children (Child D) had the same number of related searches (1) on both types of trials. She will not be included in the Wilcoxon matched-pairs test because only nonzero difference values are included. The next step is to rank the absolute values of the difference values. There are two difference values of 1. Each is given a rank of 1.5. The three children with difference values of two are given the average of Ranks 3 through 5, which is 4. The child with a difference value of three is given a rank of 6 and the child with the difference value of four is given the top rank of 7.

Once the ranks have been assigned, the sum, or total, of the ranks for the negative and positive differences can be calculated separately. There is only one negative difference score that has a rank of 1.5. Therefore, ΣR_- is equal to 1.5. The sum of the ranks with a positive difference value ΣR_+ is 26.5. The smaller value (1.5) is assigned to W.

The critical W value can be found in Table W. Using a nondirectional hypothesis with an alpha level of .05 and the row labeled 7, because there are seven difference values, the critical W is 2. The obtained W value of 1.5 is less than the critical W. Therefore, the H_0 should be rejected.

There is a significant difference between the two types of trials. DeLoache and Brown (1984) can conclude that, "For older children, there were more related searches on the surprise trials than on the error trials, $\underline{W} = 1.5$, $\underline{p} < .05$." The Wilcoxon matched-pairs test confirms the finding in the descriptive statistics. The $\overline{X}$ number of related searches on the surprise trials (2.25) is greater than the $\overline{X}$ number of related searches on the error trials (0.63). The same relationship is true if one uses the medians.

The findings from the two statistical tests in this chapter support the researchers' hypothesis. Younger children do not show a significant difference in their search strategies on surprise and error trials, but older children do. These findings support the position that older children use their memory to aid them in their search for the missing toy.

USING THE WILCOXON MATCHED-PAIRS TEST WITH A LARGE N

Table W provides the critical W values if N is equal to or less than 50. As was the case with the Mann-Whitney U test, when the sample size is large, a z score may be computed to determine whether to retain or reject H_0. The only two values needed are W, which is the smaller value of ΣR_- and ΣR_+, and N the number of difference values.

The formula for calculating the z score is

$$z = \frac{(W + .05) - [N(N + 1)]/4}{\sqrt{[N(N + 1)(2N + 1)]/24}}. \tag{44}$$

If a directional hypothesis is used, then the critical z score at the .05 level is 1.65, and at the .01 level it is 2.33. And, the difference between ranks must be in the predicted direction. If a nondirectional hypothesis is used, then the critical value at the .05 level is 1.96, and at the .01 level it is 2.58. If the absolute value of the z score equals or exceeds the critical z score, then the researcher should reject H_0 and assume that a significant difference exists between the two conditions.

SUMMARY

The nonparametric test equivalent of the t test for correlated samples is the Wilcoxon matched-pairs test. It assumes that each sample is randomly selected from a population distribution and that the values are related in pairs. Either a repeated-measures design is used with each participant providing two values, or the participants are matched in pairs on another variable. The Wilcoxon matched-pairs test makes no assumptions about the shape of the population distribution or parameters of the population. The test is appropriate when (1) the data are on the ordinal scale of measurement, such as ranks, or (2) the sample distributions indicate that an assumption of the t test may be violated and sample size is small.

The H_0 and H_1 are identical to those for the Mann-Whitney U test. The H_0 assumes that both samples were selected from the same population distribution, while H_1 assumes that the samples were selected from different population distributions. Difference values are calculated and the absolute values are then ranked. The sum of the ranks for the negative difference values ΣR_- is compared with the sum of the ranks for the positive difference values ΣR_+. The null hypothesis assumes that ΣR_- should be similar to ΣR_+. If they are dissimilar and the smaller of the values W is less than or equal to the critical W value from Table W, then the researcher may reject H_0 and assume that a difference exists between the two samples.

SUMMARY FOR USING THE WILCOXON MATCHED-PAIRS TEST

1. Develop the research hypothesis.
2. State the H_0 and H_1 and decide upon the alpha level, usually .05 or .01.

3. Calculate the appropriate measure of central tendency and variability for each sample. If the data are skewed, the median and range are recommended.

4. Calculate the difference value for each pair of values.

5. Rank the absolute values of the difference values. Differences of 0 are not included in the analysis.

6. Sum the ranks for the negative difference values ΣR_- and for the positive difference values ΣR_+. The lower value is designated as the obtained W.

7. Find the critical W value from Table W if the number of difference values is 50 or less. If the obtained W is equal to or less than the critical W, reject H_0 and assume that the samples came from different population distributions. Otherwise, retain H_0, which indicates that it is possible that both samples were taken from the same population distribution.

8. If N is greater than 50, then a z score should be calculated using the following formula:

$$z = \frac{W - [N(N + 1)]/4}{\sqrt{[N(N + 1)(2N + 1)]/24}}. \tag{44}$$

N = number of difference values.

    If a nondirectional hypothesis is used, then the critical z score at the .05 level is 1.65, and at the .01 level it is 2.33. If a nondirectional hypothesis is used, then the critical value at the .05 level is 1.96, and at the .01 level it is 2.58. The difference must also be in the predicted direction. If the absolute value of the z score equals or exceeds the critical z score, then the researcher should reject H_0 and assume that a significant difference exists between the two conditions.

9. State your conclusion in sentence form and include the necessary statistics, $\underline{W}$ = the smaller value of ΣR_- and ΣR_+, $\underline{p}$ < or > alpha level used in rejection region.

EXERCISES

1. The researchers in the chapter examples might want to combine the descriptive statistics from both examples in one graph. Construct a graph of the $\overline{X}$ number of related searches by trials for both age groups using the data from the chapter.

2. A fellow student tells you that he can complete the Wilcoxon matched-pairs test 30% faster than the t test for correlated samples. He concludes, therefore, that on any exam with two samples using the repeated-measures design, he will use the Wilcoxon matched-pairs test. Any comments?

3. Calculate the $\overline{X}$ and s for each sample in both examples to confirm the statistics reported in the text. Show your work.

4. Perhaps the researchers in the second chapter example could have used a directional hypothesis because they predicted that one trial would have

more related searches than the other. If so, what would the critical W value have been? Would they have reached the same conclusion as was reached in the text?

5. Both the Mann-Whitney U test and the Wilcoxon matched-pairs test are nonparametric tests. What is the difference between them? Is there any difference in the assumptions underlying the use of each test?

6. Six college students use two different computer keyboards in typing a paper. Half use System A first and the other half use System B first. They then switch systems. The number of words typed per minute is recorded below. Determine if there is a significant difference in the keyboards. Use a nondirectional hypothesis and an alpha level of .05.

Keyboard Used	
A	B
32	30
31	45
30	18
30	52
31	26
32	50

7. What are the independent and dependent variables in Exercise 6? What scale of measurement does the dependent variable represent?

8. Someone might argue that the values in Exercise 6 allow the use of the t test for correlated samples. Why would you not use this test?

9. A fellow student conducts a Wilcoxon matched-pairs test and finds a significant difference. Assuming that the data were in a form that would have allowed the student to use a t test (that is, none of the assumptions of the t test were violated and that data were at least on an interval scale), would the student's conclusion had been different if the t test had been used? Explain.

10. Another student does not get a significant difference when using the Wilcoxon matched-pairs test on ordinal data. She decides to increase her power by using a t test. What is your recommendation to her?

11. A teacher believes that students do not put enough time into the preparation of their term papers. To test this hypothesis, she assigns a term paper to her class of 14 students. After collecting the papers, she copies them and then returns them to the students ungraded. She tells them that they need to be improved. She gives the class one week to improve their papers and then collects them. She asks another teacher who is unaware of who wrote the papers and whether it is the first or second

copy to grade each paper. The grades assigned are shown below. Determine if there is a significant difference in performance between the first and second papers. (Hint: Grades need to be assigned numbers such as "F" = 0, "D" = 1, etc.)

Paper Submitted	
First	*Second*
F	D
F	F
D	C
D	F
D	B
C	D
C	F
C	C
C	A
B	B
B	A
B	A
A	A
A	A

12. In Exercise 11, what are the independent and dependent variables? Why was the Wilcoxon matched-pairs test used instead of the t test?

13. A researcher obtains the following results, $\Sigma R_- = 917$ and $\Sigma R_+ = 1,933$ with and N (number of difference values) of 75. Is there a significant difference using a directional hypothesis with an alpha level of .05? With an alpha level of .01?

14. Ten sixth graders, five male and five female, are tested for their IQ. They are then matched in pairs on the basis of IQ and are given a new reasoning test that is supposed to be free of sex bias. The scores on the test are shown below. Is there a difference between the boys and girls on the test? Use a directional hypothesis with an alpha level of .05.

	Sex	
Pair	*Boys*	*Girls*
a	13	21
b	40	22
c	29	20
d	65	19
e	30	20

15. Do you feel that the researcher in Exercise 14 reached the appropriate conclusion based on the findings of the test? Justify your answer in terms of the statistical findings and the descriptive statistics for each sample.

16. For each of the following cases determine if H_0 should be retained or rejected:
    a. $\Sigma R_- = 15$, $\Sigma R_+ = 30$, $N = 9$, nondirectional hypothesis, alpha level $= .05$
    b. $\Sigma R_- = 358$, $\Sigma R_+ = 107$, $N = 30$, nondirectional hypothesis, alpha level $= .01$
    c. $\Sigma R_- = 583$, $\Sigma R_+ = 320$, $N = 42$, directional hypothesis (ΣR_+ was predicted to be smaller), alpha level $= .05$

17. The overall student ratings of 10 faculty members are compared. The ratings are separated on the basis of whether it was done by a student majoring in the subject taught by the faculty member or not. The ratings on a 5-point scale are shown below. The higher the rating, the better the course was rated. Determine if student ratings are a function of whether or not the students are majoring in the course. Use a nondirectional hypothesis with an alpha level of .01.

	Type of Course	
Instructor	Major	Non-major
a	3.8	3.5
b	3.9	4.1
c	3.5	4.0
d	3.7	3.3
e	3.6	3.6
f	3.8	3.2
g	4.3	2.1
h	4.0	1.8
i	3.7	3.3
j	3.6	2.0

18. What are the independent and dependent variables in Exercise 17? Why was the Wilcoxon matched-pairs test selected rather than the t test for correlated samples?

19. Assume you did not know about the Wilcoxon matched-pairs test and used the t test for correlated samples for Exercise 17. Would your conclusion be the same as in Exercise 17?

20. Seven schools in an athletic conference are evaluated in terms of their football and basketball rankings for a given year. Their rankings are based on their final national rankings at the end of the season. The lower the rank, the better the team's performance. Determine if this conference has

a better reputation in football or basketball. Use a nondirectional hypothesis with a rejection level of .05.

School	Sport	
	Football	Basketball
a	29	18
b	45	30
c	12	15
d	20	8
e	14	13
f	35	12
g	65	43

CHALLENGE QUESTIONS

1. To test the influence of type of response mode on hemispheric processing, subjects were shown geometric stimuli that were presented to either the left visual field or the right visual field. Research has shown no difference between visual fields in the number of errors made when the subjects were required to press a button when a pair of figures were identical. In this study, subjects were required to bite on a mouthpiece. Previous research indicated that movement in the jaw and tongue may be controlled by the left hemisphere. Therefore, responses to stimuli presented to the right visual field (but processed in the left hemisphere) may be made easier and faster than those for stimuli presented to the left visual field. Each subject saw 80 pairs of stimuli (half of which were matches) presented to each visual field. The order of presentation varied randomly across trials. The number of errors made by the subjects are shown below. Using a directional hypothesis, determine if there is a significant difference between hemispheres. Use a nonparametric test because of the shape of the distribution of the difference values. (Based on Galluscio, E. H. (1983). Brain laterality: Differences in cognitive style or motor functions? *Perceptual and Motor Skills, 56,* 3–9.)

	Visual Field of Presentation	
Student	Right	Left
a	0	1
b	4	18
c	0	2
d	1	2
e	2	1
f	0	0
g	1	4
h	2	9
i	0	8
j	6	11

2. A phenomenon known as the "Ranschburg effect" describes the case in which subjects fail to recall a repeated item in a short list of items. For instance, if a person hears the sequence 6-3-2-8-3-1-7 and is asked to recall the numbers immediately, the person will be less likely to recall that 3 was presented twice than if the repeated item was replaced with a new digit within the series (e.g., 6-3-2-8-9-1-7). Research has shown that the position of the repeated item is critical. A researcher was interested in determining if the size of the set of items was an important factor for obtaining the effect. When 12 sequences of seven words were selected from a large vocabulary (78 words), then the Ranschburg effect was not obtained (there was no decrease in memory performance for the repeated item). The data listed below are based on sequences of words when they were selected from a vocabulary of 10 words. Obviously, there were repetitions of words across sequences as well as within sequences. For the repeated sequences, a word was repeated within a series at critical positions that have been shown to produce the Ranschburg effect. For control sequences, there were no repeated words within a sequence. Listed below are the number of words recalled from the critical positions for both types of sequences. Using a nonparametric test and a nondirectional hypothesis, determine if a difference exists in recall. (Based on Jahnke, J. C. (1974). Restrictions on the Ranschburg effect. *Journal of Experimental Psychology, 103,* 183–185.)

	Type of Word Sequence	
Student	Repeated	Control
a	7	9
b	5	12
c	9	12
d	10	10
e	4	2
f	2	8
g	1	4
h	11	11
i	12	10
j	12	10
k	9	10
l	10	12
m	5	7
n	9	11
o	8	12

For each question answer the following:
a. What is a plausible research hypothesis?
b. What are the H_0 and H_1?
c. Calculate the appropriate descriptive statistic for each condition.
d. Calculate the appropriate inferential statistic. Use an alpha level of .05 for Question 1 and .01 for Question 2.
e. State your findings in the proper format and provide a written conclusion about the findings (relating the inferential statistics to the descriptive statistics).

Analyzing Multiple-Condition Experiments with Ordinal Data

PROCEDURES DESCRIBED

calculating H for the Kruskal-Wallis test

calculating x for the Friedman test

Counseling juvenile delinquents is an important issue in psychology and sociology. A major goal of the counseling is the improvement of the moral reasoning of these youths. Kohlberg (1969) proposed a theory of moral development that assumed individuals pass through stages of moral reasoning. The higher the stage, the better the moral reasoning. Kohlberg hypothesized that moral development occurs as a result of conflict between one's own moral values and those of another whose moral reasoning is at a higher level.

Niles (1986) tested a group-counseling approach designed to raise the moral reasoning of juvenile boys ranging in age from 13- to 15-years-old. These boys were either enrolled at an institution or in a day-school special education program. Twenty-one boys were randomly assigned to a control group that was tested at the beginning and the end of a 16-week period. Another 19 boys were assigned to a treatment group. The treatment group consisted of twice-weekly group meetings. At each meeting, different ethical or moral dilemmas were presented to the group to discuss. A trained group facilitator was present to promote interaction among group members and to help them reach a resolution to the dilemma. Kohlberg (1969) believed that this type of interaction and reasoning process is critical to moral development. A third group, the placebo group, consisted of 19 boys who were given the same dilemmas as the treatment group but the facilitator did not seek interaction or group resolution.

Following the 16-week period, each student completed several tests including one measuring the student's stage of moral development as measured by Kohlberg's (1969) model. The students were ranked in terms of their moral development. These rankings are shown by group in Table 19.1. The higher the ranking, the higher the stage of moral development.

This study is an example of a multiple-condition experiment with ordinal data. The independent variable is the type of treatment given to the boys. There are three levels or conditions: control, treatment, or placebo. The dependent variable is the level of moral development. The values are represented in terms of rankings. Equal intervals cannot be assumed between rankings. Therefore, the dependent variable corresponds to an ordinal scale of measurement.

Much like the discussion for the *t* test for independent samples and the one-way ANOVA, there is a potential problem in conducting a series of nonparametric tests (the Mann-Whitney *U* test) that compares pairs of conditions. The experimentwise error rate, which deals with the probability of a Type I error, increases beyond the acceptable alpha level if the researcher were to conduct all possible pairwise comparisons using Mann-Whitney *U* tests.

As was the case with the one-way ANOVA, which is the accepted parametric test for a multiple-condition study with independent groups, there is a corresponding nonparametric test for multiple-condition experiments with

TABLE 19.1 Rankings for the Chapter Example		
Type of Group		
Treatment	*Placebo*	*Control*
1	2	3
22	6	4
26	7	5
27	8	11
28	9	12
36	10	13
40	14	16
45	15	18
46	17	21
48	19	23
50	20	25
51	24	30
52	29	31
53	32	35
54	33	37
55	34	41
56	38	42
57	39	43
59	58	44
		47
		49
$\Sigma R_t = 806$	$\Sigma R_p = 414$	$\Sigma R_c = 550$

independent groups. The test is called the Kruskal-Wallis test. It is the appropriate test when an independent groups design is used. Later in the chapter we will discuss a nonparametric test for multiple-condition experiments using a repeated measures design. Before discussing the tests, however, let us calculate a descriptive statistic for this example.

DESCRIBING THE DATA FOR A MULTIPLE-CONDITION STUDY WITH RANKS

The most appropriate measure of central tendency to report for this example is the median. The data in Table 19.1 are arranged in ascending order. The 50th percentile ranking (or middle ranking) for the control group is 25; for the placebo group the median is 19; and, for the treatment group it is 48.

It appears from the medians, that the treatment group has boys with higher levels of moral reasoning than the other two groups. A statistical test is needed to confirm this statement.

INFERENTIAL STATISTICS: THE KRUSKAL-WALLIS TEST

The statistical hypotheses and procedures in testing for a difference among the groups are similar to those used for the Mann-Whitney U test. The assumptions of the Kruskal-Wallis test, in fact, are identical to those for the Mann-Whitney U test. In addition, the Kruskal-Wallis test assumes that the data to be analyzed are in the form of ranks. No assumptions are made about population variances or the shape of the population distribution.

The statistical hypotheses for the Kruskal-Wallis test are identical to those for the Mann-Whitney U test. The null hypothesis describes the case in which all samples are selected from the same population distribution. The alternative hypothesis assumes that at least one sample was selected from a population distribution different from the others. As in previous examples, the research hypothesis is more similar to the H_1.

CALCULATING THE H STATISTIC

The Kruskal-Wallis test generates a statistic identified by the letter H. In order to calculate H, the sum of the ranks for each condition must be known. The sum of the ranks for each group is shown in Table 19.1. If the data are not in the form of ranks, it is necessary to rank the values without regard to group membership. This is the same procedure as described in the second example for the Mann-Whitney U test in Chapter 17.

Once the sum of the ranks is known for each group, the following formula is used:

$$H = \left[\frac{12}{N(N+1)} \Sigma \frac{R_k^2}{n_k} \right] - 3(N+1). \tag{45}$$

In this formula N refers to the total number of participants in the study. In the chapter example, N is 59. The summation involves first squaring the sum of the ranks for each group and dividing the squared sum by the number of observations within the group n_k. Then these values are added together. The number of groups or conditions in the study is represented by k. If H_0 is true, then one would anticipate the rankings to be randomly distributed among the conditions. Therefore, the sum of the ranks would be quite similar among the groups (assuming equal-sized groups).

Using the data from Table 19.1 in Formula 45 provides the following:

$$H = \left[\frac{12}{N(N+1)} \Sigma \frac{R_k^2}{n_k} \right] - 3(N+1) \tag{45}$$

$$= \left(\frac{12}{59(59+1)} \right) \left(\frac{806^2}{19} + \frac{414^2}{19} + \frac{550^2}{21} \right) - 3(59+1)$$

$$= \left(\frac{12}{3,540} \times 57,616.97 \right) - 180$$

$$= \mathbf{15.31.}$$

For this example the obtained H statistic has a value of 15.31. To interpret this value it is necessary to understand the characteristics of H statistics if H_0 is true.

INTERPRETING THE H STATISTIC

If H_0 is true, then the H statistic is distributed as a χ^2 distribution. Recall from Chapter 16 that the χ^2 distribution is a positively skewed distribution. Critical H values are the same as χ^2 values listed in Table X. For the Kruskal-Wallis test, the df is equal to the number of groups $- 1$, $k - 1$. The critical H value for this example is 5.99 (assuming an alpha level of .05).

To determine if a significant difference exists, the obtained H statistic should be compared with the critical H statistic. If the obtained statistic is equal to or greater than the critical statistic, then H_0 should be rejected. In the chapter example, the H statistic is greater than the critical H statistic. Therefore, it is unlikely that the samples were selected from the same population distribution. Niles (1986) can conclude that "the boys in the groups differed in their levels of moral reasoning, $\underline{H}(2) = 15.31$, $\underline{p} < .05$."

As was the case with the one-way ANOVA, the Kruskal-Wallis test establishes that a difference exists. Once a significant difference is found, pairwise comparison tests are necessary. A significant finding from the Kruskal-Wallis test is often followed by a series of Mann-Whitney U tests. These tests are referred to as *protected* Mann-Whitney U tests because they are performed *only* after a significant difference is found using the Kruskal-Wallis test. By first conducting a Kruskal-Wallis test, the researcher ensures that the experimental error rate is not greater than the alpha level.

Performing these tests using the data in this example reveals that the treatment group was significantly different from the other two groups, even though the other groups were not different from one another. Therefore, the use of a group facilitator who encourages interaction among the boys and a group resolution in dealing with a moral dilemma results in a higher level of moral reasoning than would be found if the counseling group did not interact or was not presented with the dilemmas.

One final comment must be made concerning the Kruskal-Wallis test. The use of the χ^2 distribution for finding critical values is not appropriate if three samples are used, with all samples having five or fewer observations. In this case, exact probability values for H statistic can be found by consulting a number of texts including Siegel (1956) or Loftus and Loftus (1982).

MULTIPLE-CONDITION EXPERIMENTS WITH REPEATED MEASURES AND ORDINAL DATA

College students often have a variety of professionals who can provide advice and counseling. Tinsley, Brown, Aubin, and Lucek (1984) surveyed 236 undergraduates about their expectancies and tendencies in seeking help. Among the questions asked were several dealing with personal problems, including sexuality, emotional stability, and self-confidence. For each of 11 problems, the students ranked seven types of professionals in terms of how likely they would seek help from the professionals. From these rankings, a "scale" ranking was obtained. The lower the ranking, the more likely the individual would be to seek help from that type of professional.

Data was generated for 24 students consistent with what was reported for the entire sample of 236 students. The rankings of the different types of professionals for these students are shown in Table 19.2. The types of professionals are listed across the top. The researchers hypothesized that there would be differences in the rankings of the types of professionals.

TABLE 19.2   Rankings for the Second Chapter Example

	Type of Professional						
Student	Counseling psychologist	Psychiatrist	Peer counselor	Clinical psychologist	College counselor	Advisor	Career counselor
a	1	2	4	3	5	6	7
b	2	3	1	5	4	6	7
c	4	1	7	2	6	3	5
d	2	7	5	3	4	1	6
e	3	1	7	2	6	4	5
f	4	2	1	5	3	7	6
g	2	1	3	5	4	7	6
h	4	2	6	3	5	1	7
i	4	1	3	2	5	7	6
j	2	3	1	6	4	5	7
k	3	2	1	4	5	6	7
l	1	2	4	3	6	7	5
m	2	3	1	4	5	7	6
n	3	1	2	4	7	6	5
o	2	6	7	5	3	1	4
p	3	4	2	1	5	6	7
q	3	7	1	4	5	2	6
r	1	3	4	2	7	6	5
s	1	4	2	6	3	5	7
t	2	6	7	5	3	4	1
u	3	5	1	7	6	4	2
v	4	6	3	5	1	2	7
w	2	3	4	1	6	5	7
x	1	4	3	2	5	6	7
Median =	2	3	3	4	5	5.5	6
$\Sigma R =$	59	79	80	89	113	114	138

This study is a multiple-condition study in which the independent variable is the type of professional. There are seven values or levels for this variable, which is on a nominal scale of measurement. The dependent variable is the preference ranking. The rankings varied from 1 (most preferred) to 7 (the least preferred). The rankings conform to an ordinal scale of measurement.

Unlike the previous example, this study uses a repeated measures design. Therefore, the rankings for the different professionals are not independent of one another. As a result, the Kruskal-Wallis test cannot be used. Rather, a nonparametric equivalent to the ANOVA for repeated measures is needed. This test is called the Friedman test. Before describing the procedures for this test, let us describe the data in Table 19.2.

DESCRIBING THE DATA

The median ranking for each type of professional was calculated. These rankings are shown at the bottom in Table 19.2. The rankings were determined using the procedures outlined in Chapter 3. Note that there appear to be differences among the professionals. For instance, students had lower median rankings for the counseling psychologist, psychiatrist, and peer counselors than for the academic advisor or career counselor. The Friedman test allows the researchers to determine if any of these differences are significant.

INFERENTIAL STATISTICS: THE FRIEDMAN TEST

The assumptions for the Friedman test are identical to those for the Wilcoxon. The statistical hypotheses can be stated in the same terms as those for the Kruskal-Wallis test. The H_0 states that the samples were selected from the same population distribution, and H_1 hypothesizes that at least one sample was selected from a different sample.

Whereas the Wilcoxon test involved ranking the difference values for each participant, the Friedman test assumes that the values for each participant are in the form of ranks. If the original data are not in the form of ranks, then the researcher must first rank the values by participant. A common practice is to assign the lowest value a rank of 1 and to assign higher ranks to ascending values.

Once the data are in the form of ranks, then the sum of the ranks for each condition should be calculated. If H_0 is true and the values were selected from the same population distribution, then differences in the ranks are the result of random selection and error. Therefore, one would expect that the sum of the ranks to be quite similar across conditions. The Friedman test examines this possibility.

The Friedman test provides a statistic identified as x. To calculate x the following formula is used,

$$x = \left[\frac{12}{nk(k + 1)} (\Sigma R_k{}^2) \right] - 3n(k + 1). \tag{46}$$

The similarities between this formula and that for the Kruskal-Wallis test should be noted. As with the Kruskal-Wallis test, k refers to the number of conditions and n is the number of participants.

The sum of the ranks for each type of professional from the chapter example is shown in Table 19.2. As a check of your summations, the sum of all the group's total should equal $nk(k + 1)/2$. In this example the sum would be 672.

Using the information from Table 19.2 in Formula 46 results in

$$x = \left[\frac{12}{nk(k + 1)} (\Sigma R_k{}^2) \right] - 3n(k + 1) \tag{46}$$

$$= \left[\frac{12}{24 \times 7 \times (7 + 1)} (59^2 + 79^2 + 80^2 + 89^2 + 113^2 + 114^2 + 138^2) \right] - 3 \times 24 \times (7 + 1)$$

$$= \left(\frac{12}{1,344} \times 68,852 \right) - 576$$

$$= \mathbf{38.75.}$$

An x statistic of 38.75 was obtained. This value must be compared with the critical x value.

As you may have already guessed, because the Kruskal-Wallis test and the Friedman test are quite similar, the x statistic like the H statistic is derived from the χ^2 distribution. Therefore, the critical x statistic can be found in Table X. The df are again defined as the number of groups (k) minus 1. For this example the df equal 6. Using Table X, a critical value of 12.59 is found for an alpha level of $p \leq .05$.

The obtained x statistic of 38.75 exceeds the critical value of 12.59. Therefore, Tinsley et al. (1984) can reject H_0 and assume that at least one of the professionals has a ranking that is significantly different from the others. They can conclude that "a significant difference exists in the preference rankings given to the different professionals for counseling of personal concerns, $\underline{x}(6) = 38.75, \underline{p} < .05$."

As was the case with the Kruskal-Wallis test, a significant difference for the Friedman test indicates that at least one sample comes from a population distribution different from the other samples. The test does not identify the sample or samples that are different. Pairwise comparisons are needed. Once a significant difference has been obtained using the Friedman test, then the researcher may conduct a series of Wilcoxon tests to determine which samples are different.

As was the case with the Kruskal-Wallis test when small samples are concerned, the χ^2 distribution is not appropriate in providing the critical value. When the design has three or four groups with fewer than 10 participants, the researcher is advised to consult either Siegel (1956) or Loftus and Loftus (1982) for procedures for calculating the exact probability.

SUMMARY   Two nonparametric tests exist that are similar to the parametric analysis of variance tests. The Kruskal-Wallis test is the nonparametric equivalent of the one-way ANOVA. It should be used with multiple-condition experiments using an independent groups design when the data are ordinal or violate assumptions of the one-way ANOVA. The test makes the same assumptions as the Mann-Whitney U test.

The Friedman test is the nonparametric equivalent of the ANOVA for repeated measures. Its assumptions are the same as those for the Wilcoxon test. The test is appropriate when each participant serves in all conditions and the responses are ranked or can be ranked.

Both tests use the same statistical hypotheses. The null hypothesis states that all samples were selected from the same population distribution. The alternative hypothesis states that at least one sample was selected from a population distribution different from the others. Both tests use similar formulas and are based on summing the ranks for each condition. The critical values for each test are based on the χ^2 distribution.

SUMMARY FOR USING THE KRUSKAL-WALLIS TEST

1. Develop the research hypothesis and determine the alpha level, usually .05 or .01.
2. Calculate a measure of central tendency for each condition; the median is often preferred.
3. State H_0 and H_1.
4. If the data are not ranked, then rank the values overall without regard to group membership.
5. Calculate the sum of the ranks (ΣR) for each condition.
6. Calculate H by using Formula 45

$$H = \left[\frac{12}{N(N + 1)} \Sigma \frac{R_k^2}{n_k} \right] - 3(N + 1), \qquad (45)$$

where N is the total number of participants and n_k is the number of participants per condition.

7. Determine the critical value by using Table X (assuming that there are more than three conditions or that if there are three conditions, one has at least 6 participants). The degrees of freedom are equal to the number of conditions (k) minus 1.
8. If the obtained H statistic is equal to or larger than the critical value, then reject H_0. Otherwise, retain H_0. State your conclusion in words and in-

clude the necessary statistics, $\underline{H}(df)$ = obtained H statistic, $\underline{p}$ < or > alpha level.

SUMMARY FOR USING THE FRIEDMAN TEST

1. Develop the research hypothesis and determine the alpha level, usually .05 or .01.
2. Calculate a measure of central tendency for each condition, the median is often preferred.
3. State H_0 and H_1.
4. If the data are not ranked by participant, then rank the values for each participant.
5. Calculate the sum of the ranks (ΣR) for each condition.
6. Calculate x by using Formula 46

$$x = \left[\frac{12}{nk(k+1)} (\Sigma R_k^2) \right] - 3n(k+1), \tag{46}$$

where n is the number of participants and k is the number of conditions.

7. Determine the critical value by using Table X (assuming that there are more than four conditions or more than 10 participants). The degrees of freedom are equal to the number of conditions (k) minus 1.
8. If the obtained x statistic is equal to or larger than the critical value, then reject H_0. Otherwise, retain H_0. State your conclusion in words and include the necessary statistics, $\underline{x}$ (df) = obtained x statistic, $\underline{p}$ < or > alpha level.

EXERCISES

1. Conduct the appropriate Mann-Whitney U tests for the first chapter problem to confirm the findings reported on page 451.
2. In the Niles (1986) study, the boys were given a pretest prior to serving in one of the three treatment groups. This pretest was given to ensure that the groups did not differ prior to the study. The pretest data for several boys are shown below. Determine if a significant difference exists among the three groups prior to the treatment. Use an alpha level of .05.

Treatment	Placebo	Control
1	3	2
7	8	4
9	11	5
10	12	6
13	14	15
18	16	20
19	17	21

3. Students rate faculty in four different disciplines in terms of their helpfulness in advising students attending a small college. Determine if there is a difference among the disciplines. Use an alpha level of .05.

Humanities	Natural Science	Social Science	Arts
6	1	2	12
8	3	5	13
9	4	10	15
11	7	14	18
19	17	16	20

4. If a significant difference were found in Exercise 3, conduct the appropriate tests to identify which disciplines differed from one another.

5. After summing the ranks for a five-condition, independent groups experiment, the following values are obtained: $\Sigma R_1 = \Sigma R_2 = \Sigma R_1 = \Sigma R_2 = \Sigma R_5 = 1010$; and $N_k = 20$. Would you expect to reject H_0? Why? Calculate the appropriate test statistic.

6. A fellow student asks your opinion concerning the wisdom of conducting a series of Mann-Whitney U tests after finding a significant H statistic. What strategy would you suggest to your fellow student if there are four conditions? Is it necessary to test the two most extreme conditions? Why?

7. Different covers of a magazine are ranked by a media critic in terms of her perceptions of their interest to readers. These covers are then grouped according to their content. The following information is obtained:

primarily political content: $\Sigma R = 140$, n = 7

movie/TV content: $\Sigma R = 140$, n = 10

recent disaster featured: $\Sigma R = 100$, n = 8

personal profile: $\Sigma R = 85$, n = 5

Conduct the appropriate test to determine if the content influenced the rankings. Use an alpha level of .05.

8. When would you use the Friedman test rather than the Wilcoxon test? When would you use the Friedman test rather than the Kruskal-Wallis test?

9. A student believes that his data violate assumptions for the t test and for the Wilcoxon. Therefore, he decides to use the Friedman test. Your comments?

10. Graph the median values for the second chapter example on students' preferences for professional help.

11. Twelve people are asked to rank four issues in terms of their importance in an upcoming election. Determine if there is a significant difference in

the rankings (use an alpha level of .01). What type of decision error might you be making?

Individual	Issue			
	A	B	C	D
a	2	3	1	4
b	3	1	2	4
c	1	2	3	4
d	1	3	4	2
e	2	3	1	4
f	3	4	1	2
g	4	3	1	2
h	2	3	4	1
i	1	3	2	4
j	1	3	4	2
k	2	1	3	4
l	1	3	2	4

12. The students from the second chapter example were also asked to rank the professionals in terms of seeking help for career problems such as choice of major and academic grades. A sample of 10 students is shown below. Determine if there is a significant difference in preference for the different professionals. Use an alpha level of .05.

Counseling Psychologist	Psychiatrist	Peer Counselor	Clinical Psychologist	College Counselor	Advisor	Career Counselor
4	7	5	6	2	3	1
3	7	6	5	4	2	1
2	6	4	5	1	7	3
5	4	6	7	3	1	2
6	5	3	4	2	1	7
3	7	5	6	4	2	1
5	7	3	6	1	4	2
4	7	3	6	2	5	1
5	6	4	7	3	1	2
6	4	3	7	2	5	1

13. Compare your findings with those for the second chapter example. Would you conclude that students seek the same types of professionals for personal as well as career problems? Support your answer.

14. How many pairwise comparisons might be needed to test all the possible comparisons for the second chapter example?

15. The second chapter example is based on an N of 24. Another student tells you that the original study was based on an N of 236. She says that the larger N would change the critical value for the test. If that is true, how?

16. An instructor asks 15 students to rank their preferences for five different types of book covers for a college textbook. The most preferred cover is given a rank of 1. The sums of the ranks for each book cover are listed below. Determine if a significant difference exists (use an alpha level of .05). If it does exist, is it necessary to conduct any further tests to explain the differences?

$\Sigma R_{cover\ a} = 25 \quad \Sigma R_{cover\ b} = 50 \quad \Sigma R_{cover\ c} = 50 \quad \Sigma R_{cover\ d} = 50$

$\Sigma R_{cover\ e} = 50$

CHALLENGE QUESTIONS

1. Locus of control refers to one's belief about what is the controlling factor in one's life, either oneself (internal) or the environment and others (external). A study was conducted to determine if locus of control was related to age. Individuals across four different age groups completed a questionnaire assessing locus of control. The individuals are ranked below. A high rank indicates a greater belief in external control. Determine if there is a difference in locus of control as it relates to age. (Based on Hale, W. D., & Cochran, C. D. (1986). Locus of control across the adult lifespan. *Psychological Reports, 59,* 311–313.)

Age of Respondent			
20 – 34	*35 – 49*	*50 – 64*	*65 – 89*
16	17	18	19
15	6	12	20
11	8	7	22
1	23	27	32
21	25	30	13
26	29	4	14
28	5	3	10
9	2	24	31

2. To study preference differences in how tests are organized, researchers asked 15 college students to rank their preferences for the sequencing of test items. Three possible sequences were offered, easy-to-hard, random order, and hard-to-easy. They gave a rank of 1 to the most preferred and 3 to the least preferred. Determine if there is a difference in the rankings. (Based on Allison, D. E., & Thomas, D. C. (1986). Item-difficulty sequence in achievement examinations: Examinees' preferences and test-taking strategies. *Psychological Reports, 59,* 867–870.)

| | Item Sequence | | |
Student	Easy-to-hard	Random	Hard-to-easy
a	1	2	3
b	2	1	3
c	1	3	2
d	1	2	3
e	2	3	1
f	2	1	3
g	1	2	3
h	3	1	2
i	2	1	3
j	2	1	3
k	1	2	3
l	1	3	2
m	3	1	2
n	1	3	2
o	2	1	3

For each question answer the following:
a. What is a plausible research hypothesis?
b. What are the H_0 and H_1?
c. Calculate the appropriate descriptive statistic for each condition.
d. Calculate the appropriate inferential statistic. Use an alpha level of .05 for Question 1 and .01 for Question 2.
e. State your findings in the proper format and provide a written conclusion about the findings (relating the inferential statistics to the descriptive statistics).

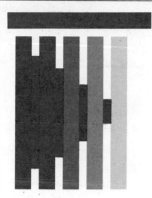

Selecting the Appropriate
Statistical Procedures

This section includes a number of diagrams that may help you in selecting the appropriate statistic or statistical procedure to report when analyzing the data from a research study. The diagrams are guidelines. They do not list all possibilities. In fact, they are limited to designs that can be analyzed using procedures described in this text. Also, there may be instances in which the researcher may want to substitute a different statistic or procedure for one listed in the diagrams. The diagrams, however, should help you in the majority of instances you will encounter in your undergraduate studies of research.

REPORTING MEASURES OF CENTRAL TENDENCY AND VARIABILITY

The first step in analyzing data often involves the use of descriptive statistics. Figure A-1 on the following page lists common measures of central tendency and variability reported in behavioral science research. The appropriate statistic to be reported is often influenced by the scale of measurement for the variable being summarized.

RESEARCH HYPOTHESES PREDICTING A LINEAR RELATIONSHIP

Figure A-2 on the following page lists the appropriate statistical procedures to be used when a researcher is testing for the existence of a linear relationship. If the researcher is using inferential statistics to determine the likeli-

A

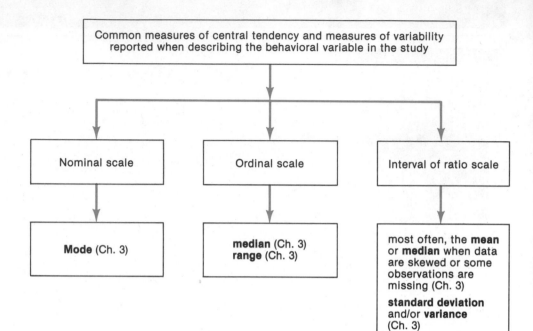

Common measures of central tendency and measures of variability reported when describing the behavioral variable in the study

Nominal scale

Ordinal scale

Interval of ratio scale

Mode (Ch. 3)

median (Ch. 3)
range (Ch. 3)

most often, the **mean** or **median** when data are skewed or some observations are missing (Ch. 3)

standard deviation and/or **variance** (Ch. 3)

FIGURE A-1

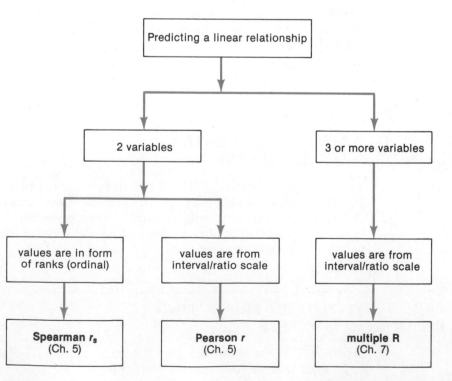

Predicting a linear relationship

2 variables

3 or more variables

values are in form of ranks (ordinal)

values are from interval/ratio scale

values are from interval/ratio scale

Spearman r_s
(Ch. 5)

Pearson r
(Ch. 5)

multiple R
(Ch. 7)

FIGURE A-2

A

hood of a relationship existing in the population, then the procedures described in Chapter 9 should be used after calculating either the Pearson r or the Spearman r_s correlation coefficients.

STATISTICAL PROCEDURES WHEN TESTING FOR A DIFFERENCE

The remaining three diagrams illustrate the steps needed in determining the appropriate statistical procedure to be used when the research hypothesis predicts a difference among conditions or levels of a variable in a research study. The diagrams differentiate among the scales of measurement for the dependent variable or the variable measuring the behavior under study.

In Figure A-3 the tests are listed for analyzing a variable on the interval or ratio scale of measurement. It is important to determine the number of variables in the study and the number of levels of the independent variable. Lastly, the researcher must differentiate between the independent groups design (a participant serves in only one condition) and the repeated measures design (a participant serves in every condition).

Figure A-4 lists the nonparametric tests. This diagram is appropriate

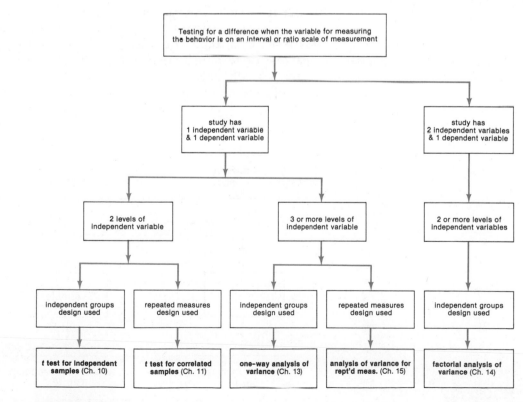

FIGURE A-3

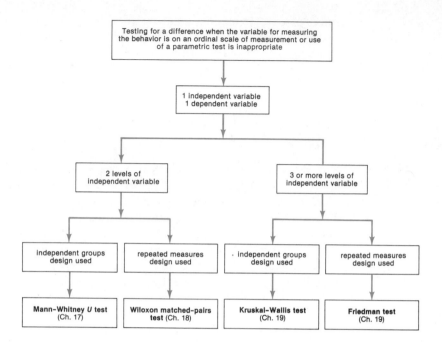

FIGURE A-4

when the dependent variable is on the ordinal scale of measurement or when the assumptions of a parametric test have been violated to the point that the researcher must use a nonparametric test. The decisions in selecting the appropriate nonparametric test are similar to those used in Figure A-4.

Lastly, Figure A-5 is a diagram for data on a nominal scale of measurement. In behavioral science research, this diagram is most often used when the data are in the form of frequencies.

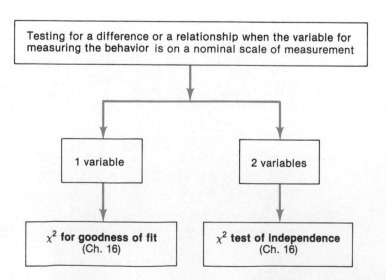

FIGURE A-5

Brief Review of Statistical Notation and Algebraic Procedures

A. Symbols Used in Arithmetic Operations

$+$ = addition
$-$ = subtraction
$\times$ or $\cdot$ = multiplication
$/$ or $\div$ = division
$>$ = greater than
$\geq$ = greater than or equal to
$<$ = less than
$\leq$ = less than or equal to
$=$ = equal to
$\neq$ = not equal to
$\sqrt{}$ = square root of

B. Basic Procedures

1. Working with fractions
   a. Convert fractions to decimals before performing any arithmetic operations.

   $$1/3 = .33 \qquad 2/10 = .20$$

   b. If you are adding or subtracting fractions that have not been converted to decimals, then find a common denominator.

   $$1/2 + 3/8 = 4/8 + 3/8 = 7/8$$
   $$2/3 - 5/13 = 26/39 - 15/39 = 11/39$$

B

c. If you are multiplying fractions that have not been converted to decimals, then multiply the values in the numerator together and then the values in the denominator.

$$3/4 \times 5/16 = 15/64 \qquad -1/3 \times 9/12 = -9/36$$

d. If you are dividing fractions that have not been converted to decimals, invert the fraction serving as the divisor and then follow the multiplication procedure in 1.c.

$$5/8 \div 2/3 = \qquad\qquad 1/10 \div 3/7 =$$
$$5/8 \times 3/2 = 15/16 \qquad 1/10 \times 7/3 = 7/30$$

2. Isolating a variable in an algebraic equation
   a. To both sides of the equation, add or subtract other terms on same side of equal sign with the variable (x) to be isolated.

$$
\begin{aligned}
x + 3y - 6 &= 2y + 5 \\
x + 3y - 6 - 3y &= 2y + 5 - 3y \quad \text{(subtract 3y)} \\
x - 6 &= -1y + 5 \quad \text{(combining terms)} \\
x - 6 + 6 &= -1y + 5 + 6 \quad \text{(add 6)} \\
x &= -1y + 11 \quad \text{(combining terms)}
\end{aligned}
$$

   b. To both sides of equation, multiply or divide by constant if variable is being divided or multiplied by constant.

$$6x = 2 \qquad\qquad x/7 = 4$$
$$(6x)/6 = 2/6 \;(\text{divide by 6}) \qquad (x/7) \cdot 7 = 4 \cdot 7 \;(\text{multiply by 7})$$
$$x = .33 \qquad\qquad x = 28$$

C. Summation Notation

1. ΣX indicates that all values associated with set X should be added together.

$$X = \{2, 6, -5, 3, 2.8\} \qquad \Sigma X = 2 + 6 + (-5) + 3 + 2.8$$
$$= 8.8$$

2. $(\Sigma X)^2$ indicates that the sum of the values associated with X is squared.

$$X = \{2, 6, -5, 3, 2.8\} \qquad (\Sigma X)^2 = [2 + 6 + (-5) + 3 + 2.8]^2$$
$$= [8.8]^2$$
$$= 77.44$$

3. ΣX^2 indicates that each value in X is squared and then added together.

$$X = \{2, 6, -5, 3, 2.8\} \qquad \Sigma X^2 = 2^2 + 6^2 + (-5)^2 + 3^2 + 2.8^2$$
$$= 4 + 36 + 25 + 9 + 7.84$$
$$= 81.84$$

4. Note that $(\Sigma X)^2 \neq \Sigma X^2$. See the calculations in the previous two sections.

$$X = \{2, 6, -5, 3, 2.8\} \qquad [(\Sigma X)^2 = 77.44] \neq [\Sigma X^2 = 81.84]$$

5. $\Sigma(c \cdot X) = c \cdot \Sigma X$. Multiplying each value in set X by a constant and then summing the values is the same as multiplying the sum by the constant.

$$X = \{2, 6, -5, 3, 2.8\}$$
$$\Sigma(4 \cdot X) = (4 \cdot 2) + (4 \cdot 6) + (4 \cdot -5) + (4 \cdot 3) + (4 \cdot 2.8)$$
$$= 8 + 24 + (-20) + 12 + 11.2$$
$$= 35.2$$

$$4 \cdot \Sigma X = 4 \cdot (8.8)$$
$$= 35.2$$

B

Appendix C

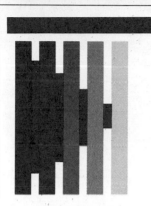

Computer Commands for Using SAS and SPSS$_x$

This appendix is an introduction to two popular computer packages used by behavioral science researchers: SAS™ (Statistical Analysis System) and SPSS$_x$™ (Statistical Package for the Social Sciences). They are most frequently used on large mainframe computers but are becoming more popular and available on microcomputers.

On the following pages, examples taken from data described earlier in this text are shown using both packages. The examples are based on procedures frequently used by researchers, but they represent only a small portion of the statistical procedures available from each package.

The following pages include an introduction to each package and specific examples based on procedures described in the text. Data from the text are reprinted followed by the necessary computer input commands and an output identifying important statistics.

The commands listed apply only to the statistical packages. You will find, however, when using a large computer, that it is necessary to know additional commands known as Job Control Language or System Control Language. These commands enable you to use the mainframe computer, to tell it which package you want to use and when you are finished. Because these commands differ widely for different computers and schools, there will be no attempt to describe them further. Your instructor will provide the necessary information.

Listed below is a table of contents for the statistical procedures described in this section. Computer commands are also listed based on their first occurrence.

Overview of the basic structures for SAS and SPSS$_x$

SAS Commands	Page	SPSS$_x$ Commands	Page
DATA;	471	DATA LIST /	473
INPUT;	472	LIST VARIABLES = ALL	474
CARDS;	472	BEGIN DATA	474
PROC PRINT;	473	END DATA	475
PROC SORT; BY;	473		

Measures of central tendency and variability (Chapter 3)

SAS Commands	Page	SPSS$_x$ Commands	Page
		CONDESCRIPTIVE	
PROC MEANS;	C-477	SORT CASES BY	C-479
VAR;	C-477	REPORT VARIABLES =	C-479
BY;	C-477	/BREAK =	C-479
		/SUMMARY =	C-479

The Pearson r correlation coefficient (Chapter 5)

SAS Commands	Page	SPSS$_x$ Commands	Page
PROC CORR;	C-482	PEARSON CORR	C-484

The t test for independent samples (Chapter 10)

SAS Commands	Page	SPSS$_x$ Commands	Page
PROC TTEST;	C-487	T-TEST GROUPS =	C-489
CLASS;	C-487		

The t test for correlated samples (Chapter 11)

SAS Commands	Page	SPSS$_x$ Commands	Page
PROC MEANS T;	C-492	T-TEST PAIRS =	C-494

The one-way ANOVA (Chapter 13)

SAS Commands	Page	SPSS$_x$ Commands	Page
PROC GLM;	C-497	ANOVA	C-499
MODEL;	C-497	STATISTIC 3	C-499
MEANS;	C-497		

The factorial ANOVA (Chapter 14)

SAS Commands	SPSS$_x$ Commands
(no new terms introduced)	

The χ^2 test of independence (Chapter 16)

SAS Commands	Page	SPSS$_x$ Commands	Page
		CROSSTABS	
PROC FREQ;	C-507	TABLES	C-509
TABLES /CHISQR;	C-507	OPTIONS 18	C-509
		STATISTICS 1,2	C-509

BASIC STRUCTURE OF SAS

There are three segments to an SAS program: the first is the creation of a data set, the second is the data itself, and the third segment is procedure statements that manipulate and analyze the data. Following are brief explanations of each. Please note that throughout this appendix, I have shown commands and information that you will provide in caps and boldface or italics. When you are actually interacting with SAS, you will not use boldface or italics.

CONSTRUCTING A DATA SET

There are three statements that are included in constructing a data set. The first statement is **DATA dataset name;** The word **DATA** is a special word for SAS and tells the computer that what follows is the construction of a data set. What follows DATA is a **dataset name** provided by the user. SAS allows you to construct several data sets in any one program and the dataset name is used to identify different sets. It can be any name you wish to create as long as it begins with a letter, is eight letters or fewer, and has no spaces within it. Therefore, CH10 or EXPER are acceptable names, but CH 10 or EXPERIMENT are not. Terms listed in boldfaced and italic print identify information or terms that you provide. They are not actually typed in italics when you are inputting information into the computer. In fact, many computers only allow you to type in capital letters. The last part of any SAS statement is the semicolon,   ;   . The ; is used to inform SAS that the statement is completed.

The next statement, which should be entered as a separate line on a video terminal or as a separate card if you are using a keypunch, is **INPUT varname1   varname2 $;** The word **INPUT** informs SAS that the terms following it identify variables in your data set. You can list as many variable names as you wish. The variable names, identified here as varname1 and varname2, can be anything you wish as long as they begin with a letter and are eight letters or fewer. As you'll see in the following examples, I often include a subject identification number or letter as the variable SUBJ followed by terms describing the relevant variables in the study. It is often helpful to arrange your data first so that each participant's information or data are listed on a separate line. Then generate a variable name to identify each of the data values you have listed for a participant. Variables that have values which are expressed as alphanumeric characters, that is letters or words, must have a $ following the variable name on the INPUT line. SAS expects a variable to be expressed as numbers on the data lines unless you inform it otherwise. (The $ need only be included on the INPUT line; SAS will remember that it identifies alphanumeric levels from that point on.)

The third statement is **CARDS;** which tells SAS that you are done identifying information about the data set and what follows on subsequent lines are the data themselves.

ENTERING THE DATA

The data then follow, with one line reserved for each participant in the study. The data can be entered in a free format, that is there is no specific spacing that must be followed. However, values should be entered in the same order as the variables listed on the input card. And, you must have a space between each value. For instance, if you were inputting a subject number and then the experimental condition and a rating value as the dependent variable, then two examples of data lines might be

1   exper   4
7   control   3.

The first line would identify the subject as Subject 1 who served in the experimental condition and had a rating of 4. The other line is for Subject 7 who served in the control condition and had a rating of 3.

There is one data line for each participant. These lines *do not* end with a semicolon because they are not SAS statements. However, after the last line of data, you should have a line with a semicolon ; by itself to inform SAS that you have entered all the relevant data.

ANALYZING A DATA SET

The last set of statements begin with the word **PROC** which is short for procedure. PROC statements perform various statistical procedures to be described on subsequent pages. You can list a number of these procedures in any one program. One common statement is **PROC PRINT.** This statement will tell SAS to print your data set for you to review. It is helpful to include this statement in all programs so that you can check your data for possible errors in entry and for a record of the original values.

Another common statement is **PROC SORT; BY varname ;** This statement will have SAS sort your data set by the variable name. This statement is useful when you want to analyze your data by groups or conditions in the study.

BASIC STRUCTURE OF SPSS$_x$

There are three segments to an SPSS$_x$ program: the first is the creation of a data set, the second is the commands for analyzing the data, and the third is the listing of the data. Following are brief explanations of each. Please note that terms shown here in caps, boldface, or italics represent commands or information you will provide to the computer. However, when you are actually interacting with SPSS$_x$, you will not use boldface type.

CONSTRUCTING A DATA SET

The primary statement for telling SPSS$_x$ that you are constructing a data set begins with **DATA LIST.** Following **DATA LIST** is a space and then a slash /. The diagonal slash / is used by SPSS$_x$ to separate information from a command within the same statement. The slash is followed by a listing of variables in the study.

If you are entering three values for each participant (a subject identification number, a value for the independent variable, and a value for the dependent variable), then DATA LIST / would be followed with three variable names such as **SUBJ 1–2 COND 4 (A) RESPONSE 6–8 .** Each term,

SUBJ, COND, and RESPONSE, are variable names constructed by the researcher to identify variables for later analysis by $SPSS_x$. They can be any name the researcher wishes as long as they are eight or fewer letters long.

Following each variable name are numbers such as 1–2, 4, and 6–8. These numbers identify the columns in which the data values will be found when the data are entered later. By identifying SUBJ with 1–2, the researcher is reserving two columns, 1 and 2, for the subject value. Column 4 will contain the value for COND, the variable name for the research condition. $SPSS_x$ expects that all values are numbers unless otherwise notified on the DATA LIST statement. Note that after the 4 the information **(A)** is presented. This informs $SPSS_x$ that the variable COND has values that are in the form of letters. In fact, because the value is in only one column (Column 4), $SPSS_x$ will expect either a single letter or number for each person's data statement in Column 4. In a simple experiment, one could use E for the experimental condition and C for the control condition.

The dependent variable is represented by the variable **RESPONSE**. $SPSS_x$ expects that the values will be up to three digits in length and that they will appear in Columns 6 through 8.

$SPSS_x$ provides methods for having more than one statement of data for each participant. However, the examples described in this appendix and in this text are designed so that the data for a participant could be contained on one line or computer card.

ANALYZING A DATA SET

Following the DATA LIST statement, $SPSS_x$ expects to be commanded to perform a statistical procedure. It will permit one procedure to be identified before expecting a list of the data. Additional procedures can then follow after the data are presented. The first example on descriptive statistics lists three procedures. The remaining examples list only one procedure. You need to remember that one procedure must be described after the DATA LIST statement and all others must be presented after the data.

A good procedure to request after the DATA LIST statement is **LIST VARIABLES = ALL.** This statement will have $SPSS_x$ print your complete data set. It is a good practice to include this statement in your program to allow you to check the accuracy of your data entries. A number of other commands for statistical procedures will be described in subsequent examples.

ENTERING THE DATA

The data set begins with the statement **BEGIN DATA .** This informs $SPSS_x$ that each line following it will contain the data for a participant in the study.

The data then follow, with one line reserved for each participant in the study. The data must be entered in the order listed on the DATA LIST statement. It is important that the data are aligned in the proper columns. Examples of data based on the DATA LIST statement described earlier could include

01   E   623
02   C   145
03   C   551.

The two-digit value is the subject number. The letter E or C represents the condition, either experimental or control, and the last three-digit value represents the value for the RESPONSE.

There is one data line for each participant. Following the last line of data, the statement **END DATA** is listed to signify the end of the data set.

C

MEASURES OF CENTRAL TENDENCY AND VARIABILITY (CHAPTER 3)

INDEPENDENT VARIABLE: Type of verb used

   Levels: Bumped, Collided, Contacted, Hit, Smashed

DEPENDENT VARIABLE: Estimated speed

   Levels: 0 to ?

SAMPLE SIZE: 9 per condition

DATA

Verb Used in the Question

Smashed	Collided	Bumped	Hit	Contacted
42	39	38	30	31
37	38	35	35	32
38	42	38	33	32
42	37	40	32	30
42	35	37	36	30
44	41	36	36	35
39	39	38	31	33
40	40	41	36	32
45	40	39	37	33

SAS Input - Measures of Central Tendency and Variability

DATA *CH3* ;	Identifies beginning of data set.
INPUT *SUBJ VERB $ SPEED* ;	Identifies three variables for each subject - a subject number , the level of the independent variable, and the value for the dependent variable.
CARDS;	
1 *SMASHED* 42	
2 *SMASHED* 37	
.	
.	
.	
10 *COLLIDED* 39	Data - one line per participant.
11 *COLLIDED* 38	
.	
.	
.	
44 *CONTACT* 32	
45 *CONTACT* 33	
;	Indicates the end of data.
PROC PRINT;	Command for printing data set.
PROC SORT; BY *VERB*;	Sorts data by values for the variable *verb*.
PROC MEANS;	Command calculates descriptive statistics.
VAR *SPEED* ;	VAR statement identifies variable to be analyzed.
BY *VERB* ;	Descriptive statistics will be done separately for each level of *verb*.

C

C

from PROC PRINT → variables, values

SAS

OBS	SUBJ	VERB	SPEED
1	1	SMASHED	42
2	2	SMASHED	37
. . .			
44	44	CONTACT	32
45	45	CONTACT	33

from PROC MEANS

SAS

$\bar{x}$ → MEAN s → STANDARD DEVIATION Σx → SUM s^2 → VARIANCE

VARIABLE	N	MEAN	STANDARD DEVIATION	MINIMUM VALUE	MAXIMUM VALUE	STD ERROR OF MEAN	SUM	VARIANCE	C.V.
---------- VERB = BUMPED ----------									
SPEED	9	38.00000000	1.87082869	35.00000000	41.00000000	0.62360956	342.00000000	3.50000000	4.923
---------- VERB = COLLIDED ----------									
SPEED	9	39.00000000	2.12132034	35.00000000	42.00000000	0.70710678	351.00000000	4.50000000	5.439
---------- VERB = CONTACT ----------									
SPEED	9	32.00000000	1.58113883	30.00000000	35.00000000	0.52704628	288.00000000	2.50000000	4.941
---------- VERB = HIT ----------									
SPEED	9	34.00000000	2.54950976	30.00000000	37.00000000	0.84983659	306.00000000	6.50000000	7.499
---------- VERB = SMASHED ----------									
SPEED	9	41.00000000	2.69258240	37.00000000	45.00000000	0.89752747	369.00000000	7.25000000	6.567

SPSS$_X$ Input - Measures of Central Tendency and Variability

DATA LIST / *SUBJ 1-2 VERB 4-12 (A) SPEED 14-15*

Statement identifies beginning of SPSS$_X$ program. Information beyond the slash / lists variables to be included in data set.

LIST VARIABLES=ALL

Statement will provide a listing of all data.

BEGIN DATA

Identifies the beginning of data listing.

01 SMASHED 42

02 SMASHED 37

One data statement per participant arranged in the order and appropriate columns as defined on DATA LIST statement.

44 CONTACTED 32

45 CONTACTED 33

END DATA

Identifies the ending of data listing.

CONDESCRIPTIVE *SPEED*

Statement calculates descriptive statistics overall.

SORT CASES BY *VERB*

SPSS$_X$ will sort data to allow for calculation of descriptive statistics for each value of *verb* .

REPORT VARIABLES=*SPEED*

Statement allows researcher to calculate specified statistics by group.

  /BREAK = VERB

Statement identifies how values should be grouped. It is important that this and other statements beginning with / begin in Column 2 on statement line.

  /SUMMARY=MEAN

calculates mean, s^2, and s for each *verb*

  /SUMMARY=VARIANCE

group in the study.

  /SUMMARY=STDDEV

C

from LIST VARIABLES=ALL

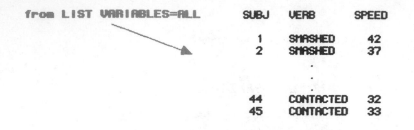

```
            SUBJ    VERB       SPEED

             1     SMASHED       42
             2     SMASHED       37
                      .
                      .
                      .
            44     CONTACTED     32
            45     CONTACTED     33
```

NUMBER OF CONDITIONS READ =   45   NUMBER OF CASES LISTED =   45

from CONDESCRIPTIVE
overall descriptive statistics

NUMBER OF VALID OBSERVATIONS (LISTWISE) =   45.00

VARIABLE	MEAN	STD DEV	MINIMUM	MAXIMUM	VALID N	LABEL
SPEED	36.800	3.952	30	45	45	

from REPORT
descriptive statistics
by condition

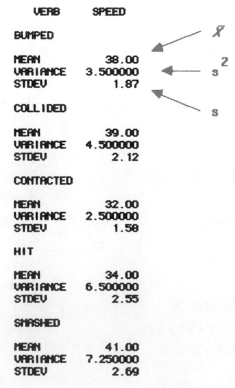

```
            VERB      SPEED

         BUMPED

         MEAN        38.00
         VARIANCE   3.500000
         STDEV        1.87

         COLLIDED

         MEAN        39.00
         VARIANCE   4.500000
         STDEV        2.12

         CONTACTED

         MEAN        32.00
         VARIANCE   2.500000
         STDEV        1.58

         HIT

         MEAN        34.00
         VARIANCE   6.500000
         STDEV        2.55

         SMASHED

         MEAN        41.00
         VARIANCE   7.250000
         STDEV        2.69
```

$\bar{X}$

s^2

s

PEARSON *r* CORRELATION COEFFICIENT (CHAPTER 5)

X VARIABLE:	Attractiveness rating
Levels:	1 to 7
Y VARIABLE:	Rating as potential date
Levels:	1 to 7
SAMPLE SIZE:	44

C

DATA

Subject	Attractiveness	Potential Date	Subject	Attractiveness	Potential Date
a	7	7	w	3	5
b	4	4	x	5	4
c	7	5	y	6	5
d	5	5	z	6	5
e	7	6	a a	3	4
f	1	2	b b	4	5
g	7	4	c c	5	4
h	2	4	dd	6	4
i	7	5	e e	7	5
j	2	1	f f	5	5
k	7	6	g g	5	4
l	2	3	h h	5	6
m	6	6	i i	2	4
n	4	3	j j	3	4
o	5	4	k k	2	1
p	3	2	ll	3	4
q	5	7	m m	4	5
r	6	7	n n	4	4
s	4	3	oo	5	7
t	6	5	p p	4	5
u	7	5	q q	4	5
v	2	3	r r	4	2

SAS Input - The Pearson r Correlation Coefficient

DATA *CH5* ;	Identifies beginning of data set.
INPUT *SUBJ* $ *ATTRACT DATE* ;	Identifies three variables for each subject - a subject ID, and the ratings for each of the two variables in the study.
CARDS;	
A 7 7	
B 4 4	
C 7 5	
.	
.	One data line per participant.
.	
PP 4 5	
QQ 4 5	
RR 4 2	
;	Indicates the end of data.
PROC CORR;	Calculates the Pearson r coefficient.
VAR *ATTRACT DATE* ;	VAR statement identifies which variables are to be included in measuring relationship.

C

Descriptive Statistics

SAS

VARIABLE	N	MEAN	STD DEV	SUM	MINIMUM	MAXIMUM
ATTRACT	44	4.56818182	1.73067707	201.00000000	1.00000000	7.00000000
DATE	44	4.40909091	1.46776498	194.00000000	1.00000000	7.00000000

PEARSON CORRELATION COEFFICIENTS / PROB > <R< UNDER HO:RHO=0 / N=44

	ATTRACT	DATE
ATTRACT	1.00000	0.65708
	0.0000	0.0001
DATE	0.65708	1.00000
	.00001	.00000

Pearson r ← 0.65708

probability that sample was selected from population distribution with no relationship (if less than alpha level, reject H_0).

C

SPSS$_X$ Input - The Pearson r Correlation Coefficient

DATA LIST / *SUBJ 1-2 (A) ATTRACT 4 DATE 6*

                                              Statement identifies beginning of SPSS$_X$ program. Information beyond the slash / lists variables to be included in data set.

PEARSON CORR *ATTRACT DATE*

                                              Statement will provide correlation coefficient for variables following CORR.

BEGIN DATA

    A 7 7

    B 4 4

       .

       .

       .

    QQ 4 5

    RR 4 2

END DATA

Identifies the beginning of data listing.

One data statement per participant arranged in the order and appropriate columns as defined on DATA LIST statement.

Identifies the ending of data listing.

C

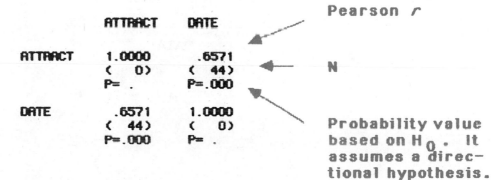

	ATTRACT	DATE
ATTRACT	1.0000	.6571
	(0)	(44)
	P= .	P=.000
DATE	.6571	1.0000
	(44)	(0)
	P=.000	P= .

Pearson *r*

N

Probability value based on H_0. It assumes a directional hypothesis.

(COEFFICIENT / (CASES) / 1-TAILED SIG)

C

THE *t* TEST FOR INDEPENDENT SAMPLES (CHAPTER 10)

INDEPENDENT VARIABLE:	Type of behavior pattern
Levels:	A or B
DEPENDENT VARIABLE:	Fatigue ratings
Levels:	1 to 11
SAMPLE SIZE:	10 per condition

DATA

Type of Behavior Pattern

A	B
1	1
2	2
2	1
3	2
3	1
2	1
3	2
1	2
2	2
3	1

SAS Input - The *t* Test for Independent Samples

DATA *CH10* ;	Identifies beginning of data set.
INPUT *SUBJ BEHAVIOR $ RATING* ;	Identifies three variables for each subject - a subject number, the level of the independent variable, and the value for the dependent variable.
CARDS;	
1 A 1	
2 A 2	
3 A 2	
.	
.	
.	
18 B 2	
19 B 2	
20 B 1	
;	Indicates the end of data.
PROC TTEST;	Command for *t* test for independent samples.
CLASS *BEHAVIOR* ;	CLASS statement identifies independent variable.
VAR *RATING* ;	VAR statement identifies dependent variable.

C

C

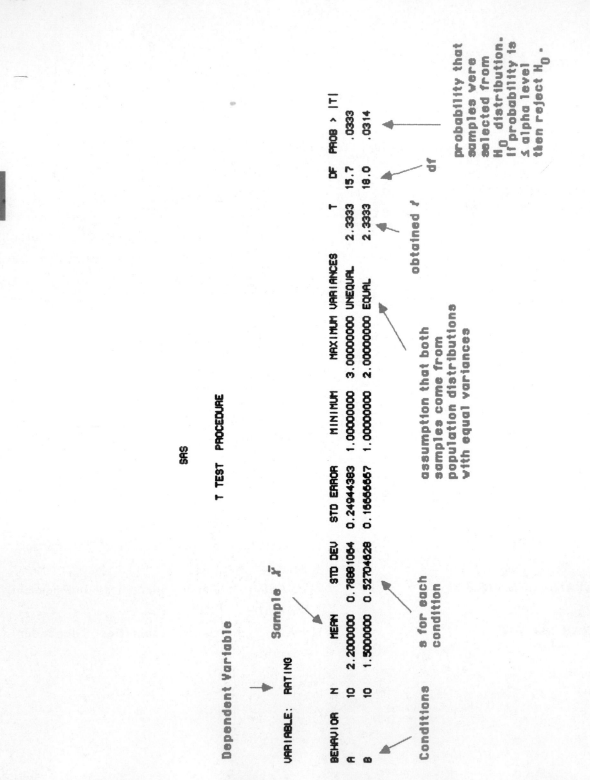

SAS

T TEST PROCEDURE

Dependent Variable

VARIABLE: RATING   Sample $\bar{X}$

BEHAVIOR	N	MEAN	STD DEV	STD ERROR	MINIMUM	MAXIMUM	VARIANCES	T	DF	PROB > |T|
A	10	2.2000000	0.78881064	0.24944383	1.00000000	3.00000000	UNEQUAL	2.3333	15.7	.0333
B	10	1.5000000	0.52704628	0.16666667	1.00000000	2.00000000	EQUAL	2.3333	18.0	.0314

Conditions   s for each condition

assumption that both samples come from population distributions with equal variances

obtained *t*

df

probability that samples were selected from H_0 distribution. If probability is ≤ alpha level then reject H_0.

SPSS$_x$ Input - The t Test for Independent Samples

DATA LIST / *SUBJ 1-2*   *BEHAV*   **4** *FATIGUE*   **6**

> Statement identifies beginning of SPSS$_x$ program. Information beyond the slash / lists variables to be included in data sct. *1* is used for Type A and *2* is used for Type B for *BEHAV* variable.

T-TEST   **GROUPS**=*BEHAV* **/**   **VARIABLES**=*FATIGUE*

> Statement will provide t value. GROUPS= defines independent variable and VARIABLES= defines dependent variable.

BEGIN DATA   Identifies the beginning of data listing.

01 1 1

02 1 2

    ·

    ·

    ·

> One data statement per participant arranged in the order and appropriate columns as defined on DATA LIST statement.

19 2 2

20 2 1

END DATA   Identifies the ending of data listing.

C

```
- - - - - - - - - - - - - - - - - - - - -  T - TEST - - - - - - - - - - - - - - -

GROUP 1 = BEHAV  EQ  1.
GROUP 2 = BEHAV  EQ  2.

                                                                    POOLED VARIANCE ESTIMATE
                                             *                *                          *
VARIABLE    NUMBER            STANDARD STANDARD*    F    2-TAIL  *    T  DEGREES OF 2-TAIL*
            OF CASES MEAN     DEVIATION ERROR  *  VALUE   PROB.  *  VALUE  FREEDOM  PROB. *

FATIGUE
   GROUP  1   10   2.2000     0.789    0.249  *                *                         *
                                             *   2.24   0.245  *   2.33    18    0.031  *
   GROUP  2   10   1.5000     0.527    0.167  *                *                         *
```

Type A = Group 1
Type B = Group 2

Descriptive statistics

obtained t

probability
value based
on H_0.

THE t TEST FOR CORRELATED SAMPLES (CHAPTER 11)

C

INDEPENDENT VARIABLE:	Visual field of presentation
Levels:	Left, Right
DEPENDENT VARIABLE:	Response time
Levels:	0 to 1000 (msec)
SAMPLE SIZE:	15 participants

DATA
VISUAL FIELD OF PRESENTATION

Subject	Left	Right
a	373	336
b	473	468
c	451	467
d	416	468
e	397	411
f	381	413
g	407	437
h	428	512
i	360	356
j	442	462
k	496	556
l	467	505
m	469	513
n	444	463
o	431	443

SAS Input - The *t* Test for Correlated Samples

DATA *CH11* ;	Identifies beginning of data set.
INPUT *SUBJ* $ *LEFT RIGHT* ;	Identifies three values for each subject - a subject ID, a value for the left condition and a value for the right condition.
DIFF = *LEFT* -*RIGHT* ;	Creates a new variable called DIFF which is a difference value based on the difference between the left response time and the right response time for each participant.

```
CARDS;
A    373    336
B    473    468
C    451    467

     .

     .                          One data line per participant.

     .

M    469    513
N    444    463
O    431    443
;                               Indicates the end of data.
PROC  MEANS  T;                 Command for t test for correlated samples.
 VAR  DIFF ;                    VAR statement identifies variable to be
                                analyzed.
```

C

from PROC MEANS T   ⟶   SAS

        VARIABLE   T

        DIFF   −3.30 ⟵ obtained *t* value

C

SPSS$_X$ Input - The t Test for Correlated Samples

DATA   LIST   / *SUBJ   1   (A)   LEFT   3-5   RIGHT   4-6*

Statement identifies beginning of SPSS$_X$ program. Information beyond the slash / lists variables to be included in data set.

T-TEST   PAIRS=*LEFT,RIGHT*

Statement will provide t value. PAIRS= defines levels of independent variable.

BEGIN   DATA

Identifies the beginning of data listing.

A   373   336

B   473   468

.

.

.

One data statement per participant arranged in the order and appropriate columns as defined on DATA LIST statement.

N   444   463

0   431   443

END   DATA

Identifies the ending of data listing.

- - - - - - - T - TEST - - - - - - -

VARIABLE	NUMBER OF CASES	MEAN	STANDARD DEVIATION	STANDARD ERROR	*	(DIFFERENCE) MEAN	STANDARD DEVIATION	STANDARD ERROR	*	2-TAIL CORR. PROB	*	T VALUE	DEGREES OF FREEDOM	2-TAIL PROB.
LEFT	15	429.0000	39.848	10.289	*				*		*			
					*	-25.0000	29.345	7.577	* 0.891	0.000	*	-3.30	14	0.005
RIGHT		454.0000	58.569	15.122	*				*		*			

Descriptive Statistics

$\bar{X}_d$ s_d $s_{\bar{d}}$ obtained t   df   probability value based on H_0.

C

THE ONE-WAY ANOVA (CHAPTER 13)

INDEPENDENT VARIABLE:	Type of word reinforced during learning phase
Levels:	Aggressive, Helpful, Neutral
DEPENDENT VARIABLE:	Level of shock intensity
Levels:	10 to 100
SAMPLE SIZE:	17 per condition

DATA

Type of Word Reinforced during Learning Phase

Aggressive	Helpful	Neutral
67	17	44
57	23	25
51	36	48
35	39	53
28	35	50
66	42	33
29	31	36
58	10	43
32	11	61
35	10	37
55	28	52
40	10	47
69	49	49
51	15	31
39	36	37
70	34	38
45	21	30

C

SAS Input - The One-Way ANOVA

DATA *CH13* ;	Identifies beginning of data set.
INPUT *SUBJ WORD* $ *SHOCK*;	Identifies three variables for each subject - a subject number, the level of the independent variable, and the value for the dependent variable.
CARDS;	
1 AGGR 67	
2 AGGR 57	
3 AGGR 51	
.	
.	One data line per participant.
.	
49 NEUT 37	
50 NEUT 38	
51 NEUT 30	
;	Indicates the end of data.
PROC GLM;	Command for analysis of variance. GLM stands for General Linear Model.
CLASS *WORD* ;	CLASS statement identifies independent variable.
MODEL *SHOCK* = *WORD* ;	Model statement lists dependent variable on left side of = and sources of systematic variability on right side.
MEANS *WORD* ;	Provides means for each condition.

from PROC GLM
info about design
and levels of
independent variable

SRS

GENERAL LINEAR MODELS PROCEDURE

CLASS LEVEL INFORMATION

CLASS	LEVELS	VALUES
WORD	3	AGGR HELP NEUT

NUMBER OF OBSERVATIONS IN DATA SET = 51

C

information for ANOVA summary table

SRS

GENERAL LINEAR MODELS PROCEDURE   obtained F ratio

DEPENDENT VARIABLE: SHOCK

SOURCE	DF	SUM OF SQUARES	MEAN SQUARE	F VALUE	PR> F	R-SQUARE	C.V.
MODEL	2	4479.56862745	2239.78431373	14.50	0.0001	0.376657	31.88188
ERROR	48	7413.41176471	154.44607843		ROOT MSE		SHOCK MEAN
CORRECTED TOTAL	50	11892.98039216			12.42763366		38.98039216

SOURCE	DF	TYPE I SS	F VALUE	PR > F	DF	TYPE III SS	F VALUE	PR > F
WORD	2	4479.56862745	14.50	0.0001	2	4479.56862745	14.50	0.0001

SRS

GENERAL LINEAR MODELS PROCEDURE

from MEANS →

MEANS

WORD	N	SHOCK
AGGR	17	48.6470588
HELP	17	26.2941176
NEUT	17	42.0000000

SPSS$_x$ Input - The One-Way ANOVA

DATA LIST / *SUBJ 1-2 WORD 4 SHOCK 6-7*

Statement identifies beginning of SPSS$_x$ program. Information beyond the slash / lists variables to be included in data set. For *WORD* variable, 1=aggressive, 2=helpful, and 3=neutral.

ANOVA *SHOCK BY WORD(1,3)*

Statement will provide ANOVA summary table.

Following ANOVA list dependent variable followed by word **BY** and then independent variable. Levels of independent variable should be included in parentheses.

STATISTIC 3

Command provides cell means as part of ANOVA.

BEGIN DATA

Identifies the beginning of data listing.

01 1 1 37
02 1 1 19

    .

    .

    .

One data statement per participant arranged in the order and appropriate columns as defined on DATA LIST statement.

43 2 2 48
44 2 2 53

END DATA

Identifies the ending of data listing.

C

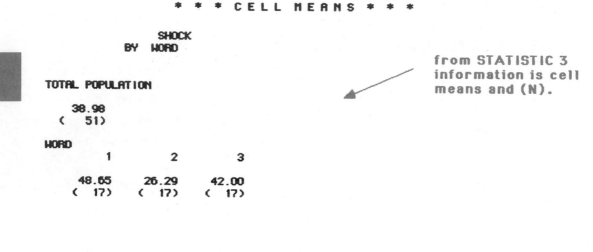

* * * C E L L   M E A N S * * *

SHOCK
BY   WORD

from STATISTIC 3
information is cell
means and (N).

TOTAL POPULATION

38.98
(51)

WORD

1	2	3
48.65	26.29	42.00
(17)	(17)	(17)

* * * A N A L Y S I S   O F   V A R I A N C E * * *

SHOCK
BY   WORD

SS_a

ANOVA Summary Table

SOURCE OF VARIATION	SUM OF SQUARES	DF	MEAN SQUARE	F	SIGNIF OF F
MAIN EFFECTS	4479.569	2	2239.784	14.502	0.000
WORD	4479.569	2	2239.784	14.502	0.000
EXPLAINED	4479.569	2	2239.784	14.502	0.000
RESIDUAL	7413.412	48	154.446		
TOTAL	11892.980	50	237.860		

F ratio

51 CASES WERE PROCESSED
0 CASES (0.0 PCT) WERE MISSING

SS_w

THE FACTORIAL ANOVA (CHAPTER 14)

INDEPENDENT VARIABLE - A:	Weight of student
Levels:	Normal, Obese
INDEPENDENT VARIABLE - B:	Speed of clock
Levels:	Slow, Fast
DEPENDENT VARIABLE:	Amount of crackers eaten
Levels:	0 to ?
SAMPLE SIZE:	11 per condition

DATA

Weight of Student

Normal		Obese	
Slow Clock	Fast Clock	Slow Clock	Fast Clock
37	34	9	18
19	0	11	61
62	0	3	25
58	34	8	33
23	0	42	53
61	0	49	8
24	8	12	44
42	22	9	23
62	4	8	47
14	37	23	48
55	37	45	53

C

SAS Input - The Factorial ANOVA

DATA *CH14* ;	Identifies beginning of data set.
INPUT *SUBJ WEIGHT* $ *CLOCK* $ *CRACKER* ;	
	Identifies four variables for each subject - a subject number, the levels of each independent variable, and the value for the dependent variable.
CARDS;	
1 NORMAL SLOW 37	
2 NORMAL SLOW 19	
.	
.	One data line per participant.
.	
22 NORMAL FAST 37	
23 OBESE SLOW 9	
.	
.	
43 OBESE FAST 48	
44 OBESE FAST 53	
;	Indicates the end of data.
PROC GLM;	Command for analysis of variance. GLM stands for General Linear Model.
CLASS *WEIGHT CLOCK* ;	CLASS statement identifies independent variables.
MODEL *CRACKERS = WEIGHT CLOCK WEIGHT *CLOCK* ;	Model statement lists dependent variable on left side of = and sources of systematic variability on right side, including main effects and interaction effect.
MEANS *WEIGHT CLOCK WEIGHT *CLOCK* ;	Provides means for each main effect and the interaction effect.

SAS

GENERAL LINEAR MODELS PROCEDURE

**from PROC GLM
info about design
and levels of
independent variables**

CLASS LEVEL INFORMATION

CLASS	LEVELS	VALUES
WEIGHT	2	NORMAL OBESE
CLOCK	2	FAST SLOW

NUMBER OF OBSERVATIONS IN DATA SET = 44

C

within group variability

SAS

GENERAL LINEAR MODELS PROCEDURE

DEPENDENT VARIABLE: CRACKER

SOURCE	DF	SUM OF SQUARES	MEAN SQUARE	F VALUE	PR> F	R-SQUARE	C.V.
MODEL	3	5299.88636364	1766.62878788	5.77	0.0022	0.302156	60.8456
ERROR	40	12240.36363636	386.00909091		ROOT MSE		CRACKER MEAN
CORRECTED TOTAL	43	17540.25000000			17.49311553		28.75000000

SS_{tot}

SOURCE	DF	TYPE I SS	F VALUE	PR > F	DF	TYPE III SS	F VALUE	PR > F
WEIGHT	1	0.02272727	0.00	0.9932	1	0.02272727	0.00	0.9932
CLOCK	1	172.02272727	0.56	0.4578	1	172.02272727	0.56	0.4578
WEIGHT*CLOCK	1	5127.84090909	16.76	0.0002	1	5127.84090909	16.76	0.0002

obtained F ratios

**SS for main and interaction
effects**

SAS

GENERAL LINEAR MODELS PROCEDURE

from MEANS

MEANS

WEIGHT	N	CRACKER

Marginal Means

WEIGHT	N	CRACKER
NORMAL	22	28.7727273
OBESE	22	28.7272727

CLOCK	N	CRACKER
FAST	22	26.7727273
SLOW	22	30.7272727

WEIGHT	CLOCK	N	CRACKER

Cell means

WEIGHT	CLOCK	N	CRACKER
NORMAL	FAST	11	16.0000000
NORMAL	SLOW	11	41.5454545
OBESE	FAST	11	37.5454545
OBESE	SLOW	11	19.9090909

C

SPSS$_x$ Input - The Factorial ANOVA

DATA LIST / *SUBJ 1-2   WEIGHT   4   CLOCK   6   CRACKER   8-9*

> Statement identifies beginning of SPSS$_x$ program.   Information beyond the slash / lists variables to be included in data set.   For WEIGHT variable, 1=normal and 2=obese. For CLOCK variable, 1=slow and 2=fast.

ANOVA   *CRACKER   BY WEIGHT(1,2)   CLOCK(1,2)*

> Statement will provide ANOVA summary table.   After ANOVA list dependent variable followed by word BY and then independent variables.   Levels of independent variables should be included in parentheses.

STATISTIC   3

> Command provides cell means as part of ANOVA.

BEGIN   DATA

> Identifies the beginning of data listing.

01   1   1   37
02   1   1   19

> .
>
> .
>
> .

> One   data   statement   per   participant arranged in the order and appropriate columns   as   defined   on   DATA   LIST statement.

43   2   2   48
44   2   2   53
END DATA

> Identifies the ending of data listing.

* * * C E L L   M E A N S * * *

CRACKER
BY WEIGHT
CLOCK

from STATISTIC 3
information is cell
means and (N).

TOTAL POPULATION

28.75
(44)

WEIGHT
        1   2

    28.77   28.73
    (22)   (22)

CLOCK

        1   2

    38.73   26.77
    (22)   (22)

            CLOCK
            1   2
WEIGHT
    1   41.55   16.00
            (11)   (11)

    2   19.91   37.55
            (11)   (11)

* * * A N A L Y S I S   O F   V A R I A N C E * * *

CRACKER
BY WEIGHT
CLOCK

SS values F ratios

ANOVA Summary Table

SOURCE OF VARIATION	SUM OF SQUARES	DF	MEAN SQUARE	F	SIGNIF OF F	
MAIN EFFECTS	172.045	2	86.023	0.281	0.756	
WEIGHT	0.023	1	0.023	0.000	0.993	Main effects
CLOCK	172.023	1	172.023	0.562	0.458	
2-WAY INTERACTIONS	5127.841	1	5127.841	16.757	0.000	
WEIGHT CLOCK	5127.841	1	5127.841	16.757	0.000	Interaction effect
EXPLAINED	5299.886	3	1766.629	5.773	0.002	
RESIDUAL	12249.364	40	306.009			
TOTAL	17540.250	43	407.913			

44 CASES WERE PROCESSED
0 CASES (0.0 PCT) WERE MISSING

C

THE x^2 TEST OF INDEPENDENCE (CHAPTER 16)

INDEPENDENT VARIABLE: Size of group

    Levels: 2, 3, 6

DEPENDENT VARIABLE: Action by student

    Levels: Helped, Did not help

SAMPLE SIZE: 13 to 26 per condition

DATA

Size of Group

2 people	3 people	6 people
11 helped	16 helped	4 helped
2 did not	10 did not	9 did not

SAS Input - The x^2 Test of Independence

DATA *CH16* ;	Identifies beginning of data set.
INPUT *SUBJ SIZE RESPONSE* **$;**	Identifies three variables for each subject - a subject number, the level of the independent variable, and the value for the dependent variable.
CARDS;	
1 2 HELP	
2 2 HELP	
.	
.	
.	
26 3 HELP	One data line per participant.
27 3 NOHELP	
.	
.	
.	
48 6 NOHELP	
49 6 NOHELP	
;	Indicates the end of data.
PROC FREQ;	Command for constructing a contingency table.
TABLES *RESPONSE * SIZE /CHISQR* **;**	Statement identifies variables for table and CHISQR tells SAS to calculate x^2.

SAS

TABLE OF RESPONSE BY SIZE

RESPONSE	SIZE			
FREQUENCY <				
PERCENT <				
ROW PCT <				
COL PCT <	2 <	3 <	6 <	TOTAL
HELP <	11 <	16 <	4 <	31
<	21.55 <	30.77 <	7.69 <	59.62
<	35.48 <	51.61 <	12.90 <	
<	84.62 <	61.54 <	30.77 <	
NOHELP <	2 <	10 <	9 <	21
<	3.92 <	19.23 <	17.31 <	40.38
<	9.52 <	47.62 <	42.86 <	
<	15.38 <	38.46 <	69.23 <	
TOTAL	13	26	13	52
	25.00	50.00	25.00	100.00

information contained in each cell

CONTINGENCY TABLE

STATISTICS FOR TABLE OF RESPONSE BY SIZE

x^2

STATISTIC	DF	VALUE	PROB
CHI-SQUARE	2	7.908	0.019
LIKELIHOOD RATIO CHI-SQUARE	2	8.295	0.016
MANTEL-HAENSZEL CHI-SQUARE	1	7.321	0.007
PHI		0.390	
CONTINGENCY COEFFICIENT		0.363	
CRAMER'S V		0.390	

SAMPLE SIZE = 52

probability value based on H_0

Cramer's ϕ coefficient

SPSS$_x$ Input - The x^2 Test of Independence

DATA LIST / *SUBJ 1-2   SIZE 4   RESPONSE 6-11*

Statement identifies beginning of SPSS$_x$ program. Information beyond the slash / lists variables to be included in data set.

CROSSTABS TABLES = *RESPONSE* BY *SIZE*

Statement will provide contingency table. Variables to be included in table are listed after TABLES.

OPTIONS 18

Command provides frequency information.

STATISTICS 1, 2

Command provides x^2 and Cramer's ϕ coefficient.

BEGIN DATA

Identifies the beginning of data listing.

01 2 HELPED

02 2 HELPED

   .

   .

   .

One data statement per participant arranged in the order and appropriate columns as defined on DATA LIST statement.

51 6 NOHELP

52 6 NOHELP

END DATA

Identifies the ending of data listing.

C

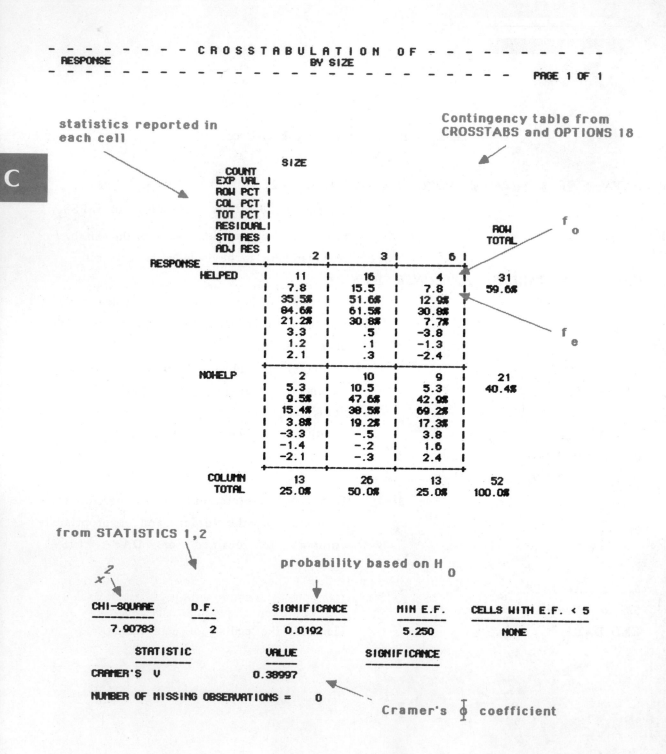

statistics reported in each cell

Contingency table from CROSSTABS and OPTIONS 18

```
                        SIZE
               COUNT
             EXP VAL  I
             ROW PCT  I
             COL PCT  I                                           ROW
             TOT PCT  I                                          TOTAL          f o
            RESIDUAL  I
             STD RES  I
             ADJ RES  I        2  I        3  I        6  I
RESPONSE -------------+---------+---------+---------+
           HELPED     I   11    I   16    I    4    I    31
                      I   7.8   I   15.5  I   7.8   I   59.6%
                      I  35.5%  I  51.6%  I  12.9%  I                          f e
                      I  84.6%  I  61.5%  I  30.8%  I
                      I  21.2%  I  30.8%  I   7.7%  I
                      I   3.3   I    .5   I  -3.8   I
                      I   1.2   I    .1   I  -1.3   I
                      I   2.1   I    .3   I  -2.4   I
                      +---------+---------+---------+
           NOHELP     I    2    I   10    I    9    I    21
                      I   5.3   I   10.5  I   5.3   I   40.4%
                      I   9.5%  I  47.6%  I  42.9%  I
                      I  15.4%  I  38.5%  I  69.2%  I
                      I   3.8%  I  19.2%  I  17.3%  I
                      I  -3.3   I   -.5   I   3.8   I
                      I  -1.4   I   -.2   I   1.6   I
                      I  -2.1   I   -.3   I   2.4   I
                      +---------+---------+---------+
           COLUMN         13        26        13        52
           TOTAL        25.0%     50.0%     25.0%    100.0%
```

from STATISTICS 1,2

x^2

probability based on H_0

CHI-SQUARE	D.F.	SIGNIFICANCE	MIN E.F.	CELLS WITH E.F. < 5
7.90783	2	0.0192	5.250	NONE

STATISTIC	VALUE	SIGNIFICANCE
CRAMER'S V	0.38997	

NUMBER OF MISSING OBSERVATIONS =   0

Cramer's ϕ coefficient

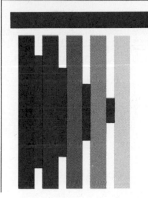

Appendix D

Answers to Odd-Numbered Exercises

CHAPTER 1

1. A researcher's observations are often more detailed and systematic than those of the layperson. They can involve naturalistic observation and observations based on one's own research and that of other researchers.

3. A theory should organize and explain findings from research studies and naturalistic observation. Theories generate testable predictions which are known as hypotheses. The researcher's prediction in a study is the hypothesis.

5. **a.** descriptive   **b.** descriptive
   c. inferential   **d.** descriptive
   e. inferential

7. No, because those students may be different from students who sit in other locations in the classroom. A random sample in which each student has the same chance of being selected would be better.

9. inferential

11. Both the confidence rating and the test score could be viewed as measures of behavior. The confidence rating may be a subjective measure in that the student's confidence is not readily observable to the researcher. The test score is an objective measure of behavior. A relationship is predicted in that the researcher predicts that confidence is related to test performance.

CHAPTER 2

1. An experiment tests for the possible existence of a causal relationship between two variables. Studying the causal effect of one variable (the independent variable) on a measure of behavior (the dependent variable) is the goal of most experiments.

3. **a.** value; color
   b. variable; 600 (or any number between 200 and 800)
   c. value; time of day
   d. value; dosage of Drug X
   e. value; Woman's name
   f. variable; 12 credit hours (usually any number between 0 and 22)

5. **a.** amount of training—ratio; self-esteem score—ratio
   b. problems in society—nominal; identification of most important problem—nominal
   c. format of essay—nominal; grade—ordinal (or interval if teachers are using equal intervals between letter grades)
   d. environment for test—nominal; response time—ratio

7. No, unless all other variables that could contribute to coffee drinking are being controlled by the researcher. One or several of the uncontrolled variables (e.g., stress level, personality variables) may be influencing both smoking behavior and coffee drinking behavior.

9. **a.** ordinal   **b.** ratio
   c. interval   **d.** ratio
   e. nominal

11. A regular frequency distribution would be used because it is unlikely that there would be so many categories (number of magazine subscriptions) that the researcher would need to group them. A histogram would be the appropriate graph.

13.

Number of Siblings	Cumulative Relative Frequency
7	100.00
6	99.96
5	99.72
4	98.80
3	95.17
2	82.81
1	44.03
0	6.88

The 50th percentile equals two siblings.

15. For four siblings, the real limits are 3.5 and 4.5. For three siblings, the real limits are 2.5 and 3.5.

17. Assuming 16 categories are used with an interval size of .06 probability units, beginning with a category from .00 to .05, the following relative frequency distribution would be obtained:

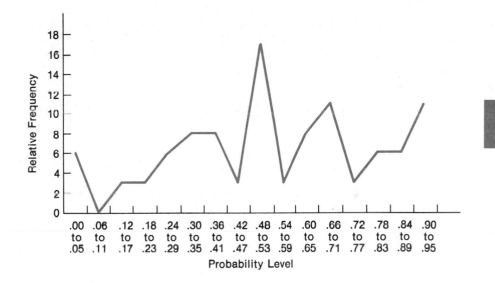

19. a.

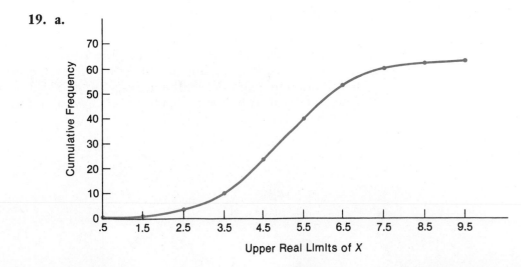

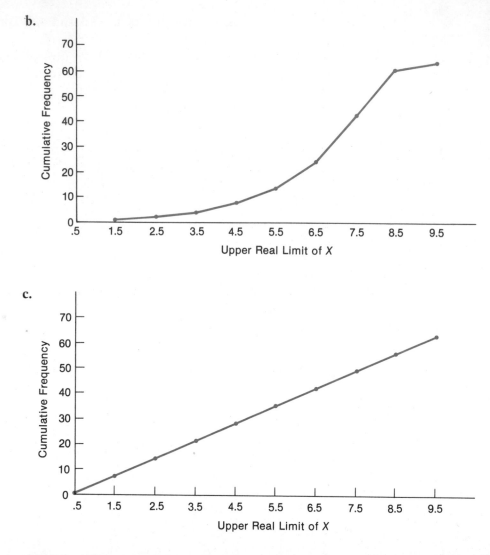

The normal distribution graphed in Figure 2.19a shows that the greatest increase occurs for the middle values of *X*. For the negatively skewed distribution in Figure 2.19b, the increase occurs for the large values of *X*. The uniform distribution in Figure 2.19c shows a uniform increase across all values of *X*.

CHAPTER 3

1. The dependent variable. In the chapter example, the independent variable is the word used in the question. The resulting behavior—the estimate of speed—is described in terms of the calculation of measures of central tendency and of variability.

3.

$A (\overline{X} = 54)$ $(X - \overline{X})$	$B (\overline{X} = 35)$ $(X - \overline{X})$	$C (\overline{X} = 3.1)$ $(X - \overline{X})$
$(95 - 54) = +41$	$(96 - 35) = +61$	$(3.8 - 3.1) = +0.7$
$(81 - 54) = +27$	$(60 - 35) = +25$	$(3.7 - 3.1) = +0.6$
$(73 - 54) = +19$	$(40 - 35) = + 5$	$(3.7 - 3.1) = +0.6$
$(45 - 54) = - 9$	$(36 - 35) = + 1$	$(3.5 - 3.1) = +0.4$
$(16 - 54) = -38$	$(14 - 35) = -21$	$(3.3 - 3.1) = +0.2$
$(14 - 54) = -40$	$(12 - 35) = -23$	$(3.1 - 3.1) = 0.0$
	$(12 - 35) = -23$	$(2.8 - 3.1) = -0.3$
	$(10 - 35) = -25$	$(2.7 - 3.1) = -0.4$
		$(2.6 - 3.1) = -0.5$
		$(2.6 - 3.1) = -0.5$
		$(2.3 - 3.1) = -0.8$
Sum of positive difference $= +87$	Sum of positive difference $= +92$	Sum of positive difference $= +2.5$
Sum of negative difference $= -87$	Sum of negative difference $= -92$	Sum of negative difference $= -2.5$

5. Every value in the set of data values contributes to the calculation of the $\overline{X}$. That is not true for the other two measures of central tendency. The $\overline{X}$ is also the only measure of central tendency that guarantees that the sum of deviations from it will equal 0. The sum of the squared deviations from the mean $\Sigma(X - \overline{X})^2$ will also be smaller than if either the median or mode is used. It is appropriate to report the M_d (1) when the data in the set are skewed, (2) when values are missing from the set of data values, or (3) when the variable is on an ordinal scale of measurement.

7. a.

	Reading Material	Film	Meet Representative
$\overline{X} =$	$1.98	$2.13	$4.70
$M_d =$	1.75	2.00	3.50

D

b.

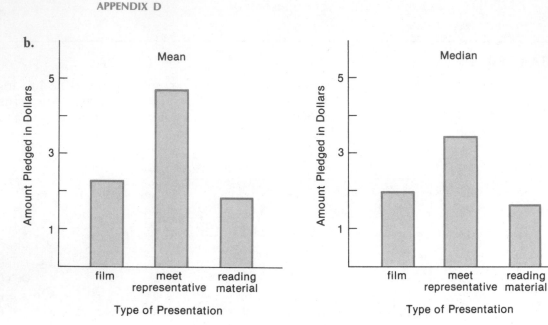

c. The graphs are a bit different because of the distribution of values for the "meet representative" condition. The contributions of $8 and $10 resulted in the $\overline{X}$ being inflated or larger than the M_d. In this condition, reporting that the "average" pledge was $4.70 is somewhat misleading because 70% of the sample pledged less than that amount.

d.

	Reading Material	Film	Meet Representative
s =	$1.11	$1.09	$3.37

The standard deviations are similar for the "reading material" and "film" conditions which indicates that the spread, or variation, in pledges is similar in the two conditions. However, the standard deviation in the "meet representative" condition is considerably larger indicating a wider range of pledges in that condition relative to the other two conditions.

9. a. independent variable—reported amount of time questionnaire took to complete
   b. the mode, because the dependent variable, shopper's response to request, is on a nominal scale of measurement (values are yes or no).

c.

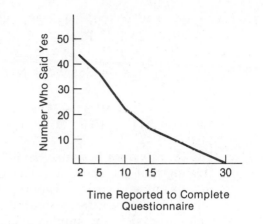

Time Reported to Complete
Questionnaire

d. As the time to complete the questionnaire increased, the proportion of shoppers willing to complete the questionnaire decreased. Whereas 90% were willing to complete the 2-minute questionnaire, no one was willing to spend 30 minutes completing it.

11. A measure of variability provides information about the range, or spread, of values within a set of data values. The measure of central tendency only provides the relative location (on a number line).

13. The deviations from the $\overline{X}$ must be squared because if the deviations themselves are summed, the resulting value will always be 0. See Box 3.1.

15.

4.672	$(4.672 - 4.950)^2 = 0.077$
8.431	$(8.431 - 4.950)^2 = 12.117$
5.008	$(5.008 - 4.950)^2 = 0.003$
5.116	$(5.116 - 4.950)^2 = 0.028$
3.924	$(3.924 - 4.950)^2 = 1.053$
2.549	$(2.549 - 4.950)^2 = 5.765$
$\Sigma X = 29.700$	$\Sigma(X - \overline{X})^2 = 19.043$
$\Sigma X^2 = 166.058$	

Conceptual Formula: $s = \sqrt{\Sigma(X - \overline{X})^2/(N - 1)}$
$= \sqrt{19.043/5}$
$= 1.952$

Computational Formula: $SS = \Sigma X^2 - \dfrac{(\Sigma X)^2}{N}$

$= 166.058 - \dfrac{(29.70)^2}{6}$

$= 19.043$

$s = \sqrt{SS/(N - 1)} = \sqrt{19.043/5}$
$= 1.952$

D

D

17. $\Sigma X = 59$; $\Sigma X^2 = 199$; $N = 20$; $SS = 199 - 59^2/20 = 24.95$
$\overline{X} = 59/20 = 2.95$ Range $= 5 - 1 = 4$
$s^2 = 24.95/19 = 1.31$ $s = \sqrt{1.31} = 1.15$

19. $\Sigma X = 3,197$; $\Sigma X^2 = 358,985$; $N = 35$; $SS = 358,985 - (3,197^2/35)$
$= 66,961.89$

   a. $\overline{X} = 3,197/35 = 91.34$; $M_d = 92$; $M_o = 95$

   b. Range $= 211 - 10 = 201$; $s^2 = (66,961.89/34) = 1,969.47$; $s = 44.38$

   c. The set of values has fairly similar measures of central tendency indicating that the set is not skewed. Smokers smoked an average of slightly more than 90 cigarettes during the 7-day period. The large values for the measures of central tendency indicated that there was a wide variation in the number of cigarettes smoked among the smokers in the group.

CHAPTER 4

1. You would know that the distribution is positively skewed in that the range of values below the $\overline{X}$ is much less than that above the $\overline{X}$.

3. He must realize that the z score is a *transformed* score. With z scores it is possible to have negative scores. If he had not taken the test, his score of 0 would probably transform to a large negative z score.

5. **a.** 7.64%   **b.** 59.87%
   c. 96.99%   **d.** 23.89%

7.

Original Values	z Scores
1	−2.01
3	−0.95
4	−0.42
4	−0.42
5	+0.11
5	+0.11
5	+0.11
6	+0.64
7	+1.17
8	+1.70
$\Sigma X = 48$	$\Sigma z = 0.004$
$\Sigma X^2 = 266$	$\Sigma z^2 = 10.00$
Mean $= 4.8$	Mean $= 0.004$ (not 0 because of rounding)
$S = 1.89$	$S = 1.00$

9. I would prefer to be from Class B. In Class A, a score of 63 transforms into a z score of −0.62 which has a percentile rank of 26.76%. On the other hand, in Class B the z score would be −0.56 and would result in a higher percentile rank of 28.77%.

11. **a.** No, a normal distribution should result in approximately the same number of positive and negative z scores. It appears that the distribution is positively skewed because there are more values below the $\overline{X}$ than above it.

   b. The median will have a negative z score because the $\overline{X}$ is "pulled" toward the extreme values, and in a positively skewed distribution the median will fall between the mode and $\overline{X}$.

13. Since he wants to change both the $\overline{X}$ and s, it will be necessary to use both multiplication and addition. He wants to reduce the s from 10 to 8. Therefore, each score in the distribution should be multiplied by .8. That will reduce the original s from 10 to 8 (original s × .80 = new s). This transformation will also change the $\overline{X}$ by .8 from an original value of 62 to 49.6 (62 × .8). To transform the $\overline{X}$ without affecting the s, he then needs to add 24.4 to each value. That will transform the $\overline{X}$ from 49.6 to 74. These two steps will result in a distribution with an $\overline{X}$ of 74 and an s of 8.

15. Top 10% would have a z score of +1.28 or higher. Using Formula 8 provides the following: 100 + [15 × (+1.28)] = 119.20

17. **a.** +1.65 **b.** −2.33 **c.** ±1.96 **d.** ±2.58 **e.** ±2.58

19. Using the guidelines that the index of skewness should be between ±0.50 and that the distribution should have at least 30 values to use z scores, you should reach the following conclusions:
   a. index of skewness = 1.00, therefore do not use z scores
   b. N is less than 30, therefore do not use z scores
   c. index of skewness = −.30 and N = 118, therefore use z scores
   d. index of skewness = 1.95, therefore do not use z scores

CHAPTER 5

1. Yes, if one assumes (1) that the research that the student is reading is based on recording different dosages of the drugs and the number of hallucinations, both of which should be on a ratio scale of measurement, and (2) that the relationship is linear. If these assumptions are met and the study was conducted correctly, then the Pearson r will reflect the direction and strength of the relationship.

3. "b" provides the weakest evidence because the absolute value of .03 is the smallest reported. "a" provides the best evidence of a linear relationship because the absolute value of .61 is the largest reported.

5. When using all values, the r is $-.92$. When restricting the relationship to X values < 5, the obtained r is $-.83$. The Pearson r is smaller because the restricted range is masking the full relationship between X and Y.

7.

X	Y	Z_X	Z_Y
91	18	$+1.47$	-1.46
17	62	-1.14	$+0.32$
46	57	-0.12	$+0.15$
92	28	$+1.50$	-1.04
14	83	-1.24	$+1.22$
34	63	-0.54	$+0.40$
70	42	$+0.73$	-0.47
53	7	$+0.13$	-1.91
76	56	$+0.94$	$+0.11$
64	59	$+0.52$	$+0.23$
8	76	-1.46	$+0.94$
27	89	-0.79	$+1.47$

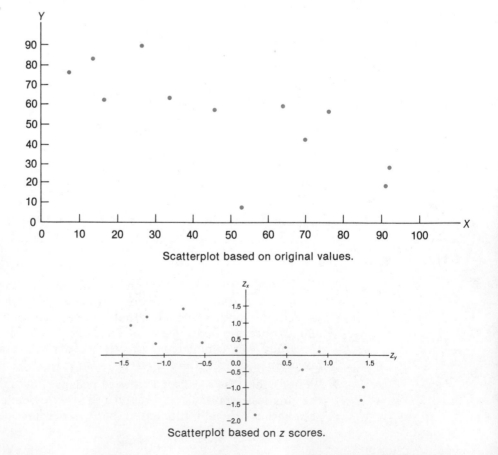

Scatterplot based on original values.

Scatterplot based on z scores.

The transformation shifted the location of the scatterplot. It did not change the nature of the relationship.

9. No, it will not change the relationship. Using the z score formula for the Pearson r, it should be obvious that any transformation will not alter the relationship because the formula will transform any set of values into one in which the $\overline{X}$ will be 0 and the s will be 1.

11. It should not be used unless the values are in the form of ranks. If the values are in the form of ranks, then the Spearman r_s should be calculated. If they are not in the form of ranks, then converting values to ranks may and probably will change the nature of the relationship between the two variables.

13. It may not be if the range of scores on the test is restricted. In all fairness to the employee, however, the personnel officer should be able to offer evidence that a relationship exists between the variables. This can often be accomplished by referring to previously published research using the screening test or preliminary studies conducted by the company designed to test the validity of the test.

15. $\Sigma X = 55$; $\Sigma X^2 = 385$; $\Sigma Y = 55$; $\Sigma Y^2 = 385$; $\Sigma XY = 344$. Using Formula 9: $r = [344 - (55 \times 55)/10]/\sqrt{82.5 \times 82.5} = +.50$

17. No, the relationship would be changed; the coefficient would not be the same. Information about the "distance" between values is lost when the original values are converted into ranks. As can be seen below, the scatterplots are not the same. Therefore, the coefficient would be different.

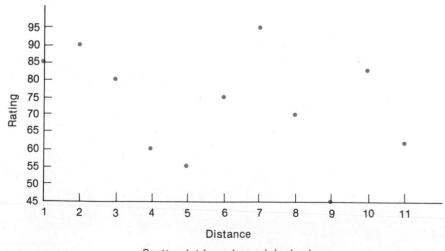

Scatterplot based on original values.

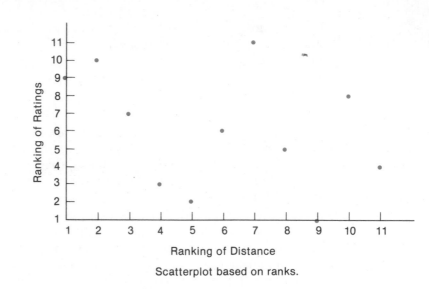

Scatterplot based on ranks.

19. The relationship would be weaker because of a restricted range problem. By reducing the range of X values, the full strength of the relationship would not be measured.

CHAPTER 6

1. $r = +.66;$ $\overline{X} = 4.57;$ $s_x = 1.73;$ $\overline{Y} = 4.41;$ $s_y = 1.47$
$Y' = (0.56 \cdot X) + 1.85$

3. $Y' = (-1.05 \cdot X) + 73.2$

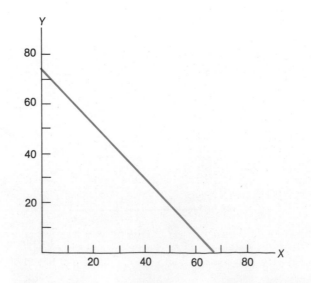

5.

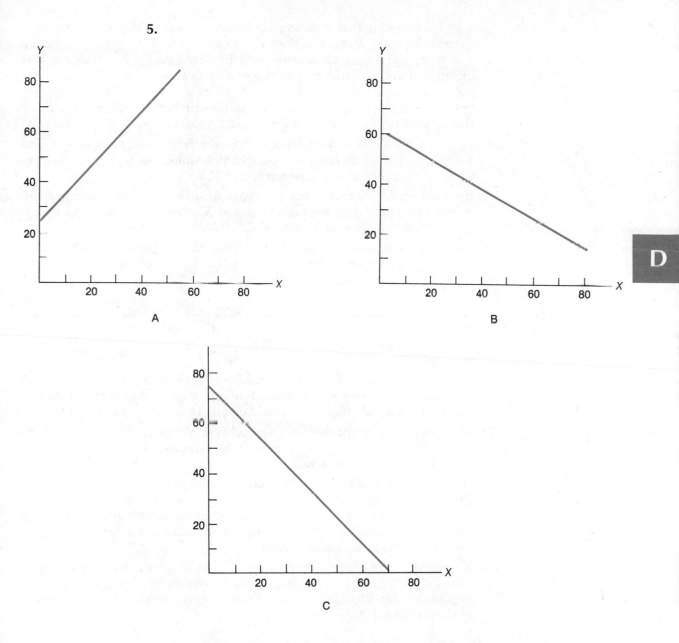

A

B

C

7. $Y' = (.05 \cdot X) + 2.57$ solving for X: $7 = (.05 \cdot X) + 2.57$; $X = 88.6$

9. $Y' = (.63 \times X) + 30.54$; $s_{est\ y} = 4.8$;   For X of 66, $Y' = 72.12$
For 68% confidence, $Y' \pm (1 \cdot s_{est\ y})$: 67.32 to 76.92

11. The lines cross at (106.19, 100.00) which is $(\overline{X}, \overline{Y})$.

13. Based on only the descriptive statistics, the best estimate for Y is the mean of $\overline{Y}$, 8. The range of possible Y values to be 68% confident includes one s_y either side of the mean, 8 ± 2. This would result in a range from

6 to 10. Knowing that a person's X score is equal to the $\overline{X}$ and the relationship between X and Y, allows you to predict that the person will have a Y score equal to $\overline{Y}$. The range will be based on $s_{est\ y}$, which for this example is 1.71. Therefore, the range of values would be 8 ± 1.71. This results in a low value of 6.29 and a high value of 9.71. The change is a reduction in the range because the relationship between X and Y reduces the variability in the range of predicted Y values.

15. $s_{est\ y} = 1.47 \times .77 = 1.13$;   Because of the relationship between X and Y the $s_{est\ y}$ is 0.77 as large as s_y. Estimates should be more accurate because of the relationship between X and Y.

17. It would tend to overestimate the range for low values of X where there is less variability than for high values of X where $s_{est\ y}$ will tend to underestimate the range of Y' values.

19. The regression lines are identical because the Spearman r_s will provide the same coefficient as the Pearson r when the values are ranks.

CHAPTER 7

1. $\beta_1 = .40$; $\beta_2 = .20$

3. $\beta_1 = .40$; $\beta_2 = .00$; The second predictor variable X_2 would not add to predicting Y because of the strength of the relationship between X_1 and X_2. R would equal .40 and R^2 would equal .16.

7. No, because the addition of the second test increases the explained variability to $(R^2 =)$ .16. This is only a 1% increase, .15 to .16, from that when the SAT is used alone.

9. No, it does not make sense to add this additional variable. Because it shares variability with the other predictor variables and is no more related to the criterion variable than the other predictor variables are; this additional variable will not contribute to accounting for unexplained variability for the criterion variable.

11. X_1 refers to the probability course; X_2 refers to the number of credit hours. $\beta_1 = .53$; $\beta_2 = -.35$; Assuming standardized values, the equation is grade in Stat. Course $= (.53 \times$ Probability Course$) - (.35 \times$ Number of Credit Hours$)$; R $= .66$

CHAPTER 8

1. Yes, because descriptive statistics can be used to summarize the data obtained from samples, whereas procedures using inferential statistics allow the researcher to generalize the findings from the samples to populations.

3. $p(\text{tails}) + p(\text{heads}) = .50 + .50 = 1.00$

5. **a.** $3/20 = .15$
   b. $3/20 + 0/20 = .15$
   c. $3/20 + 6/20 + 7/20 = 16/20 = .80$
   d. $7/20 + 2/20 + 2/20 = 11/20 = .55$

7. There are two students, A and B, with 4 siblings. There are two ways of getting a sample with an $\overline{X}$ of 4 siblings: select Student A first and then Student B, or the reverse—Student B first and then Student A:
$[p(A) \times p(B)] + [p(B) \times p(A)] = (.05 \times .05) + (.05 \times .05) = .005$

9. The mean test scores of 83 and 76 are descriptive statistics. The information $t(34) = 3.62$, $p < .05$ is new and involves inferential statistics.

11. Student B. Student A is wrong because the p refers to probability of selecting a sample and not the percentage of individuals in a population. Student C is wrong because the p values always refer to H_0 and not H_1.

13. It indicates that the probability that the groups came from the same population distribution of values is greater than .05. Statistically, the psychologist will assume that the groups could have come from the same population distribution.

15. The likelihood of selecting this sample is quite small, only 2 out of 100. There is a very good probability $p = .98$ that in randomly selecting two students from the class, I would have a sample with an $\overline{X} \neq 3.5$.

CHAPTER 9

1. The population mean μ

3. The height of the average student μ. H_1: $\mu \neq$ height of average student

5. A sample distribution consists of the frequency of individuals from a sample with particular values. The sampling distribution is based on a statistic and represents the frequency of samples with a particular statistic. There are different sampling distributions for every population distribution. Each sampling distribution is a function of N, the size of the samples. If the population consists of 20,000 individuals, then there are 20,000 possible sampling distributions, from N = 1 to N = 20,000.

7. **a.** $\mu = 32$; $s = 10.20$ **b.** $\mu = 48$; $s = 10.20$ **c.** $\mu = 32$; $s = 10.00$

9. **a.** 2.365 **b.** 1.980 **c.** 2.000
   d. 3.355 **e.** 2.878 **f.** 2.807

11. $\overline{X} \pm (t_{(.05)} \cdot s_{\overline{x}}) = 1.56 \pm (2.145 \times .21) = 1.11$ to 2.01

13. Yes, the obtained t value of -0.86 would be less within the retain-H_0 region (the critical t values are ± 2.861).

15. $\overline{X} \pm (t_{(.01)} \cdot s_{\overline{x}}) = 37.25 \pm (2.704 \times 5.09) = 23.49$ to 51.01

17. She must retain H_0 and conclude that there is a possibility that her sample was selected from the population distribution described by H_0. Her obtained t value does not exceed the critical t values of ± 2.074.

19. did; $<$

CHAPTER 10

1. Homogeneity of variance is violated in that the population variances, 1.45 and 4.11, are different.

3.

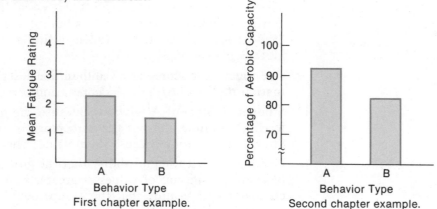

First chapter example.   Second chapter example.

Differences appear to exist in both graphs. The fatigue ratings and the percentage of aerobic capacity used, both show differences.

5. It would be better to select larger samples of equal size. Samples of approximately 25–30 each would reduce the problem associated with one of the population distributions not being normally distributed.

7. Yes, differences she gets may also be the result of differences in the sections of the course. She is unable to determine if the difference in ratings is the result of when the evaluation is given or the different sections of the course since both changed at the same time.

9. obtained $t = (5.8 - 8.4)/1.95 = -1.33$;   critical $t = \pm 3.355$
   $t(8) = -1.33$, $p > .01$;   retain H_0, no difference between men and women.

11. obtained $t = (21.64 - 19.55)/1.09 = 1.92$;   critical $t = \pm 2.048$
    $t(28) = 1.92$, $p > .05$;   retain H_0, no significant difference between the types of computer.

13. If the alpha level is .05, then H_0 is rejected (critical $t = \pm 2.042$). It would be retained if the alpha level is .01 (critical $t = \pm 2.750$).

15. The mistake is that the student did not take the square root of 9.00 to complete the calculation of $s_{\bar{x}_1 - \bar{x}_2}$. Once that is done, the obtained t of 4.01 will result in a significant difference.

17. obtained $t = (36 - 42.44)/4.06 = -1.59$;   critical $t = \pm 2.120$
    $t(16) = -1.59$, $p > .05$;   retain H_0, no significant difference in the percentage of books sold back.

19. Confidence would be lower for Case B because of the unequal N in the two samples. The assumption of the t test involving homogeneity of variance may be violated in Case B. The first sample has an s of 4.80, whereas the second sample has an s of 9.10.

CHALLENGE QUESTION 1

a. Depressed individuals will be less satisfied with life and have lower values on the scale.

b. H_0: $\mu_{depressed} = \mu_{nondepressed}$
H_1: $\mu_{depressed} \neq \mu_{nondepressed}$

c. $\overline{X}_{depressed} = 55.40$; $s_{depressed} = 15.33$
$\overline{X}_{nondepressed} = 88.62$; $s_{nondepressed} = 7.26$

d. $t = (55.40 - 88.62)/4.81 = -6.91$

e. A significant difference was found between the two groups, $\underline{t}$ (21) = -6.91, $\underline{p} < .05$. The nondepressed group had a significantly higher perceived level of life satisfaction than the depressed group.

CHAPTER 11

1. Repeated measures design was used. There is a problem in that everyone serves in Condition A first, then Condition B. It would be better to balance the order of conditions so that half of the participants serve in Condition A first then Condition B and the other half serve in the reversed order, Condition B then Condition A.

3.

Competitor's Shoe	New Shoe
b	a
e	f
i	d
c	j
h	g

5. (You need to convert seconds to proportions of a minute, sec/60.)
$\overline{X}_{competitor's} = 3.32$ min; $\overline{X}_{new\ shoe} = 3.33$ min

7. It is the denominator, $s_{\overline{d}}$ versus $s_{\overline{x}_1 - \overline{x}_2}$, because the denominator in both cases is the difference between sample $\overline{X}$s.

9. **a.** $s_{\overline{d}} = 4.74$ **b.** $s_{\overline{d}} = 5.15$

11. H_0: $\mu_{\overline{d}} = 0$; H_1: $\mu_{\overline{d}} \neq 0$; $t = 6.38/1.72 = 3.71$; A significant difference was found, $\underline{t}$(12) = 3.71, $\underline{p} < .01$.

13. Dr. Smith is wrong. He should report that the $p > .05$ in that the obtained t does not exceed the critical t value. Also, he has 19 df $(N - 1)$ not 20.

15. The obtained $t = (10.56 - 6.38)/2.00 = 2.09$. Using a nondirectional hypothesis and an α level of .05, he does reach the correct conclusion.

Although his t value is incorrect, the correct t value indicates that there is no difference in the waiting time between conditions.

17. Directional hypothesis: critical t (.05) = 1.711
    Nondirectional hypothesis: critical t (.05) = 2.064

19. It would be better to use the repeated measures design because the variability in the denominator $s_{\overline{d}}$ should be lower than if an independent groups design was used. For an independent groups design (df = 10), the critical t value is 2.228. For the repeated measures design (df = 11), the critical t value is 2.201.

CHALLENGE QUESTION 1

a. More errors will be found in essays attributed to special-education students.

b. H_0: $\mu_{\overline{d}} = 0$; H_1: $\mu_{\overline{d}} \neq 0$

c. $\overline{X}_{s-e} = 21.55$; $s_{s-e} = 4.03$; $\overline{X}_m = 19.18$; $s_m = 3.76$

d. $t = 2.36/1.27 = 1.86$

e. No significant difference was found in the number of errors the teachers found as a function of the supposed student who wrote the essay, $t(10) = 1.86$, $p > .05$.

CHAPTER 12

1. No, a Type I error is a decision error that is based on probability. When the H_0 is in fact true, there will always be the possibility that the researcher will obtain results that suggest that H_0 is false. This possibility is equal to the alpha level.

3. They are more important in detecting Type I errors—findings that suggest that a difference exists when it does not. Because the majority of studies published find significant differences, the need for replicating these studies is greater. Replicating a study with a significant difference increases the confidence that the difference is true.

5. a. more subjects, use a repeated measures design
   b. use a more stringent alpha level, .01
   c. use more subjects, use a repeated measures design; use a .05 alpha level
   d. use a more stringent alpha level, .001

7. Increasing the number of participants does not affect the probability of making a Type I error. Increasing the number of participants will increase statistical power, which will reduce the probability of a Type II error.

9. Use more students; Use an alpha level of .05 instead of .01; Use a repeated measures design; Increase the difference in rates, e.g., 1 sec and 2 sec rather than 1 sec and 1.5 sec.

11. In terms of percentage recalled, the difference of 0.90 words/30 words is 3%, which is not very large. Therefore, although a significant difference has been found, the practical significance may not be that great.

13. The professor should look at the descriptive statistics $\overline{X}$ and s to determine if the size of the difference is worth the change. A significant difference could be found that is based on a small change in performance.

15. One goal would be to provide a public outlet for experiments that attempt to replicate previous studies reporting significant differences. Experiments that do not replicate the significant findings of previous studies may indicate the possibility that a Type I error had occurred in the previous work. These experiments can also serve to provide data on the limits of the effect reported in previous studies.

17. It is possible that a study with 10 students is not sufficiently powerful to detect a significant effect. Conducting the study with more students will reduce the probability of making a Type II error.

19. The effect, although real, is small when compared with error variability.

D

CHAPTER 13

1. The number of tests is $5[(5-1)/2] = 10$. The approximate experiment-wise error rate would be $10(.01) = .10$.

3. No, that all samples come from different population distributions is only one possible alternative. It is possible that one or two or more, but not all samples come from different population distributions.

5. Independent variable: Type of therapy
   Dependent variable: Rating of presence of mood disorder

7. Yes, SS_{tot} could occur if all values are the same. SS_u would equal 0 if all sample $\overline{X}$s were the same. SS_w would equal 0 if all values within each sample equalled the sample $\overline{X}$.

9. Reject H_0 at the .05 level but not at the .01 level. The Tukey HSD test would be appropriate if the alpha level was .05. To determine the HSD we would still need the MS_w and n per sample, if the n is not the same in each condition.

11. The error is in Condition A. $SS_{cond\ A}$ results in a negative value $-300.$, which is impossible.

13. Independent variable: Age group
Dependent variable: Number of toys played with

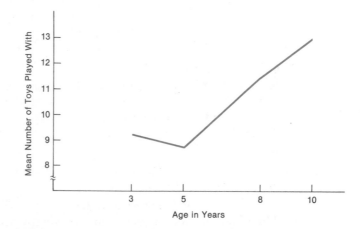

15.

Source	SS	df	MS	F
Among groups	12.08	4	3.02	3.18
Within groups	90.25	95	0.95	
Total	102.33	99		

17. Tukey HSD $= 4.04 \times \sqrt{20.17/11} = 5.47$
The 110° and 30° conditions resulted in significantly longer working times than the other conditions. And, the 90° condition had a signficantly longer working time than the 50° and 70° conditions.

19. No, that is not unexpected. It indicates that the systematic variability is 0 since the F ratio is based on (Systematic Variability + Error Variability)/Error Variability.

CHALLENGE QUESTION 1

a. Type of treatment would influence the level of anxiety reported by the women.

b. H_0: $\mu_{biofeedback} = \mu_{cogn.\ thpy.} = \mu_{no\ treat.}$
H_1: at least one sample comes from a different population

c.

	Biofeedback	Cognitive Therapy	No Treatment
$\overline{X} =$	29.00	32.00	31.86
$s =$	3.74	4.12	6.12

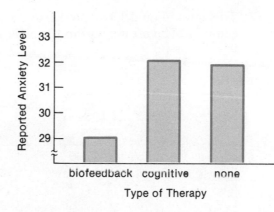

d.

Summary Table for the One-Way ANOVA				
Source	SS	df	MS	F
Among groups	37.67	2	18.84	.80
Within groups	376.86	16	23.55	
Total	414.53	18		

e. There was no significant difference in anxiety reported among the women participating in the different therapy conditions, $\underline{F}(2,16) = .80$, $\underline{p} > .05$.

CHAPTER 14

1. a. independent variables: type of format (lecture or discussion), number of tests (midterm/final or weekly)

b. dependent variable: performance on the standardized exam

3. a. The number of tests did not influence performance on the standardized exam. And, regardless of the number of tests, performance was better from the discussion classes than from the lecture classes.

b. He would have to conclude that the type of testing has different effects on performance on a standardized exam as a function of the format of the class. Generalizations would have to be limited to the type of course tested and perhaps the instructor. It would be inappropriate to generalize the findings of this study to courses with material different from that discussed in courses used in the study.

5. a. two independent variables, 2 and 3 levels, 6 conditions

b. two independent variables, 3 and 4 levels, 12 conditions

c. three independent variables, 2, 2, and 3 levels, 12 conditions

7. The rows should have the same $\overline{X}$s and the columns should have the same $\overline{X}$s. The means within the cells should be different. One possibility is

		Variable 1	
		Level A	*Level B*
Variable 2	Level A	60	40
	Level B	40	60

9. Academic year of the student and the number of students working with the subject are the independent variables. The design is a 2×3 factorial experiment.

11. The difference between the freshmen $\overline{X}$ (95.33) and the senior $\overline{X}$ (75) is not significant. However, the variable for the number of other students does reveal a significant difference. The $\overline{X}$ in the 1 condition (24) is significantly less than that in the 3 condition (106.5) and in the 5 condition (125). There is no significant interaction. Therefore, there is only one main effect, which is for the variable involving the number of other students present.

13.

Source	SS	df	MS	F
Variable 1		2		
Variable 2		4		
Interaction (1×2)		8		
Within groups		135		
Total		149		

15. Yes, it is possible. The H_0 for the interaction effect describes the case in which the pattern of differences for μs for one level of an independent variable will be the same for the other levels of that same variable. Therefore, something like the following is possible (the subscripts refer to levels for Variables A and B):
H_0: $\mu_{1,1} = \mu_{1,2} > \mu_{1,3}$ is the same as $\mu_{2,1} = \mu_{2,2} > \mu_{2,3}$
If the pattern of differences is not the same, then the H_0 for the interaction is rejected.

17. The procedures described in this chapter assume that a subject serves in only one condition in the study. The assumption of independence has been violated. The example described here is known as a mixed factorial design in that a person serves in some but not all conditions. There are procedures (not described in this text) for analyzing this type of study.

19. A factorial study allows the researcher to study how independent variables interact and combine to influence behavior. Our behavior is seldom determined by only one factor, or independent variable, but is more often the result of several factors. Therefore, a factorial design provides a clearer picture of the complex effect of various factors on behavior.

CHALLENGE QUESTION 1

a. A reasonable hypothesis would be that children would generate more uses for toys when adopting a same-sex role as opposed to an opposite-sex role. The design is a 2×2 factorial.

b. For the main effects of sex and sex role, H_0: $\mu_{boy} = \mu_{girl}$;
H_1: $\mu_{boy} \neq \mu_{girl}$
For the interaction, H_0: the pattern of μ differences found for boys and girls when adopting a same-sex role will be the same as when they adopt an opposite-sex role; H_1: the pattern of differences found for boys and girls will be different when adopting a same-sex role as compared with an opposite-sex role.

c. The mean and standard deviation for each condition is shown below:

Role adopted		Sex of the Child	
		Boy	Girl
Boy	$\overline{X}$	4.86	5.43
	s	2.27	0.98
Girl	$\overline{X}$	1.86	7.14
	s	1.35	1.35

D

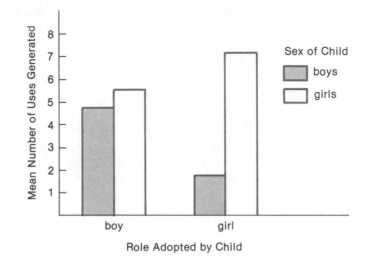

d.	Source	SS	df	MS	F
	Sex of child (S)	2.89	1	2.89	1.19
	Role adopted (R)	60.04	1	60.04	24.71
	S × R	38.89	1	38.89	16.00
	Within groups	58.29	24	2.43	
	Total	160.11	27		

e. Two significant effects were found. A significant interaction was found between sex of the child and role adopted, $\underline{F}$ (1, 24) = 16.00, $\underline{p}$ < .05. Also, a significant difference was found for the role adopted, $\underline{F}$ (1,24) = 24.71, $\underline{p}$ < .05. Relating these differences to the $\overline{X}$s shown in the figure it can be concluded that when a male role was adopted, there was no difference between boys and girls in terms of the number of ideas or uses generated for the objects. However, when a female role was adopted, girls thought of significantly more uses for the objects than boys.

CHAPTER 15

1. a. The independent variable is sex orientation of toys; the dependent variable is the amount of time the child plays with the toys.
   b. A reasonable research hypothesis would be that boys will play most with male-oriented toys, less with neutral toys, and least with female-oriented toys.

3.

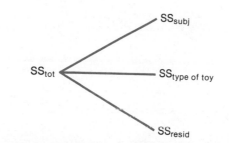

Source	SS	df	MS	F
Subjects		11		
Orientation of toys		2		
Subj × orientation		22		
Total		35		

5. If the counties are considered to be "subjects," then it may make sense to determine if there are significant differences among the counties.

7. The independent variable is the background of the screen. The dependent variable is the number of words identified. H_0: $\mu_{clear} = \mu_{letter\ parts} = \mu_{complete\ letters} = \mu_{words}$
H_1: at least one sample comes from a population distribution with a μ different from the other samples.

9. No, because the order in which the conditions were presented could have influenced performance. It would be impossible to determine if the background influenced performance or if another factor such as fatigue influenced performance.

11. a. H_0: $\mu_{phys.} = \mu_{learn.} = \mu_{devel.} = \mu_{abnormal} = \mu_{social}$
H_1: at least one sample comes from a population distribution with a μ different from the other samples

b.

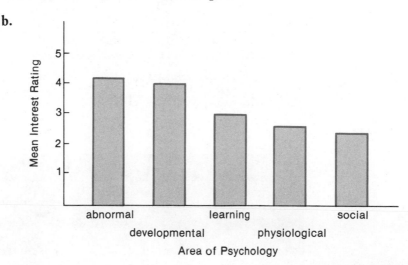

c.

Source	SS	df	MS	F
Subjects	21.84	4	5.46	—
Area of interest	10.64	4	2.66	6.05
Subj × area	6.96	16	0.44	
Total	39.44	24		

A signficant difference was found among the different areas of interest, $F(4, 16) = 6.05$, $p < .05$. A Tukey HSD test (HSD = 1.28) revealed that the abnormal and developmental areas had significantly higher levels of interest than the social and physiological areas.

13.

Source	SS	df	MS	F
Subjects	64,226.00	14	4,587.57	—
Area of interest	4,687.50	1	4,687.50	10.89
Subj × area	6,028.00	14	430.57	
Total	74,941.50	29		

The obtained F ratio is 10.89. The square root of this value is 3.30, which is equal to the obtained t of -3.30 reported in Chapter 11.

15.

Source	SS	df	MS	F
Subjects		14		—
Conditions		4		
Subj × cond.		56		
Total		74		

The critical F ratio (.01 level) for 4 and 55 df is 3.68.

17.

Source	SS	df	MS	F
Subjects	2,622.31	16	163.89	—
Type of word	4,479.57	2	2,239.78	14.96
Subj × word	4,791.10	32	149.72	
Total	11,892.98	50		

Yes, the same statistical decision is reached. The H_0 is rejected. The F ratio is slightly larger because variability resulting from individual differences has been removed from the error variability.

19. Yes, the $SS_{subjects}$ equals 0. That happened because the sum of the values for each subject is identical, 17. This indicates that there were no individual differences overall among the subjects.

CHALLENGE QUESTION 1

a. People would not rate that they liked their first, middle, and last names the same.

b. H_0: $\mu_{first} = \mu_{middle} = \mu_{last}$
H_1: at least one of the samples comes from a population distribution with a μ different from the other samples.

c.

	Name		
	First	Middle	Last
$\overline{X}$	5.72	5.22	5.33
s	1.18	1.06	1.19

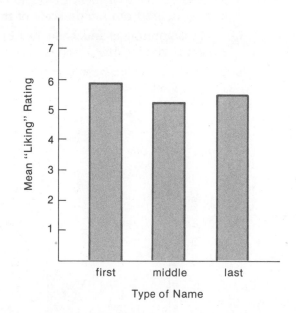

D

d.

Source	SS	df	MS	F
Subjects	38.53	17	2.27	—
Name	2.48	2	1.24	1.49
Subj × area	28.19	34	0.83	
Total	69.20	53		

e. There were no significant differences in the ratings given among the different names, $\underline{F}$ (2, 34) = .83, $\underline{p}$ > .05.

D | CHAPTER 16

1. A variable on the nominal scale of measurement has values that cannot be ordered on a number line. An example would be gender, which has two values—male and female. An ordinal-scaled variable has values that can be ordered but do not have equal intervals between values. Ranking in class is an example of an ordinal variable. The interval and ratio scale of measurements are used for variables that have values that are equally spaced. Variables without a real zero point, such as IQ scores, are from an interval scale of measurement. Variables with a real zero point, such as height, are from a ratio scale of measurement.

3. The assumption of independence of observations. In this problem each person is giving three responses, not just one.

5. Significantly more people prefer Candidate A over Candidates B and C, $\chi^2(2) = 9.60$, $p < .05$.

7.

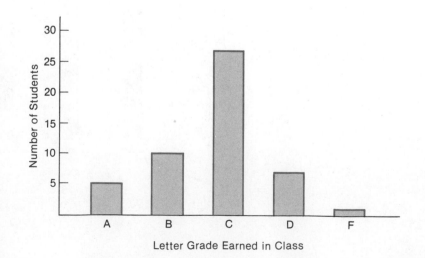

9. He is using the inappropriate test. If he surveyed both men and women and determined their desire for a coed dorm, then he should use a χ^2 test for independence with gender and desirability as variables. He needs to include the number of men and women who responded that they did not favor coed dorms. He only reported those who favored coed dorms in the problem.

11. There is a significant difference in the number of patients admitted across the various months, $\chi^2(11) = 512.36$, $p < .01$.

13. With the large sample sizes, the researchers should be careful to note that a statistical difference does not ensure a practical difference.

15. Converting to percentages makes comparisons across groups easier.

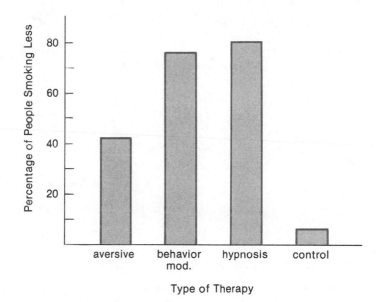

17. Type of response and gender are not significantly related to each other, $\chi^2 = 2.74$, $p > .05$.

19. There is a significant difference between the two types of individuals' preferences for the computers, $\chi^2(3) = 72.75$, $p < .01$. It appears that the business executives prefer Computer A, whereas the principals prefer Computer D.

CHALLENGE QUESTION 1

a. Men and women differ in their preferences for boys' names.

b. H_0: Gender and type of name preferred are independent of each other
H_1: Gender and type of name preferred are related to each other

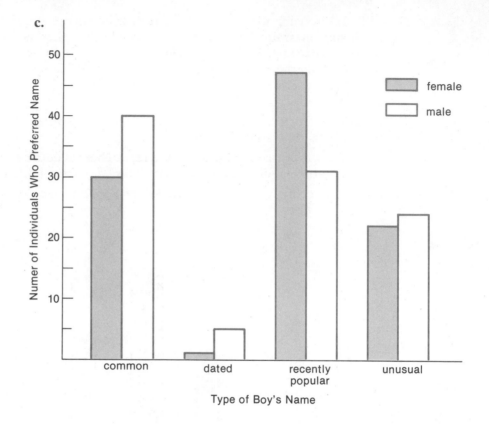

c.

(Bar chart: vertical axis "Numer of Individuals Who Preferred Name" from 10 to 50; horizontal axis "Type of Boy's Name" with categories common, dated, recently popular, unusual. Legend: female (gray), male (white).)

d. $\chi^2 = (40 - 35)^2/35 + (30 - 35)^2/35 + (24 - 23)^2/23 + (22 - 23)^2/23 + (31 - 39)^2/39 + (47 - 39)^2/39 + (5 - 3)^2/3 + (1 - 3)^2/3 = .7.46$

e. Men and women did not differ significantly in their preferences for boys' names, $\chi^2(3) = 7.46$, $\underline{p} > .05$.

CHAPTER 17

1. Because of the unequal sample size and the small sample size in one condition (N = 4) and the consequent potential violation of the assumption of normality for the shape of the population distribution, it would be best for the researcher to use the Mann-Whitney U test, which makes no assumptions about the shape of the population distribution. If the sample sizes had been larger (N = 30) and equal in both conditions, then the t test for independent samples would have been appropriate because the test is robust enough to handle the violation of the test assumptions.

3. Because if $N_1 \neq N_2$, the ΣR will be weighted toward the larger sample size. The U_1 and U_2 statistics adjust for differences in sample size between the two samples.

5. $\overline{X}_{training} = 6.50$; $\overline{X}_{control} = 2.83$. The $\overline{X}$ for each sample is larger than the M_d.

Number of Elements	Frequency for Training	Frequency for Control
9	1	1
8	1	0
7	0	1
6	2	1
5	2	0
4		1
3		2
2		8
1		3
0		1

The distribution for the control group is positively skewed.

7. In the present form, the data would not be appropriate for the Mann-Whitney U test. It is necessary for the values to be ranks without regard to group or condition membership.

9. M_d for A/B students = 12.5; M_d for D/F students = 4.5
Range for A/B students = 9; Range for D/F students = 10
$U_1 = 6$; $U_2 = 58$; There is a significant difference in the quality of notes between the two groups of students, $\underline{U} = 6$, $\underline{p} < .01$. The rankings are significantly higher for the A and B students.

11. No, because the critical U values for a nondirectional hypothesis with an alpha level of .05 would be 2 and 23, and the obtained U_1 and U_2 values of 3 and 22 would result in H_0 being retained.

13. $U_1 = 55 + 15 - 37 = 33$; $U_2 = 55 + 66 - 99 = 22$; There is no significant difference in the length of notes taken between men and women, $\underline{U} = 22$, $\underline{p} > .05$.

15. Using Formula 43, $z = (115 - 187.5)/\sqrt{(15,375/12)} = -2.03$. She should reject H_0 and assume that the two samples are different from each other.

17. a. $z = -1.23$, retain H_0 **b.** retain H_0
c. reject H_0 **d.** $z = -1.00$, retain H_0

19. $U_1 = 30 + 15 - 20 = 25$; $U_2 = 30 + 21 - 46 = 5$. She should conclude that the morning classes are not significantly preferred over the afternoon classes, $\underline{U} = 5$, $\underline{p} > .05$.

CHALLENGE QUESTION 1

a. A reasonable research hypothesis would be that the description of the defendant would influence the rating of perceived ease in defending the client.

b. H_0: both samples were selected from the same population distribution. H_1: the samples were selected from different population distributions.

c.

	Lower-Class Defendant	Middle-Class Defendant
$\overline{X}$ =	3.05	3.28
M_d =	3.65	2.95
s =	1.46	1.62

d. $U_1 = 49 + 28 - 47 = 30$; $U_2 = 49 + 28 - 58 = 19$; retain H_0

e. There is no significant difference in the ratings given by the attorneys as a function of the class of the defendant, $\underline{U} = 19$, $\underline{p} > .05$.

CHAPTER 18

1.

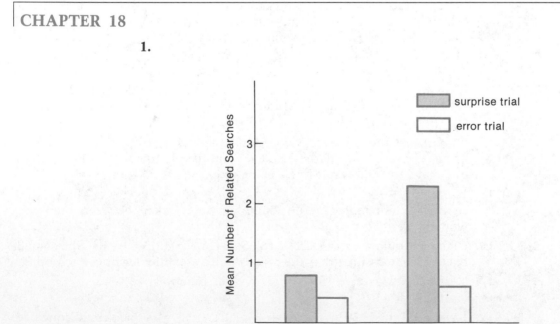

3.

$\Sigma X =$	8	4	18	5
$\Sigma X^2 =$	12	4	48	7
$N =$	10	10	8	8
$\overline{X} =$	0.80	0.40	2.25	0.63
$SS =$	5.60	2.40	7.50	3.88
$s =$	0.79	0.52	1.04	0.74

5. The main difference is that the Mann-Whitney U test assumes that an independent groups design has been used, whereas the Wilcoxon matched-pairs test assumes that a repeated measures or matched groups design was used. The other assumptions are identical for both tests.

7. Independent variable is type of keyboard. Dependent variable is the number of words typed per minute. The dependent variable is on a ratio scale of measurement.

9. No, the same conclusion should be reached. If the use of a less powerful test, the Wilcoxon matched-pairs test for instance, results in a significant difference (rejecting H_0), then the use of the t test should result in the same conclusion.

11. There is no significant change in the grades assigned to the papers, $W = 15.0$, $p > .05$.

13. $z = (917.5 - 1,425)/\sqrt{35,862.5} = -2.68$. Assuming that the difference between samples is in the predicted direction, then H_0 should be rejected at the .01 level. If the difference is not in the predicted direction, then H_0 should be retained.

15. No, the conclusion is based on too few subjects. It would be difficult to reach any conclusion given the limited sample reported in Exercise 14. There seems to be less variability in the performance of the girls than the boys, which may make any conclusions about the test suspect. It would be better to conduct the study using larger samples of subjects.

17. The student ratings do not differ between students who are majors and those who are not, $W = 6$, $p > .01$.

19. $t = 0.70/0.31 = 2.26$. With df $= 9$, the obtained t is less than the critical t value of 3.250 (alpha level is .01). Therefore, H_0 is retained, which is the same conclusion reached in Exercise 17.

CHALLENGE QUESTION 1

a. If processing is easier for stimuli presented to the right visual field, then the number of errors should be less for stimuli presented to the right visual field than for stimuli presented to the left visual field.

b. H_0: both samples were selected from the same population distribution
H_1: the samples were selected from different population distributions

c.

	Right Visual Field	Left Visual Field
$\overline{X}$ =	1.60	5.60
M_d =	1.00	3.00
s =	2.01	5.80

d. $\Sigma R_+ = 2$; $\Sigma R_- = 43$ $W = 2$; Reject H_0 (critical W value is 5)

e. Significantly more errors are made for stimuli presented to the left visual field than for stimuli presented to the right visual field, $\underline{W} = 2$, $\underline{p} < .05$.

CHAPTER 19

1. In all cases it is necessary to rerank the rankings to reflect comparisons between pairs of treatments.
Treatment versus Placebo: $U_1 = 361 + 190 - 488 = 63$; $U_2 = 361 + 190 - 253 = 298$; Reject H_0
Treatment versus Control: $U_1 = 399 + 190 - 508 = 81$; $U_2 = 399 + 231 - 312 = 318$; $(z = -3.21)$; Reject H_0
Placebo versus Control: $U_1 = 399 + 190 - 351 = 238$; $U_2 = 399 + 231 - 469 = 161$; $(z = -1.04)$; Retain H_0

3. $H = [(12/420) \times 2,425.2] - 63 = 6.29$; With df = 3, there are no significant differences among the different disciplines.

5. No, because the sum of the rankings is the same for all conditions.
$H = [(12/420) \times 2,205] - 63 = 0.00$

7. $H = [(12/930) \times 7,455] - 93 = 3.19$; With df = 3, there are no significant differences among the different contents.

9. He is not using the appropriate test because the assumptions underlying both tests are the same.

11. $x = [(12/240) \times 3,706] - 180 = 5.30$; With df = 3, there are no significant differences among the different issues.

13. Students do not appear to seek the same types of professionals. For instance, in the chapter example students were least likely to seek help from college and career counselors or advisors for personal problems. Yet, these individuals were likely to be sought when dealing with a career problem.

15. No, the critical value is based on the chi-square distribution. And, the critical value is determined by df. The df for the Friedman test is based on the number of conditions, not the number of participants.

CHALLENGE QUESTION 1

  a. Perceived locus of control is different across age groups.
  b. H_0: all the samples were selected from the same population distribution
  H_1: at least one sample came from a different population distribution

  c.

	20–34	35–49	50–64	65–89
M_d =	15.5	12.5	15.0	19.5
Range =	27	27	27	22

  d. $H = [(12/1{,}056) \times 8{,}862.5] - 99 = 1.71$; Retain H_0
  e. No significant differences were found in terms of locus of control as it relates to the age groups tested, $\underline{H}(3) = 1.71$, $\underline{p} > .05$.

D

Appendix
E

Statistical Tables

Critical values are presented for α levels of .05 (Roman type) and .01 (Boldfaced type). Obtained F ratio must be equal to or exceed critical value to reject H_0. Rows list df associated with numerator in calculating F ratio; columns list df associated with denominator.

TABLE F   Critical F Ratios

Degrees of freedom: denominator	Degrees of Freedom: Numerator														
	1	2	3	4	5	6	7	8	9	10	11	12	14	16	20
1	161	200	216	225	230	234	237	239	241	242	243	244	245	246	248
	4,052	**4,999**	**5,403**	**5,625**	**5,764**	**5,859**	**5,928**	**5,981**	**6,022**	**6,056**	**6,082**	**6,106**	**6,142**	**6,169**	**6,208**
2	18.51	19.00	19.16	19.25	19.30	19.33	19.36	19.37	19.38	19.39	19.40	19.41	19.42	19.43	19.44
	98.49	**99.00**	**99.17**	**99.25**	**99.30**	**99.33**	**99.34**	**99.36**	**99.38**	**99.40**	**99.41**	**99.42**	**99.43**	**99.44**	**99.45**
3	10.13	9.55	9.28	9.12	9.01	8.94	8.88	8.84	8.81	8.78	8.76	8.74	8.71	8.69	8.66
	34.12	**30.82**	**29.46**	**28.71**	**28.24**	**27.91**	**27.67**	**27.49**	**27.34**	**27.23**	**27.13**	**27.05**	**26.92**	**26.83**	**26.69**
4	7.71	6.94	6.59	6.39	6.26	6.16	6.09	6.04	6.00	5.96	5.93	5.91	5.87	5.84	5.80
	21.20	**18.00**	**16.69**	**15.98**	**15.52**	**15.21**	**14.98**	**14.80**	**14.66**	**14.54**	**14.45**	**14.37**	**14.24**	**14.15**	**14.02**
5	6.61	5.79	5.41	5.19	5.05	4.95	4.88	4.82	4.78	4.74	4.70	4.68	4.64	4.60	4.56
	16.26	**13.27**	**12.06**	**11.39**	**10.97**	**10.67**	**10.45**	**10.27**	**10.15**	**10.05**	**9.96**	**9.89**	**9.77**	**9.68**	**9.55**
6	5.99	5.14	4.76	4.53	4.39	4.28	4.21	4.15	4.10	4.06	4.03	4.00	3.96	3.92	3.87
	13.74	**10.92**	**9.78**	**9.15**	**8.75**	**8.47**	**8.26**	**8.10**	**7.98**	**7.87**	**7.79**	**7.72**	**7.60**	**7.52**	**7.39**
7	5.59	4.47	4.35	4.12	3.97	3.87	3.79	3.73	3.68	3.63	3.60	3.57	3.52	3.49	3.44
	12.25	**9.55**	**8.45**	**7.85**	**7.46**	**7.19**	**7.00**	**6.84**	**6.71**	**6.62**	**6.54**	**6.47**	**6.35**	**6.27**	**6.15**
8	5.32	4.46	4.07	3.84	3.69	3.58	3.50	3.44	3.39	3.34	3.31	3.28	3.23	3.20	3.15
	11.26	**8.65**	**7.59**	**7.01**	**6.63**	**6.37**	**6.19**	**6.03**	**5.91**	**5.82**	**5.74**	**5.67**	**5.56**	**5.48**	**5.36**
9	5.12	4.26	3.86	3.63	3.48	3.37	3.29	3.23	3.18	3.13	3.10	3.07	3.02	2.98	2.93
	10.56	**8.02**	**6.99**	**6.42**	**6.06**	**5.80**	**5.62**	**5.47**	**5.35**	**5.26**	**5.18**	**5.11**	**5.00**	**4.92**	**4.80**
10	4.96	4.10	3.71	3.48	3.33	3.22	3.14	3.07	3.02	2.97	2.94	2.91	2.86	2.82	2.77
	10.04	**7.56**	**6.55**	**5.99**	**5.64**	**5.39**	**5.21**	**5.06**	**4.95**	**4.85**	**4.78**	**4.71**	**4.60**	**4.52**	**4.41**

Note. Reprinted by permission from *Statistical Methods*, Seventh Edition by George W. Snedecor and William G. Cochran © 1980 by Iowa State University Press, 2121 South State Avenue, Ames, IA 50010.

Continued on next page

TABLE F   Critical F Ratios (Continued)

Degrees of freedom: denominator	Degrees of Freedom: Numerator														
	1	2	3	4	5	6	7	8	9	10	11	12	14	16	20
11	4.84	3.98	3.59	3.36	3.20	3.09	3.01	2.95	2.90	2.86	2.82	2.79	2.74	2.70	2.65
	9.65	7.20	6.22	5.67	5.32	5.07	4.88	4.74	4.63	4.54	4.46	4.40	4.29	4.21	4.10
12	4.75	3.88	3.49	3.26	3.11	3.00	2.92	2.85	2.80	2.76	2.72	2.69	2.64	2.60	2.54
	9.33	6.93	5.95	5.41	5.06	4.82	4.65	4.50	4.39	4.30	4.22	4.16	4.05	3.98	3.86
13	4.67	3.80	3.41	3.18	3.02	2.92	2.84	2.77	2.72	2.67	2.63	2.60	2.55	2.51	2.46
	9.07	6.70	5.74	5.20	4.86	4.62	4.44	4.30	4.19	4.10	4.02	3.96	3.85	3.78	3.67
14	4.60	3.74	3.34	3.11	2.96	2.85	2.77	2.70	2.65	2.60	2.56	2.53	2.48	2.44	2.39
	8.86	6.51	5.56	5.03	4.69	4.46	4.28	4.14	4.03	3.94	3.86	3.80	3.70	3.62	3.51
15	4.54	3.68	3.29	3.06	2.90	2.79	2.70	2.64	2.59	2.55	2.51	2.48	2.43	2.39	2.33
	8.68	6.36	5.42	4.89	4.56	4.32	4.14	4.00	3.89	3.80	3.73	3.67	3.56	3.48	3.36
16	4.49	3.63	3.24	3.01	2.85	2.74	2.66	2.59	2.54	2.49	2.45	2.42	2.37	2.33	2.28
	8.53	6.23	5.29	4.77	4.44	4.20	4.03	3.89	3.78	3.69	3.61	3.55	3.45	3.37	3.25
17	4.45	3.59	3.20	2.96	2.81	2.70	2.62	2.55	2.50	2.45	2.41	2.38	2.33	2.29	2.23
	8.40	6.11	5.18	4.67	4.34	4.10	3.93	3.79	3.68	3.59	3.52	3.45	3.35	3.27	3.16
18	4.41	3.55	3.16	2.93	2.77	2.66	2.58	2.51	2.46	2.41	2.37	2.34	2.29	2.25	2.19
	8.28	6.01	5.09	4.58	4.25	4.01	3.85	3.71	3.60	3.51	3.44	3.37	3.27	3.19	3.07
19	4.38	3.52	3.13	2.90	2.74	2.63	2.55	2.48	2.43	2.38	2.34	2.31	2.26	2.21	2.15
	8.18	5.93	5.01	4.50	4.17	3.94	3.77	3.63	3.52	3.43	3.36	3.30	3.19	3.12	3.00
20	4.35	3.49	3.10	2.87	2.71	2.60	2.52	2.45	2.40	2.35	2.31	2.28	2.23	2.18	2.12
	8.10	5.85	4.94	4.43	4.10	3.87	3.71	3.56	3.45	3.37	3.30	3.23	3.13	3.05	2.94
21	4.32	3.47	3.07	2.84	2.68	2.57	2.49	2.42	2.37	2.32	2.28	2.25	2.20	2.15	2.09
	8.02	5.78	4.87	4.37	4.04	3.81	3.65	3.51	3.40	3.31	3.24	3.17	3.07	2.99	2.88
22	4.30	3.44	3.05	2.82	2.66	2.55	2.47	2.40	2.35	2.30	2.26	2.23	2.18	2.13	2.07
	7.94	4.72	4.82	4.31	3.99	3.76	3.59	3.45	3.35	3.26	3.18	3.12	3.02	2.94	2.83
23	4.28	3.42	3.03	2.80	2.64	2.53	2.45	2.38	2.32	2.28	2.24	2.20	2.14	2.10	2.04
	7.88	5.66	4.76	4.26	3.94	3.71	3.54	3.41	3.30	3.21	3.14	3.07	2.97	2.89	2.78
24	4.26	3.40	3.01	2.78	2.62	2.51	2.43	2.36	2.30	2.26	2.22	2.18	2.13	2.09	2.02
	7.82	5.61	4.72	4.22	3.90	3.67	3.50	3.36	3.25	3.17	3.09	3.03	2.93	2.85	2.74
25	4.24	3.38	2.99	2.76	2.60	2.49	2.41	2.34	2.28	2.24	2.20	2.16	2.11	2.06	2.00
	7.77	5.57	4.68	4.18	3.86	3.63	3.46	3.32	3.21	3.13	3.05	2.99	2.89	2.81	2.70

Continued on next page

TABLE F Critical F Ratios (Continued)

Degrees of freedom: denominator	Degrees of Freedom: Numerator														
	1	2	3	4	5	6	7	8	9	10	11	12	14	16	20
26	4.22	3.37	2.98	2.74	2.59	2.47	2.39	2.32	2.27	2.22	2.18	2.15	2.10	2.05	1.99
	7.72	5.53	4.64	4.14	3.82	3.59	3.42	3.29	3.17	3.09	3.02	2.96	2.86	2.77	2.66
27	4.21	3.35	2.96	2.73	2.57	2.46	2.37	2.30	2.25	2.20	2.16	2.13	2.08	2.03	1.97
	7.68	5.49	4.60	4.11	3.79	3.56	3.39	3.26	3.14	3.06	2.98	2.93	2.83	2.74	2.63
28	4.20	3.34	2.95	2.71	2.56	2.44	2.36	2.29	2.24	2.19	2.15	2.12	2.06	2.02	1.96
	7.64	5.45	4.57	4.07	3.76	3.53	3.36	3.23	3.11	3.03	2.95	2.90	2.80	2.71	2.60
29	4.18	3.33	2.93	2.70	2.54	2.43	2.35	2.28	2.22	2.18	2.14	2.10	2.05	2.00	1.94
	7.60	5.42	4.54	4.04	3.73	3.50	3.33	3.20	3.08	3.00	2.92	2.87	2.77	2.68	2.57
30	4.17	3.32	2.92	2.69	2.53	2.42	2.34	2.27	2.21	2.16	2.12	2.09	2.04	1.99	1.93
	7.56	5.39	4.51	4.02	3.70	3.47	3.30	3.17	3.06	2.98	2.90	2.84	2.74	2.66	2.55
32	4.15	3.30	2.90	2.67	2.51	2.40	2.32	2.25	2.19	2.14	2.10	2.07	2.02	1.97	1.91
	7.50	5.34	4.46	3.97	3.66	3.42	3.25	3.12	3.01	2.94	2.86	2.80	2.70	2.62	2.51
34	4.13	3.28	2.88	2.65	2.49	2.38	2.30	2.23	2.17	2.12	2.08	2.05	2.00	1.95	1.89
	7.44	5.29	4.42	3.93	3.61	3.38	3.21	3.08	2.97	2.89	2.82	2.76	2.66	2.58	2.47
36	4.11	3.26	2.86	2.63	2.48	2.36	2.28	2.21	2.15	2.10	2.06	2.03	1.98	1.93	1.87
	7.39	5.25	4.38	3.89	3.58	3.35	3.18	3.04	2.94	2.86	2.78	2.72	2.62	2.54	2.43
38	4.10	3.25	2.85	2.62	2.46	2.35	2.26	2.19	2.14	2.09	2.05	2.02	1.96	1.92	1.85
	7.35	5.21	4.34	3.86	3.54	3.32	3.15	3.02	2.91	2.82	2.75	2.69	2.59	2.51	2.40
40	4.08	3.23	2.84	2.61	2.45	2.34	2.25	2.18	2.12	2.07	2.04	2.00	1.95	1.90	1.84
	7.31	5.18	4.31	3.83	3.51	3.29	3.12	2.99	2.88	2.80	2.73	2.66	2.56	2.49	2.37
42	4.07	3.22	2.83	2.59	2.44	2.32	2.24	2.17	2.11	2.06	2.02	1.99	1.94	1.89	1.82
	7.27	5.15	4.29	3.80	3.49	3.26	3.10	2.96	2.86	2.77	2.70	2.64	2.54	2.46	2.35
44	4.06	3.21	2.82	2.58	2.43	2.31	2.23	2.16	2.10	2.05	2.01	1.98	1.92	1.88	1.81
	7.24	5.12	4.26	3.78	3.46	3.24	3.07	2.94	2.84	2.75	2.68	2.62	2.52	2.44	2.32
46	4.05	3.20	2.81	2.57	2.42	2.30	2.22	2.14	2.09	2.04	2.00	1.97	1.91	1.87	1.80
	7.21	5.10	4.24	3.76	3.44	3.22	3.05	2.92	2.82	2.73	2.66	2.60	2.50	2.42	2.30

E

Continued on next page

TABLE F Critical *F* Ratios *(Continued)*

Degrees of freedom: denominator	Degrees of Freedom: Numerator															
	1	2	3	4	5	6	7	8	9	10	11	12	14	16	20
48	4.04	3.19	2.80	2.56	2.41	2.30	2.21	2.14	2.08	2.03	1.99	1.96	1.90	1.86	1.79
	7.19	**5.08**	**4.22**	**3.74**	**3.42**	**3.20**	**3.04**	**2.90**	**2.80**	**2.71**	**2.64**	**2.58**	**2.48**	**2.40**	**2.28**
50	4.03	3.18	2.79	2.56	2.40	2.29	2.20	2.13	2.07	2.02	1.98	1.95	1.90	1.85	1.78
	7.17	**5.06**	**4.20**	**3.72**	**3.41**	**3.18**	**3.02**	**2.88**	**2.78**	**2.70**	**2.62**	**2.56**	**2.46**	**2.39**	**2.26**
55	4.02	3.17	2.78	2.54	2.38	2.27	2.18	2.11	2.05	2.00	1.97	1.93	1.88	1.83	1.76
	7.12	**5.01**	**4.16**	**3.68**	**3.37**	**3.15**	**2.98**	**2.85**	**2.75**	**2.66**	**2.59**	**2.53**	**2.43**	**2.35**	**2.23**
60	4.00	3.15	2.76	2.52	2.37	2.25	2.17	2.10	2.04	1.99	1.95	1.92	1.86	1.81	1.75
	7.08	**4.98**	**4.13**	**3.65**	**3.34**	**3.12**	**2.95**	**2.82**	**2.72**	**2.63**	**2.56**	**2.50**	**2.40**	**2.32**	**2.20**
65	3.99	3.14	2.75	2.51	2.36	2.24	2.15	2.08	2.02	1.98	1.94	1.90	1.85	1.80	1.73
	7.04	**4.95**	**4.10**	**3.62**	**3.31**	**3.09**	**2.93**	**2.79**	**2.70**	**2.61**	**2.54**	**2.47**	**2.37**	**2.30**	**2.18**
70	3.98	3.13	2.74	2.50	2.35	2.23	2.14	2.07	2.01	1.97	1.93	1.89	1.84	1.79	1.72
	7.01	**4.92**	**4.08**	**3.60**	**3.29**	**3.07**	**2.91**	**2.77**	**2.67**	**2.59**	**2.51**	**2.45**	**2.35**	**2.28**	**2.15**
80	3.96	3.11	2.72	2.48	2.33	2.21	2.12	2.05	1.99	1.95	1.91	1.88	1.82	1.77	1.70
	6.96	**4.88**	**4.04**	**3.56**	**3.25**	**3.04**	**2.87**	**2.74**	**2.64**	**2.55**	**2.48**	**2.41**	**2.32**	**2.24**	**2.11**
100	3.94	3.09	2.70	2.46	2.30	2.19	2.10	2.03	1.97	1.92	1.88	1.85	1.79	1.75	1.68
	6.90	**4.82**	**3.98**	**3.51**	**3.20**	**2.99**	**2.82**	**2.69**	**2.59**	**2.51**	**2.43**	**2.36**	**2.26**	**2.19**	**2.06**
125	3.92	3.07	2.68	2.44	2.29	2.17	2.08	2.01	1.95	1.90	1.86	1.83	1.77	1.72	1.65
	6.84	**4.78**	**3.94**	**3.47**	**3.17**	**2.95**	**2.79**	**2.65**	**2.56**	**2.47**	**2.40**	**2.33**	**2.23**	**2.15**	**2.03**
150	3.91	3.06	2.67	2.43	2.27	2.16	2.07	2.00	1.94	1.89	1.85	1.82	1.76	1.71	1.64
	6.81	**4.75**	**3.91**	**3.44**	**3.14**	**2.92**	**2.76**	**2.62**	**2.53**	**2.44**	**2.37**	**2.30**	**2.20**	**2.12**	**2.00**
200	3.89	3.04	2.65	2.41	2.26	2.14	2.05	1.98	1.92	1.87	1.83	1.80	1.74	1.69	1.62
	6.76	**4.71**	**3.88**	**3.41**	**3.11**	**2.90**	**2.73**	**2.60**	**2.50**	**2.41**	**2.34**	**2.28**	**2.17**	**2.09**	**1.97**
400	3.86	3.02	2.62	2.39	2.23	2.12	2.03	1.96	1.90	1.85	1.81	1.78	1.72	1.67	1.60
	6.70	**4.66**	**3.83**	**3.36**	**3.06**	**2.85**	**2.69**	**2.55**	**2.46**	**2.37**	**2.29**	**2.23**	**2.12**	**2.04**	**1.92**
1000	3.85	3.00	2.61	2.38	2.22	2.10	2.02	1.95	1.89	1.84	1.80	1.76	1.70	1.65	1.58
	6.66	**4.62**	**3.80**	**3.34**	**3.04**	**2.82**	**2.66**	**2.53**	**2.43**	**2.34**	**2.26**	**2.20**	**2.09**	**2.01**	**1.89**
∞	3.84	2.99	2.60	2.37	2.21	2.09	2.01	1.94	1.88	1.83	1.79	1.75	1.69	1.64	1.57
	6.64	**4.60**	**3.78**	**3.32**	**3.02**	**2.80**	**2.64**	**2.51**	**2.41**	**2.32**	**2.24**	**2.18**	**2.07**	**1.99**	**1.87**

Values are presented for α levels of .05 (Roman type) and .01 (Boldfaced type). These values are used in Tukey HSD and other post hoc comparisons tests. Use the same α level as that used in analysis of variance. First column represents the *df* associated with the denominator in calculating significant *F* ratio.

TABLE Q   Studentized Range (*q*) Values

df in error term	Number of Means to Be Compared										
	2	3	4	5	6	7	8	9	10	11	12
5	3.64	4.60	5.22	5.67	6.03	6.33	6.58	6.80	6.99	7.17	7.32
	5.70	**6.98**	**7.80**	**8.42**	**8.91**	**9.32**	**9.67**	**9.97**	**10.24**	**10.48**	**10.70**
6	3.46	4.34	4.90	5.30	5.63	5.90	6.12	6.32	6.49	6.65	6.79
	5.24	**6.33**	**7.03**	**7.56**	**7.97**	**8.32**	**8.61**	**8.87**	**9.10**	**9.30**	**9.48**
7	3.34	4.16	4.68	5.06	5.36	5.61	5.82	6.00	6.16	6.30	6.43
	4.95	**5.92**	**6.54**	**7.01**	**7.37**	**7.68**	**7.94**	**8.17**	**8.37**	**8.55**	**8.71**
8	3.26	4.04	4.53	4.89	5.17	5.40	5.60	5.77	5.92	6.05	6.18
	4.75	**5.64**	**6.20**	**6.62**	**6.96**	**7.24**	**7.47**	**7.68**	**7.86**	**8.03**	**8.18**
9	3.20	3.95	4.41	4.76	5.02	5.24	5.43	5.59	5.74	5.87	5.98
	4.60	**5.43**	**5.96**	**6.35**	**6.66**	**6.91**	**7.13**	**7.33**	**7.49**	**7.65**	**7.78**
10	3.15	3.88	4.33	4.65	4.91	5.12	5.30	5.46	5.60	5.72	5.83
	4.48	**5.27**	**5.77**	**6.14**	**6.43**	**6.67**	**6.87**	**7.05**	**7.21**	**7.36**	**7.49**
11	3.11	3.82	4.26	4.57	4.82	5.03	5.20	5.35	5.49	5.61	5.71
	4.39	**5.15**	**5.62**	**5.97**	**6.25**	**6.48**	**6.67**	**6.84**	**6.99**	**7.13**	**7.25**
12	3.08	3.77	4.20	4.51	4.75	4.95	5.12	5.27	5.39	5.51	5.61
	4.32	**5.05**	**5.50**	**5.84**	**6.10**	**6.32**	**6.51**	**6.67**	**6.81**	**6.94**	**7.06**
13	3.06	3.73	4.15	4.45	4.69	4.88	5.05	5.19	5.32	5.43	5.53
	4.26	**4.96**	**5.40**	**5.73**	**5.98**	**6.19**	**6.37**	**6.53**	**6.67**	**6.79**	**6.90**
14	3.03	3.70	4.11	4.41	4.64	4.83	4.99	5.13	5.25	5.36	5.46
	4.21	**4.89**	**5.32**	**5.63**	**5.88**	**6.08**	**6.26**	**6.41**	**6.54**	**6.66**	**6.77**

E

Note. Adapted from *Biometrika Tables for Statisticians* (Vol. 1, 3rd ed., Table 29) edited by E. S. Pearson and H. O. Hartley, 1966, New York: Cambridge University Press. Copyright 1966 by Cambridge University Press. Adapted by permission of the Biometrika Trustees.

TABLE Q   Studentized Range (q) Values (Continued)

df in error term	Number of Means to Be Compared										
	2	3	4	5	6	7	8	9	10	11	12
15	3.01	3.67	4.08	4.37	4.59	4.78	4.94	5.08	5.20	5.31	5.40
	4.17	**4.84**	**5.25**	**5.56**	**5.80**	**5.99**	**6.16**	**6.31**	**6.44**	**6.55**	**6.66**
16	3.00	3.65	4.05	4.33	4.56	4.74	4.90	5.03	5.15	5.26	5.35
	4.13	**4.79**	**5.19**	**5.49**	**5.72**	**5.92**	**6.08**	**6.22**	**6.35**	**6.46**	**6.56**
17	2.98	3.63	4.02	4.30	4.52	4.70	4.86	4.99	5.11	5.21	5.31
	4.10	**4.74**	**5.14**	**5.43**	**5.66**	**5.85**	**6.01**	**6.15**	**6.27**	**6.38**	**6.48**
18	2.97	3.61	4.00	4.28	4.49	4.67	4.82	4.96	5.07	5.17	5.27
	4.07	**4.70**	**5.09**	**5.38**	**5.60**	**5.79**	**5.94**	**6.08**	**6.20**	**6.31**	**6.41**
19	2.96	3.59	3.98	4.25	4.47	4.65	4.79	4.92	5.04	5.14	5.23
	4.05	**4.67**	**5.05**	**5.33**	**5.55**	**5.73**	**5.89**	**6.02**	**6.14**	**6.25**	**6.34**
20	2.95	3.58	3.96	4.23	4.45	4.62	4.77	4.90	5.01	5.11	5.20
	4.02	**4.64**	**5.02**	**5.29**	**5.51**	**5.69**	**5.84**	**5.97**	**6.09**	**6.19**	**6.28**
24	2.92	3.53	3.90	4.17	4.37	4.54	4.68	4.81	4.92	5.01	5.10
	3.96	**4.55**	**4.91**	**5.17**	**5.37**	**5.54**	**5.69**	**5.81**	**5.92**	**6.02**	**6.11**
30	2.89	3.49	3.85	4.10	4.30	4.46	4.60	4.72	4.82	4.92	5.00
	3.89	**4.45**	**4.80**	**5.05**	**5.24**	**5.40**	**5.54**	**5.65**	**5.76**	**5.85**	**5.93**
40	2.86	3.44	3.79	4.04	4.23	4.39	4.52	4.63	4.73	4.82	4.90
	3.82	**4.37**	**4.70**	**4.93**	**5.11**	**5.26**	**5.39**	**5.50**	**5.60**	**5.69**	**5.76**
60	2.83	3.40	3.74	3.98	4.16	4.31	4.44	4.55	4.65	4.73	4.81
	3.76	**4.28**	**4.59**	**4.82**	**4.99**	**5.13**	**5.25**	**5.36**	**5.45**	**5.53**	**5.60**
120	2.80	3.36	3.68	3.92	4.10	4.24	4.36	4.47	4.56	4.64	4.71
	3.70	**4.20**	**4.50**	**4.71**	**4.87**	**5.01**	**5.12**	**5.21**	**5.30**	**5.37**	**5.44**
∞	2.77	3.31	3.63	3.86	4.03	4.17	4.29	4.39	4.47	4.55	4.62
	3.64	**4.12**	**4.40**	**4.60**	**4.76**	**4.88**	**4.99**	**5.08**	**5.16**	**5.23**	**5.29**

Note. Adapted from Table VII of Fisher & Yates: *Statistical Tables for Biological, Agricultural and Medical Research,* Published by Longman Group Ltd. London (previously published by Oliver & Boyd Ltd. Edinburgh) and by permission of the authors and publishers.

Critical r values are listed for directional and nondirectional hypotheses and for α levels of .05 and .01. Obtained r coefficient must be equal to or greater than critical r value to reject H_0. To use directional hypothesis, researcher must predict beforehand the direction of relationship $(+$ or $-)$. The first column lists df which for the Pearson r is equal to $N - 2$.

TABLE R	Critical Values for the Pearson r			
	Directional Hypothesis		**Nondirectional Hypothesis**	
df	*.05*	*.01*	*.05*	*.01*
1	.988	.9995	.997	.9999
2	.900	.980	.950	.990
3	.805	.934	.878	.959
4	.729	.882	.811	.917
5	.669	.833	.754	.874
6	.622	.789	.707	.834
7	.582	.750	.666	.798
8	.549	.716	.632	.765
9	.521	.685	.602	.735
10	.497	.658	.576	.708
11	.476	.634	.553	.684
12	.458	.612	.532	.661
13	.441	.592	.514	.641
14	.426	.574	.497	.623
15	.412	.558	.482	.606
16	.400	.542	.468	.590
17	.389	.528	.456	.575
18	.378	.516	.444	.561
19	.369	.503	.433	.549
20	.360	.492	.423	.537

E

Continued on next page

TABLE R   Critical Values for the Pearson r (continued)

df	Directional Hypothesis		Nondirectional Hypothesis	
	.05	.01	.05	.01
21	.352	.482	.413	.526
22	.344	.472	.404	.515
23	.337	.462	.396	.505
24	.330	.453	.388	.496
25	.323	.445	.381	.487
26	.317	.437	.374	.479
27	.311	.430	.367	.471
28	.306	.423	.361	.463
29	.301	.416	.355	.456
30	.296	.409	.349	.449
35	.275	.381	.325	.418
40	.257	.358	.304	.393
45	.243	.338	.288	.372
50	.231	.322	.273	.354
60	.211	.295	.250	.325
70	.195	.274	.232	.302
80	.183	.256	.217	.283
90	.173	.242	.205	.267
100	.164	.230	.195	.254

E

Critical r_s values are listed for directional and nondirectional hypotheses and for α levels of .05 and .01. Obtained r_s coefficient must be equal to or greater than critical r_s value to reject H_0. To use directional hypothesis, researcher must predict beforehand the direction of relationship $(+ \text{ or } -)$. The first column lists sample sizes (N).

TABLE Rs	Critical r_s Values for the Spearman Rank-Order Correlation Coefficient			
	Directional Hypothesis		**Nondirectional Hypothesis**	
N	.05	.01	.05	.01
5	0.900	1.000	1.000	—
6	0.829	0.943	0.886	1.000
7	0.714	0.893	0.786	0.929
8	0.643	0.833	0.738	0.881
9	0.600	0.783	0.700	0.833
10	0.564	0.745	0.648	0.794
11	0.536	0.709	0.618	0.755
12	0.503	0.671	0.587	0.727
13	0.484	0.648	0.560	0.703
14	0.464	0.622	0.538	0.675
15	0.443	0.604	0.521	0.654
16	0.429	0.582	0.503	0.635
17	0.414	0.566	0.485	0.615
18	0.401	0.550	0.472	0.600
19	0.391	0.535	0.460	0.584
20	0.380	0.520	0.447	0.570
21	0.370	0.508	0.435	0.556
22	0.361	0.496	0.425	0.544
23	0.353	0.486	0.415	0.532
24	0.344	0.476	0.406	0.521
25	0.337	0.466	0.398	0.511
26	0.331	0.457	0.390	0.501
27	0.324	0.448	0.382	0.491
28	0.317	0.440	0.375	0.483
29	0.312	0.433	0.368	0.475
30	0.306	0.425	0.362	0.467

Note. Adapted from "Significance Testing of the Spearman Rank Correlation Coefficient" by J. H. Zar, 1972, *Journal of the American Statistical Association, 67*, p. 339. Copyright 1972 by the American Statistical Association. Adapted by permission.

Critical t values are presented for directional (one-tailed) and nondirectional (two-tailed) hypotheses and for α levels of .05 and .01. Obtained t values must be equal to or exceed critical value to reject H_0.

For t tests for one sample and correlated samples, $df = N - 1$. For t test for independent samples, $df = N_1 + N_2 - 2$.

TABLE T Critical t Values Based on Student's t Distribution

df	Directional Hypothesis .05	Directional Hypothesis .01	Nondirectional Hypothesis .05	Nondirectional Hypothesis .01
1	6.314	31.821	12.706	63.657
2	2.920	6.965	4.303	9.925
3	2.353	4.541	3.182	5.841
4	2.132	3.747	2.776	4.604
5	2.015	3.365	2.571	4.032
6	1.943	3.143	2.447	3.707
7	1.895	2.998	2.365	3.499
8	1.860	2.896	2.306	3.355
9	1.833	2.821	2.262	3.250
10	1.812	2.764	2.228	3.169
11	1.796	2.718	2.201	3.106
12	1.782	2.681	2.179	3.055
13	1.771	2.650	2.160	3.012
14	1.761	2.624	2.145	2.977
15	1.753	2.602	2.132	2.947
16	1.746	2.583	2.120	2.921
17	1.740	2.567	2.110	2.898
18	1.734	2.552	2.101	2.878
19	1.729	2.539	2.093	2.861
20	1.725	2.528	2.086	2.845
21	1.721	2.518	2.080	2.831
22	1.717	2.508	2.074	2.819
23	1.714	2.500	2.069	2.807
24	1.711	2.492	2.064	2.797
25	1.708	2.485	2.060	2.787
26	1.706	2.479	2.056	2.779
27	1.703	2.473	2.052	2.771
28	1.701	2.467	2.048	2.763
29	1.699	2.462	2.045	2.756
30	1.697	2.457	2.042	2.750
40	1.684	2.423	2.021	2.704
60	1.671	2.390	2.000	2.660
120	1.658	2.358	1.980	2.617
∞(Z)	1.645	2.326	1.960	2.576

Note. Adapted from Table III of Fisher & Yates: *Statistical Tables for Biological, Agricultural and Medical Research*, Published by Longman Group Ltd. London. (previously published by Oliver & Boyd Ltd. Edinburgh) and by permission of the authors and publishers.

The obtained U_1 value must be equal to or less than the critical U_1 value and the obtained U_2 value must be equal to or greater than the critical U_2 value in order to reject H_0.

TABLE U   Critical U Values for the Mann-Whitney U Test. Use with Directional Hypothesis and α Level = .05.

Each cell shows the critical U_1 value (top) over the critical U_2 value (bottom, underlined).

N_2 \ N_1	1	2	3	4	5	6	7	8	9	10	11	12	13	14	15	16	17	18	19	20
1	—	—	—	—	—	—	—	—	—	—	—	—	—	—	—	—	—	—	0/19	0/20
2	—	—	—	—	0/10	0/12	0/14	1/15	1/17	1/19	1/21	2/22	2/24	2/26	3/27	3/29	3/31	4/32	4/34	4/36
3	—	—	0/9	0/12	1/14	2/16	2/19	3/21	3/24	4/26	5/28	5/31	6/33	7/35	7/38	8/40	9/42	9/45	10/47	11/49
4	—	—	0/12	1/15	2/18	3/21	4/24	5/27	6/30	7/33	8/36	9/39	10/42	11/45	12/48	14/50	15/53	16/56	17/59	18/62
5	—	0/10	1/14	2/18	4/21	5/25	6/29	8/32	9/36	11/39	12/43	13/47	15/50	16/54	18/57	19/61	20/65	22/68	23/72	25/75
6	—	0/12	2/16	3/21	5/25	7/29	8/34	10/38	12/42	14/46	16/50	17/55	19/59	21/63	23/67	25/71	26/76	28/80	30/84	32/88
7	—	0/14	2/19	4/24	6/29	8/34	11/38	13/43	15/48	17/53	19/58	21/63	24/67	26/72	28/77	30/82	33/86	35/91	37/96	39/101
8	—	1/15	3/21	5/27	8/32	10/38	13/43	15/49	18/54	20/60	23/65	26/70	28/76	31/81	33/87	36/92	39/97	41/103	44/108	47/113
9	—	1/17	3/24	6/30	9/36	12/42	15/48	18/54	21/60	24/66	27/72	30/78	33/84	36/90	39/96	42/102	45/108	48/114	51/120	54/126
10	—	1/19	4/26	7/33	11/39	14/46	17/53	20/60	24/66	27/73	31/79	34/86	37/93	41/99	44/106	48/112	51/119	55/125	58/132	62/138
11	—	1/21	5/28	8/36	12/43	16/50	19/58	23/65	27/72	31/79	34/87	38/94	42/101	46/108	50/115	54/122	57/130	61/137	65/144	69/151
12	—	2/22	5/31	9/39	13/47	17/55	21/63	26/70	30/78	34/86	38/94	42/102	47/109	51/117	55/125	60/132	64/140	68/148	72/156	77/163
13	—	2/24	6/33	10/42	15/50	19/59	24/67	28/76	33/84	37/93	42/101	47/109	51/118	56/126	61/134	65/143	70/151	75/159	80/167	84/176
14	—	2/26	7/35	11/45	16/54	21/63	26/72	31/81	36/90	41/99	46/108	51/117	56/126	61/135	66/144	71/153	77/161	82/170	87/179	92/188
15	—	3/27	7/38	12/48	18/57	23/67	28/77	33/87	39/96	44/106	50/115	55/125	61/134	66/144	72/153	77/163	83/172	88/182	94/191	100/200
16	—	3/29	8/40	14/50	19/61	25/71	30/82	36/92	42/102	48/112	54/122	60/132	65/143	71/153	77/163	83/173	89/183	95/193	101/203	107/213
17	—	3/31	9/42	15/53	20/65	26/76	33/86	39/97	45/108	51/119	57/130	64/140	70/151	77/161	83/172	89/183	96/193	102/204	109/214	115/225
18	—	4/32	9/45	16/56	22/68	28/80	35/91	41/103	48/114	55/123	61/137	68/148	75/159	82/170	88/182	95/193	102/204	109/215	116/226	123/237
19	0/19	4/34	10/47	17/59	23/72	30/84	37/96	44/108	51/120	58/132	65/144	72/156	80/167	87/179	94/191	101/203	109/214	116/226	123/238	130/250
20	0/20	4/36	11/49	18/62	25/75	32/88	39/101	47/113	54/126	62/138	69/151	77/163	84/176	92/188	100/200	107/213	115/225	123/237	130/250	138/262

E

Note. Adapted from "On a Test of Whether One or Two Random Variables Is Stochastically Larger than the Other" by H. B. Mann and D. R. Whitney, 1947, *Annals of Mathematical Statistics, 18*, pp. 50–60. Copyright 1947 by The Institute of Mathematical Statistics. Adapted by permission. And from "Extended Tables for the Mann-Whitney Statistic" by D. Auble, 1953, *Bulletin of Institute of Educational Research at Indiana University, 1* (2). Copyright 1953 by Indiana University. Adapted by permission. Also taken from *Fundamentals of Behavioral Statistics* (5th ed., Tables I$_1$–I$_4$, pp. 431–434) by R. P. Runyon and A. Haber, 1984, Reading, MA: Addison-Wesley. Copyright 1984 by Random House. Adapted by permission.

TABLE U (continued) Critical U Values for the Mann-Whitney U Test. Use with Directional Hypothesis and α Level = .01.

N_2 \ N_1	1	2	3	4	5	6	7	8	9	10	11	12	13	14	15	16	17	18	19	20
1	—	—	—	—	—	—	—	—	—	—	—	—	—	—	—	—	—	—	—	—
2	—	—	—	—	—	—	—	—	—	—	—	—	0 / 26	0 / 28	0 / 30	0 / 32	0 / 34	0 / 36	1 / 37	1 / 39
3	—	—	—	—	—	—	0 / 21	0 / 24	1 / 26	1 / 29	1 / 32	2 / 34	2 / 37	2 / 40	3 / 42	3 / 45	4 / 47	4 / 50	4 / 52	5 / 55
4	—	—	—	—	0 / 20	1 / 23	1 / 27	2 / 30	3 / 33	3 / 37	4 / 40	5 / 43	5 / 47	6 / 50	7 / 53	7 / 57	8 / 60	9 / 63	9 / 67	10 / 70
5	—	—	—	0 / 20	1 / 24	2 / 28	3 / 32	4 / 36	5 / 40	6 / 44	7 / 48	8 / 52	9 / 56	10 / 60	11 / 64	12 / 68	13 / 72	14 / 76	15 / 80	16 / 84
6	—	—	—	1 / 23	2 / 28	3 / 33	4 / 38	6 / 42	7 / 47	8 / 52	9 / 57	11 / 61	12 / 66	13 / 71	15 / 75	16 / 80	18 / 84	19 / 89	20 / 94	22 / 98
7	—	—	0 / 21	1 / 27	3 / 32	4 / 38	6 / 43	7 / 49	9 / 54	11 / 59	12 / 65	14 / 70	16 / 75	17 / 81	19 / 86	21 / 91	23 / 96	24 / 102	26 / 107	28 / 112
8	—	—	0 / 24	2 / 30	4 / 36	6 / 42	7 / 49	9 / 55	11 / 61	13 / 67	15 / 73	17 / 79	20 / 84	22 / 90	24 / 96	26 / 102	28 / 108	30 / 114	32 / 120	34 / 126
9	—	—	1 / 26	3 / 33	5 / 40	7 / 47	9 / 54	11 / 61	14 / 67	16 / 74	18 / 81	21 / 87	23 / 94	26 / 100	28 / 107	31 / 113	33 / 120	36 / 126	38 / 133	40 / 140
10	—	—	1 / 29	3 / 37	6 / 44	8 / 52	11 / 59	13 / 67	16 / 74	19 / 81	22 / 88	24 / 96	27 / 103	30 / 110	33 / 117	36 / 124	38 / 132	41 / 139	44 / 146	47 / 153
11	—	—	1 / 32	4 / 40	7 / 48	9 / 57	12 / 65	15 / 73	18 / 81	22 / 88	25 / 96	28 / 104	31 / 112	34 / 120	37 / 128	41 / 135	44 / 143	47 / 151	50 / 159	53 / 167
12	—	—	2 / 34	5 / 43	8 / 52	11 / 61	14 / 70	17 / 79	21 / 87	24 / 96	28 / 104	31 / 113	35 / 121	38 / 130	42 / 138	46 / 146	49 / 155	53 / 163	56 / 172	60 / 180
13	—	0 / 26	2 / 37	5 / 47	9 / 56	12 / 66	16 / 75	20 / 84	23 / 94	27 / 103	31 / 112	35 / 121	39 / 130	43 / 139	47 / 148	51 / 157	55 / 166	59 / 175	63 / 184	67 / 193
14	—	0 / 28	2 / 40	6 / 50	10 / 60	13 / 71	17 / 81	22 / 90	26 / 100	30 / 110	34 / 120	38 / 130	43 / 139	47 / 149	51 / 159	56 / 168	60 / 178	65 / 187	69 / 197	73 / 207
15	—	0 / 30	3 / 42	7 / 53	11 / 64	15 / 75	19 / 86	24 / 96	28 / 107	33 / 117	37 / 128	42 / 138	47 / 148	51 / 159	56 / 169	61 / 179	66 / 189	70 / 200	75 / 210	80 / 220
16	—	0 / 32	3 / 45	7 / 57	12 / 68	16 / 80	21 / 91	26 / 102	31 / 113	36 / 124	41 / 135	46 / 146	51 / 157	56 / 168	61 / 179	66 / 190	71 / 201	76 / 212	82 / 222	87 / 233
17	—	0 / 34	4 / 47	8 / 60	13 / 72	18 / 84	23 / 96	28 / 108	33 / 120	38 / 132	44 / 143	49 / 155	55 / 166	60 / 178	66 / 189	71 / 201	77 / 212	82 / 224	88 / 234	93 / 247
18	—	0 / 36	4 / 50	9 / 63	14 / 76	19 / 89	24 / 102	30 / 114	36 / 126	41 / 139	47 / 151	53 / 163	59 / 175	65 / 187	70 / 200	76 / 212	82 / 224	88 / 236	94 / 248	100 / 260
19	—	1 / 37	4 / 53	9 / 67	15 / 80	20 / 94	26 / 107	32 / 120	38 / 133	44 / 146	50 / 159	56 / 172	63 / 184	69 / 197	75 / 210	82 / 222	88 / 235	94 / 248	101 / 260	107 / 273
20	—	1 / 39	5 / 55	10 / 70	16 / 84	22 / 98	28 / 112	34 / 126	40 / 140	47 / 153	53 / 167	60 / 180	67 / 193	73 / 207	80 / 220	87 / 233	93 / 247	100 / 260	107 / 273	114 / 286

E

TABLE U (*continued*) Critical *U* Values for the Mann-Whitney *U* Test. Use with Nondirectional Hypothesis and α Level = .05.

N_2 \ N_1	1	2	3	4	5	6	7	8	9	10	11	12	13	14	15	16	17	18	19	20
1	—	—	—	—	—	—	—	—	—	—	—	—	—	—	—	—	—	—	—	—
2	—	—	—	—	—	—	—	0	0	0	0	1	1	1	1	1	2	2	2	2
								16	18	20	22	23	25	27	29	31	32	34	36	38
3	—	—	—	—	0	1	1	2	2	3	3	4	4	5	5	6	6	7	7	8
					15	17	20	22	25	27	30	32	35	37	40	42	45	47	50	52
4	—	—	—	0	1	2	3	4	4	5	6	7	8	9	10	11	11	12	13	13
				16	19	22	25	28	32	35	38	41	44	47	50	53	57	60	63	67
5	—	—	0	1	2	3	5	6	7	8	9	11	12	13	14	15	17	18	19	20
			15	19	23	27	30	34	38	42	46	49	53	57	61	65	68	72	76	80
6	—	—	1	2	3	5	6	8	10	11	13	14	16	17	19	21	22	24	25	27
			17	22	27	31	36	40	44	49	53	58	62	67	71	75	80	84	89	93
7	—	—	1	3	5	6	8	10	12	14	16	18	20	22	24	26	28	30	32	34
			20	25	30	36	41	46	51	56	61	66	71	76	81	86	91	96	101	106
8	—	0	2	4	6	8	10	13	15	17	19	22	24	26	29	31	34	36	38	41
		16	22	28	34	40	46	51	57	63	69	74	80	86	91	97	102	108	111	119
9	—	0	2	4	7	10	12	15	17	20	23	26	28	31	34	37	39	42	45	48
		18	25	32	38	44	51	57	64	70	76	82	89	95	101	107	114	120	126	132
10	—	0	3	5	8	11	14	17	20	23	26	29	33	36	39	42	45	48	52	55
		20	27	35	42	49	56	63	70	77	84	91	97	104	111	118	125	132	138	145
11	—	0	3	6	9	13	16	19	23	26	30	33	37	40	44	47	51	55	58	62
		22	30	38	46	53	61	69	76	84	91	99	106	114	121	129	136	143	151	158
12	—	1	4	7	11	14	18	22	26	29	33	37	41	45	49	53	57	61	65	69
		23	32	41	49	58	66	74	82	91	99	107	115	123	131	139	147	155	163	171
13	—	1	4	8	12	16	20	24	28	33	37	41	45	50	54	59	63	67	72	76
		25	35	44	53	62	71	80	89	97	106	115	124	132	141	149	158	167	175	184
14	—	1	5	9	13	17	22	26	31	36	40	45	50	55	59	64	67	74	78	83
		27	37	47	51	67	76	86	95	104	114	123	132	141	151	160	171	178	188	197
15	—	1	5	10	14	19	24	29	34	39	44	49	54	59	64	70	75	80	85	90
		29	40	50	61	71	81	91	101	111	121	131	141	151	161	170	180	190	200	210
16	—	1	6	11	15	21	26	31	37	42	47	53	59	64	70	75	81	86	92	98
		31	42	53	65	75	86	97	107	118	129	139	149	160	170	181	191	202	212	222
17	—	2	6	11	17	22	28	34	39	45	51	57	63	67	75	81	87	93	99	105
		32	45	57	68	80	91	102	114	125	136	147	158	171	180	191	202	213	224	235
18	—	2	7	12	18	24	30	36	42	48	55	61	67	74	80	86	93	99	106	112
		34	47	60	72	84	96	108	120	132	143	155	167	178	190	202	213	225	236	248
19	—	2	7	13	19	25	32	38	45	52	58	65	72	78	85	92	99	106	113	119
		36	50	63	76	89	101	114	126	138	151	163	175	188	200	212	224	236	248	261
20	—	2	8	13	20	27	34	41	48	55	62	69	76	83	90	98	105	112	119	127
		38	52	67	80	93	106	119	132	145	158	171	184	197	210	222	235	248	261	273

E

TABLE U (Continued)   Critical U Values for the Mann-Whitney U Test. Use with Nondirectional Hypothesis and α Level = .01.

E

In each cell the upper number is the first critical value and the lower (underlined in the original) number is the second critical value.

N_2 \ N_1	1	2	3	4	5	6	7	8	9	10	11	12	13	14	15	16	17	18	19	20
1	—	—	—	—	—	—	—	—	—	—	—	—	—	—	—	—	—	—	—	—
2	—	—	—	—	—	—	—	—	—	—	—	—	—	—	—	—	—	—	0/38	0/40
3	—	—	—	—	—	—	—	—	0/27	0/30	0/33	1/35	1/38	1/41	2/43	2/46	2/49	2/52	3/54	3/57
4	—	—	—	—	—	0/24	0/28	1/31	1/35	2/38	2/42	3/45	3/49	4/52	5/55	5/59	6/62	6/66	7/69	8/72
5	—	—	—	—	0/25	1/29	1/34	2/38	3/42	4/46	5/50	6/54	7/58	7/63	8/67	9/71	10/75	11/79	12/83	13/87
6	—	—	—	0/24	1/29	2/34	3/39	4/44	5/49	6/54	7/59	9/63	10/68	11/73	12/78	13/83	15/87	16/92	17/97	18/102
7	—	—	—	0/28	1/34	3/39	4/45	6/50	7/56	9/61	10/67	12/72	13/78	15/83	16/89	18/94	19/100	21/105	22/111	24/116
8	—	—	—	1/31	2/38	4/44	6/50	7/57	9/63	11/69	13/75	15/81	17/87	18/94	20/100	22/106	24/112	26/118	28/124	30/130
9	—	—	0/27	1/35	3/42	5/49	7/56	9/63	11/70	13/77	16/83	18/90	20/97	22/104	24/111	27/117	29/124	31/131	33/138	36/144
10	—	—	0/30	2/38	4/46	6/54	9/61	11/69	13/77	16/84	18/92	21/99	24/106	26/114	29/121	31/129	34/136	37/143	39/151	42/158
11	—	—	0/33	2/42	5/50	7/59	10/67	13/75	16/83	18/92	21/100	24/108	27/116	30/124	33/132	36/140	39/148	42/156	45/164	48/172
12	—	—	1/35	3/45	6/54	9/63	12/72	15/81	18/90	21/99	24/108	27/117	31/125	34/134	37/143	41/151	44/160	47/169	51/177	54/186
13	—	—	1/38	3/49	7/58	10/68	13/78	17/87	20/97	24/106	27/116	31/125	34/135	38/144	42/153	45/163	49/172	53/181	56/191	60/200
14	—	—	1/41	4/52	7/63	11/73	15/83	18/94	22/104	26/114	30/124	34/134	38/144	42/154	46/164	50/174	54/184	58/194	63/203	67/213
15	—	—	2/43	5/55	8/67	12/78	16/89	20/100	24/111	29/121	33/132	37/143	42/153	46/164	51/174	55/185	60/195	64/206	69/216	73/227
16	—	—	2/46	5/59	9/71	13/83	18/94	22/106	27/117	31/129	36/140	41/151	45/163	50/174	55/185	60/196	65/207	70/218	74/230	79/241
17	—	—	2/49	6/62	10/75	15/87	19/100	24/112	29/124	34/136	39/148	44/160	49/172	54/184	60/195	65/207	70/219	75/231	81/242	86/254
18	—	—	2/52	6/66	11/79	16/92	21/105	26/118	31/131	37/143	42/156	47/169	53/181	58/194	64/206	70/218	75/231	81/243	87/255	92/268
19	—	0/38	3/54	7/69	12/83	17/97	22/111	28/124	33/138	39/151	45/164	51/177	56/191	63/203	69/216	74/230	81/242	87/255	93/268	99/281
20	—	0/40	3/57	8/72	13/87	18/102	24/116	30/130	36/144	42/158	48/172	54/186	60/200	67/213	73/227	79/241	86/254	92/268	99/281	105/295

Critical W values are presented for samples of $N \leq 50$. The obtained W value must be equal to or less than the critical W value in order to reject H_0. First column lists sample sizes (N). Critical values are listed for directional (one-tailed) and nondirectional (two-tailed) hypotheses and for α levels of .05 and .01. Dashed lines indicate cases for which sample size is too small to conduct test.

TABLE W	Critical W Values for the Wilcoxon Matched-Pairs Test			
	Directional Hypothesis		**Nondirectional Hypothesis**	
N	.05	.01	.05	.01
5	0	—	—	—
6	2	—	0	
7	3	0	2	—
8	5	1	3	0
9	8	3	5	1
10	10	5	8	3
11	13	7	10	5
12	17	9	13	7
13	21	12	17	9
14	25	15	21	12
15	30	19	25	15
16	35	23	29	19
17	41	27	34	23
18	47	32	40	27
19	53	37	46	32
20	60	43	52	37
21	67	49	58	42
22	75	55	65	48
23	83	62	73	54
24	91	69	81	61
25	100	76	89	68
26	110	84	98	75
27	119	92	107	83
28	130	101	116	91
29	140	110	126	100
30	151	120	137	109

E

Note. Adapted from *Critical Values and Probability Levels for the Wilcoxon Ranked Sum Test and the Wilcoxon Signed Rank Test* (Table 2) by F. Wilcoxon, S. Katte, and R. A. Wilcox, 1963, New York: American Cyanamid Co. Copyright 1963 by American Cyanamid Co. Adapted by permission. And from *Some Rapid Approximate Statistical Procedures* by F. Wilcoxon and R. A. Wilcox, 1964, New York: Lederle Laboratories. Copyright 1964 by American Cyanamid Co. Adapted by permission.

Also from *Fundamentals of Behavioral Statistics* (5th ed., Table J, p. 435) by R. P. Runyon and A. Haber, 1984, Reading, MA: Addison Wesley. Copyright 1984 by Random House. Adapted by permission.

Continued on next page

E

TABLE W	Critical *W* Values for the Wilcoxon Matched-Pairs Test *(Continued)*			
	Directional Hypothesis		**Nondirectional Hypothesis**	
N	*.05*	*.01*	*.05*	*.01*
31	163	130	147	118
32	175	140	159	128
33	187	151	170	138
34	200	162	182	148
35	213	173	195	159
36	227	185	208	171
37	241	198	221	182
38	256	211	235	194
39	271	224	249	207
40	286	238	264	220
41	302	252	279	233
42	319	266	294	247
43	336	281	310	261
44	353	296	327	276
45	371	312	343	291
46	389	328	361	307
47	407	345	378	322
48	426	362	396	339
49	446	379	415	355
50	466	397	434	373

Critical χ^2 values are for α levels of .05 and .01. Obtained χ^2 value must be equal to or greater than critical χ^2 value to reject H_0. This table is used for chi-square tests and Kruskal-Wallis H test (obtained H must meet or exceed critical χ^2 value to reject H_0). First column lists df which for the different tests are,

χ^2 test for goodness of fit: df = number of categories $-$ 1

χ^2 test of independence: df = (number of rows $-$ 1)(number of columns $-$ 1)

Kruskal-Wallis H test: df = number of groups $-$ 1

Table X	Critical χ^2 Values Based on Chi-Square Distribution	
df	**.05**	**.01**
1	3.84	6.64
2	5.99	9.21
3	7.82	11.34
4	9.49	13.28
5	11.07	15.09
6	12.59	16.81
7	14.07	18.48
8	15.51	20.09
9	16.92	21.67
10	18.31	23.21
11	19.68	24.72
12	21.03	26.22
13	22.36	27.69
14	23.68	29.14
15	25.00	30.58
16	26.30	32.00
17	27.59	33.41
18	28.87	34.80
19	30.14	36.19
20	31.41	37.57
21	32.67	38.93
22	33.92	40.29
23	35.17	41.64
24	36.42	42.98
25	37.65	44.31
26	38.88	45.64
27	40.11	46.96
28	41.34	48.28
29	42.56	49.59
30	43.77	50.89
40	55.76	63.69
50	67.50	76.15
60	79.08	88.38
70	90.53	100.42

E

Note. Adapted from Table IV of Fisher & Yates: *Statistical Tables for Biological, Agricultural and Medical Research,* Published by Longman Group Ltd. London. (previously published by Oliver & Boyd Ltd. Edinburgh) and by permission of the authors and publishers.

E

Standard (z) scores are listed under Column A. Column B lists the proportion of area between the mean and the z score. Column C lists the proportion of area beyond the z. z scores can be converted to percentile ranks using the following formulas:

Percentile rank for $+z$ score $= 100 \times (.50 + \text{Proportion in Column B})$
Percentile rank for $-z$ score $= 100 \times (\text{Proportion in Column C})$

TABLE Z   Proportion of Area Under the Standard Normal Distribution

(A) z	(B)	(C)	(A) z	(B)	(C)
0.00	.0000	.5000	0.52	.1985	.3015
0.01	.0040	.4960	0.53	.2019	.2981
0.02	.0080	.4920	0.54	.2054	.2946
0.03	.0120	.4880	0.55	.2088	.2912
0.04	.0160	.4840	0.56	.2123	.2877
0.05	.0199	.4801	0.57	.2157	.2843
0.06	.0239	.4761	0.58	.2190	.2810
0.07	.0279	.4721	0.59	.2224	.2776
0.08	.0319	.4681	0.60	.2257	.2743
0.09	.0359	.4641	0.61	.2291	.2709
0.10	.0398	.4602	0.62	.2324	.2676
0.11	.0438	.4562	0.63	.2357	.2643
0.12	.0478	.4522	0.64	.2389	.2611
0.13	.0517	.4483	0.65	.2422	.2578
0.14	.0557	.4443	0.66	.2454	.2546
0.15	.0596	.4404	0.67	.2486	.2514
0.16	.0636	.4364	0.68	.2517	.2483
0.17	.0675	.4325	0.69	.2549	.2451
0.18	.0714	.4286	0.70	.2580	.2420
0.19	.0753	.4247	0.71	.2611	.2389
0.20	.0793	.4207	0.72	.2642	.2358

0.21	.0832	.4168	0.73	.2673	.2327
0.22	.0871	.4129	0.74	.2704	.2296
0.23	.0910	.4090	0.75	.2734	.2266
0.24	.0948	.4052	0.76	.2764	.2236
0.25	.0987	.4013	0.77	.2794	.2206
0.26	.1026	.3974	0.78	.2823	.2177
0.27	.1064	.3936	0.79	.2852	.2148
0.28	.1103	.3897	0.80	.2881	.2119
0.29	.1141	.3859	0.81	.2910	.2090
0.30	.1179	.3821	0.82	.2939	.2061
0.31	.1217	.3783	0.83	.2967	.2033
0.32	.1255	.3745	0.84	.2995	.2005
0.33	.1293	.3707	0.85	.3023	.1977
0.34	.1331	.3669	0.86	.3051	.1949
0.35	.1368	.3632	0.87	.3078	.1922
0.36	.1406	.3594	0.88	.3106	.1894
0.37	.1443	.3557	0.89	.3133	.1867
0.38	.1480	.3520	0.90	.3159	.1841
0.39	.1517	.3483	0.91	.3186	.1814
0.40	.1554	.3446	0.92	.3212	.1788
0.41	.1591	.3409	0.93	.3238	.1762
0.42	.1628	.3372	0.94	.3264	.1736
0.43	.1664	.3336	0.95	.3289	.1711
0.44	.1700	.3300	0.96	.3315	.1685
0.45	.1736	.3264	0.97	.3340	.1660
0.46	.1772	.3228	0.98	.3365	.1635
0.47	.1808	.3192	0.99	.3339	.1611
0.48	.1844	.3156	1.00	.3413	.1587
0.49	.1879	.3121	1.01	.3438	.1562
0.50	.1915	.3085	1.02	.3461	.1539
0.51	.1950	.3050	1.03	.3485	.1515

Continued on next page

Note. Adapted from *Statistics* (2nd ed., Table A, pp. 368–369) by R. S. Witte, 1985, New York: Holt, Rinehart & Winston. Copyright 1985 by Holt, Rinehart & Winston. Adapted by permission.

Note. Adapted from Table III of Fisher & Yates: *Statistical Tables for Biological, Agricultural and Medical Research.* Published by Longman Group Ltd. London. (previously published by Oliver & Boyd Ltd. Edinburgh) and by permission of the authors and publishers.

E

TABLE Z (Continued) Proportion of Area Under the Standard Normal Distribution

(A) z	(B)	(C)	(A) z	(B)	(C)
1.04	.3508	.1492	1.63	.4484	.0516
1.05	.3531	.1469	1.64	.4495	.0505
1.06	.3554	.1446	1.65	.4505	.0495
1.07	.3577	.1423	1.66	.4515	.0485
1.08	.3599	.1401	1.67	.4525	.0475
1.09	.3621	.1379	1.68	.4535	.0465
1.10	.3643	.1357	1.69	.4545	.0455
1.11	.3665	.1335	1.70	.4554	.0446
1.12	.3686	.1314	1.71	.4564	.0436
1.13	.3708	.1292	1.72	.4573	.0427
1.14	.3729	.1271	1.73	.4582	.0418
1.15	.3749	.1251	1.74	.4591	.0409
1.16	.3770	.1230	1.75	.4599	.0401
1.17	.3790	.1210	1.76	.4608	.0392
1.18	.3810	.1190	1.77	.4616	.0384
1.19	.3830	.1170	1.78	.4625	.0375
1.20	.3849	.1151	1.79	.4633	.0367
1.21	.3869	.1131	1.80	.4641	.0359
1.22	.3888	.1112	1.81	.4649	.0351
1.23	.3907	.1093	1.82	.4656	.0344
1.24	.3925	.1075	1.83	.4664	.0336
1.25	.3944	.1056	1.84	.4671	.0329
1.26	.3962	.1038	1.85	.4678	.0322
1.27	.3980	.1020	1.86	.4686	.0314

1.28	.3997	.1003	1.87	.4693	.0307
1.29	.4015	.0985	1.88	.4699	.0301
1.30	.4032	.0968	1.89	.4706	.0294
1.31	.4049	.0951	1.90	.4713	.0287
1.32	.4066	.0934	1.91	.4719	.0281
1.33	.4082	.0918	1.92	.4726	.0274
1.34	.4099	.0901	1.93	.4732	.0268
1.35	.4115	.0885	1.94	.4738	.0262
1.36	.4131	.0869	1.95	.4744	.0256
1.37	.4147	.0853	1.96	.4750	.0250
1.38	.4162	.0838	1.97	.4756	.0244
1.39	.4177	.0823	1.98	.4761	.0239
1.40	.4192	.0808	1.99	.4767	.0233
1.41	.4207	.0793	2.00	.4772	.0228
1.42	.4222	.0778	2.01	.4778	.0222
1.43	.4236	.0764	2.02	.4783	.0217
1.44	.4251	.0749	2.03	.4788	.0212
1.45	.4265	.0735	2.04	.4793	.0207
1.46	.4279	.0721	2.05	.4798	.0202
1.47	.4292	.0708	2.06	.4803	.0197
1.48	.4306	.0694	2.07	.4808	.0192
1.49	.4319	.0681	2.08	.4812	.0188
1.50	.4332	.0668	2.09	.4817	.0183
1.51	.4345	.0655	2.10	.4821	.0179
1.52	.4357	.0643	2.11	.4826	.0174
1.53	.4370	.0630	2.12	.4830	.0170
1.54	.4382	.0618	2.13	.4834	.0166
1.55	.4394	.0606	2.14	.4838	.0162
1.56	.4406	.0594	2.15	.4842	.0158
1.57	.4418	.0582	2.16	.4846	.0154
1.58	.4429	.0571	2.17	.4850	.0150
1.59	.4441	.0559	2.18	.4854	.0146
1.60	.4452	.0548	2.19	.4857	.0143
1.61	.4463	.0537	2.20	.4861	.0139
1.62	.4474	.0526	2.21	.4864	.0136

Continued on next page

E

E

TABLE Z (Continued) Proportion of Area Under the Standard Normal Distribution

(A) z	(B)	(C)		(A) z	(B)	(C)
2.22	.4868	.0132		2.79	.4974	.0026
2.23	.4871	.0129		2.80	.4974	.0026
2.24	.4875	.0125		2.81	.4975	.0025
2.25	.4878	.0122		2.82	.4976	.0024
2.26	.4881	.0119		2.83	.4977	.0023
2.27	.4884	.0116		2.84	.4977	.0023
2.28	.4887	.0113		2.85	.4978	.0022
2.29	.4890	.0110		2.86	.4979	.0021
2.30	.4893	.0107		2.87	.4979	.0021
2.31	.4896	.0104		2.88	.4980	.0020
2.32	.4898	.0102		2.89	.4981	.0019
2.33	.4901	.0099		2.90	.4981	.0019
2.34	.4904	.0096		2.91	.4982	.0018
2.35	.4906	.0094		2.92	.4982	.0018
2.36	.4909	.0091		2.93	.4983	.0017
2.37	.4911	.0089		2.94	.4984	.0016
2.38	.4913	.0087		2.95	.4984	.0016
2.39	.4916	.0084		2.96	.4985	.0015
2.40	.4918	.0082		2.97	.4985	.0015
2.41	.4920	.0080		2.98	.4986	.0014
2.42	.4922	.0078		2.99	.4986	.0014
2.43	.4925	.0075		3.00	.4987	.0013
2.44	.4927	.0073		3.01	.4987	.0013
2.45	.4929	.0071		3.02	.4987	.0013

z			z		
2.46	.4931	.0069	3.03	.4988	.0012
2.47	.4932	.0068	3.04	.4988	.0012
2.48	.4934	.0066	3.05	.4989	.0011
2.49	.4936	.0064	3.06	.4989	.0011
2.50	.4938	.0062	3.07	.4989	.0011
2.51	.4940	.0060	3.08	.4990	.0010
2.52	.4941	.0059	3.09	.4990	.0010
2.53	.4943	.0057	3.10	.4990	.0010
2.54	.4945	.0055	3.11	.4991	.0009
2.55	.4946	.0054	3.12	.4991	.0009
2.56	.4948	.0052	3.13	.4991	.0009
2.57	.4949	.0051	3.14	.4992	.0008
2.58	.4951	.0049	3.15	.4992	.0008
2.59	.4952	.0048	3.16	.4992	.0008
2.60	.4953	.0047	3.17	.4992	.0008
2.61	.4955	.0045	3.18	.4993	.0007
2.62	.4956	.0044	3.19	.4993	.0007
2.63	.4957	.0043	3.20	.4993	.0007
2.64	.4959	.0041	3.21	.4993	.0007
2.65	.4960	.0040	3.22	.4994	.0006
2.66	.4961	.0039	3.23	.4994	.0006
2.67	.4962	.0038	3.24	.4994	.0006
2.68	.4963	.0037	3.25	.4994	.0006
2.69	.4964	.0036	3.30	.4995	.0005
2.70	.4965	.0035	3.35	.4996	.0004
2.71	.4966	.0034	3.40	.4997	.0003
2.72	.4967	.0033	3.45	.4997	.0003
2.73	.4968	.0032	3.50	.4998	.0002
2.74	.4969	.0031	3.60	.4998	.0002
2.75	.4970	.0030	3.70	.4999	.0001
2.76	.4971	.0029	3.80	.4999	.0001
2.77	.4972	.0028	3.90	.49995	.00005
2.78	.4973	.0027	4.00	.49997	.00003

E

References

Allison, D. E., & Thomas, D. C. (1986). Item-difficulty sequence in achievement examinations: Examinees' preferences and test-taking strategies. *Psychological Reports, 59,* 867–870.

Barowsky, E. I. (1986). Effects of stereotypic expectation on evaluation of written English attributed to handicapped and nonhandicapped students. *Psychological Reports, 59,* 1097–1098.

Bransford, J. D., & Johnson, M. K. (1972). Contextual prerequisites for understanding: Some investigations of comprehension and recall. *Journal of Verbal Learning and Verbal Behavior, 11,* 717–726.

Byrne, D., Ervin, C. R., & Lamberth, J. (1970). Continuity between the experimental study of attraction and real-life computer dating. *Journal of Personality and Social Psychology, 16,* 157–165.

Camilli, G., & Hopkins, K. D. (1978). Applicability of chi-square to 2 × 2 contingency tables with small expected frequencies. *Psychological Bulletin, 85,* 163–167.

Carlson, J. M., & Dolan, K. (1985). The waffle phenomenon and candidates' image. *Psychological Reports, 57,* 795–798.

Carsrud, A. L. (1984). Graduate student supervision of undergraduate research: Increasing research opportunities. *Teaching of Psychology, 11,* 203–205.

Carver, C. S., Coleman, E., & Glass, D. C. (1976). The coronary-prone behavior pattern and the suppression of fatigue on a treadmill test. *Journal of Personality and Social Psychology, 33,* 460–466.

Craik, F. I. M., & Lockhart, R. S. (1972). Levels of processing: A framework for memory research. *Journal of Verbal Learning and Verbal Behavior, 11,* 671–684.

Craik, F. I. M., & Tulving, E. (1975). Depth of processing and the retention of words in episodic memory. *Journal of Experimental Psychology: General, 104,* 268–294.

Dambrot, F. H., Papp, M. E., & Whitmore, C. (1984). The sex-role attitudes of three generations of women. *Personality and Social Psychology Bulletin, 10,* 469–473.

Darley, J. M., & Latané, B. (1968). Bystander intervention in emergencies: Diffusion of responsibility. *Journal of Personality and Social Psychology, 8,* 377–383.

Davis, H., IV. (1986). Effects of biofeedback and cognitive therapy on stress in patients with breast cancer. *Psychological Reports, 59,* 967–974.

DeLoache, J. S., & Brown, A. L. (1984). Where do I go next? Intelligent searching by very young children. *Developmental Psychology, 20,* 37–44.

Ellis, H. C., Thomas, R. L., & Rodriguez, I. A. (1984). Emotional mood states and memory: Elaborative encoding, semantic processing, and cognitive effort. *Journal of Experimental Psychology: Learning, Memory, and Cognition, 10,* 470–482.

Galluscio, E. H. (1983). Brain laterality: Differences in cognitive style or motor functions? *Perceptual and Motor Skills, 56,* 3–9.

Galluscio, E. H., Kuehner, K. V., & VanBuskirk, A. W. (1984). Multiple resources and brain laterality. *Perceptual and Motor Skills, 59,* 815–824.

Geffen, G., Bradshaw, J. L., & Wallace, G. (1971). Interhemispheric effects on reaction time to verbal and nonverbal visual stimuli. *Journal of Experimental Psychology, 87,* 415–422.

Gordon, R. H., & Bauer, G. (1985). Social class biases of practicing attorneys. *Psychological Reports, 57,* 931–935.

Gormley, F. P., & Aiéllo, J. R. (1982). Social density, interpersonal relationships, and residential crowding stress. *Journal of Applied Social Psychology, 12,* 222–236.

Hale, W. D., & Cochran, C. D. (1986). Locus of control across the adult lifespan. *Psychological Reports, 59,* 311–313.

Holmes, T. H., & Rahe, R. H. (1967). The social readjustment scale. *Journal of Psychosomatic Research, 11,* 213–218.

Jahnke, J. C. (1974). Restrictions on the Ranschburg effect. *Journal of Experimental Psychology, 103,* 183–185.

Johnson, W. G. (1970) *The effect of prior-taste and food visibility on the food-directed instrumental performance of obese individuals.* Unpublished doctoral dissertation. Catholic University of America, Washington, DC.

Joubert, C. E. (1985a). Sex differences in given name preference. *Psychological Reports, 57,* 49–50.

Joubert, C. E. (1985b). Factors related to individuals' attitudes toward their names. *Psychological Reports, 57,* 983–986.

Keesey, R. E., & Corbett, S. W. (1983). Metabolic defense of the body weight set-point. *Psychiatric Annals, 13,* 839–842.

Keppel, G. (1973). *Design and analysis: A researcher's handbook.* Englewood Cliffs, NJ: Prentice-Hall.

Kohlberg, L. (1969). Stage and sequence: The cognitive-developmental approach to socialization. In D. Goslin (Ed.), *Handbook of socialization theory* (pp. 347–480). New York: Rand McNally.

Larson, J. R., Jr. (1985). Role of memory in the performance-evaluation process: With special reference to diary-keeping. *Psychological Reports, 57,* 775–782.

Leary, M. R., Rogers, P. A., Canfield, R. W., & Coe, C. (1986). Boredom in interpersonal encounters: Antecedents and social implications. *Journal of Personality and Social Psychology, 51,* 968–975.

Lewis, C. D., & Houtz, J. C. (1986). Sex-role stereotyping and young children's divergent thinking. *Psychological Reports, 59,* 1027–1033.

Loftus, E. F., & Palmer, J. C. (1974). Reconstruction of automobile destruction: An example of the interaction between language and memory. *Journal of Verbal Learning and Verbal Behavior, 13,* 585–589.

Loftus, G. R., & Loftus, E. F. (1982). *Essence of statistics.* Monterey, CA: Brooks/Cole.

Lovaas, I. O. (1961). Interaction between verbal and nonverbal behavior. *Child Development, 32,* 329–336.

Malloch, D. C., & Michael, W. B. (1981). Predicting student grade point average at a community college from scholastic aptitude tests and from measures representing three constructs in Vroom's expectancy theory model of motivation. *Educational and Psychological Measurement, 41,* 1127–1135.

McClain, L. (1983). Behavior during examinations: A comparison of "A," "C," and "F" students. *Teaching of Psychology, 10,* 69–71.

Milgram, S. (1965). Some conditions of obedience and disobedience to authority. *Human Relations, 18,* 57–76.

Morlock, H., Yando, T., & Nigolean, K. (1985). Motivation of video game players. *Psychological Reports, 57,* 247–250.

Niles, W. J. (1986). Effects of a moral development discussion group on delinquent and predelinquent boys. *Journal of Counseling Psychology, 33,* 45–51.

Parke, R. D., Ewall, W., & Slaby, R. G. (1972). Hostile and helpful verbalizations as regulators of nonverbal aggression. *Journal of Personality and Social Psychology, 23,* 243–248.

Rawson, J. R., Bhatnagar, N. S., & Schneider, H. G. (1985). Initial relaxation response: Personality and treatment factors. *Psychological Reports, 57,* 827–830.

Rotton, J., Kelly, I. W., & Elortegui, P. (1986). Assessing belief in lunar effects: Known-groups validation. *Psychological Reports, 59,* 171–174.

Ruch, L. O., & Holmes, T. H. (1971). Scaling of life change: Comparison of direct and indirect methods. *Journal of Psychosomatic Research, 15,* 221–227.

Runyon, R. P., & Haber, A. (1984). *Fundamentals of behavioral statistics.* Reading, MA: Addison-Wesley Publishing Company, Inc.

Sacco, P. (1985). Depression and expectations of satisfaction. *Psychological Reports, 57,* 99–102.

Schacter, S. (1971). Some extraordinary facts about obese humans and rats. *American Psychologist, 26,* 129–144.

Schachter, S., & Gross, L. P. (1968). Manipulated time and eating behavior. *Journal of Personality and Social Psychology, 10,* 98–106.

Shisslak, C. M., Beatler, L. E., Scheiber, S., Gaines, J. A., LaWall, J., & Crago, M. (1985). Patterns of caffeine use and prescribed medication in psychiatric inpatients. *Psychological Reports, 57,* 39–42.

Siegel, S. (1956). *Nonparametric statistics for the behavioral sciences.* New York: McGraw-Hill.

Stricker, G., & Huber, J. T. (1967). The graduate record examination and undergraduate grades as predictors of success in graduate school. *The Journal of Educational Research, 60,* 466–468.

Tinsley, H. E. A., Brown, M. T., de St. Aubin, T. M., & Lucek, J. (1984). Relation between expectancies for a helping relationship and tendency to seek help from a campus help provider. *Journal of Counseling Psychology, 31,* 149–160.

van Wagenberg, D., Krasner, M., & Krasner, L. (1981). Children planning an ideal classroom. *Environment and Behavior, 13,* 349–359.

Vroom, V. H. (1964). *Work and motivation.* New York: Wiley.

Vroom, V. H. (1965). *Motivation in management.* New York: American Foundation for Management Research Study.

Index

Number	Chapter	Formula
23	13	$SS_{tot} = \Sigma X_{tot}^2 - \dfrac{(\Sigma X_{tot})^2}{N_{tot}}$
24	13	$SS_a = \dfrac{(\Sigma X_1)^2}{N_1} + \dfrac{(\Sigma X_2)^2}{N_2} + \cdots + \dfrac{(\Sigma X_k)^2}{N_k} - \dfrac{(\Sigma X_{tot})^2}{N_{tot}}$
25	13	$SS_w = SS_1 + SS_2 + \cdots + SS_k$
26	13	$MS = SS/df$
27	13	$F = \dfrac{MS_a}{MS_w}$
28	13	$HSD = q\sqrt{\dfrac{MS_w}{N_k}}$
28a	13	$\tilde{n}_k = \dfrac{k}{1/N_1 + 1/N_2 + \cdots + 1/N_k}$
29	14	$SS_a = \dfrac{(\Sigma X_1)^2 + (\Sigma X_2)^2 + \cdots + (\Sigma X_k)^2}{N_k} - \dfrac{(\Sigma X_{tot})^2}{N_{tot}}$
30	14	$SS_{rows} = \dfrac{(\Sigma X_{row1})^2 + (\Sigma X_{row2})^2 + \cdots + (\Sigma X_{rowi})^2}{N\ (per\ row)} - \dfrac{(\Sigma X_{tot})^2}{N_{tot}}$
31	14	$SS_{col.} = \dfrac{(\Sigma X_{col1})^2 + (\Sigma X_{col2})^2 + \cdots + (\Sigma X_{colj})^2}{N\ (per\ column)} - \dfrac{(\Sigma X_{tot})^2}{N_{tot}}$
32	14	$SS_{r\,x\,c} = SS_a - SS_{rows} - SS_{col.}$
33	15	$SS_{subj} = \dfrac{\Sigma X_{subj}^2}{k} - \dfrac{(\Sigma X_{tot})^2}{N_{tot}}$
34	15	$SS_{resid.} = SS_{tot} - SS_{subj} - SS_a$